Effective Risk Management:
Some Keys to Success, Second Edition

Effective Risk Management:
Some Keys to Success, Second Edition

Edmund H. Conrow

American Institute of Aeronautics and Astronautics, Inc.
1801 Alexander Bell Drive
Reston, Virginia 20191-4344

Publishers since 1930

American Institute of Aeronautics and Astronautics, Inc., Reston, Virginia

1 2 3 4 5

Library of Congress Cataloging-in-Publication Data

Conrow, E. H. (Edmund H.), 1949–
 Effective risk management : some keys to success / Edmund H. Conrow.—
2nd ed.
  p. cm.
Includes bibliographical references and index.
 ISBN 1-56347-581-2
 1. Risk management. I. Title.

 HD61.C663 2003
 658.15'5—dc21

                          2003010049

Table of Contents

Preface

The purpose of this book is two-fold: first, to provide key lessons learned that I have documented from performing risk management on a wide variety of programs, and second, to assist you, the reader, in developing and implementing an effective risk management process on your program.

The lessons learned in the first edition include more than 250 tips to succeed and traps to avoid in effective risk management that I have gleaned from actual programs over a 20-plus-year period of time. Although I have worked on a variety of programs, much of my risk management experience has been on programs in the U.S. Air Force, U.S. Army, U.S. Navy, Department of Defense (DoD), and NASA, as well as other government and commercial programs with a program dollar range between less than $20 million to greater than $50 billion (life cycle cost, then year dollars) on hardware-intensive, software-intensive, and mixed programs. These programs include space, air, ground, and sea product operating environments.

For the second edition of this book I've added more than 450 tips to succeed and traps to avoid in risk management for a total of more than 700 tips and traps. Some additions are new entries, while others are enhancements to entries contained in the first edition. I've supplied corrections where warranted and also added a new section to Chapter 2 that provides some implementation guidelines for risk management and pointers to appropriate sections of this book that contain additional information. I've included a new appendix (Appendix E), written by highly respected risk management consultant and author Dr. Robert N. Charette, on the definition of risk. This appendix includes a thought-provoking discussion on differences between risk and opportunity. This discussion is particularly important and timely because many in the project management community blindly believe that opportunity should be included in the definition of risk—something that does not withstand close scrutiny.

I've also updated entries referencing DoD policy associated with acquisition and risk management that changed since the release of the first edition of this book (May 2000) through October 2002. Note: While some key DoD acquisition changes occurred in April 2002 affecting the designation of program phases, I have continued to use the previous acquisition phase nomenclature and definitions because of the vast majority of programs that will have been procured or are in development with the earlier acquisition phase nomenclature and definitions at the time that the second edition of this book was developed. See Appendix B for a discussion of both the April 2002 and previous nomenclatures.

Finally, Deputy Secretary of Defense Paul Wolfowitz canceled DoD Directive 5000.1, DoD Instruction 5000.2, and DoD 5000.2-R on 30 October 2002 when the manuscript for the second edition of this book was being finalized. In a memorandum (*Defense Acquisition*) issued on 30 October 2002, Dr. Wolfowitz indicated that revised documents would be prepared within 120 days of that date, and that in the meantime, the 5 April 2002 DoD 5000.2-R was re-issued as the "Interim Defense Acquisition Guidebook," on 30 October 2002, noting (from that document)

> "The Deputy Secretary's memorandum, *Defense Acquisition*, dated October 30, 2002, and Attachment 2 to that memorandum reference a guidebook to accompany the interim guidance. The former DoD 5000.2-R regulation will serve as the guidebook while the Defense Acquisition Policy Working Group creates a streamlined guidebook. The former DoD 5000.2-R is NOT mandatory, but should be used for best practices, lessons learned, and expectations, until replaced."

Because of potential unforeseen, future changes in these documents the most recent DoD Directive 5000.1 (23 October 2000), DoD Instruction 5000.2 (5 April 2002), and DoD 5000.2-R (5 April 2002) in place prior to 30 October 2002 are used as the primary source of relevant DoD information in the second edition of this book unless an earlier version is used because of specific policy.

While some of the material in this book may not apply to your program, and you may disagree with other material, do not "bank on" your program being the exception to the rule if potential risks exist. For example, we have "that" limitation or risk issue, but we do not need to resolve it. Doing nothing about a known risk issue will not resolve it and should not be attempted unless you are sure that the risk handling assumption option is both applicable and appropriate. And even then, you will need to set aside cost and schedule reserve to be able to address the risk issue if and when it becomes a problem

I have found that risk management on many programs is not only below the state of the art, but more importantly, *below the level needed*. Unfortunately, people are often unable or unwilling to take an unbiased and thorough look at their program's risk management process, seek outside assistance to perform a knowledgeable independent assessment, and implement suggested improvements. This occurs with industry, contractors (including the biggest in the business), and government organizations, across commercial, government, and DoD programs. It is surprising how many times I have observed inadequate risk management on programs with a life cycle cost greater than $1 billion!

For example, a company with annual sales in the multibillion-dollar range has implemented a flawed risk management process on a number of programs. A developer of the risk management process has known that critical problems exist, but has been unwilling to make changes. A few others within the company realize the process is flawed but are unwilling to notify upper management, and upper management is unaware of the issues that exist. From a company perspective this has the potential to create considerable financial problems, yet the status quo prevails.

Risk management was often historically viewed as an "ility" (e.g., like affordability) or a "nice to have." However, in the present day, the need for risk management is at least partially driven by a substantial change in the acquisition environment for commercial and government programs, characterized by shrinking budgets, often smaller development teams, and quicker time to market with the same or higher performance than a few years ago. Some companies and government organizations have "seen the light" and now openly embrace risk management. Others that do not have a corporate culture or a history of *effective* risk management may openly struggle with what good risk management is and how to implement it. Unfortunately, in some cases organizations that have no history of effective risk management or have devoted considerable effort to squash good risk management now promote themselves as risk management experts.

Recent examples exist where the government has used the contractor's proposed risk management process and evaluation of candidate risks as a key source selection discriminator in competitive procurements—in one case where the procurement totaled several billion dollars and risk management and a related process were the *sole* source selection discriminators! Thus, if performed effectively risk management may not only help a program avert potential cost, performance, and schedule impacts, but it may also help win a procurement.

In fact, I believe that the government should score proposal sections red, give a minimum award fee, etc., if poor risk management is demonstrated. The same should also be done by industry when soliciting proposals from or working with other contractors. The government should not criticize or downgrade contractors who attempt to change erroneous risk management practices, but instead it should encourage such change, provide monetary rewards where appropriate (e.g., increased award fee), and so forth. Both government, contractors, and commercial companies should also voluntarily change erroneous risk management practices where possible because this should improve design trade and risk handling prioritization results and the allocation of funds to risk handling activities, which benefits each organization.

Unfortunately, many relevant professional societies have generally taken a weak stand, no stand, or even a stand supporting poor risk management practices. Even worse, professional societies sometimes tolerate or even promote the use of flawed risk management practices: For example, one organization sells material containing a flawed methodology. In another case, a reputable professional society that should have known better uses material from another society that is both flawed and well below the state of the art. Instead, professional societies need to take a strong public stand supporting the use of good risk management practices through education, publication guidelines, or peer reviews for publications, etc. To date, this has clearly not been done for many professional societies. Hence, government, industry, and professional societies should work closely together to increase available, accurate knowledge on risk management and how it should be tailored to and practiced on actual programs.

Although I believe it very important to include risk management on a wide variety of programs, it *is not* a silver bullet or a cure all. Good risk management *will not* lead to risk-free hardware, software, or integration—not even perfect risk management will do this because much is unknown and beyond the control of the program. Hence, whereas risk management can be valuable if performed effectively, it should not be oversold because this will inevitably lead to expectations that cannot be fulfilled.

This is not an introductory text on risk management—the book assumes a working knowledge of the subject. For those readers that need to brush up on risk management, or that have limited knowledge of the subject, please carefully read Chapter 2. This chapter was specifically written to provide a common understanding and a basis for the reader to delve into more advanced aspects of the risk management process and more effective ways to implement it. [I developed Chapter 2 in large part from the most recent DoD *Risk Management Guide for DoD Acquisition* available at the time of this writing (5th ed., June 2002). *This is quite simply the best introductory document on risk management that exists!*]

Whereas DoD is implementing acquisition reform to shift some attributes of its acquisition process toward that of commercial programs, risk management is an area where DoD represents the state of the art in process theory for project management applications. I believe that the risk management process outlined in Chapter 2 widely applies to commercial, government, and defense programs, is the best process that currently exists for project management applications, and has the most features in the fewest steps, coupled with a correct, logical order.

You may obtain a complete copy of the *Risk Management Guide for DoD Acquisition* free of charge (as of the time of this writing) by downloading an electronic copy from the Defense Acquisition University Web site. The URL is http://www.dau.mil/pubs/gdbks/risk_management.asp. Note: If this URL no longer works, contact the Defense Acquisition University, and not me, about an updated URL.

Although the entirety of this book is compatible with the *Risk Management Guide for DoD Acquisition*, I do not agree with 100% of the material contained within the guide, and I did not ask for DoD's endorsement to write this book. I was one of 20 to 30 people that made key contributions in the development of the *Risk Management Guide for DoD Acquisition* and have played a major role in updating every edition of the document to date. I did this as an unpaid technical advisor to the U.S. Air Force, Office of the Secretary of Defense, Defense Systems Management College, and Defense Acquisition University. Finally, I view the *Risk Management Guide for DoD Acquisition* and this book as complementing each other, rather than as substitutes. In effect, this book discusses how to implement sound risk management on a wide variety of defense, commercial, and other programs.

In many cases inadequate risk management can be alleviated by an enhanced process linked with more capable implementation. Unfortunately, some available books and training classes are replete with many technical errors, and the information provided is often at such an introductory level that only the simplest risk management process would be possible. The net result is likely to be an ineffective risk management process. In addition, a surprisingly large percentage of risk management facilitators and trainers whom I have met have little or no experience in implementing risk management on real programs along with having long-term accountability and responsibility to make it work. As one high-technology program manager, who is also a medical doctor, said "You can't learn surgery from reading a book—you need to successfully complete (surgical) residency." Would you want to receive surgery from an unqualified person? The same answer should apply to having an unqualified risk management facilitator or trainer.

Hopefully this book will help you create and implement risk management on your program or better evaluate an existing risk management process, find at least some of the shortfalls, and develop and implement needed enhancements. I also hope that you will gain the knowledge to evaluate and challenge where necessary the efficacy of an existing risk management process; all too often inadequate processes are used over and over again within an organization. For example, are all the process steps present, are they properly implemented, is the methodology both sufficient and accurate, is the documentation adequate, and are the results being used in decision making? In addition, I have included several examples and discussions of flawed risk analysis methodologies, in the hope that you will gain sufficient insight to recognize problems of the type mentioned, as well as the ability to evaluate other methodologies that are suspect. However, this book is not a cure all or cookbook for risk management. *The material contained in this book must be tailored to your program—something that requires knowledge, desire, and experience.* The knowledge this book contains must be coupled with the desire to learn and practical experience to yield the wisdom of how to implement risk management on your program, recognize problems (including those different than discussed in this book), and take correct, decisive action in resolving them. Dysfunctional organizations will often blindly attempt to apply information to a particular program without suitable, knowledgeable tailoring.

I have also found that the overall effectiveness of a risk management process is primarily determined by two factors, namely, technical sophistication and implementation efficiency. If you consider each of these factors a number from 0 to 1, *their product yields the overall effectiveness.* On many programs both the technical sophistication and implementation efficiency are relatively modest; hence, the overall effectiveness is somewhat low. It is typically far easier to increase the technical sophistication to an adequate level than to increase the implementation efficiency by the same level. Hence, increasing the process sophistication will result in an increase in overall effectiveness. However, if the process implementation efficiency remains low, so then will the overall process effectiveness. Thus, although improvements are often made to increase process sophistication, it is just as important to improve implementation efficiency. For example, on one program a process with moderate sophistication was used and was very well implemented. The result was an effective risk management process. Simultaneously, at the same company on a different program, a more sophisticated process was developed, but not well implemented. The result in the latter case was a relatively ineffective risk management process.

One of the key implementation issues that must often be addressed is how to overcome a corporate culture that is lacking or even negative toward risk management. Typically, a corrective effort must be done at *both* the top level (e.g., upper management, preferably the program manager, his deputy, or chief engineer, etc.) and lower level (e.g., working-level engineers) to be effective. I have also observed that position within a program can be uncorrelated with the expertise and desire to effectively perform risk management. Someone that can be well trained and has the desire to *practice* risk management is typically far more effective than others who "talk the talk but don't walk the walk." Unfortunately, in some organizations the level of true risk management knowledge and ability to implement it is inversely proportional to what individuals claim. Hopefully this book will increase the available level of knowledge about risk management, expose erroneous practices that exist, and contribute to eradicating such practices.

I have tried to focus this book toward *practitioners* that include both project-management personnel and technical analysts, ranging from upper management and high-level staff to lower working levels. Some of the material included in this book may be too technical for some nontechnical managers, whereas other material may encompass too much of the "soft sciences" for some engineers. I have tried to strike a balance between too much/little in technical vs soft science information provided because both disciplines are equally important in developing an effective risk management process. However, even nonpractitioners should find information they can use to do an initial diagnosis of some aspects of risk management process health prior to bringing a more knowledgeable person into the program.

I would also be remiss if I did not say that risk management can be *very political* in some programs. This can lead to biased decisions, whether unintentional or not. People that suppress adverse risk information may not even realize that the impact of issues they avoid early in the program can grow exponentially with time and have a very adverse affect when they later surface as problems. Unresolved risk issues, either intentionally overlooked or inadvertently missed because of a weak risk management process, will often cause severe negative cost, performance, and/or schedule (C,P,S) impact later in the program when the design trade space has considerably shrunk, and the ability to efficiently trade off C,P,S greatly diminishes. Although risk avoidance may sometimes be the best risk handling approach, program managers should not expect miracles to occur on demand to resolve risk-related issues that should have been properly dealt with much earlier. When the risk issues finally impact the program, crisis management is often practiced, whereas good risk management would be more effective both in preventing the problems in the first place and resolving them when they appear.

I have *intentionally* not mentioned the names of any specific programs, company and government organizations, or individuals involved in the examples in this book unless this information has previously been published in the open literature or it represents a positive contribution that warrants credit. It is my hope that the material provided will illustrate sound risk management attributes and practices. Although I generally did not use it, the detailed, critical approach can be both appropriate and valuable. For an excellent example of this approach applied to historiography, see David Hackett Fischer, *Historians' Fallacies; Toward a Logic of Historical Thought,* Harper-Collins, New York, 1970. Fischer's book is highly recommended for those involved with risk management because it provides a framework for evaluating the validity and efficacy of lessons learned, and other considerations.

Throughout this book I have assumed a risk neutral posture, rather than one that is risk averse or a risk taker, unless specifically stated. I also weight the probability of occurrence and consequence of occurrence risk terms *equally.* Some people and texts weight consequence of occurrence higher than probability of occurrence in developing risk levels, yet do not explain the fact that this is done or the underlying rationale. I disagree with this practice.

I use the term "probability" to indicate estimates and values associated with ordinal scales and other sources not related to actual probability data. Hence, these estimates and values are not probabilities and cannot yield actual risk, which requires both probability of occurrence and consequence of occurrence terms.

I have generally used the federal government to represent the buyer and the prime contractor to represent the seller in the examples presented. However, the buyer can span a range from any level of government (e.g., local, county, state, or federal) to an individual consumer (commercial applications). In addition, a prime contractor is a buyer with regard to its subcontractors, as is a purely commercial company seeking bids from other contractors. Similarly, subcontractors, as well as prime contractors, are sellers. Hence, the material in this book can be translated rather simply to a variety of different organizations and contracting roles by understanding who the buyer and seller are and what their roles encompass.

Because the focus of this book is on project risk management, I have not discussed financial risk management, which is relevant to the finance, banking, insurance, and other industries. However, the material presented is relevant to some projects undertaken by these industries, e.g., upgrading telecommunications capability. I have also not discussed risk management as it relates to public health, and safety, and have only a brief discussion on hazards. In addition, failure modes, effects, and criticality analysis; fault trees; reliability-related risk analysis; probabilistic risk analysis as tied to event trees; and risk analysis based upon Bayes' theorem are not discussed. Decision analysis is only briefly discussed, and only some aspects of setting up and running Monte Carlo simulations are covered in Chapter 6 because excellent sources already exist.

For example, two recent texts provide a comprehensive treatment of decision analysis and its potential application to risk analysis: Robert T. Clemen, *Making Hard Decisions,* 2nd edition, Duxbury Press, New York, 1996; and John W. Pratt, Howard Raiffa, and Robert Schlaifer, *Introduction to Statistical Decision Theory,* MIT Press, Cambridge, MA, 1995. (The latter text requires a fair degree of mathematical ability.) Three recent references contain useful information on setting up and running Monte Carlo simulations: Averill M. Law and W. David Kelton, *Simulation Modeling and Analysis,* 3rd edition, McGraw–Hill, New York, 2000; David Vose, *Quantitative Risk Analysis,* 2nd edition, Wiley, New York, 2000; and Stephen Gray, *Practical Risk Assessment for Project Management,* Wiley, New York, 1995.

Most of the Monte Carlo simulations performed in writing this book were generated from commercially available products. Those commercial software packages include 1) @RISK (Versions 4.5, 4.0, and 3.5, Palisade Corporation), 2) Crystal Ball (Versions 5.2 and 4.0, Decisioneering, Inc.), and 3) RISK + (Versions 2.0 and 1.5, C/S Solutions, Inc.). Statistical results were primarily generated from Microsoft Excel (Version 5.0 and Excel 97, Microsoft Corporation) and STATGRAPHICS Plus (Version 3.0 and 4.0 Manugistics, Inc., and Statistical Graphics Corporation). (Note: Contact the referenced companies for information about these products and their copyrights and trademarks.) Finally, mention of these commercial software packages does not constitute an endorsement of their use, their accuracy, or any other claim or warranty.

I have used the phrase cet. par. (short for ceteris paribus) in this book to indicate a situation where everything else is held constant. For example, if you examine cost vs performance relationships, you should assume that schedule is held constant (or cet. par.) for the item(s) being evaluated.

In the first edition of this book I mentioned that scope could be a proxy for performance. This is incorrect—scope encompasses cost, performance, and schedule, and not simply performance. Hence, scope is not a viable proxy for performance and should not be used because of the correlation it may also have with cost and schedule.

Features, functions, and integration complexity often have similar characteristics of and result in the same risk-related problems associated with performance that are discussed in this book. Substantial cost overruns and schedule slips can occur even on relatively low-technology programs that have a high-integration complexity (e.g., civilian megaprojects such as subways), or a large number of features or functions (e.g., commercial software development projects). Hence, throughout this book, you can generally substitute the number of features and functions and the level of integration complexity as rough proxy for the level of performance relative to risk issues. [For example, as a project's integration complexity increases, the level of risk will generally increase (cet. par.).]

I use italics for emphasis. Finally, I have used the pronoun *his* for both males and females as a means to simplify the writing and editing of the text. In no instance is one sex assumed more or less capable of performing risk management than the other.

Although separate definitions are sometimes used for project vs program, I have not segregated the terms in this book. For example, the Project Management Institute *A Guide to the Project Management Body of Knowledge (PMBOK® Guide)*, 2000, p. 204 defines the word *project* as a "temporary endeavor undertaken to create a unique product, service, or result" and the word *program* as a "group of related projects managed in a coordinated way. Programs usually contain an element of ongoing work." I do not disagree with these definitions, but in risk management there can be a blurring between the terms project and program that makes the distinction in definitions difficult and somewhat artificial. For example, large-scale development activities often have a substantial time horizon (e.g., many years) and may be single items (e.g., line item) from a funding perspective. Hence, they may not be a temporary endeavor depending upon one's definition of temporary (thus leaning toward the term program). In other instances they may be viewed as a collection of items from a funding perspective (thus leaning toward the term program), yet may result in a single product (thus leaning toward the term project).

If you have examples of successful risk management tips to practice or traps to avoid beyond those given here, please e-mail them to me, and I will consider them for a future printing. Please indicate whether or not you wish to be credited for providing the information—I am perfectly willing to do so, but in some cases you may wish to remain anonymous for publication. Finally, the views expressed in this book are my own and not necessarily those of AIAA; nor the U. S. government or any of its agencies, organizations, and services; or those of any commercial organization.

Edmund H. Conrow
P. O. Box 1125
Redondo Beach, California 90278
(310) 374-7975
info@risk-services.com
www.risk-services.com
10 March 2003

Acknowledgments

I am very grateful to Arthur Alexander (Japan Economic Institute, and formerly of RAND) and Giles Smith (formerly of RAND) who helped me during 1985–1993 to develop the microeconomic framework presented in Chapter 1 and Appendix C. Giles Smith also assisted me in collecting and editing the schedule data analyzed in Appendix K.

Several people and organizations made major contributions in completing the questionnaire used for assessing probability statements discussed in Appendix I. These include Warren Greczyn (Analytical Services, Inc.), Mike Wakshull, and the Los Angeles Chapter of the Project Management Institute. I am also thankful that William Harris (formerly of RAND) informed me about the fine estimative probability work of Sherman Kent, a summary of which is included in Appendix J. Finally, I note and thank my late father and mother for introducing me to science as a child; encouraging me to create, investigate, and explore; and the support and encouragement they provided throughout my professional career.

Chapter 1
Introduction and Need for Risk Management

I. Introduction

Although there are exceptions, many development projects encounter cost overruns and schedule slippage, and some also have performance degradations. Such development problems can lead to adverse impacts during the production phase as well. For example, development-phase schedule slippage can adversely affect when rate production will occur. In addition, a hardware design that pushes the state of the art can sometimes lead to increased recurring production cost (e.g., because of problems with yield). Although such problems have historically existed on U.S. Department of Defense (DoD) and NASA programs, they are likewise common on a wide variety of commercial and other government programs. (A brief comparison of commercial vs DoD/NASA program acquisition and risk management is given in Appendix A.)

Whereas some issues that can affect risk, such as budget cuts, are beyond the control of the project team(s), others, such as initiating programs with insufficient budget and schedule for the desired level of performance and continued overoptimism during the course of the program, are often within the control of the project team(s). A very early documented example of such problems and the need for risk management follows:

> "Suppose one of you wants to build a tower. Will he not first sit down and estimate the cost to see if he has enough money to complete it? For if he lays the foundation and is not able to finish it, everyone who sees it will ridicule him, saying, "This fellow began to build and was not able to finish."[1] *Luke 14 : 28-30*

Risk management is essential for a wide variety of development and production programs because certain information about key project cost, performance, and schedule (C,P,S) attributes are often uncertain or unknown until late in the program. Risk issues that can be identified early in the program, which will potentially impact the program later, are often termed known unknowns and can be alleviated with a good risk management process. (This assumes that a technically sufficient process exists, is suitably implemented, and adequate resources can be allocated to identified issues.) For those issues that are beyond the vision of the project team(s), such as an unanticipated budget cut (often termed unknown unknowns), a good, properly implemented risk management process can help to quantify rapidly the issue's impact and develop sound plans for alleviating its effect.

"Risk management is concerned with the outcome of future events, whose exact outcome is unknown, and with how to deal with these uncertainties (e.g., a range of possible outcomes). In general, outcomes are categorized as favorable or unfavorable, and risk management is the art and science of planning, assessing (identifying and analyzing), handling, and monitoring future events to ensure favorable outcomes."[2] Thus, a good risk management process is proactive in nature and is fundamentally different than crisis management (or problem solving), which is reactive. In addition, crisis management is a resource-intensive process that is normally constrained by a restricted set of available options, which is partly because the longer it takes for problems to surface within a program the fewer options to resolve them typically exist. The adverse C,P,S impacts associated with those options are likely to be substantially greater than if the issues had been identified much earlier in the program. (This is in part because C,P,S cannot be traded perfectly in the short run.)

In the remainder of this chapter, I will 1) explore some C,P,S outcomes from historical development projects; 2) present a simplified microeconomic framework for understanding some underlying causes of many risk issues within the control of the program; and 3) discuss the need for risk management.

In subsequent chapters I will discuss a risk management process that can be used on a wide variety of commercial, government, and defense programs to help alleviate potential risk issues.

II. Some Historical Program Outcomes

C,P,S variates are often used to measure the outcomes of a variety of projects. Historically, various types of development projects typically experience cost growth and schedule slippage and can also experience performance shortfalls when actual values following completion of the development phase are compared to initial or early development estimates.

Marshall and Meckling were perhaps the first to evaluate C,P,S variations using a historical sample of DoD development programs.[3] They evaluated aircraft and missile programs with equivalent engineering and manufacturing development (EMD), see Appendix B, phase start dates in the 1940s and 1950s. They found the average ratio of the most recent and earliest production cost estimates to be between 2.4 and 3.2. [A ratio (change value) > 1 indicates cost or schedule growth or performance degradation.] This corresponds to a 140 to 220% increase in cost. They also found the average schedule change to be 1.5 between early estimates of first operational dates and the actual first operational dates (or a 50% increase in schedule). (Note:

In April 2002 the DoD introduced a change to its acquisition phases and milestones. See Appendix B for a discussion of the new and previous acquisition phases and milestones. Since at the time of this writing the majority of the historical and in-progress programs were developed and produced under the previous acquisition phases and milestones, I have continued to use the old that terminology rather than the new terminology.)

Commenting on the cost growth and schedule slippage, Marshall and Meckling said: "Availability (schedule) predictions, like cost predictions, exhibit both a decided bias toward overoptimism and substantial variation in the extent of the optimism."[3] Perry et al. estimated C,P,S change ratios for a sample of DoD programs with EMD (or equivalent) start dates in the 1950s and 1960s. They found the average C,P,S change to be 1.44, 1.05, and 1.15, respectively.[4] Dews et al. estimated these same ratios for a sample of DoD programs with EMD (or equivalent) start dates in the 1970s. They found the average C,P,S change to be 1.34, 1.00, and 1.13, respectively.[5]

I evaluated a large sample of DoD programs (primarily aircraft and missiles) that had EMD (or equivalent) start dates of the late 1950s to late 1980s and that had reached initial operational capability. Of these programs, 43 of 48 (90%) exhibited cost growth and 40 of 51 programs (78%) exhibited schedule slippage, even when the initial benchmark was taken relatively late in the development phase (start of engineering development). In this case the average cost change and schedule change ratios were 1.26 and 1.24, respectively. However, on average, there was no performance degradation (ratio of 1.00).[6] Although the average cost growth for the Conrow data set is 26%, the dollar magnitude of military program cost growth associated with this is substantial.

It was only possible to identify confidently the dollar magnitude of cost growth for 30 of the 48 programs having cost change data. Initial EMD phase cost estimates for the Conrow data set were compared to actual values recorded following the completion of this program phase. The resulting total cost growth of this sample was $10.9 billion (FY94). When projected to all military development programs over the past 35 years, including concept exploration and program definition and risk reduction phases (see Appendix B) in addition to the EMD phase, the resulting total development cost growth is likely between $40 and $80 billion (FY94)! Cost and schedule growth occurred in each of these program samples, but where performance results were evaluated, virtually no change was observed.[6]

The same preferences, interactions, and outcomes also exist for highly classified programs given the structure of their acquisition process. For example, the Government Accounting Office (GAO) found "no major difference between the cost, schedule, and performance results of the special access acquisition programs it sampled and those of non-special access DoD programs."[7]

Several insightful observations exist in the literature as to the causes of military system cost and schedule growth that also apply in some cases to commercial and other government programs. One likely cause was first identified by Marshall and Meckling:

> Typically, in weapons development great emphasis is placed on performance. Most new weapons are developed around specific detailed performance requirements laid down by the military—requirements that are taken very seriously. The penalties incurred by the contractors for not meeting performance requirements are more severe than for failure to meet availability schedules or failure to live within original cost estimates. As a result, whenever circumstances dictate a retreat from early plans, it is usually the costs and/or availability that gives ground.[3]

The government and contractors in the 1940s–1980s typically faced only weak disincentives for developing unrealistic estimates of program cost and schedule, as identified by Marshall and Meckling:

> "Contractors are anxious to have their proposals accepted by the military, and the military itself is anxious to have development proposals supported by the Department of Defense and Congress. The incentive to make optimistic estimates is thus very strong. On the other hand, the contractual penalties for having been overoptimistic are generally small."[3]

The acquisition process of U.S. military systems has been distorted in this way for many years. Hitch and McKean stated it in the following manner in 1960:

> "Excessive optimism in drawing up performance specifications can make the development so difficult that it must fail, or take much longer and cost much more than planned, or require a downgrading of the requirements. It is not unusual for weapon system requirements to be so optimistic that several inventions or advances in the state of the art are needed on schedule if the development is to succeed."[8]

The GAO identified several issues that may lead to problems in major weapons acquisition, including overly optimistic cost and schedule estimates leading to program instability and cost increases, programs that cannot be executed as planned with available funds, and programs being oversold to survive.[9]

A similar statement on the problems present in the DoD systems acquisition process was made by the GAO:

"All 12 of the missile systems we selected (for analysis) experienced cost and schedule overruns . . . These overruns can be attributed to many interrelated factors, some of which are not under DoD's direct control (e.g., changes in threat, congressional direction, etc.). However, optimistic planning assumptions by program officials were a common factor underlying major overruns. Program offices often develop cost and schedule estimates that do not adequately reflect the risks associated with the program's design, development, and production. We found that this is particularly true for technical risk assumptions, which often contribute to cost and schedule overruns."[10]

Another statement of the distorted military system development process was made by the U.S. Air Force Acquisition Process Review Team on Clear Accountability in Design:

"The contractor and government program management team overestimates technology readiness, downplays potential problems, and fails to plan and perform adequate risk management at program initiation and throughout the program, resulting in unexpected cost overruns, schedule delays, and technical compromise. Initial impacts surface as early as Dem/Val and continue throughout succeeding program phases. These effects exist on all programs to varying degrees."[11]

Some additional reasons stated by the GAO that are likely related to designs that later exhibit C,P,S problems include optimistic program projections, unrealistic C,P,S estimates, and excessive risk.[12] In summary, distortions in the military systems acquisition process that can lead to considerable cost and schedule growth have been noted for the past 35 to 40 years and validated in part by data going back to the 1940s and 1950s.

At first glance cost overruns and schedule slippage may appear to be a DoD-only problem. Unfortunately, such problems are prevalent on a wide variety of commercial and other government programs. I will now present a few examples illustrating these issues.

The average cost change and schedule change ratios for large-scale (e.g., refinery) civilian megaproject plants were 1.88 and 1.17, respectively, over roughly 46 plants.[13] The GAO examined a sample of NASA space programs and found considerable cost growth and schedule slippage.[14] Analysis of a reduced, conservative sample of 10 programs from the data set the GAO collected indicated that 9 of the 10 programs had cost growth and all 10 programs had schedule slippage. In this case the average cost change and schedule change ratios were 1.87 and 1.94, respectively, from contract initiation to first launch. Similarly, for a sample of 10 Federal Aviation Administration development programs, 7 of the 10 programs had cost growth, and the average cost change ratio was 2.6.[15] [The authors of Ref. 15 found that the major sources of cost growth were requirements uncertainty/growth, software development programs, human factors acceptability, and commercial off-the-shelf (COTS) integration complexity.] Although software development activities were included in a number of these programs, it is interesting to examine software-intensive projects to see how well their development has typically fared.

A survey by the Standish Group of 365 respondents and 8380 commercial software-intensive projects indicated that 53% of the projects were challenged: they were over budget, behind schedule, or had fewer features and functions than originally specified, and 31% of the projects were canceled. Although 16% of the sample apparently came in on budget, on schedule, and with the specified features and functions, 84% did not. On average, these challenged and canceled projects had cost change and schedule change ratios of 2.89 and 3.22, respectively, comparing original estimates vs those at the time they were completed or canceled. In addition, the completed projects had an average of only 61% of the originally specified features and functions.[16]

Other examples of substantial cost growth and schedule slippage exist for a variety of public and private sector projects. (See, for example, the President's Blue Ribbon Commission on Defense Management, "A Formula for Action," April 1986, p. 38.) Budget overruns and delays in time to market are well publicized and not uncommon in the motion picture industry. (Here, the integration complexity of the film development project is a close and suitable substitute for performance.)

Although the specific sources of C,P,S difficulty may vary from one project to the next, they are generally associated with different preferences held by the government program office and contractors, coupled with a poor understanding of the range of possible C,P,S outcomes (including risk), which themselves are conditioned by program structure.

III.   Microeconomic Framework[6,17]

The following framework is provided for government–contractor interactions in DoD, highly classified, and NASA programs.[6,17] It helps to explain several sources of risk within the control of a program and the need for risk management and can be readily modified and used for commercial and other government programs (although the results are not presented here). (Appendix C compares some predictions from the microeconomic framework to C,P,S outcomes from DoD programs.)

In acquiring U.S. defense, highly classified, and NASA systems, the government and contractor each have a set of objectives regarding the projected C,P,S outcomes. The government generally prefers lower over higher cost and schedule and higher performance. The contractor generally prefers higher over lower cost, performance, and schedule. [Note: Features, functions, and integration complexity can generally be directly substituted for performance (cet. par.). In this framework I focus on interactions at the government program office level. Tradeoffs within the government outside the program office are externalities that vary on a case-by-case basis (e.g., lead to funding fluctuations) and are not addressed here.]

Lower costs are desirable to the government to develop more military systems for a fixed budget (or the same number for a reduced expenditure). Shorter schedules that enable the system to become operational earlier enhance the force structure and military balance of power. Higher performance permits increased operational capability for the mission.

Contractors prefer higher costs because they increase profits (cet. par.). Longer schedules are also desirable to maintain a stable work force and a long-term working relationship with the government, which gives the contractor a potential competitive advantage for follow-on or future contracts. Contractors prefer high performance to improve their potential competitive advantage in the high technology arena.

The production schedule is generally set by high-level government organizations (e.g., the military services or Congress), based upon inputs from the project office and contractors (e.g., cost vs lot quantity). Hence, the production schedule can generally be characterized as a constraint externally imposed by higher-level government personnel.

Given the government and contractor preferences, the next step is to consider programmatic and technical constraints associated with C,P,S. The government will typically have in mind a maximum program cost and schedule length, along with minimum performance. The contractor will often have its own minimum cost and schedule length.

Government and contractor motivations to start and continue programs initially bias downward both parties' estimates of cost and schedule for a given level of performance, leading—later in the program—to increased cost or schedule in order to meet performance requirements. The issue faced by government and industry is how to adjust their C,P,S goals to be consistent with the technological possibilities that are being revealed to them.

Because both government and contractor utility decrease with lower performance, both parties may only reluctantly decrease performance requirements during development even when the originally chosen solution is infeasible. Hence, an unrealistic C,P,S starting point results in a C,P,S solution point that is not an unbiased or random choice between C,P,S, leading to increased cost and schedule, but little decrease in performance.

A technical possibility surface encompasses the region of feasible C,P,S

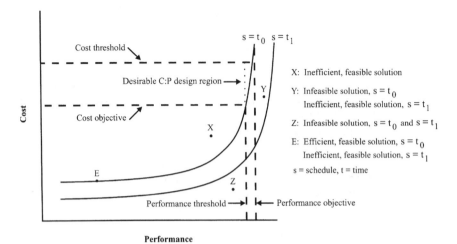

Fig. 1.1   Design feasibility—cost vs performance.

designs and is a technical program constraint. A two-dimensional slice of this surface is somewhat analogous to a production possibility curve in microeconomics. Points on the technical possibility surface or any two-dimensional slice of the surface indicate an efficient (but not necessarily optimal) design. This is given by point E on the cost vs performance (C:P) possibility curve in Fig. 1.1 (for a given schedule, $s = t_0$). Points on the C:P curve are efficient (but not necessarily optimal), such that no increase in performance can be obtained without a corresponding increase in cost, and no decrease in cost can be obtained without a decrease in performance. Points lying above a possibility curve indicate feasible, but inefficient designs. This is given by point X in Fig. 1.1. Here, the design is an inefficient combination of cost and performance because the system could be developed at the same cost but with higher performance by moving to the right (east) or at the same level of performance with less cost by moving down (south).

Those points below or to the right of a possibility curve indicate an infeasible design. This is given by point Y in Fig. 1.1. A point below or to the right of the C:P curve (Y in Fig. 1.1) is infeasible for a given set of input constraints (e.g., manufacturing processes, technology level, program structure) and for a given schedule. In effect, design Y corresponds to an inappropriate schedule length ($s = t_0$) selected for the specified cost and performance levels. At a later time the same design may either remain infeasible or become feasible efficient or feasible inefficient depending upon changes in the input constraints. For example, in Fig. 1.1 the initially infeasible design (Y) at $s = t_0$ is feasible and inefficient at a later time $s = t_1$ based upon changes in the input constraints. [However, another infeasible design (point Z) at $s = t_0$ remains infeasible at $s = t_1$.] This point (Y) will only become feasible with a shift down or to the right of the entire C:P curve, thus requiring, for example, improved yield for a manufacturing process if cost is held constant. For a given, constant range of performance, the shifted curve $s = t_1$ may also flatten somewhat because the magnitudes of the first and second derivative of cost relative to performance are potentially smaller. This will be more likely to occur as the performance region of interest corresponds to the near vertical portion of the original C:P curve ($s = t_0$).

The dashed lines in Fig. 1.1, bounded by the C:P curve, set forth the desired solution space or design region for $s = t_0$. Here, the cost threshold represents the maximum cost that the government (buyer) will pay, while the cost objective is the minimum likely contractor (seller) cost that will result. The performance threshold is the lowest acceptable level of performance acceptable to the government resulting from the requirements allocation and subsequent design activity, while the performance objective is the desired level of performance. (Note: For key performance parameters, having a resulting level of performance below the threshold value will lead to a milestone review and possible program termination. For other performance requirements, having performance below the threshold is negotiable and may be acceptable if a substantial cost savings is possible.) The resulting desirable C:P design region for $s = t_0$ is thus bounded by the C:P curve, the performance threshold and performance objective, and the cost threshold and cost objective.

Actual C:P curves are given in Fig. 1.2 for a common, commercially available microprocessor. (Although this information may appear dated, it is a valid example of the C:P relationship that exists for many different items, independent of time.) Here, data for microprocessors from the same family are plotted as normalized price vs normalized performance (clock rate). (The assumption is made here that price is a valid proxy for cost.) The only key performance attribute that affects price is the variation in microprocessor clock rate. In all cases the lower limit of normalized performance presented (0.54) corresponds to a 90-MHz clock rate. Data for April, June, and August 1996 include an upper limit of performance (1.00) corresponding to a 166-MHz clock rate, whereas that for September and November 1996 has an upper limit of performance (1.20) corresponding to a 200-MHz clock rate. The 200-MHz processor was initially offered in September 1996. Data were obtained from the same wholesale vendor during this time to eliminate potential pricing variations between sources. Finally, all price data were normalized against the April 1996 166-MHz microprocessor price.

The first and second derivatives of price vs performance are positive in each case for the microprocessor data set in the normalized performance range between 0.80 to 1.00 for the April through August 1996 data (corresponding to 133- to 166-MHz clock rates). Similarly, the first and second derivatives of price vs performance are positive in each case for the micro-

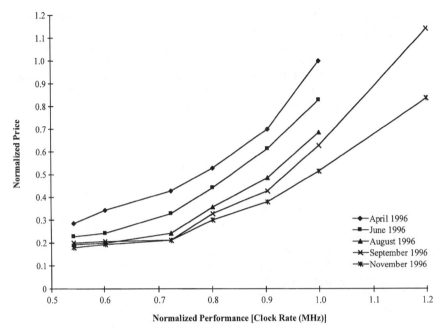

Fig. 1.2   Normalized microprocessor price vs performance.

processor data set in the normalized performance range between 0.80 to 1.20 for the September and November 1996 data (corresponding to 133- to 200-MHz clock rates). (Positive first and second derivatives of price vs performance commonly occur near the upper limit of achievable performance for a wide variety of commercial, government, and DoD items. See Appendix D for a summary of some results.)

Note also that there is a tendency for the C:P curve to shift downward vs time in this range—clearly evident for microprocessors with normalized performance ≥ 0.80 (corresponding to a clock rate ≥ 133 MHz). The curves can also be viewed as shifting to the right when higher performance parts are introduced (e.g., when the 200-MHz microprocessor was introduced in September 1996). This is consistent with the theoretical discussion just presented. (Note: For microprocessors with normalized performance ≤ 0.72, corresponding to a clock rate of ≤ 120 MHz, economic considerations associated with reduced demand contributed to parts having only small reductions in price with time, although the first and second derivatives of price vs performance are positive even in this range for most cases.)

The last few percent of the maximum performance possible will lead to increasingly greater program risk as well as cost and schedule length because the first and second derivatives of cost and schedule with respect to perform-ance are positive. (This is consistent with the C:P curves in Fig. 1.2 for normal-ized performance ≥ 0.80.) This potential cost and schedule growth can lead to major problems in commercial and military systems when relatively high levels of performance are specified for development programs, yet insuffi-cient cost and/or schedule are typically allocated to achieve the desired level of performance.

The postulated characteristics of the C:P slice of the technical possibility surface are also evident in an elegant figure developed by Norman Augustine. The figure includes a number of highly diverse commercial and military items that have similar normalized C:P curve shapes and positive first and second derivatives of cost with respect to performance to the data given in Fig. 1.2 (Ref. 18). Augustine states that, "A disproportionate share of the cost of most purchase is concentrated in a very small fraction of the features sought. So-called extras are particularly flagrant contributors to cost in both the commercial and government marketplaces."[18] A discussion of Augustine's results, including additional data points supplied by this author, is given in Appendix D.

Knowledge of the technical possibility surface, or even two-dimensional slices of the surface (such as the C:P curves in Fig. 1.2), is often unknown or highly uncertain for key subsystems until late in the development phase or even the production phase. An uncertain technical possibility surface can lead to severe program risk when performance levels approach or exceed the highly uncertain state of the art, particularly when program cost and sched-ule characteristics are not considered in an unbiased fashion. When ambi-tious performance requirements are set and the design process is dominated by performance, pressure exists on the government and contractor alike to meet these requirements, even if program cost and schedule are adversely affected as a result.

By the time the problem is usually recognized, a considerable investment has already been made in the existing system design. Hence, the flexibility to alter the design may be limited, leading to higher program risk and even greater cost or schedule growth than if the true situation had been recog-nized at the beginning of the program when performance requirements were specified and the initial C,P,S design was set.

In addition, there is a common underestimation bias in estimating the likely level of C,P,S that can be achieved. The net result may be $C\uparrow$, $S\uparrow$, and $P\downarrow$. (For aerospace programs this typically translates to $C\uparrow$ and/or $S\uparrow$, and P held nearly constant given the preferences discussed in this section and Appendix C.) This effect is generally more pronounced for "bottoms-up" estimates (e.g., engineering cost estimates) vs those derived by other methods; particularly for programs that require relatively high levels of performance.

If the C,P,S design lies in the infeasible region, such as point Y in Fig. 1.1, resolution of this unsustainable situation requires upward (north) movement of the design until the C:P curve is crossed, which leads to increased cost, to the left (west) with decreasing performance or a combination of the two. Because the utility of both parties decreases with decreasing performance, this will generally not occur unless it is externally mandated. Hence, design change will tend to be toward the north (increasing cost) rather than toward the west (decreasing performance), bounded by the technical possibility curve, and the resulting design will also generally be inefficient (e.g., lying above this curve, as point X in Fig. 1.1).

Because both government and contractor utility increase with increasing performance and this has historically often dominated the design choice process, the magnitude of program risk can be substantial when the initial C,P,S design is relatively high up on the technical possibility surface (e.g., a normalized performance ≥ 0.80 in the C:P curves in Fig. 1.2). Such a design may cause large development, and even production, cost, or schedule growth if the initial design is unrealistic, particularly if impractical performance requirements are not relaxed.

True shifts in the technical possibility surface can occur with time because of technological changes, such as the availability of an improved technology, improvements in manufacturing process yield, redesigns, and other considerations. However, these shifts may be unrelated to the initial development phase C,P,S design, which is typically set without detailed analysis or consideration by high-level government and contractor decision makers.

In summary, the government and contractor may have little knowledge of the feasibility of the initial C,P,S design nor the technical possibility surface during the early to midpart of the development phase, particularly for complex systems. This relatively large uncertainty, thus risk, results from both random and bias components associated with government and contractor preferences, which typically lean toward increasing performance, as well as uncertainty associated with the surface itself. The concept exploration and program definition and risk reduction program phases of DoD programs represent that part of the military system acquisition process where design changes are relatively easy to accommodate (in terms of C,P,S). Hence, foregoing detailed, unbiased, C,P,S trade studies and failing to implement the results into the design in the early portion of the development phase can propagate potential C,P,S issues (e.g., an infeasible design) into actual problems (e.g., increased cost, schedule, and risk) later in the program's development and production phases.

The performance-driven choice process becomes all the more troublesome when the starting point is relatively high up on the technical possibility surface. Such a choice may increase program risk and lead to large subsequent cost or schedule growth if the C,P,S starting point is unrealistic, particularly if impractical performance requirements are not relaxed. The resulting cost and schedule growth will generally lead to increased contractor profit. Because contractor utility increases with increasing profit, they have little reason to decrease cost and schedule, particularly when in a sole source role late in the development phase.

Enhancing risk management and placing equal or near-equal emphasis on meeting program cost and schedule, as well as performance objectives, will be necessary to eliminate the strongly ingrained government and contractor program management bias favoring performance that has existed since at least the 1940s in U. S. military systems. This is particularly important given the substantial dollar magnitude associated with cost growth during this time. No appreciable change in program outcomes is likely to occur without a reoriented C,P,S emphasis.

IV. Need for Risk Management

Several other considerations exist that warrant increased emphasis on risk management in addition to those related to uncertainty in trading C,P,S plus historical biases toward performance just discussed. (Although the material in this section was developed independently, some of the ideas were also mentioned by Dana Spears and Ron VanLaningham.)

Since the early to mid-1990s, substantial cuts have occurred in the overall DoD budget for development and procurement of weapon systems. Some government organizations that traditionally have had large budgets which often increased in times of need have, in the last several years, experienced budget cuts causing the stretchout and even termination of some programs. [As one high-level manager of such an organization said: "The wheelbarrows of cash are now going in the opposite direction" (meaning that instead of additional funds arriving to cover cost overruns, budget cuts are now occurring).] Such problems are not limited to the DoD, its services, and certain government organizations.

Other government organizations and commercial industry have also been substantially affected. During the 1990s, there has been an overall industry trend toward consolidation and downsizing, which has sometimes resulted in fewer qualified people and smaller budgets to develop new programs often with challenging performance and schedule requirements. This trend is exasperated when coupled with increased shareholder expectations in the market place (e.g., the need for sustained, high return on investment). For example, NASA is also facing a changing acquisition environment and has instituted a number of acquisition reforms. Some changes in the NASA acquisition process (extracted from Ref. 19) in the late 1990s include but are not limited to:

1) "the use of full-cost accounting,"
2) "performance-based contracting,"
3) "life-cycle-cost decision making,"
4) "the use of COTS for products and services,"

5) "a renewed emphasis on past performance in source selection,"
6) "emphasis on best value in source selections,"
7) "a shift to voluntary and consensus standards," and
8) "the use of a single process initiative."

One acquisition strategy embraced by the NASA director is the desire to acquire many of its key systems for planetary and interplanetary observations in a faster, better, cheaper manner. Far from an esoteric mantra, there is considerable pressure on many NASA programs to implement a shorter development and production schedule, have equivalent if not greater performance than in the past, and reduce development and production costs. Commercial industry has also recognized that reducing development cost and time to market are key considerations for profitability, and even survival. (A brief comparison of commercial vs DoD/NASA program acquisition and risk management is given in Appendix A.)

Given this situation, it is clear that performance-dominated designs may no longer be accepted carte blanche at any cost and schedule for both government and industry. For example, the DoD and its services are implementing Cost as an Independent Variable (CAIV)—an initiative to rebalance the trade space away from a performance-dominant position toward one where cost, performance, schedule, and risk are evaluated.[20] CAIV principles are required on all major defense programs.[21] Additional emphasis is also being placed on reducing total ownership cost and reducing the development time of DoD programs. These activities by the DoD and its services mirror characteristics of good commercial practices used for some time by industry.

One result of such trends is an increase in program risk (cet. par.) and the need for enhanced risk management, both in terms of a more viable process and one that is more effectively implemented. For example, NASA management has recognized that their desire for faster, better, cheaper systems makes enhanced risk management a necessity, not just a "nice to have."[22] On programs where there are strong cost and schedule constraints, yet high performance requirements, there is typically a high opportunity cost and little ability to correct mistakes (e.g., dealing with risks late in the development phase that should have been identified much earlier). Whereas enhanced risk management is desirable for a wide variety of projects to better allocate scarce resources, it is particularly important for high-performance projects where large, adverse impacts can occur. Nobel Laureate Richard Feynman made the following observation, as part of the Presidential Commission on the Space Shuttle *Challenger* Accident. It directly applies to the need for risk management on almost all programs with high performance, including those with a large number of features or functions, and high integration complexity.

"They must live in reality in comparing the costs and utility of the shuttle to other methods of entering space. And they must be realistic in making contracts, in estimating costs, and the difficulty of the projects. Only realistic flight schedules should be proposed, schedules that have a reasonable chance of being met. If in this way the government would not support them, then so be it. NASA owes it to the citizens from whom it asks support to be frank, honest, and informative, so that these citizens can make the wisest decisions for the use of their limited resources. For a successful technology, reality must take precedence over public relations, for nature cannot be fooled."[23]

If you don't have time to perform effective risk management you will often later have to find additional time (and budget) to develop and implement changes to the program. Regardless of the contract type used and cost sharing arrangements for funding changes, the impact of failed opportunities to effectively perform risk management early in the program will typically be much more detrimental to the buyer and/or seller later in the program. This is in part because the ability to resolve cost, performance, and/or schedule issues tends to diminish as a product matures in its development cycle because the trade space between these variables tends to shrink with time. Hence, it is often better to resolve potential issues when they are identified rather than "betting" that they can be solved later in the development cycle. Often, on moderate to large programs one or two averted risks (issues dealt with that don't become problems later in the program) may pay for all risk management on the program.

An effective risk management process can potentially improve an organization's reputation by assisting it to better trade and meet C,P,S objectives. Conversely, organizations that practice poor risk management increase the likelihood of functioning in a crisis management mode (cet. par.). In the long run this may lead to reduced contract awards, decreased market share, lost revenue, etc. As members of one large corporation that develops and manufactures air conditioners for home use stated: "It is hard to sell air conditioners in September in the Northern Hemisphere," meaning, if they miss the critical summer delivery date to retail sellers, they have effectively missed the entire market year in the Northern Hemisphere. An effective risk management process can also improve the accuracy of management reports used both internal and external to the organization. Conversely, poor risk management can introduce considerable uncertainty, if not errors, into such reports. This can lead to faulty projects that in the worst case can adversely affect the entire organization.

While specific implementation details may vary across industries, effective risk management is needed on a large variety of development and production projects. For example, many construction projects are relatively "low tech," yet cost growth and schedule slippage of 100% or more is not uncommon for one-of-a-kind projects. Thus, do not assume that some industries have less need for project risk management based upon the degree of technological advancement needed, or the relative degree of maturity that the industry appears to possess.

Risk management can also be a key tool when competitive situations exist, and can contribute to winning a source selection. In one case a higher performance, but higher risk, design existed. Here, an excellent risk management process including risk handling plans, demonstrated a credible risk reduction path and contributed to the team with the higher performance and risk design win. When competitive development exists risk management can be a key insight tool for the buyer as well as demonstrating competence by the seller, and building confidence for both parties. Conversely, a poor risk management process may provide the buyer with little confidence or reason to select a seller, and when one seller has a superior risk management process over another, this can be a key advantage in source selection.

When done properly, risk management can be a key process that can provide valuable program insight. But, as discussed in Chapter 3, this requires that cost, performance (technical), and schedule risk management activities be effectively performed and integrated. It also requires that risk management be effectively integrated with other key top-level program processes (program management and systems engineering) lower-level processes (e.g., cost analysis, design, and schedule analysis to name a few), and a fundamental shift in the attitude of both program management from reactive problem solvers to proactive risk managers to be effective. The following statement is a telling indication of this shift in position: "Unfortunately, in the past, some program managers and decision makers have viewed risk as something to be avoided. Any program that had risk was subject to intense review and oversight. This attitude has changed. DoD managers recognize that risk is inherent in any program and that it is necessary to analyze future program events to identify potential risks and take measures to handle them."[2] Likewise, risk management should be considered by working-level program personnel on a day-to-day basis as part of their job function. *This does not suggest that everyone should become a risk manager, but that risk management should be considered and performed by all program personnel.* Unless these and other considerations are properly executed, the value of risk management performed on a program will be substantially reduced.

Risk management principles are required on all major defense programs.[24] *However, this does not guarantee that an effective risk management process will exist on any program.* In 1986 the GAO developed five criteria that they considered essential in the assessment of technical risk. These criteria include the following:[25]

1) "prospective risk assessments" (consider possible future technical problems),
2) "planned and systematic risk assessment,"
3) "attention to technical risk,"
4) "documentation of procedures and results," and
5) "reassessment in each acquisition phase."

Of the 25 programs examined by the GAO only 3, or 12% had adequately performed all 5 items.[25] Although this study is now between one and two decades old and the criteria are somewhat simplistic, I still routinely see deficiencies with items 2, 3, and 4 (in the previous list) to this day!

Under Secretary of Defense Paul Kaminski's 4 December 1995 memo that promulgated CAIV also recognized the need for enhanced risk management—without an effective risk management process, CAIV would not be successful. This, and other considerations, led to a substantial effort to upgrade risk management capability within the DoD and Services during 1996–1997.[2] The result, published in the Defense Acquisition Deskbook and Department of Defense *Risk Management Guide for DoD Acquisition,* is a world-class risk management process and a substantial enhancement over prior DoD risk management processes. [The risk management team was comprised of personnel from the Office of the Secretary of Defense, U.S. Air Force, U.S. Army, U.S. Navy, Defense Acquisition University, Defense Systems Management College, Institute of Defense Analysis, consultants, other relevant organizations and included inputs from the aerospace and commercial industry. The material published in the Defense Acquisition Deskbook and the March 1998 Department of Defense *Risk Management Guide for DoD Acquisition* is a substantial upgrade over previous DoD positions on risk management, which included Department of Defense, "Risk Assessment Techniques," Defense Systems Management College, 1st ed. July 1983; and Department of Defense, "Risk Management Concepts and Guidance," Defense Systems Management College, March 1989. (This material was released to the public in 1998 and updated in 1999, 2000, 2001, and 2002 as the Department of Defense, *Risk Management Guide for DoD Acquisition,* Defense Acquisition University, currently 5th ed. June 2002.)] Although some commercial and international organizations might shy away from using this DoD risk management guide, *it is the best introductory document on risk management that exists.*

While the need to perform effective risk management is great, there will likely be a decline in the credibility of project risk management over the next few years that will continue as long as the project management community tolerates it. This is in large part related to overblown promises of promoters coupled with flawed research methodology and limited implementation experience. Often these characteristics are found in the same individuals. In addition, most risk management trainers have had no credible long-term risk management implementation experience, and they propagate existing misconceptions and errors as well as introducing new ones themselves. "One evidence of the decline of project risk management as a credible discipline is the all too frequent errors that exist in published papers and presentations, including those in refereed journals ... Assertions are frequently made without any substantiating evidence." This sorry situation reminds me of a joke I heard many years ago (unknown source). There were three people stranded on a desert island, a chemist, a physicist, and an economist. One day a food crate washed up on shore. Taking out a can of food, the chemist said: "I can calculate the amount of heat, and thus size of the fire, needed to pop the can open." The physicist said: "I can estimate the trajectory of the food shooting out of the can so we can catch it on the fly." The economist said: "Assume a can opener!" Why is the economist in this joke far more disciplined and professional than many project risk management authors? Because the economist used the qualifier "assume!" "The typical presentation of hypothesis, outline of experiment, collection of data, analysis of data, and conclusions often jumps straight to assertions without any supporting ground rules and assumptions, data, analysis of data, etc., nor any disclosure on the part of authors' that such information even exists. While such behavior is clearly unacceptable in scientific and engineering publications, it is all too common in many programs and in project management and related publications involving risk management." [26]

It is the purpose of this book to provide suggestions that will help enhance risk management on a wide variety of programs. The material contained in this book is compatible with that in the Department of Defense *Risk Management Guide for DoD Acquisition* and focuses on hundreds of lessons learned from having implemented this process on a wide variety of defense, other government, and industry programs. Hopefully, this material will help contribute to a reduced likelihood and impact of cost, performance, and/or schedule issues before they become problems and adversely affect the program. In some cases, an effectively implemented executed risk management process using the principles outlined in this book may make the difference between program failure/termination and success. (For example, on one high-technology, high-risk program I worked on, the sponsoring government agency credited the effective risk management process outlined in this book with helping the program achieve its high degree of success and preventing program termination on more than one occasion.)

References

[1]Luke 14:28–30, *Holy Bible: New International Version*, International Bible Society, 1984.

2Department of Defense, *Risk Management Guide for DoD Acquisition*, 5th ed., Defense Acquisition Univ., Ft. Belvoir, VA, June 2002, p. 1.

3Marshall, A. W., and Meckling, W. H., "Predictability of the Costs, Time, and Success of Development," RAND, Santa Monica, CA, P-1821, Oct. 1959, pp. 17, 20–22.

4Perry, R., Smith, G., Harman, A., and Henrichsen, S., "System Acquisition Strategies," RAND, Santa Monica, CA, R-733-PR/ARPA, Vol. 2, No. 3, June 1971, pp. 199–212.

5Dews, E., Smith, G., Barbour, A., Harris, E., and Hesse, M., "Acquisition Policy Effectiveness: Department of Defense Experience in the 1970s," RAND, Santa Monica, CA, R-2516-DR&E, Oct. 1979.

6Conrow, E. H., "Some Long-Term Issues and Impediments Affecting Military Systems Acquisition Reform," *Acquisition Review Quarterly*, Vol. 2, No. 3, Summer 1995, pp. 199–212.

7Comptroller General of the United States, "Defense Acquisition: Oversight of Special Access Programs Has Increased," U. S. Government Accounting Office, GAO/NSIAD-93-78, Washington, DC, Dec. 1992, p. 10.

8Hitch, C. J., and McKean, R. N., *The Economics of Defense in the Nuclear Age*, Antheneum Press, New York, 1978, p. 252.

9Comptroller General of the United States, "Weapons Acquisition: A Rare Opportunity for Lasting Change," U. S. Government Accounting Office, GAO/NSIAD-93-15, Washington, DC, Dec. 1992, pp. 18–24, 44,45.

10Comptroller General of the United States, "Tactical Missile Acquisitions: Understated Technical Risks Leading to Cost and Schedule Overruns," U. S. Government Accounting Office, GAO/NSIAD-91-280, Washington, DC, Sept. 1991, p. 1.

11U. S. Air Force, "U. S. Air Force Acquisition Process Review Team: Clear Accountability in Design," Final Rept. April 1991, p. 3.

12Comptroller General of the United States, "Defense Weapon System Acquisition," U. S. Government Accounting Office, GAO/HR-97-6, Washington, DC, Feb. 1997, pp. 10, 17.

13Merrow, E. W., Chapel, S. W., and Worthing, C., "A Review of Cost Estimation in New Technologies," RAND, Santa Monica, CA, R-2481-DOE, July 1979, p. 73.

14Comptroller General of the United States, "NASA Program Costs: Space Missions Require Substantially More Funding Than Initially Estimated," U. S. Government Accounting Office, GAO/NSIAD-93-97, Washington, DC, Dec. 1992.

15Fenton, R. E., Cox, R. A., and Carlock, P. G., "Incorporating Contingency Risk into Project Cost and Benefit Baselines: A Way to Enhance Realism," *Proceedings of the Ninth Annual International Symposium*, International Counsel on Systems Engineering, June 1999.

16"Charting the Seas of Information Technology," The Standish Group International, Dennis, MA, 1994.

17Conrow, E. H., "Some Considerations for Design Selection in Commercial, Government, and Defense Programs," *1997 Acquisition Research Symposium Proceedings*, Defense Systems Management College, Ft. Belvoir, VA, 1997, pp. 195–217.

[18]Augustine, N. R., *Augustine's Laws,* AIAA, New York, 1983, p. 46.

[19]Newman, J. S., "Life Cycle Risk Mitigation for NASA Programs," presented at the Aerospace Corporation and Air Force Space and Missile Systems Center Risk Management Symposium, 2–4 June 1997.

[20]Kaminski, P., Under Secretary of Defense (Acquisition and Technology), "Reducing Life Cycle Costs for New and Fielded Systems," memorandum, plus two attachments, 4 Dec. 1995.

[21]Department of Defense, "Mandatory Procedures for Major Defense Acquisition Programs (MDAPs) and Major Automated Information System (MAIS) Acquisition Programs," Regulation No. 5000.2-R Sec. 1.3, "Cost as an Independent Variable," 5 April 2002.

[22]David, L., "Is Faster, Cheaper, Better?," *Aerospace America,* Sept. 1998, pp. 42–48.

[23]Feynman, R. P., "Personal Observations on Reliability of Shuttle," Appendix F, *Report of the Presidential Commission on the Space Shuttle Challenger Accident,* Vol. 2, June 1986, p. F-5.

[24]Department of Defense, "Mandatory Procedures for Major Defense Acquisition Programs (MDAPs) and Major Automated Information System (MAIS) Acquisition Programs," Regulation No. 5000.2-R, Sec. C5.2.3.4.3, risk management paragraph associated with "System Analysis and Control," 5 April 2002.

[25]Comptroller General of the United States, "Technical Risk Assessment: The Status of Current DoD Efforts," U. S. Government Accounting Office, GAO/PEMD-86-5, Washington, DC, April 1986, pp. 35–41.

[26]Conrow, E. H., "Achieving Effective Risk Management by Overcoming Some Common Pitfalls," *Cutter IT Journal*, Vol. 15, No. 2, Feb. 2002, p. 22.

Chapter 2
Risk Management Overview*

I. Introduction to Risk Management

A. *Risk Management Structure and Definitions*

Although each risk management strategy depends on the nature of the system being developed, good strategies contain the same basic structure and processes shown in Fig. 2.1. (Note: Feedback from the risk monitoring step should be a direct input to the risk handling and risk analysis steps and may also impact the risk identification and risk planning steps. The solid feedback lines in Fig. 2.1 indicate a direct, typical interaction, while the dashed lines indicate a possible interaction.) Of course, other risk management structures and processes are possible, and some are discussed in Chapter 3. The application of risk management varies with acquisition phases and the degree of system definition, but it should be integrated into the program management or systems engineering function.

Some basic definitions for the elements of risk management include the following:

1) **Risk** is a measure of the potential inability to achieve overall program objectives within defined cost, schedule, and technical constraints and has two components: 1) the probability (or likelihood) of failing to achieve a particular outcome and 2) the consequences (or impact) of failing to achieve that outcome. [Most sources, including reputable unabridged dictionaries of the English language, define risk primarily or solely in terms of loss. Others consider that risk includes the possibility of loss and gain. For example, losses and gains can both occur with gambling and business risk. What is generally not credible is the position that risk can purely be related to gain without the possibility of loss. Although the primary perspective of this book is that risk is related to loss, the risk management process, methodologies, and approaches can also be used where both losses and gains are possible (e.g., risk included as part of a design trade process and evaluating different risk handling strategies). See Chapter 3, Sec. I.C and Appendix E for additional information.] To avoid obscuring the results of an assessment, the risk associated with an issue should be characterized in terms of its two compo-

---

*Primarily extracted and edited from Ref. 1. Some additional material has been included in this introductory chapter.

21

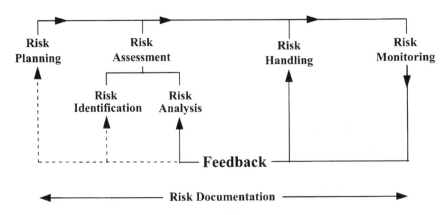

Fig. 2.1   Risk management process structure.

nents. Other factors that may significantly contribute to the importance of risk issues, such as the frequency of occurrence, time sensitivity, and interdependence with other risk issues, can also be noted and used either directly or indirectly in the risk rating methodology used.

2) **Risk management** is the act or practice of dealing with risk. It includes planning for risk, assessing (identifying and analyzing) risk issues, developing risk handling options, monitoring risks to determine how risks have changed, and documenting the overall risk management program.

3) **Risk planning** is the process of developing and documenting an organized, comprehensive, and interactive strategy and methods for identifying and tracking risk issues, performing continuous risk assessments to determine how risks have changed, developing risk handling plans, monitoring the performance of risk handling actions, and assigning adequate resources.

4) **Risk assessment** is the process of identifying and analyzing program areas and critical technical process risks to increase the likelihood of meeting cost, performance, and schedule objectives. *Risk identification* is the process of examining the program areas and each critical technical process to identify and document the associated risk. *Risk analysis* is the process of examining each identified risk issue or process to refine the description of the risk, isolating the cause, and determining the effects.

5) **Risk handling** is the process that identifies, evaluates, selects, and implements options in order to set risk at acceptable levels given program constraints and objectives. This includes the specifics on what should be done, when it should be accomplished, who is responsible, and what are the associated cost and schedule. Risk handling options include assumption, avoidance, control (also known as mitigation), and transfer. The most desirable handling option is selected and a specific approach is then developed for this option.

6) **Risk monitoring** is the process that systematically tracks and evaluates the performance of risk handling actions against established metrics throughout the acquisition process and provides inputs to updating risk handling strategies, as appropriate.

7) **Risk documentation** is recording, maintaining, and reporting assessments, handling analysis and plans, and monitoring results. It includes all plans, reports for the program manager and decision authorities, and reporting forms that may be internal to the program.

B. Some Characteristics of Acquisition Risk

Acquisition programs tend to have numerous, often interrelated, risks. They are not always obvious: relationships may be obscure, and they may exist at all program levels throughout the life of a program. To manage risk, the risk management process should be focused on the critical areas that could affect program outcomes. Work breakdown structure (WBS) product and process elements and engineering and manufacturing processes may contain many of the significant risk issues. Risk issues are determined by examining each WBS element and process in terms of sources and areas of risk. (Note: Various types of acquisition processes or models exist. However, the risk management structure given in Fig. 2.1 is generally applicable, albeit with tailoring to the individual program. Some common acquisition processes are given in Appendix F.)

Some common risk categories for both DoD and non-DoD programs may include, but are not limited to the following:

1) **Cost** is the ability of the system to achieve the program's life-cycle support objectives. This includes the effects of affordability decisions and the effects of inherent errors in the cost estimating technique(s) used (given that the technical requirements were properly defined). (Note: Cost is within the control of the program, whereas budget is not.)

2) **Design/engineering** is the ability of the system configuration to achieve the program's engineering objectives based on the available technology, design tools, design maturity, etc. (Note: Design/engineering risk is sometimes interrelated and/or confused with technology risk.)

3) **Functional** is the level of uncertainty in the ability to perform and test a critical program capability. Functional risk involves the ability to meet each designated requirement, or at least key requirements, for the program. (Note: Although a design may be generated based upon the flowdown of requirements, it is not sufficient to simply estimate the design/engineering risk and then claim that this presents an accurate picture of functional risk.)

4) **Integration** is the level of uncertainty in the integration of hardware/ hardware, hardware/software, and/or software/software items. Hardware/ hardware integration risk is indicated by the level to which the interfaces

have been previously demonstrated, the level of complexity of the components involved, and the anticipated operating environment. Hardware/software integration risk is characterized by the successful demonstration of interfaces between increasingly more mature hardware and software components. Software/software integration risk is characterized by the number and types of interfaces among the software units. The likelihood of integration risk varies with the number of interfaces, quality of interface definitions, ability to perform early prototyping and testing, etc. (cet. par.).

5) **Logistics/Support** is the ability of the system configuration to achieve the program's logistics objectives based on the system design, maintenance concept, support system design, and availability of support resources.

6) **Manufacturing** is the ability of the system configuration to achieve the program's fabrication (e.g., production) objectives based on the system design, manufacturing processes chosen, and availability of manufacturing resources (such as facilities and personnel).

7) **Schedule** is the adequacy of the time allocated for performing defined tasks. This factor includes the effects of programmatic schedule decisions, the inherent errors in the schedule estimating technique used, and external physical constraints.

8) **Technology** is the degree to which the technology proposed for the program has been demonstrated as capable of meeting all of the program threshholds and possibly objectives. (Note: Technology risk is sometimes interrelated and/or confused with design/engineering risk.)

9) **Threat** is the sensitivity of the program to uncertainty in the threat description, the degree to which the system design would have to change if the threat's parameters change, or the vulnerability of the program to adverse intelligence collection efforts (sensitivity to threat countermeasure). (Whereas this risk category may not apply to all non-DoD programs, it may be critical for some information technology and physical security applications.)

In addition, key program processes and resources (e.g., manpower) should also be considered as potential risk categories.

A number of other possible risk categories may also exist. Those listed next may exist on both DoD and non-DoD programs. However, whereas each may potentially be an important risk category, they are also typically difficult to evaluate accurately and objectively, even if they do apply:

1) **Budget (funding)** is the availability and adequacy of funding for the system. This includes the effect of budget decisions on the program. (Note: Cost is within the control of the program, whereas budget is not.)

2) **Concurrency** is the sensitivity of the program to uncertainty resulting from the combining or overlapping of life-cycle phases or activities. (This risk category may require performing a quantitative cost and/or schedule risk analysis.)

3) **Capability of developer** is the ability of the developer to design, develop, and manufacture the system. The contractor should have the experience, resources, and knowledge to produce the system. This may also apply to the government program office, particularly in cases where key personnel have limited, relevant experience.

4) **Management** is the degree in which program plans and strategies exist and are realistic and consistent. The government and contractor acquisition team should be qualified and sufficiently staffed to manage the program.

5) **Modeling and simulation (M&S)** is the adequacy and capability of M&S to support all phases of a program using verified, valid, and accredited M&S. [This risk category may be better treated by evaluating the capability of specific M&S tools as part of other risk categories (e.g., performance simulations for meeting requirements).]

6) **Requirements** are the sensitivity of the program to uncertainty in the system description and requirements except for those caused by threat uncertainty.

7) **Test and evaluation** is the adequacy and capability of the test and evaluation program to assess attainment of significant performance specifications and determine whether the systems are operationally effective and suitable.

Additional areas, such as environmental impact, operational, political, systems safety and health, systems engineering, and others that are analyzed during program plan development, may provide indicators for additional risk issues. In some cases these areas may also warrant being examined as separate risk categories (e.g., environmental impact for a planned large-scale construction project involving the generation of hazardous waste). These areas should generally be examined very early on and the results used as part of the architecture and systems trade process because of the potential for large adverse impact later in the program's acquisition cycle. (Although several of these potential risk categories, such as political risk, may be difficult to assess accurately they should nevertheless be examined carefully. For example, Jimmy Carter, while campaigning for the presidency in 1976, made the cancellation of the B-1A bomber a campaign promise. Less than seven months after his inauguration, he canceled the program on 30 June 1977.)

II. Risk Management Process Steps

A. Risk Planning

1. Purpose of Risk Plans
Risk planning is the detailed formulation of a program of action for the management of risk. It is the process to develop and document an organized, comprehensive, and interactive risk management strategy; determine the

methods to be used to execute a program's risk management strategy; and plan for adequate resources. Risk planning is iterative and includes the entire risk management process, with activities to assess (identify and analyze), handle, and monitor (and document the risk associated with a program). The result is the risk management plan (RMP).

2. Risk Planning Process

Planning begins by developing and documenting a risk management strategy. Early efforts establish the purpose and objective, assign responsibilities for specific areas, identify additional technical expertise needed, describe the assessment process and areas to consider, define a risk rating approach, delineate procedures for consideration of handling options, establish monitoring metrics (where possible), and define the reporting, documentation, and communication needs.

The RMP is the road map that tells the government and/or contractor team how to get from where the program is today to where the program manager wants it to be in the future. The key to writing a good RMP is to provide the necessary information so the program team knows the objectives, goals, and the risk management process. Because it is a road map, it may be specific in some areas, such as the assignment of responsibilities for government and contractor participants and definitions, and general in other areas to allow users to choose the most efficient way to proceed. For example, a description of techniques that suggests several methods for evaluators to use to assess risk is appropriate because every technique has advantages and disadvantages depending on the situation.

B. Risk Assessment

1. Purpose of Risk Assessments

The primary objective of risk assessments is to identify and analyze program risks so that the most critical among them may be controlled. Assessments are factors that managers should consider in setting cost, performance (technical), and schedule objectives because they provide an indication of the likelihood of achieving the desired outcomes.

2. Risk Assessment Process

Risk assessment is the *definition* stage of risk management that identifies and analyzes and quantifies potential program issues in terms of probability and consequences, and possibly other considerations (e.g., the time to impact). The results are a key input to many subsequent risk management actions. It is often a difficult and time-consuming part of the risk management process. There are no quick answers or shortcuts. Tools are available to assist evaluators in assessing risk, but none are totally suitable for any program and are often highly misleading if the user does not understand how to apply them or interpret the results. Despite its complexity, risk assessment is one of the most important phases of the risk management process because the caliber and quality of assessments can have a large impact on program outcomes. The components of assessment, identification and analysis, are performed sequentially with identification being the first step.

Risk identification begins by compiling the program's risk issues. The government and/or contractor should examine and identify program issues by reducing them to a level of detail that permits an evaluator to understand the significance of any risk and identify its causes (e.g., risk issues). This is a practical way of addressing the large and diverse number of potential risks that often occur in acquisition programs. For example, a WBS level 4 or 5 element may be made up of several risk issues associated with a specification or function.

Risk analysis is a technical and systematic process to examine identified risks, isolate causes, determine the relationship to other risks, and express the impact in terms of probability and consequence of occurrence (sometimes termed consequence of failure).

a. Risk identification activity. To identify risk issues, evaluators should break down program elements to a level where they can perform valid assessments. The information necessary to do this varies according to the phase of the program. During the early phases, requirement, threat documents, and acquisition plans may be the only program-specific data available. They should be analyzed to identify issues that may have adverse consequences. Another method of decomposition is to create a WBS as early as possible in a program and use this in a structured approach to evaluate candidate risk categories against candidate system or lower level designs.

b. Risk analysis activity. Analysis begins with a detailed study of the risk issues that have been identified. The objective is to gather enough information about the risks to judge the probability of occurrence and the impact on cost, performance, and schedule if the risk occurs. Risk analyses are often based on detailed information that may come from the following: comparisons with similar systems, relevant lessons-learned studies, experience, results from tests and prototype development, data from engineering or other models, specialist and expert judgments, analysis of plans and related documents, modeling and simulation, and sensitivity analysis of alternatives.

c. Risk assessment by risk category. Each top-level risk category (e.g., cost, technical, and schedule) includes a core set of evaluation tasks and is related to the other two categories. This relationship requires supportive analysis among areas to ensure the integration of the evaluation process. For example, a technical evaluation should typically include a cost and schedule analysis in determining the technical risk. Some characteristics of the evaluations are listed here:

1) Cost evaluation characteristics are as follows:
    a) builds on technical and schedule evaluation results;
    b) translates technical and schedule risks into cost;
    c) derives cost estimate by integrating technical risk, schedule risk, and cost-estimating uncertainty impacts to resources; and
    d) documents cost basis and risk issues for the risk evaluation.
2) Schedule evaluation characteristics are as follows:
    a) evaluates baseline schedule inputs;
    b) reflects technical foundation, activity definition, and inputs from technical and cost areas;
    c) incorporates cost and technical evaluation and schedule uncertainty inputs to program schedule model;
    d) performs schedule analysis on program schedule; and
    e) documents schedule basis and risk issues for the risk evaluation.
3) Technical evaluation characteristics are as follows:
    a) provides technical foundation;
    b) identifies and describes program risks (e.g., technology);
    c) analyzes risks and relates them to other internal and external risks;
    d) prioritizes risks for program impact;
    e) quantifies associated program activities with both time duration and resources;
    f) quantifies inputs for cost evaluation and schedule evaluation; and
    g) documents technical basis and risk issues for the risk evaluation.

d. Risk rating. Risk ratings are an indication of the potential impact of risks on a program. They are typically a measure of the likelihood of an issue occurring and the consequences of the issue and are often expressed as low, moderate, and high or low, low moderate, moderate, moderate high, and high. (Other factors that may significantly contribute to the importance of risk issues, such as frequency of occurrence, time sensitivity, and interdependence with other risk issues, can also be noted and used either directly or indirectly in the rating methodology used.) The prioritization should be done based on a structured risk rating approach using relevant expert opinion and experience.

Program managers can use risk ratings to identify issues requiring priority management (moderate or higher risk). Risk ratings also help to identify the areas that should be reported within and outside the program. Thus, it is important that the ratings be portrayed as accurately as possible.

C. Risk Handling

1. Purpose of Risk Handling

Risk handling includes specific methods and techniques to deal with known risks, identifies who is responsible for the risk issue, and provides an estimate of the cost and schedule associated with handling the risk, if any. It involves planning and execution with the objective of handling risks to an acceptable level. The evaluators that assess risk should begin the process to identify and develop handling options and approaches to propose to the program manager, who selects the appropriate one(s) for implementation.

2. Risk Handling Process

The risk handling phase must be compatible with the RMP and any additional guidance the program manager provides. A critical part of risk handling involves refining and selecting the most appropriate handling option(s) and specific approach(es) for selected risk issues (often those with medium or higher risk levels).

Personnel that evaluate candidate risk handling options may use the following criteria as a starting point for evaluation:

1) Can the option be feasibly implemented and still meet the user's needs?

2) What is the expected effectiveness of the handling option in reducing program risk to an acceptable level?

3) Is the option affordable in terms of dollars and other resources (e.g., use of critical materials and test facilities)?

4) Is time available to develop and implement the option, and what effect does that have on the overall program schedule?

5) What effect does the option have on the system's technical performance?

Risk handling options include: assumption, avoidance, control, and transfer. Although the control option (often called mitigation) is commonly used in aerospace and high technology programs, it should not automatically be chosen. All four options should be evaluated, and the best one chosen for each risk issue.

3. Risk Assumption

Risk assumption is an acknowledgment of the existence of a particular risk situation and a conscious decision to accept the associated level of risk, without engaging in any special efforts to control it. However, a general cost and schedule reserve may be set aside to deal with any problems that may occur as a result of various risk assumption decisions. This risk handling option recognizes that not all identified program risks warrant special handling; as such, it is most suited for those situations that have been classified as low risk.

The key to successful risk assumption is twofold:

1) Identify the resources (e.g., money, people, and time) needed to overcome a risk if it materializes. This includes identifying the specific management actions (such as retesting and additional time for further design activities) that may occur.

2) Ensure that necessary administrative actions are taken to identify a management reserve to accomplish those management actions.

4. Risk Avoidance

Risk avoidance involves a change in the concept, requirements, specifications, and/or practices that reduce risk to an acceptable level. Simply stated, it eliminates the sources of high or possibly medium risk and replaces them with a lower risk solution. This method may be done in parallel with the up-front requirements analysis, supported by cost/requirement trade studies, which can include Cost as an Independent Variable (CAIV) trades. It may also be used later in the development phase when test results indicate that some requirements cannot be met, and the potential cost and/or schedule impact would be severe.

5. Risk Control

Risk control does not attempt to eliminate the source of the risk but seeks to reduce or mitigate the risk. It manages the risk in a manner that reduces the likelihood and/or consequence of its occurrence on the program. This option may add to the cost of a program, and the selected approach should provide an optimal mix among the candidate approaches of risk reduction, cost effectiveness, and schedule impact. A summary of some common risk control approaches includes the following:

1) **Alternative design** is a backup design option that should use a lower risk approach.

2) **Demonstration events** are points in the program (normally tests) that determine if risks are being successfully reduced.

3) **Design of experiments** is an engineering tool that identifies critical design factors which are sensitive, therefore potentially medium or higher risk, to achieve a particular user requirement.

4) **Early prototyping** is used to build and test prototypes early in the system development.

5) **Incremental development** is initiated to design with the intent of upgrading system parts in the future.

6) **Key parameter control boards** are appropriate when a particular fea-

ture, such as system weight, is crucial to achieving the overall program requirements.

7) **Manufacturing screening,** including environmental stress screening, can be incorporated into test article production and low-rate initial production to identify deficient manufacturing processes for programs in engineering and manufacturing development (EMD).

8) **Modeling/simulation** can be used to investigate various design options and system requirement levels.

9) **Multiple development efforts** are used to create systems that meet the same performance requirements. (This approach is also known as parallel development.)

10) **Open systems** are carefully selected commercial specifications and standards whose use can result in lower risk levels.

11) **Process proofing** is selecting particular processes, especially manufacturing and support processes, that are critical to achieve system requirements.

12) **Reviews, walkthroughs, and inspections** are three actions that can be used to reduce the likelihood and potential consequences of risks through timely assessment of actual or planned events.

13) **Robust design** is the approach that uses advanced design and manufacturing techniques which promote quality and capability through design.

14) **Technology maturation efforts** are normally used when the desired technology will replace an existing technology, which is available for use in the system.

15) **Test-analyze-and-fix (TAAF)** is the use of a period of dedicated testing to identify and correct deficiencies in a design.

16) **Trade studies** are used to arrive at a balance of engineering requirements in the design of a system. Ideally, this also includes cost, schedule, and risk considerations.

17) **Two-phase engineering and manufacturing development** consists of incorporation of a formal risk-reduction phase at the initial part of EMD.

18) **Use of mockups,** especially man-machine interface mockups, can be used to conduct early exploration of design options.

19) **Use of standard items/software reuse,** where applicable, can potentially reduce risks.

6. Risk Transfer

Risk transfer may reallocate risk during the concept development and design processes from one part of the system to another, thereby reducing the overall system and/or lower-level risk, or redistributing risks between the government and the prime contractor or within government agencies or between members of the contractor team. It is an integral part of the functional analysis process. Risk transfer is a form of risk sharing and not risk abrogation on the part of the government or contractor, and it may influence cost objectives. An example is the transfer of a function from hardware implementation to software implementation or vice versa. (Risk transfer is also not deflecting a risk issue because insufficient information exists about it.) The effectiveness of risk transfer depends on the use of successful system design techniques. Modularity and functional partitioning are two design techniques that support risk transfer. In some cases risk transfer may concentrate risk issues in one area of the design. This allows management to focus attention and resources on that area. Other examples of risk transfer include the use of insurance, warranties, and similar agreements.

7. Resource Allocation

Risk handling options and the implemented approaches have broad cost implications. The magnitude of these costs are circumstance dependent. The approval and funding of handling options and specific approaches should be done by the Risk Management Board (RMB) (or equivalent) and be part of the process that establishes the program cost, performance, and schedule goals. The selected handling option and approach for each selected risk issue should be included in the program's acquisition strategy.

Once the acquisition strategy includes the risk handling strategy for each selected risk issue, the cost and schedule impacts can be identified and included in the program plan and integrated master schedule, respectively.

D. Risk Monitoring

The monitoring process systematically tracks and evaluates the effectiveness of risk handling actions against established metrics. Monitoring results may also provide a basis for developing additional risk handling options and approaches, or updating existing risk handling approaches, and reanalyzing known risks. In some cases monitoring results may also be used to identify new risks and revise some aspects of risk planning. The key to the risk monitoring process is to establish a cost, performance, and schedule management indicator system over the program that the program manager and other key personnel use to evaluate the status of the program. The indicator system should be designed to provide early warning of potential problems to allow management actions. Risk monitoring is not a problem-solving technique, but rather a proactive technique to obtain objective information on the progress to date in reducing risks to acceptable levels. Some techniques suitable for risk monitoring that can be used in a program-wide indicator system include the following:

1) **Earned value (EV)** uses standard cost/schedule data to evaluate a program's cost performance (and provide an indicator of schedule perform-

ance) in an integrated fashion. As such, it provides a basis to determine if risk handling actions are achieving their forecasted results.

2) **Program metrics** are formal, periodic performance assessments of the selected development processes, evaluating how well the development process is achieving its objective. This technique can be used to monitor corrective actions that emerged from an assessment of critical program processes.

3) **Schedule performance monitoring** is the use of program schedule data to evaluate how well the program is progressing to completion vs the baseline schedule.

4) **Technical performance measurement (TPM)** is a product design assessment, which estimates, through engineering analysis and tests, the values of essential performance parameters of the current design as effected by risk handling actions.

The indicator system and periodic reassessments of program risk should provide the program with the means to incorporate risk management into the overall program management structure. Finally, a well-defined test and evaluation program is often a key element in monitoring the performance of selected risk handling approaches and developing new risk assessments.

E. Risk Management Documentation and Communication

Successful risk management programs include timely specific reporting procedures that accurately communicate plans, data, results, and other relevant information. Normally, documentation and reporting procedures are defined as part of the risk management strategy planning before contract award, but they may be added or modified during contract execution as long as the efforts remain within the scope of the contract or are approved as part of a contract change.

The need for good documentation is well recognized, but it may be lacking on a program. Some important reasons for having sound risk management documentation include the following:

1) It provides a good baseline for program risk assessments and updates as the program progresses.

2) It tends to ensure a more comprehensive risk assessment than using less formal documentation.

3) It provides a basis for monitoring risk handling actions and verifying the results.

4) It can assist in tracking the progress of supporting technology programs vs a baseline.

5) It provides a management tool for use during the execution of the program, including permitting a more objective assessment of how additional funds or potential budget cuts should be allocated.

6) It provides the rationale for why program decisions were made.

7) It provides program background material for new personnel.

Draft documentation should be developed by those responsible for planning, collecting, and analyzing data. The number and types of risk management reports will typically depend on the size, nature, and phase of the program. Examples of some risk management documents and reports that may be useful to the program manager and other key personnel are risk management plan, risk information form, risk assessment report, risk handling plan for selected risks, and risk monitoring documentation for selected risks.

The need for properly communicating risk results is often an overlooked facet of risk management. It is of little value to perform risk management functions if the information generated cannot be properly shared with participants both within and outside the program. As stated by the National Research Council[2]:

> "Risk communication is an interactive process of exchange of information and opinion among individuals, groups, and institutions. It involves multiple messages about the nature of risk and other messages, not strictly about risk, that express concerns, opinions, or reactions to risk messages or to legal and institutional arrangements for risk management. . . . Successful risk communication does not guarantee that risk management decisions will maximize general welfare; it only ensures that decision makers will understand what is known about the implementations for welfare and the available options."

III. Some Risk Management Implementation Guidelines

A. Introduction

This section provides a set of guidelines for performing risk management on a variety of programs. It is not meant to be all inclusive, but a relatively simple starting point that you should tailor to your program. I have included references to chapters and appendices from this book and the fifth edition of the Defense Acquisition University's *Risk Management Guide for DoD Acquisition* (Ref. 1) that provide additional information where appropriate.

B. Risk Planning

1) If you don't have an RMP, consider developing one using information contained in Chapter 4, Sec. IV and Ref. 1 (Fig. 5.2 and Appendix B). If you do have an RMP, consider evaluating it and improving it with this material.

2) Ideally the risk manager develops the RMP with the assistance of key program personnel. However, regardless of who writes the RMP, the RMB, or equivalent, should approve it.

3) If you can't develop an RMP, at least develop: a) a set of ground rules and assumptions that the program will use for performing risk management (Chapter 4, Sec. IV.B.4); b) a structured methodology for performing risk identification (Chapter 5, Sec. II.B), analysis (Chapter 6), handling (Chapter 7, Sec. II), and monitoring (Chapter 8, Sec. II); and c) an agreed-upon set of organizational roles and responsibilities (e.g., RMB or equivalent, IPT leads, risk focal points) (Chapter 3, Secs. VII and XII).

4) Once you have a suitable RMP, then perform risk management training within the program. Both upper management and working level personnel should be exposed to risk management principles, but the focus of the material and extent of coverage will vary with each category of people.

C. Risk Identification

1) Consider the six techniques and use appropriate one(s) for risk identification (WBS, WBS with ordinal scales, top-level, key processes, program requirements, and mission capability) (Chapter 5, Sec. II.B) coupled with methods for eliciting expert opinion (Chapter 6, Secs. VII.E and VII.F, and Ref. 1, Sec. 5.4.7).

2) Consider using the guidelines given in Chapter 5, Sec. II.H for documenting candidate risks.

3) The RMB should approve all candidate risks. Note any comments and changes from the RMB in the risk identification documentation. After a risk issue has been approved by the RMB, the IPT lead should assign a risk focal point to the risk issue.

D. Risk Analysis

1) For those risks approved by the RMB, the risk focal point, with the assistance of the IPT lead, performs a risk analysis.

2) For cost and schedule risks use a Monte Carlo simulation. Define the structure of the simulation model, identify elements that have estimating uncertainty and risk, estimate the necessary probability distribution critical values (e.g., mean and standard deviation for a normal distribution), perform the Monte Carlo simulation, and evaluate the results at the desired confidence level (e.g., 50th percentile). (See Chapter 6, Secs. IV.G, VII, and VIII for additional information.)

3) For technical risks and other risks (e.g., management), estimate the probability of occurrence term, estimate the consequence of occurrence term, and convert the results to risk level using a risk mapping matrix. (See Chapter 6, Secs. IV, V, VII, VIII, and IX; and Appendices H, I, and J for additional information. If calibrated ordinal scales are used, select the threshold value associated with risk level boundaries.)

4) If you have multiple risk facets for a given item (e.g., a cost risk,

schedule risk, and technical risk estimate for an electronics box), integrate the different risk results into a cohesive "picture."

5) The RMB should approve all risk analysis results, clearly identify all medium and higher risks, and where possible prioritize risks within a risk level (e.g., rank all high risks). Record any comments and changes from the RMB in the risk analysis documentation you develop.

E. Risk Handling

1) For those risks authorized by the RMB (e.g., medium and higher plus some specified low risks), the risk focal point develops a Risk Handling Plan (RHP) with the assistance of the IPT lead.

2) Consider using the guidelines given in Chapter VII to develop the RHP. Be particularly conscious of developing the risk handling strategy and the type and resources needed to implement the risk handling strategy (option and implementation approach). Develop the risk handling strategy by first selecting the option (assumption, avoidance, control, transfer), then picking the best implementation approach for the chosen option. This is the primary risk handling strategy. (For additional information on the four risk handling options see Sec. II.C; Chapter 7, Sec. II.O; and Ref. 1, Sec. 5.6.)

3) Develop one or more backup risk handling strategies as appropriate (e.g., for all high risks and other risks specified by the RMB). Also determine whether the backup strategy(ies) will be implemented in parallel or later in the program. If later in the program, pick a decision point with specific criteria for choosing the backup strategy(ies).

4) Select the cost, performance, and schedule metrics you will use to monitor risk during the risk monitoring step. Consider using earned value (cost), Technical Performance Measurements (TPM) (performance), and variation in schedule from the Integrated Master Schedule or equivalent (schedule). In addition, consider using other metrics as warranted for the monitoring function. (Note: TPMs must be developed individually for each risk issue and should be selected before the RHP is approved.)

5) The RMB should approve all RHPs. Note any changes from the RMB in the RHP you develop.

6) The IPT lead and RMB allocate resources and the IPT lead and risk focal point implement the RHP.

F. Risk Monitoring

1) Perform both the monitoring and feedback functions. For monitoring, use the metrics identified as part of risk handling and included in the RHP. (See Chapter 8, Sec. II for additional information.) The risk focal point should collect the risk monitoring data, integrate the data into a cohesive "picture," and review it with the IPT lead.

2) Make sure that you update and evaluate the monitoring tools (e.g., earned value) at the same time and use them at the same WBS level else the results may be inconsistent.

3) Consider updating all existing risks monthly—there is no set time period (and sometimes it's on contract), but quarterly is too long and substantial changes may occur. The RMB should meet as often as needed, including "special sessions" as warranted.

4) RHPs should be adjusted as warranted (e.g., unanticipated changes in risk level or a plan far behind schedule). These adjustments or replans should be developed by the risk focal point and IPT lead and implemented after RMB approval.

5) Risk analysis results should be updated monthly or as otherwise appropriate (as previously noted) by the risk focal point and IPT lead and approved by the RMB.

6) Risk identification documentation should be updated as warranted (e.g., a new facet of the risk appears) by the risk focal point and IPT lead and approved by the RMB.

7) Risk planning updates, including revisions to the RMP, should be performed anytime there is a major change to the program (e.g., change in baseline, program phase, budget change), substantial change in ground rules and assumptions, or when a new risk category is identified. Updates to the RMP should be approved by the RMB.

G. Closing Thoughts

1) Strive to create a climate where risk management is viewed as a key process and a "plus" to use. Risk management is not, however, the "be all, do all, end all" process, but is a contributor to good project management and systems engineering.

2) Risk management needs to be implemented top-down (upper management to workers) and bottom-up (workers to upper management); otherwise risk issues will likely not be properly identified or dealt with.

3) Everyone on the program should be aware of risk management and use its principles. (This does not mean that everyone on the program should become a risk manager.) Risk management is not just for a selected "few" on the program—-this will lead to ineffective results.

IV. Risk Management Activities During DoD Acquisition Phases

Risk management activities should be applied continuously throughout all acquisition phases. (See Appendix B for additional information on DoD acquisition phases, including the DoD acquisition changes, including program phases and milestones, that occurred in April 2002. (I have continued to use the previous acquisition phase nomenclature and definitions because the vast majority of programs will have been procured or are in development with the earlier system at the time that the second edition of this book was developed.) Note that the acquisition phases of other industries may vary from the DoD model and are not discussed here. However, because of the difference in available information, the level of application and detail will vary for each phase. In Concept Exploration (Phase 0) risk management focuses on assessing the risks in the alternative concepts available to satisfy users' needs and on planning a strategy to address those risks. For each of the subsequent phases [Program Definition and Risk Reduction (Phase 1), EMD (Phase 2), Production, Fielding/Deployment, and Operational Support (Phase 3)], all four risk management process steps (planning, assessing, handling, and monitoring) may be applied with increasing focus on risk handling and monitoring plus developing more comprehensive risk assessments. The program manager and other key personnel identify objectives, alternatives, and constraints at the beginning of each phase of a program and then evaluate alternatives, identify sources of project risk, and select a strategy for resolving selected risks. The program office updates the acquisition strategy, risk assessments, and other aspects of program planning, based on analyses, in a manner consistent with the program's acquisition phase.

Developers should become involved in the risk management process at the beginning, when users define performance requirements, and continue during the acquisition process until the system is delivered. The early identification and analysis of critical risks allows risk handling approaches to be developed and to streamline the program definition and the Request for Proposal [or similar government (buyer) requests] around critical product and process risks.

The following paragraphs address risk management in the different DoD acquisition phases in more detail.

A. Concept Exploration

DoD 5000.2R describes Concept Exploration (Phase 0) as normally consisting of studies that define and evaluate the feasibility of alternative concepts and provides the basis for the assessment of these alternatives in terms of their advantages, disadvantages, and risk levels at the Milestone I decision point. In addition to the analysis of alternatives, the program manager develops a proposed acquisition program baseline (APB) and criteria for exiting Concept Exploration and entering Program Definition and Risk Reduction (Phase 1).

The APB documents the most important cost, performance, and schedule objectives and thresholds for the selected concepts. The parameters selected are such that a reevaluation of alternative concepts is appropriate if thresholds are not met. Exit criteria to the next program phase are events or accomplishments that allow managers to track progress in critical risk categories. They must be demonstrated to show that a program is on track and permit the program to move to the next program phase.

In defining alternative concepts program managers should pay particular attention to the threat and the user's requirements, which are normally stated in broad terms at this time. Risks can be introduced if the requirements are not stable, or if they are overly restrictive and contain specific technical solutions. Requirements can also be significant cost and schedule risk drivers if they require a level of performance that is difficult to achieve within the program budget and time constraints. Such drivers need to be identified as early in the program as possible and evaluated as part of system level cost, performance, schedule, and risk trades.

The acquisition strategy should address the known risks for each alternative concept, and the plans to handle them, including specific events, intended to reduce the risks. Similarly, the test and evaluation strategy should reflect how test and evaluation, with the use of modeling and simulation, will be used to assess risk levels and identify new or suspected risk issues.

A risk management strategy, derived in concert with the acquisition strategy, should be developed during this phase and revised and updated continually throughout the program. This strategy should include risk planning that clearly defines roles, responsibilities, authority, and documentation for program reviews, risk assessments, risk handling, and risk monitoring.

B. Subsequent Phases

During Phase 1 and beyond, concepts, technological approaches, and/or design approaches (selected at the previous milestone decisions) are pursued to define the program and program risks. Selected alternative concepts or designs continue to be analyzed, and the acquisition strategy, and the various strategies and plans derived from it, continue to be refined.

Risk management efforts in these phases focus on understanding critical technology, manufacturing, and support risks, along with cost, performance, schedule, and other risks, and demonstrating that they are being controlled before moving to the next milestone. Thus, particular attention should be placed on risk handling and monitoring activities. Planning and assessment should continue as new information becomes available, and new risk issues are identified. Also note that the accuracy of risk analyses should improve with each succeeding program phase (cet. par.).

During Phase 1 and beyond, the risk management program should be carried out in an integrated government-contractor (buyer-seller) framework to the extent possible that allows the government to manage program level risks, with the contractor responsible to the government for product and process risks and for maintaining design accountability. Both the government and contractors need to understand the risks clearly and jointly plan management efforts.

C. *Risk Management and Milestone Decisions*

Before a milestone review, the program manager should update risk assessments, explicitly addressing the risks in the critical areas (e.g., design and technology), and identify areas of moderate or higher risk. Each critical assessment should be supported by subsystems' risk assessments, which should be supported by design reviews, test results, and specific analyses. The program manager should present planned and implemented risk handling plans for medium or higher risk issues plus results to date in reducing risk levels to the desired values at the milestone review.

References

[1]Department of Defense, *Risk Management Guide for DoD Acquisition,* 5th ed., Defense Acquisition Univ. , Ft. Belvoir, VA, June 2002. Additional material from Department of Defense, *Risk Management Guide for DoD Acquisition*, 3rd ed., Defense Acquisition Univ. and Defense Systems Management College, Ft. Belvoir, VA, Jan. 2000.

[2]National Research Council, *Improving Risk Communication,* National Academy Press, Washington, DC, 1989, p. 21.

Chapter 3
Some Risk Management Implementation Considerations

I. Introduction

In this chapter we will briefly look at some key features of the how to implement the risk management process, including some recommended approaches and traps to avoid.

A. Some Top-Level Considerations

Carefully examine any definition of risk management to make sure that it is consistent with the risk management process steps supplied in other material. I recommend that you review graphics, other process flow representations, and text to make sure that the risk management process steps are consistent among these sources. Inconsistencies are surprisingly common and point to sloppy work. For example, a graphic representing a risk management process included: identify, assess, handle, and control steps, while another graphic in the same document showed the process as: identify, analyze, handle, track, and control. (Note that neither process graphic included the risk planning step.) In addition, descriptions often do not match the process steps that exist. For example, one discussion indicated that risk management is a process focused on the identification and management of events, yet included a risk management process that included far more and explicit steps than identification and management. In another case a risk management process included planning, identification, analysis, handling, and monitoring steps, yet was summarized as the systematic process of identifying, analyzing, and responding to project risks. Here, the descriptive statement omits the planning and monitoring steps and thus introduces confusion into what steps exist, and which ones are important. Clearly, in both cases above the risk management definition did not match the risk management process steps.

Carefully examine any definition of risk management to make sure that it is consistent with the risk management process steps provided.

In some cases a risk management process with specific steps is given in program documentation [e.g., risk management plan, (RMP)], then a different risk management process is used. This is often indicative of fundamental project management and configuration control problems on the program.

Verify that the risk management process that is claimed to be used on the program is actually the process that has been implemented.
Risk management is not a "cure all" and it should never be viewed as such. Having a good, or even a great, risk management process will not in and of itself lead to project success. And risk management success should not solely be measured against how well specific project objectives should be accomplished because there are many other processes that come into play, and external or other unplanned events often occur.

Risk management is not a "cure all" and it should never be viewed as such.
Your risk management best practices may not correspond to your customer's risk management best practices. At a minimum, you should demonstrate how your process and best practices map to your customer's process and best practices and address any disconnects. Do this as early as possible to help prevent any misunderstandings and potential problems. Don't just say without providing substantiating information that your process and best practices are better than those of your customer's. I've witnessed multiple instances of this behavior directed at a customer in a public forum, including twice from the same individual. The net result was a substantial loss of credibility at the company-wide level in the eyes of a very important customer. Instead, even if you have a superior risk management process and best practices vs your customer, work with the customer to the extent possible to help them understand your process and best practices and to upgrade theirs as appropriate.

Your risk management best practices may not correspond to your customer's risk management best practices. At a minimum, you should demonstrate how your process and best practices map to your customer's process and best practices and address any disconnects.
A balance must be achieved between having a risk management process that is unstructured vs one that can not be changed. Neither extreme is conducive to effective risk management. The risk management process should be formal enough to have suitable structure but flexible enough to change with a changing program (e.g., program phase or major restructuring).

A balance must be achieved between having a risk management process that is unstructured vs one that can not be changed. Neither extreme is conducive to effective risk management.
If risk balancing across entities [e.g., integrated product teams (IPT), organizations] is done with risks whose levels are subjectively estimated, then the results may contain an unknown level of uncertainty that can adversely impact risk ranking, allocation of resources for Risk Handling Plans (RHP), etc. If, however, the risk balancing is performed on results from a structured risk analysis methodology, then at least some uncertainty will be eliminated (and even more if the uncertainty associated with the results are known).

Do not perform risk balancing with risks whose levels are subjectively estimated because the results may contain an unknown level of uncertainty that can adversely impact risk ranking, allocation of resources for RHPs, etc.

Developing a detailed flow diagram of your risk management process, such as Fig. 3.1, can be helpful to identify missing process steps, steps out of order, functions not performed in a given process step, and management actions not properly taking place. However, this understanding will only occur if the analyst is willing to take an objective look at the existing risk management process no matter how many shortcomings may exist.

Developing an objective, detailed risk management process flow diagram can be helpful to identify missing process steps, steps out of order, functions not performed in a given process, and management actions not properly taking place.

Do not confuse risk management process steps with Risk Management Board (RMB) actions, resources, and other criteria. For example, appointing a risk manager is part of risk management organizational implementation and not a risk management process step or a risk handling action.

Do not confuse risk management process steps with RMB actions, resources, and other criteria.

The risk management process and how it is implemented are separate but interrelated items. The process steps themselves should stand on their own, but the mechanism for implementing the steps may vary on a step-by-step basis. For example, on some programs the risk manager may play a key role in developing the RMP, all program personnel should (be encouraged to) perform risk identification, the risk issue point of contact (POC) with the assistance of the IPT lead and risk manager should analyze approved risk issues, the risk issue POC with the assistance of the IPT lead and risk manager should develop draft RHPs, the risk issue POC with the assistance of the IPT lead should implement approved RHPs, and the risk issue POC with the assistance of the IPT lead should develop risk monitoring information. Note that the roles and responsibilities are different across most of the process steps in the above example.

The risk management process and how it is implemented are separate but interrelated items. The process steps themselves should stand on their own, but the mechanism for implementing the steps may vary on a step-by-step basis.

Testing does not reduce the level of risk present but can assist in performing risk management by: 1) pointing to risk issues, 2) generating data that may lead to a change in risk level, and 3) providing information about an item that may/may not be related to risk management.

Testing does not reduce the level of risk present but can assist in performing risk management.

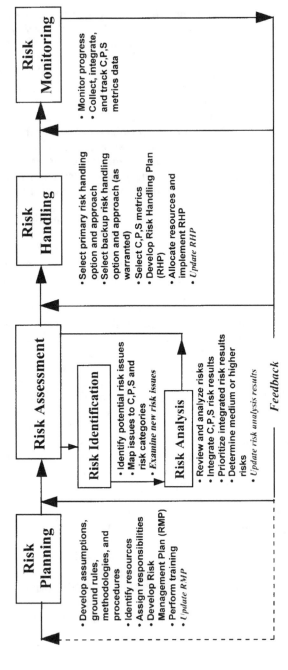

Fig. 3.1 Enhanced risk management process structure.

B. Risk and Probability and Consequence of Occurrence

Risk is a function of both probability of occurrence and consequence of occurrence. It is not appropriate to discuss risk in terms of one of these two terms only. For example, it is not appropriate to say that risks are grouped in terms of probability of occurrence. It is also not correct to say that a risk can range from severe (e.g., loss of a mission) to minor (little or no damage) because this only includes the consequence of occurrence term and excludes probability of occurrence.

Risk is a function of both probability of occurrence and consequence of occurrence. It is not appropriate to discuss risk in terms of one of these two terms only.

Avoid phrases such as "likelihood of a risk" or "risk probability" and "impact of a risk" or "risk impact" since this mixes risk with *either* probability *or* consequence, when in reality, risk is composed of *both* probability *and* consequence terms. The intermixing of risk with a component of risk (e.g., probability) should be avoided since it is confusing, redundant, and may lead to misinterpretation, confusion, and erroneous results by different people. Note also that likelihood and risk are part of an overlapping set and risk is not independent of likelihood since risk = f (probability, consequence). The same is also true of impact and risk—they are part of an overlapping set and risk is not independent of impact since risk = f (probability, consequence).

Avoid phrases such as "likelihood of a risk" or "risk probability" and "impact of a risk" or "risk impact" since this mixes risk with either probability or consequence, when in reality, risk is composed of both probability and consequence terms.

Risk includes both probability of occurrence and consequence of occurrence terms, and is often represented by: Risk Factor = P * C. The probability of occurrence is only one of two components of risk—the other being consequence of occurrence. Hence, probability of occurrence is related to risk in a nonconstant manner that varies with the consequence of occurrence term present. In the narrower sense, uncertainty represents the variability around estimates of probability of occurrence, consequence of occurrence, and thus risk. It is often not expressed in a standalone manner but as the variation, represented by say a distribution or ± bounds, around the value. A broader view of uncertainty is related to states of knowledge [e.g., certainty to chaos as proposed by Arthur Alexander (see Chapter 6, Sec. II.C)]. While the broader view is helpful for structuring the nature of risk-related problems and the applicability of certain methodologies, the narrower view is often used to estimate specific levels of variation.

A narrow view of uncertainty represents the variability around estimates of probability of occurrence, consequence of occurrence, and thus risk. A broader view of uncertainty is related to states of knowledge.

Values associated with calibrated or uncalibrated ordinal "probability" scale levels are only an indicator of probability, not risk. Such values do not imply a level of risk occurring because risk is composed of both probability and consequence of occurrence terms, and consequence of occurrence information does not (or should not) exist in probability of occurrence scales.

Values associated with calibrated or uncalibrated ordinal "probability" scale levels are only an indicator of probability, not risk.

Avoid falling into the trap of accepting sloppy work as adequate for risk management—something, for example, which is quite common in risk analysis methodologies. While in most cases an unknown uncertainty exists, this is not justification to use a number of poor assumptions or approximations, and then to say for example, "It does not matter if it introduces a 10% error, that is well within the uncertainty range of our analysis." The reason why this attitude should be avoided is that several poor assumptions will usually exist and can have a nontrivial impact on the results. Such carelessness often manifests itself as deficiencies in other parts of the risk management process as well.

Avoid falling into the trap of accepting sloppy work as adequate for risk management—something, for example, which is quite common in risk analysis methodologies.

Risk management and crisis management are opposites. "Hopefully risk management will supersede and displace crisis management, which is routinely practiced on a wide variety of programs."[1] And those that practice risk management can one day comment that there are "few takers for a career in crisis management."[1] Unfortunately, this will likely not happen anytime soon in many organizations.

Risk management and crisis management are opposites. "Hopefully risk management will supersede and displace crisis management which is routinely practiced on a wide variety of programs."[1]

C.   A Brief Discussion of Opportunities, Risk, and Hazards

While some people argue that risk includes both opportunities and losses, there is rarely if ever an opportunity without the possibility of loss, while often there is the chance of loss without opportunity. (See Appendix E for a comprehensive discussion of risk and opportunity.) Also, while risk is often to the individual affected, opportunities may pass to others, not the individual in question. Two simple examples follow. The first example is a sign posted in front of two major corporations that I sometimes pass that states: "Unauthorized vehicles will be towed at the owner's risk and expense." Clearly there is no opportunity for gain for the vehicle driver, unless they want to practice their legal skills in court, but there are potential negative outcomes. On the other hand, there is a potential opportunity for gain for the tow truck driver that would likely impound the vehicle. The second example is a sign posted at the entrance to an ecological reserve that states: "Warning—Mountain Lion Country—A Risk. Mountain lions may be present and are unpredictable. They have been known to attack without warning. Your safety cannot be guaranteed." In this case, there is no possibility of opportunity for the hiker, but there is potential opportunity for the mountain lion!

While some people argue that risk includes both opportunities and losses, there is rarely if ever an opportunity without the possibility of loss, while there often is the chance of loss without opportunity.

There are at least three different classes of opportunity that may exist on projects. In some cases the outcome may be positive (e.g., a net gain), while in other cases the outcome will likely be negative but ideally less negative. In addition, the outcomes of potential opportunities may be beyond the control of the participants at the time the estimates are made.

The first class is a gamble, such as a new concept or technology. Here, the sign of the outcome can be positive or negative and is often uncertain, if not unknown, at the time the action is taken. The second class involves project management actions (e.g., risk handling activities), which often involve a cost, but lead to a less negative outcome. For example, if an RHP is implemented, expenditures of resources take place and the risk ideally is reduced to an acceptable level. From an impact perspective, when the benefit/cost ratio > 1, or if it prevents other negative events from occurring (e.g., program cancellation), then this can be viewed as an opportunity. The assumption risk handling option is not applicable here because no action is taken and management reserve should be set aside to cover potential risk occurrence. For the avoidance risk handling option relative opportunities may exist if the intent is to change a requirement or a design. [The opportunity is not absolute since some cost, performance, and schedule (C,P,S) degradation will likely occur to reduce the risk.] Here, a relative opportunity is one where a "less negative" outcome will result than if no action is taken at all, yet the outcome will not be positive. For example, cost increases but may be less than another course of action. In this case the cost is still a negative item, not a positive item. For the control risk handling option, relative opportunities may exist to reduce risk by undertaking actions that ideally result in a lower C,P,S expenditure than if the risk actually occurs. For the transfer risk handling option, whether or not an opportunity exists varies with the application but it may be relative (e.g., insurance, guarantees, warranties, transfer between organizations, transfer between different sides of an interface). The third class is related to uncertainty. Here, if the event occurs on the left side of the probability distribution mode, median, or mean (as appropriate to the distribution in question) and no specific risk handling action is taken, then a relative opportunity may occur. For example, if the cost of a widget is estimated to be $3.00 but actually is $2.00 then a relative opportunity may exist (cet. par.) due to cost estimating uncertainty. Whether or not this class applies depends on if: 1) there is true uncertainty in stating the parameter (e.g., information quality), 2) the optimistic estimate represents a different solution (e.g., using widget "X" instead of widget "Y"), or 3) a risk handling strategy is used, etc. In cases where true uncertainty does not exist the second class, previously stated, more likely applies and a relative opportunity may exist.

At least three different classes of opportunity may exist on different projects. In some cases the outcome may be positive, while in other cases the outcome will likely be negative. In addition, the outcomes of potential opportunities may be beyond the control of the participants at the time the estimates are made.

Although I do not cover hazards in this book, I would like to note that people are often unaware of the risks, if not danger, that are directly in front of them. This can lead to very unwise decision making and potentially tragic consequences. For example, those that participate in high-altitude mountain climbing are well aware of some potential risks known as "objective hazards," while other people in seemingly more mild settings may be completely unaware of such risks. An example of the latter case, sometimes known as "day hiker syndrome," is that often people die from going on short hikes—even those that are experienced hikers—because they underestimate the risks present by thinking "I'm only going to be gone for a few hours," or "It's just the local mountains." Of course, then there are the truly foolish that are totally unaware of the danger present even when directly confronted with it. In one case I was returning from a hike in the appropriately named "Icehouse Canyon" when a woman wearing a dress and three-inch, high-heeled shoes insisted on going up the trail to meet some friends. After some debate and complaining on her part, I chopped some steps in the ice with an ice axe and she went on her way—oblivious to the sharp drop off the side of the three-foot wide trail and the rocks below that could have led to serious injury or death if she had fallen. (Had I not chopped the steps she would have gone anyway and possibly fallen as I watched her.)

But even the most experienced mountain climbers who know, or at least should know, the risks often continue to take them. A summation of this lifestyle is given by Babu Chiri (1966-2001) who held the record for the number of most successful Mt. Everest summits (10), and the fastest ascent of Mt. Everest (16 hours, 56 minutes). In an interview conducted the day before he died from a fall into a crevasse on Mt. Everest, Babu Chiri said: "No pain, no gain. If I'm scared of the mountain, I'm not going to reach my goal. Risk is essential. You can't do without risk."[2] Similarly, two climbers I met—and one that I knew—who had eight successful summits of Mt. Everest between them, died on their last attempt to summit Mt. Everest. Each of their lives had been spared many times yet they continued this activity. One climber told me that he should have died several years earlier after reaching the summit of K2 (the world's second highest peak and generally regarded as the world's most difficult mountain to climb), had it not been for a summit team member who found the route down despite deteriorating light and blowing snow. In this case, the climbers violated their preset turnaround time by several hours and were very fortunate to return alive. It was another violation of a preset turnaround time that later contributed to the death of this climber while descending from the summit of Mt. Everest.

Serial thinking (A leads to B, but not realizing that B may lead to C) is somewhat common with decision makers, but whether or not it may lead to serious or even life threatening results depends upon the operating environment and other considerations. For example, serial thinking coupled with hypoxia (oxygen depravation) and other degenerative ills from high altitudes can increase the likelihood that even experienced climbers will take moderate to high risks (e.g., violating their preset turnaround times), and may prevent them from clearly thinking through the potential consequences of their actions. This chain of thinking has led to some tragedies on high-altitude peaks. (For example, see Kurt Diemberger, "The Endless Knot: K2, Mountain of Dreams and Destiny," The Mountaineers, Seattle, 1990 for a frank account and causes of the tragic 1986 climbing season on K2 when 13 climbers perished.) [I have not forgotten a memorial stone in a small cemetery at a staging point for a high altitude peak. The marking on one stone said "Conqueror of Mt. Everest." I privately asked one high altitude climber who had climbed Mt. Everest twice at that time whether or not anyone ever "conquers" a mountain—even Mt. Everest. His response, and that of other famous climbers has been a humble and soft spoken "no": you are fortunate to summit, but the key is to descend the peak alive.]

A personal example of serial thinking in mountain climbing follows. I was intent on reaching a 2700-meter summit whose trails were clogged with snow and ice. (While only a modest sized mountain, the climbing conditions later proved hazardous.) Having ascended this summit a number of times before, I prepared by bringing appropriate gear for the environment (e.g., plastic climbing boots, crampons, ice axe) and notified an acquaintance, Nick, who worked in the mountain range that if I had not returned back by 6:00 p.m. to call the Sheriff's Department Search and Rescue Team. Nick said that if I could look at the face of the peak and not see specular reflections, then ice was likely absent. A half mile from the base of the peak I did so, and not seeing specular reflections I left the crampons at that location. This was my first mistake. I then proceeded to the base of the mountain and found the trail covered in snow rather than ice. I left the plastic climbing boots at that location. This was my second mistake. I then proceeded towards the summit with the ice axe, chopping steps while traversing across 45-degree slopes. Not realizing that ice was under the snow until some time afterward and that the snow would become slushy later in the day (and thus form a slippery and potentially hazardous combination) was my third mistake. At about 100 meters below the summit and a half mile of lateral distance I realized that I might not possibly make the summit and return back before 6:00 p.m. At that point, I made the conscious decision to descend and return to the starting point. Nick was puzzled at why I was back at 2:30 p.m. and I proceeded to analyze my actions. I should have first realized that there was no way that I could have seen specular reflections in a deeply shaded and partially tree covered slope from a half mile away. But by leaving the crampons I had now made the plastic climbing boots potentially less effective and traversing the subsequent ice fields more hazardous. Dropping off the plastic climbing boots at the start of the ascent was also unwise because the boots were superior in terms of edging ice and snow, adhering to wet surfaces, and being waterproof rather than leather hiking boots. Furthermore, the descent proved more difficult and hazardous than the ascent because the snow had became wet and quite slippery on top of the ice. Hence, I did not look ahead to estimate possible outcomes at the time I made the first decision (leaving the crampons), or did I when I made the second decision (leaving the plastic climbing boots), or the third decision (estimating the difficulty of the descent). However, I broke the serial thinking by realizing that under no circumstances would I place myself in a situation of returning later than 6:00 p.m. and thus initiating a search and rescue at the expense of the taxpayers and possible danger of the team members. [This was despite the fact that I estimated I had a 70 percent chance of reaching the summit and returning before 6:00 p.m. Had I retained the crampons and plastic climbing boots I could easily have reached the summit and returned well before 6:00 p.m. (e.g., 100 percent chance by 6:00 p.m. and perhaps an 85 percent chance by 4:00 p.m.).] This personal lesson led me to be more conscious of recognizing attributes of serial thinking and how to break out of it. I went back to the same mountain once more a month later. At that time there was no snow or ice present and I ascended and returned without incident before 2:00 p.m. After this experience I became more appreciative of those who experience serial thinking under other stressful situations, regardless of the altitude or other environmental considerations, as well as climbers at 8000+ meters where every decision can mean life or death. (As my former trainer, renowned climber Jim Bridwell, said when you are climbing a "giant" mountain, the mountain is the hunter and you are the hunted, *all the time*![3])

How then can you prevent serial thinking? As Peter Habeler [who along with former partner Reinhold Messner were the first people to summit Mt. Everest without supplemental (bottled) oxygen in May 1978] told me, well before you begin a high altitude climb you have to understand your strengths and limitations, develop a plan, take decisive action (implement the plan), and stick to that plan unless it is essential to change it. And if you must change your plan, understand the potential risk of each and every action to avoid falling into serial thinking.[4] While program managers and other key decision makers are rarely in life threatening situations, Mr. Habeler's sound advice directly applies to risk handling: 1) understand the strengths and limitations of the team (e.g., resources and capabilities), 2) develop a suitable (risk handling) plan, 3) implement the plan, and 4) only change the plan if necessary. [Here, any competent high altitude mountain climber will first have prepared for the climb (risk planning), identified potential issues (risk identification), and analyzed these issues (risk analysis) before developing a climbing strategy.]

People are often unaware of the risks, if not danger, that is present. This can lead to very unwise decision making and potentially tragic consequences.

II. Risk Management Process

A. Process Comparison

There is no single best risk management process for any given program, let alone one that can be universally applied to all programs. However, a very good risk management process structure and flow that is suitable for a variety of programs, developed from 1996 through 1998 by the U.S. Department of Defense (DoD 1998), is discussed in Chapter 2. Another representation of the risk management process (Fig. 2.1) is provided in Fig. 3.1, which includes some functions performed for each process step. These functions are discussed in Chapters 2, 4, 5, 6, 7, and 8.

Because terminology varies from industry to industry, and even program to program, it is far less important what the individual process steps are termed than the function(s) they represent and their order. However, it is remarkable that risk management processes published by even reputable organizations often have one or more steps missing, and in some cases several process steps may be absent.

I will now briefly examine some published risk management processes to show which process steps are included and which are missing, vs the recommended steps [DoD 1998: risk planning, assessment (identification and analysis), handling and monitoring]. The example risk management processes evaluated were developed by institutions, such as the DoD, and professional societies. These examples should give the reader sufficient information to evaluate almost any risk management process structure in terms of what steps are present and missing, plus their ordering of performance. A summary of the steps missing from the risk management processes evaluated is given in Table 3.1.

The 1989 Defense Systems Management College (DSMC) *Risk Management Concepts and Guidance* includes planning, assessment, analysis, and handling steps.[5] (The risk management process structure published by the Defense Systems Management College in 1989 is superseded by the DoD 1998 process and published in the 1998 version of the Defense Acquisition University/Defense Systems Management College *Risk Management Guide for DoD Acquisition.* The current, enhanced fifth edition of this guide was published in June 2002.) Here, the planning and handling steps correspond directly to those discussed in Chapter 2 (representing DoD 1998), the analysis step is equivalent to the analysis portion of the assessment step, and the

Table 3.1 Risk management process steps

Risk Management Process	Missing Process Steps[a]
DSMC (DoD, 1989)	Monitoring
DoDI 5000.2 (2002)	Planning, Handling (mentioned 0 of 4 options), and Monitoring
DoD 5000.2-R (2002)	Handling (mentioned 0 of 4 options)
Software Engineering Institute (1996)	Planning, Handling (mentioned 2 of 4 options)
Project Management Institute (2000)	None, but splits risk analysis into qualitative and quantitative steps

[a]Missing steps when compared to DoD 1998 risk management process.

assessment step is equivalent to the identification portion of the assessment step (Chapter 2). In addition, the risk handling step encompasses assumption, avoidance, control (mitigation), and transfer options. Feedback is shown from the risk handling step to all other steps, but there is no risk monitoring step. Consequently, this risk management process includes three of the four steps [planning, assessment (identification and analysis), handling and monitoring] (as discussed in Chapter 2). Except for the lack of the risk monitoring step, the remaining steps and the available documentation[5] are acceptable. It is unfortunate to see how many defense and commercial programs have risk management processes largely inferior to the DSMC 1989 process, particularly because it has been documented, widely circulated, and is readily available to the public.

The most recent version of DoD Directive 5000.1 (change 1, January 2001) does not include mention of risk management, so this reference, which was included in the first edition, is dropped.

The 2002 Department of Defense Instruction (DoDI) 5000.2 states, "Risk management is an organized method of identifying and measuring risk and developing, selecting, and managing options for handling these risks."[6] There are no definitions provided discussing the risk management process steps. No risk planning step is specified. Risk analysis is mentioned indirectly ("measuring risk"). Similarly, although risk handling is mentioned, there is no mention of specific risk handling options; thus zero risk handling options can be accounted for. Consequently, this risk management process includes one of the four steps (Chapter 2).

The 2002 Department of Defense Regulation 5000.2-R states, "The establishment of a risk management process (including planning, assessment (identification and analysis), handling, and monitoring) to be integrated and continuously applied throughout the program, including, but not limited to, the design process. The risk management effort shall address risk planning, the identification and analysis of potential sources of risks including but not limited to cost, performance, and schedule risks based on the technology being used and its related design, manufacturing capabilities, potential industry sources, and test and support processes; risk handling strategies, and risk monitoring approaches."[7] There are no definitions provided discussing the risk management process steps. Although risk handling is mentioned, there is no mention of specific risk handling options; thus zero risk handling options can be accounted for out of the four stated. Consequently, this risk management process includes three of the four steps (Chapter 2). (Note: Although this process does not discuss specific risk handling options, at the top-level it is nevertheless consistent with the DoD 1998 process.)

The Software Engineering Institute (SEI) risk management process includes these steps: identify, analyze, plan, track, and control.[8] (The SEI process has been included in a number of other documents, such as "NASA Procedures and Guidelines: Risk Management Procedures and Guidelines," NPG 8000.4, NASA, 25 April 1998. Substantial funding to develop the SEI risk management process was provided in part by the DoD and concluded in December 1997.) No risk planning step exists in this process. Here, the identify step is equivalent to the identification portion of the assessment step (Chapter 2), and the analyze step is equivalent to the analysis portion of the assessment step. In addition, the plan step is equivalent to the risk handling step, but the only options discussed are assumption and control (mitigation). The track step is equivalent to the monitoring step (Chapter 2), and the control step is equivalent to feedback (Chapter 2). Consequently, this risk management process includes 2-1/2 of the 4 steps (Chapter 2).

The available SEI documentation (including Ref. 8 used here) contains many good project management and risk management insights. However, it contains little material on risk analysis methods (e.g., ordinal risk scales and Monte Carlo simulations) and risk handling options and potential implementation approaches for each option (e.g., discussion of transfer option and some different candidate implementation approaches for this option). In addition, although the SEI risk management process is generic, some of the supporting documentation primarily focuses on nonspecific software technical risk (e.g., not identified as technology or design/engineering risk). Finally the available SEI documentation has little or no treatment of hardware and integration risk; and cost, schedule, and other risk categories (see Chapter 2, Sec. I.B).

In the first edition of this book I discussed the risk management process contained in the 1998 San Francisco Bay Area Chapter of the International Council on Systems Engineering (INCOSE) *Systems Engineering Handbook*.[9] I have omitted this discussion in this edition because the process does not represent an overall INCOSE risk management process, but only a process of a single chapter.

The 2000 Project Management Institute (PMI) *A Guide to the Project*

Management Body of Knowledge (PMBOK® Guide) includes planning, identification, qualitative risk analysis, quantitative risk analysis, response planning, and monitoring and control steps.[10] Discussion is presented on all four risk handling options. Consequently, this risk management process includes four of the four steps (Chapter 2).

Although the PMI 2000 process contains all four process steps (and is an improvement worth mentioning vs the PMI 1996 process), it nevertheless has content limitations vs the 1998 DoD process. For example, the PMI 2000 process documentation contains no discussion of organizational and behavioral considerations associated with risk management. In addition, the performance dimension and technical risk are not discussed except for a very short mention of technical risk (one sentence, Sec. 11.2.1.3) and technical performance measurement for risk monitoring (two sentences, Sec. 11.6.2.4). [In fact the term "performance" in the 2000 PMI *Project Management Body of Knowledge (PMBOK® Guide)* appears to be unrelated to technical matters, except perhaps for the single sentence on technical risk.] In addition, risk analysis is split into qualitative and quantitative process steps without any convincing argument, errors exist in the discussion of ordinal and cardinal numbers, risk scales, and the risk mapping (Probability-Impact) matrix as part of qualitative risk analysis (Sec. 11.3.2.3), and quality and scope are identified as consequence of occurrence components without any information to support this assertion (Sec. 11.3.2.3). (See Chapter 6, Sec. V.H for a brief discussion of why quality and scope are not suitable consequence of occurrence dimensions.) There is also very little discussion on measuring actual vs planned progress associated with an implemented RHP as part of risk monitoring.

Table 3.1 shows clearly that many risk management processes focus on risk assessment (identification and analysis) and to a slightly lesser extent risk handling (although an insufficient number of handling options may exist, which weakens the process). It is surprising that the risk planning and/or monitoring steps are often not included. Although this might at first seem nothing more than a formality, without good risk planning and monitoring the overall risk management process will be greatly weakened. [Note: The risk management processes just evaluated do not represent the most deficient case I have encountered, where cost risk analysis was coupled with the risk handling control option. This process includes 5/12 of the 4 steps. (Here, cost risk analysis is 1/3 of the three top-level risk analysis categories with the others being technical performance and schedule.)]

A variation of the problem of missing risk management process steps is that the steps (planning, assessment, handling and monitoring) may be listed, but one or more may not actually be performed. For example, the risk management process structure may show a risk planning step, but it is never actually performed.

Finally, do not be swayed by the mistaken claims of seemingly informed people regarding what risk management process steps should exist. In one case, a DoD support contractor stated to a DoD audience in June 1999 that: "current DoD thinking regarding risk management identifies five elements of an effective risk management process—risk identification, risk analysis, risk assessment, risk mitigation, and risk management." This is *clearly wrong* given the 1998 DoD risk management process, and includes 1-1/4 of the four steps (Chapter 2)—risk assessment (1) and the control (mitigation) option of risk handling (1/4).

For risk management to be effective, planning, assessment, handling and monitoring steps must be continuously performed.

B.   Some Additional Process Considerations

Another problem that sometimes exists is that risk management process steps may be not be well integrated, or even worse, decoupled. The result will often be decreased effectiveness for the overall process as well as for the individual steps because outputs from one step will likely not be properly carried over as inputs to the next step (e.g., not all identified risks may be properly analyzed). On the surface this may seem trivial, but the problem is severe on some programs. For example, when cost, performance (technical), and schedule risk analysis is performed by different groups within the program, there is, for example, an increased likelihood that risk issues identified through a performance (technical) risk analysis are not considered as part of cost risk analysis.

Outputs from the risk planning step are inputs to the assessment (iden-tification and analysis) and handling and monitoring steps. The outputs from risk identification should be inputs to risk analysis, risk analysis outputs should be inputs to risk handling, and risk monitoring results (of implemented RHP) should be inputs to risk handling and risk analysis (as well as possibly risk identification and planning). Cost, performance (tech-nical), and schedule aspects of risk management must be tightly integrated within the risk management process.

Another common problem is an excessive emphasis on risk analysis, and typically numerical risk analysis scores, over developing and implementing viable RHPs. The greatest risk analysis methodology in the world will not really help the program unless viable methods of handling the risk exist, are implemented, and the progress in reducing the risks is accurately monitored.

No one step should dominate the overall risk management process— strong implementation of all steps is generally necessary to ensure success.

Although less common, it is possible that the risk management process steps may be performed out of logical order, which will reduce the effective-ness of the overall process. For example, in one case risk identification, then risk handling, then risk analysis was performed. Several problems exist with this type of implementation, not the least of which is the need to develop a preliminary RHP for each potential risk issue, rather than those that warrant it (e.g., medium- or higher-risk issues). In this case there was not an effective risk analysis methodology, further weakening the risk management process.

In some cases the risk management process steps may be out of order by more than one process step. For example, in one case the program's RMP was developed after the initial, comprehensive risk identification and risk analysis were performed. Here, there was no initial risk planning and the RMP was effectively developed two steps out of sequence (should have been before risk identification, not before risk handling). Yet without a set of formalized ground rules and assumptions, likely risk categories, and identification and analysis methodologies, the initial risk identification and analysis activities were likely inefficient and potentially ineffective. Similarly, performing initial risk handling evaluations as part of risk identi-fication is also inefficient and potentially ineffective because it is unclear whether or not the risk threshold level needed for performing risk han-dling has been broached because risk analysis has not been performed, and the initial risk handling observations may be incorrect vs those more systematically derived as part of a more formal evaluation. [It is possible that these initial observations may bias the judgment of the risk issue POC by anchoring (see Sec. XIV) who must later develop risk handling strate-gies.]

Unfortunately, the degree to which risk management process steps are out of order cannot be underestimated. In one risk management process devel-opment of the RMP occurred after risk monitoring had been performed when it should have been the output of the very first process step (risk planning). The analyst should carefully evaluate each process step and the functions associated with it to determine the existing vs appropriate risk management process order.

In some cases the risk management process steps may be out of order by more than one process step. The risk planning, assessment, handling, and monitoring steps should be performed in consecutive order (with feedback present).

Somewhat similarly, it is possible to have valid functions assigned to the wrong risk management process step. When this occurs the result can be more than just an annoyance. In some cases it may introduce inefficiency that requires additional resources, while in other cases it may increase the likelihood of generating erroneous results. For example, risk ranking may be performed as part of risk handling when it is actually a risk analysis function. Another example is performing at least part of the risk analysis evaluation (e.g., estimating the consequence of occurrence for a risk issue) as part of risk identification. A third example is developing initial RHPs as part of risk identification when RHPs would only be needed for risk issues evaluated to be medium or higher risk (determined by risk analysis). While there is no universal set of correct functions to perform for each risk management process step on each program, consider using the functions listed in Fig. 3.1 (and discussed in Chapters 2, 4, 5, 6, 7, and 8) as a starting point.

Attention should be paid to the functions performed in each risk management process step to reduce potential inefficiency and the likelihood of generating erroneous results.

The most important element of risk management is to develop and implement a suitable risk management process, including all key process steps and the necessary behavioral considerations to make the process "work." Without this, there is little chance of having effective risk management. For example, you can collect "perfect" risk data but still have an ineffective risk management process unless the steps are comprehensive and tailored to the program and a suitable behavioral environment exists to perform risk management.

The most important element of risk management is to develop and implement a suitable risk management process, including all key process steps and the necessary behavioral considerations to make the process "work."

Risk management is not a separate process step or group of steps, it is the entire risk management process that includes all process steps; how the process is implemented; existing and retired risks, how information is documented and communicated; and so forth.

Risk management is not a separate process step or group of steps; it is the entire risk management process.

Some risk management process steps may be represented by more than one step. This may have the appearance of being "more complete" but this typically adds nothing of substance and may lead to additional nonessential work being performed. For example, in one case risk analysis was split into qualitative and quantitative components—each a separate process step. This is potentially inappropriate since either one or both may be used and in either order—hence there is no flow that necessarily exists between the two steps. In another case risk handling was split into selection of the primary option and development of the implementation approach for the selected option. In reality, the two steps, while they flow together, should be merged into one and the candidate risk handling strategy reviewed by the RMB (or equivalent). Having risk handling split into two steps requires two screening sessions by the RMB (or equivalent)—one for the risk handling option and one for the implementation approach. Of course, rejected or other nonselected options and implementation approaches may be reviewed by the RMB (or equivalent) as necessary. In some cases the RMB (or equivalent) may select one or more other options and implementation approaches as backup strategies.

Some risk management process steps may be represented by more than one step. This may have the appearance of being "more complete" but typically adds nothing of substance and contributes an additional layer of work being performed.

All risk management process steps are equally important. If you do not do one or more steps, or you do them poorly, you will likely have an ineffective risk management process. In one case, three different divisions of the same organization said that a different process step was most important. One said risk identification, the second said risk analysis, and the third said risk handling. In reality, each group needed a noticeable degree of improvement in its "most important" risk management process step. In addition, none of the groups performed risk planning, the risk handling control option appeared to be selected with little or no consideration of the other three options (assumption, avoidance, and transfer), and each had only a weak risk monitoring process step. Hence, each group had ~ 1 1/4 to 2 1/4 of the 4 risk management process steps (vs DoD 1998), and they should have been focusing on correcting the substantial weaknesses present in their own processes rather than magnifying the importance of a single process step.

All risk management process steps are equally important. If you do not do one or more steps, or you do them poorly, you will likely have an ineffective risk management process.

The reason for performing a risk assessment is not to attempt to handle risks but to identify candidate risk issues, and for those risk issues approved by the RMB, estimate the level of risk present. For example, in some cases candidate risk issues will not be approved and in other cases a risk issue may be analyzed to be low risk and no formal risk handling action taken. Thus not every candidate risk issue will undergo formal risk handling.

A risk assessment is performed to identify candidate risk issues, and for those risk issues approved by the RMB, estimate the level of risk present. It is not performed to handle risks.

Having a simple risk management process is not sufficient in and of itself—the process must include all steps, be structured, repeatable, the steps must be in the correct order, have sufficient sophistication, etc. Of course, having an overly complicated risk management process is not beneficial, but that is not a justification to use a simplistic process, particularly when it will be inadequate to properly perform risk management on the program.

Having a simple risk management process is not sufficient in and of itself—the process must include all steps, be structured, repeatable, the steps must be in the correct order, have sufficient sophistication, etc.

It is important to realize that the risk management process and each process step is iterative, not just a single process step (e.g., risk analysis). If process steps are static, important updates may be missed and the effectiveness of the risk management process can be greatly diminished.

The risk management process and each process step is iterative, not just a single process step (e.g., risk analysis).

Continuously evaluating risk issues and exploring potential, new risk issues is not limited to a single risk management process step, but should be performed in all risk management process steps (including risk planning).

The entire risk management process should be implemented in a continuous manner, not just a single process step.

Risk indicators and triggers should ideally be evaluated as part of risk planning and, if appropriate, used for risk identification. Indicators and triggers are not generally suitable tools and techniques for performing a risk analysis.

Risk indicators and triggers should ideally be evaluated as part of risk planning and, if appropriate, used for risk identification.

When multiple, related risk issues exist (e.g., four issues associated with the same component), it is generally better to treat the risk issues separately rather than evaluate them and report a composite score. The reason for this is that the nature of each underlying risk issue may be lost, including the probability and consequence of occurrence values, different RHPs may be needed, critical schedule milestones may be different, etc. This is particularly true when the individual risk issues diverge from each other rather than being closely related (e.g., same predominant risk category and dominant consequence of occurrence component).

When multiple, related risk issues exist, it is often better to treat the risk issues separately rather than evaluate them and report a composite score.

Don't casually rebaseline risk issues—this should only be done on a case-by-case basis with the authorization of the RMB. Rebaselining a risk issue may lead to changes in 1) relevant risk categories, 2) likelihood and/or consequence of occurrence and risk score, 3) relative ranking among program risks, 4) risk handling strategy and necessary resources, and/or 5) risk monitoring approach. Of course, rebaselining should be performed when warranted (e.g., revelation that the existing risk handling strategy is no longer suitable), but only after carefully evaluating the ramifications of such an action before enacting the change(s).

Don't casually rebaseline risk issues—this should only be done on a case-by-case basis with the authorization of the RMB.

If you do not have a well estimated and fixed baseline and/or do not initially estimate/plan risk handling milestones vs time, then it may be difficult, if not impossible to perform quantitative risk monitoring on RHPs and their implementation approach tasks. For example, all you have is a single risk step-down chart time and you do not know whether or not you are on, ahead, or behind the plan. In such cases, fix a baseline as soon as possible and get risk handling tasks agreed upon and inserted into the integrated master schedule (IMS) (or equivalent) which provides a basis for estimating actual vs plan progress checks.

A well estimated and fixed baseline and an initial estimate/plan risk of handling milestones vs time are needed to perform quantitative risk monitoring on RHPs and their implementation approach tasks.

The inclusion of related-risk issues for risk identification, analysis, and handling should include a two-tier approach. In the first tier, simply list the interrelated risk issues. In the second tier, probe and discuss the specifics of the interrelationship (e.g., the types and level of shared resources), quantitative considerations, etc. Don't just use the top-level, first tier approach—it is generally too simplistic to be beneficial in estimating the affect of risk issue interrelationships on the program.

When evaluating interrelated risk issues use a two-tier approach. In the first tier, simply list the interrelated risk issues. In the second tier, probe and discuss the specifics of the interrelationship.

Do not arbitrarily change risk scales ("probability" and consequence) during a program phase when the primary goal is to show progress vs time in reducing risk via implementing RHPs. In the worst case this is nothing more than gaming the risk levels, and in the best case may introduce confusion. Also, the risk ranking may change with different scales which may be of some importance if full funding is not available, and only a limited number of RHPs can be fully funded.

Do not arbitrarily change risk scales ("probability" and consequence) during a program phase when the primary goal is to show progress vs time in reducing risk via implementing RHPs.

Avoid situations where confusing methodologies are proposed, then re-proposed despite flaws associated with them having been identified and agreed upon by participants. This can lower morale associated with performing risk management, especially when the methodology is moderately to severely flawed. In one case a risk issue POC continued to bring forth a methodology numerous times after being told by upper management that the methodology was confusing and should not be used. This had the potential to weaken the program's risk management process and how it was implemented on the program.

Avoid situations where confusing methodologies are proposed, then re-proposed despite flaws associated with them having been identified and agreed upon by participants.

In some cases risk issues are ranked by the ability to manage an effective response. Even worse, this may be done as part of risk identification. Risk issues should ranked by the level of risk that exists (and from highest to lowest), and performed as part of risk analysis, not identification. In addition, the ability to manage an effective response should be part of every risk handling strategy developed and included in RHPs.

Risk issues should ranked by the level of risk that exists (and from highest to lowest), and performed as part of risk analysis, not identification.

Stop light charts (e.g., red, yellow, green) can be very subjective and should only cautiously be used. In addition, scoring rules for the resulting colors must be clearly explained. There is considerable potential for misclassifying results into such charts (e.g., two scores of yellow and one score of green being scored green rather than yellow), the same way, as for example, misclassifying results from multiple probability scales into a single-scale level. This is made all the more critical if the number of stop light levels is small (particularly if three), since a misclassification of a single level can have a large impact on the results.

Stop light charts (e.g., red, yellow, green) can be very subjective, should only cautiously be used, and if used scoring rules for the resulting colors must be clearly explained.

A key question to ask after performing a risk assessment (identification and analysis) is "do the results make sense?" In one case the number of medium- and high-risk issues was seemingly inversely related to the "true" risk level associated with several risk items (e.g., a higher risk item had fewer risk issues analyzed to be medium and high than a lower risk item). While this was not identified by the seller organization, it was detected by the buyer organization. This should have been detected by the seller as part of a "sanity check" performed on the results, but was not.

After performing a risk assessment, step back and examine the results to see if they "make sense."

Communication, like documentation, is not a separate risk management process step, but an implicit process and set of procedures that apply to each process step.

Communication, like documentation, is not a separate risk management process step.

C. Risk Planning

If you perform risk planning, then make it a formal process step and include it in the risk management process. In such cases, don't just list risk planning as an input to risk identification since this may unwittingly suggest that risk planning is less important than other risk management process steps.

If you perform risk planning, then make it a formal process step and include it in the risk management process.

D. Risk Identification

Do not include risk analysis as part of risk identification. For example, "risk cues" that include word definitions for low, medium, and high risk should not be part of risk identification. This confuses the level of a risk with whether or not the risk is a valid issue to explore on the program. Similarly, each risk issue should not be explored to develop one or more cues that then are fitted as low, medium, or high as part of risk identification. Risk scoring into levels should only be performed as part of risk analysis on RMB (or equivalent) approved risk issues from risk identification, not just as part of risk identification.

Do not include risk analysis as part of risk identification.

E. Risk Analysis

Risk analysis is not risk management but only one substep (part of risk assessment) of four risk management process steps. Risk management can help the project manager as an input to his decision making, while risk analysis by itself is of little or no value. For example, if you do not have valid ground rules and assumptions (risk planning), have not correctly identified risk issues (risk identification), have not developed and implemented viable RHPs (risk handling), and do not perform risk monitoring (risk monitoring), even a "perfect" risk analysis methodology will have little or no value to the program manager and his risk management needs.

Risk analysis is not risk management but only one substep (part of risk assessment) of four risk management process steps.

Risk analysis should refer only to the risk analysis process step, not identification and analysis. If a superset term is desired, risk assessment should be used for identification and analysis, not analysis.

Risk analysis should refer only to the risk analysis process step, not identification and analysis.

Prioritize risks should not be a separate process step as it is a function performed in risk analysis. Making it a separate process step is inefficient and may introduce confusion (e.g., who performs the prioritization, is prioritization as important as analysis?).

Prioritize risks should not be a separate process step as it is a function performed in risk analysis.

Reevaluate risk exposure is not a risk management process step. At best it refers to performing the risk analysis again, at worst it is a gross over-simplification of the feedback portion of the risk management process flow that examines actual vs planned progress in implementing RHPs, reanalyzes risk issues, reevaluates risk identification documentation to ensure that the nature of the risk has not changed, and reexamines the underlying process as warranted (e.g., if scope changes occur) as part of risk planning.

Reevaluate risk exposure is not a risk management process step.

Risk scores should be objectively generated and not used as a political tool between organizations. For example, on one program risk estimates appeared to be artificially high for a particular subcontractor, and the subcontractor did not readily supply suitable backup data to explain its estimates. (It is also interesting to note that the level of estimated management reserve that could be allocated to an organization was proportional to risk level on this program.) The net effect was to irritate other teammates on the program and cause concern on the part of the buyer, particularly given the exaggerated nature of the representation. The higher-level organization reevaluated the lower-level organization risk scores and estimated that they were roughly X% too high. While this X% factor was not out of line, rather than having the lower-level organization reevaluate the risks and provide acceptable backup, the higher-level organization reduced the risk scores by X%. Thus, in this case the risk analysis process had likely been violated twice—once by the lower-level organization who overestimated risk scores and a second time by the higher-level organization who directed an X% reduction.

Risk scores should be objectively generated and not used as a political tool between organizations.

Risks that are analyzed to be medium or higher should also be mapped to program requirements where possible in addition to budget and schedule to ensure that sufficient resources will be focused on meeting critical performance requirements.

Risks that are analyzed to be medium or higher should also be mapped to program requirements where possible.

Risk analysis results should be an input to the risk handling process step, but they should not generally be used to "drive" the risk handling strategy perhaps beyond 1) a floor where if you are below it, placing the item on the watchlist may be acceptable and no RHP is needed; and 2) having multiple risk handling strategies for high risks. Most other relationships between risk analysis and risk handling (e.g., high risk requires the risk handling control option) are generally flawed and can lead to erroneous results.

Risk analysis results should be an input to the risk handling process step, but they should not generally be used to "drive" the risk handling strategy.

Another instance of mixed up risk management functions in different process steps is including an evaluation of the "ease of mitigation" as part of risk analysis. Not only was this a subjective assessment, but it was limited to the mitigation option of risk handling. Similarly, the same risk management process included no risk planning step and only the control and assumption options of risk handling. In addition, a primary means of risk analysis in this risk management process was a subjective evaluation of probability (1 to 10) and impact (1 to 10), which yields a risk factor with a range of 1 to 100 and one that is unstructured and purely subjective without any guidelines for its generation. Rather amazingly, this risk management approach has been used to evaluate a number of systems with high life-cycle costs.

Do not reference risk mitigation (handling) as part of risk analysis. Risk analysis and risk handling are two separate risk management process steps.

Another example of intermixing risk analysis and risk handling is when risk levels are tied to the degree of difficulty to employ "risk mitigation." Not only are risk handling and risk analysis uncorrelated (except for the desire to perform risk handling on risk issues with, say, medium- or higher-risk levels), but the optimal risk handling options are also uncorrelated with the risk level for a given risk issue. Simply stated, there is no correlation between the risk level and the "best" risk handling strategy—it varies on a case-by-case basis with each risk issue, or the "ease of mitigation" that will exist.

Do not tie risk levels to the degree of difficulty to employ risk mitigation (handling). Risk analysis and risk handling are two separate risk management process steps.

Risk analysis should not be viewed as the "front end" of risk management—it is the second part of the risk assessment step and should follow after risk planning and identification.

Risk analysis should not be viewed as the "front end" of risk management—it follows risk planning and risk identification in order of application.

Quantitative risk analysis results for a given risk issue are of little or no value in selecting risk handling strategies. However, they should be considered as one of many tools for evaluating candidate risk handling strategies on selected risk issues. For example, risk analysis results for a given risk issue will generally provide no information about the viability of risk handling strategies. But once the decision has been made to develop and implement an RHP for a given risk issue, the candidate risk handling strategies to address that risk issue should include risk analysis to determine likely risk levels vs milestones, thus time, and other techniques (e.g., benefit/cost ratio) as well.

Quantitative risk analysis results for a given risk issue are of little or no value in selecting risk handling strategies. However, they should be considered as one of many tools for evaluating candidate risk handling strategies on selected risk issues.

In one risk management process risk ranking was an output of risk handling, however, this is generally ineffective. Risk ranking should be an output of risk analysis and thus an input to risk handling in case full funding is not available to cover all RHPs, etc. Risk ranking is part of risk analysis, not risk handling.

Risk ranking should be an output of risk analysis, not risk handling.

F. Risk Handling

Placing a risk issue on a watchlist is not a risk handling option. This is an RMB function, not a risk handling option. The risk handling options are assumption, avoidance, control, and transfer.

Placing a risk issue on a watchlist is not a risk handling option.

Do not include risk handling information (e.g., risk handling strategy tasks) as part of the documentation of rationale for developing risk analysis probability and consequence of occurrence scores. Risk handling strategies and the detailed tasks that will be implemented should be included as part of the RHP, not risk analysis results to prevent confusion between the two risk management process steps. In addition, the RMB should determine which approved risk issues will have corresponding RHPs developed—not all issues that are evaluated as part of risk analysis will require RHPs (e.g., while it varies on a program-by-program basis, the RMB might set a threshold of a medium- or higher-risk level to develop an RHP).

Do not include risk handling information (e.g., risk handling strategy tasks) as part of the documentation of rationale for developing risk analysis probability and consequence of occurrence scores. Risk analysis and risk handling are two different risk management process steps.

Risk alternatives should be evaluated as part of risk handling, not risk identification (although alternatives may in and of themselves introduce risks).

Risk alternatives should be evaluated as part of risk handling, not risk identification.

Questions pertaining to existing and potential risk handling strategies should not be included as part of risk identification, but part of risk handling for those risk issues where development of an RHP is appropriate.

Questions pertaining to existing and potential risk handling strategies should not be included as part of risk identification, but part of risk handling.

Initial risk handling planning should not be performed as part of risk identification or analysis. This is because a number of candidate risk issues will not be approved by the RMB, and in some cases only risk issues that are analyzed to be medium or higher will have RHPs developed. Thus, developing draft risk handling information as part of risk identification or analysis may waste scarce resources and not even be used.

Initial risk handling planning should not be performed as part of risk identification or analysis.

III. Risk Management Process Integration

A. Some Integration Considerations

Risk management should be either part of the program's program management or systems engineering processes and linked to both of these processes. (Both program management and systems engineering can be viewed as top-level program processes. In commercial programs risk management is often part of the program management process, whereas in many defense programs it is often included as part of the systems engineering process.)

A key consideration is that risk management should have both a focal point and a group that takes ownership responsibility within the government and contractor program offices. (Of course, this is in addition to the program manager who is ultimately responsible for risk management, but not for routine activities.) A key goal, regardless of how risk management is integrated into a higher-level process, is to make all program personnel aware that risk should be a consideration in the design, development, production, fielding/deployment, and operational support of a system. "It should not be treated as someone else's responsibility."[11]

Risk management should also be well integrated with a number of other key processes that exist in the program. These include, but are not limited to 1) contracting (presolicitation through program execution), 2) configuration management, 3) cost analysis, 4) cost as an independent variable (and design to cost), 5) design, 6) manufacturing, 7) quality assurance, 8) reliability, 9) schedule analysis, 10) support (e.g., maintainability), and 11) test and evaluation. If the risk management process is not well integrated with each of these processes, then key program decisions may be adversely affected. In addition, risk management should be closely coupled with the program's acquisition strategy (e.g., budget, number of competitors, and goals). For example, the risk management process should be aligned with the program's acquisition strategy to help the program pass major milestones in the most cost effective and timely manner possible.

B. Relationship to Program Management and Systems Engineering

Risk management should be viewed as a program management or systems engineering process; and thus a subset of one of these top-level processes. It is not a separate unrelated process, nor a complete overlap of either program management or systems engineering. Similarly, risk management is a subset of either the program management or systems engineering processes, not the complete process by itself.

Current DoD guidance says that risk management "should be integral to a program's overall management." In addition, this guidance says that risk management should be considered a "vital integrated program management tool that cuts across the entire acquisition program, addressing and interrelating cost, performance (technical), and schedule risk."[11]

There are pros and cons of integrating risk management with program management vs systems engineering. In reality, the quality of the implementation is generally more important than the higher-level process that risk management is integrated with—both good and bad examples exist for program management and systems engineering. For example, regardless of the higher-level process that risk management is integrated with, the program manager and other key program personnel should take an active role in the risk management process to ensure that their approach leads to a balanced use of program resources, reflects their overall management philosophy, and includes government and contractors.

Risk management should be viewed as a program management or systems engineering process, and thus a subset of one of these top-level processes.

The risk management process should be owned by program management or systems engineering organizations within the program, not other organizations such as cost estimating, because their focus will often not adequately span the program, and the resulting process can be, and often is, flawed.

The risk management process should be owned by program management or systems engineering organizations within the program.

While risk management is a potentially important facet of project management, it should not be viewed as equivalent to and the sole process associated with project management (e.g., good risk management is good project management). Good project management includes a number of other important characteristics, including but not limited to, budgeting/cost, communication, configuration control, contracting, human resources, management, scheduling, etc. Focusing on risk management at the expense of other key project management disciplines is unwise and will likely contribute to problems in the program. Similarly, risk management is a component of good systems engineering, but not the sole or necessarily the most important part of systems engineering. For example, risk management is a component of the systems analysis and control function of systems engineering, but this function may also include such things as configuration management, data management, effectiveness analysis, interface management, performance-based progress management, and tradeoff studies. Likewise, the systems analysis and control function is but one function of systems engineering, the others being functional analysis/allocation, requirements analysis, and synthesis (design).[12]

While risk management is a potentially important facet of project management and systems engineering, it should not be viewed as equivalent to and the sole process associated with project management and systems engineering.

Risk management is not, and should never be viewed as, a "Band-Aid®" for poor project management or systems engineering. Good project management and systems engineering should be practiced by all program personnel to the extent possible otherwise the number of risk issues will likely increase as will the number of problems that impact the program (cet. par.)

Risk management is not, and should never be viewed as, a "Band-Aid®" for poor project management or systems engineering.

IV. Risk Management Process Effectiveness

A. Some Desirable Process Attributes

The risk management process should be tailored to each program. Although this seems obvious and trivial, it is surprising how many programs attempt to copy and use an existing process, including its tools and techniques. Although the same risk management process steps should be used [planning, assessment (identification and analysis), handling, and monitoring], how the steps are implemented in *your program* must be carefully considered to ensure that it is the right fit and will yield acceptable results. Some of the considerations for tailoring risk management to a program include, but are not limited to 1) program budget, performance (or integration complexity, etc.), and schedule (e.g., key milestones); 2) contractual requirements; 3) buyer, seller, and stakeholder expectations; 4) structure of buyer and seller organizations; 5) organizational and corporate culture toward risk management; 6) knowledge, experience, and attitude of the program manager toward risk management; 7) program phase; 8) communication mechanisms and reporting techniques; 9) likely risk categories; 10) implementation experience with various tools and techniques; and 11) resource availability (e.g., number and training of personnel).

What will almost guarantee an ineffective risk management process, if not failure, is taking the RMP and lessons learned from a program where risk management was effective and blindly attempting to apply it without expert tailoring to your program. This is all the more unwise when the people attempting to perform the implementation do not have credible risk management training and experience, or suitable behavioral or management science skills. Unfortunately this cookie-cutter behavior is surprisingly common, particularly in organizations that do not have a history of effective risk management. Such organizations often attempt to copy previous work to a new program—winding up with a square peg in a round hole—rather than obtain the necessary expert assistance to help perform the tailoring process. This is not only wastes resources early in the program because of inefficiency in initially implementing the process, but may lead to substantial trouble throughout the remainder of the program because of the increased likelihood of an ineffective process. This practice is truly penny wise and pound foolish.

When a risk management process that was successful on one program is transferred to others, be cautious of claims by the personnel in the recipient programs that they have correctly implemented the process, including tailoring it to their particular program. Successful risk management process transfer from one organization to another will generally not happen without "glitches" and issues having to be resolved. All too often the resulting risk management process will be degraded on the recipient project compared to the original project. While this can be the result of faulty tailoring, it is often common that the recipient project injects other changes into the process and its implementation beyond what is needed for tailoring. Such attempts to "improve" the process may well lead to the opposite result and lower the effectiveness. Dealing with this situation can be complicated when the recipient organization does not perform, or even worse does not permit, independent evaluations of its risk management process to be performed. Independent evaluations are often helpful, if not essential, to ensure that the recipient organization has properly implemented the risk management process, to verify that the tailoring it performed is suitable, and that erroneous information has not been injected.

Similarly, a tendency exists for those that participated on a program where risk management was effective to simply copy the process to another program. This is unwise as tailoring, at a minimum, is needed. Beyond that it may be necessary to have a substantially different process that cannot be efficiently derived from tailoring the previous process. Yet this may not even be recognized. Participants in such cases are looking through a microscope when they should initially be viewing through a wide-angle lens.

Another variant of this problem is that organizations without a history of effective risk management will take an RMP from a program that was successful and apply it to another program. The reason sometimes given for doing this is that if the program was successful, then the RMP is suitable for use on another program. However, this rationale is faulty—the program may have been successful for reasons unrelated to the RMP or even the implemented risk management process. And in some cases the RMP may be substandard and should not be used on any other program without substantial modifications and enhancements.

The risk management process should be tailored to each program. This tailoring should be performed by personnel with credible training and experience. Attempting to blindly use an RMP and lessons learned from another program will almost guarantee an ineffective risk management process and increases the likelihood that adverse events will occur later in the program. When a risk management process that was successful on one program is transferred to others, be cautious of claims by the personnel in the recipient programs that they have correctly implemented the process; including tailoring it to their particular program.

Risk management is implemented in a weak or ad hoc manner on many programs. This may contribute to a wide variety of problems associated with the individual process steps, the results generated, and the effectiveness of the overall process.

"A structured risk management process, which is applied early, continuously, and rigorously, provides a disciplined environment for decision making and for the efficient use of program resources."[11] By performing risk management in this manner, program personnel can potentially uncover and resolve risk issues that would otherwise become problems and have a major adverse cost, performance, and/or schedule impact later in the program.[11]

"The need for a formal risk management process arises from the nature of risk and the complexity of acquisition programs. The numerous risks in an acquisition program are often interrelated and obscure and change in the course of the development process. A formal approach is the only effective method to sort through numerous risk issues, to identify the risks and their interrelationships, to pinpoint the truly critical ones, and to identify cost, performance, and schedule effective ways to reduce those risks, consistent with overall program objectives."[11]

"A structured (risk management process) can reduce the complexity of an acquisition program by defining (and planning) an approach to assess, handle, and [monitor (and communicate)] program risk. The systematic identification, analysis, handling, and (monitoring) of risks [also (helps)] to ensure objectivity [(cet. par.)], that is, minimize unwarranted optimism, prejudice, ignorance, or self-interest. Further, structure tends to reduce the impact of personnel turnover and provides a basis for training and consistency among all of the functional areas of a program. A structured risk program may also promote teamwork and understanding and improves the quality of the risk products."[11]

Risk management should be implemented as a structured process whereby planning occurs and risks are systematically assessed (identified and analyzed), handled, and monitored.

Effective risk management is also based on the premise that program personnel must identify risk issues, long before they occur and become problems, and develop strategies that increase the likelihood of a favorable outcome to these problems. "Typically, the early identification of risk issues is concerned with two types of events. The first are relevant to the current or imminent acquisition phase of a program [(near or) intermediate term]," such as using risk as part of the design trade process or satisfying a technical exit criteria in time for the next milestone review.[11] "The second are concerned with the future phase(s) of a program (long-term) such as potential risk (issues) related to transitioning a system from development to production."[11] In both cases the risk issue is or should be known but has not yet impacted the program.[11]

There is a tendency on some programs to be less concerned about risk issues that have a moderate- to long-time horizon vs those with a short-time horizon. Although this is understandable, program personnel must not fall into the trap of crisis management of near-term issues or present problems vs effective risk management. A better way to implement risk management is to identify and analyze risks for each candidate risk issue per program phase, develop suitable risk handling strategies, and fund the approved RHPs based upon overall program priority determined by risk ranking and the necessary RHP initiation date. (Note: The frequency of occurrence of the risk issue and interdependence with other risk issues can also be used either directly or indirectly in the risk rating methodology.)

Risk management should be forward looking to identify potential, future risk issues. Risk issues should be analyzed for each program phase, suitable risk handling strategies developed (for medium or higher risks), and RHPs funded based upon overall program priority determined by risk level ranking and the necessary RHP initiation date.

B. Risk Management Process Sophistication

The necessary sophistication of the risk management process may be related to the industry of the project but is often more related to the level of performance, integration complexity, etc. that is required. (Of course, some industries also have considerable regulatory oversight, which may add to the needed level of risk management process sophistication. In industries without considerable regulatory oversight, projects that are well within the performance or integration state of the art may not require a sophisticated risk management process.)

For example, a representative of a commercial aircraft manufacturer stated that little formal risk management was needed on a particular aircraft development project. (After being briefed on the project, it appeared that the risk management process was both weak and ad hoc.) The development project required changing the shape of the wing—well within the state of the art, fairly far down the cost/performance curve, and low risk. However, as an observer in the audience later commented, if the aircraft also needed to be nearly invisible to radar a considerable increase in the required level of risk management and its sophistication would have been warranted because the resulting design would have been near or at the state of the art and on the steep part of the cost vs performance curve—potentially indicative of high risk.

Even a very high-visibility, large-budget program may have an inadequate risk management process. For example, on one very large program with numerous, highly publicized cost increases and schedule slips, the risk management process was woefully inadequate [e.g., no risk planning step, overly simplistic and erroneous risk analysis methodology, inadequate risk handling (control option pushed, transfer option not discussed, and avoidance option not mentioned—thus only control and acceptance or two of the four handling options were in use), and no risk monitoring was performed].

The degree of sophistication and completeness of the risk management process is often uncorrelated with the budget, performance, schedule, and priority and visibility of the program. Simply stated, do not assume that a large, "high tech" program has a superior risk management process to say a smaller program even in the same organization. For example, a simple comparison of the risk management processes on two different programs (A, B) revealed the following. Program "A" (the smaller program) and program "B" (the larger program) had comparable, risk management processes from a process sophistication and completeness perspective. Program "A" had better risk planning, somewhat better risk analysis, and a better risk handling selection criteria, while program "B" had better risk monitoring. (The two programs had comparable risk identification and risk documentation.) Programs "A" and "B" had roughly equal, and exceptional, risk management implementation and both had a positive culture to perform it. Programs "A" and "B" were very different acquisitions in different organizations, but overlapped in time. Yet the budget for program "B" was ~ 2,500 times greater than that for program "A" over the life cycle and the schedule for program "B" was ~ 10 times longer than program "A." This in no way is a criticism of program "B," but only an illustration that effective risk management is possible even on relatively small programs so long as program management and higher management within the organization want to properly perform risk management. If the reverse is true, there may be no amount of budget or schedule that may lead to effective risk management.

Similarly, the size of an organization and its programs is not necessarily correlated with risk management effectiveness. It is not uncommon to find large organizations with numerous high-value projects using substandard risk management that is years behind available best practices. For example, in one case risk management practices being used by a large organization with numerous multibillion dollar projects relied on published risk management guidance that was 10 years old and one to two major revisions out of date. This was despite the fact that updates to the guidance were available free and widely published.

I have also noted on many programs that risk management process sophistication is practically uncorrelated with its effectiveness. Sophisticated processes (e.g., using quantitative risk analysis methods including simulations) can be poorly implemented, and the resulting effectiveness can be very low. Conversely, a relatively unsophisticated risk management process (e.g., one that does not use any simulations) may have very good organizational implementation, where management and workers are performing risk management as part of their regular job function. In this case the resulting risk management process effectiveness may be fairly high.

The overall risk management process effectiveness is a combination or product of two factors: namely, the technical sophistication coupled with the level of its organizational implementation. Assume that each of these terms is a decimal number from zero to one, with the product of the two terms representing the overall effectiveness. A low score for either term can substantially reduce the overall risk management process effectiveness, and in many cases the degree of difficulty to improve the level of organizational implementation is several times greater than that to achieve the same incremental improvement in technical sophistication. However, whereas it may be easier to obtain marginal improvements in process sophistication over organizational implementation, both areas must be satisfactory to have an effective risk management process.

Risk management process effectiveness is often uncorrelated with company size and market share. On several occasions I have observed large companies using a risk management process that is neither sophisticated nor well implemented, and the overall effectiveness is low. Company personnel sometimes said they were using a corporate process, which was particularly disappointing because the same flawed approach was likely being used on a large number of programs. However, in other cases I have observed a wide variation in both risk management process sophistication and the level of organizational implementation on different programs within the same division and location of a company.

The degree of sophistication and completeness of the risk management process is often uncorrelated with the budget, performance, schedule, and priority and visibility of the program. Simply stated, do not assume that a large, "high tech" program has a superior risk management process to say a smaller program even in the same organization. Similarly, the size of an organization and its programs is not necessarily correlated with risk management effectiveness. When risk management process improvements are considered, those associated with technical sophistication usually gain greater support than those associated with organizational implementation. While it may be easier to obtain marginal improvements in process sophistication over organizational implementation, both areas must be satisfactory to have an effective risk management process.

For military or proprietary commercial projects the overall effectiveness of the risk management process is typically uncorrelated with the sensitivity of the project (cet. par.). Simply stated, high security provides no guarantee or even indication that the project's risk management process is adequate and that the project itself will be successful. In some cases, I have observed that the effectiveness of the risk management process is inversely proportional to the security level of the program. This is often related to an acquisition environment that has historically been insulated from outside scrutiny and controls, coupled with problem solving (e.g., crisis management) being practiced rather than risk management by key program personnel (see Secs. XIII and XIV in this chapter for additional information).

The effectiveness of the project's risk management process is typically uncorrelated with the sensitivity of the project. High security provides no guarantee or even indication that the project's risk management process is adequate and that the project itself will be successful.

Every project should not have the same level or depth of risk analysis or even risk management. The level or depth of each risk management process step should be tailored to the project—one size does not fit all—and is dependent upon a number of considerations (e.g., budget, performance, schedule, contractual requirements, available tools and techniques). Attempting to use the "one size fits all" approach will generally lead to an inefficient use of resources.

Every project should not have the same level or depth of risk analysis or even risk management. This will vary on a program-by-program basis and is dependent upon a number of considerations.

The level of sophistication associated with the approach used to develop improved risk management methodologies can be readily compromised by faulty decision making during the course of the development activity. For example, in one case considerable effort was made to develop a set of ordinal "probability" scales and the within-scale calibration was performed.

However, there was substantial disagreement among the participants as to what the between scale calibration coefficients should be. A meeting involving key personnel was planned, and the software was in-place and available to record data from participants. Unfortunately, the risk manager discarded this approach, did not invite key personnel to the meeting, and resolved the matter by deciding that the three scale categories should be weighed equally (e.g., 1/3, 1/3, and 1/3), when no evidence existed to support this approach. This eliminated the agreed upon methodology and its advantage of a structured, repeatable process in favor of a subjective guess, and due to the "flip-flop" behavior, potentially diminished the credibility of the risk management process implementation.

The level of sophistication associated with the approach used to develop improved risk management methodologies can be readily compromised by faulty decision making during the course of the development activity.

C. Known Unknowns vs Unknown Unknowns

Although the risk management process should focus on known unknowns (e.g., an immature manufacturing process for a high-performance sensor detector chip), it should be responsive to potential unknown unknowns (e.g., an unannounced budget cut), even if these issues are external to the program. After the possibility of a specific event is identified, the issue should be rapidly evaluated in a risk management context. This can potentially assist key program personnel to make more objective decisions than otherwise possible. Having an effective risk management process in place can also help identify some issues that might otherwise slip through the cracks and later surface as problems. (Actual risks that have occurred or are occurring are problems, while potential risks are risk issues.) It may also help key personnel make more intelligent decisions by providing them with accurate inputs associated with potential risk issues after they are identified (even if they were initially unknown unknowns).

A related issue is that comprehensive risk assessments involving the program's work breakdown structure (WBS) (to at least Level 5) and key program processes are infrequently performed on many programs. This can lead to some risk issues not being detected in a timely fashion causing potentially serious problems later in the program when risk issues surface. However, in many cases at least some of these unknown unknowns should have been previously identified, analyzed, and handled. Comprehensive risk assessments should be done at the beginning of a program phase, and then once a year or even more frequently—particularly for fast-paced programs. (On one very fast-paced program that I worked on, the RMB formally met once a month. However, the daily program engineering–management meeting included the same participants as the RMB. Risk-related decisions were sometimes made daily to ensure that suitable risk handling approaches were developed or updated and implemented on a timely basis.) In addition, periodic updates should also be performed (e.g., once a quarter or more frequently as warranted) to ensure that no new risk issues exist or the status of identified issues has not substantially changed.

Comprehensive risk assessments can help identify some potentially significant risk issues that might otherwise remain undetected until later in the program when they can have substantial cost and/or schedule impact to resolve.

V.   Risk Management, the Program Life Cycle, and Time-Frame Considerations

The risk management process should exist over the life cycle of the program, not simply during the tenure of a given program manager. Requirements for risk assessment and risk handling steps will likely change somewhat during the program, and this should be reflected in the risk management process and documented in the RMP. For example, it may not be possible to perform a detailed analysis of manufacturing risks during the Concept Exploration program phase but this should be done as part of the detailed design trade process early in the Program Definition and Risk Reduction program phase.

Risk management should be tailored to the specific program phase.

On some programs the philosophy is to start risk management when it is necessary to "build something." This is often too late to implement risk management, and the effectiveness of risk management in such cases will typically be low. If this approach is used, then risk management will not be properly included in the architecture, system, and detailed design trade processes, and will not provide support to upper management for the myriad decisions that must be made prior to production activities. Starting risk management late in the development phase or early in the production phase will almost ensure that risk issues that could have been identified and resolved relatively early in the program will surface later in development or production as problems and have considerable adverse impact because of the large opportunity cost that already exists, and the relative inability to trade cost, performance, schedule, and risk at that time. Such a philosophy is actually akin to problem solving or crisis management, not risk management, which should be started at the beginning of the conceptual development phase and continued throughout the program.

On some programs the philosophy is to start risk management when it is necessary to "build something." This is often too late to implement risk management, and the effectiveness of risk management in such cases will typically be low.

Risk management should generally be started long before hardware is fabricated, software is coded, and integration, assembly, and test are performed. While on some programs risk management is begun part-way during these activities, this is generally not the desired course of action, because by that time risk issues that should have been identified may become problems, and optimal risk handling strategies may not be possible because some options will have become foreclosed. In addition, risk management should be viewed as a tool to assist the design trade process (e.g., cost, performance, schedule, and risk trades). If not begun until say hardware fabrication, the potential benefit of involving risk as part of the design process will be reduced, if not foreclosed. Hence, while in some cases it may be necessary to postpone risk management from the beginning of the program, this is often penny wise and pound foolish because of the potential leverage that it may be available if performed properly.

Risk management should generally be started long before hardware is fabricated, software is coded, and integration, assembly, and test are performed.

Risk management is often not effectively implemented until midway in the development phase instead of early in the development phase when it potentially can have much greater leverage. For example, risk assessments should be performed as early as possible in the life cycle to ensure that critical cost, performance (technical), and schedule risks are addressed and RHPs incorporated into program planning and budget projections.[11]

Waiting until midway in the development phase to implement an effective risk management process can greatly reduce the potential benefit to the program for the design and other key processes. It will also likely lead to increased program cost and/or schedule growth, which may occur later in the development phase, and even the production, fielding/deployment, and operational support phase.

Implemented the risk management process at the start of the development phase and update it as needed during the course of the program.

Risk issues and risk management objectives may vary with program phases. If risk management is tracked across program phases, it is important to identify risk issues separately, analyze risk levels, develop RHPs, and monitor the implemented RHPs for each program phase. This is particularly important if products of different designs or capabilities are fabricated during different program phases or if the program's risk management ground rules and assumptions strictly separate the program's development, and Production, Fielding/Deployment, and Operational Support phase. The tendency is often to examine one phase or the other or to blur the phases together, rather than examining each phase and the potential interrelationships between phases (e.g., shared technologies and designs that may be enhanced in a subsequent phase).

Ensure that risk issues are representative and risk management objectives are suitable for each program phase.

There may be a tendency to avoid dealing with risk issues in a prompt manner. In many cases, and even in some instances where the assumption option would eventually be selected, the resulting delay in addressing the risk issue can have substantial adverse impact on the program. This delay in dealing with risk issues can be unintentional, accidental or the result of 1) inadequate risk management skills (e.g., a risk issue that should have been identified but was not); 2) a form of denial (e.g., the risk issue does not really exist even when relevant data is available to the contrary), or 3) a conscious decision to wait even though there is no indication that information helpful to resolving the risk issue will exist in the future. The latter issue may entail early warning trends being tolerated and not acted upon—in effect a form of procrastination, or the expectation that resolution of the risk issue will occur at any moment (even if this is not likely true). In one case, a program manager on a large development program failed to acknowledge the serious nature of a risk issue and routinely over-rode his own technical experts who pleaded to begin implementing an RHP that involved using the development of an alternate item. The eight-month postponement in eventually dropping the primary development approach and selecting the alternate item, lead to more than a $10-million cost increase on the program. And at no time during this eight-month period of time was data available that supported maintaining the primary development approach—all theoretical and actual test data were either inconclusive or pointed to the failure of the primary development approach and the need to select the alternate item. In another case the consequences of this type of action were far worse—literally tragic. Here, a highly touted drug was given a "fast track" approval to be sold in the U. S., but led to at least 63 confirmed deaths and thousands of injured patients. "As the death toll mounted, the U. S. Food and Drug Administration recommended a monitoring program involving multiple regimens of blood testing to safeguard patients. Yet, no scientific proof existed at that time or even later that such a monitoring approach would offer patients taking the drug any substantial protection."[13]

There may be a tendency to avoid dealing with risk issues in a prompt manner. In many cases, and even in some instances where the assumption option would eventually be selected, the resulting delay in addressing the risk issue can have substantial adverse impact on the program.

Don't artificially constrain how long it will take to develop effective risk management on a program. While I don't recommend an open-ended implementation activity, having an artificially constrained one will generally lead to ineffective risk management. For example, if it is estimated to take six months on a given program, and implementation support is withdrawn in six weeks, the resulting process will likely be ineffective. What is often needed is a reasonable implementation plan with clear objectives, milestones, and support and commitment from key management personnel.

Don't artificially constrain how long it will take to develop effective risk management on a program.

When discussing time frame in risk management care should be taken to adequately define what is being represented. For example, there are at least three attributes of time frame that should be considered in ranking risk analysis results and in performing risk handling. First, when is the risk issue likely to occur? Second, if the risk issue requires an RHP or suitable management reserve (assumption option), then when must the RHP be implemented or when must the management reserve be made available? Third, when must one or more backup risk handling strategies be selected and implemented?

When discussing time frame in risk management care should be taken to adequately define what is being represented.

VI. Risk Management Training

A. Need for Risk Management Training

Inadequate training to implement and perform risk management may exist and reduce risk management process efficiency. In some cases this may be present on a single project, whereas in others it may point to an across-the-board deficiency in a given organization.

If the program's risk manager (or equivalent) has a weak program management and/or systems engineering background, the amount of instruction needed to overcome this deficiency may be substantial. Similarly, if personnel responsible for generating risk assessments or RHPs do not have sufficient training, the validity of their output may be suspect.

One cannot safely assume that program management or systems engineering personnel have adequate experience or knowledge about risk management. For example, some engineering specialists I have interacted with considered themselves risk management experts, which was not only a delusion, but dangerous to the projects they worked on. In other cases, system engineers knew very little about probability theory, which permitted the introduction of substantial risk-related issues. Belonging to a functional organization (e.g., systems engineering) does not guarantee that you have sufficient knowledge to implement risk management nor make you a good risk management leader.

Similarly, most program managers have some risk management experience, but this does not guarantee that they have suitable skills to implement properly an effective risk management process. For example, in some cases they had used a risk management process on earlier programs with substantial deficiencies (e.g., a process without a risk planning or monitoring step) and were unaware of the deficiencies that existed.

Working-level engineers should also be given risk management training. This is important because many engineers are never adequately exposed to cost, schedule, and risk-related issues while in college. Once in the workforce, their job reviews are often dominated by technical performance-related items. Ideally, working-level engineers should recognize potential risk issues, then surface these issues through the proper channels (e.g., directly, through IPT leads). The goal is not to turn every engineer on the program into a risk manager, but to sensitize engineers to potential risk issues, methodologies for evaluating them, and approaches for handling them.

In summary, training should be tailored to different groups that need it—upper program management, IPT leads, risk facilitators, working-level engineers, etc. One risk management training course will generally not be appropriate for all.

Training should be given to most of the program team, from senior management through working-level engineers, to increase the likelihood of more effectively implementing risk management on the program. Separate training can be developed for management and engineering personnel to provide them with information tailored to issues that they will likely face. In addition, training should be tailored to different groups that need it.

B.   Quality of Risk Management Training

In many cases inadequate risk management can be alleviated by an enhanced process linked with more capable implementation. Unfortunately, some available books and training classes include little or no information on how to 1) enhance an existing process or create an improved one, 2) overcome existing operational problems, and 3) implement risk management on an actual program. Similarly, discussions of common mistakes associated with the risk management process and each of its steps are typically limited. Also, the information provided is often at such an introductory level that only the simplest risk management process would be possible. The net result is likely to be an ineffective risk management process.

Unfortunately, many risk management facilitators and trainers have knowledge well below the state of the art, or have little or no experience in implementing risk management on real programs along with having long-term accountability and responsibility to make it work. (In one high-technology organization a facilitator is described as providing risk management expertise to the program, as well as leading training sessions. However, the role and job description of the facilitator: "is trained in meeting skills, conflict resolution, tools, etc." Rather amazingly, the facilitator was expected to help lead risk management activities on the program, yet no risk management qualifications or credentials were required for the position!) The risk facilitator and risk trainer should have adequate statistical and social science skills, in addition to relevant technical knowledge. Simply having a job title does not qualify an individual to facilitate risk management or perform risk management training, yet it is not uncommon for risk trainers and facilitators to have little or no risk management knowledge and experience. In many cases risk management trainers are simply chart readers—presenting material developed by others and not having any real understanding or relevant experience about the subject. Although this might seem shocking in the sense that most people would not want surgery from someone who had only read surgery books or never successfully completed surgical residency, there are a surprisingly large percentage of risk management facilitators and trainers with inadequate credentials. (Based upon discussions with numerous project risk management facilitators and trainers over the years, I estimate that about 90% have 1) knowledge well below the state of the art, 2) little or no experience in implementing risk management on real programs, or 3) little or no long-term responsibility and accountability to make it work. For example, of the last 10 risk management facilitators and trainers with whom I have interacted, 3 had a knowledge base 10 to 15 years behind the state of the art, 5 had zero real world implementation experience, and 2 had no long-term accountability and responsibility to make risk management work on actual programs.) (See Chapter 6, Secs. VII. E and VII. F for additonal information.)

Having long-term responsibility and accountability on previous and/or the current program should be key requisites for any people performing risk management training. Only spending a few equivalent man weeks at a facility, or by performing only a limited portion of the risk management process (commonly a risk analysis) generally provides insufficient responsibility and accountability. A number of questions should be asked of any risk management trainer, including but not limited to

1) If initial training was performed, did the trainer play a major, minor, or negligible role in then implementing the risk management process?

2) For an in-place process, what recommendations were delivered and did the trainer play a major, minor, or negligible role in then implementing the recommended changes that were approved?

3) What was the relative state of the art of the risk management process being propagated or suggested improvements (e.g., when compared to the 1998 OSD risk management process)?

4) Which process steps did the trainer have responsibility to implement?

5) How did the trainer implement these process steps (e.g., level of interaction with program personnel)?

6) Was the trainer responsible for preparing contractual or otherwise binding risk management documentation (e.g., RMP, risk evaluation reports, and RHPs)?

7) How long a period of time (calendar months and percent of program phase) did the trainer assist in implementing the process or improvements?

8) What level of responsibility and accountability did the trainer have in this implementation?

9) What level of authority did the trainer have regarding project management (e.g., did the trainer routinely brief multiple levels of upper management or have little responsibility for doing so)?

10) Was the trainer's performance recognized by project management and upper management as having made substantial positive contributions?

When only a few of the previous items are met or yield a strong desirable response, key project managers should ask themselves if it is worth gambling the outcome of their project on such limited experience because it may be difficult, if not almost impossible, to undo the effects of inadequately applied risk management later in the program. Rather surprisingly, an executive at one well-known training company mused this issue and said: "You mean it actually matters that a trainer has real-world experience?" Let the buyer beware!

In addition, the focus of some risk management courses is on performing Monte Carlo simulations, yet this is far down on the list of things necessary to create an effective risk management process (e.g., probably not even in the "Top 10"). I say this having run *thousands* of cost, performance, and schedule Monte Carlo simulations since the 1970s. Simply stated, having an excellent Monte Carlo simulation to perform a risk analysis is almost irrelevant if the risk management process is missing one or more key steps, if the process is poorly implemented, etc. (One former government acquisition manager who dealt with the problem repeatedly commented that his tolerance for those in love with risk analysis tools was very low because they typically cannot see the "big picture" needed to get risk management to work on a real program. Similarly, at one risk management conference I heard several people talking, who worked for a risk analysis tool vendor with less than a first-rate reputation. They had no credible risk management experience, yet they agreed they should teach a risk management course as a better way to sell their tools and services. Months later I received a copy of a presentation outline that one of the individuals gave. It had little or nothing to do with risk management, and it was clearly a lure for the purpose of selling their software tool.)

Risk management training should include information on how to tailor and implement the process as well as sufficient material on each process step. However, it is also important that training be obtained from people that have state-of-the-art knowledge and substantial hands on experience in making risk management work on actual programs to help avoid problems later in the program. In addition, having long-term responsibility and accountability on previous and/or the current program should be key requisites for anyone performing risk management training.

C. Use of Risk Management Mentors for Developing Risk Managers

In many large organizations there are few programs that have adequate or better risk management, and simply conducting training will not necessarily lead to a large increase in risk management effectiveness. One method that can potentially help quicken the pace that risk management effectiveness is increased is through the use of competent mentors. Here, a mentor is a very knowledgeable risk management practitioner, not simply someone who is a risk management facilitator or trainer. Mentors should also possess suitable cost, design, requirements, schedule, and systems engineering knowledge if possible and have a relevant background associated with the product under development or production so they can provide rapid and sound inputs.

Initially, mentors should provide hands-on guidance beyond the risk management course for a given project. However, a primary goal should be to assist in the grooming and development of a qualified risk manager (and perhaps a backup) for each program. Mentors should work with candidate risk managers on more than one program at a time (which will also increase the mentor's expertise). Although the exact number depends on the programs, a practical upper limit might be two to four at a time.

After a candidate risk manager is suitably trained, both in terms of book knowledge and practical experience, he becomes the program risk manager. The mentor for that risk manager then transitions off of the program and is assigned to another program with its candidate risk manager(s). The now-qualified risk manager continues with the project, then carries this knowledge to another program after the current one is completed.

This strategy may greatly increase risk management effectiveness in many government and industry organizations and also substantially shorten the time needed to raise risk management effectiveness to the desired level.

Consider using risk management mentors (a very knowledgeable risk management practitioner) to train candidate risk managers in large organizations where numerous programs exist. This strategy may greatly increase risk management effectiveness in many government and industry organizations and also substantially shorten the time needed to raise effectiveness to the desired level.

VII.　Risk Manager

The program may have no risk manager (or risk focal point), or if a person is identified, it may be only on paper. Until and unless the risk manager can provide capable leadership; thoroughly understand the characteristics of a good risk management process; assist in performing a detailed independent cross-check of all risk assessment results, risk handling options, and risk monitoring results generated by other personnel; have true insight into program risk issues and risk management implementation problem areas; and take a proactive stance for risk management, the effectiveness of the risk management process will be impaired, if not severely limited. However, even if the risk manager has these desirable characteristics, this does not guarantee success because some programs and their underlying culture are focused more on crisis management than risk management.

A risk manager should be identified who understands and practices risk management, has the power to help enact sound risk management implementation, enforces the quality of the implemented process and results produced, and is an active champion for risk management within the program.

Don't underestimate how much damage a poor risk manager can cause. In such cases the risk manager may not only weaken risk management effectiveness by missed opportunities, etc., and damage the reputation of the organization itself by poor performance, but also give risk management a poor reputation within the organization.

A poor risk manager can cause a variety of problems on a program that may be difficult to overcome.

Be wary of new risk managers (or those who assume the role of risk manager) that have little or no training and experience performing risk management on actual programs and make widespread changes to the risk management process and its implementation. Such changes will often be flawed or without merit, lead to disruption and reduce risk management effectiveness. Another example of flawed behavior is the new risk manager that does not understand the existing risk management process and refuses to consult relevant documentation. This can lead to both misinterpretation of the existing process and information pertaining to existing program risks.

Be wary of new risk managers that have little or no training and experience performing risk management on actual programs and make widespread changes to the risk management process and its implementation.

A person is sometimes designated the risk manager without regard to the risk management qualifications of that person or the desire to learn and practice risk management. Just because someone is smart and "nice" does not make them anymore qualified to become the risk manager than anyone else on the program. And putting the wrong person in the risk manager position will tend to degrade risk management effectiveness and may have a lasting negative impact beyond the tenure of the person in question because most organizations do not have a history of effective risk management.

Candidates for the risk manager should have suitable risk management qualifications and the desire to learn and practice risk management.

The program's risk manager may have no prior risk management experience. At best this contributes to a delay in implementing an effective risk management process. At worst, this may contribute to a weak process implementation or its failure. Another variant of this problem is that the risk manager may have demonstrated an unproductive attitude and actions toward risk management in past work assignments. Short of a marvelous transformation, it is unlikely that the person will be an effective risk manager.

The risk manager should have both suitable training and credible prior risk management experience.

The risk manager may be knowledgeable about some parts of the risk management process, but not other parts. This will often lead to concentration of effort on the risk manager's stronger areas, but inadequate treatment of the weaker areas. For example, on one program the risk manager had good working experience in risk analysis and the control aspect of risk handling. However, this is only equivalent to 3/4 of one of the four risk management process steps (risk analysis is one of two risk assessment process substeps, and control is one of four risk handling options).

To be successful, the risk manager must have experience in each of the four risk management process steps (planning, assessment, handling, and monitoring), and the ability to stretch himself to learn additional information in those areas where he has limited experience.

A single risk manager should exist on the program. Multiple risk managers assigned to key personnel or organization within the program (e.g., IPTs) should be avoided because it generally sets up a bureaucracy and dilutes the overall authority of the position.

A single risk manager should exist on the program.

Different personnel may be assigned as the risk manager in a short period of time, which can substantially weaken the effectiveness of the risk management process. For example, on one large program four risk managers existed in seven months (and the last three had no prior risk management experience). This is particularly critical during the early- to mid-development phase when risk management can have a substantial positive affect on system design and development, and the lack of stable staffing can have an adverse impact on the overall management process effectiveness. If the risk manager does not remain until the project's completion, a transition plan and training covering the entire risk management process, its implementation, and key risk issues will be necessary for the next risk manager. In addition, any medium- or higher-risk issues, issues with imminent key decision points, or issues with pending tests should be identified and briefed to the new risk manager.

The risk manager position should not be staffed as a short-term job. Doing so will likely diminish the overall effectiveness of the risk management process.

On programs with a relatively small budget and/or short schedule it may not be practical to have a full-time risk manager. In such cases, risk management should be led part-time by someone with suitable risk management training and experience. Various approaches can be explored to select a part-time risk manager, including but not limited to 1) a risk management consultant, 2) an individual from a functional or product group assigned to the program part-time, or 3) someone within the program. (Note: In the latter two cases the individual will typically be in a program management or systems engineering organization.) Regardless of which approach is used, a key challenge for the risk management focal point is to 1) rapidly tailor and implement risk management principles (e.g., process steps and relevant activities) on the program, 2) ensure that it is suitably performed, and 3) ensure that risk management information and results are used by key personnel in decision making.

On programs with a relatively small budget and/or short schedule it may not be practical to have a full-time risk manager. In such cases, risk management should be 1) led part-time by someone with suitable risk management training and experience, 2) tailored to the program, and 3) used by key personnel in decision making.

The risk manager should be more than just an integrator of the risk management process—he must assist the risk issue POC, IPT leads, RMB, etc. in implementing and practicing risk management on the program. In some cases the risk manager may be nothing more than an information collector or chart reader receiving inputs from other personnel and then transmitting these inputs to other parties. This will often contribute to the risk management process being unfocused and inefficient. In cases where I have observed this practice, the effectiveness of the risk management process is generally not high. While cause and effect cannot be proven, making the risk manager nothing more than an information hub is not a useful means to increase risk management effectiveness.

The risk manager should be more than just an integrator of the risk management process—he must assist the risk issue POC, IPT leads, RMB, etc. in implementing and practicing risk management on the program.

The risk manager should be able to work with program personnel and help them apply risk management principles to assist in their responsibilities. Limiting this interaction either intentionally or unintentionally to risk management statusing (e.g., charts, reports) will tend to reduce risk management effectiveness on the program.

Risk management statusing (e.g., charts, reports) should not be the primary or sole focus of the program risk manager.

The risk manager should have a clear reporting relationship within the project; failure to do so can lead to reduced effectiveness both in interacting with other managers and with other project personnel.

The risk manager should have a clear reporting relationship within the project.

Beware of the "ivory tower" risk manager who, not understanding risk management, avoids interaction with program personnel, does not attend regularly scheduled status meetings, and makes little attempt to understand the technical and organizational aspects of the project or people working on it. This type of behavior sets a bad example for others on the project and does not contribute to effective risk management.

Beware of the "ivory tower" risk manager who avoids interaction with program personnel, does not attend regularly scheduled status meetings, and makes little attempt to understand the technical and organizational aspects of the project or people working on it.

I've noted two bad extremes for how a risk manager acts on a program—in the first he does almost nothing, in the second he tries to do everything. Neither approach is generally effective. In the latter case it is important that the program manager and other key personnel participate to provide proper support and send the "proper message" toward risk management to all program personnel. Another issue to avoid is a situation where the risk manager takes credit for "everything" when other key program personnel made substantial contributions. This type of behavior will dissuade program personnel from taking active part in risk management and diminish its effectiveness.

The risk manager should neither do too little nor attempt to do everything to implement risk management.

Wholesale changes of risk managers across organizations on a given program should be avoided whenever possible unless necessary (e.g., due to lack of performance). Changing risk managers in a short time horizon on multiple seller organizations that interact on the same program will often lead to a loss of continuity and tend to decrease risk management effectiveness.

Wholesale changes of risk managers across organizations on a given program should be avoided whenever possible unless necessary.

It is generally helpful for the risk manager (or risk management lead) to be included in the organization that has ownership of the risk management process [e.g., program management or the systems engineering IPT (SEIPT)]. When this is not the case, there can be conflict between the risk manager and the head of the organization owning the process. The net result can be a decrease in risk management effectiveness because there may be no direct management relationship between the risk manager and the owning organization. In one case this permitted the risk manager to implement the process in a weak, somewhat confusing manner, despite the fact that the original process developed within the SEIPT was well defined in terms of both technical attributes for each process step and organizational roles and responsibilities.

It is generally helpful for the risk manager (or risk management lead) to be included in the organization that has ownership of the risk management process. When this is not the case, there can be conflict between the risk manager and the head of the organization owning the process.

The risk manager along with the risk issue POC and IPT leads should report significant changes in existing risk issues to the RMB. This responsibility should not solely fall on the risk manager otherwise ownership issues will likely exist.

The risk manager along with the risk issue POC and IPT leads should report significant changes in existing risk issues to the RMB.

Generally, the risk issue POC and the IPT leads should monitor actual vs planned progress for implementing RHPs. While the risk manager can assist in performing this task, it should not be solely assigned to the risk manager.

Generally, the risk issue POC and the IPT leads should monitor actual vs planned progress for implementing RHPs, not the risk manager.

Developing risk management lessons learned from other programs or previous program phases is not solely the function of the risk manager, although the risk manger should assist in this activity. This is because the risk manager will often not have a broad enough perspective to collect and evaluate lessons learned; particularly from other programs.

The risk manager should not solely be responsible for developing risk management lessons learned.

Everyone on the program should participate in risk identification, not just the risk manager. The risk manager should not be the sole person that identifies candidate risks. If so, this will lead to risk issues being missed, create an ownership issue, and does not encourage other project personnel to get involved in performing risk management.

The risk manager should assist in performing risk identification, but not be either the sole party involved or be responsible for each and every risk issue.

VIII.   Cost and Benefits of Risk Management

The quantification of risk management cost and benefits (for cost, performance, and schedule) may range from a fairly straightforward process to one that is very difficult to achieve. Potential cost and benefits can sometimes be estimated for a specific program change, such as a change in subsystem design or the risk assessment methodology used. However, it is often difficult to estimate the potential cost and benefits associated with the impact a particular risk issue would have had if not identified, analyzed, and properly handled. (A program's outcomes are somewhat akin to one iteration through a coupled simulation. Hence, it is often difficult, given the lack of certain information, to look back in time accurately and identify how outcomes would have changed had certain decisions been made.) In some cases though it is possible to identify the nature of problems that would have occurred had risks not been identified and risk handling plans not been implemented.

When cost and benefit calculations are performed, key ground rules and assumptions to help interpret the results may not be included, and it is sometimes difficult to separate normal development activities from risk handling activities unless specific records are kept, particularly because multiple funding accounts may be involved across several fiscal years. In addition, risk management is typically not included in the program's WBS; hence, its administration is often charged to program management, systems engineering, or other activities. Finally, potential cost and noncost savings from risk management are often not calculated until after the fact, and may be little more than guesses in some cases.

The following is a simple, condensed example associated with cost and benefits derived from an actual spacecraft payload program.

The item in question was the development of a dichroic filter (beamsplitter) for a complex, high-performance electro-optical imaging system. The dichroic filter is quite complex, with approximately 50 layers of different materials to shape the reflectance/transmittance of the incident light over a broad spectral bandpass, even though the filter area is smaller than a microscope slide. Without a very high-performance filter the resulting payload performance would suffer (e.g., the intensity and spectral tailoring of light would be degraded).

The optical subsystem subcontractor selected a vendor they had worked with extensively to develop the coating and fabricate the filter (the primary strategy). The prime contractor had no direct evidence that the vendor would fail, but was concerned with potential manufacturing process control issues at the vendor facility. The prime contractor assessed the risk for this filter to be moderate–high due to its complexity (performance) and the cost that would be incurred to the program if the initial vendor failed because the dichroic development task was on the program's critical path. The risk handling option selected was control, and the specific approach was to fund in parallel a backup development activity with a vendor selected by the prime contractor (termed the backup strategy). (The primary and backup represented the same dichroic filter—made by different vendors.)

As it turned out, the primary development strategy (vendor selected by the optical system subcontractor) failed—a substantial performance degradation would have existed. However, the backup strategy succeeded: the second vendor produced a filter on time and met performance specifications.

The primary strategy was included as part of the development estimate and correctly not charged to risk management. The entire backup strategy cost $15,000, including subcontractor management. (Note: All dollars in this example are FY99.) Without the backup strategy in place and funded for parallel development, the entire sensor development program would have slipped X weeks while the filter was developed (because the filter was on the program's critical path). This period of time coupled with a burn rate of $Y per week leads to a potential cost of $1.8 million. Hence, we have the cost of risk handling activity is $15,000 (FY99), savings from risk handling activity is $1.8 million (FY99), and return on investment (ROI) is $1.8 million/$15,000 or 120:1. In addition, the 120:1 ROI is conservative because the program could have been canceled by the government had it exhibited the potential schedule slip.

Finally, the savings from this one risk handling activity ($1.8 million) is 6:1 to 10:1 greater than the cost of all risk management activities during the course of the baseline development phase (for those items and their risk handling activities not included in the development plan).

The ROI on risk management will vary on a case-by-case basis even within a single program. Not all cases will have an ROI = 120:1, most will be much lower. In some cases a small ROI (even < 1:1) may be acceptable if there are substantial potential performance and schedule consequences that could adversely affect the program (or keep the program from being canceled).

The program that this example was drawn from had an effective risk management process that was duly recognized by the government. In fact, government managers said that on more than one occasion the program was kept alive and received continued funding because of the effective risk management process coupled with excellent program management. Without this combination, the government said the program would have been terminated. Thus, while you consider the cost of risk management, realize that the *benefits* from having an effective process may far exceed simple ROI calculations for a given risk issue.

It is also possible that a technically sound and well-implemented risk management process may make the difference between a program being canceled or allowed to continue. This was the case on the highest risk program that I have worked on. In a four-week period of time, I tailored a risk management process to the program, developed an RMP, led the initial risk assessment, led development of draft RHPs, formulated and attended the first RMB meeting, and successfully briefed members of the government program office and numerous high-level government representatives from the sponsoring agency. This series of actions was credited in part by the government as reason to continue the program and fully fund it through completion.

Funding and priorities for risk management are often diminished or abandoned in favor of crisis management (problem solving) when unanticipated problems occur. This should not be the case, and in fact, the reverse may be warranted because a good, implemented risk management process can help provide structure when evaluating unanticipated problems as well as a framework to assist in their resolution. This is all the more important when the program's life-cycle cost is large—else a penny wise, pound foolish result may occur.

To the extent possible, fence funds allocated for risk management activities. ROI and similar measures can be useful in quantifying the cost and benefits of risk management actions.

IX. Some Risk Management Implementation Considerations

A. Top-Level Considerations

The starting point on many programs is that risk management won't be effective, that is it won't be neutral, or that it will be effective, because the organization has either a poor culture toward risk management or no history of effective risk management. If this climate exists it must be overcome in order to provide the opportunity to develop effective risk management.

The starting point on many programs is that risk management won't be effective. This will often require focused attention and resources to eliminate.

A number of common excuses exist for avoiding performing risk management. None of these excuses are generally valid and will often lead to problems occurring later in the program. Some common excuses for avoiding risk management include, but are not limited to 1) risks already identified earlier in the program (yet the program has entered a new acquisition phase with emphasis on different risk categories or the program has been re-baselined), 2) do not have time to perform risk management (if you do not perform risk management and risk issues become problems later in the program, there can be a very large, adverse C,P,S impact, which among other things, will take much more time to resolve), 3) it is a management function (risk management principles should be performed by all program personnel), 4) there is too much work already so why get involved [added responsibilities associated with risk issues should be recognized by management (e.g., additional personnel assigned and financial compensation), and in the long-run may reduce the level of work needed to be performed by resolving risk issues before the affect the program as problems], 5) what is in it for me (good performance using risk management should be recognized by management, and it can contribute to program success), 6) we already won the competition, so why should we do it [poor program performance is often used as a source selection criteria in future competitions, and may be an award fee (or similar evaluation) criteria for the current contract], 7) it's not specifically called out in the contract (this may be so, but if it helps to better manage the program it may lead to increased program success), and 8) it is just a buyer initiative (risk management can help both the buyer and seller better manage a program).

A number of common excuses exist for avoiding performing risk management. None of these excuses are generally valid and will often lead to problems occurring later in the program.

Some organizations perform risk management in a "check the box" or similar fashion. In such cases risk management is not a key process and its principles will not be used by decision makers beyond routine matters associated with its constrained implementation. Even if the lead buyer or seller organizations behave in this manner, lower-level organizations should explore ways, to the extent possible, to have an effective risk management process. In such cases the higher-level organization may impose a process to use, but it is often possible to improve a poor risk management process via enhancements in process steps, tools and techniques, etc. that will lead to a better process, yet one that can still map back to the imposed process. Similarly, some implementation aspects may be imposed by the higher-level organization (e.g., the risk management process owner and nature of the RMB), but there is often considerable latitude as to how upper management in lower-level organizations create a culture to implement risk management and how risk management will be used in decision making. Hence, even when an inferior risk management process and/or implementation approach is imposed by a higher-level organization, lower-level organizations will often have sufficient latitude to at least partially correct these deficiencies, *but only if they are willing to do so.*

Some organizations perform risk management in a "check the box" or similar fashion. In such cases risk management is not a key process nor will its principles be used by decision makers beyond routine matters associated with its constrained implementation.

The buyer may often strongly resist updating its risk management process. This situation is made all the more worse when it then develops poorly worded RFPs that references a risk management process well below the state of the art, as well as one that does not contain the necessary process steps [risk planning, assessment (identification and analysis), handling, and monitoring], and/or where the process steps overlap (e.g., mitigation and control). Because the buyer often is uninterested in updating its risk management process, let alone correcting an erroneous process, this type of problem may be very difficult to solve, and it clearly sends the wrong, negative message to the seller.

The buyer may often strongly resist updating its risk management process even when parts are erroneous. This type of problem may be very difficult to solve, and it clearly sends the wrong, negative message to the seller.

Whether or not the risk management process should be improved must be evaluated on a program-by-program basis, and the outcome may depend upon a number of considerations, including: 1) effectiveness of the existing process, 2) available resources, 3) time available for the enhancements, 4) inputs from upper management and other stakeholders, 5) potential benefit/cost of the enhancements, and 6) contractual requirements. Regardless of whether or not a risk management process should be improved an organization may choose in some cases not to enhance its risk management process because of existing constraints or guidance. (For example, if the need for a better process or a process that includes particular characteristics is not contractually required the organization may be reluctant to enhance an existing risk management process.)

Whether or not the risk management process should be improved must be evaluated on a program-by-program basis.

Do not assume that simply because good initial progress is made toward implementing risk management that this will continue or improve with time. It will not generally continue unless a conscious effort is expended; particularly in organizations without a history of effective risk management. In one case the risk management process was initially well received and the implementation was proceeding quite well. A year later the risk management process was less well implemented, and certainly less well practiced than it had been initially. In addition, during that year not a single comprehensive risk assessment was performed (not even for risk identification), while management routinely discussed how the project was not yet mature enough. In such situations, risk management effectiveness may decrease precipitously unless key managers within the program begin to practice risk management principles as part of their decision making, and both require and reward other program personnel for using it.

Do not assume that simply because good initial progress is made towards implementing risk management that this will continue or improve with time. It will not generally continue unless a conscious effort is expended, particularly in organizations without a history of effective risk management.

In some cases a big improvement in risk management process effectiveness might be, going from an informal process to one that includes risk assessment (identification and analysis), handling, and monitoring. While this may truly be a relative improvement, and commendable, it still falls short because in this case there is no risk planning step. Hence, do not believe that just because you have made an improvement in your risk management process that the resulting process is necessarily effective or even adequate for your program.

Just because you make an improvement in your risk management process the resulting process may still not be effective or even adequate for your program.

In general, technical improvements to the risk management process should be evaluated and improvements implemented that offer the greatest potential benefit with the least likely cost. In this case, benefits and costs can represent a variety of things, including but not limited to 1) budget, 2) schedule, 3) accuracy, and 4) confidence of results. The output from such an analysis should be a rank ordered list of improvements. (While it is desirable that such an analysis can be performed quantitatively, in many cases it can only be performed qualitatively.) From this, the RMB (or equivalent) can then evaluate and approve the results, request implementation plans for the selected improvements, allocate resources to accomplish the implementation, and monitor the results of the implementation (particularly when they extend over a period of time). [In effect, this should parallel the risk management process being applied (risk planning, identification, analysis, handling, and monitoring).]

If the above approach is used it may be more difficult to apply it to organizational and behavioral implementation issues than to technical process improvements in terms of evaluating the costs and benefits of potential improvements because such improvements may be difficult to quantify (even if only a qualitative analysis is performed).

In general, technical improvements to the risk management process should be evaluated and improvements implemented that offer the greatest potential benefit with the least likely cost.

Ineffective risk management can blind its proponents to the point of causing damage to the reputation of the firm. In one case, members of a prime contractor that had implemented a severely flawed risk management process were oblivious to its considerable flaws. Thinking instead that it was a great risk management process (and one that they wanted to disseminate company wide), they provided it to a government organization in the hopes that the government would approve, and perhaps even use this process. What happened instead was that a government analyst saw that the process was severely flawed. The net result to the contractor was a potential "black eye." This could have been easily avoided if the contractor had performed an objective evaluation of this risk management process rather than being intoxicated by its own (self-generated) praise reports. And despite the private upbraiding that the contractor received, there is no indication that they learned from this lesson or performed an independent assessment of the process to improve its shortcomings.

Ineffective risk management can blind its proponents to the point of causing damage to the reputation of the firm.

B. Risk Issue Classification, Tracking, and Closure

Management may be reluctant to approve risk issues—instead either closing them or placing them into other categories. A true risk issue is still a risk issue no matter what you choose to call it. Closing a risk issue before it has been satisfactorily resolved invites problems to occur. Calling a candidate risk issue something else does nothing in and of itself to resolve it. At a minimum, what is generally needed is a specific course of action, including a plan with milestones, point of contact, and "drop-dead date" for completion else it should be treated as a risk issue to prevent it from becoming a problem later in the program.

Management may be reluctant to approve risk issues—instead either closing them or placing them into other categories. Prematurely closing a risk issue before it has been satisfactorily resolved invites problems to occur. And calling a candidate risk issue something else does nothing in and of itself to resolve it.

Unresolved issues usually propagate during the program with time—they generally do not solve themselves. And unless the assumption risk handling option is the best option possible, it is often not wise to defer an issue indefinitely. At a minimum, if deferral is used to postpone dealing with the issue (rather than explicitly using the assumption risk handling option), then a plan including a responsible party and one or more milestones as to when the issue needs to be re-evaluated, should be developed and implemented.

Unresolved issues usually propagate during the program with time— they generally do not solve themselves.

Typical RMB outcomes for a given candidate risk issue should be: approve, deferred, pending, need more information, engineering process/practice action, management action, and closed. ("Need more information" can be a valid RMB action for any process step.) The RMB can choose to "bin" the issue as a risk issue or other type of an issue. But in any event, if an issue is approved, regardless of the type (e.g., risk, management action), this should initiate specific steps delineated in the RMP (e.g., risk analysis for risk issues) with accountability in terms of a focal point and due date(s). What you do not want to have happen is that an issue is approved, but no "clear cut" action with accountability occurs. This type of response will increase the likelihood that the issue will become a problem later in the program.

Typical RMB outcomes for a given candidate risk issue should be: approve, deferred, pending, need more information, and closed.

In addition to classifying an issue as a risk, also consider treating issues as engineering process/practice and management actions. However, be careful not to allow risk issues to "slip through the cracks" or let engineering process/practice and management actions become risk issues because they have not been successfully closed.

Distinctions are sometimes made between normal engineering development issues and risk issues. One perspective is that only the "important" issues should be evaluated for risk management purposes. This approach has the potential to let a number of risk issues "slip through the cracks" and not be recognized until much later in the program when they surface as problems. The converse approach should also bring caution that routine engineering issues are all risk issues. If this occurs, then the risk management process, including the risk identification step, will become overly burdensome. Another set of bounds that is sometimes used ranges from risk management to management actions—in the former case a risk handling plan is developed and implemented, while in the latter case a management action item is taken to resolve the issue. Clearly, some middle ground between these categories must exist, *yet a different middle ground will exist for each program and must be found by tailoring to that program.* One approach is sometimes to use a list of carefully constructed risk trigger questions (based in part upon historical evidence from similar programs) and related techniques for risk identification to help separate out normal engineering issues from risk issues. Likewise, if an issue can be clearly defined, quickly closed, and entails a small number of readily defined steps, then a management action may be a suitable approach so long as formal monitoring of actual vs planned progress is made. (And, if for example, actual progress lags planned progress by a pre-defined amount, then this serves as a trigger for risk identification purposes.) However, it is *almost always* far better to err on the side of conservatism—that all issues should be considered as candidate risk issues and evaluated by the program's RMB. The reason for this is that even a single risk issue that "slips through the cracks" and is not identified until much later in the program when it surfaces as a problem, can have a very large adverse impact on the program. A single risk-related problem that is averted late in the program's development phase may pay for much, if not all risk management that is performed during the entire development phase.

In addition to classifying an issue as a risk, also consider treating issues as engineering process/practice and management actions. However, be careful not to allow risk issue to "slips through the cracks" or let engineering process/practice and management actions become risk issues because they have not been successfully closed.

Be wary of approving a risk issue simply because a similar issue was a risk on another program. While lessons learned from analogous programs can provide valuable insights to your program, that does not mean that you will have identical risks, let alone identical risk levels unless the same item is used, in the same operating environment, at the same time, and under the same acquisition environment. Be particularly cautious of situations where there is no evidence that the issue in question is a risk (e.g., no satisfactory risk definition can be developed)—only that an issue may exist in the future. This may be fine as a placeholder, to declare it a management action or engineering process/practice action, or to put it on the watchlist, but it does not mean that the issue should be approved as a risk. (Note: I am not suggesting that the issue be given insufficient attention; else it may well reemerge as a risk or even problem later in the program.) Be particularly cautious of situations where the "pet issue" has been identified by a stakeholder, and where the stakeholder specifies the risk level without even performing a risk analysis. Even if the resulting conjecture proves accurate, the end result can be harmful because it often bypasses the implemented risk management process, thus providing a negative model to others on the program.

Be wary of approving a risk issue simply because a similar issue was a risk on another program. While lessons learned from analogous programs can provide valuable insights to your program, that does not mean that you will have identical risks, let alone identical risk levels unless the same item is used, in the same operating environment, at the same time, and under the same acquisition environment.

Labeling an item a "work in progress" or some other nomenclature does not necessarily mean that the item is not a risk issue. It is unwise to arbitrarily term potential risk issues with other names, particularly if the implication exists that an issue is "being worked" and is thus categorically not a risk issue. (This is different than the RMB deferring a risk issue.) The danger here is that the issue may be segregated for an extended period of time and if and when it is finally recognized as a risk it may have a far greater impact to the program than if it had been identified, analyzed, and handled earlier. Instead, evaluate all potential issues to determine whether or not they may be candidate risk issues.

Labeling an item a "work in progress" or some other nomenclature does not preclude the item from being a risk issue. Instead, evaluate all potential issues to determine whether or not they may be candidate risk issues.

Avoid being caught up in a frenzy to eliminate candidate or approved risk issues. While careful screening is necessary, and elimination of nonrisks prudent, a philosophy to drive down the number of risks on a program without performing suitable risk analysis and risk handling is a potentially unwise practice that can lead to genuine risk issues being mistakenly eliminated, and then coming back as problems later in the program.

Avoid being caught up in a frenzy to eliminate candidate or approved risk issues because genuine risk issues being mistakenly eliminated, and then coming back as problems later in the program.

When risk issues are overly broadly defined, it is possible that some aspects of a risk issue may be closed or reduced to watchlist status before others (sometimes long before others). In such cases, consider removing the closed or watchlist portion of the risk issue and redefining the risk issue to capture the remaining risk. This also goes hand-in-hand with carefully defining the risk issue in the first place so it is not overly broad.

Redefine the risk issue as needed after key aspects are successfully closed.

It is not sufficient to close a risk issue simply by saying that only a single source is capable of performing the work when that source has not yet demonstrated any ability to develop and deliver the item in question. If anything, this suggests that a higher level of risk may exist than had previously been estimated. In one case a risk retired with this rationale came back later in the program as a problem with adverse impact. Instead of retiring a risk issue for such a reason, a second source should have been more vigorously pursued (control risk handling option). While the assumption risk handling option may be used in such cases sufficient management reserve must exist, both in terms of C,P,S. This clearly did not happen in the program in question.

Risk issues should not be closed simply by saying that only a single source is capable of performing the work when that source has not yet demonstrated any ability to develop and deliver the item in question. If anything, this suggests that a higher level of risk may exist than had previously been estimated.

Be careful about arbitrarily removing risk issues from the program watchlist either because it has been on the watchlist for some time, no one formally objects to taking it off the watchlist, or it is assumed to have been transferred to another area (where it may slip "through the cracks"). Removing a risk issue from the watchlist should be a conscious decision of the RMB and suitably documented to so that all program personnel may be aware of this decision.

Do not arbitrarily remove risk issues from the program watchlist.

Just because a risk issue has been reduced to a low risk level, do not automatically assume that the risk should be closed. This can be a bad mistake on development programs, because for example, additional testing may reveal unforeseen difficulties even after the item was judged to be mature enough to warrant a reduced risk rating, and potentially low risk level. It is often wise in such cases to place the risk issue on a "watch list" or similar mechanism until it has passed all appropriate tests and been accepted. Placing the item on a "watch list" will provide a mechanism for routine monitoring which may alert the program to potential changes in its risk level, rather than perhaps being caught off guard if the risk issue had been closed. Only after the RHP objectives are met should a risk issue be closed.

Just because a risk issue has been reduced to a low risk level, do not automatically assume that the risk issue should be closed.

A closed risk issue should remain closed unless there is a compelling reason for the RMB to reopen it.

Don't arbitrarily reopen a closed risk issue.

C. Process-Level Issues

Don't use unsubstantiated statements to sell risk management because this can be counter-productive for the team and may decrease risk management morale. For example, statements such as "the risk identification sessions are always effective" are nothing more than marketing statements, and have no inherent creditability.

Don't use unsubstantiated statements to sell risk management because this can be counter-productive for the team and may decrease risk management morale.

Claims are sometimes made that an initial project risk identification, analysis, and handling session can address risk issues in a matter of hours to a few days. While this may well be true it says nothing about the completeness, accuracy, or level of uncertainty of such information. For example, if there is no risk planning step that includes ground rules and assumptions, how can the participants have a common baseline for identifying candidate risks, analyzing those that are approved, and developing risk handling strategies for selected risks? While it is desirable to perform risk management in an acceptable amount of time, overly simplistic promises of rapid risk management may lead to unrealistic expectations, flawed results and create substantial problems later in the program.

Claims are sometimes made that an initial project risk identification, analysis, and handling session can address risk issues in a matter of hours to a few days. While this may well be true it says nothing about the completeness, accuracy, or level of uncertainty of such information.

It is extremely unwise to think that anyone will master risk management following a day or so of intensive study. At best the individual will learn some fundamentals to help evaluate an existing risk management process or begin to plan a new risk management process. However, a detailed process evaluation or implementation is something that will often take six months to a year or more of hands-on experience, coupled with a suitable academic background and risk management training. People that think that a day is sufficient time to become proficient in risk management are sorely mistaken and have unrealistic expectations no matter how good the instruction is.

It is extremely unwise to think that anyone will master risk management following a day or so of intensive study. This is something that will generally take implementation experience as well a suitable academic background and risk management training.

While it may be desirable to limit the number of participants for performing a risk analysis on a particular approved risk issue, it is generally not desirable to limit the number of those performing risk identification. In cases where a subset of program personnel must perform an initial risk assessment, great care must be taken to select people with appropriate technical and management skills to ensure that both a suitably broad and detailed evaluation be performed. Setting arbitrary limits on those that participate without considering their potential contribution will likely lead to missed candidate risk issues that may surface as problems later in the program. (For example, in a program with strong IPTs, you should consider having a key member from each IPT as a participant along with one or more upper management personnel to achieve a satisfactory balance across the program.)

While it may be desirable to limit the number of participants for performing a risk analysis on a particular approved risk issue, it is generally not desirable to limit the number of those performing risk identification.

A risk management process should always be evaluated on its merits, not in terms of what organization developed it. For example, if a risk management process is created by a predominantly hardware development organization, that does not mean that the process is necessarily superior to another risk management process for hardware development, or even satisfactory for that purpose. Similarly, if an organization funds the development of a risk management process, it will be highly reluctant to change it, let alone move away from it, even if the process is clearly inferior to other processes available. This can occur at relatively low levels in an organization (e.g., a company's systems engineering department) up to and including very high level organizations (e.g., a government agency). Each risk management process should be independently evaluated to determine its suitability (including process steps included/excluded, supporting reference material, etc.) and how it can be tailored to a program.

A risk management process should always be evaluated on its merits, not in terms of what organization developed it.

The risk management process should not be "dumbed down" for users no more than it should be made artificially complex. Grossly oversimplifying the process in terms of methodologies, inputs and outputs will contribute to ineffective, rather than effective, risk management.

The risk management process should not be "dumbed down" for users no more than it should be made artificially complex.

D.   Some Personnel Considerations

A decrease in risk management effectiveness may occur when program management personnel frequently change priorities, and there is no accountability for completing work assignments. This situation is sometimes related to key program personnel operating in a crisis management (problem solving) mode rather than using generally accepted project management principles. [Frequent changes in program management priorities can also be the result of external events (e.g., stakeholder instability).] However, when key management personnel operate in this manner it can contribute to 1) schedule slips, 2) increased cost to complete the work, 3) a lower quality product, and 4) decreased program morale. It will also certainly decrease risk management process effectiveness—sometimes to the point that risk management is not practiced despite what documentation may exist (e.g., RMP, RHPs, etc.).

A decrease in risk management effectiveness may occur when program management personnel frequently change priorities, and there is no accountability for completing work assignments.

In some cases program personnel may have a greatly biased viewpoint of their risk management process such that they will not have any understanding of the errors and other limitations that are present, and be resistant to change. Attempts to enhance the risk management process under such circumstances will likely be inefficient or ineffective. In one case the program had no satisfactory risk planning or RMP, and had never performed a comprehensive risk identification; it used poorly worded, three-level ordinal scales, performed mathematical operations on the results, and had subjective threshold levels to convert scores to risk. In addition, their risk handling did not consider all four options (focusing on control), there were no RHPs, risk step-down charts were subjective and did not synchronize with risk handling actions; and there were no risk monitoring except for reevaluating risk scores. Yet despite the weak management process, and how poorly it was implemented, the program manager refused to improve the process and steadfastly believed it was adequate. This was despite the fact that his program was in a competitive procurement and risk management was a source selection criteria.

In another case a high-level engineer working on an advanced program for the prime contractor told a large group of government personnel that he was so enthusiastic about the risk management process on his program that he transferred it to two other programs and was going to recommend that it become the corporate risk management process. This was not only biased but foolish thinking. The process was lacking a risk planning step, used an erroneous risk analysis methodology, had a limited risk handling methodology ("the control option was preferred"), and only used informal risk monitoring. Hence, of the four risk management process steps, only risk identification was likely done properly. And deploying this poor risk management process at the corporate level would have been a disaster.

In some cases program personnel may have a greatly biased viewpoint of their risk management process such that they will not have any understanding of the errors and other limitations that are present, and be resistant to change. Attempts to enhance the risk management process under such circumstances will likely be inefficient or ineffective.

Beware of program personnel who talk about risk management but know nothing about the subject. This is particularly harmful when the people are assigned to a program and blindly copy material and have no idea what it represents or how to apply it. Poorly developed or inaccurate risk management applied in these situations can be very difficult to displace by more effective and accurate risk management if the inferior process has been inculcated across the program.

Similarly, it is exceedingly unwise to have a risk management spokesman that knows little or nothing about risk management. This will increase the likelihood that faulty risk management processes will be propagated and will lower the credibility of risk management in general. It can also set back the progress made over a period of years. In such cases it is much better to remove the person than continue to allow damage to occur.

Beware of program personnel who talk about risk management but know nothing about the subject. The program risk management spokesman should be knowledgeable about the subject else substantial loss of credibility may result.

Risk management process steps should not be assigned to individual program personnel (e.g., the program manager is in charge of prioritizing risk issues or is in charge risk handling). This is an oversimplification and compartmentalizes risk management rather than encouraging team members to participate and perform it. In addition, possible assignments will often be incorrect. For example, in the case of the program manager being in charge of risk handling, the risk issue POC and their IPT should be in charge of developing draft RHPs and the IPTs and RMB should be in charge of reviewing the draft RHPs, the RMB (chaired by the program manager) should have responsibility for approving the RHP, the IPTs should have authority to implement the RHP, and the risk issue POC should have responsibility for leading the RHP implementation. Similarly, the responsibility for prioritizing program risks should rest with the program's RMB (or equivalent) to provide a broader perspective on risk issues and their potential affect on the program. Using the RMB in this role also sends a positive message to other program personnel—both management and working level engineers, that varied perspectives are encouraged and included in the risk management process.

Risk management process steps should not be assigned to individual program personnel. This is an oversimplification and compartmentalizes risk management rather than encouraging team members to participate and perform it.

E. Resources Needed

Risk management should be expected to cost money up front but savings may well exist later in the development, production, and/or support phases. Up-front cost should be the norm, not the exception to the rule, and the funding level for risk management should be anticipated from the beginning of the program phase.

Risk management should be expected to cost money up front but savings may well exist later in the development, production, and/or support phases.

Consistent underestimates of the budget, schedule and other resources needed by management to develop a variation on an existing risk management methodology are common. For example, management had not attempted a project of this type before, but assumed it could be done quickly and with adequate quality. This often times is not true, and the opportunity cost to the program can be huge. [Here, opportunity cost can be both direct (e.g., budget growth and schedule slips) and indirect (e.g., decreased morale that weakens risk management implementation and its use).] Putting artificially short dates on developing methodologies is especially foolish since the adverse affects can hurt the remainder of the program. For example, in one case it was estimated to take $2\frac{1}{2}$ to $3\frac{1}{2}$ months to develop a risk management methodology. Lower management first agreed, then buckled to upper management that it had to be done *much quicker.* However, substantially shortening the schedule could only be accomplished if 1) the priority given to the methodology development was very high, 2) the number and thoroughness of the validation steps was reduced (which increases risk to successfully deliver a quality product), and 3) the number of iterations to closure was decreased from three to two (which also increases risk). Given these caveats, the time to complete was estimated at about $1\frac{2}{3}$ months. Lower management then dictated that it would have to be finished in three weeks! Well, the number of iterations was reduced to one, verification was reduced to a bare minimum, and while the priority was initially increased, it shortly dropped back to its historic low level. Two weeks later one lower level manager said, "Well, it looks like we won't get done in three weeks" when they were less than 25% complete. In the process the shortcuts mentioned above that were taken to initially speed things up led to a situation that could not be undone at a later point in time, and the overall quality suffered because of reduced verification and a single iteration, despite a substantial schedule slip. The actual time to complete was 13 months! All the management posturing about completing the methodology faster had no effect at all in terms of developing a product of suitable quality. Although the resulting methodology was acceptable the development process was quite painful, to say the least.

It is essential that a realistic budget, schedules, and other resources be included for proposed risk management activities because a high-opportunity cost may result if the work does not meet expectations.

F. Some Implementation Constraints

An insufficient budget and/or schedule may prevent adequate development of the risk management process (e.g., accurate, high in quality, and sufficient in scope) or how it is implemented (e.g., not iterated frequently enough or performed in a closed-loop fashion). For example, on one program insufficient funds existed to develop the desired risk analysis methodology. This led to the use of an incomplete and flawed risk analysis methodology, which produced erroneous results.

Accurate, realistic estimates of budget and schedule should exist to develop the desired risk management process. Once approved, a high program priority should exist to ensure that these resources are protected, applied, and the necessary personnel are available.

Insufficient budget (may translate to cost), performance margins, or time (schedule) may exist as part of a contingency plan within the program. The results can be a reduced number of potentially viable risk handling options and/or approaches, an inadequate performance reserve to meet essential requirements, or insufficient time to permit proper risk resolution. Furthermore, when inadequate funds exist, the risk management process may be undermined, and crisis management becomes standard operating procedure rather than proactive risk management.

Sufficient budget, performance margins, and time should be maintained to the extent possible for a given design to preserve risk management options during the course of the program.

X. Documenting and Communicating Risk Management Results

As mentioned in Chapter 2, Sec. II.E, risk management documentation is vital for both understanding the nature of risk issues vs time and communicating this information to program personnel.

Documentation is needed for each risk management process step. Having insufficient documentation or no documentation can precipitate a variety of problems later in the program that otherwise could have been avoided.

On some programs documentation is marginal or nonexistent for risk assessment results, risk handling approaches, and risk monitoring status. (For example, it is uncommon to find documentation that adequately explains how technical risk analysis scores were derived—typically only the scores are reported, or there is insufficient rationale to allow recreation of the risk analysis results.) If documentation exists, it may not effectively communicate key information associated with risk issues and results. I have reviewed documentation in some cases that did not accurately convey results (e.g., risk levels were presented when only the probability term of risk was computed). In other cases the documentation prevented issues from being clearly understood (e.g., why a potential problem is a candidate risk issue and what will the program impact be).

Risk management documentation should be clearly written. It should provide sufficient rationale to inform the reader why risk issues exist and what their potential impacts are, what are the risk scores and the rationale for assigning them, key characteristics of RHP, and risk monitoring results.

Risk documentation and communications should include, not exclude uncertainty that exists. Almost all risk analysis results and RHPs include uncertainty, yet uncertainty is rarely estimated, documented, or communicated to decision makers. Some indication of the level of confidence of estimates and the significance of uncertainty should generally be conveyed in risk documentation and communications. "In addition, data gaps and areas of significant disagreement among experts should also be disclosed."[14]

Estimates of uncertainty should be documented and communicated with risk analysis results and RHPs.

Risk management documentation should include a method to alert decision makers of impending impacts from issues analyzed to have medium or higher risk. This can include such things as potential drop-dead dates for implementation and selection of risk handling options, risk triggers that identify when the level of a risk issue increases (e.g., low to medium risk), and risk monitoring results that indicate insufficient progress being made between the plan (e.g., information in the RHP) and actual results. On large programs this may be more easily accomplished if an electronic risk management database is used. Prioritized risk summaries can by very beneficial, but should also clearly indicate the nature of each risk and who is responsible for resolving it.

Risk management documentation should include warnings when adverse changes occur in issues analyzed to have medium or higher risk.

On many programs risk management documentation may not have wide distribution and use. In the worst case the products and results may have virtually no use or impact on the key program decisions and plans. For example, in some cases key program personnel made important decisions contrary to what existing risk documentation indicated. If documentation is prepared, but not used in decision making, the overall effectiveness of the risk management process will often be greatly diminished.

Another related problem is that inadequate communication between participants (government-prime contractor, prime contractor subcontractor), including the flow of information, may exist, which will tend to reduce risk management process effectiveness. A balance must be reached between requiring excessive documentation that becomes a resource burden and insufficient documentation that does not provide sufficient information to understand risk issues accurately. The resulting level of documentation must also be freely available to program personnel. (One program I worked on had an extensive on-line information archive, but only a small fraction of the personnel could actually access key databases because of software design and implementation issues.)

Risk management documentation should be widely distributed and used by program personnel, including government-prime contractor and prime contractor subcontractor.

No prioritized top-level summary of risk issues (e.g., high risks or similar list) may exist, or if it does exist it may not be frequently updated. Top-level risk lists are valuable to focus upper management's attention, particularly when tied to key program milestone dates. They can become particularly important when either funding shortfalls or bonuses exist that can impact the number of risk issues that can be resolved. For example, if a program is faced with a $20-million budget cut, having such a list (coupled with the cost of risk handling activities for each item on the list) will allow the program manager to identify which risk handling activities can no longer be fully funded. If funding is terminated or modified for a given risk handling activity, the potential impact to the program can be estimated. This is far more persuasive than discussing such matters with personnel attempting to cut budgets without substantiation. (This approach was successfully used by one program manager to fight off potential budget cuts on his program.)

In some cases a prioritized top-level summary of risk issues may exist, but it may contain a variety of risks whose type and ownership are not clearly delineated. For example, system- and lower-level risks and government and contractor risks should not be mixed in the same list without clearly identifying each issue and organizational risk owner. In such cases it may be helpful to maintain separate risk lists for system and lower level risks and government and contractor risks in addition to a single master list. This may help prevent confusion associated with the risk issues and their ownership. If a single prioritized risk list exists, it is important to identify the nature of each risk and the organization responsible for resolving it.

A prioritized top-level summary of risk issues should be maintained and frequently updated. The nature of each risk (e.g., system level or lower level) and its ownership (e.g., government or prime contractor) should be clearly identified.

Do not just presuppose a fixed number of risk issues should exist for risk handling and monitoring purposes (e.g., the "Top N" list). This may be unwise if there are more risk issues than the value of "N;" particularly if they are issues with a high risk level. A much better approach is to handle and monitor all medium or higher risk issues. In addition, "Top 10" or similar risk lists are only effective for risk monitoring if the risk list is dynamic, where it is updated vs time, and not static. A static risk list used during the course of a program is generally not meaningful and should not be used.

Do not just presuppose a fixed number of risk issues should exist for risk handling and monitoring purposes (e.g., the "Top N" list). A much better approach is to handle and monitor all medium or higher risk issues.

The "Top N" risk issues or any other set of risk issues (e.g., high risks) should not be updated and reported either too frequently or too infrequently. The proper balance will vary on a case-by-case basis for each program and program phase (although contractual requirements may dictate the frequency). If done too frequently it will waste resources and diminish the level of enthusiasm of program personnel. If done too infrequently, either new risks may emerge that are not identified or substantial changes may occur for existing risk issues. (Note: Risks should generally not be updated and reported daily on almost any project.)

The "Top N" risk issues or any other set of risk issues (e.g., high risks) should not be updated and reported either too frequently or too infrequently. The proper balance will vary on a case-by-case basis for each program and program phase.

A method should be available that avoids possible retribution to permit program personnel to anonymously provide information on potential risk issues. (Ideally, this approach will not be needed, but the interpersonnel climate on some programs is sufficiently hostile to warrant its use.) Ideally, a bidirectional communication channel should exist between the risk manager and other program personnel to permit collecting additional information as needed. Of course, the nature of the messages and their content requires a balance to be struck between security (for anonymity) and sufficiency (for content).

It may be necessary to have a method to anonymously transmit adverse risk information between program personnel and the risk manager. As with any sensitive information, there may be a reluctance on the part of the government and/or contractors to share openly adverse risk management information. This can involve a wide range of information from specific risk issues to the effectiveness of the risk management process.

The following examples at the risk management process level are derived from observing the prime contractor and government on several programs. Similar observations have also been made for prime and subcontractors and at the risk issue level vs the process level illustrated here.

The prime contractor may be reluctant to communicate known problems about the government's risk management process even if it is substantially flawed. Similarly, if the government thinks that the contractor's risk management process is great, then the contractor may strongly resist changing its process even if it knows that it is flawed and how to correct the problems. This situation will become amplified when more than one prime contractor is competing with the government on the same program. In such cases the contractor will generally be very reluctant to send any bad news relating to its or the government's risk management process to the government, even if it is having an adverse impact on the program. This may improve the contractor's position in the short run, but may adversely impact the program in the long run.

It is essential that the prime contractor and government and prime contractor and subcontractors be able to exchange risk information honestly, or the effectiveness of all party's risk management activities will likely suffer.

Even if information generated by the risk management process is accurate, *recipients must view it as credible, otherwise the information may be discounted or misinterpreted.* As stated by the National Research Council,

> "The most important factors affecting the credibility of a source and its messages relate to the *accuracy* of the messages and the *legitimacy* of the process by which the contents were determined, *as perceived by the recipients.* Recipients' views about the accuracy of a message are adversely affected by 1) real or perceived advocacy by the source of a position in the message that is not consistent with a careful assessment of the facts; 2) a reputation for deceit, misrepresentation, or coercion on the part of the source; 3) previous statements or positions taken by the source that do not support the current message; 4) self-serving framing of information in the message; 5) contradictory messages from other credible courses; and 6) actual or perceived professional incompetence or impropriety on the part of the source. The perceived legitimacy of the process by which the contents of a message are determined depends on 1) the legal standing of the source with respect to the risks addressed; 2) the justification provided for the communica-

tion program; 3) the access afforded affected parties to the decision making process; and 4) the degree to which conflicting claims are given fair and balanced review."[14]

Recipients must view information generated by the risk management process as credible, otherwise it may be discounted or misinterpreted. Recipient concerns about the accuracy of the messages and the legitimacy of the process by which the contents were determined should be carefully considered and actions taken to correct potential problems to help ensure viable communication.

If insight on a risk issue is injected into the program, the method that the information is brought into the program and communicated may be critical to whether or not the information is accepted, no matter how correct it is. If, for example, the information is brought in through the noncognizant IPT, it may not be given an unbiased evaluation which may limit its use and effectiveness.

If insight on a risk issue is injected into the program, the method that the information is brought into the program and communicated may be critical to whether or not it is accepted.

XI. Risk Categories

Cost, performance (technical), and schedule risk represent fundamental top-level risk analysis categories. In some cases one or more of these categories may only be assessed infrequently, if at all, which can substantially weaken the risk management process. For example, on one large program there was no effective cost risk analysis or schedule risk analysis capability implemented. By the time the program was canceled, however, both cost growth and schedule slippage had occurred, which were both related to technical risk issues. No effective risk analysis methodology existed on the program to evaluate this potential impact. Monte Carlo cost risk and schedule risk simulations incorporating technical risk could have provided estimates of the impact of known technical risks on both cost and schedule.

Cost, performance (technical), and schedule risk should be adequately evaluated whenever possible. Failure to evaluate each of these risk categories and use of the resulting information to help shape key program decisions increases the possibility of problems occurring later in the program with potentially severe impacts.

The prescribed risk categories may be overly broad (e.g., programmatic risk), leading to difficulty in identifying risk issues, analyzing their level and developing and implementing a viable, measurable risk handling strategy.

Risk categories should be narrowed to specific risk issue areas whenever possible.

While it is important to identify high-level categories that describe risk issues, using such categories may not provide sufficient information to help "get to the heart" of the risk issues. For example, if high-level risk categories such as technical and programmatic are used, it is also important to evaluate potential lower-level risk categories associated with candidate risk issues. This can readily be done using the following two-stage approach. First, identify whether the risk issue is programmatic and/or technical. Second, from the programmatic branch determine which risk categories are applicable (e.g., cost, schedule, other as discussed in Chapter 2, Sec. I.B). Similarly, from the technical branch determine which risk categories apply (e.g., design/engineering, manufacturing, other as discussed in Chapter 2, Sec. I.B).

While it is important to identify high-level categories that describe risk issues, using such categories may not provide sufficient information to help "get to the heart" of the risk issues.

A variety of risk categories should be considered for both risk identification and analysis evaluations. Risk categories that should be examined will vary not only with the project but the acquisition phase. While some risk categories will apply to all programs (e.g., cost and schedule), others will only apply on a case-by-case basis. (The evaluation of potential risk categories should be performed as part of the risk planning process. See Chapter 4, Sec. IV.B.5 and Chapter 2, Sec. 1.B for additional information.) The following are relevant acquisition phases for some of the key risk categories discussed in Chapter 2 that should be evaluated. Cost, schedule, and threat risk should be examined for each acquisition phase. Performance risks related to technical issues (e.g., design/engineering and technology) should be examined during the entire development phase [e.g., concept exploration, program definition and risk reduction (PDRR), and engineering and manufacturing development (EMD)], but not generally during production. (Systems typically do not enter production until required performance levels have been achieved.) Manufacturing risk should be examined from relatively early in development to the production phase. (In some cases insufficient design detail may exist in concept exploration to perform a manufacturing risk assessment, but this should be possible during the PDRR phase.) Logistics/support risk should be examined from relatively early in development to the production, fielding/development, and operational support phase. (In some cases insufficient system deployment and design detail may exist in concept exploration to perform a logistics/support risk assessment, but this should be possible during the PDRR phase.)

Finally, the fidelity of the risk analysis process should increase with acquisition phase for many risk categories. For example, estimates of most likely cost, cost-estimating uncertainty, schedule risk, and technical risk that are included in a cost risk analysis should be more accurate during EMD than during concept exploration (cet. par.).

Each risk category should be evaluated during relevant acquisition phases, and the fidelity of the risk analysis process should increase with acquisition phase for many risk categories.

An inappropriate number (too few or too many) of risk categories may be used to describe technical/performance risk. Performance risk cannot be readily reduced to a single risk category, whereas cost and schedule risk can. However, including a large number of performance categories in a risk analysis may lead to questions of how the performance categories are weighted so that they do not dominate the overall assessment, as well as requiring excessive resources to perform the assessment and interpret and report the results.

Consider using three to five categories to describe technical risk. (These categories may be different for hardware and software items.) For example, for hardware items, design/engineering, manufacturing, and technology should typically be evaluated. (The exact categories, however, will vary on a program-by-program basis.)

A single risk category may dominate the evaluation of all others in a biased fashion. When this occurs, the overall risk management process may become ineffective in assessing and handling key program risks. (In such cases, it may be appropriate to evaluate other risk categories in greater detail and/or give them a higher degree of weighting in developing risk results.)

Do not weight the results from one risk category over another without solid rationale.

A single risk category may drive the entire risk management process (center of the universe syndrome), whereas it should only be one of n risk analysis categories, and risk analysis being only one of two risk assessment steps, and risk assessment is only one of four risk management process steps. This typically occurs when risk evaluations are primarily performed by a group of people that have a narrow focus in the program (e.g., design) coupled with the program having a weak risk management process.

The risk management process should not be dominated by a single process step or substep (e.g., analysis) or by a single risk category (e.g., design/engineering). All candidate risk categories should be evaluated and the results included in a balanced risk management process.

Risk issues associated with an item may be mapped to a single risk category (e.g., schedule), when in reality they represent and should be included in more than one risk category (e.g., design/engineering and schedule). This may propagate through risk assessment, risk handling, and risk monitoring steps and mask the true nature of the risk that exists.

Objectively evaluate a risk issue against all likely risk categories that apply to the item.

One or more major risk categories may be properly evaluated, but never effectively included in the program's risk management process. In some cases cost, performance (technical), and schedule risk are assessed, handled, and monitored in isolation from each other, and the results are never effectively integrated and included in the risk management process. For example, cost and/or schedule risk analysis results may be estimated but never really integrated into the program's risk management process because these risk categories are typically considered outside of technical risk (which often dominates the risk management process). This may lead to an ineffective risk management process, potentially weak engineering design analysis function (e.g., evaluating cost, performance, schedule, and risk trades and cost as an independent variable), and potential budget and schedule problems for some WBS elements and/or risk issues.

The risk management process should include and integrate results associated with cost, performance (technical), and schedule risk.

There is often a tendency to focus on hardware over software and integration risk issues, when in reality the reverse may be appropriate. The magnitude of potential cost growth and schedule slippage associated with software risk issues is often considerably greater than for hardware risk issues on moderate to complex or high-tech development programs. (The former program control director for a very high-technology government agency told me that if he could have been assured of *only* having 200% cost growth and schedule slippage on his software-intensive projects, he would have immediately requested that contractors sign firm fixed-price contracts!) Although I do not have detailed data, the magnitude of cost and schedule growth associated with integration risk issues can also be substantial, particularly because they often occur relatively late in the development process when a small to very limited solution space typically exists for the selected design, and many related activities are on the program's schedule critical path.

Hardware, software, integration, and programmatic WBS elements should be evaluated with a risk assessment methodology that is tailored to these items. When software and/or integration are a nontrivial part of the development activity, additional emphasis should be placed on the assessment of potential risk issues, development of suitable risk handling plans, and monitoring the results achieved in reducing the level of risk present because of the possibility of moderate-to-large cost and/or schedule growth.

System-level risk issues (e.g., the availability of a booster to launch the program's satellite) are often not considered or are relegated to a low priority for evaluation. Although sometimes difficult to address, system-level risk issues should be assessed, handled, and monitored with a priority and thoroughness given to lower WBS level issues.

There are three general classes of system-level risks. The first type of system-level risk represents the summed impact over a number of identical fabrication units. For example, a substantially greater risk may exist if an annual production rate of 20 satellites per year is required vs one per year. This type of risk can be captured by a risk assessment that uses a thorough set of ground rules and assumptions that state such things as the annual production rate and total production quantity. Hence, when a manufacturing risk assessment is performed, the required annual production rate and total quantity becomes the assessment baseline, not a single unit.

The second type of system-level risk is the roll up of lower-level risks through the WBS structure. In theory, if the roll up is done correctly, then the impact of a low-level WBS item can be measured at the system level. One method of computing this for values derived from uncalibrated ordinal scales (see Chapter 6 and Appendix H) is to take the largest risk being carried upward through the WBS structure and keep it undiminished. In effect, this results in a system-level risk equal to the highest risk at a lower WBS level. If calibrated ordinal scales are used (see Chapter 6 and Appendix H), then a mathematical roll up can be performed. However, there is a tendency that the contribution of even high-risk scores at low WBS levels (e.g., WBS Level 6) will be substantially diminished after being rolled up three or four levels. Consequently, a separate tracking of individual WBS level risks should always be maintained to prevent a potentially high risk at a low WBS level from slipping through the cracks following a roll up.

The third type of system-level risks are top-down risks that affect a high WBS level [e.g., Level 1 (program or architecture) or Level 2 (e.g., segment)] and only indirectly impact lower WBS levels. An example of this type of system-level risk is the impact of launch vehicle availability or failure on a satellite. If the launch vehicle is not available (e.g., because of production or development problems) or if it fails, then all lower-level WBS elements on the spacecraft are equally affected (cet. par.).

It is the third type of system-level risk (the top-down risk) that is more commonly not properly assessed in medium- and large-scale projects vs the first and second types. This is because different risk categories may exist, and different methodologies for risk identification and analysis may be needed for top-down system-level risks than for lower-level risk identification and analysis (e.g., particularly vs WBS Levels 4 or 5). Hence, although the project's existing risk identification and analysis methodology may suitably capture the first and second types of system-level risks, it will generally not adequately capture the third type.

System-level risks that enter the program at WBS Levels 1 or 2 may require a different risk assessment methodology than lower WBS level risks. Because of the potential for wide cost, performance, and schedule impact, such system-level risks should be evaluated, handled, and monitored with a priority no less than that for lower WBS level risks.

XII.   Organizational Considerations and Risk Management Process Implementation

A.   Organizational Considerations

Risk management responsibility should be a balance between being too centralized and too decentralized, and will require tailoring on each program (e.g., due to contractual requirements, organizational culture, best practices). If it is too centralized it will tend to discourage participation by others, and this may introduce errors of various types (e.g., overlooked risk issues). But if risk management is too decentralized, it will tend to lack overall project management focus and also include other types of errors (e.g., improperly prioritized risks).

Risk management responsibility should be a balance between being too centralized and too decentralized, and will require tailoring on each program.

If an organization develops a good risk management process and is then forced to integrate it into an inferior process at a higher-level organization, the result may be a decrease in risk management effectiveness for the lower-level organization. This is particularly true when the higher-level organization is not interested in hearing about issues with their own process and/or enhancing their own process to make it more effective.

If an organization develops a good risk management process and is then forced to integrate it into an inferior process at a higher-level organization, the result may be a decrease in risk management effectiveness for the lower-level organization.

A potential benefit of getting IPTs or groups of technical experts with a common understanding to evaluate a risk issue (e.g., check or perform a risk analysis) is that they may have information that a single person does not, thus potentially providing a fuller perspective to examine. (This does not mean hiding or suppressing risk issues via a group, engaging in "group think," or other unhelpful behaviors, but using additional information to evaluate the risk issue.)

It is helpful to have IPTs or groups of technical experts with a common understanding to evaluate a risk issue is that they may have information that a single person does not, thus potentially providing a fuller perspective to examine.

In the era of corporate consolidation, great care should be taken in transferring a risk management process from one company to another because of cultural issues and the possibility that the selected risk management process may be substandard or contains substantial errors. In one case a very poor risk management process was transferred across three other large, high-tech companies following consolidation activities where the host company acquired the other three.

In the era of corporate consolidation, great care should be taken in transferring a risk management process from one company to another because of cultural issues and the possibility that the selected risk management process may be substandard or contains substantial errors.

Organizations that have ineffective risk management practice may sometimes cite a reference document or even a version of a reference document that acknowledges or supports the process in question, even when a more recent reference document or version of the document no longer supports the flawed practice. For example, it is fairly commonplace for organizations incorrectly performing mathematics on the results from ordinal scales to cite the DSMC "Systems Engineering Management Guide," 2nd ed., Chapter 15, 1986; but not cite the DSMC "Systems Engineering Management Guide," 3rd ed., Chapter 15, 1990 where this material was withdrawn; or the DSMC "Systems Engineering Fundamentals," Chapter 15, 2001, where this material was refuted. (See Chapter 6, Sec. IV.A for additional information.)

Organizations that have ineffective risk management practice may sometimes cite a reference document or even a version of a reference document that acknowledges or supports the process in question, even when a more recent version of the documentation no longer support the flawed practice.

In some organizations that have a flawed risk management process, internal risk management standards documents may be adequate and not cite external reference documents that are obsolete or include flaws. However, the process used within the organization may use a flawed or an obsolete version of the external reference document. Thus, the existing risk management process, while supposedly based upon the organization's risk management standard, may instead be based in part on an external document that is flawed and/or obsolete, and not cited within the organization's standard. Rather amazingly, this type of problem is not uncommon with very large organizations engaged on programs with life-cycle costs far in excess of $1 billion!

If external reference documents are used ensure that they are not obsolete or flawed, particularly if they contradict adequate internal risk management standards documents.

If organizations and personnel selected to develop an RMP or perform an independent risk management assessment have no credible risk management experience, the resulting products will generally be flawed. Making such selections will range from unwise to exceedingly foolish and the opportunity cost may be very large because of lost time and decreased "good will" toward risk management. For example, on a program with a life-cycle cost exceeding $20 billion, a small contractor was chosen do write an RMP, yet neither the company nor the personnel assigned to the program had any comprehensive risk management experience.

If organizations and personnel selected to develop an RMP or perform an independent risk management assessment have no credible risk management experience, the resulting products will generally be flawed and the opportunity cost may be very large because of lost time and decreased "good will" toward risk management.

B. Process Implementation

Effective risk management requires early and continual involvement of all of the program team as well as outside help from subject-matter experts, as appropriate. Risk management must be implemented at all levels of the organization: it must work both top down from upper management to bottom up from working-level engineers to be successful.

However, it should come as no surprise that how the risk management process is best implemented on a particular program will vary on a case-by-case basis. In fact, attempting to force fit the same process implementation into a variety of different programs (e.g., with different contract types, schedule, and scope) will almost certainly lead to suboptimal results.

Within DoD programs there appear to be two common schools of thought for risk management organizational implementation, both using IPTs and both involving the program manager. In the first case a top-level IPT [often known as the Overarching IPT (OIPT) or WBS Level 1 IPT] takes on the responsibility for making key risk management decisions. In the second case, a separate RMB is responsible for these decisions. Although, in my opinion the second approach is desirable, both approaches can yield suitable outcomes assuming that they are well implemented.

A typical implementation involving the RMB approach is now discussed. [Note: The implementation of the OIPT or Level 1 IPT approach is virtually identical to the RMB approach in terms of the functions performed by the RMB (OIPT/Level 1 IPT), risk manager, and IPTs.] In the RMB case the RMB or systems engineering IPT owns the risk management process, and the risk manager (who reports to the systems engineering lead, or chief engineer) is the program's day-to-day risk management focal point.

The RMB (or equivalent) should be chartered as the program group that evaluates all program risk issues, draft risk analyses, and risk handling plans and progress. It is a decision-making board that includes the program manager (or designated alternate), the systems engineering lead (or chief engineer), the risk manager, IPT leads, and other key management personnel approved by the RMB (e.g., a customer or user representative).

It is important that at least one member of the RMB in addition to the risk manager have credible risk management training and experience. Without this knowledge decisions may be made that are contrary to good risk management practices that can later have a substantial adverse impact on the program. Some detailed considerations for implementing and sustaining RMBs are now given.

The program manager (or deputy program manager) should both establish and chair the RMB, not the risk manager. If the risk manager is the responsible party, then key program personnel may not be motivated to participate and dedicate their time, and this will "send a message" to other program personnel that risk management is not an important program process, which may lead to decreased risk management effectiveness on the program.

The program manager should both establish and chair the RMB, not the risk manager.

A single RMB should exist for each organization on a given program, not one per IPT or product unless the IPT or product is effectively a separate program or nontrivial geographic separation exists. Otherwise the risk management activity will not accurately span the work being done in individual areas in terms of necessary knowledge and resources. Be wary of having multiple levels of RMBs for a given program and organization. This type of risk management implementation is generally not helpful and can lead to a substantial risk management bureaucracy that does not necessarily improve risk management effectiveness and may actually diminish it. A better approach is to have the risk manager and cognizant IPT lead review risks with the risk issue POC, then pass the results to the RMB. On large programs a risk management working group (RMWG) may exist as an intermediate group/step between the IPT and risk issue POC and the RMB, and on very small programs the risk manager may directly review risks with the risk issue POC. The key here is that no single risk management organizational implementation is suitable for all programs, and the risk management process and how it is implemented must be tailored to each and every program.

A single RMB should exist for each organization on a given program unless the IPT or product is effectively a separate program or nontrivial geographic separation exists. Multiple levels of RMBs for a given program and organization are generally not helpful and can lead to a substantial risk management bureaucracy that does not necessarily improve risk management effectiveness and may actually diminish it.

The RMB should be a formally constituted board at the program-level. Unless this occurs it will send the "wrong message" to program personnel that risk management is not important enough to warrant high-level program attention.

The RMB should be a formally constituted board at the program-level.

Constituting an RMB but not giving it the authority to approve risk management products will diminish its stature within the program and lead to decreased effectiveness.

Risk management products should be approved by the RMB.

It is important for risk management related items to be filtered by the RMB rather than simply being implemented because they appear to be valid. In more than one instance I've heard suggestions that any item on the program critical path should be declared a risk issue. This was inadequate, inaccurate, and a potential waste of time because 1) an accurate schedule did not exist, 2) no schedule risk analysis had been performed, and 3) any potential issue—even on the probabilistic critical path—must first be evaluated by the RMB to become an approved risk issue.

It is important for risk management related items to be filtered by the RMB rather than simply being implemented because they appear to be valid.

One RMB function that is often needed on programs that involve different organizations and risk analysis methodologies is to "level" the resulting risk scores and prevent biasing (up or down) from skewing risks across the entire program.

Leveling of risk scores is one RMB function that is often needed on programs that involve different organizations.

The RMB should prioritize risks, not the risk manager who will generally not have the authority or vision to properly do this across the program. Also the results may not be fully accepted by other program personnel if the prioritization is performed by the risk manager.

The RMB should prioritize risks, not the risk manager.

Even when the program has a formally designated risk manager, risk management-related decisions should be made by or with the concurrence of the RMB (or equivalent). This is because the risk manager may not have a program-wide perspective on potential risk issues and may not represent all key management personnel within the project. In addition, this sends the "wrong message" to other personnel—even if an RMB exists risk management decisions that potentially cut across the entire program can be made without its concurrence. Thus, independent of the accuracy of the decisions made by the risk manager, such unauthorized actions will tend to weaken the effectiveness of the risk management process.

Even when the program has a formally designated risk manager, risk management-related decisions should be made by or with the concurrence of the RMB (or equivalent).

The RMB should define risk management roles and responsibilities within the program, not the risk manager who does not have adequate authority or position to do so.

The RMB should define risk management roles and responsibilities within the program, not the risk manager.

It is generally very unwise for the RMB as an entity to perform day-to-day risk management except on very small programs. The risk issue POC, with the assistance of the risk manager and cognizant IPT lead, should be the primary source to perform risk analysis, handling, and monitoring. (All program personnel should perform risk identification.) Otherwise, if the RMB is viewed as the group that performs risk management it will discourage other program personnel from participating.

The RMB as an entity should not be perform day-to-day risk management except on very small programs.

While it is possible that risk issues may be worked outside of the program's RMB this practice should be avoided. Three reasons for not permitting this practice are now given. First, feedback from different key program management personnel (RMB members) may provide different insights into how to best resolve the risk issue, and interrelationships between this issue and others. Second, resources may be needed outside of the sphere of influence associated with the person(s) attempting to deal with the risk issue, and the RMB often would be able to provide both a better knowledge base of what those resources are, and to commit them. Third, dealing with risk-related issues outside of the RMB sends the wrong message to the project—as if the RMB is only a "figurehead" organization and "real" risk-related decisions do not require it. This attitude will weaken the credibility of the RMB and the entire risk management process on the program, and not only should it be discouraged, but immediately eliminated.

While it is possible that risk issues may be worked outside of the program's RMB this practice should be avoided.

While members of the RMB may disagree about risk-related matters, it is important that it reach a consensus on how to address such matters. This does not mean that a "hard-line" position should exist to force a result (which may reflect an autocratic management style) or that a unanimous decision should always be reached immediately (which may indicate the presence of "group think" or other undesirable behaviors), because both of these actions are indicators of potential problems and can greatly weaken the RMB and its ability to promulgate risk management-related direction to the program. Risk management ground rules and assumptions, located in the RMP, should be used to help set boundaries on risk-related discussions. And constructive disagreement in a nonretribution environment can sometimes lead to additional information being made available that can form the basis for consensus. However, in many cases it is the program manager who chairs the RMB that must offer guidance to the other members and help achieve a consensus.

While members of the RMB may disagree about risk-related matters, it is important that it reach a consensus on how to address such matters.

C. Roles and Responsibilities

The roles of some of the RMB personnel are discussed next, followed by considerations for the risk issue POC and a discussion of RMB and IPT responsibilities.

The program manager (PM) is the chair of the RMB and has final risk management responsibility and authority. The PM, as chairman of the RMB, approves the RMP, the prioritized list of risks within the program, and the RHPs, and allocates resources to the IPTs to implement RHPs. The PM should not be (solely) responsible for identifying risks or developing RHPs and performing risk management training unless the program is small in scope or simple in complexity—these functions should be led by the program IPTs and the risk manager.

The systems engineering lead (or chief engineer) serves as a technical advisor for the program's risk management activities. The systems engineering lead recommends the elimination or reduction of unaffordable and/or high-risk program requirements and acts as the interface between the risk manager and other key program focal points.

The risk manager (or risk focal point) is the program's day-to-day risk management focal point. The risk manager, who reports to the systems engineering lead, should perform a variety of activities, including, but not limited to 1) preparing and submitting the draft RMP to the PM for approval, 2) providing risk management training as needed to program staff (the risk manager may use qualified outside personnel to develop and perform the training), 3) integrating and verifying risk identification inputs and risk analysis updates, 4) performing an initial evaluation of the feasibility of proposed risk handling strategies developed by IPTs, and 5) evaluating the risk monitoring reports developed by the IPTs on enacted risk handling strategies and reporting status and variances to the RMB. (For additional considerations for the risk manager, see Sec. VII.)

The risk issue POC is generally not a member of the RMB, although it is possible that RMB members may become in some cases a risk issue POC. Some considerations associated with risk issue POC are now given.

The risk issue POC should "own" a given risk, not the program manager. While the program manager has ultimate responsibility for risk management on the program (e.g., "the buck stops here"), the specifics of individual risk issues should be managed on a day-to-day basis by the risk issue POC.

One POC should be assigned to each risk issue, not one for each process step (e.g., handling); else the resulting implementation may be inefficient and increase the likelihood of errors occurring because 1) several risk management activities will be performed in parallel as part of the risk monitoring feedback activity, 2) the process step focal point may not be knowledgeable about all relevant aspects of the risk, and 3) continuity issues may exist. Also, having a single focal point for each process step is likely an inefficient organizational approach, and one that implements a substantial bureaucracy.

Risk issue POC should participate in and be responsible for risk analysis on a given risk issue, not the risk manager. While the risk issue POC should work with the risk manager (and cognizant IPT lead), the risk manager himself should not be responsible for risk analysis on each and every risk issue. Doing so will overburden the risk manager and lead to diminished interest towards risk management and involvement of others on the program and a decrease in risk management effectiveness.

The risk issue POC should be assigned the entire RHP and individual RHP implementation steps should not be given to different people. Using the former approach is desirable, if not necessary, to ensure continuity and prevent activities from "slipping through the cracks" and becoming issues or problems.

Risk issue POC should not select their own methodologies (including risk analysis methodology). This is made even worse when different risk issue POC choose different methodologies. In such a case, not only will the results be suspect, but there could be a substantial degree of uncertainty and variability between results even when the same risk issue is being analyzed using the same ground rules and assumptions.

RMB responsibilities include, but are not limited to 1) approving the RMP and subsequent revisions (which should be signed by the program manager), 2) approving candidate program risks (identification) and subsequent risk analysis results, 3) prioritizing program risks, 4) approving risk handling strategies and RHPs, and 5) approving metrics used for risk monitoring.

On a very small scale program the RMB (or equivalent) may perform risk planning, identification, analysis, handling, and monitoring. However, this is both inefficient and unwise on moderate to large-scale programs.

Program IPTs should have the authority and resources to successfully accomplish their portion of the program, including all risk related activities. The IPTs implement the risk management process following the approved RMP. IPT responsibilities should include, but are not limited to (working together with the risk issue POC) 1) performing draft risk analyses of approved risk issues using the methodology given in the approved RMP, 2) preparing draft RHPs for each candidate issue, 3) implementing the RMB approved risk handling strategy, and 4) developing risk monitoring progress reports.

Finally, on large-scale multiyear programs a modification to the implementation structure just discussed may be desirable. This is because a large amount of risk management-related material may be generated, that warrants evaluation and screening by a group of people (not just the risk manager) prior to reaching the RMB. In such a case it may be beneficial to include an advisory risk organization to the RMB. Such a risk working group might meet weekly and, together with the risk manager, evaluate and prepare material for the RMB. This is a working-level group, which could be composed of the risk manager, IPT leads, and others as desired. It also serves as an advisory group to the RMB because it passes its recommendations onto them along with their normal inputs. (Of course, dissenting opinions should always reach the RMB to guard against intentionally or unintentionally biasing the information they receive.) Some additional considerations for IPT involvement with risk management are now given.

Risk issues crossing more than one IPT or functional organization should be dealt with by program management or systems engineering to ensure that a sufficiently broad view of the risk exists in how it is identified, analyzed, handled, and monitored.

Whenever possible, the IPT lead should perform the role of an IPT risk coordinator since this is the only person typically with both the authority and broad knowledge needed to evaluate risk management practice and products within the IPT (e.g., draft risk analyses, draft RHPs, risk monitoring results).

IPTs do not in and of themselves lead to effective risk management. Effective risk management is much more related to the culture and how risk management is implemented and used than whether or not IPTs exist. This is an example of organizational behavior being far more important than organizational structure.

IPTs should not approve candidate risks, risk analyses, and risk handling plans. This is a key function of the RMB. Similarly, the RMB, not the IPT, should approve the risk handling strategy.

XIII. Support for Risk Management Within the Program

Risk management may not have support or participation from upper management within the program, which will contribute to reduced efficiency in its implementation and operation. This also sends a message to the technical staff and working-level engineers that risk management is not an important activity.

Extensive top-down management support and participation are generally required to ensure an effective risk management process.

The program manager often has considerable influence on both the nature and effectiveness of risk management on his program. The best type of program manager I have worked with to implement risk management is what I would call a leader and learner. He was a leader because he was willing to play a key role in making risk management work on his program. For example, the program manager, deputy program manager, and I together performed the first evaluation of a candidate risk issue. The program manager then briefed the results of the example to the entire engineering management team and incorporated their feedback. This program manager was a learner because he was willing to listen, ask questions, accept constructive criticism, educate himself, and embrace far more comprehensive risk management than he had previously used. (It is no coincidence that he has been recognized by peers at his company, as well as by a relevant professional society, as an excellent program manager.) It was also very fortunate that the deputy program manager had many of the same leader and learner characteristics toward risk management as the program manager. Thus, the two top managers on the development program were very positive models for risk management to the remainder of the managers and working-level engineers.

In addition, this program manager 1) encouraged all personnel to embrace risk management, and identify risks and assisted in developing RHPs; 2) strongly supported the risk consultant and carefully listened to and incorporated his recommendations; 3) regularly evaluated potential program issues from a risk management perspective; 4) included risk management in his daily decision-making process; 5) chaired the RMB; 6) competently briefed risk identification, risk analysis, and risk handling results to contractor and government managers; and 7) rewarded program personnel for effective risk management performance. The program manager also made key risk management information associated with the process, how each step was implemented, approved risk issues and their risk level, and approved RHPs available on line and gave all program personnel access. [Because I was the risk management consultant on this program, I cannot completely evaluate it in an unbiased fashion. Nevertheless, I would grade the process sophistication as a C+ (relative)/A− (normalized to program), whereas the implementation was an A−. The process sophistication was tailored to the program and was about as good as could be done for the budget, schedule, and scope present (e.g., a 4:1 schedule compression existed with a total development time of one year). The only process improvement I can suggest in retrospect is a more detailed examination of assembly and integration tasks for potential risk issues. (Here the relative C+ rating indicates the level of sophistication across programs I have worked on, while the A− rating indicates how much more sophisticated the process could have been for this particular program.) The one implementation feature that might have been improved was the program manager pushing risk management a bit more. (For example, attendance at RMB meetings was sometimes below desirable levels. However, this was compensated by the RMB members attending the daily engineering management meetings that occurred.) The program delivered, one week ahead of schedule, a very-high-technology product within budget, which met or exceeded all performance requirements. (It was the fastest development time ever recorded for an item of its type and complexity.)

In many government and industry organizations, there is almost a critical need to foster a culture of risk management (e.g., planning to prevent problems) *to overcome an existing culture of problem solving* (e.g., crisis management). This behavior is generally different from, and even contrary to, good risk management practices. This predicament exists, in part, because problem solvers are often promoted while those that practice sound project-management skills, including risk management, are overlooked. Thus, key program personnel are often unaware of good risk management practices, and in some cases may even be hostile to developing and implementing effective risk management. [One limited indication of the insufficient use of risk management by key program personnel follows. A survey of cost risk analysis methods and usage was performed that asked in part, "to what degree is (cost) risk analysis accepted by management?" Of the 61 responses from 35 government and industry aerospace organizations, only 28% of the responses indicated that cost risk analysis was fully or unconditionally accepted by management (e.g., "unqualified acceptance, integral part of analysis, required"). Whereas this was about the same proportion of responses that did not accept the results (26%), the remaining 46% of the responses indicated only marginal acceptance at best.[15]]

Ideally, the attitude toward risk management should be as one program manager said: "It's a tool that helps me manage the program." Although this may seem obvious and trivial, it is important and not routinely practiced. It is also very important that the program manager or deputy program manager (or perhaps the chief engineer, mission systems engineer, or technical director under clear authority from the program manager) has this viewpoint and believes it otherwise the risk management process will likely be weak or ineffective.

I have observed a wide variety of attitudes about risk management from other program managers. A small but representative sample of positive attitudes from actual programs (with a brief example for each case) include the following:

1) Interested and recognized its value (demonstrated leadership in risk management)

2) Student (did not thoroughly understand risk management but was willing to listen to and learn from more knowledgeable program personnel)

3) Curious (did not thoroughly understand risk management but recognized that it could help the program)

4) Delegation of authority (delegated responsibility to the deputy program manager who was a good leader. (Of course, just because a deputy program manager leads risk management does not insure a positive attitude towards it or success.)

5) Warmed up to it (initially was guarded about participating but became supportive and openly demonstrated the use of risk management principles in decision making during the course of the program)

A representative, but not exhaustive sample of negative program manager attitudes about risk management from actual programs (with a brief example for each case) include the following:

1) Procrastination (realized it is important but waited too long before finally embracing it)

2) Indifference (it is important but I will not make it a priority, or it is important but I will not make key decisions using it)

3) Sometimes I will use it and sometimes I will not (yes I have monthly RMB meetings but I make the big decisions on my own, followed by I guessed wrong, followed by time to retire)

4) I need to do it immediately (I have not done risk management to date but my program may be canceled if I do not start right now)

5) Big talker (lots of talk but no real action)

6) Telling everyone it is important but actions are contrary (not his cup of tea and too busy to learn, but permitted incompetent people to lead key risk management activities)

7) What me worry? (I am not concerned with potential qualitative or quantitative risk analysis errors—we use a subjective methodology and do not formally document the results)

8) Politician (I will tell the customer exactly what they want to hear, or this is not a high-risk program so do not tell me about any high risks)

9) Suspicious (it may mess up my program)

10) Lip service (I have to do it, I will do it, but I will not invest the necessary resources to do it comprehensively)

11) Check the box (I will only do as much as we are contractually required to do)

12) If the customer does not ask for it we will not do it (we will not do risk management unless the customer includes it as part of the next program review)

13) We will only report a few risks (we do not want the customer to know the number of risks we have, followed by why is this program in trouble)

14) Doubtful of the ability of others [the risk management work was done before I took over the program, so it is likely not acceptable (despite consistent praise from the customer)]

15) I do not have time to do it (this is a fast-paced program and I do not have the time to really implement it, followed by why did we not find the risk issues much earlier)

16) I do not need it (I will perform analysis, testing, and characterize the design and environment—whatever I feel or think today—and never mind that I do not have enough resources to evaluate all possibilities)

17) This is just an incremental program so it is not necessary (we are just modifying an existing design and do not need it, followed by why did we have 40% cost growth which almost bankrupted the company)

18) We have a great process (our risk management process is great—it had to be—we won the contract, followed by how could anyone question how good our process is, followed by so what if we consistently misanalyzed risk issues—how could this mistake almost kill our program)

19) A waste of time (I am a good problem solver—it does not matter that this is a high-risk program)

20) Against risk management (it did not solve *all* of my problems on the last program)

21) I want it free. ("I'll do risk management as long as it doesn't cost me anything." In such cases, as soon as RHPs require funding and implementation or if major process upgrades were needed, then there may be a retreat away from risk management.)

22) In denial (A program manager has been in denial for years. A poor risk management process has contributed to problems on two different programs yet the program manager will not change or improve the risk management process.)

23) It can't happen to me (not interested in understanding the risk drivers on a relatively high risk development activity)

24) On then off (A program manager uses risk management in spurts—on

then off. There is no consistency in the usage and it sends an inharmonious and potentially negative message to other program personnel.)

25) Huff and puff (talks about having a valid risk management process but then does nothing to remove fundamental, obvious technical errors from the process, or to correct the people that continued to propagate the erroneous information).

26) Bull in a china shop (doesn't participate in risk management-related activities very often, makes decisions that appear to be independent of risk management considerations, then tries to silence anyone with a contrary opinion).

27) Gun slinger (shoots from the hip on risk management, and while his insights are sometimes very good, he often overrules the structured, well implemented process without any rationale that can be substantiated)

28) Gun-shy (knows risk management can be helpful and makes tepid commitments to it, but won't take a strong stand for its implementation and daily use on the program)

29) Omniscient—I know all the risks (claims he knows all the risks on the program, despite the fact that the program involves complex, state-of-the-art development and is early in development)

30) Mildly interested (wanted assistance to evaluate and improve the risk management process, but then did little to implement recommended changes)

As you can see, all of the behaviors in this 30-item list are detrimental to risk management implementation, and thus to its effectiveness. Unfortunately, the behaviors illustrated do occur. And it is somewhat frightening to realize that several of these 30 behaviors existed on programs with a life-cycle cost greater than $1.0 billion.

Some program managers say they are interested in increasing risk management effectiveness but their actions are contrary to it. In one case the manager repeatedly said he wanted to improve the risk management process and had a valid and pressing reason to do so (an impending competition) but continued to settle for substandard, mediocre work that was inconsistent with the organization's need and below the minimum likely required for the forthcoming competition.

In other cases the program manager and deputy program manager may have vastly different views and experience on risk management. This generally leads to reduced risk-management process effectiveness, particularly when an unclear allocation of responsibilities between the parties' or personality clashes exists. Ideally, the most experienced of the two individuals should take responsibility for risk management on the program (cet. par.), although the program manager is ultimately responsible for key decisions. However, in organizations without a history of effective risk management or in dysfunctional organizations, subtle or even overt conflict between the program manager and deputy program manager may occur and lead to an ineffective risk management process.

For example, the "lead" individual for risk management may interfere with the other individual's desire to effectively implement the process. This interference may be unintentional and result from a lack of knowledge or a difference in "style" between the individuals. However, in other cases it may be intentional and due to a variety of factors, such as a power struggle or personality conflicts between the individuals. The potential damage to the program from such unintentional, and particularly intentional, behavior should not be underestimated—it may lead to very serious problems—so much so that upper management should immediately intervene.

The program manager and other key personnel may discourage effective risk management implementation through either subtle or overt methods. In the former case the program manager may, for example, make it clear that he is very busy and does not wish to be disturbed by anything but urgent matters. This can have the indirect effect of reducing the number of risk issues identified and the urgency in which they should be resolved. In the latter case the program manager may directly damage the atmosphere for performing risk management. For example, in one case the program manager stated in an RMB meeting (according to the RMB secretary's official minutes) that "all whining would be cut" from the risk list. This not only castigated RMB members but resulted in a number of risk issues being dropped without proper evaluation. (Several of these risk issues were reinstated and approved one month later when the program manager was replaced.)

Also, the program manager or deputy program manager may engage in micromanagement, which when coupled with a controlling behavior can limit the flow of information (including risk management information) to other program participants. (Bi-directional free flow of information between workers and management is an essential ingredient for risk management success.) This can have a substantial adverse impact on the ability to perform risk identification and adequately develop and implement risk handling plans. The result of such actions will likely be a decrease in the overall effectiveness of the risk management process, and an increase in the number of risk issues not adequately dealt with that will later become problems.

Finally, the program manager (and other key personnel) has the ability to greatly influence the effectiveness of the risk management process. Unfortunately, the behavior exhibited toward risk management may unintentionally or intentionally limit its effectiveness. For example, managers may game a risk analysis to yield the desired results. This practice damages the credibility of not only the risk analysis, but the entire risk management process, and can contribute to substantial problems later in the program. Given that such problems do sometimes exist on actual programs, it is important that the organization's upper management monitor, and in some cases attempt to independently evaluate, the effectiveness of the risk management process to identify and work with the program manager to correct deficiencies before they translate into major program problems.

The effectiveness of the program's risk management process is often highly correlated with the attitude of the program manager and other key personnel toward it. For risk management to be effective, the program manager (or deputy program manager) should have an honest, unbiased attitude toward it; have the desire to learn and participate; encourage the free flow of information between workers and management; and have some active involvement in leading, or at least guiding, its implementation and operation. It is also important that the organization's upper management monitor, and in some cases attempt to independently evaluate, the effectiveness of the risk management process to identify and work with the program manager to correct deficiencies before they translate into major program problems.

Key decision makers have often long left the program before the outcomes of their risk management strategy can be evaluated. There may be insufficient incentive for a program manager to develop and implement an unbiased, objective risk management process if he will leave long before the validity of identified risk issues, the number of unidentified risk issues that should have been identified, assessed levels of risks, suitability of risk handling approaches, and effectiveness of risk monitoring approaches are known.

Key decision makers will often leave a program before the effectiveness of the risk management process is accurately known. When possible, the tour of duty for top performing program managers should be extended to provide continuity for risk management and other activities. If the program manager is replaced, and an effective risk management process already exists, the existing process should be maintained to the extent possible to prevent unforeseen problems from occurring later in the program.

Although the program manager may be ultimately responsible for risk management, unless it is performed on a daily basis by both management and working-level personnel, its effectiveness will greatly diminish or even vanish. For risk management to be effective, program personnel must consider it in daily decisions. This is not to say that each member of the program becomes a risk manager, but that they are conscious that risk management is something to consider in their decision-making process. For example, on one software-intensive project, the software developers noted when potential problems were identified whether or not these problems could be resolved in three hours or less. If they could quickly solve the problem, they did so without reporting it to management. If the anticipated solution would likely take more than three hours to implement, then the issue was surfaced as a candidate risk. (Of course, the three-hour threshold could be adjusted to any value appropriate to the program.) This procedure helped identify potential problems early, when the resources needed to correct them were small, without overburdening the working-level engineers or management. *For risk management to be effective, working-level personnel must consider it as part of their daily decision-making process.*

The program manager should approve the RMP. This is essential to convey the proper message to program personnel that the program manager stands behind the risk management process and how it should be implemented. If anyone else approves the RMP it sends the wrong message to program personnel (e.g., risk management is not important enough for the program manager to be involved or the program manager is too busy to be involved). This is even more important if the person with final approval authority for the RMP is a mid to low-level manager on the program, such as the risk manager.

The program manager should approve the RMP. This is essential to convey the proper message to program personnel that the program manager stands behind the risk management process and how it should be implemented.

The program manager, not risk manager, should lead efforts to foster an open atmosphere and facilitate risk communication within the project. The risk manager does not command the respect of program personnel to the degree that the program manager does. Hence, while the risk manager should assist the program manager in this activity, the program manager should be in charge of it.

The program manager, not risk manager, should lead efforts to foster an open atmosphere and facilitate risk communication within the project.

XIV.   Some Behavioral Issues Associated with Implementation

A.   Organizational Level

Many organizations do not have a history of effective risk management, and the ability to develop effective risk management in such organizations is often more closely related to behavioral issues associated with culture change and resistance to a paradigm shift than to more logical or straightforward considerations related to training, development of a suitable RMP, etc. (For a classic study in how organizations and individuals change and resist change, see Thomas S. Kuhn, *The Structure of Scientific Revolutions*, University of Chicago Press, Chicago, 1962.)

Just because an organization has a successful, high-tech background does not mean that risk management is correctly or properly performed. For example, if the organization's culture has been to perform the best design work possible without using a structured risk management process, attempts to introduce effective risk management to existing or new programs will typically require a paradigm shift to be successful and will likely be ineffective without it. This is also generally true for organizations that promote problem solvers rather than individuals with sound project management skills because principles of sound risk management will often be alien to key program personnel.

Even when seeing the obvious need for change, it is all together too common for organizations to blindly continue their historical way of doing business, despite the fact that the world has changed around them. For example, one organization has an indisputable history of developing and deploying successful, very high-technology systems, yet was previously immune from budget cuts and outside scrutiny. Now that they face budget cuts, program terminations, and increased scrutiny like many other organizations, it would be logical to expect them to embrace risk management; cost, performance, schedule, and risk trades; and other processes to help them more effectively manage their programs. Yet the results of one in-house study this organization performed indicated the following (in almost these exact words): in the past we did not do risk management, in the present we will think about risk management, and in the future we may actually have to implement risk management!

On the surface this type of behavior may seem illogical, but it is fairly common and is closely related to the way organizations view themselves (and in a biased fashion), their long-term culture, and how they resist change. Many of these patterns are highly predictable and repeatable, but nevertheless they are either not seen or are discounted by those internal to the organization. Visionaries that initially push to incorporate risk management in such dysfunctional organizations often meet strong resistance and may well pay a *substantial* personal price. (As in many cases where paradigm shifts take place, if a dysfunctional organization later embraces risk management, contributions made by the visionaries are often greatly discounted or forgotten and the visionaries have been expelled.)

In some cases the resistance to implementing a better risk management process is so severe that failure results. In addition, I have observed that suggestions made for improving a program's risk management process are sometimes dismissed out of hand. Even worse, people that attempted to improve the process are sometimes removed—despite the fact that their comments may have considerable merit. In some organizations and on some programs with a dysfunctional risk management implementation, the degree that corrective action recommendations are accepted appears to be inversely proportional to the true level of expertise the individual possesses. (A close corollary in such cases is that the true level of risk management knowledge is inversely proportional to what people claim.) This type of behavior is exceedingly unwise and can lead to substantial problems later in the program's development cycle when unanticipated issues surface as problems that should have been identified and handled much earlier.

Unfortunately, because dysfunctional organizations often reward engineering and management problem solvers rather than people with good project management skills, this may feed another cycle of crisis management leading to promotions that subsequently bias key program personnel against sound risk management practices ("Catch 22"). As one project management consultant wisely said: "Rewarding fire fighters breeds arsonists." This truly applies to promoting problem solvers who then impede risk management on future programs. (Another consultant provided a different interpretation of this statement. Here people create a problem that they know they can solve, solve the problem, get promoted, then create and solve even more problems with the hope of getting another promotion. This situation greatly damages the ability to perform risk management. However, this type of behavior does occur—so much so that on one high-technology program a specific name was created for those engaged in this practice.)

Finally, it is exceedingly unwise to think that such problems can be solved by the stroke of a pen via some directive or initiative. It will generally take considerable time and resources to correct years of neglect or antagonism toward risk management—it almost never will occur overnight. As mentioned in this chapter, if upper management provides viable and visible support for risk management (e.g., leadership by example) both at the program level and above, this will often greatly increase the likelihood that positive change will occur and lead to increased risk management effectiveness.

Many organizations do not have a history of effective risk management, and the ability to develop effective risk management in such organizations is often more closely related to behavioral issues associated with culture change and resistance to a paradigm shift than to logical or straight forward considerations related to training, development of a suitable RMP, etc. If upper management provides viable and visible support for risk management (e.g., leadership by example) both at the program level and above, this will often greatly increase the likelihood that positive change will occur and lead to increased risk management effectiveness.

An organization without a history of successful risk management may attempt to justify an informal, unstructured, weak, or undocumented risk management process as adequate after the fact rather than improve the existing process. This may not only be a delusion, but the ruse may be penetrated by others outside the organization in question. The net result will often be unhelpful to the developing organization on the project in question, but may also adversely affect its ability to obtain future projects. For example, in one case the seller presented information on its risk management process following completion of the development phase, yet the buyer program manager strongly believed that the seller was without a clue as to what good risk management is.

An organization without a history of successful risk management may attempt to justify an informal, unstructured, weak, or undocumented risk management process as adequate after the fact rather than improve the existing process.

In organizations without a history of effective risk management, people, including the program manager, may revert to a subjective, ad hoc risk management process even when a superior, structured, risk management process exists, is in use, and is adequately documented. This type of problem is surprisingly common and may be very difficult to eliminate. One method I've used is to continue to guide discussions, using the existing risk management process, gently point out when that process is being violated, and offer suggestions as to how to revert back to the superior risk management process.

In organizations without a history of effective risk management, people, including the program manager, may revert to a subjective, ad hoc risk management process even when a superior, structured, risk management process exists, is in use, and is adequately documented.

In organizations without a history of effective risk management there may be a tendency to revert back to crisis management (problem solving) when risk issues arise (even when the time horizon needed to resolve them is mid-to-long term) and to turn away from risk management. (This will likely occur until and unless risk management is firmly entrenched into the program.) Upper management in such cases may not have any hesitation in making such a switch, because they are typically more familiar with "fire fighting" than using risk management principles to resolve issues. Here, the tendency is to reduce cognitive dissonance between the two fundamentally conflicting approaches by selecting crisis management, which they are more familiar with.

In organizations without a history of effective risk management there may be a tendency to revert back to crisis management when risk issues arise and to turn away from risk management.

Organizations that do not have a history of effective risk management will often cling to old, inferior risk management process rather than changing to a better one, even in a competition for a new program. In some cases this holds for competitive source selections involving formal RFPs, where in theory, the better the risk management process, the better the score for that portion of the evaluation. Yet it is remarkable how often inferior risk management processes that are well below the state of the art are maintained and included in proposals, and attempts to enhance the level of process sophistication as well as the overall risk management effectiveness are often rebuffed.

Organizations that do not have a history of effective risk management will often cling to old, inferior risk management process rather than changing to a better one, even in a competition for a new program.

After an ineffective risk management process is entrenched in a program, it may be very difficult to supplant, even when a superior risk management process is developed. In some cases it may appear that the cost or schedule needed to improve the risk management process may be excessive. However, substantial risk management process enhancements can often be achieved with limited funding and calendar time. In fact, the rationale to retain a flawed risk management process, even if it is the process always used or a process from corporate headquarters, often rests upon behavioral considerations relative to resisting change rather than evidence that the chosen process is superior or even adequate for the program.

For example, in one case the program's risk manager was heavily involved in developing the initial risk management process. Whenever he had the opportunity to use the improved risk management process (which was noticeably superior to the initial process), he continued to cling to the initial process despite being counseled on the detriments of the original process and the benefits of the new one. This behavior continued over an extended period of time and led to the risk manager being replaced.

For an enhanced risk management process to supplant an existing one, a behavioral paradigm shift will often be needed. Attempts to effectively implement the enhanced process will likely fall short or fail if its proponents primarily or solely focus rationale for its use on technical merit without considering and addressing relevant behavioral issues associated with program personnel.

Organizations without a history of effective risk management may act indecisively when asked or directed to implement a more comprehensive risk management process. While some degree of indecisiveness may be expected, such organizations will often waste considerable time both resisting implementing risk management, then generally doing so poorly.

In other cases, organizations without a history of effective risk management may resist, even strongly, improving a risk management process once a weak to modestly good process is in place. Attempts to improve the risk management process in such cases are likely to be unsuccessful without expending considerable political capital.

Organizations without a history of effective risk management may act indecisively or resist improving a risk management process once a weak to modestly good process is in place.

In some cases an organization without a history of effective risk management may initially need to improve its risk management process and target deficiencies that are (ideally) both the most substantial and easiest to remedy. For example, an initial evaluation for such an organization may reveal that one or more process steps is missing and/or out of order with the others, and it may thus be desirable to focus improvement activities on remedying such a situation. Here, there is little to be gained and potentially much can be lost by attempting to implement improvements that are likely to have only a small marginal gain on the process effectiveness, and may in some cases be completely lost because of larger overriding flaws. For example, it would be a waste of resources to implement a schedule risk analysis using a Monte Carlo simulation on a program does not perform risk planning nor have a structured risk identification process. [And even if a schedule risk analysis using a Monte Carlo simulation is a contractual requirement on the program, it should still not be attempted until more fundamental issues are resolved (e.g., implementing risk planning and a structured risk identification process).]

In some cases an organization without a history of effective risk management may initially need to improve its risk management process and target deficiencies that are (ideally) both the most substantial and easiest to remedy rather than implement improvements that are likely to have only a small marginal gain on the process effectiveness.

In organizations without a history of successful risk management, and particularly in dysfunctional organizations, do not underestimate the level or type of problems that may occur in response to attempts to improve the existing risk management process. In some cases the resulting behaviors may be irrational or even worse in nature. For example, in one organization, a manager with risk management oversight responsibility voluntarily said to the customer that the team would turn over its proprietary methodology, and the customer was free to circulate the methodology to the competition. This not only would have been a major blunder, but would have provided the competition (and likely other organizations) with an improved methodology to compete with it on other existing and future programs. Fortunately this offer was never carried out. Shortly thereafter, a member of the risk analysis methodology team was caught hampering the development of an improved approach, and management did nothing to alleviate this problem.

In organizations without a history of successful risk management, and particularly in dysfunctional organizations, do not underestimate the level or type of problems that may occur in response to attempts to improve the existing risk management process.

In organizations without a history of effective risk management it is not uncommon for risk management to be reduced whenever budget uncertainties exist. In such cases, cutbacks may include all aspects of risk management and not be limited to a small portion of the process and its implementation.

In organizations without a history of effective risk management it is not uncommon for risk management to be reduced whenever budget uncertainties exist.

Organizations without a history of effective risk management will often select a risk manager without any formal risk management experience, then be reluctant to properly support or train the person or remove him if unacceptable performance is demonstrated. This indecisive action will contribute to ineffective risk management.

Organizations without a history of effective risk management may not select a suitable risk manager candidate, then be reluctant to either support or train him.

The academic or experiential grounding of an organization may play a strong role in shaping the resulting risk management process produced by such an organization. For example, one organization without strong leadership in technical disciplines developed a risk management process that was devoid of the performance dimension and did not address technical risk. When challenged on this accord, representatives defended their position by stating that it was "hard to define" performance and technical risk. While this may be the case for the organization in question, it does not serve as a sufficient reason to dismiss this component of risk. Put another way, it doesn't matter what you believe if reality is contrary to your opinion. Yet avoiding the performance dimension and technical risk has no credibility when they clearly exist in many cases.

The academic or experiential grounding of an organization may play a strong role in shaping the resulting risk management process produced by such an organization.

Organizational bureaucracy can adversely affect risk management process selection and implementation, and its potential impact should not be underestimated. In one case an adequate risk management process existed but key management personnel insisted that they go to a higher-level organization to obtain insights about that organizations risk management best practices. What the program personnel did not realize is that the risk management process and implementation that already existed and was being used was consistent with the best practices of their own organization and was superior in some regards to that of the higher-level organization. In both this and another related case the program office misjudged the quality of the risk management best practices of the higher-level organization with those in their own organization, and wasted scarce resources and potentially diminished risk management effectiveness on the program.

Organizational bureaucracy can adversely affect risk management process selection and implementation, and its potential impact should not be underestimated.

Organizations that do not routinely implement a structured risk management process will generally not benefit from lessons learned on past programs. For example, if commercial off-the-shelf (COTS) development exists they may continue to underestimate the risk associated with hardware, software, and hardware/software integration activities despite difficulties on previous programs. This is because while the issues may be similar, there is no formalized mechanism with how to plan, identify, analyze, handle, and monitor the issues.

Organizations that do not routinely implement a structured risk management process will generally not benefit from lessons learned on past programs.

Behavioral issues may need to be examined and evaluated at a number of different levels to assist in implementing risk management, ranging from "people to people" to organization to organization (e.g., one IPT to another, project to program, program to larger organization, subcontractor to prime contractor, contractor to government).

Behavioral issues may need to be examined and evaluated at a number of different levels to assist in implementing risk management.

When the buyer says that a risk score or level is "X" and the methodology used by the seller yields a much different risk level, the seller should not arbitrarily agree to the buyer's viewpoint. This is a clear case when discussion between the buyer and seller should occur and the rationale presented for why a risk issue was scored the way it was rather than blindly accepting unsubstantiated assertions.

When the buyer and seller arrive at a much different risk score or level for a given risk issue discussion should occur between the buyer and seller should occur rather than one party arbitrarily conceding to the other.

Pushing a new tool or technique on an organization without a history of risk management or a dysfunctional organization will generally be met with covert, if not overt resistance, and the resulting effectiveness will often times be poor. As one systems engineering manager said "you have to show the working-level engineers what is in it for them" in order to have the tool or technique successfully assimilated. Without this, resistance will often be strong and the resulting effectiveness will suffer.

Pushing a new tool or technique on an organization without a history of risk management or a dysfunctional organization will generally be met with covert, if not overt resistance, and the resulting effectiveness will often times be poor.

Once a risk management process is implemented, there will likely be one or more groups within the program that will either limit the use on their portion of the program, change the process, or attempt to oversimplify the process to the point that it no longer resembles what is required (e.g., on contract). Such actions will tend to reduce risk management effectiveness, both directly via a degraded process and/or its use, and indirectly by "sending a signal" to others on the program that the risk management process can be tailored in somewhat of an unbounded manner to suit each particular group and/or individual. Be aware that such acts may occur and be prepared to provide correction action as warranted.

Once a risk management process is implemented, there will likely be one or more groups within the program that will either limit the use on their portion of the program, change the process, or attempt to oversimplify the process to the point that it no longer resembles what is required. Be aware that such actions may occur and be prepared to provide correction action as warranted.

The behavior of people in one organization was such that it greatly inhibited the dissemination of effective risk management practices. This included a number of detrimental activities, caused by a group of program personnel that did not actually perform risk management but bypassed upper management and the customer organization. This harmful practice went on for a considerable period of time without upper management knowing (or not wanting to know) and led to considerable difficulty on the program.

It is very important that once management makes a commitment to program personnel regarding risk management that it keep this commitment, otherwise trust will diminish and the effectiveness of the process may suffer greatly. This is often the case because many organizations do not have a history of effective risk management (or even worse are dysfunctional toward project management skills), and working level personnel may view risk management as just one more "thing to do" without any management support. If management initiates risk management implementation on a program and workers observe, or even sense, that the draft products that they are generating (e.g., risk identification, analysis, handling) are not being objectively evaluated by management in a timely fashion, then the barriers to having effective risk management on the program will continue to grow in height and may become exceedingly difficult to overcome.

It is very important that once management makes a commitment to program personnel regarding risk management that it keep this commitment, otherwise trust will diminish and the effectiveness of the process may suffer greatly.

How much people in an organization know about risk management is often not so important. What may be more important is how much they are willing to learn and implement about risk management.

How much people in an organization are willing to learn and implement about risk management may be more important than what they currently know about risk management.

B.   Organizational Structure, Roles, Responsibilities

Situations may exist when a program manager inherits a program that does not have an effective risk management process and there is insufficient budget and other resources to adequately support risk management. Here, the program manager may have very little flexibility to substantially improve the risk management process, especially if RHPs need to be funded, and may have to approach upper management to request additional funding if it can not be located within the project (e.g., management reserve, reallocate from other activities). The likelihood of improving risk management effectiveness in such situations will generally be low and may only be overcome if the program manager or deputy program manager invest considerable personal capital.

If a program manager inherits a program that does not have an effective risk management process and there is insufficient budget and other resources to adequately support risk management, the likelihood of improving risk management effectiveness in such situations will generally be low and may only be overcome if the program manager or deputy program manager invest considerable personal capital.

It is very important that risk management have a high-level sponsor within an organization in order to assist lower-level personnel who are implementing the process, as well as to help overcome biases against risk management (should they exist). While ideally the high-level sponsor would be the program manager, this may not always be possible due to commitments to other program activities. In such cases it is still assumed that the program manager (or deputy program manager) is the final risk management authority, but may not be its daily champion. Typically the risk manager is a mid-level manager and sometimes may not have sufficient organizational rank to serve as an effective champion for risk management. Practically speaking, someone between the rank of risk manager and program manager (e.g., chief engineer, assistant program manager, or deputy program manager) may make a suitable risk management champion. In organizations where risk management is not firmly rooted, switching key management sponsors often leads to a diminished level of risk management effectiveness that is difficult to overcome. If the current risk management champion takes on additional responsibilities or leaves the program, it is very important that a suitable replacement be identified and trained by working with the champion, risk manager, and other program personnel to avoid a loss of risk management effectiveness. It is also very important that the new champion desire to take an active role in seeing that risk management is properly implemented on the program.

It is very important that risk management have a high-level sponsor within an organization in order to assist lower-level personnel who are implementing the process, as well as to help overcome biases against risk management (should they exist).

An all too common situation regarding implementing risk management is that those given the *responsibility* to implement the process do not have the *authority* to do so, and key program management personnel either do not have the time or interest to support the implementation. This will almost always contribute to an ineffective risk management process because process steps will not be properly implemented, the direction given by upper management to implement and routinely use risk management will often be both weak and contradictory, and the commitment to perform risk management by upper management will be inadequate (which will be observed and modeled by working level engineers as well).

Those given the responsibility to implement risk management should also have the authority to do so.

Risk organizational roles and responsibilities should be consistent with management philosophy disseminated to the project team. For example, individuals may be encouraged by management to be risk management leaders by involvement in daily activities. However, in some cases IPT leads identify candidate risk issues, perform the risk analysis and/or develop the RHP. In this case there is a disconnect between management philosophy and risk management assignments which sends an unclear message to program personnel and will not contribute to effective risk management.

Risk organizational roles and responsibilities should be consistent with management philosophy disseminated to the project team.

Responsible parties may not be assigned to issues surfaced by risk identification, nor exist in subsequent process steps (analysis, handling, and monitoring). This will reduce the chance that the risk issue will be resolved efficiently.

A responsible party should be assigned to each risk issue that is approved by the RMB (as part of risk identification) by the cognizant IPT lead. If the same individual cannot remain as the risk issue POC during the course of the program, then a smooth transition should occur to prevent key knowledge from being lost. In some cases it may be appropriate to change the risk issue POC for a given risk issue during RHP development or while it is being implemented, but this should be done on a case by case basis, rather than automatically.

The risk issue POC should generally be assigned based upon the type of risk issue and the level of expertise associated with available personnel. For example, a working-level engineer may be a suitable POC for technical risk issues, while an appropriate manager may be needed for a program management risk issue.

The risk issue POC should have the ability to analyze, handle and monitor each risk issue that is assigned. This includes 1) supplying additional information on risk issues approved by the RMB, 2) developing a draft risk analysis, 3) developing a suitable risk handling strategy and draft RHP for risk issues with a medium or higher level of risk, and 4) performing an initial evaluation of risk monitoring data associated with implemented RHPs.

An appropriate responsible party should be assigned for each approved risk issue. Ideally, the same point of contact will exist until the risk issue is resolved.

Organizational units within the program should be empowered to perform and implement risk management within the bounds defined in the RMP and approved by the RMB. For example, when a program's structure incorporates IPTs, they should have a major responsibility for implementing the risk management process. However, as several program managers have told me, IPTs that exist in name only (e.g., historical functional organizations with just a name change) may not be capable of effectively implementing risk management.

IPTs should possess cohesiveness, leverage, and breadth of knowledge to implement risk management effectively.

While IPTs and related teaming structures can be helpful in implementing risk management their effectiveness can be diminished in cases where multiple stakeholders exist that have conflicting objectives or positions on risk management. For example, in one program the SEIPT was the risk management owner. Direction given to the risk management focal point within the SEIPT by the focal point's functional managers within the organization's systems engineering department was often contrary to the recommendations of key program personnel (e.g., chief engineer). In this case, the chief engineer had a much better understanding of risk management and its implementation than anyone in the systems engineering department. Yet the risk management focal point was torn between direction from the functional organization (who also gave him performance reviews) and the desires of key program personnel This led to considerable inefficiency in implementing risk management on the program and a much less effective process than would have occurred had the functional organization not interfered. In another case, the functional organization had more risk management knowledge than the program office. But again, there was often conflict between the functional organization and the program office on the risk management process, how to implement it, and roles and responsibilities both for the organization and individuals. These conflicts should come as no surprise, and are surprisingly common whenever multiple sponsors for risk management exist within a program. This can be due to the organizational structure used (e.g., strong matrix where the functional department heads have considerable control and the program manager has limited authority) or the behavior of key program personnel. In either case such conflict can greatly weaken risk management effectiveness and should be addressed and eliminated at the beginning of a program phase.

While IPTs and related teaming structures can be helpful in implementing risk management their effectiveness can be diminished in cases where multiple stakeholders exist that have conflicting objectives or positions on risk management. Such differences should be addressed and eliminated at the beginning of a program phase.

A common tendency is to focus on the risk management process implementation structure (e.g., the number and responsibility of IPTs) rather than the more important behavioral characteristics associated with it. For example, having a risk manager is a positive step toward process implementation. However, if the risk manager is isolated from the rest of the program, not active in daily design or other key trades, or does not interact with key personnel in the program's IPTs, then the effectiveness of the risk management process will likely be low.

The effectiveness of a risk management process is almost always much more closely tied to the behavior of participants than the specific organizational structure associated with the implementation.

C. Heuristics

People often rely on a limited number of heuristic principles that reduce complex tasks of assessing probabilities and predicting values to simpler judgmental operations. These heuristics can lead to biased assessments of probability. Three such heuristics, first discussed by Amos Tversky and Daniel Kahneman, include adjustment and anchoring, availability, and representativeness.[16] (For a broader discussion of these and related topics, see D. Kahneman, P. Slovic, and A. Tversky, eds., *Judgment Under Uncertainty: Heuristic and Biases,* Cambridge University Press, New York, 1982.) Although the heuristics are most directly associated with the risk analysis step, they can also influence risk identification (e.g., developing candidate risk issues) and risk handling (developing risk handling strategies) decisions.

As stated by Tversky and Kahneman: "In many situations, people make estimates by starting from an initial value that is adjusted to yield the final answer."[16] This judgmental heuristic is called *adjustments.* Adjustments are typically insufficient—different starting points yield different estimates, which are biased toward the initial values (hence the term *anchoring*).[16]

Consequently, adjustment and anchoring can lead to an underestimation bias of potential minimum and maximum values associated with the likelihood of an event occurring (or the resulting probability distribution).

As stated by Tversky and Kahneman, in some situations, people "assess the frequency of a class or the probability of an event occurring by the ease with which instances or occurrences (of past events) can be brought to mind."[16] This judgmental heuristic is called *availability.* Availability can contribute to an underestimation bias (smaller than the likely probability) if the analyst or manager has little or no knowledge of a potential event. Conversely, if the analyst or manager is familiar with past occurrences of a potential event, then an overestimation bias (higher than the likely probability) can result. (Note: It is also possible that availability can affect estimation of consequence of occurrence.)

As stated by Tversky and Kahneman,

> "Many of the probabilistic questions with which people are concerned belong to one of the following types: What is the probability that object A belongs to class B? What is the probability that event A belongs to process B? What is the probability that process B will generate event A? In such cases, people often rely on representativeness, in which probabilities are evaluated by the degree to which A is representative of B, that is, by the degree to which A resembles B."[16]

This judgmental heuristic is called *representativeness.* Representativeness can affect risk related decisions in several ways, including 1) insensitivity to prior probability of outcomes, 2) insensitivity to sample size, 3) misconceptions of chance, 4) insensitivity to predictability, 5) the illusion of validity, and 6) misconceptions of regression.[16]

In addition to these heuristics, at least three others are common that can adversely impact the risk assessment process.[14] The first of these heuristics is the tendency to fit ambiguous evidence into predispositions. "When faced with ambiguous or uncertain information, people have a tendency to interpret it as confirming their preexisting beliefs; with new data they tend to accept information that confirms their beliefs but to question new information that conflicts with them."[14] The second is the tendency to systematically omit components of risk. "In analyses of complex technological systems, certain features are commonly omitted, possibly because they are absent from operating theories of how the technological systems work. In particular, analysts are prone to overlook the ways human errors or deliberate human interventions can affect technological systems."[14] The third is overconfidence in the reliability of analyses. Except in special cases (e.g., weather forecasters), people performing risk analyses generally do not 1) "make numerous forecasts of the same kind,"[14] 2) have "extensive statistical data available on the average probability of the events they are estimating,"[14] and 3) receive accurate feedback that provides a "quick and unambiguous knowledge of results"[14] (e.g., would require completion of development). Because of these and other considerations, the likely result is overconfidence among experts performing risk analyses.[14]

Biased assessments of probability (and in some cases consequence of occurrence) can occur when people rely on a limited number of heuristic principles that reduce complex tasks of assessing probabilities and predicting values to simpler judgmental operations. Although common heuristics are most directly associated with the risk analysis step, they can also influence risk identification (e.g., developing candidate risk issues) and risk handling (developing risk handling strategies) decisions. Key personnel involved with implementing and administering risk management should be aware of these heuristics and develop safeguards to prevent them from adversely influencing results.

Heuristics are generally not applicable to risk, but to the underlying probability and consequence of occurrence terms. Heuristics, such as availability and representativeness are more often relevant to the probability term, not the consequence term. While adjustment and anchoring can be applied to both the probability and consequence terms, they are typically most often related to the probability term. Hence, while these heuristics primarily affect the probability term, the resulting impact on risk will vary on a case-by-case basis. For example, it is possible that estimates of both the probability and consequence terms could be affected by adjustment and anchoring, but to a different extent in a given case. Here, there may be no simple a priori way to estimate the resulting impact on risk.

Heuristics are generally not applicable to risk, but to the underlying probability and consequence of occurrence terms.

Be wary of individuals that assert that heuristics do not apply to them or their organizations because they are often blind and subject to the very problem they claim is absent. In one case I was collecting data to enhance a risk analysis methodology for an organization. Anchoring was a potential issue because the risk manager forced the data collection form to be structured in a certain way. The more I explained anchoring and how it applied in this case, the more people resisted. More than one person said they were not affected by anchoring—even after I brought in copies of a highly regarded article from the relevant literature. The risk manager refused to accept that anchoring existed in this case, and would not permit the data collection to be refocused to eliminate the anchoring that could lead to biased results (even though the alternate approach had already been developed and could have been implemented immediately). Finally, the risk manager stormed out of his office saying, "Your anchoring is biased." This is not only an oxymoron, since anchoring is biased, but both denial and delusion on the part of the risk manager.

Be wary of individuals that assert that heuristics do not apply to them or their organizations because they are often blind, subject to, and entrenched in the very problem they claim is absent.

D. Stakeholders

The government and contractor organizations are not singular in nature or monolithic in opinion. For a defense program a variety of stakeholder organizations will exist, including, but not limited to, the user command, Service hierarchy, Office of the Secretary of Defense, Government Accounting Office, and Congress (and its staff). (A stakeholder is defined by the Project Management Institute as "individuals and organizations that are actively involved in the project, or whose interests may be positively or negatively affected as a result of project execution project completion. They may also exert influence over the project and its the results."[17]) Similarly, for the prime contractor stakeholders can include the division and group management over the program and corporate staff and executives. Each of these organizations, let alone individuals within the organizations, can have different viewpoints on key program issues. Hence, program stakeholders can have a substantial impact on activities and outcomes. In some cases their actions may substantially reduce program risk, whereas in other instances may greatly increase program risk.

A classic example of laudatory stakeholder influence is that of Dr. William Perry, then Under Secretary of Defense for Research and Engineering (USDR&E), who established and chaired the Executive Committee (EXCOM) to provide programmatic and fiscal direction for the first generation

U. S. cruise missile program. "The EXCOM (established in 1977 and disbanded in 1981) was not a voting group; rather its purpose was to review and discuss issues in an attempt to establish a consensus."[18] "In the absence of a consensus, the USDR&E acted as required and reported dissenting opinions to the Secretary of Defense along with recommendations for action. Normal communication channels remained open to the military services to express dissent."[18] Another feature of the EXCOM was that it provided a forum for an expeditious review of problem areas. For example, the "several elements of the cruise missile project were being developed, integrated, and tested on a tight schedule, and in those conditions it was inevitable that funding shortages would appear from time to time. EXCOM members usually resolved such shortages."[18] In addition, through its high-level Office of the Secretary of Defense and service membership, and the use of action item assignments, EXCOM interaction with the Joint Cruise Missile Project Office substantially reduced program cost and schedule risk.[18]

"The EXCOM was officially referred to as an advisory body, but it seems clear that Dr. Perry, EXCOM chairman and USDR&E, acted as the senior authority whenever it became necessary to resolve disputes between the services."[18] This was highly desirable because the inevitable intra- and interservice bureaucratic complexity of a joint project office may make necessary a consolidated reporting mechanism—namely a strong, high-level member of the office of the Secretary of Defense to encourage the services to come together and to adjudicate conflicts.

Unfortunately, the behavior of key stakeholders can sometimes have a significant adverse impact on a program's risk via budget perturbations, changes in scope, schedule variations, etc. Risk management process inputs, analysis procedures, or outputs may be biased by key stakeholders that are external to the program. The likelihood of this occurring increases with a number of factors, including 1) unresolved contractual issues, 2) an uncertain budget, 3) unstable requirements, 4) competing systems (particularly if they are close substitutes), and 5) competing organizational elements for a given mission.

In some instances stakeholders will promote risk management, yet their actions are contrary to its principles. Such behavior can be harmful when the stakeholders have limited accountability coupled with little grasp of the project's technical difficulty or scope. This type of behavior can have a substantial adverse impact, particularly when it occurs on a high-profile program. (Here, stakeholders may behave in a reactionary manner because of political pressure or perceived public perceptions rather than evaluating the program's attributes, such as schedule length, in an objective fashion). In addition, such stakeholder behavior can be extremely trying to the government and prime contractor program managers and is unfortunately not uncommon.

Although stakeholder behavior can sometimes adversely impact a program, having a well-implemented risk management process can often be helpful in assessing the impact of potential program changes before they actually occur. This may assist the program office in developing suitable response strategies (e.g., reallocating resources) to at least somewhat reduce potential impacts.

Finally, stakeholders may view risk issues, assigned risk levels (e.g., medium), risk handling strategies, and risk monitoring results differently than those within the government and/or contractor program office. For example, right or wrong, stakeholders may identify risk issues not considered by the program office, recommend a different risk prioritization, or interpret risk monitoring results differently. It is often prudent to discuss such differences with the stakeholders. However, even if the program office believes that its position is correct, it may have to yield to stakeholders on some issues to prevent a lack of support (or worse) from occurring.

The risk management process should be responsive to stakeholder inputs. Stakeholder influence can run the gamut from extremely helpful to adverse. In some cases changes in stakeholder position may lead to substantial program perturbations. However, the outcome of these perturbations can sometimes be reduced by having an effective risk management process to assess proactively the impact of potential program changes and develop suitable response strategies. Finally, stakeholders may view risk related information differently than those within the program office.

Stakeholder influence can sometimes directly inject itself into the risk management process, not just the outputs of risk management. While this may be beneficial in some cases, it often is not. For example, in one case a key stakeholder changed a 5 × 5 risk mapping matrix to a 3 × 3 matrix in order to "keep it simple." While this may be an admirable attempt at assisting in the development of the risk analysis methodology, the rationale provided for using the 3 × 3 matrix is not convincing and potentially harmful to effectively performing risk management. (For example, it may well be acceptable to take five level ordinal "probability" and consequence scales used and map the results to a 3 × 3 matrix, but it is generally not meaningful to use a 3 × 3 mapping matrix if only three-level ordinal "probability" and consequence scales are used, or if "probability" and consequence scores are nothing but guesses.)

Stakeholder influence can sometimes directly inject itself into the risk management process, not just the outputs of risk management. While this may be beneficial in some cases, it often is not.

Stakeholders may, in some cases "push" an inferior risk management process and resist changing the process even when presented with evidence of the inferior nature of the process and when superior risk management processes are available. This will likely be all the more difficult to overcome if the stakeholders had a personal or financial interest in funding development of the inferior process. For example, one large organization provided funding to assist in the development of a risk management process and continually rejected feedback to use a superior risk management process that was available free of charge and in the public domain. This is a classic example of the "not invented here" syndrome. Unfortunately, the inferior risk management process contained so many deficiencies that the impact to the many programs using it were likely substantial.

Stakeholders may, in some cases "push" an inferior risk management process and resist changing the process even when presented with evidence of the inferior nature of the process and when superior risk management processes are available.

E. People-Level Considerations

On moderate- to large-scale programs, the participation of working-level engineers is typically essential for effective risk identification, analysis, and handling. In some programs, these functions are performed by an outside group or an individual without the active participation of appropriate personnel (e.g., the risk issue POC). However, this can lead to evaluations that are missing key information, or include erroneous results, which may lead to problems occurring later in the program. It may also contribute to a lack of ownership by program personnel that may affect how the risk issue is managed.

The participation of working-level engineers is generally essential for effective risk identification, analysis, and handling.

Friction may exist between working-level engineers and management in identifying and analyzing potential risk issues and developing suitable risk handling options and approaches. For example, one group may believe that the risk level for a particular issue is lower than the other. It is particularly important that management not overrule working-level engineers carte blanche, because working-level engineers may have more insight into the nature of the potential risk than management. Conversely, management may have more insight into the potential program-wide impact of a risk issue than working-level personnel.

Expertise from both working-level personnel and management is often needed to obtain an accurate picture of the nature of risk issues and their potential impact on the program.

Adverse risk information (risk assessment, handling, or monitoring) is often suppressed due to disincentives that are present. These disincentives may be overt or subtle, and discourage personnel from reporting adverse risk information. Unless upper management is committed to and receptive toward receiving adverse risk information, this will have a chilling effect on the type and quantity of such information flowing up to their level.

Disincentives should be removed that may limit adverse risk information from being reported and flowing to upper management. When disin-

centives exist, risk issues will likely surface later in the program as problems, with increased cost and/or schedule needed to address them.

Appropriate motivation should be given to program personnel to perform effective risk management. Negative motivation should be eliminated whenever possible, regardless of how it is stated. For example, one program manager who is supportive of risk management used the following approach to "encourage" its use. Continue to encourage program personnel to identify risk issues—no negative repercussions. Provide negative inducements for those that "sit on" risk issues and do not report them. While the latter approach is the opposite of "shoot the messenger," it is still not appropriate motivation to perform effective risk management.

Appropriate motivation should be given to program personnel to perform effective risk management. Negative motivation should be eliminated whenever possible, regardless of how it is stated.

A variety of methods should be considered to reward personnel for identifying potential risk issues. Such methods can run a broad gambit from direct financial reward, positive impact on yearly performance reviews, positive recognition by management, etc. Without such rewards there may be insufficient incentive for personnel to perform risk management, particularly in a hostile program environment.

Motivational ideas to support risk management on a program do not have to involve large sums of money to be effective. In fact, surprisingly inexpensive items can be used to help foster a positive atmosphere toward risk management on a program. For example, the risk manager for a large company recommended to management that outstanding examples of risk management be rewarded by providing the engineer and spouse (or guest) with an all-expense paid dinner at a good, local restaurant. (This idea was suggested by Steve Waddell.[19]) For a cost of less than $100, both the engineer and spouse would be recognized for the quality of the work performed—a small price to pay to encourage engineers to be more aware of risk management (particularly on a multibillion dollar program where this idea was applied).

Suitable incentives should be developed and implemented within the program that reward personnel for identifying potential risk issues. Motivational ideas to support risk management on a program do not have to involve large sums of money to be effective.

While nonintrinsic motivators, such as public recognition and awards, can increase risk management effectiveness, intrinsic motivators are often more potent and should be used whenever possible. For example, in one very fast paced program, an early risk management success occurred associated with identifying a risk issue, properly analyzing it, and developing and implementing a risk handling plan. This not only had a large ROI in terms of the cost (and associated schedule) impact, but more importantly it demonstrated to the entire team that risk management greatly assisted the program. As the program manager astutely said, early risk management successes helped to motivate the entire team to think in terms of risk management and to continue to apply risk management principles to other potential issues (which the team did with success). This type of motivation can not be dictated by memo or assumed to occur on its own—it must be encouraged and nurtured by the program manager and other key personnel else it will not happen.

While nonintrinsic motivators, such as public recognition and awards, can increase risk management effectiveness, intrinsic motivators are often more potent and should be used whenever possible.

A program should consider using risk management "success stories" that it has obtained during the course of the program to build team enthusiasm for risk management. (Here, a "success story" may involve a risk issue that was reduced to an acceptable level that would have had a major adverse impact on the program if not suitably handled.) This will often inspire the team to "try" risk management more often, thus more effectively implementing it on the program. This is somewhat self-growing—the desire to use it continues to grow with the number of "success stories."

Risk management "success stories" obtained during the course of the program can be used to build team enthusiasm for risk management.

Beware of situations where an individual or group exasperates a risk issue, then goes on their own in an attempt to "fix" the risk issue. The net result of such behavior can be very detrimental to the program, both in terms of increasing the level of risk for the specific issue, as well as demoralizing program personnel which can lead to decreasing risk management effectiveness.

Beware of situations where an individual or group exasperates a risk issue, then goes on their own in an attempt to "fix" the risk issue.

Some individuals that claim to see the value of risk management never really adopt it in their project management style despite claims to the contrary. For example, in one case an individual had a propensity for underestimating the amount of time needed to complete a task. This coupled with less than adequate communication skills (including limited written communications) created substantial difficulties on a program because the work this person was responsible for was on the critical path for a key project. The program risk manager was consistently more correct ("realistic") in estimating durations for key tasks (e.g., 80+%) vs the individual in question. Despite the fact that this person claimed to recognize that their most valuable lesson learned was the need for good risk management, the individual continued to exhibit the same poor project management characteristics for an extended period of time, leading to substantial schedule slips. Unfortunately, in some cases you simply cannot "teach an old dog new tricks," and you need to recognize individuals that this applies to quickly, particularly when they hold key project positions, to see if upper management can either improve their education and performance level, or remove them from their position.

Some individuals that claim to see the value of risk management never really adopt it in their project management style despite claims to the contrary.

To the extent possible, it is desirable to maintain continuity in personnel assigned to risk issues across risk management process steps and during the course of the program. Of course, a change in personnel may be unavoidable due to unforeseen factors, but routinely changing personnel during risk analysis, handling, and/or monitoring will contribute to a lack of ownership (e.g., "why should I get involved?"), decrease effectiveness in managing the particular risk and increase the likelihood that important aspects of the risk are not properly dealt with in a timely manner.

To the extent possible, it is desirable to maintain continuity in personnel assigned to risk issues across risk management process steps and during the course of the program.

The loss of one or more key personnel may increase the level of risk for a particular issue; particularly if the individual(s) is making a contribution and then dismissed from the program. While in some cases a one-for-one replacement may be possible on purely objective grounds (e.g., both have equivalent knowledge), the trauma caused by a team member being removed may lower morale and lead to reduced effectiveness in addressing a particular risk issue at least in the near-term.

The loss of one or more key personnel may increase the level of risk for a particular issue; particularly if the individual(s) is making a contribution and then dismissed from the program.

Following major program changes or wholesale personnel turnover, a situation may exist whereby remaining personnel may be wary to hostile of any attempt to change an existing risk management process even if the process needs major enhancement to be effective. Management should recognize that such resistance may exist and respond accordingly. For example, in one case the person assigned to risk management assumed that he would become the risk manager, although he was not slated to do so. His assistance was often "what couldn't be done" rather than "what could be done" and he was closely tied to the previous regime that used a weak risk management process, and one that was not well implemented. In the long run keeping such a person involved may be detrimental to performing effective risk management unless they have a suitable "conversion experience" and become a help rather than a hindrance. Otherwise it is best to remove any risk management responsibilities from such a person.

Following major program changes or wholesale personnel turnover, a situation may exist whereby remaining personnel may be wary to hostile of any attempt to change an existing risk management process even if the process needs major enhancement to be effective.

Personnel with substantial responsibilities for performing risk management, such as the risk manager, should be careful not to take on project management functions and decisions without authorization of relevant project management personnel. Otherwise, risk management may be viewed as interfering with project management functions, which may cause a loss of interest by other project personnel and decrease risk management effectiveness.

Personnel with substantial responsibilities for performing risk management, such as the risk manager, should be careful not to take on project management functions and decisions without authorization of relevant project management personnel.

Key management personnel may sometimes make arbitrary risk management-related decisions that are contrary to risk management inputs. When this routinely occurs it greatly undercuts the value and validity of performing risk management and can lead to the perception that risk management is not seriously practiced on the project. For example, in one case "probability" of occurrence and consequence of occurrence ordinal scales existed but risk results were obtained by a subjective management decision. Clearly this sent a negative "signal" to other program personnel (e.g., the existing risk management process did not have to be followed) and contributed to ineffective risk management. (Here, if the ordinal scales were unsuitable, they should have been improved, not bypassed.)

Key management personnel may sometimes make arbitrary risk management-related decisions that are contrary to risk management inputs. When this routinely occurs it greatly undercuts the value and validity of performing risk management and can lead to the perception that risk management is not seriously practiced on the project.

In some cases working-level engineers may tend to underestimate the level of risk for a given item, whereas managers may overestimate the level of risk. (This behavior has been observed in civilian space programs with leading-edge technologies.) However, on some programs, managers may exert pressure on working level personnel that suppresses risk issues from being identified and/or artificially biases downward risk scores for known risk issues. In the worst case, this may contribute to termination of the program manager or even program cancellation. Potential management-induced problems associated with risk assessment can range from overt to subtle. An example of overt pressure is a statement from management that "this is a low-risk program." (I've heard upper management make statements like this on several programs, only to later realize that this was a big mistake.) An example of subtle pressure is using ordinal "probability" scales to assist in risk identification and having a column on the scale indicating the resulting risk level (e.g., low, medium, or high). (Here the analyst may feel "pressured" to prescribe a lower than actual "probability score," particularly if the slightest hint of management pressure exists. Note also that this is a risk analysis not a risk identification function, and having risk levels assigned to a "probability" scale is not correct since the combination or product of probability and consequence of occurrence yields risk, not either term separately.)

Subtle or overt management pressure can potentially lead to biased risk assessments, including missing risk issues and assigned risk scores that are artificially low. Although this may appear in management's best interest in the short run, in the long run it can have a disastrous effect.

Contributions should be invited from a variety of personnel, if not all program personnel, in at least the risk identification and risk handling steps. This will improve the likelihood that more risk issues will be identified and viable RHPs will result. Both managerial and nonmanagerial personnel, as well as personnel across a broad variety of functional areas (e.g., budget, design, test, etc.) should be encouraged to provide inputs for risk identification and risk handling steps. At a minimum all program personnel should be encouraged to identify potential risk issues. In addition, development of risk handling approaches or workarounds should not necessarily be limited to traditional methods, especially when the program faces nontrivial cost or schedule constraints. (Of course, the risks associated with risk handling or workaround failure must also be considered, and necessary procedures should not be arbitrarily short cut.) For example, failures occurred in two different units of a high-technology spacecraft subsystem. In the first case the manager made arrangements with the local coroner's office, transported the equipment to that location, and performed tests to help pinpoint the failure mechanism. In the second case part of an epoxy joint had to be removed without contaminating other components. The manager made arrangements to hire a local dentist to drill out the epoxy joint. His reasoning was although he and his staff were novices to such a procedure, dentists do precision drilling daily. The manager exhibited what is currently termed out of the box thinking—devising clever approaches that saved budget and time, yet did not compromise performance. Such thinking will have a much greater chance of flourishing when company policies encourage, rather than stifle, worker creativity and participation in the risk management process.

Contributions should be invited from a variety of personnel, if not all program personnel, in at least the risk identification and risk handling. Creative thinking to develop innovative risk handling approaches should be encouraged and rewarded.

F. Need for Independent Evaluation

The lack of risk management skills on a given program may range from personnel assigned to the project to one where inadequate risk management exists throughout a large segment of the organization. In addition, the scope and effectiveness of the risk management process is sometimes overestimated by participants and may be criticized by uninformed nonparticipants. This often occurs because key engineering and management personnel do not to take an objective look at the quality and level of maturity of risk management implemented on their program (e.g., they may have a biased perspective). In some cases key program personnel don't know what they don't know. They may think they are knowledgeable about risk management or even risk management experts, yet their actual level of knowledge may be very low and resulting decisions are often flawed.

An independent evaluation of the risk management process and how it is implemented on the program may provide valuable insights to increase process effectiveness and have a very high benefit/cost ratio. However, when independent evaluations are performed by people without sufficient knowledge and experience, the resulting risk management effectiveness may actually decrease because the evaluation results and recommendations may be erroneous, and the resources spent may be wasted. Hence, it is very important that the independent assessor(s) have considerable risk management knowledge and credible, relevant experience.

Independent methods of evaluating the risk management process are needed to ensure that the process is effective and results are unbiased and accurate. However, this does not typically exist on many programs. One key to getting risk management to succeed on your program is perform a thorough and truly independent evaluation of the risk management process and carefully review and incorporate the recommended changes.

When an outside independent evaluator (or group of evaluators) goes into an organization, it will take time to understand and document the risk management process and how it is implemented, plus additional time to perform risk management activities. The amount of time involved will vary on a case-by-case basis, but it is clear that evaluations involving anything more than an initial diagnosis and set of recommendations to enhance the process and its implementation will take far more than a man week of time—particularly if the evaluator(s) help implement the recommended enhancements and apply it to the program (e.g., facilitate performing a risk assessment). What project management should clearly avoid is when independent evaluators make unsubstantiated promises in terms of what they can deliver over a given period of time then fall woefully short in meeting these promises. Such "foot in the door" tactics are unethical and unfortunately not uncommon, and the result is that key project personnel will be duped into performing the evaluation while it takes a much greater level of resources (funds, personnel, and schedule) to conduct than initially promised. In addition, the degree of cooperation that the evaluator obtains is sometimes related to whether or not they already work for the organization (or higher-level organization) performing the assessment, and the degree to which stakeholders or key management personnel impress on project personnel the need to perform the evaluation, rules of engagement for the evaluation, and the anticipated output. Without such stakeholder or key management personnel support, the ability to perform the evaluation will diminish and the resources needed to perform it will increase (cet. par.).

Be wary of claims that an independent evaluation of a given risk management process can be performed in a short period of time. Such claims usually underestimate the amount of time necessary, and sometimes represent an intentional bias on the part of those desiring to perform the evaluation.

Ideally, a group of people within the program, knowledgeable of potential risk issues and including but not solely limited to the risk manager, should serve as facilitators who assist IPT personnel in performing risk assessments and developing risk handling options and approaches. Without this capability the risk assessment and handling steps may be led by personnel with little or no risk management training or responsibility, which will increase the likelihood of inaccurate and biased results occurring.

The use of facilitators, knowledgeable of potential risk issues and trained in performing risk assessments and developing risk handling options and approaches, can increase the effectiveness of the risk management process.

G. Some Additional Considerations

It is unwise to believe that because industry has a financial bottom line key personnel on a given program will perform risk management in an acceptable or even rational manner. In some cases key personnel, including the program manager, may behave in a manner inconsistent with good risk management principles. This problem is all the more likely to occur when risk management is not strong in the corporate culture.

For example, in one case the prime contractor program manager believed claims made by a subcontractor program manager that the item being developed by the subcontractor would meet all specifications despite the fact that the item had failed more than one key test and its design could not be readily modified to meet one key requirement. In addition, pleas made by technical personnel to the program manager regarding the item's inherent risk fell on deaf ears. The program manager continued to postpone eliminating the troubled item and replacing it with a lower-risk alternate unit. (The longer the decision was postponed, the greater the resulting development cost became because of personnel cost plus software that would have to be rewritten.) The program manager said that he was "banking on a miracle." This level of faith may have some credence when sound theoretical and design considerations are not contrary to the position taken, when the subcontractor is making good progress and providing timely, unbiased information, and when the best inputs from key program personnel and independent assessors agree with you. However, that position borders on being foolish when the contrary situation is present, which existed here.

In this particular case the subcontracted item was eventually dropped, a substantial cost was borne by the prime contractor (which had to proceed with an alternate development), the schedule margin was eroded on the program, legal action was threatened between the prime and subcontractor, and the prime contractor program manager left long before the development phase was completed.

It is unwise to assume that industry managers will behave in a rational manner pertaining to risk management and other key processes simply because they must answer to a financial bottom line.

There may be a tendency to suppress identifying some potential risk issues because they are being worked within the program. This is sometimes a management position—after an issue is identified and action is being taken to solve the problem, then the issue is no longer treated as a risk. However, this faulty logic presupposes that the strategy employed will effectively eliminate or substantially reduce the risk issue to an acceptable level.

Risk reduction should never be presumed or credit taken for it until the risk reduction has been suitably demonstrated and verified against preselected criteria through the risk monitoring step.

There may be a tendency to delete a potential item from consideration of risk or even classes of items (e.g., risk for all hardware components) based on having particular personnel or a certain contractor as part of the program team. Even if the personnel or contractor have developed or produced items of this type before, unless an identical item to the one needed on the current program has been built, the risk issue does not warrant being summarily dismissed. For example, on one high-technology program (life-cycle cost greater than $1 billion) key prime contractor technical personnel attempted to delete a complex hardware subsystem from a risk assessment (stating that it would have very low risk) because a certain contractor was part of its team. This occurred before the prime contractor personnel knew what the specific requirements were for the item, and whether or not the specific item needed by the current program had ever been built. In this case even if the requirements existed, there was no guarantee that the item needed by the current program had ever been built, nor that there would be negligible risk resulting from integrating the item with other parts of the system.

Potential risk issues associated with a single item (e.g., focal plane array) or classes of items (e.g., all hardware components) should never be summarily dismissed unless an identical, proven item can be used on the current program without modification.

Catchy buzz words, phrases, or unsupported and exaggerated claims may be used to sell the risk management process when the terms may be overly broad or may not even apply. For example, stating that an improved process for the risk assessment step yields improved management information may be correct, but not due to the availability of more proactive management tools and the use of insight rather than oversight. (In this case potentially better results may aid the management decision-making process, but proactive management tools and insight vs oversight really do not apply.) The unjustified use of such jargon or unsupported and exaggerated claims can actually impede effective risk management or oversell the results to a level that will likely never be achieved.

Catchy buzz words, phrases, or unsupported and exaggerated claims should not be used to implement or sell the risk management process or else the effectiveness can be impaired or expectations can exist that cannot be met.

The potential accuracy of information generated by the risk management process may be oversold to upper management internal or external to the program. (This overselling may occur intentionally or unintentionally.) This can lead to less accurate and/or more uncertain information being forwarded to key decision makers than what was promised. It can have a wide potential range of adverse impacts on the program and its risk management process (e.g., large opportunity cost, erroneous decisions being made, and subsequent disillusionment or lack of overall trust with risk management).

For example, in one case an engineering specialist temporarily assigned to a program promised key program personnel that he could develop a certain methodology in one week, but had no prior experience developing such a methodology. (A more realistic estimate to develop this methodology with acceptable quality would be two to three months.) Unfortunately, the engineer's unsubstantial claims were accepted. Several weeks later the team had finished its first iteration and found the methodology wanting. The engineer then greatly simplified the approach used to derive the methodology and claimed victory despite the fact that the approach used and the resulting methodology were flawed, and it would likely have taken another two months to correct these problems. The deficiencies were not stated to upper management at that time, yet flawed risk analysis results were generated. In the process the engineer substantially damaged morale toward risk management and alienated program personnel who would eventually be needed to correct the flawed methodology.

Do not oversell the potential accuracy of information generated by the risk management process to key decision makers. Even if the overselling is unintentional, there are generally more issues associated with the underlying methodologies and larger uncertainty in the results than what analysts realize, which can lead to key program personnel making erroneous decisions.

No single person, whether from within or outside the program, should perform the entire risk assessment because 1) diverse viewpoints that are often necessary to properly identify and analyze risks will be absent, 2) a variety of errors may be introduced (both intentional and unintentional), and 3) this reduces the level of support the results will have within the program. In some cases, such as when the available time to perform a risk assessment is short, it may be desirable for two or three knowledgeable program personnel to perform a draft risk assessment. This provides a strawman for others to evaluate without being constrained by the limitations of a single person. However, if this approach is used, it must done in such a manner as to openly invite inputs from other program personnel who may have valid additions, deletions, and corrections to the draft results.

The development of a strawman risk assessment by a small number of program personnel can sometimes prove helpful, but if done, it should always be coupled with a critique from other program personnel with detailed knowledge of specific risk issues, programmatic considerations, WBS items, and key program processes.

It is important to identify instances early on where an individual responsible for key program activities (e.g., IPT lead) is not interested in being part of the risk management process implementation, considers risk management a waste of time, or will actually work to thwart successful implementation. This situation becomes increasingly more important and urgent to resolve as the number of issues and level of their risk increases, coupled with relatively short need dates or other critical milestones. What you do not want to have happen is to find a number of key risk issues under the control of such an individual who will not be helpful in properly implementing risk management, coupled with insufficient time to devise suitable backup options. (For example, this could include an individual who oversees relatively high-risk issues that fall on the program's critical path.)

Identify key program individuals whose behavior is not conducive to effective risk management implementation. Use training and other methods as needed to modify their behavior to one that is proactive toward risk management.

When in a crisis, key program personnel will sometimes accept risk management on a temporary basis to help keep their program alive. (This may occur via external direction from key stakeholders or from within the program.) However, their desire to continue risk management often greatly diminishes when threats to cancel the program have subsided. In such cases risk management is only a device for crisis management not a proactive management tool. Not surprisingly, the program may still be canceled because fundamental, necessary changes, such as implementing a viable risk management process and continuing it for the duration of the program, are typically not made.

If risk management is implemented as a stop-gap measure to keep a program alive, and not earnestly implemented and continued, it will generally be ineffective. In such cases risk management will not substantially help a struggling program.

On multinational programs, language, corporate culture, national cultural, contracting, legal, and other differences may be substantial management risk issues that must be evaluated and handled to avoid difficulties.[20] (On one overseas project that I worked on these issues were a *substantial* management risk and eventually led the principals to terminate the business arrangement. In this case there were language, corporate culture, national cultural, contracting, infrastructure, legal, and other key differences that could not be readily overcome.) Whereas the recognition of such differences can help planning and acceptance of the differences that can boast team spirit, the failure to recognize and properly accommodate these variations and differences can potentially lead to serious problems, if not program termination.

On multinational programs, language, corporate culture, national cultural, and other differences may be substantial management risk issues that should be addressed.

XV. Government/Contractor Risk Management Processes

Incompatible risk management processes may exist between the government and prime contractor (generically, the buyer and seller). This may make it difficult to compare risk analysis results and RHPs generated by the different organizations. Typically, the government and prime contractor risk management processes will have one or more steps missing relative to the other party [e.g., planning, assessment (identification and analysis), handling and monitoring] or be implemented differently so that key risk management functions (activities) cannot be mapped from one organization to the other.

To the extent possible, the government and prime contractor should have compatible risk management processes, including process steps.

A subset of this problem is that different risk analysis methodologies may be used within the government or contractor organizations for somewhat similar activities, thus making comparison of results difficult. For example, the prime contractor may use different risk analysis approaches for hardware items than the government.

To the extent possible, a single risk identification and single risk analysis approach should be used for similar categories of items (e.g., hardware, software, integration, and programmatic) in the government and contractor organizations.

Incompatible risk management processes may also exist between the prime contractor and subcontractors making it difficult to compare risk analysis results generated by the different organizations. Although a single process may be the official one, the fact that other risk management processes exist and are sometimes used is potentially problematic because it can lead to confusion as to what process steps exist, which methodology should be used, or what actions should be taken, etc. This is particularly troublesome when weak risk management processes are being used and when the personnel examining them do not understand enough about risk management to sift the wheat from the chaff. In one case I observed *four different* risk management processes in use at the prime contractor's facility on a single program besides the prime contractor's official risk management process. In addition, these nonapproved processes were being used by people that could not make accurate judgments about the quality of the material and should have been using the program's approved process. The atmosphere that existed on this program can accurately be described as chaos.

A single, agreed-upon risk management process should be used within the government team and the contractor team, and ideally by both teams.

A related cause of concern is that a subcontractor's risk management process may be inadequate, and the prime contractor, and likely the government, may have little or no insight into the process. This is particularly critical when key product components or key parts of the project are developed and produced by subcontractors.

In one such case a highly complex radio was under development. A subcontractor was in charge of developing the most complex board in the radio (complex based upon technology and engineering considerations). The subcontractor did not appear to have an effective, formalized risk management process, and the prime contractor and subcontractor were unable to suitably deal with the inherent risk and underlying development issues. In addition, the government had limited visibility and insight into the potential problems until after they surfaced because the risk issue was at the subcontractor level. This contributed to a schedule slip on the subcontractor's board, as well as the entire radio. In such cases the prime contractor should consider flowing down risk management requirements to its subcontractors so that compatible risk analysis methodologies exist and other key risk management information is collected and can be exchanged.

The prime contractor should be required to monitor actively the risk management activities of subcontractors. However, it should be rewarded (if contractually possible) by the government for having current insight into the subcontractors' risk management processes and assisting the subcontractors to the extent possible, practical, and contractually feasible in managing its risks (particularly in the areas of risk identification, risk analysis scoring, development of RHPs, and reviewing risk monitoring results).

XVI. Some Contractual Considerations

A. Risk Management in the Request for Proposal and Source-Selection

Both government and industry may use an RFP, or similar device to elicit proposals from prospective sellers of goods and services. These RFPs may include instructions for risk management, either as stand-alone text, or as part of a larger section (e.g., program management). It is unfortunately common that the text used to describe the desired and/or required risk management process and its implementation is vague or inadequate. In some cases I have observed statements pertaining to risk management that were clearly written and/or reviewed by individuals without sufficient knowledge on the subject. For example, in one RFP for a program with a life-cycle cost greater than $1 billion, a sentence was so scrambled that I developed eight feasible interpretations for the proposal manager. Although some interpretations were more likely what the buyer wanted than others, I could not rule out any of the eight! Clearly, in this case, no one screened the final text that was knowledgeable about risk management. (This text also contained numerous errors beyond the problems in this single sentence.) Unfortunately almost every RFP I have ever reviewed has contained flawed text pertaining to risk management. Thus, a more effective screening process is needed, particularly from the perspective that if the text is put on contract, can both the buyer and seller live with it?

No single set of text will be universally acceptable for inclusion into an RFP for risk management (or practically any other subject). Candidate text for Proposal Preparation Instructions, Evaluation Criteria, and Standards is given in Appendix G. This text is provided as a starting point for including risk management in an RFP or similar request by the buyer and evaluating proposal responses in a subsequent source selection. (Note: This text should be tailored to both the program and the program phase.)

Including a well-reasoned statement for risk management in the RFP is potentially beneficial because risk management may not be otherwise performed or an ineffective risk management process may exist. As demonstrated in Appendix G, information included in an RFP does not have to be voluminous to probe the seller's (e.g., prime contractor's) level of risk management knowledge and implementation experience. However, simply having a brief description about risk management in the RFP or subsequent Statement of Work (SOW) will not guarantee the buyer (e.g., government or prime contractor) an effective risk management process and implementation. (For example, on one high-risk program the SOW included only a single sentence about risk management, "Develop a comprehensive, proactive RMP." Although brevity of this statement is noteworthy, there is not enough substance to be beneficial to either the buyer or seller.)

In addition, unless there is a contractual requirement to generate specific risk management deliverables and a viable means to evaluate and reward seller progress (e.g., via award fee), the resulting post-award risk management process will tend to be weak or ineffective. (As one former government program manager and contracting official stated, "If it ain't on contract, it ain't worth XXX.")

However, just because risk management is required in the proposal, evaluated in source selection, and put on contract, there is no guarantee that it will be successfully implemented after the program phase is initiated. For example, many proposal writers are not involved with the project after the next program phase begins.

The buyer should not expect any better risk management process to be put on contract than that it asks for in the RFP and evaluates in seller proposals. Improvements to the seller's risk management process may occur after contract award. However, it is often far better to initiate a program phase having the seller understand what risk management requirements will likely be needed to successfully complete that part of the program. In addition, it may be desirable to have a contractual mechanism available to reward the seller for having an effective risk management process as it relates to the products being developed or produced.

Once selected for the next program phase, the offeror (e.g., contractor) may be reluctant to enhance the risk management process given in the proposal. This reluctance may exist despite considerable shortcomings and errors associated with the proposal risk management process and sound recommendations made to the offeror to correct these deficiencies following the offeror's selection. (As one contractor mid-level manager said: "If our proposal was good enough to win, why should we change anything?")

The best time to enhance the risk management process is at the beginning of a program phase, not later in the phase when unanticipated problems may appear that have substantial cost and/or schedule impact to resolve (cet. par.).

The comment is sometimes made pertaining to risk management, "how will it help me win the next program phase," or "how will it help me capture more market share in the future?" Many organizations without a history of effective risk management (or in some cases even project management) tend to focus on immediate issues vs those with a longer time horizon. However, even if time frame was not an issue, a potential problem for the seller in a development project is whether or not they want the buyer (customer) to potentially adjust the seller outputs if the buyer is unhappy with the seller (e.g., they do not believe or understand the seller methodology, or the seller methodology is sloppy). The consequences of the buyer adjusting the seller's results in such cases may be very painful in the long-run (e.g., may not accurately represent the seller's situation). Consequently, it is incumbent on the seller to understand the buyer's need for risk management, along with the buyer's cost, performance, schedule, and risk objectives where possible, and to accurately and carefully communicate this information to the buyer, to prevent misinterpretation by the buyer and any subsequent arbitrary adjustment that may occur.

It is incumbent on the seller to understand the buyer's need for risk management, along with the buyer's cost, performance, schedule, and risk objectives where possible, and to accurately and carefully communicate this information to the buyer.

B. Risk Management and Contract Type

It should come as no surprise that the sharing of and responsibility for risk experienced on a program is related to the contract type between the government and prime contractor (or prime contractor and subcontractor). Generally, cost-type contracts (e.g., cost plus fixed fee) place more risk on the government (buyer) than the prime contractor (seller), whereas the reverse is true for fixed-price-type contracts (e.g., firm fixed price). (Of course, there are gradations between these two extremes depending upon which specific type of contract is used, e.g., cost plus fixed fee, cost plus award fee, or cost plus incentive fee). The preceding guidance is applicable to many, but certainly not all programs, *and it is foolish to apply it blindly.*

For example, if the prime contractor performs poorly on a cost-type contract, this may jeopardize its position for future procurements, whether for the same item (e.g., a production competition) or similar items (follow-on phase to a competitive development program). Similarly, the government is not absolved of risk when it uses a fixed-price-type contract. If the contractor performs poorly, the government may not receive the promised item on time, or it may not meet necessary performance specifications. When there are no close substitutes, the government may be stuck without any desirable, if not viable, options.

Consequently, regardless of the contract type used both the government (buyer) and prime contractor (seller) should generally have an effective risk management process implemented and used continuously. What will tend to change among contract types is the level of responsibility of one party vs another, reporting requirements, etc. However, in almost no case should this discharge one party from performing risk management. (There are low-tech examples, such as the repeated procurement of production lots of ammunition from the same company, where risk management is effectively replaced by quality control. The absence of risk management should be the exception, not the rule.) In general, the level and sophistication of risk management needed for a program have little to do with the contract type in place and more to do with the program's 1) budget, 2) performance requirements, 3) schedule, 4) type of program (e.g., high-tech development vs low-tech production), 5) phase of the program, and 6) experience of the government and contractor personnel, and other considerations.

What I have observed is that the government may be complacent about the prime contractor's risk management process when a fixed-price contract exists. (The same can be true between a prime contractor and subcontractor when the subcontractor is under a fixed-price contract.) As just mentioned, conventional wisdom says the contractor bears the risk when a fixed-price contract exists, whereas the government bears the risk when a cost-plus contract is in place. However, this type of thinking is overly simplistic and can lead to substantial problems.

In the worst case, for a fixed-price contract, the government may not obtain the item it contracted for—either it may not be delivered on time or it may not meet performance requirements. The contractor may even default, and lose substantial funding. However, the government can be stuck in this situation, not having units that meet its delivery schedule or requirements.

I will now provide a more detailed example of risk management on a development program that used a fixed-price contract to show some of the pitfalls of one-dimensional thinking about responsibility for risk.

On one high-tech development program the government program manager continued to think that because the prime contractor was under a fixed-price contract the government did not have to be especially concerned about schedule or performance issues, nor active in risk management. However, he did not fully consider the harm to the government that the potential inability to meet a key operational performance parameter would have. (The contractor design would likely fall short of meeting this performance parameter by more than a factor of 10, and the operational impact would have truly been substantial.) When the contractor realized that it could not meet the performance parameter, it requested a waiver from the government, which the government rightly denied. The prime contractor finally instituted a redesign that permitted meeting the performance parameter— something that cost the contractor several million dollars and substantially reduced schedule margin.

This was a particularly interesting case from a risk perspective because the item that caused the design to fall short of meeting the performance requirement had been scored at the *lowest risk level possible*. This was, of course, erroneous, and something that should have been recognized perhaps a year earlier by the prime contractor. In effect, based upon subcontractor claims, the prime contractor *assumed* the item (which was under development) would pass all performance tests, and thus meet all requirements. However, the key error from a risk analysis perspective was that credit was given in terms of meeting performance requirements before the tests for these requirements were performed. After the tests were performed, the prime contractor realized that the item would not meet at least one key requirement, and it could not be easily redesigned to do so. (Thus, an alternate design was necessary that required a major development.) Hence, the lowest risk item in the program became the program's single highest-risk issue overnight.

In reality, a much smaller change in the risk level should have occurred if the risk analysis had been properly conducted in the first place because the "probability" of occurrence score should have remained the same (no change in the state of the item), whereas the cost and schedule consequence of occurrence scores should have increased with time (reflecting the increasing opportunity cost associated with delayed implementation of the design change). (The performance consequence of occurrence score should have remained constant.) In effect, the item should never have been rated lower than a medium risk, and thus warranted far more management attention than occurred until it failed key performance tests. (I pointed out several errors in risk analysis and risk handling associated with this item about 10 months before the prime contractor finally took decisive action to correct these problems. However, neither my comments nor those of technical specialists within the program were able to sway upper management's contention that everything would be fine.)

It is also important for the government to realize that a somewhat similar situation is possible when a fixed-price-type contract exists—the potential cost impact it faces may not be zero. At first glance the cost impact to the government appears to be zero when a firm fixed-price contract type is used, thus corresponding to minimal cost risk. However, if scope changes occur, then the cost impact to the government will likely be greater than zero, and the cost risk may not be minimal (or at the lowest ordinal scale level). Because the source of most development and production program cost growth is generally from contract growth (scope changes) rather than overruns (from a 1993 unpublished manuscript by the author), then a nonzero level of cost risk will likely exist even when fixed-price-type contracts are used. This also points to the need that on most programs both the government and prime contractor have an effective risk management process implemented and used continuously.

The sharing of and responsibility for risk experienced on a program is related to the contract type between the government and prime contractor (or prime contractor and subcontractor). Generally, the government (buyer) is more at risk for cost-type contracts, and the prime contractor (seller) is more at risk for fixed-price-type contracts. However, this does not absolve the other party from having an effective risk management process because neither party will ordinarily face zero risk on most programs. Both the government and prime contractor should generally have an effective risk management process implemented and used continuously. Failure to do this can lead to substantial adverse impacts, regardless of the contract type used.

XVII.   Some Additional Considerations

A.   User Involvement

The lack of user involvement may lead to inefficiency in identifying, analyzing, and prioritizing risk issues and risk handling options. Ideally, user involvement should be synchronized with other government and contractor personnel in the design and systems engineering processes to reduce the number and magnitude of design and requirements changes. User involvement is critical during the early to mid-development stages, especially when potentially unaffordable and/or high risk requirements are being evaluated.

To the extent possible, the government program office and contractor team should routinely interact with the user community to better understand and evaluate program requirements. If the program has a user representative, consider inviting him to be a member of the RMB.

B. Use of Commercial Off-the-Shelf Items

COTS items are increasingly being evaluated in the design trade process and incorporated in military and space systems because they *may* lead to lower program cost and schedule and reduce risk. [For example, COTS Integrated Circuits (IC) may cost one or more orders of magnitude less than a similar radiation hardened part.] However, to assume this always true, rather than on a case-by-case basis, is unwise. I will now briefly list some potential issues associated with COTS software and provide a specific example for COTS hardware.

Some potential COTS risk issues for software intensive projects include, but are not limited to 1) business risks of dealing with vendor companies, 2) inconsistencies in interfaces (human and technical), 3) incompatibilities among different packages, 4) phasing of upgrades among multiple packages on different release schedules, 5) obscure features of the packages, 6) features present in one release and deleted in a subsequent release (e.g., not backwards compatible), 7) failure to adapt the development process to the characteristics of COTS-based development, 8) dependencies on particular vendors, and 9) insufficient package and/or operating system lifetime vs the project life cycle.[21] (Some of the items listed were provided by this author.)

An example of potential hardware problems is the use of COTS ICs in space systems. The reliability of COTS ICs has generally increased over the last 10 to 15 years, thus making them more desirable for space applications. However, increased reliability may be uncorrelated with radiation hardness, which may also be necessary for space applications. This is particularly important for certain types of radiation-induced problems—one example is a single event upset.

"Single event upsets (SEU), or soft errors, are mainly logic upset errors that almost always occur in high-density ICs."[22] Whereas some types of radiation can be shielded (e.g., solar wind protons), others cannot (e.g., the heavy ion component of galactic cosmic rays). Thus, SEU hardening must primarily be done at the circuit and systems level.[22] Hardening at the circuit level requires inherently hardened parts—something that cannot be accomplished after the fact with soft parts. In some cases the redesign of soft parts to increase radiation hardness may be difficult, if not impossible. (In one instance this led to substantial cost and schedule impact at the program level.)

Even when COTS electronic components from one lot successfully pass radiation survivability tests, there is no guarantee that parts from another lot will pass the same test. This is because slight manufacturing process variations can lead to noticeable changes in the radiation hardness levels of some electronic components. The manufacturing parameters that affect radiation hardness may not be well controlled for commercial parts, whereas they are tightly controlled for parts designed to have high radiation hardness. (In addition, the design and layout of a part with high inherent radiation hardness will typically be different than the otherwise identical commercial part.) Because the malfunction of a critical part can lead to mission failure, it is highly desirable to measure the hardness level of electronic components and use this information together with shielding options in the design process. Failure to do so can increase risk and lead to substantial, if not enormous, cost and schedule impact later in the program.

Finally, COTS items, even simple commercial items, can have a relatively high risk if they aren't available in time (schedule), have poor quality (performance), ship with reduced features/functions (performance), regardless of their cost. For example, in one case it took six months to get processor chips mounted on a commercial board with secondary (L2) cached memory. A comedy of errors resulted—multiple iterations had boards that were "dead on arrival," the wrong version of the processor chip used (so that it was incompatible with other system hardware), etc. The simple bottom line: don't discount potential risk issues associated with COTS items!

COTS items are increasingly being evaluated in the design trade process and incorporated in military and space systems because they may lead to lower program cost and schedule and reduce risk. However, to assume this is generally true, rather than on a case-by-case basis, is unwise. Prior to using a COTS approach, a suitable analysis should be conducted to ensure that the item will meet necessary performance requirements (e.g., availability, operational environment, and reliability) and Operations and Support requirements to avoid unanticipated problems later in the program. Don't discount potential risk issues associated with COTS items.

C.   Work Breakdown Structure

Risk management is sometimes not implemented with an available and accurate low-level WBS (e.g., Levels 4–6), and in the worst case no WBS is used. Often the result is that potential risk issues are not identified or analyzed until later in the program until they have become problems and their cost and/or schedule impacts may be substantial. The WBS level at which a risk assessment is performed will vary with the design selected and potential risk categories that exist.

The program risk assessment is sometimes performed at a very low WBS level (e.g., Level 6 or lower). A very low-level risk assessment may be expensive and time consuming to conduct. It can also generate a large amount of information that may require excessive resources to evaluate, develop RHPs, and conduct risk monitoring. In this case the RMB should evaluate candidate risk issues and consider eliminating some that are likely low risk, particularly when they are being satisfactorily addressed. (This will often help reduce the candidate risk issues to a manageable number.) Conversely, if the risk assessment is implemented at a very high WBS level (e.g., Level 3), then potential risk issues will likely be undetected until later in the program when they become problems and adversely impact the program. Risk assessments should typically be performed at WBS levels five and lower (e.g., the box level) and go down to even lower levels as warranted (e.g., for medium- or higher-risk issues a CPU chip or a focal plane array detector chip). RHPs should be developed for medium- or higher-risk issues, and risk monitoring should occur at the WBS level of the risk issue to help ensure that a focused effort will exist to reduce the risk to an acceptable level. However, for some possible risk categories, such as mission operations (one aspect of requirements risk) and threat, the resulting risk assessment will likely be at a much higher WBS level (e.g., Levels 1 or 2). Consequently, the WBS level that the risk assessment is performed at will vary with the potential risk categories as well as the risk issues that exist for a program.

When ordinal "probability" of occurrence scales are used in risk analysis, it may be unclear at what WBS level they should be applied. Using ordinal "probability" scales at the wrong WBS level can clearly lead to erroneous results. Risk categories including, but not limited to, mission operations and threat are generally best handled at higher WBS levels [e.g., program (Level 1) or segment (Level 2, if a segment level exists)]. At lower WBS levels it is better to adjust the design to meet potential requirements and threat changes, rather than attempting to evaluate each WBS element specifically against these risk categories. This will reduce the chance that an erroneous risk assessment will be performed. (Of course, different candidate designs can be developed that reflect different requirements and threats; therefore, the potential impact of requirements and threat are evaluated at lower WBS levels by more appropriate risk categories, e.g., design/engineering.) Risk categories such as cost, design/engineering, manufacturing, schedule, and technology should be evaluated at an appropriate WBS level where risk issues exist without substantial aggregation (e.g., Level 5 or lower). For other risk categories, such as logistics/support, it may be necessary to evaluate different aspects of the risk category at different WBS levels. For example, this may range from a relatively high WBS level (e.g., WBS 2 or 3) for some items (e.g., how a support concept impacts field maintenance of a system, such as a missile procured as a wooden round) to a lower level (e.g., WBS 5 or lower) for other items (e.g., software upgrades for a particular processor box).

A suitable WBS is required to perform an accurate risk assessment. An WBS down to Level 5 (box level) is typically needed for many risk assessments. However, it may be necessary to evaluate certain items at WBS Level 6. When ordinal "probability" scales are used, they should be applied at an appropriate WBS level to measure this term of risk accurately.

D. Risk Management Information Collection

A variety of techniques can be used to collect information, which is particularly helpful in performing risk assessments (identification and analysis) and developing risk handling options and approaches. These include, but are not limited to 1) diagrammatic methods, e.g., Fishbone (cause and effect) diagrams; 2) direct methods, e.g., one on one expert interviews; 3) betting, 4) Modified Churchman/Ackoff Technique; and 5) Delphi Approach.[23] Whatever approach is used, it should be implemented in a nonthreatening manner for respondents, so that individuals will clearly state their position without intimidation or fear of reprisal. This will provide a greater chance that different positions are reported that are generally helpful for risk assessment and developing risk handling options and approaches. When information is collected in a group environment, facilitators should guard against a variety of potential problems occurring, such as 1) a single person dominating the discussion (particularly when that person is not knowledgeable about the risk issue being examined), 2) group think, and 3) grooved thinking, which can adversely impact the development and fair consideration of ideas for risk identification, analysis, and handling. Unless this is done, potential risk issues may not be identified, the level of analyzed risk may be incorrect, and the resulting risk handling option and specific implementation approach selected may not be the best possible one.

Various techniques can be used to collect information for risk assessments and to develop risk handling options and approaches. However, a key to collecting accurate risk information is to collect data in a nonthreatening manner. When risk information is collected in a group environment, special precautions are needed to ensure that potential risk issues are identified, the level of analyzed risk is correct, and the resulting risk handling option and specific implementation approach selected are the best possible ones.

E. Subjective Criteria

Subjective criteria are the predominant means of evaluation used in some risk management processes. This can lead to flawed results in risk assessment (both identification and analysis) and risk handling and risk monitoring steps that can have a substantial adverse impact on the program. For example, risks may not be identified, analyzed, or prioritized in a consistent manner, the resulting assigned risk levels may be incorrect, RHPs may not be developed for all necessary issues (e.g., medium or higher risks), the best risk handling option may not be selected, and uncertain risk monitoring information may exist. This can lead to inaccurate decisions made by key program personnel. Some risk categories (e.g., programmatic) may require subjective criteria for assessment, but the broad use of this approach should be avoided.

The use of subjective criteria for risk identification, analysis, handling, and monitoring should generally be avoided. On the surface, subjective criteria are appealing—their development cost is minimal, and they are easy to use. However, the results obtained are often nonrepeatable, unsubstantiated, and cannot be easily documented. Some risk categories (e.g., programmatic) may require subjective criteria for assessment, but the broad use of this approach should be avoided.

F. Problems, Risks, and Their Time Frame

A question that sometimes arises is how a program (e.g., its RMB) handles problems vs risks. Here, problems are assumed to already be affecting the program vs risks that have not yet occurred. The potential danger on some programs with risk issues is that they may not receive the proper level of attention through a structured risk management process. If not properly resolved, this may later adversely impact the program as problems. However, even if a problem is actively being worked, it is still generally wise to examine it from a risk management perspective. For example, several questions should be asked relative to how the problem is being or will be resolved, such as

1) Have the appropriate ground rules and assumptions been developed and documented (risk planning)?
2) Is the specific problem cause and likely effect clearly understood (risk identification)?
3) Are the potential likelihood and C,P,S consequence of occurrence confidently known (risk analysis)?
4) Has the best option and approach for resolving the problem been developed, suitable resources applied, and implemented, and do backup strategies exist (risk handling)?
5) Do suitable metrics exist to objectively evaluate the progress being made to resolve the problem (risk monitoring)?

I have found that at least in some cases asking these questions will reveal that one or more important steps or activities is missing that should be added to properly resolve the problem (e.g., a suitable backup strategy may not have been devised). Finally, as when dealing with risk issues, it is unwise to assume a problem will be satisfactorily resolved prior to its actual closure, because as some car bumper stickers say, "stuff happens."

Another potential concern involves risk issues that will not affect the program for some time. In some cases the risk may be analyzed to be medium (or higher), yet can potentially be resolved fairly easily at a later date. An RHP may exist, may be in place, but will not be executed in the foreseeable future. A temptation in this situation may be to assume that the issue is low risk, to close it, or defer doing anything to resolve it for a substantial period of time. This is generally unwise because without satisfactory progress being made it will likely become a problem and adversely impact the program. For example, if a medium-risk issue (e.g., a piece of specialized test equipment) is critical to program success, can probably be built without substantial difficulty, but not needed for a year, the issue should generally be carried as an open risk to ensure that the necessary resources will be programmed and later allocated to acquiring the necessary item. (What sometimes happens if the issue is brushed aside is that resources are allocated to more immediate issues and/or problems, insufficient attention may then be given to the issue with the longer time horizon, and it later surfaces and adversely affects the program.) Although this may increase the number of program risks, it is often far better to include such issues than to exclude them because of the considerable adverse impact that may result later in the program if they are not properly addressed. (If necessary, they can be placed in a separate category to distinguish them from other issues that require resources over a long period of time to resolve.)

A variety of issues will likely surface on many programs, including problems (issues already affecting the program) and risks (issues that have not yet occurred). It may be tempting to deal with problems or risk issues that do not have to be addressed for a relatively long time, outside of the risk management process. Doing so may offer some near-term convenience, but it may also lead to substantial difficulties later in the program if the issues are not properly and thoroughly addressed and/or necessary resources are no longer available.

G.   Accurately Interpreting and Portraying Risk Levels

A balance is needed when using ordinal scales (particularly when maturity-based "probability" scales are used) between routine issues being rated as medium or higher risk because risk handling has not yet started and/or the issue is part of the normal design process and cases where something has not been done before where the experience base of the contractor is limited. On the one hand this can force or lead to the need for risk handling being performed on a large number of issues, which can be excessive. On the other hand, it aids a structured response to potential risk issues. Not performing risk handling will enhance the odds of problems occurring later in the development process (or even during production) where fixes may be much more expensive. One should be wary of statements like "we know how to do that," when a mistaken level of confidence exists. This mentality may contribute to delaying development activities (including risk handling), and the result may be unanticipated surprises or a much more difficult development process than anticipated, which generally leads to increased cost and/ or schedule.

Any issue analyzed to have a medium or higher risk should have an RHP developed. If the underlying issue is a simple matter to resolve, then this should be noted in the plan, along with the start date of the activity (assuming the control option or transfer option is selected) and funding and other resources required. If the issue is a routine one (e.g., buying another piece of commercially available test equipment) and the start date is some time away, then the issue can potentially be transferred to a watch list or equivalent. (A simplified RHP may also be sufficient for routine issues.) However, for issues that are not routine specific action should be taken, particularly if the needed start date is close and the required level of technical sophistication or integration is nontrivial. Attempting to subjectively discount risk issues solely based on experience will increase the odds of problems occurring later in the program when the potential cost and/or schedule impact can be large.

Representations and projections of risk (probability and consequence) vs time are often imprecise, if not subjective, in nature. Often a flawed risk analysis approach is used to project risk levels vs time for risk handling planning purposes. Although this may provide the appearance of having an accurate assessment of both risk and risk reduction vs time, it often includes both an unknown error from the risk analysis methodology (e.g., mathematics performed on uncalibrated ordinal scales—see Chapter 6) and an unknown uncertainty associated with the risk issue itself because it is typically estimated as a point value. These errors and uncertainty can greatly diminish the value of the information portrayed and provide a false level of confidence in the results. In addition, risk projections are sometimes not tied to a particular risk analysis methodology (they may just be subjective guesses) and/or to a detailed analysis of planned risk handling steps and the anticipated product maturity, testing, and outcome of these tests.

In general, avoid portraying numerical representations of risk vs time for risk analysis, handling, or monitoring purposes if the data are subjective because people often ascribe a higher degree of accuracy and a lower degree of uncertainty to the results than actually exist. This includes cases where the data are derived from subjective assessments and uncalibrated ordinal risk scales. When calibrated ordinal risk scales are used, the data can be portrayed, but recognize that uncertainty levels are generally unknown. A safer approach is to define bands on the ordinate as low, medium, and high and portray risk reductions against specific actions/ milestones vs time.

H.   Technical Performance Measurement

Technical performance measurement (TPM) is a technique that compares estimated values of essential technical performance parameters with achieved values and determines the impact of any differences on the system effectiveness. An example of a TPM is software source lines of code (SLOC), measured during the development cycle (thus vs time). (This TPM is also an example of a software risk metric.) Earned value is an analogous metric to TPMs for cost and includes measures for cost variance (budgeted cost of work performed minus the actual cost of work performed) and schedule variance (budgeted cost of work performed minus the budgeted cost of work scheduled). Similarly, estimates derived from actual vs planned schedule progress measured on the program's IMS can be used for schedule (e.g., change in delivery date and change in slack).

TPMs should be identified and measured at the same WBS level where potential or actual risk issues exist—measurements made at too high or too low a level may not adequately point to the source of potential technical problems, and TPMs should be carefully selected for the item in question so that they represent essential performance parameters, not unimportant or irrelevant ones. TPMs are relevant to risk identification, handling, and monitoring. For risk identification, TPMs can be used to assess the technical characteristics of the system and to identify and flag design deficiencies impacting the ability of the system to satisfy a performance requirement. Often, the performance level anticipated or achieved is compared with performance values allocated or specified in contractual documents. Measured values that fall outside an established tolerance band (or worse than a predetermined trigger level) should be treated as pointing to a candidate risk issue that requires review and potential corrective action by management. After a candidate risk issue has been approved by the program's RMB (or equivalent), it enters the program's risk management process for evaluation purposes (e.g., risk analysis, then if deemed necessary, risk handling and risk monitoring). For those risks judged by the RMB to require risk handling (e.g., medium or higher risks), one or more relevant TPMs should be identified and included in the draft RHP, approved by the RMB and implemented. TPMs can be useful in risk monitoring by comparing planned and achieved values of parameters in areas of known risk. The regular monitoring of TPMs can provide early and continuing predictions of the effectiveness of risk handling actions and/or the detection of new risks before substantial cost and schedule impacts occur. Risk monitoring TPM values that fall outside the tolerance band or that are worse than a predetermined trigger level should be quickly investigated, and appropriate corrective action taken. [In some cases this may necessitate fine tuning the risk handling strategy or even updating the strategy (e.g., selecting the backup strategy) and RHP as needed.]

TPMs, however, have absolutely no inherent risk analysis capability; they are merely indicators of risk even if trigger levels are attached to them by the analyst. Attempts have been made to relate TPM results to risk levels by several techniques. Such approaches are generally highly subjective, contain unknown uncertainty, and should be avoided unless they can be tied to relevant historical data from analogous 1) items (e.g., the identical subsystem), 2) TPMs (preferably the same TPM), and 3) risk analysis results (e.g., growth in SLOC by 50% corresponded to a medium risk). Similarly, attempting to assign probability distributions to TPMs, performing a Monte Carlo simulation, and using the simulation results for risk analysis purposes will also yield highly subjective and uncertain results and should be avoided without substantial carefully screened analogous data for comparison purposes.

TPMs are a valuable tool for risk identification, handling, and monitoring. However, TPMs should not be used for risk analysis purposes unless relevant carefully screened analogous historical data exists because the results will often be subjective and contain unknown uncertainty.

I. Risk Management Tools and Techniques

Risk management tools that used by one organization may not be a good "fit" or even applicable for another organization. In once case the risk management tool used by a program was supplied by another organization and was "broken." This required the risk manager to spend a considerable amount of time to manipulate the risk tool so that it would generate correct results and took precious time away from performing more critical risk management activities on the program. Realistically estimate resources for any risk management tool prior to accepting it, and understand the limitations of each risk tool before you use it on your program.

Risk management tools used by one organization may not be a good "fit" or even applicable for another organization.

A risk management tool should never impose a risk management process on a program. For example, in one case the process had to be adapted to fit the risk tool, rather than the program having the flexibility and capability to adapt the risk tool to the existing risk management process. In addition, a risk tool based upon a sub-standard risk management process may actually promote ineffective, rather than effective, risk management because errors and sloppiness propagated in the tool will often be carried over into day-to-day risk management by program personnel.

A risk management tool should never impose a risk management process on a program.

Define the risk management process before selecting specific tools for each process step. It is OK to discuss general tools and techniques that might be applicable, but selection of specific tools and techniques should follow the definition of the process and how each process step will be implemented. For example, if a specific tool is selected to perform a Monte Carlo schedule risk analysis, yet there is no contractual requirement to perform such a simulation, there is insufficient time to implement the simulation, and it unclear whether or not upper management would even desire such a simulation (e.g., it may not be practical given potential resource constraints), it is premature to specify the tool in this case.[24]

Define the risk management process before selecting specific tools and techniques for each process step.

Risk tools are simply part of the risk management process' tools and techniques that apply to each process step. They are not another risk management process step in and of themselves. Such a view is "tool centric" and as stated by one astute risk management practitioner, often results in the risk management process suffering for the sake of promoting and promulgating one or more risk tools.

Risk tools are simply part of the risk management process' tools and techniques that apply to each process step. They are not another risk management process step in and of themselves.

In some cases the tools and techniques actually used on a project may vary considerably from those documented in the RMP and elsewhere. This type of disconnect is very unwise and should be dealt with immediately because it can decrease risk management effectiveness and contribute to a host of problems on the program. For example, in one case the program manager used a methodology for risk analysis that was very different from that contained in the RMP and the monthly risk reports. Surprisingly, he was apparently unaware that any other risk analysis methodology existed on the program. (This was disturbing since he was the ultimate signatory on the RMP.)

In some cases the tools and techniques actually used on a project may vary considerably from those documented in the RMP and elsewhere. This type of disconnect is very unwise and should be dealt with immediately because it can decrease risk management effectiveness and contribute to a host of problems on the program.

Risk management tools should strike a balance between sophisticated/not easy to use and simple/easy to use. Do not assume that a simple tool is easy to use, as there may be substantial limitations or traps associated with such tools, and tool simplicity should not be the key criteria for tool selection. Of course, a complex tool can also have a number of limitations, and may not be easy to use. The important thing here is to conduct a thorough, unbiased evaluation of candidate tools recognizing their strengths and weaknesses.

Risk management tools should strike a balance between sophisticated/ not easy to use and simple/easy to use.

The sophistication of a risk tool should be tailored and appropriate to the program, particularly given cost, schedule, and other resource constraints that the program has. A risk tool may be as simple as word processing and spread sheet templates on a small and/or very short duration program, and something as sophisticated as an intranet-based tool for a larger and longer-duration program.

The sophistication of a risk tool should be tailored and appropriate to the program, particularly given cost, schedule, and other resource constraints that the program has.

The technical characteristics of a risk tool (e.g., the nature of an ordinal "probability" scale) should be based upon correct risk management principles. A risk tool should also be compatible with an organization's best practices to the extent possible. However, if an organization's existing best practices are flawed, that is no reason in and of itself to develop a flawed risk management tool. Note though that the effective use of a candidate risk tool may often depend upon organizational culture as well as training. For example, if checklists are infrequently used for risk identification, then introducing one, even a checklist that is very accurate for a particular risk category, may require additional training and trial use with feedback to relevant personnel before it is adopted across the program. If this is not performed then the tool may not be properly used by program personnel, or a bias may exist that suppresses its use on the program.

The technical characteristics of a risk tool should be based upon correct risk management principles. However, the degree to which a tool is effectively implemented will depend upon organizational culture as well as training.

Several risk analysis tools exist that include risk management databases which may be used on a variety of programs. One such risk analysis tool is Risk Radar™ (Version 3.2, December 2002 at the time of this writing). (While I generally do not discuss specific risk tools, Risk Radar™ is sometimes flowed-down to contractors by the government and thus warrants evaluation and comment.) Here, the user is requested to provide a probability of occurrence value for a given risk issue from 10% (remote) to 90% (nearly certain).[25] [Note: The probability statements (remote, unlikely, likely, highly likely, and near certainty) and corresponding scale levels (a, b, c, d, and e) are identical to those given in Table 2-2 of Ref. 11. The only change was to add percentiles associated with probability statements. The pedigree of these percentiles is unknown and likely not derived from a statistical analysis of survey results (as was performed for Appendix J of this book).] There are no guidelines provided to assist the user in estimating the probability value. (See Appendix J, Sec. I for a discussion of why a subjective, particularly unstructured, probability assessment *should be last choice, not the first choice*, for performing a risk assessment.) The user is also requested to provide a consequence of occurrence value for a given risk issue from 0 to 5, which includes a subjective ranking of 0 = does not apply, plus five additional levels of increasing consequence of occurrence. [25] (Note: The remaining five consequence of occurrence levels are highly similar to those given in Table 2-3 of Ref. 11, and even include the same overlapping cost consequence of occurrence inequality errors contained in Ref. 11. These C,P,S consequence of occurrence scales are only an "example"[11] and as discussed in Appendix I of this book, they should not be used on a specific program.) The resulting product [risk exposure (factor)] is computed and then converted to risk levels by a risk mapping matrix. The risk mapping matrix uses symmetric boundaries between probability and consequence for high risk, but asymmetric boundaries for low and medium risk and no rationale is provided as to why asymmetric boundaries are used. (It does not appear possible for the user to specify a different risk mapping matrix.) Very limited documentation and input capability exist for risk identification and risk handling within Risk Radar™ and the risk handling discussion is particularly weak and contains errors. In summary, while the Risk Radar™ tool contains an easy to use database to document risk issues, it has substantial limitations associated with its 1) risk analysis methodology, 2) very limited documentation and input capability for risk identification and risk handling, and 3) errors in the risk handling discussion. These limitations weaken the effectiveness of this tool and should be corrected.

The Risk Radar™ tool (Version 3.2, December 2002) contains an easy to use database to document risk issues, but has substantial limitations associated with its 1) risk analysis methodology, 2) very limited documentation and input capability for risk identification and risk handling, and 3) errors in the risk handling discussion. These limitations weaken the effectiveness of this tool and should be corrected.

A risk management tool that requires more than one-quarter of the time for the risk manager to use and generate reports is potentially resource intensive. In such cases, a separate person rather than the risk manager should be designated to use and generate charts; else the tool will take away valuable time from the risk manager actually performing risk management on the program.

Additional support should be provided to the risk manager if a resource intensive risk tool is used. Otherwise, the risk manager's effort to perform risk management on the program will be diluted.

No risk tool, even the "best" one is effective itself. How effective the risk tool is in practice depends on how "good" it is coupled with the degree to which it is efficiently and effectively used by the team and assists in performing risk management. In several instances I've observed that a bad (e.g., weak) risk tool adversely impacted the entire program. As philosopher William Carton said: "Man must be the slave of his machine."[26] This is particularly apropos to ineffective and/or inefficient risk tools.

No risk tool, even the "best" one is effective itself. How effective the risk tool is in practice depends on how "good" it is coupled with the degree to which it is efficiently and effectively used by the team and assists in performing risk management.

J. Risk Management Databases

An electronic risk management database should be used when practical that contains key risk planning information (e.g., the RMP), known risk issues (risk identification), as well as risk analyses, risk handling strategies, and risk monitoring results for these issues.

The nonrecurring cost to develop such a database is typically ≤ $0.1 million. Although this may be impractical for a program with a $1.0 million budget, it is potentially a wise investment for multiyear programs with funding on the order of $10 million or more per year because it can improve the efficiency of implementing and maintaining the risk management process.

All program personnel should have access to this database and be encouraged to provide comments—anonymously if necessary. However, configuration control should be maintained and enforced to ensure that any changes do not occur without proper screening, evaluation, and permission.

An electronic risk management database should be used when practical, particularly on multiyear programs with a sufficient budget.

Risk management databases are generally shells that integrate data and may have relational capability but are not tools—they may encompass existing tools and techniques but often they are not a tool or technique, or do not include any new tools and techniques themselves.

Risk management databases are generally shells that integrate data and may have relational capability but are not tools in and of themselves.

Using or being forced to use an existing risk management database may bring a considerable amount of unanticipated and undesirable baggage to a program. In several instances on large programs I've observed a risk management database being used that implied or mandated a risk management process that was considerably different than that already in use on the program. Of greater concern, the risk management process associated with the database was often inferior to that in use on the program. Clearly, the risk management process, along with relevant contractual, programmatic, organizational, and behavioral considerations; should dictate or at least suggest the type of risk management database to be used on a program—the risk management database should never impose a risk management process on a program—particularly where its process is inferior to that already in use.

Existing risk management databases may bring a considerable amount of unanticipated and undesirable baggage to a program. In addition, the risk management database should never impose a risk management process on a program.

On small programs it maybe more cost and schedule effective to use a simple reporting mechanism with forms entered via a word processing program than to "force fit" a risk management database. Existing risk management databases are often unsatisfactory for large programs because of the amount of tailoring that must be done. On programs with a life cycle exceeding one to one and a half years, it may be prudent to develop a risk management database using a standard relational database software package to encompass desired inputs and required documentation outputs than to attempt to revise an existing database.

On small programs it maybe more cost and schedule effective to use a simple reporting mechanism with forms entered via a word processing program than to "force fit" a risk management database.

References

[1]Grant, J., "Few Takers for a Career in Crisis Management," Financial Times, 15 May 2000, p. 17.

[2]Matson, B., interview with Babu Chiri, "National Geographic Explorer," 2001, National Geographic Society, Inc.

[3]Bridwell, J., private communication, 1995.

[4]Habeler, P., private communication, 1992.

[5]Defense Systems Management College, *Risk Management Concepts and Guidance*, Ft. Belvoir, VA, 1989, p. 5-2.

[6]Department of Defense, Department of Defense Instruction 5000.2, Sec. 4.7.3.2.3.4.1, 5 April 2002.

[7]Department of Defense, "Mandatory Procedures for Major Defense Acquisition Programs (MDAPs) and Major Automated Information System (MAIS) Acquisition Programs," Regulation No. 5000.2-R, Sec. C.5.2.3.4.3, 5 April 2002.

[8]Dorofee, A. J., et al., *Continuous Risk Management Guidebook,* Software Engineering Institute, Carnegie Mellon Univ., Pittsburgh, PA, 1996, pp. 230, 231.

[9]International Council on Systems Engineering, *Systems Engineering Handbook*, San Francisco Bay Area Chapter, Release 1.0, Jan. 1998, p. 4.5–16.

[10]Project Management Institute, *A Guide to the Project Management Body of Knowledge (PMBOK® Guide)*, Newtown Square, PA, 2000, p. 127.

[11]Department of Defense, *Risk Management Guide for DoD Acquisition,* Defense Acquisition Univ., 5th ed. June 2002, pp. 5, 18, 19, 36, 37.

[12]Air Force ASC/EN and SMC/SD, "Systems Engineering Guide," Version 1.1, 5 April 1996, p. 4.

[13]Willman, D., "The Rise and Fall of the Killer Drug Rezulin," Los Angeles Times, 4 June 2000, pp. A1, A16.

[14]National Research Council, *Improving Risk Communication*, National Academy Press, Washington, DC, 1989, pp. 6, 7, 17, 46, 47, 170.

[15]Derived from the "U.S. Aerospace Risk Analysis Survey," Society of Cost Estimating and Analysis, International Society of Parametric Analysts, Space Systems Cost Analysis Group, 1998 Toronto Joint Conference, p. 5.

[16]Tversky, A., and Kahneman, D., "Judgment Under Uncertainty: Heuristics and Biases," *Science*, Vol. 185, 27 Sept. 1974, pp. 1124–1131.

[17]Project Management Institute, *A Guide to the Project Management Body of Knowledge (PMBOK® Guide)*, op. cit., 2000, p. 208.

[18]Conrow, E. H., Smith, G. K., and Barbour, A. A., "The Joint Cruise Missiles Project: An Acquisition History," RAND, Santa Monica, CA, R-3039-JCMPO, Aug. 1982, pp. 13–15; and Conrow, E. H. Smith, G. K. and Barbour, A. A. "The Joint Cruise Missiles Project: An Acquisition History—Appendixes," RAND, Santa Monica, CA, N-1989-JCMPO, Aug. 1982, pp. 8–10.

[19]Steve Waddell, private communication, 2001.

[20]Gardiner, D. A., and Phaneuf, D. H., "Risk Management in Evolutionary Large System Development," *3rd Software Engineering Institute Conference on Software Risk*, April 1994, pp. 7, 8, 12.

[21]Fairley, R. E., "Risks and Opportunities in Developing COTS-Based Software Systems," *Software Engineering Institute Conference on Risk Management*, April 1997.

[22]Messenger, G. C., and Ash, M. S., *The Effects of Radiation on Electronic Systems,* 2nd ed., Van Nostrand Reinhold, New York, 1992, pp. 416, 417.

[23]Department of Defense, *Risk Management Concepts and Guidance,* Defense Systems Management College, Ft. Belvoir, VA, 1989, pp. F-2–F-11. An edited form of this material is provided in Department of Defense, *Risk Management Guide for DoD Acquisition,* Defense Acquisition Univ., 5th ed., Appendix A, June 2002.

[24]Based upon a suggestion by Chadbourne, B. C., "Put Risk Management Training Wheels on Your Project Support Office," presentation at Project Management Institute Connections 2000, Houston Texas, 11 Sept. 2000.

[25]Risk Radar™ 3.2 Users Guide, Version 1.2, American Systems Corporation, December 2002, pp. 11-13, 18-25.

[26]Carton, W., private communication, 1970.

Chapter 4
Some Risk Planning Considerations

I. Introduction

In this chapter, I will briefly look at some key features of how to implement risk planning, including some recommended approaches and traps to avoid.

II. Need for Risk Planning

Risk planning is possibly the least practiced risk management process step but may be the most important one. If you can't specify risk categories, document inputs, outputs, tools and techniques, and key functions for each process step; specify key ground rules and assumptions; and describe organizational implementation and associated roles and responsibilities, then how will you perform risk management on your program? Generally in such cases where insufficient risk planning exists, the resulting risk management process is at least somewhat unstructured, ad hoc, and poorly implemented, all of which contributes to ineffective risk management. Similarly, in organizations without a history of risk planning (which is, unfortunately, common), there is a tendency for risk planning to show up on a risk management process flow diagram, yet it is never formally and/or properly performed.

Surprisingly, little or no formal risk planning typically exists in many programs. This can weaken risk management process effectiveness by causing risk issues to be missed, analyses to be inaccurate or inconsistent, poor risk handling approaches, and subjective risk monitoring.

The lack of risk planning can sometimes be traced to the risk management process implementation itself. For example, from Table 3.1, the DoDI 5000.2 (2002) and Software Engineering Institute (1996) risk management processes do not contain a formal risk planning step. In other cases the risk management process contains a risk planning step, but it is often not practiced, or the step is so informal that it effectively does not exist.

Without a fairly formal risk planning step people may spend months to a year or more attempting to add new features and capabilities to their risk management process. In most cases a couple of weeks to a month or so of reasonable, deliberate risk planning activity early on, followed by institution of a Risk Management Board (RMB) and its meeting would have identified and permitted resolution of many of the issues associated with the risk management process that otherwise continued to pop up as problems and surprise program management later in the program. The typical counter for having a risk planning step is that "we don't have time to do it—we have to perform a risk assessment." This mentally is generally related to crisis management and problem solving on many programs and often points to inadequate program management or systems engineering. (As discussed in Chapter 3, Secs. XIII and XIV, this may point to larger problems.) Beyond that, when people directly plunge into performing a risk assessment the methodology is typically wanting, some key ground rules and assumptions are generally missing, some key risk categories may not be included, and a suitable work breakdown structure (WBS) may not exist. Thus, the risk assessment results are often flawed, yet this may not be known for some time, and the resulting opportunity cost can be very large. Simply stated, in every situation I have heard people say they did not have time to perform initial risk planning, the end results proved them wrong, and the time spent on risk planning would have by far been the best use possible of initial resources applied to risk management.

Simply stated, it is your choice how you will implement risk management in your program. You can skip the planning step because you are in a crisis mode and go straight to risk assessment and likely pay a big price later, or you can take some time earlier in the program to agree on what you need for a risk management process and how you will implement it. But the advantages of formalized risk planning are somewhat similar to shooting—if you do not aim at the target, you will likely miss it.

Risk planning is possibly the least practiced risk management process step but may be the most important one. Little or no formal risk planning typically exists on many programs. This can weaken risk management process effectiveness by causing risk issues to be missed, analyses to be inaccurate or inconsistent, poor risk handling approaches, and subjective risk monitoring. Formal risk planning should be performed on most programs and will aid overall risk management process effectiveness.

III. Some Risk Planning Considerations

Given that you want to include risk planning as part of the risk management process, here are three things to consider. First, it is very important to develop a specific set of goals that you want to accomplish. Although this may seem trivial, one reason why risk planning is sometimes not successful is that key inputs and outputs, as well as implementation considerations, have not been well thought out. Key inputs to risk planning typically include program requirements documents (including threat documents for DoD programs), an accurate WBS, funding profile, relevant acquisition and systems engineering documents, and the program schedule (e.g., Integrated Master Schedule). The primary output of risk planning is the development and implementation of the risk management plan (RMP) and risk training for management and working-level personnel. (Note: The RMP *is not* the risk planning step, but only one of its outputs. This is unfortunately a common mistake on many programs.)

Second, there may be a tendency to finalize risk planning and hold it static, when updates should be performed during the course of the program to ensure that the risk management process adequately matches the nature of the program (e.g., potential risk categories are reevaluated to see which ones are applicable, and lessons learned applicable to the risk management process are incorporated). Risk planning should be performed at program initiation and revisited at the beginning of each program phase. This includes developing an RMP and updating it as appropriate. Some level of risk planning should also be performed prior to the initiation of each program phase, but the level of available resources may preclude developing and implementing a comprehensive approach and/or RMP. Risk planning should be reexamined whenever substantial changes to the program's acquisition process or scope occur.

Third, risk planning should not be rigid in nature. Although it is desirable to presuppose particular end results, such as a specific risk category to focus on, do not foreclose or reduce opportunities to identify and analyze potential risk issues outside of previously identified risk categories or limit the number and scope of potential risk handling or monitoring options. Common issues related to an overly rigid risk planning process include 1) adopting the risk management process from another program without suitable tailoring; 2) failing to recognize potential risk categories outside of prespecified ones (e.g., security risk); 3) focusing on the control (mitigation) option almost exclusively for risk handling; 4) assuming the control option is selected, limiting the number of candidate approaches evaluated to ones previously used in the program; and 5) selecting an insufficient number or inadequate metrics to monitor the progress of reducing technical risk issues.

IV. Some Risk Management Plan Considerations

Perhaps the best spent funds in risk management are in developing and implementing a good RMP. Development of a suitable RMP and implementing the documented process will increase the likelihood of achieving effective risk management. When key management personnel know that an RMP is required yet choose not to adequately fund its development, associated training, and implementation, they greatly increase the likelihood that the risk management process will be ineffective because, among other things 1) ground rules and assumptions and risk categories are not specified, 2) key inputs are not present (e.g., a suitable WBS), 3) risk identification and risk analysis methodologies will not be suitable or adequately defined, 4) a structured method for selecting the risk handling strategy will be absent, 5) ad-hoc risk monitoring will likely exist, 6) roles and responsibilities will not be well defined, and 7) products and due dates will not be well defined.

A weak RMP, on the other hand, may have little or no practical value to the program. The RMP should include, at a minimum, a balance of 1) introductory material (e.g., program overview), 2) ground rules and assumptions, 3) process information (e.g., steps, inputs, tools and techniques, and outputs), 4) organizational implementation (e.g., structure, roles, responsibilities), and 5) documentation and reporting. RMPs that only focus on a few of these items will generally be deficient and not particularly helpful to implementing risk management on the program. Finally, if you develop an RMP, use it—do not let it sit on a shelf and gather dust, or acknowledge its existence and then either not use it or implement a risk management process different from that described in a recently written RMP. Surprisingly, both of these considerations do occur in actual programs.

A common problem on many programs is that no formal RMP [or equivalent document(s)] may exist, which will reduce the effectiveness of the program's risk management process. In other cases an RMP may exist, but it does not adequately lay out the program's risk management process. You might wonder how developing an RMP will help the program's risk management process. In several instances it was the act of putting together a comprehensive RMP that forced a number of important issues to the surface associated with the risk management process (e.g., how many technical risk categories should be used and how often should risk assessments be performed). To resolve these issues, key program personnel made decisions that affected the structure and implementation of the risk management process. Without initial resolution of these issues, they would likely not have appeared until during process implementation, or even later in the program, which would have led to decreased morale and effectiveness. (On some programs morale for implementing and using risk management will not be high to begin with, so it is important to avoid false starts and stop/restart conditions. This will prevent morale from plunging and the subsequent process effectiveness from dropping to unacceptably low levels.)

It is important that if you perform risk planning and develop an RMP that it be *comprehensive* to encompass likely key characteristics of the risk management process and its implementation. For example, in one case a number of important components were not included, such as: anticipated risk categories, risk assessment ground rules and assumptions, key program documents (and other inputs for each process step), and buyer vs seller roles and responsibilities (treating the buyer and seller as a monolith). A simplistic RMP may have the appearance of documenting the risk management process, but it may not be helpful for implementing risk management on the program. Similarly, if a weak or poor RMP exists, there may be no reference or source that program personnel can access to understand and help implement risk management. Additionally, in cases where the buyer and seller have a distorted view of what constitutes a "good" RMP, the RMP may be judged adequate, yet still include little or no information on the risk management process and its implementation. In such cases, program personnel may collect inputs from various sources to "fill the void" of an inadequate RMP, yet this often leads to ineffective risk management because the quality of the sources was varied and often times not very high.

The RMP should contain key risk management information, including (but not limited to) a description of 1) purpose, 2) program summary, 3) program acquisition and contracting strategies,4) key definitions, 5) key requirements documents, 6) process steps, 7) inputs, tools and techniques, and outputs for each process steps, 8) linkages of risk management with other program processes, 9) ground rules and assumptions (used for all risk management process steps), 10) relevant risk categories, 11) contractor (or seller) and government (or buyer) responsibilities and guidelines for interaction, 12) general approach, 13) specific organizational roles and responsibilities, and 14) personnel roles and responsibilities. (Another related viewpoint of RMP contents is given Ref. 1.)

Some RMPs (or similar risk documents) have little or no internal consistency when it comes to documenting and discussing the risk management process. The process should be consistently described in the document from the introduction through the discussion of each process step, plus organizational roles and responsibilities. For example, if the RMP says that tools and techniques are first introduced after being approved by the RMB at the beginning of the program and updated as needed, they should not be discussed in another part of the RMP as being developed and approved outside of the RMB and allocated to a single process step.

Similarly, when reviewing an existing RMP carefully examine the risk management process that it contains. In one case I discovered two different and contradictory risk management processes within a single RMP! At best this is confusing and at worst indicative of poor risk management. If more than one risk management process must be used, then meld them together or use a single process together with a translation table showing how process steps from one process map into another.

When reviewing an RMP it is important to check the validity of sections of the document that have not yet been performed by its author and on the program in question to insure that the information is both accurate and relevant. In such situations it is often not uncommon to find substantial technical and implementation errors in the material that require correction prior to their being used.

In general, if suitable configuration control procedures do not exist, particularly in a culture without a history of effective risk management, the RMP may degrade with time. In one situation the RMP degraded in both quality and content. People that had no risk management knowledge and experience turned it into a "warm fuzzy" document with no detail and no indication of what people should do (e.g., no responsibilities stated). Active safeguards (e.g., a vigilant RMB) should be employed to maintain both the quality and content of the RMP with time.

Be careful of situations where an RMP is developed, which becomes an input to another risk management document (especially a standard or guide within the organization) because a divergence may exist between the risk management material contained in the two documents vs time. The RMP should be the governing source of risk management process information used on the program regardless of how the information is used and modified in other documents. What can be troublesome in situations where the organization does not have a history of effective risk management, or if it is a dysfunctional organization, is when the organization's risk management standard or guide is then fed back to the program and used to influence the existing RMP. In such cases, it is possible that the next iteration of the RMP may be substantially degraded vs the original version, and it is possible that the more iterations that exist between the RMP and the organization's standard or guide the more degraded the RMP may become. In one case, important material contained in the RMP later appeared in the organization's risk management guide and was then deleted in the next edition of the RMP. Unfortunately, the material deleted from the RMP, was not referenced by the RMP in the organization's guide, and thus became "lost." This was clearly a case where a useful, superior document became a far less useful, marginal document within a short period of time. To make matters worse, the RMB which should have had configuration control over the RMP, did not exercise any control over the RMP. In addition, the RMB did not even realize that the degradation had occurred.

Finally, don't include risk identification, analysis, handling, and monitoring results in the RMP. This will lead to a very voluminous document! For example, it is not relevant to include risk handling information in an RMP for program risk issues. This would dilute the quality of the RMP and require frequent updates to revise progress on risk handling information. (Risk handling plans (RHP) and progress made in implementing them should be documented outside the RMP.) Include results in a separate database or document (e.g., a monthly or quarterly Risk Evaluation Report).

A. Introduction

1. Purpose

The purpose serves as an overview to the RMP, the risk management process, and how it will be implemented on the program.

2. Program Summary

A brief description of the program is provided. It should include a short historical introduction, key mission areas for the system, detailed government objectives for the current program phase, and anticipated government objectives for succeeding program phases.

3. Program Acquisition and Contracting Strategies

A brief summary of the government acquisition strategy (e.g., number of contractors, number of years per program phase, key milestones and dates for the current acquisition phase, any other constraints facing the program beyond key milestones and dates, and key products per program phase) and contracting strategy (e.g., contract type and value) is provided.

4. Key Definitions

Definitions for key items associated with the risk management process and its implementation are provided. Definitions might include risk management process steps, risk categories, risk levels (e.g., medium), organizational roles and responsibilities (e.g., RMB and risk manager), plus others as needed.

5. Key Requirements Documents

A summary of key technical requirements and threat documents and how they impact program objectives and the risk management process is provided. (For example, a change in the threat may impact the needed missions, which may result in a change in design, which may require different technologies, which may lead to changes in required manufacturing processes and support procedures.)

B. Risk Management Process

1. Process Steps

An overview of the program's risk management process and a detailed discussion of each process step are provided.

2. Inputs, Tools and Techniques, and Outputs for Each Process Step

For each process step identify key inputs (which will generally include outputs from previous steps plus other items); tools and techniques [e.g., interviews, charting, models (qualitative and quantitative) and databases (manual and automated)]; outputs [training, results, (e.g., schedule risk analysis with cumulative distribution functions for key activity durations and finish dates)]; and documentation (e.g., RMP, risk identification lists, prioritized risk lists, RHP, and risk monitoring reports). Also, include to the extent practical, a step-by-step set of instructions for performing and documenting key actions, particularly risk identification, analysis, and handling activities. (Note: The risk analysis methodology may sometimes be so extensive that a separate appendix is warranted.)

3. Linkages of Risk Management with Other Program Processes

Describe how risk management is linked with higher-level processes (program management and systems engineering) and other processes [e.g., contracting (presolicitation through program execution), configuration management, cost analysis, Cost as an Independent Variable (and Design to Cost), design, manufacturing, quality assurance, reliability, schedule analysis, support (e.g., maintainability), and test and evaluation]. This should include information on how process steps and key inputs and outputs are interrelated.

4. Risk Management Ground Rules and Assumptions

A good set of ground rules and assumptions developed as part of the risk planning process step can help increase overall risk management effectiveness since this information can and should be used during risk identification, risk analysis, and risk handling. Performing risk identification, analysis, or handling with an incomplete or poorly documented set of ground rules and assumptions will almost guarantee errors and inconsistencies in any data that are collected and results that are generated.

Specific ground rules and assumptions that describe the program and are used for performing risk assessments (both identification and analysis) and developing RHPs are provided. On the surface this may not seem warranted, but the lack of viable ground rules and assumptions is a consistent stumbling block on many programs. This is because without the entire program team employing common information about important program characteristics (e.g., the design freeze date), the resulting risk identification and analysis results will include a noise term that can be substantial. Similarly, this information is also needed for developing RHPs to ensure that key acquisition characteristics and milestones are incorporated. (See Chapter 5, Sec. II.A and Chapter 6, Sec. II.B for some additional considerations.)

Program ground rules and assumptions should be developed, documented, and made available to participants before performing an initial risk assessment. Attempting to identify key ground rules and assumptions during the risk assessment meeting will almost certainly lead to some key information (e.g., program requirements) being omitted. The specific nature of candidate risks identified may well contain errors, thus increasing the potential that erroneous risk analysis results may later occur. In addition, this may also contribute to some candidate risk issues not being identified while others are included that may not warrant consideration.

5. Relevant Risk Categories

Anticipated risk categories for hardware (e.g., technology maturity), software (e.g., algorithm definition), integration (e.g., hardware/software), and programmatic items are described. As a starting point, consider risk categories given in Chapter 2 (e.g., cost, design/engineering, functional, integration, logistics/support, manufacturing, schedule, technology, and threat), tailored to hardware, software, integration, and programmatic items. In addition, key program processes and resources should also be considered as potential risk categories. (Note: Not all risk categories will apply to each item. For example, manufacturing is not a feasible risk category for software items. A matrix of feasible risk categories vs items vs program phase should be developed.)

C. Risk Management Implementation

1. Contractor and Government Responsibilities and Guidelines for Interaction

A description of what aspects of risk management the prime contractor team and the government are responsible for and how the parties interact with each other is provided. This should also provide a description of risk management- related documentation that will be transferred and appropriate channels for communication between the contractor and government organizations. (Although it may seem strange to talk about guidelines for interaction, on some programs that are in competitive development or production there may be very strict and substantially limiting rules on how the prime contractor teams and government can interact.)

2. General Approach

A brief discussion of the charter for risk management (e.g., authorization to perform it and an overview of the organizational structure), risk management policies (e.g., what the risk management process attempts to do in the program), and overall risk management strategy (e.g., how often risk assessments are performed) within the program is provided. (This section may be related to Sec. IV.A.1, but provide more detailed information.)

3. Specific Organizational Roles and Responsibilities for Contractor and Government

A discussion of the prime contractor team and government organizational implementation and key responsibilities is provided. (If the RMP is authored by the prime contractor, then the primary emphasis should be on its organizational implementation and key responsibilities. If the government authors the RMP, then the emphasis should be on its implementation and responsibilities.) A brief discussion of some organizational roles and responsibilities associated with risk management is given in Chapter 3, Sec. XII.

4. Personnel Roles and Responsibilities

Specific roles and responsibilities of key personnel beyond the program manager, systems engineering lead, risk manager, and integrated product team leads (which should be discussed under specific organizational roles and responsibilities) are provided.

V. Risk Management Training

Risk management training is often considered an output of the risk planning process. While this may or may not be absolutely true, suitable risk management training will increase the likelihood that effective risk management occurs on your program. Training and education coupled with on-the-job experience is a key consideration for working personnel to accurately perform risk management. Similarly, good training and education is also critical to help managers to correctly interpret risk management data and use it in their decision making process. Consequently, at least some level of suitable, high quality risk management training is desirable for both managers and working-level personnel at the beginning of a program (or program phase) as well as during the course of the program to assist in implementing and effectively performing the risk management process. (See Chapter 3, Sec. VI, for additional information.)

Reference

[1]Department of Defense, *Risk Management Guide for DoD Acquisition,* 5th ed., Defense Acquisition University, Ft. Belvoir, VA, June 2002, p. 56.

Chapter 5
Some Risk Identification Considerations

I. Introduction

In this chapter I will briefly look at some key features of how to implement risk identification, including some recommended approaches and traps to avoid.

II. Some Risk Identification Considerations

A. Top-Level Considerations

Ground rules and assumptions developed as part of risk planning are a key input for risk identification for two reasons. First, they should be used to help "set the stage" for risk identification. This is important because different people may be thinking about different program characteristics (e.g., milestones such as the technology freeze date, radiation environment), and this will affect which candidate risk issues are identified. Put another way, if everyone used the same set of ground rules and assumptions, there would be less chance that at least some risk issues might remain unidentified. Second, they may also contribute to or counteract a potential risk issue (e.g., level of threat present). In a more stressing case, key ground rules and assumptions may form program constraints and drive a risk assessment. For example, a very compressed development schedule may lead to increased schedule risk (cet. par.), as well as increased schedule consequence of occurrence for technical risks (cet. par.).

Ground rules and assumptions developed as part of risk planning are a key input for risk identification, both to help "set the stage," and because they may also contribute to or counteract a potential risk issue.

When performing risk identification, it is important to examine 1) the item to be developed and/or produced, 2) capability and maturity of the processes, and 3) availability of personnel and other resources (e.g., facilities) needed because risk issues may exist in each area. For example, a missile may require complex computer software to perform real-time targeting. The likely software design (e.g., architecture) should be examined for possible risk, as well as the maturity of the software development process to be used, and the availability of a suitable number of trained software developers. (If the software development process has never been applied to this type of complex real-time problem, it may not have sufficient capability or maturity for the required task and thus introduce risk. Likewise, if insufficient trained personnel exist, this will also introduce risk.)

When performing risk identification, it is important to examine 1) the item to be developed and/or produced, 2) capability and maturity of the processes, and 3) availability of personnel and other resources (e.g., facilities) needed because risk issues may exist in each area.

When examining candidate risk issues it is sometimes helpful to consider an "if, then" approach for clarifying and documenting the risk. Here, "if" corresponds to the potential event, and "then" corresponds to the potential impact. Another helpful approach to use in conjunction with the "if, then" method is to consider "how can the risk issue occur?" This may better help to focus the participants on the source and nature of the risk issue.

Relatively simple approaches for structuring initial activities associated with identifying candidate risks include evaluating issues with an "if, then" approach, and considering "how can the risk issue occur?" These methods are often helpful in overcoming mental "roadblocks" during risk identification activities.

Even if a program member believes a risk to be low, it may still be important to submit the risk issue and have it evaluated. The reason for this is the risk issue may be interrelated to other risk issues (e.g., shared resources) and the combined effect (e.g., risk level) of the two risk issues may be greater than either issue individually [e.g., two separate low risk issues may form one medium risk issue relative to the availability of shared resource (e.g., personnel, facilities, or equipment)]. Similarly, management may have a broader perspective on a particular candidate risk issue, and, in some cases the risk issue may have a higher level of risk than anticipated by the person that submitted it.

Candidate risk issues should be documented then evaluated by the Risk Management Board (RMB) regardless of what risk level the originator believes the risk to be.

When a comprehensive risk identification is performed it is important to determine which issues 1) require additional information (e.g., are similar to another risk issue because of missing information), 2) are interrelated with other risk issues, and 3) overlap with other risk issues.

When additional data is obtained in the first case, the risk issues may either diverge, in which case they may have little relationship with other risk issues (and thus warrant being treated as separate candidate risk issues), or converge with either the second or third cases. In the second case, the candidate risk issues should be separately maintained but reference should be made to their interrelationship as part of the risk identification documentation. In the third case it may be possible to eliminate at least one of the overlapping candidate risk issues (e.g., one issue when two issues totally overlap). Here we need to first understand what the source of the overlap is. For example, one source is due to different groups simultaneously performing risk identification on the same items. This type of overlapping issue is relatively easy to spot and eliminate. A second source of overlapping risk issues is when different aspects of interrelated items (e.g., hardware and/or software) are evaluated. This type of overlapping issue may be more difficult to spot and eliminate. Also note that while combining risk issues that do in fact overlap will reduce the number that exist in some cases to a far more management level, the potential danger from doing this is that while some aspects of a risk issue may overlap with another, other aspects may not. The result in the latter case is often that either 1) one or more key aspects of the individual risk issues have inadvertently been eliminated, or 2) some risk issues will not fully overlap and the resources required to deal with the differences may be larger than that to deal with the risk issues separately. Hence, when the disconnects between overlapping risk issues are nontrivial it may be better to treat each as a separate risk issue.

After performing a comprehensive risk identification activity, determine which issues 1) require additional information, 2) are interrelated with other risk issues, and 3) overlap with other risk issues. Obtain additional information as needed, note interrelationships with other risk issues, and carefully reduce overlapping risk issues as warranted.

Once a comprehensive risk identification activity is performed, do not assume that all program risk issues have been identified—even at that time—because it is likely that one or more key risk issues will be overlooked. At a minimum, have the program team take another look after the risk issues have been collected to identify "missing" risk issues (as well as incomplete data). Even then, do not have a false sense of security that all risk issues have been identified at that time.

After completing a comprehensive risk identification activity is performed, do not assume that all program risk issues have been identified—even at that time.

B. Some Risk Identification Approaches

A variety of different approaches exist for performing a structured risk identification activity to develop candidate risk issues. Six different methods are now briefly described for risk identification, plus one method for clustering results. These approaches are not all inclusive, and each has pluses and minuses that you should evaluate for your project in order to help you to select which method(s) to use.

The first approach is to perform the risk identification by work breakdown structure (WBS) element. Although it may seem obvious, an accurate, up-to-date, WBS is essential. With this approach a selected number of WBS elements are evaluated to see what, if any, candidate risks may exist. Here, all items in the WBS are systematically evaluated to a predetermined level, with care given to not set the level too high, which will lead to risks being missed, or to set it too low, which may provide too many items to evaluate and attempt to identify potential issues for each item. The plus side of this approach is that it is product driven, whereas the minus side is that it may be difficult to select the lower WBS threshold for evaluation.

The second approach examines the WBS and uses available ordinal risk analysis scales to identify candidate risk issues (whose level of "probability" and consequence can later be readily determined as part of risk analysis if warranted). The plus side of this approach is that specific risk categories (e.g., design/engineering) are examined, whereas the minus side is that underlying issues may not be transparent, plus risk categories may be unintentionally eliminated unless appropriate ordinal scales are selected.

The third approach involves a top-level look at the program for items not associated with lower WBS levels. Some candidate risks may exist at higher WBS levels (1–3) that may not manifest in an easily recognizable manner to lower WBS levels. (Note: A synergistic combination is to use the first and third methods discussed: the WBS element approach coupled with the top-level evaluation.)

The fourth approach examines key processes (e.g., design, manufacturing, test) to evaluate their maturity, available resources, etc. to what candidate risks may exist. The results from this approach may also span a large portion of the program since each process may cut across a number of integrated product teams (IPT). This approach may be difficult to perform in the early development phase of a program when insufficient detail exists about key processes.

The fifth approach is a top-down method that maps program requirement(s) to potential risk issues. Here a specific requirement may drive one or more candidate risk issues. The benefit of this approach is that the most important program requirements can potentially be evaluated. The difficulty with this approach is that it may affect a diverse set of WBS elements that may not be obvious to the participants.

The sixth approach is mission capabilitybased, which somewhat ties the WBS-based, process-based, and the requirements-based approaches together. In the mission capability approach, consider defining the mission in terms of, say, 1) the minimal mission, 2) acceptable mission, and 3) full mission. [This could also be minimal acceptable capability (or features, functions, etc.), moderate capability, and full capability for a commercial product.] Then determine which requirements, key processes, and WBS elements map to each mission category. From this, corresponding risk categories associated with the allocated requirements, WBS elements, and key processes can be determined and mapped to mission capability. (For example, a new technology, with unproven design and manufacturing process is needed for WBS element XXX to satisfy allocated requirement YYY in order to meet the minimal mission.) The benefit of this approach is that in some respects it bridges the WBS-based, process-based, and requirements-allocations–based approaches. The difficulty with this approach is that it may not apply to a given program (e.g., one with a point design) and is potentially resource-intensive to set up.

A common method for clustering risk identification results from the six methods mentioned above is commonly called affinity. Here candidate risks are clustered by an intrinsic similarity among the issues, and this association is then used to develop a group identifier for each cluster (e.g., similar risk descriptions for several candidate risks may then lead to a common risk heading, such as personnel availability). (I used the affinity approach to develop the 6 software risk groupings and 17 unique software risk issues derived from 150 total software risk issues contained in 10 surveys as given in Table 5.1. I also used the affinity approach to develop the 6 risk analysis methodology groupings and 33 evaluation criteria given in Table 6.1.)

Ideally, each candidate risk identified should also be mapped to one or more specific risk categories. This may not be performed initially since it may be an impediment to some people involved in the risk identification activity, but it should be performed prior to the candidate risk being evaluated by the RMB.

While none of the six approaches is consistently the easiest to use, and it is possible that contractual requirements or stakeholder expectations may necessitate using a specific approach, I've found the WBS element approach together with the top-level approach to be a good combination. If you use this strategy it may also be helpful to evaluate how key program requirements and key program processes contribute to candidate risks to reduce the likelihood that important candidate risks will be omitted. (This is particularly important if a relatively small number of WBS elements are under evaluation.) Finally, you can use the affinity approach to initially cluster candidate risk issues into possible groupings before they are mapped to specific risk categories.

Six different methods to perform a structured risk identification include: WBS, WBS coupled with ordinal risk scales, top-level evaluation (WBS levels 1–3), requirements, mission capability, and key processes. Each method should be considered and used as appropriate. Map the resulting candidate risk issues into risk categories. (This also serves as good input to the subsequent risk analysis evaluation). Provide this information to RMB, or equivalent.

C. Some Tools and Techniques

A variety of tools and techniques should be considered for risk identification purposes, including, but not limited to 1) lessons learned (historical data on similar projects and other studies), 2) templates and checklists, 3) expert opinion, 4) risk metrics [e.g., technical performance measurements (TPM) and earned value], 5) diagramming (e.g., Fishbone diagram of cause and

Table 5.1 Summary of some key risk issues for software-intensive projects, with permission from IEEE Software; Vol. 14, No. 3, May/June 1997, p. 84. ©1997 IEEE

Risk grouping	Software risk issue
Project-level	Excessive, immature, unrealistic, or unstable requirements
	Lack of user involvement
	Underestimation of project complexity or dynamic nature
Project attributes	Performance shortfalls (includes errors and quality)
	Unrealistic cost or schedule (estimates and/or allocated amounts)
Management	Ineffective project management (possible at multiple levels)
Engineering	Ineffective integration, assembly, and test; quality control; specialty engineering; systems engineering or (possible at multiple levels)
	Unanticipated difficulties associated with the user interface
Work environment	Immature or untried design, processes or technologies selected
	Inadequate work plans or configuration control
	Inappropriate methods, tool selection, or inaccurate metrics
	Poor training
Other	Inadequate or excessive documentation or review process
	Legal or contractual issues (e.g., litigation, malpractice, ownership)
	Obsolescence (includes excessive schedule length)
	Unanticipated difficulties with subcontracted items
	Unanticipated maintenance and/or support costs

effect), and 6) requirements flowdown. Lessons learned, templates, checklists, and expert opinion should all be based on experience with similar items from relevant (analogous) programs, otherwise they may inadvertently bias the risk identification activity (e.g., candidate risks identified that are not risks to the current program and some risk issues that are missed). A variety of risk metrics can be used for risk identification purposes. Common metrics include TPMs tailored to the items in question (see Chapter 3, Sec. XVII.H) and earned value (e.g., cost variance). Although there are no firm guidelines as to when a measurement value becomes a candidate risk issue, one consideration is when the actual value exceeds the planned value (where an actual value greater the planned value is not the desired outcome).

No single tool or technique is likely to be sufficient given the broad scope of most development projects. For example, templates or sets of risk related questions can be helpful for risk identification if they are focused to potential causes of or issues associated with 1) specific WBS categories (e.g., hardware, software, and integration), 2) potential risk categories (e.g., design/engineering), and 3) possible correlation between WBS categories (e.g., software and integration) for a given WBS element or between WBS elements. Issues identified from templates should then be evaluated in a risk analysis to determine the likely magnitude of the probability of occurrence and consequence of occurrence risk terms. I will now briefly discuss templates, checklists, and requirements flowdown for risk identification in a bit more detail.

An example template developed for candidate software risk issues is given in Table 5.1 (Ref. 1). This was derived by evaluating 10 different studies that reported key software risk issues. Here, 150 total software risk issues were identified among the 10 surveys representing different sets of software-intensive projects. The 150 risk issues were clustered into 6 risk groupings and 17 unique risk issues. The very high degree of overlap present between risk issues (17 unique vs 150 total) supports the contention that highly common problems typically exist among software-intensive projects.

This template should provide a starting point for evaluating the presence of some software risk issues, assuming the project uses traditional software development techniques (e.g., no object oriented programming). (When the program manager of a high-performance $250 million software development activity saw this template, he said that he would apply it to his program the next day!) However, this and other templates should be tailored to each program and used to ask probing questions that may uncover either more clearly defined or additional risk issues. For example, poor training may be an indicator of potential risks, but it is often more important to understand what part(s) of the development activity may be affected and the likely cost, performance, and schedule impacts.

Similarly, although templates can be valuable for risk identification, great care should be taken not to assume that templates represent the sole potential risk sources for a given program and design. This will almost always lead to at least some risk issues not being identified. The analyst must also consider whether or not the templates apply to the program in question because of potential changes in key processes associated with product design and manufacturing, because of age, fundamentally new ways of doing business (e.g., IPTs), etc. (In fact, these are some concerns associated with using Ref. 2.)

Checklists may also be helpful for risk identification purposes. In some cases a response to a carefully worded question may be sufficient to indicate a medium or higher risk on a program, thus warranting performing a risk analysis on the item in a timely manner. (Note: Although templates, checklists, and similar tools may prove very helpful for risk identification, they should almost never be the sole methodology used because at least some risk issues will be missed.) In this latter instance the questions must be carefully worded and written in such a manner that any answer, "no" (vs "yes"), points to something that has proven to be a risk issue with similar items from other relevant programs. Vaguely worded questions may point to potential risks but elicit unclear or ambiguous answers and thus reduce the value of conducting such an exercise. (For example, does the design exceed the current state of the art?)

I will now give examples of a possible checklist question with inadequate, marginal, and adequate wording:

1) Inadequate—Are sufficient software personnel available?

2) Marginal—Are sufficient software personnel trained and in place prior to the program's Software Readiness Review?

3) Desirable—Six months prior to the program's Software Readiness Review are at least 75% of the necessary software development personnel trained and in place?

It is also important that templates (e.g., Table 5.1) and checklists are applied at a representative WBS level. Ideally, the WBS level used to derive the templates and checklists should be the same WBS level that the tools are used to identify candidate risks on the program in question. If this is not possible, then it is important that the templates and checklists not be used several WBS levels above or below that used to derive them to prevent risks from being overlooked because risks at much higher or lower WBS levels may be quite different than at the WBS level used to derive the tools.

Another approach for risk identification takes potentially stressing requirements and allocates them to the subsystems that they will likely affect. The potentially affected subsystems are then evaluated to see if risk issues will likely be present. This provides an indication of potential risks, but like the other tools and techniques discussed here it is not a stand-alone, sufficient risk identification procedure. For example, if an aircraft is required to have Mach 3 speed, some likely risk areas will include the propulsion system and vehicle thermal control. The propulsion system may include risk issues associated with thrust, weight, and fuel consumption whereas the vehicle thermal control system will include issues associated with choice of materials and method of cooling. This is far from an exhaustive list, but given as an example of some stressing requirements can be mapped to some potential risk issues. As in the template case, the analyst should not assume that requirements allocation will identify all key risk issues for a given design approach.

A variety of tools should be considered for risk identification, including, but not limited to 1) lessons learned (historical data on similar projects and other studies), 2) templates and checklists, 3) expert opinion, 4) risk metrics (e.g., TPMs and earned value), 5) diagramming (e.g., Fishbone diagram of cause and effect), and 6) requirements flowdown. No single tool or technique is likely to be sufficient given the broad scope of most medium and large-scale programs.

D. Examine Candidate Issues for Both the Probability and Consequence Terms

Risk identification should consider both the risk probability and consequences terms, not just one or the other. I am not suggesting that a (risk analysis) probability or consequence evaluation be performed, but that both terms of risk should be considered when evaluating a given item for risk identification purposes. For example, assume that a moderate performance sensor focal plane array (FPA) based on an existing design is required, but six months of schedule slack exists between the completion of its development and when it is required for sensor integration. In this case the FPA might not be identified as a risk issue, and in particular a schedule risk issue. However, if zero schedule slack existed for the FPA development and the item was on the program's critical path, then the potential schedule and cost impact of any development problems could be very substantial, and FPA development may be identified as a risk issue (cet. par.).

In addition, key "probability" of occurrence components which are often related to risk categories (e.g., technology maturity associated with technology) and consequence of occurrence components (e.g., cost, performance, schedule) should be noted and documented as part of risk identification. Here, identify the components that may be dominant as part of risk identification, but do not quantify these components until risk analysis. For example, cost impact may be a key consequence of occurrence component for a given risk issue but do not attempt to estimate the cost until performing a risk analysis.

Risk identification should consider both the risk probability and consequences terms, not just one or the other. Key "probability" of occurrence and consequence of occurrence components should be noted and documented as part of risk identification.

E. Additional Risk Identification Information to Collect

In addition to considering probability and consequence of occurrence information, the risk identification activity should examine for each risk issue 1) the cause(s) and outcome(s) possible, 2) the frequency of occurrence, and 3) any interdependence of the risk issue under evaluation with any other risk issue.

A clear statement of the potential cause(s) and outcome(s) for each risk issue should be developed. Without this information the risk issue may not be accurately identified, and subsequent action(s) taken may not be properly focused. In addition, a weakly defined risk issue can lead to a risk analysis result that contains substantial uncertainty. In addition, if a risk handling strategy is needed (for medium or higher risks), it may not be suitably focused to resolve the underlying risk issue.

Because some risk events can occur more than once, the frequency of occurrence of the potential risk issue should be estimated. This should become an input to the risk analysis step and at a minimum used for risk prioritization purposes. (For example, if two items had the same risk score, the item with the higher frequency of occurrence should be assigned a higher risk prioritization than the other.)

Because some risk issues may be interrelated with other issues, such interrelationships should be noted. This should become an input to the risk analysis step and at a minimum used for risk prioritization purposes. (For example, if two items had the same risk score, the item with the larger number of interrelationships might be assigned a higher risk prioritization than the other.) Whereas it may be possible to quantify the affect of the interrelationships in some cases (e.g., in Monte Carlo simulations), there is often substantial uncertainty in the results unless the correlation can be accurately modeled. In other cases it may not be possible to quantify the affect because a qualitative risk analysis methodology is used.

Additional risk identification outputs should include for each risk issue 1) a clear statement of the cause(s) and outcome(s) possible, 2) the frequency of occurrence, and 3) any interdependence of the risk issue under evaluation with any other risk issue.

F. Risk Categories to Consider

The matrix of feasible risk categories (e.g., design/engineering) vs items (hardware, software, integration, and programmatics) included in the risk management plan (RMP) should be used to evaluate potential risk issues during risk identification. By doing this in risk identification, risk categories that do not apply to a given item can be eliminated from the more resource intensive risk analysis step.

No single set of risk categories will apply to all programs, but the following, given in Chapter 2, should be routinely considered for risk identification purposes: cost, design/engineering, functional, integration, logistics/support manufacturing, schedule, support, technology, and threat. (Cost, design/engineering, logistics/support manufacturing, schedule, technology, and threat risk categories were given in Ref. 3 to be evaluated by all DoD programs, but were deleted from subsequent revisions to this Directive.[4]) (Whereas threat may seem to only apply to DoD programs, it should also be considered for non DoD, including commercial, programs, e.g., computer security, physical security, and industrial espionage.) In addition, key program processes and resources should also be considered as potential risk categories.

(See Chapter 2, Sec. I.B and Appendix A, Sec. III, for additional risk categories to consider for risk identification. Please realize that these risk categories may not form a complete or even suitable set for *your* program.)

In general, stressing requirements in any of the preceding risk categories can lead to substantial program risk. For example, a constrained budget, a high-performance level, and a short schedule will often lead to cost, performance (technical), and schedule risk (cet. par.). In effect, this may tend to drive parts of a design (if not the entire system) that might not otherwise have substantial risk.

When ordinal scales are used to perform a subsequent risk analysis, it is usually best to evaluate all three consequences of occurrence components (cost, performance, and schedule) as part of the risk analysis step, rather than screening out components that may not apply in risk identification. The distinction here between risk categories and consequence of occurrence components may seem subtle, but it is important. When ordinal scales are used, risk categories are often related to the probability term (except for cost and schedule risk), whereas consequence of occurrence components are solely related to the consequence term (again except for cost and schedule). Whether or not a risk category applies is often binary (yes or no). For example, (hardware) manufacturing risk does not apply to software items, and (software) algorithm risk does not apply to hardware items. However, for consequence of occurrence whether a given component applies is often not binary, and typically more a gradation between the upper and lower bounds of the scale.

The matrix of feasible risk categories vs items (hardware, software, integration, and programmatics) included in the RMP should be used to evaluate potential risk issues.

G. Some Organizational Considerations

Risk identification should not just be performed by individuals that are uninvolved in the potential risk issue—this can lead to a number of risk issues not being identified until later in the program when the surface as problems because key knowledge is missing. It may also weaken the overall risk management process effectiveness because key personnel were not permitted to identify candidate risks, and thus may not have a sense of "ownership" for these issues and the process itself.

Do not limit those that perform risk identification to individuals that are uninvolved in the potential risk issue. This increases the likelihood that key information associated with a risk issue will be omitted, which may lead to problems later in the program.

It is important that when candidate risk issues are evaluated by the RMB (or equivalent), that no preconceived notions exist as to the fraction of those candidate issues that should be declared risk issues or a total number of risk issues that should result. The result in such cases is likely to be risk issues that are overlooked and will surface later in the program as problems.

The RMB should evaluate candidate risk issues without bias toward the number or type of issues that should exist on the program.

Every person on the program should have the ability to submit a candidate risk issue. In some cases IPT leads act as an initial management layer to evaluate candidate risk issues. This may affect the risk identification process by directly (filtering) or indirectly (discouraging) diminishing inputs from working level personnel. While IPT personnel together with the risk manager can be used to screen frivolous issues or request more information, all suitably prepared candidate risk issues should be evaluated by the RMB.

All suitably documented candidate risk issues should be submitted to the RMB for evaluation.

H. Documentation of Risk Issues

Risk identification documentation should include a number of items discussed below. It is not sufficient to limit such documentation to the nature of the potential risk and possible impact(s)—this is generally necessary but not sufficient to permit program personnel to understand the risk issue. Insufficient documentation describing candidate risk issues is commonplace. One simple solution is to use a short form (less than one page) that lists key risk identification information, including, but not limited to 1) risk title; 2) date identified; 3) item (e.g., product description and WBS number); 4) allocated requirements (e.g., via requirements flowdown) where available; 5) nature of the potential risk issue, including cause(s) and outcome(s); 6) applicable risk categories; 7) possible correlation with other risk issues; 8) any relevant historical information; 9) responsible individual (and relevant manager), 10) actions taken to date; and 11) recommendations for disposition. This information should be forwarded to the appropriate personnel for review and disposition (e.g., the IPT lead, then RMB).

A key consideration in developing the risk identification documentation is that the information should clearly and accurately describe the nature of the risk issue so that other program personnel can examine the issue and the RMB can make informed decisions based upon this data. To this end the person completing the risk identification documentation may also include additional relevant information as warranted to help others further understand the risk issue. For example, the risk title should be included in the risk identification form. The risk title should be descriptive and clearly relate to the nature of the risk otherwise it will tend to be confusing.

Finally, although it is possible to classify risk issues based on the risk categories they possess, I generally do not recommend this unless the risk identification information is entered into an electronic database and this classification is provided as a secondary view. The primary view should be, for example, by WBS element and/or risk issue, with applicable risk categories listed for each WBS element. Although it may be helpful to know which WBS elements contain a specific risk category, this is generally less important than knowing which risk categories relate to a given WBS element for a particular risk issue. This is because Risk Handling Plans must be implemented on a WBS element basis across relevant risk categories for the item, not by risk category across WBS elements. (In cases where key program processes and resources are evaluated, risk identification information can be tied back to relevant WBS elements and/or treated as a separate risk category with ties to affected WBS elements. For example, in one case a potential shortage of trained manufacturing labor existed. A separate risk identification entry was made for this issue, and the WBS elements this potential problem affected were noted.)

Document candidate risk issues with sufficient information, clarity, and accuracy to permit RMB members to evaluate the issues and determine whether or not to approve them. This information may also prove useful to other program personnel who may have additional data to share about candidate risk issues. It is also generally better to portray risks by WBS element and/or risk issues, with applicable risk categories listed for each WBS element, rather than by classifying risks by risk category across WBS element(s) and/or risk issues.

References

[1]Conrow, E. H., and Shishido, P. S., "Implementing Risk Management on Software-Intensive Projects," *IEEE Software,* Inst. of Electrical and Electronics Engineers, Vol. 14, No. 3, May/June 1997, p. 84. (For some useful insights into underlying causes of software risks, see C. Jones, *Assessment and Control of Software Risks,* Yourdon Press Computing Series, Prentice–Hall, Upper Saddle River, NJ, 1994.)

[2]Department of Defense, "Transition from Development to Production," DoD 4245.7-M, Sept. 1985.

[3]Department of Defense, DoD Directive 5000.1, Pt. 1, Sec. C.2, 23 Feb. 1991.

[4]Department of Defense, DoD 5000.1, March 15, 1996, 21 May 1999 (incorporating change 1), 23 Oct. 2000, and 4 Jan. 2001 (incorporating change 1).

Chapter 6
Some Risk Analysis Considerations

I. Introduction

Oftentimes risk analysis is the most detailed methodology of the entire risk management process. Unfortunately, substantial errors exist in a surprisingly large amount of the methodology used in project management and published in the literature. In this chapter I will briefly look at some key features of how to implement risk analysis, including some recommended approaches, common errors, and traps to avoid.

A. Some Top-Level Process Considerations

Several different risk analysis methods are discussed in this chapter, including decision analysis [expected monetary value (EMV) and payoff matrices], risk scales, and Monte Carlo simulations. While there are no simple rules for determining which of these methodologies should be used in a given situation, Table 6.1 provides a framework for you to consider in evaluating these approaches on your program. Thirty-three evaluation criteria were developed and grouped into six categories in this table using an affinity approach. These criteria should be considered as a starting point for your evaluation and not all inclusive; tailor this information to your needs. The same criteria may also help assist you in preparing to implement a risk analysis methodology (e.g., it may help you think through potential issues that may occur by using a particular methodology). While a number of these criteria may apply to your program, please remember that a single criteria may be so important that it may necessitate that a particular methodology be used (e.g., if a particular methodology is specified as a contractual requirement). Note: I do not recommend segregating risk analysis into qualitative risk analysis and quantitative risk analysis. This distinction is somewhat artificial because there is often a high degree of overlap between the two categories in terms of procedures to obtain inputs (e.g., interviews), resources required (e.g., analysts to collect data), and desired results (e.g., risk level for a given issue).

There are no simple rules for determining which risk analysis methodology should be used in a given situation, but a framework is provided to consider in evaluating these approaches on your program.

While it is desirable for quantitative risk analysis tools to be simple, and relatively easy to learn and implement, this should not be the primary

Table 6.1   Risk analysis methodology evaluation criteria

Group	Evaluation Criteria
Nature of risk	Risk category (e.g., technical, cost, schedule, other)
	For technical risk, which type (e.g., manufacturing, technology)?
Program characteristics	Buyer or seller performing analysis
	Knowledge and certainty of all organizations' utility functions
	Program size and duration
	Program phase and fraction into current phase
	Type of program (e.g., industry, sector)
	Need date for initial risk analysis results
Requirements and expectations	Contractual requirements or incentives
	Customer expectations and/or requirements
	Noncustomer (e.g., stakeholder, user) expectations and/or requirements
Best practices, tools and techniques, resources	Organizational best practices and procedures
	Risk Management Plan and other documentation
	Existing tools/techniques (prior or current program)
	Availability of additional tools and techniques
	Ability to modify or tailor tools and techniques
	Stability of tools and techniques (e.g., obsolescence with computer-based systems)
	Ability of tools and techniques to directly generate results needed (e.g., level of post-analysis processing required)
	Relevancy of methodology to risks being evaluated
	Personnel skill level necessary to perform risk analysis
	Training necessary prior to performing risk analysis
	Non-recurring resources necessary to perform risk analysis (e.g., people, computers, software)
	Recurring resources necessary to collect data, perform risk analysis, document results, and communicate results (e.g., people, computers, software)
	Time to perform risk analysis and generate results (initial and subsequent analyses)
Data characteristics	Data availability (historical, current)
	Structure of data
	Relevancy of data to performing risk analysis (e.g., level of pre-processing needed)
	Data accuracy and uncertainty
Results and their use	Type of results needed (e.g., statistical, risk levels)
	Fidelity of results (e.g., accuracy vs precision)
	Evaluation and validation of results
	How will results be documented and communicated?
	How will results be used?

consideration for selecting the tool. In some cases a tool may be too simple, which can and often will lead to errors that may often go undetected for some time. Using inferior risk analysis tools simply because they are easier to learn to use or may be somewhat easier to use on a recurring basis is flawed logic and may adversely impact both the accuracy of the results and the resources needed to generate them. While tool training and ease of use are certainly factors that should be investigated and considered in the selection process, they *should not* be the primary considerations. In one case an inferior tool was selected for unconvincing reasons, yet it was incapable of accepting anything other than a small set of input types, incapable of estimating more than one desired output, forced the users to manually edit the output, and prevented other, more desirable output reports from being generated. While more capable software to perform this same type of analysis is not without problems, it is clear that a poorly defined evaluation criteria contributed to an inferior product being selected and led to long-term issues associated with its use and generation of necessary results and reports. In addition, the comparison performed by the organization of candidate software tools was clearly biased toward the one that they selected; strengths of other tools were not included and weaknesses of the chosen tool were omitted. This type of biased analysis is foolish, especially when used by lower level workers to justify their decision to upper management.

While it is desirable for quantitative risk analysis tools to be simple, and relatively easy to learn and implement, this should not be the primary consideration for selecting the tool. Using inferior risk analysis tools simply because they are easier to learn to use or may be somewhat easier to use on a recurring basis is flawed logic and may adversely impact both the accuracy of the results and the resources needed to generate them.

No "best" set of overarching risk categories exists, but cost, performance (technical), and schedule is a good, small set. In addition, a given risk category may contain a number of widely varying subcategories. For example, the technical category may include everything other than cost and schedule risk categories. What is of primary importance is that regardless of how top-level categories are selected, all of the likely risk issues to be encountered on the program should clearly and unambiguously map to the tier 2 (second level) or tier 1 (top-level) risk categories used. If this is not the case, then one or more subcategories or top-level categories should be edited (modified or added) to properly accommodate the risk categories that result from these risk issues.

No "best" set of overarching risk categories exists, but cost, performance (technical), and schedule is a good, small set.

When several risk issues are interrelated, it may be helpful to draw a "wiring diagram" or figure showing the interrelationships between the risk issues. This can be particularly helpful for a risk analysis when the interrelationships between the risk issues are numerous and/or complex.

When several risk issues are interrelated, it may be helpful to draw a "wiring diagram" or figure showing the interrelationships between the risk issues.

Generally, one risk issue doesn't *cause* another risk issue to occur (cet. par.), but it may *contribute to* another risk issue occurring. In effect, the correlation coefficient between the likelihood term of risk issues is generally less than 1.0. Thus, calculations should generally not be performed linking risks unless an accurate understanding of the probability and consequence levels for each risk exists. (Of course, such calculations should not be attempted on results from uncalibrated ordinal scales.)

Generally, one risk issue doesn't cause another risk issue to occur (cet. par.), but it may contribute to another risk issue occurring.

There is often a tendency for project personnel to fallback on subjective estimated probability (likelihood) values (0.0 to 1.0) when performing analysis, even when high-quality ordinal scales or other methods are in place on the program. This is a bad practice for at least three reasons. First, there is no indication that the personnel will accurately estimate the probability of occurrence. Second, there is an unknown uncertainty associated with such ad hoc evaluations. Third, it diminishes the credibility of the documented and implemented risk analysis process. This method of evaluating probability of occurrence should generally be the last resort, not the first choice as exists in many programs.

Do not use subjective estimated probability values in a risk analysis; particularly if higher quality, more certain methodologies exist and are in place.

While risk analysis results will have different levels of accuracy, subjective, direct methods of quantifying risk (e.g., directly to low, medium, and high based upon expert opinion) should not be used. Similarly, L, M, and H risk definition statements (e.g., see Fig. 6.2) may be used as a cross-check to a structured risk analysis methodology, but should not be the sole risk analysis methodology.

Subjective methods of quantifying risk should not be used in a risk analysis.

Data is often grouped into subjective and objective, and quantitative and nonquantitative (or qualitative) categories. While some data are typically subjective (e.g., estimates without ties to actual, relevant data) or objective (e.g., actual historical data or measured data from the current project), many other types of data (e.g., interview results, lessons learned, and available studies) require careful analysis to determine which is the appropriate category. In addition, quantitative data can be derived from subjective assessments (e.g., the estimative probability information given in Appendix J) or objective assessments (e.g., measurements), and objective data may be nonquantitative (e.g., some project decisions) or quantitative (e.g., actual costs from historical projects). The key here is to examine the type, nature, and quality of the data, not just its source, before attempting to categorize it into subjective and objective, and quantitative and non-quantitative bins. For example, a scenario analysis can be either subjective or objective depending upon the source of the data. A scenario analysis based upon guesses without ties to actual data will likely be subjective, while an analysis based upon experiences with analogous systems (or programs, etc.) or where data obtained from measurement exists can be objective. Similarly, a scenario analysis based upon cardinal probability and consequence of occurrence information will likely be quantitative, while an analysis based upon decisions made by a project manager may be qualitative.

Before attempting to categorize data into subjective and objective, and quantitative and non-quantitative bins, examine the type, nature, and quality of the data, not just its source.

"Probability" and consequence of occurrence ordinal scale definitions should not exist that include, let alone are solely related to, a risk handling strategy. For example, for a medium "probability" level definition: "without mitigation, a program milestone is at risk." Here, the definition is vague and subjective and is framed in terms of risk handling [mitigation (control option)] and risk. This definition gives the analyst no objective or structured means to evaluate the "probability" level present and confuses the potential cause ("without mitigation") with the potential effect ("a program milestone is at risk") rather than evaluating the "probability" state of the issue itself. Also, in this case the word "risk" is used which is incorrect for a "probability" definition. (In fact, in this case the definition is really a risk-level definition and not a "probability"-level definition.) (See Appendix H, Sec. I for additonal information.)

"Probability" and consequence of occurrence ordinal scale definitions should not exist that include, let alone are solely related to, a risk handling strategy.

High, medium, and low levels should not be assigned to "probability" of occurrence and consequence of occurrence scores, particularly when ordinal scale definitions are given in terms of *risk*, not probability and consequence.

Do not assign high, medium, and low levels to "probability" of occurrence and consequence of occurrence scores.

The probability associated with a risk issue can sometimes be measured (or compared to actual data), estimated via expert opinion, derived from ordinal scales (as an approximation), etc. No one procedure is universal and all inclusive, and the risk management practitioner should not artificially limit the tools and techniques used to estimate the probability associated with a risk issue, so long as the results will be accurate and with an acceptable degree of uncertainty.

Do not artificially limit the tools and techniques used to estimate the probability associated with a risk issue, so long as the results will be accurate and with an acceptable degree of uncertainty.

Probability of occurrence should not be stated in terms of percent chance that a problem will occur. This is because the term "problem" may imply an adverse event to some readers, and even if true, may bias their response up or down depending upon whether they are risk averse or risk takers. *Probability of occurrence should not be stated in terms of percent chance that a problem will occur.* A risk analysis should include an estimate of the consequence of occurrence if the risk occurs, hence probability = 1.0, not if it likely occurs or any other descriptor that assumes or implies a probability < 1.0.

A risk analysis should include an estimate of the consequence of occurrence if the risk occurs.

For technical risk, consequence of occurrence is a function of cost, performance, and schedule (C,P,S) components. Consequence of occurrence does not, nor should it, include a time to impact (or time frame) term. Time frame can be used by the Risk Management Board (RMB) as part of risk prioritization using expert opinion rather than mathematical formulation, but it should not directly be incorporated into the risk factor, or consequence of occurrence term. A good, but not necessarily "best" method to include time frame is to 1) score the risk issues, 2) prioritize the risk issues based upon risk score, and 3) use time frame (or other considerations) as a tie-breaker among risk issues that have the same risk level (e.g., high).

For technical risk, consequence of occurrence is a function of cost, performance, and schedule components. Consequence of occurrence does not, nor should it, include a time to impact (or time frame) term.

When a poor risk analysis methodology exists it increases the likelihood that results will have substantial uncertainty and not "make sense." In one case a risk analyzed as high was re-analyzed as low only a short period of time later, while a key risk driver pointed to increased, not decreased, risk. The cause of the problem in this case was due to several factors, including: 1) inadequate, poorly worded three-level ordinal "probability" and consequence of occurrence scales; 2) misscoring when originally performed; and 3) management pressure to "reduce risk." In reality, no risk handling occurred to lower risk during this time and key management personnel could not provide the customer with a satisfactory explanation of how this "miracle" occurred.

A poor risk analysis methodology increases the likelihood that results will have substantial errors, uncertainty, and/or not "make sense."

Top-level definitions of risk (e.g., low, medium, and high) may contain an imbalance between levels that makes their application difficult and uncertain. For example, high risk includes "personnel, resources, and descoping considerations;" medium risk includes "cost/benefit estimate of risk management and the use of contingency plans," and low risk includes "items left to project personnel to solve." In another case, high risk is defined as "implement new process(es) or change baseline plan(s), medium risk as "aggressively manage and consider alternative process," and low risk as "monitor." The common thread between these two sets of definitions is that they are related to *desired risk management actions* rather than appropriate definitions of risk on the program itself. This is particularly interesting since in both cases structured risk analysis methodologies were developed, yet they were not apparently consulted in developing the top-level risk definitions for the program.

Top-level definitions of risk (e.g., low, medium, and high) may contain an imbalance between levels that makes their application difficult and uncertain.

B. Some Top-Level Implementation Considerations

A risk analysis should only be performed on approved risks; else a waste of resources may occur. This is because some risks will be closed, others deferred (e.g., for more information), others translated to management actions, others judged to be engineering process/practice items, etc. And a risk analysis, which takes time and personnel to perform, is not meaningful in such cases and should only be performed on approved risks.

Only perform a risk analysis on approved risks.

Two teammates used different risk criteria for thresholds vs the "official level" for categorizing risks into L, M, and H. This may have contributed to noticeable differences in risk results even if the same risk analysis scores had existed. Here the resulting differences ranged from about 10% to 40% depending upon the level of the risk and were sufficient to cross a risk boundary (e.g., low to medium). Consequently, it is important that a consistent risk analysis methodology be used by teammates, or at the very least an accurate method to map risk scores from one teammate to another must be employed to avoid generating erroneous results.

A consistent risk analysis methodology should be used by teammates, or at the very least an accurate method to map risk scores from one teammate to another must be employed to avoid generating erroneous results.

If you wait to get the last 10% of the quality of inputs needed to perform a risk analysis, you may wait too long and "pay the price" or the value of performing the risk analysis may be lost (e.g., insights from the output will not be available in a timely manner). Obviously, poor quality and/or highly uncertain inputs should be avoided, but postponing a risk analysis indefinitely, particularly when the participants are "afraid" of the possible outcomes, can have a large opportunity cost. Even worse, if procrastination is then followed by a "crash program" to fill the gap, then the quality of the output will likely suffer.

If you wait to get the last 10% of the quality of inputs needed to perform a risk analysis, you may wait too long and "pay the price" or the value of performing the risk analysis may be lost.

A single risk assessor should generally not be used on a program and perform risk assessments in a vacuum; otherwise this can lead to erroneous results (e.g., misscored risk issues) and/or potential ownership issues due to a lack of involvement from risk issue POC.

A single risk assessor should generally not be used on a program and perform risk assessments in a vacuum; otherwise this can lead to erroneous results.

The use of anonymous identification group software may be helpful for generating risk analysis information. While this may not be practical on a limited budget program, it can be valuable on larger programs because it helps break down barriers associated with group dynamics, etc.

The use of anonymous identification group software may be helpful for generating risk analysis information.

Do not simply assume that a methodology provided by a customer organization is acceptable for use on your project or any other project—it may be unacceptable and lead to erroneous results. For example, in one case an ordinal "probability" scale contained clearly defined C,P,S consequence of occurrence information. This was not only wrong, but just as bad, the cost and schedule boundaries were not meaningful and the performance consequence description was incomplete.

Do not simply assume that a methodology provided by a customer organization is acceptable for use on your project or any other project—it may be unacceptable and lead to erroneous results.

All too frequently sloppy scholarship leads to a flawed risk analysis methodology, and the methodology is not corrected when convincing evidence is presented that it is flawed. Prior to using any risk analysis methodology, the reader should ascertain whether or not it is valid and appropriate for his program. For example, in one case an estimative probability table was published without any discussion as to how the information was derived. (Lacking measurements or a statistical analysis of survey data, the resulting data is at best expert opinion that possesses severe limitations and at worst not credible.) The author, rather than correcting the flawed data or providing a disclaimer, simply cited an early paper published in a somewhat obscure journal as the source of the data, as if this brings credibility to a flawed set of information. In another instance an author incorrectly attributed non-linear decimal values to an ordinal "probability" scale, and a second author used the flawed scales in a subsequent paper citing the first author. While this was a correct method of citation, it does nothing to resolve the flawed coefficients that existed. (A cursory evaluation of the coefficients together with the scale definitions showed that the coefficients were incorrect vs values that may have resulted had the scales been calibrated by an accepted procedure. Thus, using the incorrect values could lead to substantial errors in a risk analysis.)

All too frequently sloppy scholarship leads to a flawed risk analysis methodology, and the methodology is not corrected when convincing evidence is presented that it is flawed. Prior to using any risk analysis methodology, the reader should ascertain whether or not it is valid and appropriate for his program.

C. Risk-Related Behavior of Decision Makers

Assumptions about risk-related behaviors associated with decision makers are often times not stated, sometimes oversimplified, and other times clearly erroneous. Yet these assumptions can influence both risk analysis results and how they are reported and interpreted. For example, if an asymmetric matrix mapping probability and consequence scores to risk levels is appropriate for your program, then by all means use it. (See Sec. IX.A for examples of symmetric and asymmetric risk mapping matrices.) What I object to is the arbitrary use of an asymmetric matrix when there is no convincing objective or quantitative proof it should be used, coupled with no statement to the reader that it is being used and why it is being used. In such cases a symmetric risk mapping matrix should be utilized along with a disclaimer that there is insufficient empirical data to warrant an asymmetric matrix. I also object to "fluff" statements without any substantiation that support the use of an asymmetric risk mapping matrix (e.g., "recent trends in project risk management"). Some suggest that a matrix favoring consequence over probability is appropriate for a decision maker that is risk averse, but this is not very convincing since the risk mapping matrix (probability of occurrence and consequence of occurrence) is being compared to utility vs consequence of occurrence that defines the risk nature of the decision maker. In addition, if an asymmetric matrix is used, what "real world" quantitative data do you have on *your program* to justify the degree of skew, hence matrix boundaries? [Here, a decision maker is risk averse if the first derivative of his utility vs consequence of occurrence plot is positive and the second derivative is negative, risk neutral if the first derivative of his utility vs consequence of occurrence plot is positive and the second derivative is zero, and a risk taker if the first derivative of his utility vs consequence of occurrence plot is positive and the second derivative is positive. Note also that probability levels, such as scores attached to levels in an estimative probability or consequence of occurrence scale, *do not* indicate whether or not the scale and those that derived it are risk averse, risk neutral, or risk takers. This can only be determined by examining utility vs consequence of occurrence plots which rarely if ever are generated. In addition, probability of occurrence and consequence of occurrence scale coefficients have nothing to do with risk preferences, let alone risk handling option at any given risk level. (For example, the following type of statement is meaningless: "the program desires to avoid risk with high consequence scores.")]

Simple assumptions about the behavior of personnel on a given project will sometimes not yield accurate or meaningful results about the risk preferences of the participants. For example, pursing a risk issue does not necessarily indicate that the person behaves as a risk taker. A key risk issue may require handling and the behavior exhibited may be a risk neutral or even risk averse position. Similarly, arriving at a risk neutral position is not just simply averaging a series of behaviors including those that are risk averse, risk neutral, and risk taker. [Note also that *people* exhibit risk averse, risk neutral, and risk taker behaviors, *organizations* do not! Also recognize that people generally attempt to obtain an adequate value and utility for a given outcome, not just one type (e.g., risk neutral) or another.]

It is also not reasonable to assume that if a project manager is risk averse (or even a risk taker), this forms the justification for employing an asymmetric risk mapping matrix. For example, it is erroneous to justify the use of an asymmetric risk mapping matrix by saying that a "risk issue is medium to an organization that is averse to risks with high consequence of occurrence." Such statements and rationale are meaningless and do not incorporate information associated with utility.

The utility preference of decision makers may vary considerably at a minimum 1) with the variable being examined (e.g., C,P,S), 2) with the structure of the organization (e.g., the buyer and seller are not monolithic organizations), and 3) between buyer and seller for the variable being examined (e.g., buyer and seller preferences for cost and schedule are often different). On some large-scale development projects (life-cycle cost > $1 billion), I have witnessed project managers make decisions indicative of a risk taker behavior and others indicative of a risk averse behavior *in the same day!*

If decision makers were risk averse then many moderate- to large-scale development projects would not even get started because there is typically insufficient budget and schedule for the required level of performance. Hence, often both the buyer and seller exhibit a risk taker attitude from the very beginning of a project (even if the budget and schedule are set by higher level stakeholders outside the project) and try to play "catch up" during the course of the development. Analysis of the outcomes of a large number of complex development projects given in Appendix C (many with life-cycle costs far in excess of $1 billion) indicates that the utility preferences of the buyer and seller continue to be unbalanced even late in the development phase. If this was not the case, then there would be a symmetrical distribution of variations in cost and schedule at project completion versus project initiation (cet. par.). Yet this clearly is not true for many different industries; the distributions are often right-skewed even when the benchmark for comparison is late in the development phase! However, even here, there is typically insufficient information to indicate how much a risk mapping matrix should be skewed to account for the risk-related behavior of key decision makers.

There are far more elegant and sophisticated procedures that can be employed vs a risk mapping matrix—some involve estimating the utility function of decision makers for a given set of variables and conditions. While

I have used such tools/techniques over a number of years, these methodologies are often complicated to implement, involve complex mathematics that are beyond the reach of many decision makers, and still result in a fairly wide dispersion of data. For example, in one utility vs performance analysis I conducted, results from 9 "experts" I surveyed routinely yielded a coefficient of variation [(standard deviation/mean)*100] of > 40, and in some cases ~ 100 indicating a large difference of opinion in their preferences; and this evaluation was on a narrow set of homogeneous items! In addition, some procedures published in the literature are severely flawed in terms of the mathematical constructs used, along with how they are implemented. Pity the decision maker that has been convinced by an analyst that the "new and improved" method to map probability and consequence of occurrence values to risk should be used, but it actually contains a number of limitations and errors. And these problems are almost never stated by the proponents of such tools/techniques nor adequately discussed in the literature.

Another observation to note is that performing expected value computations (e.g., EMV) in decision (tree) analysis invokes the assumption that the parties are risk neutral. Yet, this assumption is typically not stated. The interesting point here is that an asymmetric risk mapping matrix is sometimes used along with EMV computations *on the same program, at the same time, yet both techniques require fundamentally different and potentially contradictory assumptions about the risk attributes of key decision makers!*

Assumptions about risk behaviors associated with decision makers are often times not stated, sometimes oversimplified, and other times clearly erroneous. Yet these assumptions can influence both risk analysis results and how they are reported and interpreted.

II. Risk Analysis Process

A. *Comparison of Risk Analysis Results*

As mentioned in Chapter 3, the government and contractors may use different risk management processes. (The same is often true between prime contractor and subcontractors.) This is unfortunately common with risk analysis methodologies, where incompatible approaches can make comparing results difficult and error prone. If different methodologies exist, it is essential to have a way of evaluating the results so that accurate comparisons can be made between the approaches. At a minimum, this requires a clear understanding of how the probability of occurrence, consequence of occurrence, and risk results are generated. (In some cases a more structured translation of results may be possible, such as mapping risk scores between approaches, but this may not be universally possible.)

If the government and prime contractor (or prime contractor and subcontractors) use different risk analysis methodologies, it is essential to have a way of evaluating the results so that accurate comparisons can be made between the approaches.

B. Inadequate or Undocumented Ground Rules and Assumptions

If inadequate ground rules and assumptions are used in performing the risk analysis, widely varying and potentially erroneous results can occur for the same risk issue evaluated by different people or for different risk issues evaluated by the same people. For example, if the snapshot in time is not identified for the risk analysis, one person may assume that it represents the current (today's) state of the item, whereas another may assume that it represents the state of the item one year in the future. If this occurs, the estimated level of risk may be different.

Be very wary of comments from analysts or management that state or imply "we all know that information." For example, one time, when I heard this through a government program engineer, I challenged him to press the contractor's engineers to state some simple ground rules and assumptions that should apply to their development program (e.g., technology freeze date). Needless to say, the contractor's engineers were unable to consistently answer these simple, fundamental questions, and the results from a recent risk analysis they performed were suspect.

On most programs relevant ground rules and assumptions can be listed in one to two pages, yet such documentation typically does not exist. After assisting in the development of comprehensive ground rules and assumptions on one program, the program's technical director and systems engineering director remarked with pleasant surprise that such a small amount of text was able to describe adequately the key characteristics of their program. The ground rules and assumptions should be updated as necessary (e.g., when changes in program acquisition or scope occur). Assuming that the ground rules and assumptions are suitably documented, they must be distributed to and used by each person that will perform the risk analysis.

Key ground rules and assumptions needed to perform a risk analysis are typically not adequately identified, documented, and/or distributed. This can lead to erroneous risk analysis results.

C. Classes of Uncertainty

An overly simplistic set of assumptions often exists pertaining to identifying the type of uncertainty that is present and the impact that this may have on a given risk analysis methodology. There are five general classes of uncertainty: 1) certainty; 2) probability distributions of known form embedded in known models, covering known possible states; 3) probability distributions of unknown form embedded in known models; 4) uncertain models (strong uncertainties); and 5) chaos.[1]

A military system in the development phase is typically representative of uncertainty classes 3) and 4). Imperfect information typically exists for a given program of risk category (e.g., threat) attributes; hence, classes 1) and 2) are unlikely. Conversely, some knowledge of possible risk category trends typically exists; hence, class 5) is unlikely. In the Production, Fielding/Deployment, and Operational Support phase, classes 1), 2), and 3) are possible, depending upon the item and its production and Operations and Support history. For items just entering into production, the likely classes of uncertainty are 2) and 3). For items with a long production history but with limited production quantities and annual production rates (e.g., many space programs), the likely classes are 2) and 3). For items with a long production history and with substantial production quantities and annual production rates (e.g., some commercial items), the likely classes are 1) and 2).

Ordinal risk scales ("probability" or consequence) are typically used in situations where uncertainty classes 3) and 4) exist and detailed quantification is not typically possible (see Sec. IV and Appendix H for additional information). Of course, ordinal risk scales can be used with uncertainty classes 1) and 2), but they may not accurately estimate the risk present because there is often insufficient granularity for definitions at the lower scale levels of "probability" scales.

The basis for quantitative analytic or stochastic risk analysis (e.g., Monte Carlo simulations) is class 2), where probability distributions of known form are embedded in known models, covering known possible states. However, a match is unlikely to occur between the true program probability distributions and those used in quantitative risk analysis procedures (e.g., cost or schedule) for programs in the development phase, where classes 3) and 4) are typical. A match may not even occur for items just entering into production or for items with a long production history, but with limited production quantities and annual production rates where classes 2) and 3) are common.

Thus, in most programs in the development phase and for those entering production or with limited production history, even the results of quantitative risk analysis will be at least somewhat uncertain and unreliable.

Different classes of uncertainty will exist for military programs, typically depending upon the acquisition phase of the program. To reduce uncertainty in the results, the selected risk analysis approach should be matched to the program phase and the level of uncertainty present.

D.   Inherent Errors in the Risk Analysis Methodology

The risk analysis methodology may contain errors, whose likelihood and impact do not generally diminish as the level of mathematical sophistication increases. Consequently, risk analysis results may be faulty and/or be far more uncertain than what is believed or touted. For example, the accuracy of risk analysis results is often uncorrelated with, and sometimes inversely proportional to, the number of decimal places reported. (In more than one case I have seen risk analysis results reported to three decimal places that had substantial uncertainty in the first decimal place. Even worse, these problems occurred on programs with a life-cycle cost > $1 billion.)

It is not uncommon to find risk analysis methodologies that on first glance appear to be reasonable, but on closer examination are unsound. In the worst case the underlying basis for the methodology is highly flawed, and the results will be meaningless or erroneous. The opportunity cost associated with using such a methodology may be substantial because of errors, wasted resources, and foreclosed options that can never be recovered.

For example, a methodology was developed by a large high-tech organization for estimating the critical values of probability distributions for use in Monte Carlo simulations. I stopped counting after I had identified *eight different erroneous assumptions and errors* associated with this methodology on a single page!

In another case, a flawed methodology was developed by Ph.D. mathematicians and used by others at a high-tech organization. In other instances the organizations employed those with Ph.D. in mathematics, statistics, and engineering who should have unmasked flawed methodologies developed in house but did not. This was typically because key personnel wanted answers and wanted them quickly and/or did not permit an independent, objective evaluation of the methodology. (The expression "you want it bad, you get it bad" is very appropriate in such cases.) Often, the flawed methodologies are still being used years later!

Whatever risk analysis methodology is used, it should be impartially evaluated to ensure that

1) It has a valid mathematical and probabilistic basis regardless of whether or not it is published in the literature and what its proponents say (e.g., performing mathematical operations on uncalibrated ordinal risk scales will yield erroneous results, yet this is commonly practiced).

2) It can be suitably tailored to a given program (one size does not fit all).

3) Resources needed to successfully implement and use the methodology are well understood (otherwise it may not be adequately implemented or used).

4) The outputs directly support overlaying cost, performance (technical), and schedule risk for a given issue and risk prioritization for that issue (a three-dimensional risk picture is highly desirable for each risk issue).

5) It is possible to identify a level of uncertainty associated with the results (point estimates are rarely correct).

6) Limitations associated with the methodology are well understood (e.g., does it yield risk or an approximation to risk).

Risk analysis methodologies often contain flaws that can lead to degraded or misleading results. In the worst case the results can be meaning-

less or erroneous. An impartial evaluation should be performed of the proposed risk analysis methodology to verify its suitability and identify its limitations. Any errors or substantial limitations identified should be corrected to prevent the results generated from having an adverse impact on the program.

E. Probability vs Consequence of Occurrence Risk Terms

Risk analysts may be confused between what is the probability of occurrence term and what is the consequence of occurrence term for a particular risk issue. In some cases this can lead to results being reversed. As mentioned in Chapter 2, the consequence term relates to the *impact* the issue can have if it fails or the event occurs, whereas the probability term relates to the *likelihood* associated with failing to achieve a particular outcome or the likelihood of an event occurring.

This error can be either overt or subtle. For example, one set of ordinal "probability" scales has wording that begins with "negative outcome is likely (or not likely)" for the definition of each of its levels. Although the error in this case is subtle, negative outcome represents an impact rather than a likelihood, and the wording may confuse the analyst in terms of scoring or how the results are used.

Care should be taken to not confuse methodologies used to estimate the probability and consequence of occurrence risk terms, nor the resulting values.

The emphasis of risk analysis is often on the probability of occurrence term over the consequence of occurrence term. However, equal emphasis should be placed on estimating each risk term, and if either risk term is estimated by a weak or flawed methodology, the resulting risk level will be suspect.

Often detailed methodologies exist for estimating the probability term, while simple and potentially inaccurate methodologies are used for the consequence term. For example, in one case more than 50 uncalibrated ordinal scales used to estimate the "probability" term, yet only three simple four-level scales were used to estimate the consequence term (one scale each for C,P,S).

Equal emphasis should be placed on accurately estimating the probability of occurrence and consequence of occurrence risk terms.

F. Evaluate the Probability and Consequence of Occurrence Risk Terms

The probability and consequence of occurrence terms of risk should be evaluated, then correctly combined to form risk. Failure to do so can lead to erroneous risk analysis results. For example, I've observed in several cases requirements to estimate either the probability of occurrence or consequence of occurrence for risk issues without there being a requirement to determine the level of risk present. (This can be particularly confusing when risk, probability and consequence are used somewhat interchangeably.)

Some risk analysis methodologies directly incorporate both probability and consequence of occurrence terms, such as Monte Carlo simulations, and yield results that are risk. However, results from other approaches may not actually represent risk.

If ordinal risk scales are used, separate scales representing the "probability" and consequence terms must be used, and the results combined using a risk mapping matrix to yield risk (see Sec. IX.A). (However, *risk* cannot be estimated from ordinal scales because the "probability" of occurrence scales is almost never derived from actual probability data. This is independent of the question of whether risk can be estimated from ordinal numbers.) In one large program great care was taken to correctly evaluate the risk "probability" term, yet the consequence term was not examined. While this maybe acceptable for trading highly similar items that have identical function [e.g., different cryogenic coolers that would cool the same focal plane array (FPA)—hence the performance consequence of occurrence term would be the same], it is inadequate when comparing items that have different cost or schedule consequence of occurrence, or when comparing items across the system because different levels of consequence would typically exist (e.g., ranging from none to catastrophic). Thus, the result of only evaluating the "probability" risk term might be incorrect risk prioritization and allocation of funding for risk handling activities.

In another large program the risk analysis methodology used four uncalibrated ordinal scales that were labeled risk, but in actuality three of the scales were related to the "probability" term of risk (e.g., technology maturity) and the other scale was related to the consequence term of risk (potential for cost growth). Although this simplistic approach may be appealing for immature programs (e.g., ones performing system level trades), erroneous results will likely occur because none of the scales actually represented risk.

In another case ordinal "probability" of occurrence scales were inadvertently labeled risk, which led to some confusion as to how they should be applied. In several programs I've also observed one or more ordinal scales whose definitions contain attributes of both "probability" and consequence of occurrence—sometimes within a single scale definition. This is not only incorrect, but potentially confusing to the analyst and may lead to erroneous results.

If a subjective risk analysis is used, the participants should clearly understand whether they are estimating risk, or only a single risk term (probability of occurrence or consequence of occurrence). Without clear ground rules and guidance it is quite possible that a mixture of results may occur among participants—some estimating risk and others estimating only a single risk term. When this occurs, some of the estimates may be erroneous, yet the problem may not be obvious to the participants.

The probability and consequence of occurrence terms of risk should be evaluated, then correctly combined to form risk. Failure to do this can lead to erroneous risk analysis results.

G.   Performance vs Technical Risk

Confusion sometimes exists between estimating performance risk and technical risk. The two risks are interrelated by the underlying design, but substantial differences may otherwise exist.

Assume that the same method of estimating consequence of occurrence can be used for both performance and technical risk. (This is commonly the case in many situations.) In such cases the difference between risk types will be related to the probability risk term.

Performance risk typically assesses how well a given design will operate, whereas technical risk often examines the design and technology implementation associated with meeting performance requirements. In many cases technical risk is evaluated when examining specific hardware or software components (e.g., the availability of a suitable FPA), but in some cases the evaluation of performance risk is necessary (e.g., is the FPA sensitive enough to separate two objects of certain sizes and radiances?). Ordinal scales can often be used to evaluate technical risk, but may not be well suited to evaluate performance risk unless tailored to specific issues (e.g., dark current noise levels for a given FPA) by a requirements flowdown process.

The distinction between technical and performance risk is sometimes clouded when technical ordinal probability scales include phrases such as "meets performance requirements." Often, however, technical risk is evaluated by using ordinal risk scales, whereas performance risk is determined from Monte Carlo simulations. Here, both the probability and consequence of occurrence terms are estimated from different methodologies and may not be readily comparable.

Performance and technical risk are often assumed the same but actually represent different risk categories. Performance risk typically assesses how well a given design will operate, whereas technical risk often examines the design and technology implementation associated with meeting performance requirements.

H.   Estimating the Performance Component of Consequence of Occurrence

A variety of different performance consequence of occurrence dimensions are possible, including, but not limited to 1) overall mission success of the individual system (e.g., spacecraft); 2) the degree that specific requirements can be met (e.g., Can the objective value of all key performance parameters be achieved?); 3) the degree that the given item (e.g., payload) functions properly during operation; 4) the degree that the given item affects overall mission success; and 5) the degree of redesign needed to ensure meeting performance requirements. Because there is no single best way to measure the performance component of consequence of occurrence, the analyst, working with program management, should ensure that the measure(s) chosen are compatible with the system being evaluated and the desires and requirements of the users. In addition, there are a variety of different performance consequence of occurrence orientations and subsequent measurement techniques (e.g., ordinal scales, subjective assessments, and test results). Consequently, the analyst and program management should weigh the pluses and minuses of each of these approaches against its value to the program, ease of use, and the ability to track changes during the course of the program (vs a static approach that will always give the same result), then select the approach(es) best suited to the program.

Various measures of the performance component of consequence of occurrence are possible, and no single measure may be best for all programs. Each candidate approach should be evaluated and approach(es) selected that are best suited to the program.

I.   Some Different Measures of Cost and Schedule in Risk Analysis

Three different measures of cost are common in risk analysis and prioritization. None is universally superior, and each is best suited for specific types of analysis. First, the level of cost risk can be estimated using a Monte Carlo simulation, given an estimate of cost estimating uncertainty, schedule risk, and technical risk. Cost risk derived from a Monte Carlo simulation encompasses both probability and consequence of occurrence and is typically reported as cost at a given cumulative distribution function (CDF) percentile. Second, cost consequence of occurrence is sometimes separately derived from an uncalibrated or calibrated ordinal scale and often measured in terms of percent cost growth (e.g., 5% cost increase) or in dollars (e.g., $5 million cost growth). This information is typically used in estimates of technical risk, which involve separate ordinal "probability" and consequence of occurrence scales. Third, an estimate of the cost consequence can be used in other risk calculations, such as EMV (see Sec. III.D of this chapter).

Four different measures of schedule are common in risk analysis and prioritization. First, the level of schedule risk can be estimated using a Monte Carlo simulation, given a most likely schedule estimate, plus estimates of schedule uncertainty, cost risk, and technical risk. [This assumes that a schedule network exists and activities can be mapped into the work breakdown structure (WBS) used to identify risk issues.] Schedule risk derived from a Monte Carlo simulation encompasses both probability and consequence of occurrence terms and is typically reported as a duration or finish date at a given CDF percentile. Second, schedule consequence of occurrence is sometimes separately derived from an uncalibrated or calibrated ordinal scale and often estimated in terms of percent schedule change (e.g., 5% schedule slip) or time change (e.g., five months schedule slip). This information is typically used in estimates of technical risk, which involve separate ordinal "probability" and consequence of occurrence scales. Third, an estimate of the schedule consequence can be used in other risk calculations such as the schedule equivalent of EMV (see Sec. III.D of this chapter). Fourth, the risk handling plan (RHP) initiation date is the time that exists to begin implementation of the selected RHP and is sometimes called the *"drop dead date."* A refined estimate of this initiation date should be included in the subsequent, approved RHP and the program's integrated master schedule (IMS). On short duration programs or where weak risk management implementation exists, the RHP initiation date may be soon or even immediate. In such cases a rough estimate of the RHP initiation date may become a key metric used as part of risk prioritization.

Finally, estimation of cost and schedule risk using ordinal scales or subjective measures is generally not effective and often yields highly uncertain, if not erroneous, results. However, estimates of cost and schedule risk derived from quantitative risk analysis techniques (e.g., Monte Carlo simulations) can also contain large, uncertain errors unless the methodology is properly developed and implemented and applied in a precise and consistent fashion.

Several different measures of cost and schedule are common in risk analysis and prioritization. None of these measures are universally superior, and each is best suited for specific types of analysis. Each approach can yield erroneous and uncertain answers unless the methodology is properly applied.

J. Risk Related to Items on or near the Program's Schedule Critical Path

In cases where activities are on the program's schedule critical path or on the probabilistic critical path (the critical path developed by a Monte Carlo simulation), a slip in schedule not only induces schedule consequence to the activity itself, but may also impact the schedule and/or cost of other activities. Consequence of occurrence ordinal scales that capture potential cost and schedule impact can be applied at the WBS element or activity under evaluation. However, in some cases an estimate of project-wide cost and schedule impact may be needed to capture the magnitude of the potential problem. For a single WBS element or activity this reduces to the trivial solution—it is just the WBS element or activity in question. For an item on the critical path or on the probabilistic critical path, the potential exists to affect a much larger number of activities (e.g., a schedule slip for an item on the critical path may adversely impact the cost associated with numerous WBS elements). In some cases a schedule slip associated with *a single activity* on the critical path may cause the *entire program* to slip by the same amount. In such cases the financial impact to the program can be substantial, in addition to the schedule impact that will exist.

For activities on or near the program's schedule critical path, a slight slip in schedule can have substantial adverse impact to the program. The risk associated with such activities should be carefully evaluated, along with the resulting program effect, and suitable risk handling strategies developed as warranted prior to problems actually surfacing.

K. Some Helpful Information for Risk Prioritization

Risk prioritization should not be viewed as a separate risk management process step, but part of risk analysis.

Risk prioritization is part of risk analysis and not a separate risk management process step.

Estimates of an issue's probability of occurrence and consequence of occurrence should be made as part of the risk analysis. The resulting risk score should be used as an input to RMB risk prioritization.

Other information that should be estimated and considered for risk prioritization purposes includes the potential RHP initiation date, the risk issue frequency of occurrence (particularly if the issue can occur more than once), and interdependence with other risk issues.

Probability and consequence of occurrence information is essential for computing risk and for subsequent risk prioritization. Also consider the potential RHP initiation date, the risk issue frequency of occurrence, and interdependence with other risk issues for risk prioritization.

While a number of methods can be used to prioritize risk issues, the primary one involves risk level, with probability and consequence terms, and potentially modified by such things as time sensitivity, frequency of occurrence, and interdependence with other risk issues. It is not meaningful to develop a list of prioritized risks based upon risk category or consequence of occurrence component, because the interrelationship between the possible groupings are typically unknown. For example, if you prioritize risk by C,P,S consequence of occurrence, the results will not be meaningful because: 1) cost consequence, for example, is only one of three components of consequence of occurrence, and 2) the relative weight of cost vs performance vs schedule consequence components is almost always unknown [and not likely equal (1/3, 1/3, 1/3)]. Similarly, if risks are prioritized by risk category (e.g., technology vs design vs manufacturing for hardware), each category is only one of "n" components of the probability term of risk, and the relative weight of one probability term vs the others is unknown (and generally not equal).

Do not develop a list of prioritized risks based upon risk category or consequence of occurrence component because the interrelationship between the possible groupings are typically unknown.

Risk categories should not directly be used to rate resulting risk levels. For example, it is not correct to presume that risk issues within a certain risk category (e.g., technology) should automatically have a higher risk level than risk issues within a different risk category (e.g., manufacturing). This type of subjective weighting may lead to both uncertain and erroneous results and should not be used. [Note: This is different than risk = probability * consequence where probability and consequence are a weighted average of different probability and consequence terms, as with between-scale weights for calibrated ordinal scales. Here the risk category coefficients are only used to estimate a weighted average risk level, performed actually at the "probability"-term level (e.g., technology, design, manufacturing), rather than at the risk level. Risk-level weighting is incorrect, as is probability-term weighting unless calibrated ordinal scales or some similar methodology is used.]

Do not use risk categories as a criteria for rating resulting risk levels.

In cases where ordinal risk scales are used, ranking risk issues should be based upon the resulting risk levels (e.g., L, M, H), plus additional considerations as warranted [e.g., the potential RHP initiation date, the risk issue frequency of occurrence (particularly if the issue can occur more than once), interdependence with other risk issues], not just the consequence of occurrence term of risk. The resulting risk score will generally be unitless, but when risk is derived from other methodologies it may not be unitless. For example, with a Monte Carlo simulation, EMV, or some other quantitative approaches the resulting risk score will often have units (e.g., dollars for cost risk).

Risk scores derived from ordinal scales will generally be unitless, but when risk is derived from other methodologies it may not be unitless.

It is not meaningful to rank risks by data quality for several reasons. First, it is often difficult, if not impossible, to accurately bound the potential range of uncertainty around a risk level, particularly when subjective assessments are performed. Even when quantitative evaluations are performed, actual results can be far outside of the bounds thought possible (even the anticipated 0 and 100 percentile values). Second, even if you could accurately bound the uncertainties, unless the risk levels estimated were cardinal, there is typically no meaningful way to combine the uncertainty and risk level data. Subjectively combining uncertainty data with risk level data will in and of itself introduce an unknown uncertainty term despite the appearance of both accuracy and precision! (This is made all the worse when both the risk levels and uncertainty estimates are based upon subjective assessments, then you may have nothing more than one set of guesses obscuring another set of guesses!)

Do not rank risks by data quality; the results may be subjective, uncertain, and meaningless.

L. Validation of Risk Analysis Methodologies

Risk analysis methodologies should be validated before widespread use on a program to identify and correct approaches that yield erroneous results and are too resource intensive. The former problem can lead to erroneous decisions being made, whereas the latter problem can prevent the full implementation of the methodology. Unfortunately, the validation that is performed is typically not done in an objective, structured fashion.

In addition, validation of a new or enhanced risk analysis methodology cannot always be performed by comparing the results to those generated from the existing methodology. The existing methodology is never perfect and rarely without defect, yet generally not totally imperfect or defective. Hence, direct comparison of results between the existing and enhanced methodologies will typically not yield an objective measure of how much better the enhanced methodology is compared to the existing methodology.

For example, in one case the enhanced methodology was presumed to be more accurate, but the risk score variation or spread among issues believed to be medium and high risk was actually less than that achieved with the previous (existing) methodology. More than a year later the participants still had not identified that one substantial source of this reduced variation was caused by not having properly normalized the calibrated ordinal scales used to estimate the "probability" and consequence of occurrence risk scores. (Thus, the resulting product of "probability" and consequence tended to be lower and have a smaller range than would otherwise be reasonable.)

The validation should also constitute a trial run of the risk analysis methodology to estimate the 1) level of training desired, 2) resources needed, 3) aspects of the methodology that are confusing and require correction, and 4) number of iterations typically required to yield acceptable results. This validation process also provides the opportunity for management to approve the risk analysis process and its methodology before it is implemented on a full-scale basis.

In addition, an independent analysis is often needed to determine the degree to which the existing methodology and the new or enhanced methodology are sound. Results from each methodology must also pass a "sanity check" indicating that they are credible. The independent analysis is also needed because there is generally no best way to develop a methodology for a given risk category (including its probability risk of occurrence terms) or across categories (e.g., how results should be aggregated for multiple risk categories).

Risk analysis methodologies should be validated before widespread use to prevent errors from adversely affecting program decisions and to ensure the methodology is suitable to be implemented (e.g., resources needed are not excessive). An independent analysis should also be performed to determine the degree to which the risk analysis methodology is sound.

M. Uncertainty Associated with Risk Analysis Results

Any risk analysis is likely to be based on incomplete knowledge combined with assumptions, each of which is a source of uncertainty that limits the accuracy that should be ascribed to the results.[2]

In the best case, risk analysis results will be at least somewhat uncertain and should not be blindly accepted. Even when an accurate risk analysis methodology exists and is properly implemented, the results should be used as an indicator to management of potential problems and progress to resolve them. In most cases it is delusional to think that a risk rating of 0.85 is any different than another of 0.80, particularly because the level of uncertainty around the point estimates is typically not quantified and hence is unknown. Yet on numerous occasions I have witnessed both technical specialists and key program management personnel having almost blind faith in numerical risk scores without considering the level of uncertainty present. The result can be poor decision making that can have a strong adverse impact on the program. In the preceding example the proper perspective should be that both risk ratings (0.85 and 0.80) likely indicate high-risk issues and require substantial management attention to address the underlying problems, rather than debating the merits of a score of 0.85 vs 0.80.

Risk analysis results should be used as an indicator to management of potential problems and progress to resolve them. They should not, however, be blindly accepted because the level of uncertainty present is typically not quantified and hence is unknown. It is particularly important not to make key decisions based upon slight differences in numerical risk scores without carefully investigating the credibility of the results.

An unknown level of uncertainty often exists for probability of occurrence, consequence of occurrence, and, thus, risk results. This can be true for results generated from ordinal "probability" and consequence scales, subjective assessments, or Monte Carlo simulations. In effect, the probability, consequence, and other key values selected (e.g., scores from ordinal scales or critical values for the risk distribution associated with the critical values for a given WBS) are typically chosen as if no uncertainty exists, when in effect nonzero uncertainty almost always exists.

Even worse, no attempt is typically made to quantify the level of uncertainty present through sensitivity analyses or other techniques in conjunction with the risk analysis. The lack of an uncertainty analysis will not always invalidate risk analysis results, but in some cases it can lead to faulty decisions being made because the true level of confidence is less than the anticipated level.

For example, when probability distributions are selected for use in Monte Carlo simulations, rarely if ever does the analyst consider that the critical values that describe the distribution for a given item (e.g., optimistic, low; pessimistic, high; and most likely values for a triangle distribution) themselves contain uncertainty, which unfortunately is almost never quantified. (Assuming that the uncertainty was known, then a distribution of values associated with each critical value could be identified, and the simulation performed using draws from separate probability distributions for each critical value per iteration. See Secs. VII.H and VII.D for additional information.) Similarly, when ordinal risk scales are used, the analyst rarely estimates the uncertainty associated with "probability" of occurrence and consequence of occurrence scores.

Although implementing uncertainty into a Monte Carlo simulation or other forms of quantitative risk analysis is sometimes impractical, not implementing uncertainty may lead to diminished accuracy and decreased confidence in the results vs the true values.

Some questions developed by the National Research Council that analysts and decision makers should ask regarding uncertainty in risk analysis results include the following: [2]

"1) What are the weaknesses of the available data? Information needed to estimate the risks . . . of an activity . . . often do not exist. Sometimes experts dispute the accuracy or reliability of the data that are available. And often not enough is known to extrapolate confidently from those data to estimates of risk.

2) What are the assumptions and models on which the estimates are based when data are missing or uncertain or when methods of estimation are in dispute? How much dispute exists among experts about the choice of assumptions and models?

3) How sensitive are the estimates to changes in the assumptions or models? That is, how much would the estimate change if it used different plausible assumptions . . . or different methods for converting available data into estimates? What are the boundaries or confidence limits within which the correct risk estimate probably falls? What is the basis for concluding that the correct estimate is not likely to lie outside those bounds?

4) How sensitive is the decision to changes in the estimates? That is, if, because of uncertainty, an estimate of risk . . . were wrong by a factor of 2 or more, would the decision maker's choice be any different?

5) What other risk assessments have been made, and why are they different from those now being offered?"

Risk analysis results often contain uncertainty. In many cases no attempt is made to quantify the uncertainty present in probability of occurrence, consequence of occurrence, and/or risk results. The uncertainty associated with risk analysis results should be estimated and presented to key program personnel, particularly when critical program decisions are being made.

III. Representation of Risk

A. *Some Common Representations of Risk*

When suitable, meaningful probability and consequence of occurrence quantitative data is available, it is often desired to compute risk via a mathematical equation. There is no perfect mathematical representation of risk, but some approaches are more suitable than others for project risk management applications. Two forms widely used to represent risk (often termed risk factor) include the following:

$$\text{Risk Factor} = P * C \qquad (1)$$

and

$$\text{Risk Factor} = P \cup C = P + C - P \cap C \qquad (2)$$

where

$$P \cap C = P * C \qquad (3)$$

Thus,

$$P \cup C = P + C - P * C \qquad (4)$$

where P is the probability of occurrence and C the consequence of occurrence. The second representation is mathematically known as the union of P and C ($P \cup C$) and is related to the algebra of sets (collection of objects). Although I have not identified the first citation for this risk factor form, an early one in DoD literature occurred in 1983.[3] Formally, $A \cup B$ represents the set of all elements that belong to at least one of the sets A and B (Ref. 4). This is the equivalent of saying that $A \cup B$ is the set of all elements in A or B or in both A and B. (This last term "in both A and B" is also known as the intersection of A and B, which is denoted as $A \cap B$.) Pictorially, if you have two overlapping circles, A and B, $A \cup B$ is the area of circle A + the area of circle B − the overlapping (intersecting) area that is common to circles A and B.

There are two serious problems with the $P \cup C$ risk factor. First, although $P \cup C$ may not be incorrect from a purely mathematical perspective, its use raises difficult questions without apparent, convincing answers. How can probability of occurrence (which is unitless) and consequence of occurrence (which typically has units, e.g., dollars) be added, as required by the additive term $P + C$ in Eq. (4)? In addition, $P \cup C$ requires that probability and consequence of occurrence intersect [$P \cap C$ Eq. (3)]. This requires that P and C overlap [more formally the set of all elements that belong to each of the sets P and C (Ref. 4)—the overlapping set of values that is common to P and C]. Yet how can probability and consequence of occurrence overlap when they represent completely different entities and they are independent of each other? There are no convincing arguments that either of these difficulties can be satisfactorily resolved. Thus, there is no persuasive basis to permit the use of the $P \cup C$ risk factor [(Eq. (2)].

The second problem with $P \cup C$ is that a high P and low C or low P and high C can give the same results as a high P and high C. This form of the risk factor can yield misleading results that can adversely impact design trades and allocating funding for risk handling based on risk prioritization. For example, items that do not require development but have a critical impact on mission performance can have a large resulting risk factor because they have a high performance component of consequence of occurrence despite the fact that they are well understood and proven items.

I will now present three related examples from an actual spacecraft development program to illustrate the second problem with the $P \cup C$ risk factor. The spacecraft risk assessment identified 54 risk issues that were analyzed with calibrated ordinal "probability" and consequence of occurrence scales.

An electrical power system (EPS) battery with a well-proven technology, design, and manufacturing process might have a low P, yet because of its criticality to the spacecraft it may have a high performance component of C. [The actual level of performance consequence of occurrence depends on how this component is defined. If it is defined as the degree that the given item affects overall mission success, then the resulting score will be very high. However, if it is defined as the degree that the given item, (e.g., payload), functions properly during operation or the degree of redesign needed to ensure meeting performance requirements, then the resulting score will be noticeably lower.] In the risk analyses performed for this program, the performance component of consequence of occurrence was related to how the item affects overall mission success. A normalized calibrated ordinal scale was used for the performance component of consequence of occurrence, and the coefficients between levels and scales were determined by the Analytical Hierarchy Process (AHP, see Appendix H, Sec. VII).

In the risk analyses performed for this program, the "probability" of occurrence included technology maturity, design/engineering maturity, and five forms of manufacturing maturity. A normalized calibrated ordinal scale was used for each of these categories, and the coefficients between levels and between scales were determined by AHP.

The resulting EPS battery P and C scores were 0.06 and 1.00, respectively.

(Although there is likely uncertainty in the first, and certainly the second decimal place, the P and C scores are reported here to two decimal places for illustration purposes only.) The resulting EPS battery risk factor values are

$$\text{Risk Factor (EPS Battery)} = P * C = 0.06 * 1.00 = 0.06$$

$$\begin{aligned}\text{Risk Factor (EPS Battery)} &= P + C - P * C \\ &= 0.06 + 1.00 - 0.06 * 1.00 = 1.00\end{aligned}$$

When using the first risk representation, the EPS battery risk is 17 times lower than the $P \cup C$ form and much more reasonable from a technology maturation and operational perspective. When the $P \cup C$ form is used, the EPS battery risk is unrealistically large—as large as any other item on this program.

Using the first risk representation, the maximum risk value for the entire program was the mid-wave infrared/long-wave infrared (MWIR/LWIR) sensor integration, assembly, and test (IA&T). The P and C values for this item are 0.30 and 1.00, respectively. Hence, the resulting risk factor values are

$$\text{Risk Factor (Sensor IA\&T)} = P * C = 0.30 * 1.00 = 0.30$$

$$\begin{aligned}\text{Risk Factor (Sensor IA\&T)} &= P + C - P * C \\ &= 0.30 + 1.00 - 0.30 * 1.00 = 1.00\end{aligned}$$

When using the first risk representation $(P * C)$, the risk rating is 3 times lower than the $P \cup C$ form and also more reasonable from a technology maturation and operational perspective. When the $P \cup C$ form is used, the MWIR/LWIR sensor IA&T risk factor is also unrealistically large.

Comparing the MWIR/LWIR sensor IA&T and EPS battery risk factor values when using the second representation $(P \cup C)$, *there is no difference in scores;* while using the first representation $(P * C)$, the risk factor for MWIR/LWIR sensor IA&T is *over five times larger than that for the EPS battery!*

Of the 54 issues contained in the spacecraft risk analysis, there were 12 issues having a risk factor value of 1.0 with $P \cup C$ (the EPS battery was one of the 12). Hence, the risk factor associated with the EPS battery was tied for having the highest risk on the program. However, when the first representation was used, the EPS battery was ranked as the 31st highest risk.

I realize that the preceding example was somewhat extreme: the results would be less dramatic if the cost and schedule consequence of occurrence components were included because they would likely have a lower magnitude than the performance component. Thus, the weighted average of the three consequence of occurrence components estimated from calibrated ordinal scales would be lower than 1.00, and the resulting P ∪ C value would be < 1.00.

Although it was not done at the time the program generated the risk analysis, I have included a second example that shows the resulting risk factor from the two different risk factor representations. Here, the only difference is the use of a modified performance component of consequence of occurrence (which reflects the degree of redesign needed to ensure meeting performance requirements, rather than the degree that the given issue affects overall mission success, which was used in the first example). As before, the coefficients between levels and between scales were determined by AHP.

The resulting EPS battery P and C scores were 0.06 and 0.07, respectively. The resulting EPS battery risk factor values are

$$\text{Risk Factor (EPS Battery)} = P * C = 0.06 * 0.07 = 0.004$$

$$\begin{aligned}\text{Risk Factor (EPS Battery)} &= P + C - P * C \\ &= 0.06 + 0.07 - 0.06 * 0.07 = 0.13\end{aligned}$$

When using the first risk representation (P * C), the EPS battery risk is 30 times lower than the P ∪ C form and more reasonable from a technology maturation and performance consequence of occurrence perspective. When the P ∪ C form is used, the EPS battery risk is considerably lower than the P ∪ C form in the first example because of differences in the performance consequence of occurrence risk scale.

The P and C values for sensor IA&T are 0.30 and 0.15, respectively. Hence, the resulting risk factor values are

$$\text{Risk Factor (Sensor IA\&T)} = P * C = 0.30 * 0.15 = 0.05$$

$$\begin{aligned}\text{Risk Factor (Sensor IA\&T)} &= P + C - P * C \\ &= 0.30 + 0.15 - 0.30 * 0.15 = 0.41\end{aligned}$$

When using the first risk representation, the risk rating is 9 times lower than the P ∪ C form and also more reasonable from a technology maturation and performance consequence of occurrence perspective.

The results from the second example also illustrate the effect that a single risk scale can have on the results. In this case only changing the performance consequence of occurrence scale led to a change in the first risk representation of 14 times (EPS battery) and 6 times (sensor IA&T) vs the first example. Using the P ∪ C representation, the change in performance consequence of occurrence scale led to a change of about 8 times (EPS battery) and over 2 times (sensor IA&T) versus the first example. These risk factor changes are quite substantial and should serve as a caution to the analyst who might somewhat arbitrarily select ordinal scales for a risk analysis, particularly when the scale can have a substantial impact on the overall risk score.

A third and final example is also provided that shows the resulting risk factor from the two different risk factor representations. This example uses the modified performance component of consequence of occurrence introduced in the second example. It also includes cost and schedule components of consequence of occurrence as well. The coefficients between levels and between scales for the C,P,S consequence ordinal scales were determined by AHP.

The resulting EPS battery P and C scores were 0.06 and 0.14, respectively. (The C,P,S consequence components were 0.18, 0.07, and 0.23. The weighting between components was not uniform, e.g., not 1/3, 1/3, and 1/3.) The resulting EPS battery risk factor values are

$$\text{Risk Factor (EPS Battery)} = P * C = 0.06 * 0.14 = 0.008$$

$$\text{Risk Factor (EPS Battery)} = P + C - P * C$$
$$= 0.06 + 0.14 - 0.06 * 0.14 = 0.19$$

When using the first risk representation (P * C), the EPS battery risk is 23 times lower than the P ∪ C form and more reasonable from a technology maturation and consequence of occurrence perspective. When the P ∪ C form is used, the EPS battery risk is considerably lower than the P ∪ C form in first example because of differences in the consequence of occurrence risk scale.

The P and C values for sensor IA&T are 0.30 and 0.39, respectively. Hence, the resulting risk factor values are

$$\text{Risk Factor (Sensor IA\&T)} = P * C = 0.30 * 0.39 = 0.12$$

$$\text{Risk Factor (Sensor IA\&T)} = P + C - P * C$$
$$= 0.30 + 0.39 - 0.30 * 0.39 = 0.57$$

When using the first risk representation (P * C), the risk rating is about 5 times lower than the P ∪ C form and also more reasonable from a technology maturation and consequence of occurrence perspective.

The results from the third example illustrate the effect that using a single consequence of occurrence component can have on the results. In this case adding the cost and schedule consequence of occurrence scales led to a change in the first risk representation of 2 times (EPS battery) and over two times (sensor IA&T) vs the second example where only the performance consequence of occurrence component was included. Using the P ∪ C representation, adding the cost and schedule consequence of occurrence scales led to a change of about 1.5 times (EPS battery) and about 1.4 times (sensor IA&T) vs the second example. These risk factor changes are also fairly substantial and should serve as a caution to the analyst who might select only a single consequence of occurrence component for a risk analysis, rather than using C,P,S components.

In the three examples just given (and six different risk factor computations), the first risk factor representation (P * C) value was considerably lower (3 to 30 times) than the P ∪ C value. In addition, if either the P or C risk term is high, then the resulting risk factor value will be high with the P ∪ C representation (as illustrated in the first example). Given these issues, when suitable quantitative data are available, it is recommended that the first risk factor representation be used (P * C), and the P ∪ C form not be used.

Of course, neither the first (P * C) nor the second (P ∪ C) risk factor can be used with data from uncalibrated ordinal "probability" and consequence of occurrence scales or the results will be meaningless (see Sec. IV.B of this chapter).

*Risk values can vary considerably depending upon the equation used to calculate the risk factor, as well as the source of the probability (P) and consequence of occurrence (C) terms. When suitable quantitative data are available, it is recommended that risk be computed via P * C, and not from the union of probability and consequence (P ∪ C = P + C − P * C). The analyst is also cautioned not to arbitrarily select ordinal scales for a risk analysis, nor estimate risk using only a single consequence of occurrence component, rather than using C,P,S components.*

B. Some Risk Representations to Avoid

I have also come across several other different representations of risk besides the two common ones mentioned in Sec. III.A. Four additional representations are outlined next. The one thing they all have in common is that there is no persuasive basis to permit their use.

The first risk factor representation is one variation of P ∪ C sometimes used in software risk analysis:

$$\text{Risk Factor} = P \cup C = P + C - 0.1\,(P \cap C)$$

where $0 \le P \le 10$ and $0 \le C \le 10$. Here, both P and C were computed from uncalibrated ordinal scales whose possible values were 1, 3, 5, 7, and 9. Note that in this case the risk factor was not properly normalized—with P = 9 and

C = 9, the risk factor = 9.9. (Instead of using 0.1 as the normalizing term, 0.111 should have been used to obtain the risk factor of 10.) Having a risk factor > 1 is also somewhat counterintuitive, but this is a minor problem compared to the erroneous assumption associated with performing mathematics on values obtained from uncalibrated ordinal "probability" and consequence of occurrence scales.

The second risk factor representation simply adds probability and consequence of occurrence values to obtain risk (e.g., Risk Factor = P + C). This is equivalent to $P \cup C$ [Eq. (2)], but where $P \cap C = 0$ [Eq. (3)]. (Note: The assertion that $P \cap C = 0$ in this case is typically not stated, yet it is a necessary condition.) In addition as just given, how can probability of occurrence (which is unitless) and consequence of occurrence (which typically has units, e.g., dollars) be added and what does the result represent? In addition, if this risk factor is used with data from uncalibrated ordinal "probability" and consequence of occurrence scales (which was the case in the actual application), the results will be meaningless (see Sec. IV.B of this chapter).

The third risk factor representation employs an equation beyond simple multiplication (or $P \cup C$) to combine probability and consequence of occurrence terms into risk. For example, in one case risk was given by $(X*Consequence^2 + Probability^2)^{0.5}$ where $X > 1.0$, yet no convincing basis exists for its use. Another error with this approach is that the equation weights one term of risk more than the other (e.g., consequence of occurrence has a higher weight than probability of occurrence). However, there is no logical basis for having such weights. (For example, the preceding representation does not imply a risk averse, risk neutral, or risk taker position.) In addition, if this risk factor is used with data from uncalibrated ordinal "probability" and consequence of occurrence scales (which was the case in the actual application), the results will be meaningless (See. Sec. IV.B of this chapter).

The fourth risk factor representation involves using multiple probability scales. In this illustration I have chosen two such scales:

$$\text{Risk Factor} = [P(A) + P(B) - P(A) * P(B)] * [a * C_c + b * C_p + c * C_s],$$

where: A = Probability scale 1 score
       B = Probability scale 2 score
       C_c = Cost consequence of occurrence score
       C_p = Performance consequence of occurrence score
       C_s = Schedule consequence of occurrence score
       a = weight for C_c
       b = weight for C_p
       c = weight for C_s

This representation is never valid from results from uncalibrated ordinal scales, since the "probability" terms are not probabilities and the weights associated with the C,P,S consequence scales are almost certainly (unstructured) guesses. Similarly, even with calibrated ordinal scales, unless the calibration was performed using actual probability values (which is very rare), then again, the "probability" terms are not probabilities. Hence, this risk factor form should not be used.

There are innumerable representations of risk possible, but most do not appear to have a convincing mathematical or probabilistic basis. Computation of risk should generally be performed using a simple multiplicative representation (P * C), assuming the underlying data do not violate any other mathematical or probabilistic principle.

Several other variants of incorrect risk representations are possible, including those that use weighting coefficients and time frame.

Using weighting coefficients will not make an invalid risk representation valid. For example:

$$\text{Risk Factor} = P + C$$

is just as invalid as:

$$\text{Risk Factor} = a * P + b * C$$

regardless of how a and b are estimated and constrained (e.g., $a + b = 1$).

Another representation of risk to avoid is one that attempts to directly include a term such as the time to impact in estimating the risk score, such as:

$$\text{Risk Factor} = a * P + b * C + c * T$$

where T refers to the time frame needed to begin risk handling, regardless of how a, b, and c are estimated and constrained (e.g., $a + b + c = 1$).

Similarly, even if a correct representation for estimating the risk factor existed (e.g., P * C), adding a term associated with time frame will often lead to erroneous results. Four different representations of the risk factor are now given that includes a time-frame term:

$$\text{Risk Factor} = P * C + a * T$$

$$\text{or Risk Factor} = a * (P * C) + b * T$$

$$\text{or Risk Factor} = P * C * (a * T)$$

$$\text{or Risk Factor} = a * (P * C) * (b * T)$$

In the above four cases, it is unclear which representation is correct/incorrect or best/worst, and how the weighting coefficients can accurately be estimated. For example, even if P, C, and T can be accurately estimated, how would you estimate the weighting coefficients and which form of the representation including time frame would you choose? If you say that you will estimate the coefficients from utility theory, how would you balance risk against time frame, what form of the equation would you use (multiplicative or additive), and how many coefficients would you include (e.g., one or two from above)? Here, it is not sufficient to say that decision makers can accurately balance risk against time frame, and thus choose suitable coefficients for a given form of the equation, since the entities are fundamentally different, as with P and C since they represent different sets. Even if the coefficients are carefully estimated you may thus develop precise risk factor scores that are highly inaccurate.

Note: For calibrated ordinal and ratio scales the resulting "probability" term will be a * P and the consequence term will be b * C where a and b are estimated coefficient values. Hence, in these cases the (valid) risk factor is given by

$$\text{Risk Factor} = (a * P) * (b * C)$$

In the simplest representation, which should generally be used unless convincing evidence exists to select another set of coefficients, assume that a = b = 1 and the risk factor = P * C.

Variants of incorrect risk representations including those that use weighting coefficients and time frame will almost always lead to incorrect results and should not be used.

C. Range of Risk Factor Values

Although there is no rule or mathematical requirement to do so, it is often desirable that risk values have an upper bound of 1.0 when they are obtained from ordinal "probability" and consequence of occurrence scales. An upper-bound risk > 1.0 may be psychologically difficult to assess or interpret even though it may not be numerically incorrect. Whereas probability data are clearly bounded from 0.0 to 1.0, no such constraint exists for consequence of occurrence data. (However, for consequence of occurrence data an upper limit of 1.0 can readily be achieved by normalizing the scale to the upper-bound value.)

Whatever the resulting risk scale bounds are, they should be documented and clearly stated. For example, in one case the lower-bound risk as derived from the equation used was 0.0 whereas upper bound was > 1.0. However, the analyst was not informed that the upper-bound level was > 1.0, and the implication was that a maximum level of 1.0 existed. This situation could adversely affect the decision-making process. For example, if the analyst or decision maker presumed risk values were bounded from 0.0 to 1.0, but the upper bound was actually 2.0, then this could affect how thresholds were set separating low, medium, and high risk.

For some applications and sources of probability and consequence of occurrence data, it is desirable for risk that the bound of risk values be from 0.0 to 1.0. In any event the bound of risk values should be clearly documented to prevent decision making from being adversely impacted.

D. Use of Decision Analysis

In some cases multiple outcomes are possible for a given risk issue. Here, it may be possible to evaluate the risk events (and the resulting strategies) using decision analysis. Ideally, the analyst would have a defined probability associated with each outcome. Given C,P,S outcome information (e.g., consequence of occurrence), then the expected C,P,S outcomes could be computed for each branch. [When a decision tree only involves defined probabilities and cost outcomes, it is sometimes termed "expected monetary value" (EMV). Equivalent terms can be developed for performance and schedule variants.]

I will now present a very simple example of EMV. An extended discussion of decision analysis techniques is beyond the scope of this book, but numerous good references are available.[5-9] (The treatment here of the application of decision analysis to risk analysis is very brief and limited to some risk analysis considerations. References 5 and 6 provide a comprehensive treatment of decision analysis and its potential application to risk analysis.) The decision tree representing this problem is given in Fig. 6.1. (For a discussion of decision making under certainty and uncertainty involving payoff matrices, see Sec. III.E. Other good concise discussions of decision making under uncertainty involving payoff matrices are given in Refs. 7 and 8. For a game theory treatment of decision making under certainty and uncertainty involving payoff matrices and much more, see Ref. 9.)

Assume a case with a single node that leads to two possible outcomes, and only the cost outcome is nonzero. If the probability associated with the first branch occurring is 0.90 and the cost outcome is $500, then the resulting cost EMV is $450. For the second branch the probability of occurrence is 0.10 (the branch probabilities must sum to 1.00), while the cost outcome is $9000, then the resulting EMV is $900. In this example the second branch has a 100% higher EMV even though it is only 11% as likely to occur as the first branch.

EMV (or the performance and schedule equivalent) is typically used when relatively accurate estimates exist for the probabilities and outcomes. Unfortunately, probabilities of events occurring, and even the C,P,S outcomes, may be difficult to quantify and may be fairly uncertain when real world data are absent. This is particularly disappointing because many key

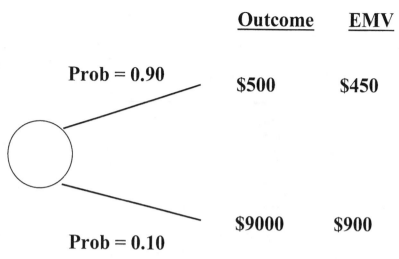

Fig. 6.1   Example decision tree.

decisions are made that affect the system's ultimate design and life-cycle cost during the early portions of the development phase. Thus, although EMV (or equivalent) can potentially be helpful, it should be cautiously used because an unknown level of uncertainty may exist for the defined probabilities even if the outcomes (e.g., cost) are highly certain.

Ordinal "probability" and consequence of occurrence scales are generally not helpful in estimating likely outcomes in decision analysis. In almost all cases, ordinal "probability" scales do not represent true probability, but some other characteristic (e.g., development maturity) and cannot be accurately used. [Also, ordinal estimative "probability" scales that appear to represent probabilities are generally poorly developed and often inadequate for evaluating an issue represented by a probability value. (See Sec. IV.C of this chapter for additional information.) Similarly, many ordinal consequence of occurrence scales are also inadequate unless they are adjusted to represent actual values rather than percentages, e.g., a cost impact of $100,000 should be used instead of a 10% increase in cost.]

A Monte Carlo simulation can be performed when there is uncertainty in the branch probabilities and/or outcomes, assuming of course that the distributions can be accurately identified. When outcomes can be clearly defined, yet there is a range of potential probabilities, it is sometimes possible to approximate a continuous probability CDF with a discrete distribution consisting of only a few values and use this in a decision-tree analysis.[10]

In cases where reasonably accurate estimates of the branch probabilities cannot be made, yet the EMV (or equivalent) for each branch may be relatively high, it may be necessary to develop RHPs for each branch. If funding and time permit, the RHPs can be implemented in parallel. Otherwise, one should be designated the primary plan and the others backup plans with a decision date defined as to when the backups must either be selected or rejected. (Of course, the backups should be prioritized and used as needed. Also note that each backup may have its own "drop dead date" for successful implementation.)

Decision analysis techniques can be used to select optimal strategies when relatively accurate estimates exist for the probabilities and C,P,S outcomes. However, probabilities of events occurring, and even the C,P,S outcomes, may be difficult to quantify and fairly uncertain when applicable real world data are absent. In some cases it may be possible to overcome this limitation by performing a Monte Carlo simulation of the decision tree with the probability values and/or potential outcomes modeled as distributions, or by the use of other statistical approaches.

The EMV and similar calculations may not represent an average value that the decision maker would achieve if they evaluated the probability and consequence values a given number of times. At a minimum, this presupposes knowledge of the underlying probability distribution(s). For example, does the probability value selected represent the mean, median, mode, or some unspecified percentile value? In addition, EMV and similar calculations require the assumption that the parties are risk neutral—something that may or may not be true at any given period of time and may change during the course of the program.

The EMV and similar calculations may not represent an average value that the decision maker would achieve if they evaluated the probability and consequence values a given number of times.

E. Payoff Matrices

Payoff matrices are sometimes used to estimate possible outcomes. They represent a two-person game against an opponent with no known utility function. Four commonly used payoff matrices include 1) Laplace criterion, 2) Wald's maximin, 3) Hurwicz optimism criterion, and 4) Savage's minimax regret.

For the examples presented here, assume the simple payoff matrix given in Table 6.2.

Table 6.2 Payoff matrix

Strategy	Nature (State 1)	Nature (State 2)
Option 1	100	−50
Option 2	50	50

For the Laplace criterion, if the probabilities are unknown, assume all are equal. Then pick the option with the maximum expected value. Hence:

Expected value (Option 1) = 0.5 * 100 + 0.5 * −50 = 25

Expected value (Option 2) = 0.5 * 50 + 0.5 * 50 = 50, and

Choose option 2 (50)

For Wald's maximin, find the minimum payoff for each option, then pick the maximum of the minimum payoffs. Hence:

Option 1 = −50

Option 2 = 50, and

Choose option 2 (50)

For the Hurwicz optimism criterion (also known as the maximax criterion), find the maximum payoff for each option, then pick the maximum of the maximum payoffs. Hence:

Option 1 = 100

Option 2 = 50, and

Choose option 1 (100)

For Savage's minimax regret, take the maximum of any column minus its other entries (this is a regret). Then pick the minimum of the (maximum) regrets. The resulting regrets for each option and state are given in Table 6.3.

Choose option 2(50)

Payoff matrices representing a two-person game against an opponent with no known utility function are sometimes used to estimate possible outcomes. Four commonly used payoff matrices include 1) Laplace criterion, 2) Wald's maximin, 3) Hurwicz optimism criterion, and 4) Savage's minimax regret.

IV. Risk Analysis Methodology

A. Scales Used in Risk Analysis

Scales that relate (word) definitions for a given level to a resulting score are often used as a methodology for estimating the risk probability and

Table 6.3   Savage minimax regret matrix

Strategy	Nature (State 1)	Nature (State 2)	Maximum Regret
Option 1	0	100	100
Option 2	50	0	50

consequence of occurrence terms. Six types of scales are common, and only some are suitable for use in risk analysis. (Reference 11 contains a good introductory discussion of nominal, interval, ordinal, and ratio scales. It does not, however, contain information on calibrated ordinal scales or estimative probability scales. The material presented on ordinal scales is not from Pariseau and Oswalt, but from my own original research first published in a contract report in 1991 and continuing through the present time.)

The first scale type is a nominal scale. Here, the numerical values are only placeholder numbers (such as the numbering of freeways). The values have no mathematical meaning or relationship and are not ordinal or cardinal. Mathematical operations performed on the values are meaningless. Nominal scales are not used in risk analysis.

The second scale type is ordinal. (I call ordinal scales uncalibrated, also known as "raw," through much of this chapter and Appendix H to differentiate them from calibrated ordinal scales, the fourth scale type.) Ordinal scale levels are actually only rank-ordered values, and the scale levels whether 1, 2, 3, and so on or 0.1, 0.2, 0.3, and so on are no different than A, B, C, and so on. (In fact, using letters to represent ordinal scale values rather than numbers has considerable merit because it tends to discourage people from attempting to perform mathematical operations on the results.) This is because the true increments between adjacent scale levels are unknown. Ordinal scale values are not cardinal values, and there is no probabilistic or mathematical justification to perform common math operations (e.g., addition, multiplication, or averaging) on scale values. Similarly, more elaborate mathematical operations on values obtained from these scales also have no basis. For example, in one case, the root sum square $[x = (a^2 + b^2 + c^2)^{0.5}]$ was applied to results from ordinal "probability" and consequence of occurrence scales to combine values. Mathematical operations performed on values derived from ordinal scales will almost always yield meaningless results, unless the scales have been calibrated (the fourth type of scale) or in the exceedingly rare instance where the ordinal scale was derived from actual probability data. (See Appendix H for a discussion of different types of ordinal scales.) Meaningful mathematical operations cannot be performed on a combination of cardinal and ordinal numbers, and the results in most cases will still be ordinal. For example, you cannot multiply a cardinal probability of occurrence times an ordinal consequence of occurrence value and get meaningful results. A simple example illustrates this point.

Assume that for risk issue one, the probability of occurrence = 0.8, while for risk issue two, the probability of occurrence = 0.4. Assume B and A are both ordinal cost consequence of occurrence scale level values, where B > A, and for risk issue one, the cost consequence = B, while for risk issue two, the cost consequence = A. Multiplying the probability and consequence of occurrence values for risk issue one yields 0.8*B, and for risk issue two yields 0.4*A. The comparison between risk issues one and two is thus: (0.8*B)/(0.4*A) = (0.8/0.4)*(B/A) = 2*(B/A). Since the true interval values for B and A are unknown, the product of the (cardinal) probability and (ordinal) consequence is still ordinal.

Ordinal scales are commonly used in DoD and commercial program risk analyses, and there is nothing incorrect about this. Unfortunately, performing mathematical operations on values obtained from uncalibrated ordinal scales is wrong and also common, having been promoted by the industry and the DoD in the 1980s to mid-1990s and even the general commercial industry and professional societies.

Although numerous examples from the 1980s and 1990s exist that were published by DoD and its services, perhaps the earliest source of performing mathematics on results from uncalibrated ordinal scales is Department of Defense, *Systems Engineering Management Guide,* 1st ed., Defense Systems Management College (DSMC), 1983, pp. 12:4-10. (Note: While this document was published by DSMC it was developed under contract by a major aerospace company.) Material on mathematics performed on uncalibrated ordinal scales in the first edition and the subsequent 1986 DSMC *Systems Engineering Guide* (effectively the 2nd edition of the document), pp. 15:9-11, is erroneous and was eliminated by DoD in the third edition of the *Systems Engineering Guide* (1990). (The chapter on risk management contained in the third edition, Chapter 15, contains no reference to performing mathematics on uncalibrated ordinal scales, or even any mention to ordinal scales.) In addition, the 2001 version of the DoD *System Engineering Fundamentals* does not contain this flawed methodology, and indeed refutes it. For example:

> "Most of all, beware of manipulating relative numbers, such as 'risk index' or "risk scales," even when based upon expert opinion, as quantified data. They are important information, but they are largely subjective and relative; they do not necessarily define risk accurately. Numbers such as these should always be the subject of a sensitivity analysis."[12]

Note, however, that since the relative ordering of true scale level coefficients for "probability" and/or consequence of occurrence scales may vary between scales, even sensitivity analysis results may not be very meaningful when mathematical operations have been performed.

Conversations with the DSMC risk management focal point in 1991 indicate that the material contained in previous editions of the *Systems Engineering Guide* (1983 and 1986) on mathematics performed on results from uncalibrated ordinal scales was intentionally removed from the third edition (1990) because of the likelihood that erroneous results would occur. The detailed observations I provided in 1991 to DSMC confirmed the DSMC risk management focal point's own concerns that the methodology was severely flawed and should not be included.

[A discussion of ordinal scales, or performing mathematical operations on results from such scales, was never included in DoD (DSMC) risk management guides. For example, there is no reference to this methodology in Department of Defense, *Risk Assessment Techniques,* 1st ed., Defense Systems Management College, July 1983. In addition, there is no reference to this methodology in Department of Defense, *Risk Management Concepts and Guidance,* Defense Systems Management College's March 1989. This guide "updates and expands the Defense Systems Management College's 1983 Risk Assessment Techniques Guide," per the DoD Form 1473 contained in the back of the March 1989 version. Hence, the March 1989 version is often known as the second edition even though its title is different than the July 1983 version. A final footnote to this saga is that the contractor who developed the March 1989 risk management guide version attempted to include isorisk contours and risk factor computations commonly used with results from ordinal scales in the final draft (1 Aug. 1988) to this document (p. 3-3). However, this material was specifically eliminated by DSMC from the final, published version. Subsequent versions of the DoD (DSMC) *Risk Management Guide* 1st through 5th editions (March 1998 through June 2002) have included specific, strong language refuting this flawed methodology (as mentioned next).]

Another widely circulated document that contained mathematics on results from uncalibrated ordinal scales was Air Force Materiel Command, "Acquisition Risk Management Guide," AFMC Pamphlet 63-101, 15 Sept. 1993, pp. 22–26. This material was deleted from the next (final) edition of AFMC Pamphlet 63-101, 9 July 1997, although erroneous examples relating to ordinal scales and mathematics performed on results from them still exist on pp. 20–22. Another document that presented ordinal scales and indicated that the scale values were cardinal (e.g., probability scales with decimal ranges such as probable = 0.4 to 0.6) was "Software Risk Abatement," AFSC/AFLC Pamphlet 800-45, 30 Sept. 1988.

DoD officially denounced this methodology beginning in 1997 in strong terms. The initial DoD refutation occurred in 1997 in internal documents. (The first DoD source generally available to the public that contained this information was Department of Defense, *Risk Management Guide for DoD*

Acquisition, Defense Acquisition University and DSMC, March 1998, pp. 16 and 17.) This author contributed to writing the cited passage that appeared in both the 1997 internal documents and the March 1998 public document.

The DoD position has since been updated and continues the refutation of this faulty methodology:

> "There is a common tendency to attempt to develop a single number to portray the risk associated with a particular event. This approach may be suitable if both likelihood (probability) and consequences have been quantified using compatible cardinal scales or calibrated ordinal scales whose scale levels have been determined using accepted procedures (e.g., Analytical Hierarchy Process). In such a case, mathematical manipulation of the values may be meaningful and provide some quantitative basis for the ranking of risks."

> "In most cases, however, risk scales are actually just raw ordinal scales, reflecting only relative standing between scale levels and not actual numerical differences. Any mathematical operations performed on results from ordinal scales, or a combination of ordinal and cardinal scales, can provide information that will at best be misleading, if not completely meaningless, resulting in erroneous risk ratings. Hence, mathematical operations should generally not be performed on scores derived from ordinal scales. [Note: Risk scales that are expressed as decimal values (e.g., a five-level scale with values 0.2, 0.4, 0.6, 0.8, and 1.0) still retain the ordinal scale limitations discussed.]"[13]

However, commercial industry and some DoD programs continue to perform mathematical operations on uncalibrated ordinal scales today. Analysts often conveniently cite early DoD sources (generally the 1986 DoD *Systems Engineering Guide,* 2nd ed.) as justification for this methodology, without admitting that the methodology has both been withdrawn and refuted in later documents that are readily accessible to the public without charge. Of great concern is that this defective methodology has been used on a large number of programs whose combined life-cycle cost is several hundred billion dollars. On just two of numerous programs where I observed this flawed methodology in use, the combined life-cycle cost was almost $100 billion!)

The danger in performing mathematics on results from ordinal scales is that erroneous risk analysis results are being used in design trades and for allocating risk handling dollars, thus having a negative impact on a large number of very high cost commercial and defense development and production programs.

A simple example of estimating risk from uncalibrated ordinal "probability" and consequence of occurrence scales is given in Appendix I as an illustration of how to correctly use this approach. An extensive discussion of ordinal scales and some of their limitations is given in Appendix H.

The third scale type is interval. Values on interval scales are cardinal. However, the scales have no meaningful zero point, and ratios between similar scales are not equivalent. Hence, limited mathematical operations are possible that yield valid results. Well-known examples of interval scales are the Celsius and Fahrenheit temperature scales. Limited mathematical operations are possible that yield valid results (e.g., $F = 1.8 * C + 32$). However, many common mathematical operations will not yield valid results. For example, if $C_1 = 100°$ C and $C_2 = 50°$ C and if $D = C_1 / C_2$, $D \neq 2.0$. Believe it or not, the correct answer in this case (although it may not make sense initially) is $D = 1.15$. [Celsius temperature values cannot be divided by each other. Only temperatures from an absolute (ratio) scale (e.g., Kelvin) can be divided and yield meaningful results. Hence, the Celsius temperature values must first be converted to Kelvin, then mathematical operations performed. In this case $C_1 = 100°$ C $= 373.15°$ K, $C_2 = 50°$ C $= 323.15°$ K, and $D = 373.15/323.15 = 1.15$.] Interval scales are not common in risk analysis.

The fourth scale type is calibrated ordinal. Here, scale-level coefficients are commonly estimated by evaluating an additional utility function and replace ordinal values (mentioned in scale type two). Calibrated ordinal scales are not commonly used in risk analysis, in part because of the difficulty in accurately calibrating them. Calibrated ordinal scales should be used whenever the analyst wants to perform mathematical operations on resulting values. However, both "probability" of occurrence *and* consequence of occurrence scales must be calibrated. Only calibrating either the "probability" or consequence ordinal scales will lead to meaningless results.

Limited mathematical operations are possible that yield valid results. This is in part because the resulting scale coefficients are cardinal, but relative in nature unless actual values separately existed and were used as part of the calibration process. Similarly, "probability" of occurrence scales calibrated by such techniques are not probability values, just cardinal relative values, unless actual probability values separately existed and were used as part of the calibration process. Thus, risk, the product of probability and consequence of occurrence, *cannot* generally be derived from calibrated ordinal scales. Instead, a weighted value of relative importance to the program exists. Here, a value of 0.6 is twice as important to the program as another value of 0.3 (cet. par.) even though neither value is actually risk. In addition, the resulting calibrated scales have no true zero value (unless one separately existed and was used as part of the calibration process). The intervals between scale values are estimated (e. g., through evaluating an additive utility function) and are typically not perfect. Unless they are carefully derived, the scale coefficient values may have substantial uncertainty (including both a random and bias noise term) that may greatly diminish their usefulness. "Probability" and consequence of occurrence scales that are poorly calibrated will generally be of far less value in performing risk analysis than using the (underlying) uncalibrated ordinal scales together with a suitable risk mapping matrix. (An illustration of this approach is given in Appendix I.)

A nonlinear, but not necessarily well-defined, relationship between scale levels is common, particularly for scales used in risk analysis. Hence, results from performing mathematical operations on scores from calibrated ordinal scales are only accurate within the bounds of estimated scale values. Extrapolating scores beyond the scale boundaries or even interpolating scores between scale levels may be unwise. A brief discussion of calibrating ordinal scales and some of their limitations is given in Appendix H.

The fifth scale type is ratio. With ratio scales the coefficient values are cardinal, indicate absolute position and importance, and the zero point is meaningful. In addition, intervals between scales are consistent, and ratio values between scales are meaningful. In addition, the zero point for a ratio scale exists. Prevalent examples of ratio scales are the Kelvin and Rankine temperature scales. Mathematical operations can be performed on ratio scales and yield valid results. However, as with calibrated ordinal scales, the results are subject to uncertainty that may be present in some cases (e.g., possibly from data measurement). Although ratio scales are the ideal scales for use in project risk analysis, they will rarely exist.

The sixth type of scale is based on subjective estimates of probability for different probability statements (e.g., high), termed here "estimative probability." In the worst case the probability estimates are point estimates or ranges developed by the scale's author with no rigorous basis to substantiate the values. In the best case the probability estimates are derived from a statistical analysis of survey data from a substantial number of respondents and include point estimates and ranges around the estimate for each probability statement. Scales based on estimative probabilities are typically presented as one of two types. The first is an uncalibrated ordinal scale (e.g., Table H.5, Appendix H, derived from statistical results discussed in Appendix J), and the second is a probability table (e.g., Table 6.12). (See Sec. IV.C and Appendix J for some limitations of estimative ordinal scales and probability tables.)

Often, the values contained in estimative probability scales (both ordinal scales and probability tables) have unknown uncertainty, regardless of whether they are given as point estimates or ranges because they are not based on any real world data, but rather guesses. Values contained in estimative probability scales may have a known level of uncertainty if the values, which include ranges, were carefully derived from a statistical analysis.

Estimative probability scales will often yield poor results unless three conditions are met. First, the relationship between the word descriptors and probability values must be derived through a carefully conducted, extensive survey with thorough statistical analysis of the results. Often, the word descriptor and probability value for a given scale level have little or no credible linkage or supporting documentation. Second, a suitable measure of uncertainty derived from a statistical analysis of the survey information should be presented along with the probability point estimate. (For example, from Table 6.12 "high" corresponds to a median value of 0.85 with third and first quartile values of 0.85 and 0.75, respectively.) In effect, the probability values are not point estimates, and it is erroneous to present them that way. Third, estimative probability scales should only be applied to risk issues where sufficient information is available to estimate accurately the probability of the issue. This often means that the associated risk issue is a very close analogy to a risk issue on an existing item, or where a number of units have been produced so that a statistical data sample is available. *Unfortunately, in many cases where estimative probability scales are used in project management, none of the three conditions are met.*

Estimative probability scales should generally include ranges around each point value, but only when the point values and ranges are *derived from a statistical analysis of survey information—not guesses.* In some cases probability values are presented as ranges, yet there is generally no greater confidence in the values than for point estimates because the estimates are typically guesses and not based upon a statistical analysis of survey data. In some cases the point value (again a guess) is converted to a range, yet the values bounding each scale level are simply derived from the number of scale levels (n) by creating intervals of 1/n (e.g., see Table H.8, Appendix H). In other cases seemingly arbitrary probability ranges are selected with no justification or supporting rationale. [For example, one common five-level scale in defense programs uses the following five probability ranges: $0.0 \leq$ Probability ≤ 0.10 (Level 1), $0.11 \leq$ Probability ≤ 0.40 (Level 2), $0.41 \leq$ Probability ≤ 0.60 (Level 3), $0.61 \leq$ Probability ≤ 0.90 (Level 4), $0.91 \leq$ Probability ≤ 1.0 (Level 5). There is no apparent basis for using these probability ranges.] Still in other cases word descriptors are deleted, and only probability point estimates or ranges are presented. The probability point estimates or ranges have no documented justification. This may eliminate the first problem already mentioned, but the second and third problems remain.

Mathematical operations should not be performed on estimative probability ordinal scales or probability tables based on guesses because of the typically unknown uncertainty present. Limited mathematical operations are possible on values from estimative probability tables, so long as statistically derived range information is present. In this case the analyst must decide how to incorporate range information in the calculations.

Scales that relate (word) definitions for a given level to a resulting score are often used for estimating risk probability and consequence of occurrence terms. Of six common scale types only ordinal, calibrated ordinal, and tables statistically derived from subjective estimates of probability are generally suited and used for risk analysis. Uncalibrated ordinal "prob-

ability" and consequence of occurrence scales are commonly used. However, erroneous results will generally occur if mathematical operations are performed on the values generated from these scales. Ordinal "probability" and consequence of occurrence scales can be calibrated by evaluating an additive utility function. Although results from such scales will not yield risk, they are indicators of risk and potentially valuable to the program. Probability tables based on subjective estimates of probability statements can be used in risk analysis, but only if the values are derived by a statistical analysis of survey results, and not simply guesses by the scale's author.

1. Some Additional Risk Scale Considerations

When collecting risk analysis data, be careful not to confuse ordinal and cardinal data. The key consideration in most cases is the underlying nature of the data rather than its numerical representation. For example, the data: 0.05, 0.10, 0.20, 0.40, 1.00 may appear to be cardinal or even probabilities, *but the true nature of the data is unknown.* Here, if the information was obtained from a five-level ordinal scale, then the data are ordinal, not cardinal. A test for cardinal data is that it indicates absolute position and importance, and the zero point is both meaningful and exists. (Data of this type is also necessary for ratio scales, as discussed in Sec. IV.A.) On the other hand, ordinal data are only rank ordered or monotonic (as discussed in Sec. IV.A). Given that the criteria for cardinal data are stringent, numbers that are monotonic should be treated as ordinal unless compelling information exists to the contrary.

What makes a number nominal, ordinal, and so on may have little to do with how the value is represented vs what the number was derived from. For example, measured probabilities of 0.1, 0.3, and 0.5 have cardinal meaning, but assigning the same values to three ordinal items does not give them cardinal meaning. Similarly, assume three ordinal values A, B, and C, where C > B > A. These same three ordinal values can be represented as 5, 3, 1; or 0.5, 0.3, 0.1, and so on, but the fact is that both of these representations are ordinal, not cardinal in nature because the underlying data was ordinal (in effect, the true coefficients associated with A, B, C were unknown and it was not possible to estimate them). As mentioned in Appendix H, I recommend assigning letters to ordinal values to dissuade individuals from attempting to perform mathematical operations on the results. While I don't encourage the use integer number designators (e.g., 5, 3, 1), this is preferable than decimal values (e.g., 0.5, 0.3, 0.1) and especially decimal numerical ranges (e.g., ≥ 0.5, < 0.5 to ≥ 0.3, < 0.3 to ≥ 0.1) which tend to imply precision when none is warranted. Similarly, using subjective probability statements (e.g., high, medium, low) to describe ordinal scale levels should generally be avoided, because 1) the terms might connote risk levels to some people when risk is not represented, 2) the terms are subjective statements, and 3) individuals may disagree with the rating for a particular scale level (e.g., high corresponds to Level 4 when they believe that high = Level 5) and thus through cognitive dissonance choose a different and possibly incorrect level because of this.

An ordinal value does not require a particular type of designator, nor does it exclude practically any type of designator. For example, the sequences 0.9 and 0.8; 2 and 1, E and D (E > D), and high and medium (high > medium) are all potentially valid ordinal representations because the first item has a greater value than the second item listed. To say that cardinal values follow only examples of the first case (0.9 and 0.8), while ordinal values follow only examples of the fourth case [high and medium (high > medium)] is blatantly incorrect. [Note: I prefer not to use subjective probability statements (e.g., high) as ordinal designators since they may impart numerical meaning in the mind of the reader (and this may vary on a case to case basis as shown in Appendix J, Sec. IV).]

In summary, the nature of the data, not its representation is generally a key determinant factor of whether or not a value is ordinal or cardinal. (However, note that the third and fourth cases given above will always be non-cardinal. Again, note the limitation associated with the fourth case mentioned previously.)

Don't confuse the representation of a number with the underlying nature of the data it was derived from. Doing so may lead to erroneous results (e.g., if mathematical operations are performed on ordinal data).

Combinations of ordinal and cardinal values will often yield uncertain, if not meaningless, results and should generally not be attempted. Consider the case where a probability value (0 to 1) is combined with a consequence term that has a value of 0 to 10. Here, the 0 to 1 probability value is based upon an estimative probability scale whose values do not appear to have been developed from a statistical survey. The consequence value of 0 to 10 is only an ordinal value (because in almost no case can cardinal consequence be expressed by a range of 0 to 10), and was also highly subjective because the reader did not have a structured ordinal scale to use. The resulting risk factor is given by probability * consequence and bounded by 10 (P = 1 and C = 10) and 0 (P = 0 and C = 0). However, a score of say 5 is "Y" times higher risk than a score of 2.5, where "Y" is unknown and almost certainly not equal to 2.0. It is particularly meaningless to present results this way and include decimal values (e.g., 5.5) because of the above limitations coupled with the inherent uncertainty that is present in both the "probability" and consequence terms. Since the ordinal consequence values can be replaced by letters, such as E, D, C, B, and A where E > D > C > B > A, then probability * consequence in this case is an ordinal value [e.g., 0.4B vs 0.6C = 0.6/0.4 (C/B) = 1.5 (C/B) where C and B are typically unknown], and a value that in this case has an unknown degree of uncertainty.

Combinations of ordinal and cardinal values will often yield uncertain, if not meaningless, results and should generally not be attempted.

In some cases what appears to be cardinal results may in effect represent an erroneous outcome from performing mathematical operations on results obtained from ordinal scales. Evaluate the underlying methodology used to determine if any results are valid before accepting them. In one example, a number of three-level ordinal "probability" scales were developed where L = 1, M = 6, and H = 10. (There is no basis for assigning such values to these three scale levels—they are only rank ordered and C, B, and A where C > B > A is just as appropriate.) Also, a consequence term ranging from 1 to 10 is used and is only a subjective guess. Risk for each scale category (e.g., technology) is then estimated by multiplying the "probability" term (with a value of 1, 6, or 10) by the consequence term (1 to 10). The overall risk score is then computed by determining the arithmetic average across the risk scores for the individual (probability) categories. In this case the resulting overall risk score is just an ordinal value, and given the faulty methodology used for both the "probability" and consequence terms, plus the averaging performed, one that is likely highly uncertain. Remarkably, the average risk score is reported to three significant digits (e.g., 41.9%) where there is substantial uncertainty in the first digit!

In some cases what appears to be cardinal results may in effect represent an erroneous outcome from performing mathematical operations on results obtained from ordinal scales. Evaluate the underlying methodology used to determine if any results are valid before accepting them.

If "n"-level ordinal "probability" and consequence of occurrence scales are used, do not multiply the "probability" and consequence values and assume that the resulting scores from 1 to n^2 are cardinal values or even "relative" cardinal values. As with results from any uncalibrated ordinal scales, they are only ordered. In addition, they should be converted to risk using a risk mapping matrix (or similar approach) with appropriate level boundaries.

Results obtained from ordinal "probability" and consequence of occurrence scales are not cardinal but ordinal.

When using summary-level risk rating definitions (e.g., see Fig 6.2), be sure to include either a general statement about risk or a specific reference to C,P,S. Do not, for example reference one or two of the three consequence dimensions without referencing all three. For example, a definition for medium risk such as cost or technical concern may require management attention says nothing about schedule risk. What if the particular item being evaluated had a major schedule risk? There would be an incompatibility between the risk level and the summary-level definitions in this case. Similarly, avoid including risk handling actions in summary-level risk rating definitions as the simplistic reference to risk handling will almost always be either inadequate or incorrect.

When using summary-level risk rating definitions, be sure to include either a general statement about risk or a specific reference to all three consequence dimensions.

Unclear or ambiguous ordinal scale definitions can lead to substantial uncertainty and error in scoring risk issues. For example, in one case a five-level consequence of occurrence scale had definitions for each level that were difficult to interpret by users (and the risk manager). While the scale's author may have understood the definitions, users often could not identify which level was appropriate and variations in score of up to three levels sometimes existed when scored at the same time by different users.

Unclear or ambiguous ordinal scale definitions can lead to substantial uncertainty and error in scoring risk issues.

Make sure that ordinal scale definitions are not "out of synch" with the scale levels. For example, on a three-level "probability" scale where Level 1 = low, Level 2 = medium, and Level 3 = high, it would almost never be appropriate to have a scale definition for Level 1 as "some software modifications necessary." Such a definition more likely points to Level 2 given potential problems exhibited on many projects related to almost any non-trivial software modifications that are made.

Make sure that ordinal scale definitions are not "out of synch" with the scale levels.

Not all risk scales may apply to a given risk issue, and only those "probability" of occurrence scales that do apply should be used. In some cases this will be simple to identify—such as not using a manufacturing risk scale for a software issue. In other cases this may be less clear cut, such as not using a hardware/hardware integration scale for a hardware item where technology development, but not integration is necessary. Using nonapplicable or marginally applicable "probability" of occurrence scales may lead to incorrect risk scoring as well as wasting resources and should be avoided. (Note: C,P,S consequence of occurrence scales should all be used when evaluating a risk issue.)

Not all risk scales may apply to a given risk issue, and only those "probability" of occurrence scales that do apply should be used.

If uncalibrated ordinal scales are used for a risk analysis and aggregation is necessary there is no "best way" to compute risk, but some ways are better than others. The conservative approach is to take the highest "probability" of occurrence score and the highest consequence of occurrence score and convert these values to risk using a risk mapping matrix. Erroneous approaches include making an assessment of the individual scores and subjectively averaging the results or performing mathematics on the individual scores since the true coefficients of each scale will likely be both unknown and nonlinear.

If uncalibrated ordinal scales are used for a risk analysis and aggregation is necessary there is no "best way" to compute risk, but some ways are better than others.

The wording of ordinal scale definitions may be so subjective that even if the relationship between adjacent scale levels *must be* monotonic, it may not be or it may not be interpreted as monotonic.

Ordinal scale definitions must lead to monotonic relationships between adjacent scale levels and should not be subjective.

Even when using carefully worded ordinal scales, variations in scores will almost always exist in "probability" and consequence of occurrence scales due to differences in attributes associated with the item for both different measures (e.g., maturity, availability, complexity) and different risk categories being evaluated (probability, such as technology and manufacturing) or different consequence of occurrence terms. However, if the upper- and lower-scale level definitions for ordinal "probability" scales correspond to different "states of the world" even within a single-scale type (e.g., maturity), then there will likely be an imbalance between the scales that can lead to variations in scoring (cet. par.). For example, if the upper scale level in one "probability" scale corresponds to scientific research ongoing, while in another it refers to a brassboard passing relevant tests, then scores across the two scales will not be compatible, and comparison of results across the scales may not be meaningful.

Even when using carefully worded ordinal scales, variations in scores will almost always exist due to differences in scale characteristics between risk terms and risk categories.

A single "probability" or consequence of occurrence scale should not be used to perform a risk analysis, no matter what the circumstances, as it clearly will not yield results that are risk. In one case an ordinal risk analysis scale was developed by a customer organization that only evaluated schedule consequence. This in and of itself might not have been troubling, except the schedule consequence scale was the sole risk analysis scale that was to be used for performing an upcoming risk analyses. Unfortunately, when apprised of this situation, and the severe limitations of this approach, the customer organization did nothing to remedy the situation.

A single "probability" or consequence of occurrence scale should not be used to perform a risk analysis, no matter what the circumstances, as it clearly will not yield results that are risk.

In some cases ordinal scales contain nonuniform levels (a change in interval value), without any apparent reason, for example, 0.1, 0.1, 0.1, 0.1, 0.1, 0.2. And in other cases this change may occur more than once (e.g., 0.2, 0.2, 0.1, 0.2, 0.1, 0.1). In both examples given here the change in the interval values are simply guesses, and interval scores of $G > F > E > D > C > B > A$ would be just as meaningful, if not more so, because the certainty of the interval values would not be overstated and there would less of a tendency to perform mathematical operations on the resulting values. Ordinal scales with nonuniform levels should generally not be used.

In some cases ordinal scales contain nonuniform levels (a change in interval value), without any apparent reason. Ordinal scales with nonuniform levels should generally not be used.

In general, keep specific program milestones (dates) out of ordinal scale definitions when possible. That way if a rebaseline in the program occurs the scales won't have to be changed.

Do not include specific program milestones (dates) in ordinal scale definitions.

When developing and reviewing draft ordinal scales, there is often a period of divergence on the scale definitions before consensus is achieved on the final definitions. It is important that people attempting to develop such scales realize that this will likely occur and that it will take some time to resolve the issues and achieve consensus.

When developing and reviewing ordinal scales, a nontrivial amount of time may be needed to achieve consensus.

A balance is needed between ordinal scale definitions that are too specific and too vague for a given "probability" category. If the definitions are too detailed and specific, then only a few people may have the knowledge to perform the analysis. If the definitions are too vague, they may be interpreted differently by different people leading to scoring errors.

A balance should be developed between ordinal scale definitions that are too specific and too vague for a given "probability" category.

The definition for the upper level (e.g., least mature) of an ordinal "probability" scale must represent a feasible, achievable activity, complexity, maturity, etc. For example, scientific research is ongoing. If the definition leaves no exit to the next lower level (higher maturity), then an unacceptable discontinuity exists. For example, scientific research is ongoing but technology development is not possible. This leaves no exit from the upper-scale level. And if the scale is calibrated, the resulting coefficient value may be very large as well and possibly equal or greater in magnitude than the sum of the other coefficient levels. Depending on the number of scale levels present, this can have an adverse effect of (greatly) compressing the coefficient values of the remaining scale levels so that the contribution from lower (e.g., more mature) scale levels likely for many risk issues is made relatively small (e.g., instead of say 0.1 to 0.25, it may be 0.025 to 0.1).

The definition for the upper level (e.g., least mature) of an ordinal "probability" scale must represent a feasible, achievable activity, complexity, maturity, etc.

The use of ranges based upon percentiles of actual survey results around the median for an estimative probability scale permits an uncertainty analysis to be performed. However, ranges that are developed from unsubstantiated guesses are not useful for this purpose and may introduce considerable error into the results.

If an uncertainty analysis is desired from estimative probability scales, the ranges should be based upon percentiles of actual survey results rather than guesswork.

Subjectively estimating fractional values using ordinal "probability" or consequence of occurrence scales will lead to unsubstantiated and potentially incorrect results (e.g., instead of scoring an item as Level 3 or 4, scoring it as 3.7). First, there is generally no basis whatsoever for selecting a fractional score. Second, because the true coefficients of each scale are generally both unknown and nonlinear, the resulting fractional value will likely be erroneous. It is far better in such cases to take the conservative approach and select the higher (e.g., less mature) of the two values (in this case 4) than to arrive at an erroneous fractional score.

Subjectively estimating fractional values using ordinal "probability" or consequence of occurrence scales will lead to unsubstantiated and potentially incorrect results.

Binary or two-level ordinal "probability" or consequence of occurrence scales should not be used because ± one level could change a risk level from say low to high (cet. par.). In addition, binary scale definitions are often quite poor (e.g., subjective), which makes it relatively easy to misscore risk issues.

Do not use two-level ordinal "probability" or consequence of occurrence scales to perform a risk analysis.

It is generally far easier for decision makers to work with ordinal "probability" and consequence of occurrence scales that are ordered from highest level to lowest level (e.g., Level "E" first and Level "A" last where E > D > C > B> A for a five-level scale) than the reverse. This may prevent the user from subconsciously interposing two scale levels (e.g., erroneously thinking that Level "A" is Level "E" on a five level scale) and arriving at incorrect results. Also, note that the use of numbers does not increase discipline in performing a risk analysis using ordinal scales—letter designators are usually superior because they lead to a disciplined, repeatable approach and at the same time dissuade the user from attempting to perform mathematical operations on the results.

It is generally far easier for decision makers to work with ordinal "probability" and consequence of occurrence scales that are ordered from highest level to lowest level (e.g., Level "E" first and Level "A" last where E > D > C > B> A for a five-level scale) than the reverse.

Do not let program personnel arbitrarily choose which ordinal "probability" of occurrence scales apply to their particular risk issue, or how scores are converted into risk levels. This can lead to a wide variation in potential results across different people with similar knowledge analyzing the same risk issue depending upon which scales are used and how results from multiple "probability" scales are converted into risk levels (e.g., choosing the maximum of the "probability" scores with uncalibrated scales or the weighted average of scores from calibrated scales). The risk manager working with the IPTs should select which "probability" scales are appropriate to avoid injecting this variation into the results.

Do not let program personnel arbitrarily choose which ordinal "probability" of occurrence scales apply to their particular risk issue, or how scores are converted into risk levels. This can lead to a wide variation in potential results.

2. Some Additional Probability of Occurrence Scale Considerations

Do not intermix different types of "probability" scale information in a single-scale type. This may lead to confusion on the part of the analyst and results that are misscored. For example, in one case, a single five-level ordinal "probability" scale was developed and used on a program with a life-cycle cost exceeding $20 billion. The scale employed five subjective probability word descriptors (very high, high, moderate, low, very low), as well as five definitions describing the maturity of a current process. Here, neither scale subset was suitable in a standalone manner. For example, the subjective probability portion was being applied to risk issues where probabilities were typically not known by the reader. And the process-related scale definitions were couched in terms of whether or not the process could prevent the event from occurring, coupled in several instances with risk handling actions that may be needed. (Here, the process definitions were worded in such a manner as to imply one minus the probability. Including information pertaining to risk handling actions further clouded estimating the process "probability;" especially since the wording was vague and only included on three of the five scale levels.) Hence, in this instance, neither "probability" scale was sufficient and the combination of the two widely varying scales into a single "probability" scale resulted in an even less adequate methodology.

Another example is provided as an illustration of what is not an acceptable ordinal "probability" scale. (The scale is given in Table 6.4.) Here, there are a number of issues that require correction prior to using the scale. First, the heading designation, "probability scale," is invalid. This represents the scale level, not a probability scale. Second, the scale definitions are linked to a subjective probability statement—something that is fundamentally flawed. This is because the ordinal scale definitions to not apply to a subjective probability statement in any specific manner, and because different readers will assume a different level of probability for each equivalent technology maturity level. Hence, the analyst attempting to use the scale may misscore results because of cognitive dissonance (e.g., a scale level definition may

Table 6.4   Example unacceptable "probability" of occurrence ordinal scale

Technology Maturity	Probability Scale	Color
Basic principles observed	Very high	Red
Concept design analyzed for performance	High	Red
Breadboard or brassboard validation in relevant environment	Medium	Yellow
Prototype passes performance tests	Low	Green
Item deployed and operational	Very Low	Green

conflict with the subjective probability statement and lead to misscoring). In effect this scale includes two disparate types of ordinal "probability" scales— namely a maturity-based scale and an estimative probability scale, yet with the worst characteristics of both. What is needed is a column in the scale that relates to the scoring level, preferably E, D, C, B, A, where E > D > C > B > A for an ordinal representation. If however, the goal is to create an estimative probability scale, then the scoring designators should be replaced by probability values (preferably median, 25th percentile and 75th percentile values) obtained from the statistical analysis of survey results. Third, it is inappropriate to include a color (often a risk indicator) as part of an ordinal scale, or in general any probability or consequence scale. This too may lead to misscoring on the part of the analyst due to cognitive dissonance.

Do not intermix different types of "probability" scale information in a single scale. This may lead to confusion on the part of the analyst and results that are misscored.

The number of ordinal "probability" scale levels should generally be odd, and the middle level should typically represent the mid-point of possible outcomes. When this is not the case and the scale definitions are skewed toward one extreme or the other then biased scores may result. (This biasing may be removed by setting the boundaries of the risk mapping matrix, but this should not be viewed as the first resort, but as the last resort.) When an even number of scale levels exist, the scale definitions above and below the theoretical midpoint should similarly be balanced.

The number of ordinal "probability" scale levels should generally be odd, and the middle level should generally represent the mid-point of possible outcomes.

Do not use skewed, and especially highly skewed, estimative probability values when defining an ordinal scale because this increases the likelihood that the descriptors associated with the probability levels will not be a good match and may lead to misscoring due to cognitive dissonance. For example, low: $P < 0.05$, medium: $0.05 < P \leq 0.50$, and high: $0.50 < P$ can lead to disconnects in scoring. Instead, I recommend using the data presented in Appendix J, which in this case would be for the median (plus 25th and 75th percentiles), low: 0.15, (0.15, 0.25); medium: 0.45 (0.45, 0.55); and high: 0.85 (0.75, 0.85).

Do not use skewed, and especially highly skewed, estimative probability values when defining an ordinal scale because this increases the likelihood that the descriptors associated with the probability levels will not be a good match and may lead to misscoring due to cognitive dissonance.

When developing an ordinal or estimative probability table, do not include words such as low, medium, high, etc. as part of the table as this may at best confuse the reader and at worst cause the reader to misscore the probability level because of cognitive dissonance. [For example, if Level 4 of a 5-level scale is termed medium and the reader agrees with the definition associated with the scale level but disagrees with "medium," the reader may chose a different scale level (e.g., 3) which he believes is consistent with "medium" even if he may disagree with the definition for this scale level.]

When developing an ordinal or estimative probability table, do not include words such as low, medium, high, etc. as part of the table.

Do not develop an ordinal scale where words of subjective probability (e.g., possible) are provided with a word definition (e.g., may occur), without any numerical estimates for the probability level and range involved (e.g., median = 0.55, third quartile = 0.65, first quartile = 0.35, as given in Table J.2, Appendix J). The problem with an ordinal scale of this type is that it is highly subjective; not only are the words of subjective probability given without any numerical value and range, but the word definition provided is also subjective and again does not include any numerical value and range.

Do not develop an ordinal scale where words of subjective probability (e.g., possible) are provided with a word definition (e.g., may occur), without any numerical estimates for the probability level and range involved.

If data included in a probability table is derived from actual data or analysis of survey results (estimative probability), then the coefficients can be treated as calibrated probability data for the purpose of mathematical operations, and the resulting scale can be considered a calibrated ordinal scale. (Of course, the underlying uncertainty present should be included in a sensitivity analysis.) Otherwise, the resulting coefficients are ordinal, and the scale should be viewed as an ordinal scale. In this case, coefficients associated with scale levels in a probability scale (e.g., high = 0.9 = Level 5) are ordinal and the scale should be viewed as an ordinal scale.

Coefficients included in a probability table should be viewed as ordinal unless it is derived from actual data or analysis of survey results (estimative probability).

When ranges are given for estimative probability scales, there is no more guarantee that the data will be any more meaningful than when point values or point values coupled with a range are given unless the underlying data was derived from a statistical analysis of survey results. For example, Table 6.5 includes data in the first two columns that is highly similar to data used by an organization on a multibillion dollar program. The origin of the data is unknown, but it was almost certainly not derived from a statistical analysis of survey results. [Note: Levels 4 and 5 (low likelihood and not likely) used by the organization are reversed vs the survey results. I corrected this inconsistency, otherwise the computations would have yielded even more dramatic results.] The third, fourth, and fifth columns of Table 6.5 are results from the survey conducted for this book (provided in Appendix J) and serve as a comparison to the data used on the large-scale program.

In order to perform this analysis it was assumed that the organization's data endpoints corresponded to the 75th and 25th percentile values of the survey. (Had a wider bound been selected, say the 90th and 10th percentiles,

Table 6.5 Comparison of data for five probability statements

Probability Statement	Organization	Median (from Survey)	25th Percentile (from Survey)	75th Percentile (from Survey)
Near certainty	0.8–1.0	0.95	0.95	0.95
High likelihood	0.6–0.8	0.85	0.75	0.85
Possible	0.4–0.6	0.55	0.35	0.65
Low Likelihood	0.2–0.4	0.15	0.15	0.25
Not likely	0.0–0.2	0.25	0.15	0.30

the results would have been even more pronounced than for the 75th and 25th percentiles.) Given these assumptions, I then computed the difference between the organization's lower bound value and the 25th percentile, and the organization's upper bound value and the 75th percentile for each probability statement, as given in Table 6.6. I then computed the percent deviation between this difference and the corresponding survey value at both the 25th and 75th percentile values, as given in Table 6.6.

Several observations follow from the data analysis. First, the organization's scale levels are 0.2 wide, yet deviations of | 0.15 | existed on either the high or low scale bound (organization − survey) for four of the five probability statements and intervals used. Second, a considerable range existed among the deviation results for the five probability statements, from an absolute deviation of 5% to 60% (75th percentile) to 16% to 100% (25th percentile). Third, the average of the absolute deviations was 37% (75th percentile) and 22% (25th percentile). Fourth, for the lower two probability statements (low likelihood and not likely), the average of the absolute deviation was 47% (75th percentile) and 67% (25th percentile). In summary, the results of this analysis show that arbitrarily selecting values to provide a

Table 6.6 Organization vs survey deviations for five probability statements

Probability Statement	Organization − Survey (25th percentile)	Organization − Survey (75th percentile)	% Deviation vs Survey (25th percentile)	% Deviation vs Survey (75th percentile)
Near certainty	−0.15	+0.05	−16%	+5%
High likelihood	−0.15	−0.05	−20%	−6%
Possible	+0.05	−0.05	+14%	−8%
Low Likelihood	+0.05	+0.15	+33%	+60%
Not likely	−0.15	−0.10	−100%	−33%

range for estimative probability statements may lead to considerable error (as evident from Table 6.6).

When ranges are given for estimative probability scales, there is no more guarantee that the data will be any more meaningful than when point values or point values coupled with a range are given unless the underlying data was derived from a statistical analysis of survey results.

3. Some Additional Consequence of Occurrence Scale Considerations

When estimating consequence of occurrence the analyst should first understand to whom the consequence of occurrence will apply. For example, is it a seller (e.g., vendor, prime contractor); or what WBS level will it occur at (e.g., total program or a subsystem); etc.? This is particularly important if absolute values, not percentages are used for cost and schedule consequence of occurrence, and also for performance consequence of occurrence if the ordinal scale definitions are not carefully worded.

When estimating consequence of occurrence the analyst should first understand to whom the consequence of occurrence will apply.

Do not use consequence of occurrence scales where the fundamental nature of the definition changes between levels. For example it is best not to include definitions that include a quantitative value for schedule slip for some levels, while qualitatively discussing the amount of slack for other levels. This mixture of scale definitions can be confusing to the reader and lead to interpretation errors even if it is technically correct.

Do not use consequence of occurrence scales where the fundamental nature of the definition changes between levels.

Do not intermix definitions in C,P,S consequence of occurrence ordinal scales else the resulting scale may be confusing to the reader. For example, in one case a *schedule* consequence of occurrence scale was developed, yet the lowest level of the scale discussed impact on element and system *performance.*

Do not intermix definitions in C,P,S consequence of occurrence ordinal scales else the resulting scale may be confusing to the reader.

If a structured methodology exists for estimating C,P,S consequence of occurrence, don't simply assume that one or more of the consequence components may not be important and can be neglected without performing a rigorous evaluation. On one program a manager believed that the technical consequence of occurrence, measured by an ordinal scale tied to the level of performance reduction coupled with the type of workaround needed, was sufficient relatively late in the development program. However, he did not realize that any design changes made would have considerable cost and schedule impact to the program, and he recommended not estimating the impact of such changes. Here, as in most cases, it was necessary to estimate the impact of C,P,S impact to the program.

If a structured methodology exists for estimating C,P,S consequence of occurrence, don't simply assume that one or more of the consequence components may not be important and can be neglected without performing a rigorous evaluation.

Single word consequence of occurrence definitions, such as: negligible, marginal, critical, and catastrophic should generally be avoided, because they are subjective and will likely impart a considerable response range from those attempting to use this information (just as in the case of subjective probability terms). Even worse in this case is that such wording cannot be readily tied, as in the case of estimative probability, to specific levels, unless separate, detailed definitions are available.

Do not use single word consequence of occurrence definitions because they are subjective and may elicit a different understanding from different readers.

Consequence of occurrence measures should not just be a subjective scale from 1 to 5 where the user guesses the value—this is both erroneous and will often introduce considerable uncertainty into the results. This practice should not be used.

Do not use a subjective, unstructured estimate for consequence of occurrence.

Be cautious about using constrained statements in consequence of occurrence scale definitions. For example, "requires use of management reserve," particularly when a small number of scale levels exist (e.g., three). Here, there is no gradation in the scale level vs the amount of management reserve used and the same score could result whether a management reserve was employed that was 10% of the program budget as $1.00 more than the initially allocated funding for the item.

Be cautious about using constrained statements in consequence of occurrence scale definitions.

Schedule estimates for ordinal consequence of occurrence scales are often one of two types, including the schedule length extension for a given activity (e.g., months or percent) and an issue regarding impact to the project, which depends on the network logic and milestones. In effect, the schedule consequence of occurrence reflects both the potential variation in the activity or group of activities being evaluated, along with relevant constraints (e.g., finish by or start no later than). Unfortunately, these types of information are not compatible in a single ordinal scale and generally can only be properly treated in a schedule risk analysis via a Monte Carlo simulation. One approach is to take the two types of ordinal schedule consequence of occurrence scales, then select the "worst case" result (highest scale level) of the two and report this value.

Schedule estimates for ordinal consequence of occurrence scales generally do not accurately reflect both duration and milestones and may be difficult to apply.

B. Results Derived from Mathematical Operations on Ordinal Scale Values

When mathematical operations are performed on the values from ordinal "probability" and consequence of occurrence scales, the resulting values and even relative rankings may be erroneous. I will first provide two simple illustrations that show how even relative rankings can be erroneous, then give some specific results from actual risk analyses.

Suppose you have two different "probability" scales and one consequence scale (e.g., performance only), and risk is computed as Risk Factor = P * C. It is entirely possible that for two different WBS elements (A and B) you have

WBS A:

$$\text{Risk Factor (A)} = P(\text{scale1,A}) * C(A) + P(\text{scale2,A}) * C(A)$$

WBS B:

$$\text{Risk Factor (B)} = P(\text{scale1,B}) * C(B) + P(\text{scale2,B}) * C(B)$$

The problem even in this simple case is that unless all values achieved for either WBS A or WBS B are consistently greater than the other (here WBS B or WBS A), then you cannot make any statement as to whether the risk factor is higher for WBS A or WBS B. Only when all three inequalities for A > B, or when two inequalities for A > B and the third inequality is A = B, or when one inequality for A > B and the other two inequalities are A = B can you say Risk Factor(A) > Risk Factor(B). [For example, P(scale1,A) must be > P(scale1,B), C(A) must be > C(B), and P(scale2,A) must be > P(scale2,B) to say WBS A has a higher risk factor than WBS B.] If any of the three inequalities does not hold, e.g., C(B) > C(A), then you cannot say that Risk Factor(A) > Risk Factor(B) because you do not know the correct interval values for the underlying (uncalibrated) ordinal scales. It is entirely possible that if two inequalities hold, but the relationship for the third inequality is reversed, e.g., C(B) > C(A), then Risk Factor(B) may be > Risk Factor(A). As just mentioned, only when all three inequalities for A > B, or when two inequalities for A > B and the third inequality is A = B, or when one inequality for A > B and the other two inequalities are A = B can you say Risk Factor(A) > Risk Factor(B). (For any other combination of A and B based upon >, = and < you cannot prove that A > B—the relationship of A vs B is unknown.) The more ordinal "probability" and consequence scales you are working with, the more complicated the underlying inequality. This is the case whether or not the "probability" and consequence scales are normalized (e.g., to 1.0) or unnormalized.

However, the same problems exist with the simplest case possible, one "probability" scale and one consequence scale:

WBS A:

$$\text{Risk Factor (A)} = \text{P(scale1,A)} * \text{C(A)}$$

WBS B:

$$\text{Risk Factor (B)} = \text{P(scale1,B)} * \text{C(B)}$$

If P(scale1,A) > P(scale1,B) but C(B) > C(A), you cannot prove that Risk Factor(A) > Risk Factor(B) without knowing the correct interval values for the underlying (uncalibrated) ordinal scales. Without this information the resulting inequality is simply unknown, e.g., Risk Factor(A) could be >, =, or < Risk Factor(B). That is the danger in trying to do any math with (uncalibrated) ordinal scales. [In this case only if P(scale1,A) > P(scale1,B) and C(A) > C(B), or P(scale1,A) > P(scale1,B) and C(A) = C(B), or P(scale1,A) = P(scale1,B) and C(A) > C(B) can you conclusively say that Risk Factor(A) > Risk Factor(B), and so on.]

The reader might wonder what the potential impact of performing mathematics on uncalibrated ordinal scales is. For example, if the effect is small, the preceding discussion may be nothing more than academic. Unfortunately, the effect can be very large. As already mentioned, when erroneous risk analysis results derived with this flawed methodology are used in design trades and for allocating risk handling dollars, it can and does have a negative impact on a large number of very high cost commercial and defense development and production programs.

I will now present three examples that show that performing mathematics on scores derived from uncalibrated ordinal scales can indeed lead to substantial errors.

The first example, given in Table 6.7, compares the coefficients from a single ordinal technology "probability" scale with seven levels. The results indicate the difference in values between equivalent scale levels for uncalibrated and calibrated scale coefficients. The average difference between the uncalibrated and calibrated scale coefficients is 188% with a standard deviation of 139%! This somewhat underestimates the actual deviation that exists because few risk issues will score at the highest scale level (7, which in this case had a 0% deviation because of the normalization technique used).

This and similar technology ordinal "probability" scales have been calibrated several times by different groups. Deviations in the resulting scale coefficients have typically been relatively small and much, much less than the 188% average difference between the uncalibrated and calibrated scale coefficient values given in Table 6.7. Average differences between uncalibrated

Table 6.7 Percent differences between uncalibrated and calibrated ordinal technology scale values

Uncalibrated scale level[a]	Uncalibrated scale value[b] normalized to upper level	Calibrated scale value[c] normalized to upper level	Percent difference, [(uncal.-cal.)/cal.]*100
7	1.00	1.00	0
6	0.857	0.551	+56
5	0.714	0.321	+122
4	0.571	0.184	+210
3	0.429	0.106	+305
2	0.286	0.058	+393
1	0.143	0.043	+233
Average difference, %	N/A	N/A	**+188**
Standard deviation of Difference, %	N/A	N/A	**139**

[a]Uncalibrated scale level: Ordinal scale level for a seven-level scale.
[b]Normalized uncalibrated scale value = uncalibrated scale level divided by 7.
[c]Calibrated scale value: Scale values estimated by the AHP and normalized to the upper level value. The internal inconsistency ratio for this calibration is 0.080, which is small and indicates high consistency in deriving the coefficients.

and calibrated scale coefficients for other risk categories (e.g., design/engineering and manufacturing) also typically range from 100 to 200+%.

An irrefutable example is now provided that illustrates the potential magnitude of errors associated with assigning coefficients to ordinal scales. Table 6.8, includes seven U. S. currency bills of $1, $2, $5, $10, $20, $50, and $100. Here, the seven bills are rank ordered according to value and given ordinal scale levels of 1 ($1.00) through 7 ($100.00). The raw scale value normalized to the upper level ($100.00) is then computed. (Here, the scale level is normalized by dividing it by 7.) Similarly, the calibrated scale value normalized to the upper level is also computed. (Here, this corresponds to the value of each bill normalized by $100.00.) The percent error is then computed between the normalized raw and calibrated values, along with the average error and standard deviation of error for the results. Both the average error (+602 percent) and standard deviation of the error (557 percent) are so large that they would render any risk analysis *totally meaningless*. And in this case the deviations are truly errors—there is no question since the currency valuations are cardinal, and have zero error and uncertainty.

While I cannot say that by performing mathematical operations on results from uncalibrated ordinal scales errors of this magnitude will exist in your case, *how can anyone say that such errors will be absent (e.g., what is the magnitude of the error present on your program)*? Performing mathematical operations on results from uncalibrated ordinal scales is a clear example of a flawed approach, regardless of who developed it and who is using it. No one has yet to develop and provide me with a convincing argument backed by theoretical considerations (e.g., a proof like the one contained in this subsection) coupled with actual results that such a methodology is accurate. *While this example does not contain the largest (or smallest) average error possible, it decimates any assumption that mathematical operations can be accurately performed on results from uncalibrated ordinal scales.*

A risk analysis that uses ordinal scales will typically have several "probability" of occurrence scales and one or three consequence of occurrence scales, with risk computed using Risk Factor = P * C. Given the magnitude of the deviations between the uncalibrated and calibrated scale coefficients, erroneous results will likely exist when derived by performing mathematics on scores from uncalibrated ordinal scales.

To examine the severity of the potential problems, I took an actual program risk analysis and compared results obtained using calibrated and uncalibrated ordinal "probability" and consequence of occurrence scales. Here, 54 risk issues were evaluated for a long design life, low-earth-orbit satellite. Seven "probability" scales were used (technology, design/engineering, and five manufacturing scales), along with a single consequence of occurrence scale (related to performance). The calibrated coefficients for each scale were determined using AHP (see Appendix H, Sec. VII), and the

EFFECTIVE RISK MANAGEMENT

Table 6.8 Percent error between uncalibrated and calibrated scale values for some U. S. currency

Item	Raw Scale Level[a]	Raw Scale Value Normalized to Upper Level[b]	Calibrated Scale Value Normalized to Upper Level[c]	Percent Error, ((Raw-Cal)/Cal)*100
One Hundred Dollars	7	1.00	1.00	0
Fifty Dollars	6	0.86	0.50	+71
Twenty Dollars	5	0.71	0.20	+257
Ten Dollars	4	0.57	0.10	+471
Five Dollars	3	0.43	0.05	+757
Two Dollars	2	0.29	0.02	+1329
One Dollar	1	0.14	0.01	+1329
Average Error (%)	N/A	N/A	N/A	**+602**
Standard Deviation of Error (%)	N/A	N/A	N/A	**557**

[a]Raw Scale Level: Ordinal scale level for a seven level scale.
[b]Normalized Raw Scale Value = Raw scale level divided by 7.
[c]Calibrated Scale Value: Currency scale value normalized to hundreds of dollars.

resulting risk factor was computed taking the weighted average between scales (whose coefficients were also determined by AHP) using Risk Factor = P * C. A large number of schemes for normalizing uncalibrated ordinal "probability" scale scores and weighting one "probability" scale vs another were explored and used to compute the risk factor using the same equation as in the calibrated scale case (P * C).

Two results were of interest for this comparison: first, the number of Top 5 risk issues estimated by calibrated scales not included in results derived from uncalibrated ordinal scales; and second, the number of Top 5 risk issues derived from calibrated scales vs those in the wrong order in the results derived from uncalibrated ordinal scales (includes those Top 5 risk issues derived from calibrated scales not present in results from uncalibrated scales).

A summary of some of the comparison results is given in Table 6.9. Here, three of the Top 5 risk issues determined from the calibrated scales were not estimated in the Top 5 by the uncalibrated scales. In addition, the ordering for the Top 5 risk issues was different for at least four of the five issues when comparing the calibrated ordinal scale results to the uncalibrated ordinal scale results. From this analysis it is clear that not only will key risk issues be missed when performing mathematical operations on ordinal scales, but even the relative rankings will be substantially impacted! (Note: Because the space system under development was not near deployment, there is no way to prove that the Top 5 risks determined from using the calibrated ordinal scales were the correct Top 5 risks.)

A summary of results from seven different comparisons is given in Table 6.10. Only one uncalibrated case had results not substantially dissimilar from the calibrated ordinal scales (with two of the Top 5 risks wrong and 3 misordered Top 5 risks). However, this was related to the way the weighting between scale categories was performed and was likely unique to the specific risk analysis performed and might not be repeatable on other analyses.

The results given in Tables 6.9 and 6.10 are not the worst case because two of the seven "probability" scales had minimal contribution (e.g., consistently low numerical scores), and two others often had low scores. Although it cannot be proven simply, it is likely that if these four scales had a larger contribution to the overall risk factor score the resulting ordering for the uncalibrated results would likely have diverged even further from the calibrated results (e.g., more wrong Top 5 risks).

The number of Top 5 risk issues that are excluded or in the wrong order when comparing results derived from uncalibrated ordinal scales vs those from calibrated ordinal scales often understates the severity of the problem associated with using values obtained from performing mathematical operations on results from uncalibrated ordinal scales when risks with smaller scores are compared. This is because the variation in scores among the program's highest risks are often larger or even much larger than the scores

Table 6.9 Comparison of Top 5 risk issues—calibrated vs uncalibrated ordinal scales

Risk rank	Risk issue calibrated scales[a]	Risk issue, uncalibrated scales, wt. avg. #1	Risk issue, uncalibrated scales, wt. avg. #4
1	Waveband #2 sensor IA&T	Waveband #2 sensor IA&T	Spacecraft/sensor IA&T
2	Rad-hard computer Mmicroprocessor chip set	Spacecraft/sensor IA&T	Waveband #2 sensor IA&T
3	Waveband #2 cryocooler (mechanical)	Comm. 60 GHz transmitter	Comm. 60 GHz transmitter
4	Spacecraft/sensor IA&T	Comm. payload IA&T	Comm. payload IA&T
5	Waveband #2 cryocooler (electrical)	Waveband #3 sensor IA&T	Waveband #1 sensor IA&T
Number wrong Top 5 risks[b]	N/A	3	3
Number Top 5 risks in wrong order[c]	N/A	4	5

[a]Calibration performed via the AHP on ordinal "probability" design/engineering, manufacturing, and technology scales widely used for risk analysis (seven scales total) and one performance consequence of occurrence scale.

[b]Number of Top 5 risks derived from calibrated scales not included in the results derived from uncalibrated ordinal scales.

[c]Number of Top 5 risks derived from calibrated scales vs those in wrong order in the results derived from uncalibrated ordinal scales (includes those Top 5 risks derived from calibrated scales not present in results from uncalibrated scales).

**Table 6.10 Number of wrong and misordered
Top 5 risks between uncalibrated and calibrated
ordinal technology "probability" scale values**

Number of wrong top 5 risks	Number of misordered top 5 risks
	5 (2 of 7 cases)
3 (6 of 7 cases)	4 (3 of 7 cases)
2 (1 of 7 cases)	3 (2 of 7 cases)

for risks with a lower resulting risk level. Hence, a variation in the results from even a single "probability" or consequence of occurrence scale can strongly influence the overall risk score. For example, the variation among the Top 5 risk scores may be 0.20 based upon the highest minus the lowest score (normalized to 1.0). Yet the risk score for say the 25th highest risk in the program may be less than 0.20 and the variation among risk scores from say the 20th to 30th highest risk scores may be less than 0.10. Thus, even if three of the Top 5 risk scores are missed and/or out of order, an even larger percentage of scores representing risks with lower levels may be missed and/or out of order.

Consequently, based on both theoretical and actual risk analyses, performing mathematical operations on values obtained from uncalibrated ordinal scales will often lead to erroneous results. [For example, on one multibillion-dollar program the average value derived from 10 uncalibrated ordinal probability scales is multiplied by the average value of 3 uncalibrated ordinal consequence of occurrence scales (C,P,S). In another case involving multibillion-dollar programs, the average value derived from 5 to 10 uncalibrated ordinal "probability" scales is multiplied by the average value of 3 uncalibrated ordinal consequence of occurrence scales. As one government senior manager remarked, "who knows what you get when you do this?"] Any subsequent mathematical analyses performed using values derived from uncalibrated ordinal scales will also yield erroneous results, *no matter how elaborate or sophisticated the methodology.*

Do not perform mathematical operations on scores obtained from ordinal "probability" and consequence of occurrence scales because the resulting specific numerical values as well as the relative rankings are typically erroneous.

Scales used in risk analysis at the top level are either ordinal or cardinal, they cannot be both. (If cardinal, then they are either interval, calibrated ordinal, ratio, or estimative probability.) In addition, it is not credible to treat the same risk analysis scale as ordinal in one breath, then cardinal in the next.

Scales used in risk analysis at the top level are either ordinal or cardinal, they cannot be both.
There is no basis to compute an average risk level for a given project unless calibrated ordinal or ratio scales are used, or true probability and consequence values exist, and some measure of the uncertainty associated with the results can be captured. Even if appropriate data exists an average risk value may not be particularly meaningful. For example the average risk level can be skewed by the number and/or magnitude of high risks or low risks. While I don't recommend it, a median value coupled with the 25th percentile and 75th percentile values would be more meaningful. Performing such calculations with results obtained from ordinal scales will likely lead to erroneous results and should not be attempted.

There is no basis to compute an average risk level for a given project unless calibrated ordinal or ratio scales are used, or true probability and consequence values exist, and some measure of the uncertainty associated with the results can be captured.

Performing mathematical operations on results from uncalibrated ordinal scales may lead to a larger error if used for estimating probability distribution critical values than a direct subjective estimate for the distribution critical values. While the ordinal scale approach is at least potentially structured and repeatable, it may lead to large errors, possibly even larger than just an expert opinion of the critical values.

Do not perform mathematical operations on results from uncalibrated ordinal scales to estimate probability distribution critical.

It is not correct to take a five-level uncalibrated probability scale result and multiply it by a five-level uncalibrated consequence of occurrence scale result and assume that there are 25 resulting possible risk levels. That says that every square in a 5×5 risk mapping matrix has a unique entry if done, for example, as $(0.05, 0.25, 0.50, 0.75, 0.95)$ and $(1, 2, 3, 4, 5)$. The results vary between 0.05 and 4.75 or a ratio of maximum/minimum $= 4.75/0.05 = 95$, when in reality only $5 + 10 = 15$ unique values exist. Here, 5 unique values exist along the diagonal and 10 unique values exist in the upper or lower triangle of the square minus the diagonal. This can be verified using letters (a, b, c, d, e) or numbers $(1, 2, 3, 4, 5)$ for the x and y axes because the upper and lower triangle of the matrix are symmetrical. Thus, in this case, 10 of the 25 possible risk levels are not unique, which can lead to erroneous results 10/25 or 40% of the time on average! Also, even to have 15 risk boundaries is far too granular for almost any program and the 5×5 matrix given above should be reduced to probably no more than five risk levels (e.g., low, low medium, medium, medium high, high). Further refinement to yield a potentially valid set of 25 risk scores would involve, for example, calibrating both the five-level ordinal "probability" and consequence scales. But then too, care should be given not to blindly believe the 25 possible values for rank ordering due to potential errors and uncertainty in both the calibration process and the risk scoring process.

When using uncalibrated ordinal scales, the number of risk levels should never equal the number of cells in the risk mapping matrix. This is not only far too granular for practical use, but erroneous as well.

Even performing relatively simple mathematical operations on results from uncalibrated ordinal scales may yield erroneous results. An example is now provided that illustrates some of potential problems with summing risk scores. A risk analysis methodology included several three-level ordinal scales (where high = 3, medium = 2, and low = 1). Candidate activities are then evaluated against the risk scales, and scores are summed both "down" an activity (against all relevant risk scales) as well as "across" all activities for each risk scale. The risk level for each activity is then estimated by mapping the scores summed "down" an activity against a table delineating risk boundaries (e.g., medium = 3). There are a number of problems with this risk analysis methodology beyond using ordinal scales with three levels. First, each ordinal scale was assumed to represent risk, yet several of the scales were related to maturity and availability issues, and thus only an indicator of the "probability" term of risk, not risk itself. (In addition, some of the three-level scale definitions were subjective or mixed potential risk issues.) In addition, those scales that represented uncertainty did not have a clearly defined consequence of occurrence dimension, and thus were also primarily related to the "probability" term of risk. Second, the presumption is that the scores for low, medium, and high across all scales were equal (1, 2, and 3, respectively). This is not reasonable, since the scales are only ordinal, the given coefficient values (1, 2, 3) are only placeholders and the actual coefficient values for each scale are unknown. Third, because a variety of risk scales were mixed, and as mentioned above each scale represented a different degree of pedigree relative to risk, "probability" and consequence of occurrence; there is no clear basis for summing the results since different entities are being combined. (However, even if such a basis existed, it would still yield incorrect results since the coefficients used are only placeholders and the actual scale level coefficients are unknown.) Fourth, the presumption is that between scale coefficient values are equal, hence all scales are weighted the same. This may or may not be reasonable, since the scales are only ordinal and no formal methodology was used to estimate the between scale coefficients (e.g., an additive utility approach). Fifth, there is no apparent basis to map the summed values derived from ordinal scales (which themselves are erroneous) to risk scores delineating boundaries (e.g., low, medium, and high). The mapping that was performed is subjective with no documented rationale for its use.

Even performing relatively simple mathematical operations on results from uncalibrated ordinal scales may yield erroneous results.

Do not start off with a risk factor, then artificially "work backward" or reverse engineer to estimate separate probability of occurrence and consequence of occurrence terms (e.g., as Risk Factor = P * C). This may lead to erroneous results; particularly when uncertain information exists for the probability and/or consequence of occurrence terms.

Do not estimate separate probability of occurrence and consequence of occurrence terms given a risk factor. This may lead to erroneous results.

It is not valid to map geometric ratios of actual probability or consequence of occurrence values onto ordinal scales. This is because ratioing values derived from ordinal scales still do not lead to correct values since the underlying intervals are almost always nonlinear even if they are monotonic. Hence, the resulting coefficients may, and often will, contain large errors.

Do not map geometric ratios of actual probability or consequence of occurrence values onto ordinal scales. The resulting coefficients may, and often will, contain large errors.

While it is unwise to assign decimal values to risk mapping matrix cells, it is foolish to then use these values in subsequent calculations because this amounts to performing mathematical operations on subjective values associated with the results from ordinal "probability" and consequence of occurrence scales.

Do not assign decimal values to risk mapping matrix cells, or use such values in any subsequent mathematical operations.

C. Probability Values Derived from Subjective Estimates

In some cases subjective estimates, often nothing more than guesses, that appear to represent probability values may be used in a risk analysis. These scales are sometimes known as estimative probability scales and are typically represented by ordinal probability scales and probability tables. Such probability scales are generally not derived from actual probability data. In addition, because of the subjective definitions used, considerable uncertainty will generally exist among potential analysts as to what probability corresponds to a given level. This can lead to misscoring results when the definition for the probability level does not match the numerical score anticipated by the analyst. When this occurs, the resulting probability level chosen may be wrong, and often not much more than a guess.

For example, consider the estimative probability table given in Table 6.11. The method used to derive the probability scores is unknown, but is likely a subjective assessment by the table's author.

Next consider another set of results using the same definitions used in Table 6.11. The probability value levels for this set of results were derived from an extensive survey, using data from 151 respondents. (See Appendix J for a discussion of the survey and a summary of the statistical results.) The median (50th percentile), upper quartile (3rd quartile, the value above which

**Table 6.11   Example of probability
values derived from subjective estimates,
sources of probability levels unknown**

Definition	Probability score
Certain	1.00
High	0.75
Medium	0.50
Low	0.25
Almost no chance	0.05

25% of the data will lie; the 75th percentile), lower quartile (1st quartile, the value below which 25% of the data will lie; the 25th percentile), percent of survey respondents whose scores where above the third quartile, percent of survey respondents whose scores were below the 1st quartile, and the percent of survey respondents whose scores were either above the 3rd quartile or below the 1st quartile for the same scale definitions used in Table 6.11 are given in Tables 6.12a and b.

Table 6.12a   Example of estimative probability table

Definition	Median (50th percentile)	3rd quartile (75th percentile)	1st quartile (25th percentile)
Certain	0.95	0.95	0.95
High	0.85	0.85	0.75
Medium	0.45	0.55	0.45
Low	0.15	0.25	0.15
Almost no chance	0.05	0.15	0.05

Table 6.12b   Example of estimative probability table

Definition	Percent > 3rd quartile (75th percentile)	Percent > 1st quartile (25th percentile)	Percent > 3rd quartile and < 1st quartile
Certain	0	24	24
High	13	13	26
Medium	13	20	33
Low	15	9	24
Almost no chance	11	0	11

It is *strongly recommended* that any estimative probability tables derived from the data given in Appendix J include the variables just mentioned and illustrated in Tables 6.12. (Note: The information contained in Table 6.12b is backup data for Table 6.12a, but nevertheless should be available to both analysts and decision makers to help them understand the range of underlying survey responses.) *It is inappropriate to solely use the median value—it is tantamount to refusing to recognize that a range of responses exists and can lead to erroneous results.* Solely using the median value is particularly inappropriate given the broad range of responses for each probability statement, as given in Appendix J. It is also recommended that the percent of responses outside the third and first quartiles be separately reported, along with the sum of these two values.

The median values in Tables 6.12 agree to ≤ 0.1 with the same definitions in Table 6.11. An interquartile range (75th percentile–25th percentile) of 0.1 was present in four of the five cases (all but certain). Between 11 and 33% of the respondents were either above the upper quartile or below the lower quartile for the five definitions in Tables 6.12. Thus, a notable fraction of potential analysts may assess the subjective estimate of probability *differently* than given by the median value or the median value bounded by the upper quartile and the lower quartile! In addition, the high and low values for each level often represent considerable deviations from the median value. From Appendix J the smallest range (high to low) for the five probability statements evaluated here in Table 6.12 was 0.7 (medium), whereas the largest range was 0.9 (certain) and the average of the 5 ranges was > 0.8!

Several problems exist with developing and using ordinal scales or tables derived from estimative probability data. (See Appendix J, Sec. I for a fuller discussion.)

First, as just discussed, the definitions are interpreted differently by different analysts. If, for example, high is defined as 0.75, but the analyst believes that it is much lower, say 0.45, and medium is defined as 0.50, the analyst may choose to score an issue as having a medium probability level because of the potential contradiction between the word definition and the numerical score provided. The broad range of values given by survey respondents for the definitions in Table 6.12 indicates that a considerable level of variation will exist for a group of analysts in scoring issues based upon subjective probability, which may lead to erroneous results.

Second, results obtained from using estimative probability information will typically have a high degree of uncertainty. For example, when estimative probability data is used to construct an ordinal scale, the increment values between adjacent (scale) levels are generally unknown or highly uncertain *unless the scale values are derived from a statistical analysis of survey information, not guesses.* When probabilities are given as point values, this can convey a false sense of accuracy. *Hence, a range around the median (or mean) value, should always be reported (e.g., quartiles). (Median values are preferable to the mean because the distribution of responses will typically be skewed and nonnormal.)* Note: A range around the median (or mean) that is contrived (e.g., guess) or devised without the use of a statistical analysis of underlying data should never be used because it too conveys a false sense of accuracy.

Third, candidate risk issues often evaluated with such probability data (e.g., an ordinal scale or a probability table) may be related to maturity (e.g., potential development status of an item) or some other criteria different than probability. *This forces the analyst to choose a probability level that may not at all apply, or one where the analyst has little confidence in the results.*

Fourth, probability data of this type almost never represents probabilities associated with *actual measured values* (e.g., real-world data or survey results), but typically only subjective estimates made by the author of the estimative probability ordinal scale or probability table, and later the analyst attempting to use it. Thus, a subjective evaluation is often made by the author to generate the probability values associated with a statement, and a subjective interpretation is made by the analyst using the statements and their associated probability values.

Fifth, in cases where the probability representation of a risk issue may actually be valid, the analyst often has little or no knowledge how to score the given issue. (For example, the analyst may have to rate the reliability of an item that has not been developed, nor where reliability predictions exist.) Thus, without relevant supporting data, the result will typically be nothing more than a guess.

Probability values derived from subjective estimates should not be used in risk calculations unless they are based on real world data or extensive, carefully constructed surveys. Data from surveys should not be treated as a point estimate and should include a range around the reported score (e.g., upper and lower quartile values around the median value).

D. Purely Subjective Risk Analysis Methodology

On some programs the risk analysis methodology is primarily or solely based on a subjective evaluation with little or no supporting rationale as to why certain choices were made. The danger with this approach is that when no objective or even measurable criteria for comparison are used the results may be highly uncertain or erroneous unless 1) expert opinion is available, 2) very close analogy systems both technically and programmatically are used for comparison purposes, and 3) lessons learned from highly analogous programs are well documented and used. Although some subjectivity will exist in most risk analyses performed, the primary basis for the methodology should generally not be unstructured guessing.

The risk analysis methodology should not be based solely upon a subjective evaluation unless expert opinion is available, very close analogy systems are used for comparison purposes, and lessons learned from highly analogous programs are well documented and used.

E. Components Included in Estimating C,P,S Risk

Different approaches are commonly used for estimating C,P,S risk on a variety of programs. Often an imbalance exists pertaining to what variables are included in the methodology when analyzing risk for these variables.

Technical risk is often estimated subjectively or from ordinal scales whereas performance risk is generally modeled in a Monte Carlo simulation. When estimating technical risk, cost and schedule risk components are typically only directly considered through the consequence of occurrence term (e.g., where separate ordinal scales may exist for C,P,S consequence of occurrence), although they may be indirectly present through the candidate design (which reflects the program budget or cost and schedule). Approaches for estimating performance risk do not directly include cost or schedule components, although they also may be indirectly present through the candidate design.

Generally the components modeled for schedule risk in a Monte Carlo simulation include estimating uncertainty and/or technical risk modeled in one or more probability distributions. A cost risk component should be included, but typically is not. Cost risk analysis using a Monte Carlo simulation should include cost estimating uncertainty and schedule risk and/or technical risk modeled in one or more probability distributions.

Thus, an imbalance often exists between C,P,S risk analysis in terms of the components directly included in the methodology.

One position sometimes advanced is that technical risk does not directly depend on cost risk or schedule risk, but schedule risk depends on technical risk and cost risk depends on schedule and technical risk. However, this position is not strongly defensible because, for example, changes in cost can impact schedule risk via a fixed program budget (cet. par.), just as technical risk can impact schedule risk. Similarly, when work packages are developed in part from cost estimates [e.g., usually based on an engineering (bottoms-up) estimate], then cost risk (or at least cost estimating uncertainty) associated with labor rate can potentially translate into a schedule impact.

At the total program level changes in development cost are typically only weakly correlated with changes in development schedule. Although changes in cost and schedule should intuitively be highly correlated, the missing dimension is the change in performance. When changes in performance are not controlled, then a simple relationship between the change in cost and the change in schedule will typically not exist at the total program level (as discussed in Chapter 1). In effect, C,P,S are interrelated in a complex manner for a given design. The same can be said for C,P,S (as well as technical) risk.

Many projects do not have the available knowledge, resources (e.g., personnel and budget), or time to evaluate adequate these issues prior to making key decisions early in the development phase. Using simplistic assumptions associated with C,P,S interrelationships plus how risk associated with each variable will be modeled in terms of other variable risk may simplify the risk analysis process. However, it will lead to results that typically include an unknown level of uncertainty via random and perhaps bias noise terms related to how risk components are estimated even if the methodology used contains no other errors.

When estimating C,P,S risk, consciously decide which variables to include in the risk analysis methodology. Do not simply assume that the methodology you are using is sufficient and includes all appropriate variables—often one or more variables are absent.

F. Use of Checklists for Risk Analysis

In a limited number of cases, it may be possible to use checklists or lists of attributes to identify medium or higher risk issues so long as a very close analogy both technically and programmatically exists with historical data, and expert opinion is available. However, checklists or lists of attributes should not be used as a quantitative risk analysis tool because even the simplest form of mathematical operations can lead to erroneous results.

First, even simple mathematical operations performed on checklists results (e.g., summing the number of "yes" answers) almost always assume that the questions (items) are weighted equally, which may not be the case. Second, some of the questions may be posed as probability or consequence of occurrence-related, when in reality, risk should be addressed. Third, unless the questions are carefully worded and subjective phrases are absent (e.g., moderate difficulty), it is possible that an erroneous response may result. Fourth, there is no basis to perform mathematical operations on checklist scores and doing so may lead to erroneous results. For example, there is no rigorous method to relate the sum of the checklist scores (e.g., assume yes = 1 and no = 0) to a specific risk level (e.g., medium). Conversely, risk factors derived from the sum of the checklist scores divided by the total possible score (e.g., 30 scores = yes out of 50 total scores yields a risk factor of 0.60) or similar methods are not rigorous and may lead to erroneous results. Fifth, items in the checklist may not be uncorrelated, or the checklist may be heavily weighted (in terms of the number of items) to a particular issue. The net result can be a bias toward a certain answer (e.g., a particular issue, such as hardware development, and an associated response, such as yes or no), which can be compounded when the questions are not carefully worded. Sixth, and conversely, the questions included may not capture the totality of potential risk issues that exist (e.g., design/engineering risk may be covered but not manufacturing risk). Seventh, it is not valid to develop ranges of answers (either "yes" or "no") that correspond to high, medium, and low risk. To illustrate this point, if the checklist contains 40 questions, and you define high risk as 30 or more questions answered "yes," medium risk to be 15 to 29 questions answered "yes," and low risk to be 14 or fewer questions answered "yes," then results may not be meaningful for several reasons. (For simplicity in this example, a "yes" response corresponds to a risk condition, while a "no" response does not.) Although it is possible that the risk level will increase with the number of questions answered "yes," a "yes" answer to even a *single question* may indicate a risk issue that warrants more detailed evaluation, and may in turn point to a high, medium, or low risk. Eighth, it is not clear how the analyst develops numerical boundaries separating high-, medium-, and low-risk levels. For example, what evidence exists in the previous (hypothetical) example that a high risk corresponds to 30 or more questions answered with a "yes" response? In general, there will be insufficient substantiation to confidently develop such risk level boundaries.

In a limited number of cases, it may be possible to use checklists or lists of attributes to identify medium or higher risk issues so long as a very close analogy both technically and programmatically exists with historical data and expert opinion is available. However, checklists or lists of attributes should not be used as a quantitative risk analysis tool because even the simplest form of mathematical operations can lead to erroneous results.

G.   Brief Discussion of Monte Carlo Simulations

It is not my intention to provide an exhaustive discussion of Monte Carlo simulations here—good references are available that describe how to setup and run such simulations.[14-16] I will now briefly discuss the use of Monte Carlo simulations for C,P,S risk analysis.

1.   Cost Risk Analysis[13]

This technique provides a cost estimate at completion (EAC) typically at WBS Level 1 that is a function of cost estimating uncertainty, schedule risk, and technical risk. (This section was developed in part from Ref. 13.) It uses separately determined cost reference point estimates for each WBS element and probability distributions developed for each of the elements. (Typically, each element will have at least a cost estimating uncertainty, and some will have both schedule risk and technical risk.)

Although the details of implementing the Monte Carlo simulation will vary between applications, most cost risk analyses use the following procedures:

1) "Identify the lowest WBS level for which cost probability distribution functions will be constructed. The level selected will depend on the program phase."[13] For example, during Phase 0, it may not be possible to go lower than WBS Level 3 simply because a representative design and an accurate WBS has not yet been developed for lower levels. "As the program advances into subsequent phases, the design is matured, and the WBS is expanded, it will be possible and necessary to go to WBS Levels 4, 5, and possibly lower."[13]

2) Develop the reference point estimate for each WBS element contained within the model.

3) Identify cost estimating uncertainty, schedule risk, and technical risk for these WBS elements. (As just mentioned, schedule risk and technical risk may not apply to all WBS elements.)

4) Develop suitable probability distributions for each WBS element being investigated.

5) Aggregate the WBS element probability distributions functions using a Monte Carlo simulation program. The results of this step will typically be an WBS Level 1 cost EAC and CDF of cost vs probability. "These outputs are then analyzed to determine the level of cost risk and to identify the specific cost drivers."[13] (The CDF of the output distribution is evaluated to identify the risk dollars that exist at a given confidence interval. For example, if the CDF median, which is the 50th percentile value, is $1.5 million and the sum of the reference point estimates without risk is $1.0 million, then the risk dollars are $1.5 − $1.0 million = $0.5 million at the 50th percentile of confidence.)

The use of probability distributions at individual cost WBS elements results in a more realistic EAC than simply using and aggregating reference point estimates for the WBS elements because risk is included in the resulting Monte Carlo simulation output.

2. Performance Risk Analysis

Although the details of implementing the Monte Carlo simulation will vary between applications, most performance risk analyses use the following procedure:

1) Define the performance model that will be evaluated.

2) Identify model elements that contain risk.

3) Estimate the level of risk for these elements.

4) Develop suitable probability distributions for each element being investigated.

5) Aggregate the WBS element probability distributions functions using a Monte Carlo simulation program. The results of this step will typically be one or more measures of performance (e.g., aircraft velocity) and a CDF

of performance vs probability. These outputs are then analyzed to determine the level of performance risk and to identify the specific performance drivers.

3. Schedule Risk Analysis[13]

This technique provides a means to determine schedule risk at a desired level of aggregation (often WBS Level 1) as a function of schedule estimating uncertainty, cost risk, and technical risk. (This section was developed in part from Ref. 13.) It uses separately determined schedule estimates for each activity and probability distributions developed for selected activities. (Because of the large number of activities present in many development programs, probability distributions may be developed for only a subset of the total number of activities. These distributions should at least include schedule estimating uncertainty, and some will have both cost risk and technical risk.)

A schedule risk analysis expands the commonly used Critical Path Method (CPM) of developing a program schedule to obtain a realistic estimate of schedule risk. ("The basic CPM approach uses single point estimates for the duration of program activities to develop the program's expected duration and schedule."[13])

Although the details of implementing the Monte Carlo simulation will vary between applications, most schedule risk analyses use the following procedures:

1) Identify the lowest activity level for which duration estimates and probability distributions will be developed. "The WBS should be used as the starting point for identifying activities and constructing a network of activities. The WBS level selected will depend on the program phase."[13] As in the cost risk analysis case, during Phase 0, it may not be possible to go lower than WBS Level 3. As the program advances into subsequent phases, the design is matured, and the WBS is expanded, it will be possible and necessary to go to WBS Levels 4, 5, and possibly lower.

2) Construct a CPM schedule for the activities at the desired WBS level. This includes determining and analyzing start and finish dates and the duration for each activity being investigated.

3) Identify schedule estimating uncertainty, cost risk, and technical risk for these activities. (Schedule estimating uncertainty, and especially cost risk and technical risk, may not apply to all activities.)

4) Develop suitable probability distributions for each activity being investigated.

5) Aggregate the activity probability distributions functions using a Monte Carlo simulation program. The results of this step will be a schedule at the desired (WBS) level and CDFs of schedule vs probability. The CDFs will typically represent duration and finish date at the desired activity level, but can include other variables as well. "These outputs are then analyzed to

determine the level of schedule risk and to identify the specific schedule drivers."[13] (The CDF of the output distribution is evaluated to identify the duration or finish date that exists at a given confidence interval. For example, if the CDF median, which is the 50th percentile, value is 100 days and the deterministic duration is 85 days, then the added duration caused by risk is 100 days − 85 days = 1 = days at the 50th percentile of confidence.)

The use of probability distributions at selected activities results in a more realistic schedule assessment than simply using point duration estimates for the activities because risk is included in the resulting Monte Carlo simulation output.

Another issue that can potentially be overcome by using a Monte Carlo schedule simulation is related to path convergence. (Path convergence is the node in the schedule where parallel paths merge or join. At that node, delays or elongation or any converging path can delay the project.[17]) Path convergence causes most project scheduling software to compute optimistic completion dates vs what will likely be achieved. Schedule compression adds to this potential problem as more and more activities have similar durations and are performed in parallel. One approach to resolving this issue is to identify schedule activities with potential uncertainty and/or risk, include appropriate schedule estimating uncertainty, cost risk, and technical risk distributions for these activities, and perform a Monte Carlo simulation. The resulting output will provide a probabilistic estimate (e.g., CDF) of the impact of uncertainty, risk, and path convergence on key schedule milestones.

H. Estimating Risk by Monte Carlo Simulation vs Ordinal Scales

In some cases it is acceptable to have C,P,S consequence of occurrence terms derived from ordinal scales. However, because ordinal "probability" scales are typically not derived from probability values, the risk factors computed from the "probability" and consequence of occurrence values will often be erroneous. In addition, it is generally not appropriate to estimate cost and schedule risk using cost and schedule ordinal "probability" scales. Because the scale definitions are often subjective, the resulting "probability" scores may not be meaningful. Unless the "probability" scales are calibrated, the result is an ordinal scale which cannot be combined with technical "probability" attributes (e.g., design/engineering and technology).

When feasible, it is often better to analyze C,P,S risk in a Monte Carlo simulation because estimates of risk will result, which are typically not possible with ordinal scales. Risk values can be derived via Monte Carlo simulations because both cardinal probability and consequence values exist. (Of course, this is not to say that there is no uncertainty in the simulation results, quite the contrary in most cases.)

Another reason that a Monte Carlo simulation may be preferable is that a CDF of consequence units [e.g., dollars (cost) and time (schedule)] plus risk can be developed—something not possible with ordinal scales or estimative probabilities.

Although Monte Carlo simulations can provide very useful information for analysts and decision makers, they do have some key limitations.

First, as would seem obvious, the results from a simulation are only as good as the inputs. Some key considerations that affect simulation accuracy include, but are not limited to 1) identifying elements believed to contain risk; 2) the most likely costs (cost), performance level (performance), and duration (or finish date, etc.) (schedule) for identified elements; 3) the variables that contribute to risk (e.g., cost estimating uncertainty, schedule risk, and technical risk contribute to cost risk); 4) the distribution types selected and their critical values; 5) the degree of uncertainty associated with selecting the distribution types and their critical value; 6) the degree of correlation (if any) between the model elements; 7) simulation settings (e.g., the number of iterations the simulation is run and the type of sampling performed); 8) how risk is estimated from the CDF and the confidence level that the simulation CDF is evaluated; 9) attempts to allocate risk back to individual model elements; and 10) how the results are portrayed for decision makers.

As evident from the preceding list, numerous factors can affect the accuracy and certainty of results obtained from a Monte Carlo simulation. In one vernacular of modeling, the potential for "garbage in, garbage out" is very real for simulations. Finally, it is exceedingly important that both analysts and decision makers not get trapped into placing more credibility into simulation results than they warrant. This is often quite tempting because the complex nature of the calculations may preclude detailed independent evaluation of the results coupled with the information rich nature of the potential output (e.g., a CDF plot).

Second, to carefully set up a Monte Carlo simulation requires an investment of resources, both in terms of trained analyst(s), plus program personnel needed to 1) obtain the deterministic estimate for each element (e.g., reference point estimate for cost); 2) identify model elements containing risk; 3) select and quantify distribution types and their critical values; 4) determine the degree of correlation (if any) between the model elements; and 5) interpret the model output. In effect, running the simulation on a computer generally requires far less resources than developing the inputs and interpreting the outputs.

There are a number of Monte Carlo simulation packages available commercially and many, many more that have been written for internal use. Unfortunately, even popular commercial packages sometimes contain substantial bugs and limitations that are often not publicized ("let the buyer beware"). Whereas simulation tools that are add-ins to spreadsheet or scheduling software packages often have refined input settings and output options, they may be held hostage by changes to the interface and capabilities of the host spreadsheet or scheduling packages. In the worst case this can render the add-in inoperative until a debugged upgrade is available. In other cases features contained within the host package must not be used to prevent the add-in from crashing, or even worse, generating inaccurate results. Finally, the time needed to perform a simulation may vary by one to two orders of magnitude on the same computer platform depending whether the simulation is performed by an add-in to a spreadsheet or hand coded using an optimized compiler using a mid- to low-level programming language. (Tests I have run indicate code produced from an optimized compiler routinely runs 20 to 40 times faster than a similar simulation run from a spreadsheet add-in.) Even worse is the case for add-ins to some project scheduling packages because of the inefficiency in how the host package performs floating point mathematics. The equivalent throughput speed may be up to one to two orders of magnitude slower than for a spreadsheet add-in for a model with the same number of identical probability distributions.

I. Comparison of Results from Ordinal Risk Scales and Monte Carlo Simulations

Ordinal scales and Monte Carlo simulations are sometimes used to evaluate cost or schedule risk for a given WBS element or activity. This begs the question of whether or not the results will be compatible. Unfortunately, the two sets of results often cannot be directly compared.

Results obtained from ordinal scale(s) are generally not risk. If technical "probability" scales (e.g., design/engineering) are used with cost or schedule consequence of occurrence scales, the results will not be compatible with those from Monte Carlo simulations because different risk categories are being modeled. If estimative probability scales are used with cost or schedule consequence of occurrence scales, the results will also not be compatible because the probability scale score will at best represent a range with generally unknown uncertainty rather than a point estimate on almost all such scales (see Appendix J for additional information), whereas the Monte Carlo simulation result will be the deterministic estimate plus risk at the desired confidence level (albeit with uncertainty also present). If cost or schedule consequence of occurrence scales are used, this only yields one term of risk—probability of occurrence is missing—hence the results will be incompatible.

Several other considerations will tend to make comparing results from ordinal scales and Monte Carlo simulations difficult, including 1) the methodology used to estimate the level of potential cost or schedule impact for ordinal consequence of occurrence scales; 2) methods used to estimate the probability distribution critical values used in a Monte Carlo simulation; 3) the number and types of probability distributions used in the Monte Carlo simulation for a given WBS element or activity; 4) the confidence level selected for estimating cost or schedule risk from a Monte Carlo simulation may be different than that used to estimate the likely "probability" level and dollar or schedule impact with ordinal scales; 5) the approach used to allocate cost or schedule risk back to individual WBS elements or activities will impact the resulting risk allocation (and because no methodology is likely optimal, then results will vary with the algorithms considered); and 6) different personnel developing information used for the two analyses.

It is generally difficult, and it may not be possible, to compare accurately cost and schedule risk estimates obtained from ordinal scales and Monte Carlo simulations for a given WBS element or activity.

J. Use of Ordinal Scales to Adjust C,P,S Values

Values derived from ordinal scales are sometimes used to adjust estimates of C,P,S but the results may be erroneous. A simplified example of this procedure follows where a risk factor is used to adjust a baseline cost to yield a risk adjusted cost.[18] (The example presented here is simplified vs that given by Ref. 18, but is sufficient to illustrate the point being made in this subsection.)

$$RC = BC * (1 + RF)$$

where RC is the risk adjusted cost, BC the baseline cost, and RF the risk factor. Assume that we want to estimate the potential development cost for a computer board. Also, assume at the present time the computer board is at the brassboard development stage. Here, the risk factor is derived from one or more normalized uncalibrated ordinal scale and effectively increases the baseline cost to yield the risk adjusted cost. For example, if the baseline cost is $100,000 and the risk factor is 0.5, then the risk adjusted cost is

$$RC = \$100,000 * (1 + 0.5) = \$150,000$$

Despite the attractiveness to do so, *uncalibrated ordinal scales should not be used to provide risk (adjustment) factors,* or "probability" or maturity levels to adjust C,P,S outcomes because 1) the resulting scale level values are generally only indicators of "probability" and consequence and almost never lead to risk, 2) increments between successive levels are almost never equal in value and are often strongly nonlinear (e.g., see Tables 6.7 and 6.8), and 3) it is unclear whether such scales can accurately adjust C,P,S values even if calibrated.

Using ordinal scales for this purpose is appealing because it provides structure for adjusting potential C,P,S values vs some parameter (e.g., technological maturity). However, uncalibrated ordinal "probability" and consequence scales are typically used, and the results will have an unknown uncertainty because incorrect interval, thus scale values, exist.

If an ordinal "probability" scale is used and has been accurately calibrated with a suitable technique, then the results may be of value even though it is not risk. However, in many cases a single ordinal scale will not accurately describe the development, or Production, Fielding/Deployment, and Operational Support phase for the candidate item, and the results will be flawed. For example, hardware product development generally encompasses, at a minimum, design/engineering, manufacturing, and technology considerations. Combining these three areas into a single "probability" scale can lead to incorrect results, or using one ordinal "probability" scale (e.g., focused on design/engineering) while eliminating the other risk categories (e.g., technology and manufacturing) will also lead to incorrect results. Similarly, using a single ordinal "probability" scale (e.g., manufacturing) may capture some aspects of a risk category (e.g., manufacturing production equipment), but not include others (e.g., availability of sufficient numbers of trained personnel). In addition, using ordinal "probability" scales focused on a particular risk category (e.g., manufacturing) may only capture the potential impact of a single C,P,S variable (e.g., cost), while implicitly requiring that the other variables are held constant (e.g., performance and schedule), which may not be a reasonable assumption. For example, assume recurring cost is related to the item's performance requirements (e.g., FPA detector chip sensitivity), then higher performance leads to lower chip yield, which results in higher recurring cost (cet. par.). In this case it is not reasonable to assume that a manufacturing ordinal "probability" scale can accurately adjust recurring cost over a wide range of potential chip performance.

Using multiple calibrated ordinal scales with calibrated weighting factors between the scales will generally provide more accurate results. However, the fundamental question exists as to whether even calibrated ordinal scales can be accurately used to adjust C,P,S values. Unless the calibrated interval values were derived using closely analogous data to the item(s) to be adjusted, then nontrivial uncertainty will likely exist in the coefficients. In addition, as just mentioned, the scale levels typically do not represent risk, but instead product maturity or an indication of probability (even through not true probability). Hence, it is unclear whether any valid mathematical and probabilistic basis exists for adjusting cost or schedule with such scales.

Even if calibrated ordinal scales can be developed that represent risk (or at least a weighted value of relative importance to the program), the scales should generally be used to only adjust the *variable component* of cost or schedule, not total cost and schedule, which has a fixed component (e.g., nonrecurring cost). For example, a manufacturing ordinal "probability" scale may include both nonrecurring items (e.g., adequate facilities) and recurring items (e.g., item is currently produced at the necessary rate). However, the nonrecurring items should only be applied to the nonrecurring portion of cost and/or schedule, and the recurring items against the recurring portion of cost and/or schedule.

Finally, when using risk (adjustment) factors derived from ordinal "probability" scales, if the lowest scale level has a value of 0.0 assigned to it this does not imply zero risk (or "probability") but a risk (or "probability") of low level. This consideration may become important if the definition of the ordinal scale level assigned a rating of 0.0 does not imply a thoroughly proven item that meets all C,P,S requirements.

Despite the attractiveness to do so, uncalibrated ordinal scales should not be used to adjust C,P,S outcomes. Similarly, calibrated ordinal scales can only be considered for this application if the coefficients were derived using closely analogous data to the item(s) to be adjusted. Even if this is the case, great care should be taken to ensure that the scales are properly applied and the results are not blindly used.

K. Mapping Consequence of Occurrence into a Single Component

In some cases, estimative probability values (see Appendix J) are used in conjunction with cardinal consequence of occurrence data to compute risk. (This will generally lead to an uncertain estimate of risk unless carefully developed guidelines are used with the estimative probability values, e.g., how to include probability range information in the calculations, and the analysts are very familiar with the issue being assessed.)

The approach used by one organization for consequence of occurrence is to estimate cardinal cost (e.g., dollars), performance (e.g., level of redesign needed), and schedule (e.g., time). The consequence of occurrence results are then translated into a single component (e.g., cost), and the other two consequence components are not reported. The argument is sometimes made that two of the relevant components (e.g., performance and schedule) can be mapped into the third component (e.g., cost), and this is a sufficient measure of consequence of occurrence. However, this argument is generally wanting for two reasons.

First, it assumes that accurate and certain relationships exist between the three consequence of occurrence components, which is often not true. Second, when potential impacts are required between risk issues or over a period of time, separate C,P,S consequence of occurrence information may be needed by decision makers. For example, even if all impacts can be translated into cost, schedule impacts may be important for program planning purposes (e.g., integration of tasks), and technical impacts may be important to understand the magnitude of potential redesign activities needed.

Estimate and report C,P,S consequence of occurrence information for each risk issue even if these data can be accurately combined into a single consequence component.

L. Seemingly Enhanced Methodologies May Not Improve Accuracy

The risk analysis methodology may contain a mixture of methodologies that may appear to increase the accuracy or precision or results but may not actually do so. For example, a set of three-level ordinal scales are used to estimate the "probability" of occurrence term. Once the "probability" level is determined, then the analyst estimates the subjective probability value (guess), where the issue would fall within the particular "probability" of occurrence category. An example of this flawed methodology follows.

An ordinal "probability" of occurrence scale defines low to be a "probability" between $0.0 < P \le 0.4$, medium to be a "probability" between $0.4 < P \le 0.7$, and high to be a probability between $0.7 < P \le 1.0$. (However, as already mentioned, an ordinal scale cannot represent a probability or probability range unless originally derived from probability-related data. Because this was not the case in this implementation, the "probability" ranges for each scale level are meaningless.) Assume that the analyst correctly selects the ordinal scale level (e.g., low) by matching the state of the issue in question against the appropriate ordinal scale level definition. (However, as mentioned in Appendix H, Sec. III, a three-level ordinal scale is not desirable because a miscalculation of a single level can change risk results from low to moderate, etc.) The analyst then (incorrectly) defines a "probability" value or range within the ordinal scale level that is believed to represent the issue being evaluated (e.g., a value of perhaps 0.17 or $0.10 < value \le 0.20$, within the low range of $0.0 < P \le 0.4$). Here, a subjective probability analysis without any known basis is applied against a three-level ordinal "probability" scale level whose incorrect "probability" range has no known basis. Although this approach appears to imply added accuracy, the results are virtually meaningless beyond the original ordinal scale value selected (low, medium, and high) because of the unknown uncertainty that exists in the results. (Using a three-level "probability" scale, let alone an ordinal estimative "probability" scale with broad scale value ranges and lacking in supporting documentation, is *extremely unwise.*)

The risk analysis methodology may contain a mixture of methodologies that may appear to increase the accuracy or precision or results but may not actually do so. An independent examination of the risk analysis methodology should be performed to determine its soundness and validity.

M.   Validity of a Risk Analysis Methodology

There may be no documented rationale why the proposed risk analysis methodology for a given risk category is valid, and in some cases the methodology is definitely invalid. For example, blindly using probability ratings derived from subjective estimates as point values will likely lead to errors because there is often substantial uncertainty around the point values, both in the initial derivation of the estimates then later when they are used in a risk analysis (see Sec. IV.C). In addition, performing mathematical operations on the scores obtained from uncalibrated ordinal scales will lead to erroneous results (see Sec. IV.B).

Errors in the methodology can range from overt to very subtle. Consequently, an independent examination of the risk analysis methodology should be performed to help ensure its validity.

I now give three examples of risk analysis methodologies that may yield erroneous results. The underlying cause of the problem(s) for each methodology is sometimes subtle, and I give these examples to provide some insights into how to evaluate candidate methodologies, as well as to look at the issues each contains.

The first case represents an immeasurable cause and effect between ordinal "probability" scale definitions and the risk category the scale represents. (A related problem not discussed here is an invalid cause and effect.) The "probability" scale was developed for requirements volatility (risk category). Scale-level definitions included statements such as, at least 5% but less than 15% of the design is altered because of modifications to the threat documents. This scale definition represents an immeasurable cause and effect. Here, the cause is modifications to the threat documents, and the effect is at least 5% but less than 15% of the design is altered. In reality, the percent change range for the degree that the design is altered likely cannot be confidently measured nor validated. (Similarly, ordinal "probability" scales for alternate items, correlation or dependency or interaction, and concurrency also represent an immeasurable cause and effect between scale definitions and the risk category the scale represents.)

The second case represents a methodology that may be valid at one WBS level, but not valid at another WBS level. Here, an ordinal "probability" scale was developed based on the total program (WBS Level 1) schedule length for a number of similar programs. (The procedure for deriving this type of scale is given in Appendix K.) The use of an ordinal schedule "probability" scale may be acceptable so long as it is applied at the same WBS level as the database it was derived from to classify the likelihood that a similar program could be completed within a certain period of time. However, it is not acceptable to apply this scale at a different WBS level than it was derived from. For example, you cannot accurately apply such a scale to WBS Level 5 if the database used to derive the scale only includes information at the total program level (WBS Level 1).

A presumption for the correct use of a schedule probability scale derived from WBS Level 1 data is that *all* elements in the program, including those at the level evaluated by the scale (e.g., Level 5), must have a schedule length identical to the total program schedule length. Although this may be correct for evaluating a similar, current program at WBS Level 1, it is not likely to be correct when applied at say WBS Levels 4 or 5.

For example, assume that the planned (total program) schedule length from Milestone II to first delivery for a given item is 3.6 years, and this corresponds to say the 40th percentile of similar programs in the database (see Table K.1, Appendix K for additional information.) This indicates that there is a 40% chance of achieving this schedule and a 60% chance that a longer schedule will exist (cet. par.). This is the correct use for such an ordinal schedule probability scale. Now assume that the scale is used to evaluate the probability term of schedule risk at lower WBS levels, and say you evaluate a 2.4-year task at WBS Level 4. Using the total program (WBS Level 1) database, you cannot say what the schedule probability value is for the WBS Level 4 task. It is clearly not simply the 20th percentile at the total program level that is 2.4 years (see Table K.1, Appendix K)—*the value is unknown!* (Also, in some cases I have examined the schedule values for specific scale levels that are often purely subjective with no specific reference or application to the program being evaluated.)

In addition, an ordinal schedule probability scale derived at the total program level cannot be applied to lower WBS levels because the schedule at the total program level cannot generally be related by any analytically quantifiable measure to lower WBS levels (e.g., it, is not the mean of the lower-level tasks). The total program schedule length is influenced by a host of considerations at lower WBS levels that vary on an activity-by-activity basis, including, but not limited to 1) individual activities having different durations independent of the risk present, 2) constraints (e.g., start no earlier than a specific date), 3) planned start and finish dates, 4) path convergence, 5) slack, 6) uncertainty vs the plan, 7) cost risk, and 8) technical risk.

Because these various conditions will never be met except in the most trivial instances, an ordinal schedule probability scale derived with data at the total program level should not be applied to lower WBS levels.

Similarly, cost or schedule data, including change data, derived at the total program level *should not be used* to adjust cost or schedule at lower WBS levels because values at the total program level are often not representative of values at lower WBS levels (e.g., schedule risk that contributes to schedule change is aggregated at the total program level and often far different for the activities associated with lower WBS levels).

The third case is a combination of immeasurable cause and effect coupled with a methodology that *may be* valid at one WBS level, but not valid at another WBS level. Here, an attempt is made to map technical characteristics or risk scores obtained at lower WBS levels to historical cost or schedule data, such as change data, at the total program level for a given program phase [e.g., engineering and manufacturing development (EMD)]. The appeal of this procedure is that more strenuous technical characteristics or higher risk scores might correspond to larger cost and/or schedule change (final outcome divided by initial estimate) by some quantifiable amount. For example, a higher risk score might be related to larger cost growth or schedule slippage. However, there are at least two substantial problems with this approach that cannot be easily resolved and eliminated. (These problems are in addition to those previously discussed with using risk scores derived from uncalibrated ordinal scales, which is part of this methodology.)

First, if you compare technical characteristics or risk scores to total program cost change or schedule change, you have not properly constrained the relationship between cost change, performance change, schedule change, and risk. For example, even if you could map lower WBS level performance to total program cost change and assume that performance change is negligible, the necessary assumption is that schedule change and risk are held constant, which is rarely the case across a sample of historical programs when such computations are performed. (Similarly, mapping between lower WBS level performance to total program schedule change requires that performance change is negligible and cost change and risk are held constant, which is also rarely the case.)

Second, you must assume that the historical program(s) contain subsystems, components, and other items with equal technical characteristics and/or risk scores, and this will almost never be the case. Typically on many development programs a handful of subsystems or components will push or exceed the current state of the art and/or will be high risk, more of these approach the state of the art and/or are medium risk, and there are more below the state of the art and/or are low risk. Thus, the variation in performance relative to the state of the art and/or risk score will be nonzero across the subsystems and components within the system and will also vary between programs. In effect, there are unique distributions of performance relative to the state of the art and risk scores for each program. *However, these distributions are typically unknown for many historical programs.*

But, even if the distributions of performance relative to the state of the art and risk scores were known and you could correctly map performance and/or risk score information associated with a specific subsystem or component for a current program to the distribution of values for a historical program, there is no convincing, correct way to 1) map this information to historical total program cost change and/or schedule change data for a single program and 2) map this information to a distribution of historical total program cost change and/or schedule change data. Finally, although it may be possible to devise a methodology to perform such a mapping, there is no convincing proof that it will yield accurate or even meaningful results. Without such a proof any such methodology should be rejected. (Surprisingly, this methodology has been used in government cost risk analyses on numerous high-value programs, yet no convincing justification exists for its use.)

The validity of a risk analysis methodology should never be blindly accepted because it may contain nontrivial errors. These errors can range from overt to very subtle, but in some cases they can potentially have a large adverse affect on the results. Consequently, an independent examination of the risk analysis methodology should be performed to help ensure its validity prior to its use.

V. Methodologies and Issues for Some Risk Categories

A. Evaluation of Software Items

The computer software configuration item (CSCI) may be at too high a level of integration to identify and analyze software risk issues—they can become aggregated and smoothed over. For example, on several large-scale software intensive development programs (with life-cycle costs exceeding $1 billion), there were only 5 to 10 CSCIs defined for the entire program! In these programs as in others, a lower level of integration than the CSCI (e.g., computer software component or even the computer software unit) is often needed to properly identify, analyze, handle, and monitor software risks.

When evaluating software risk, risk identification and analysis performed at the CSCI may be at too high a level of integration to yield meaningful results. Consider evaluating software risk at the computer software component or even the computer software unit level. Similarly, for risk issues that are medium or higher, develop RHPs and identify and implement risk monitoring metrics at the same level as the risk issues.

B. Probability Term for Some Risk Categories

The evaluation of some risk categories is often better left to a subjective risk analysis by key program personnel rather than attempting to develop ordinal "probability" scales. These risk categories include, but are not limited to, management, programmatic, requirements changes, and contractor capability. Every ordinal "probability" scale I have examined for these risk categories has had substantial deficiencies because of the inability to relate a specific issue to a given probability level clearly and uniquely.

For example, potential risk issues associated with management, programmatics, requirements changes, and contractor capability often 1) do not follow a structured, repeatable process or pattern; 2) do not easily relate to the number and quality of available personnel or tools; 3) are not related to complexity; 4) have substantial uncertainty as to how they should be quantified; 5) cannot be quantitatively measured to determine probabilities; and 6) may be outside the control of the program (e.g., requirements changes). In addition, these risk categories generally do not represent events that have true ordinal ranking on a consistent basis (e.g., event 1 is always less mature or less probable than event 2, event 2 is always less mature or less probable than event 3, and so on).

Given these limitations, the probability term of management, programmatics, requirements changes, and contractor capability risk should not be estimated via uncalibrated or calibrated ordinal scales developed for these risk categories. A subjective analysis of the probability term, perhaps using a carefully constructed estimative ordinal probability scale or probability table, coupled with an evaluation of applicable C,P,S ordinal consequence of occurrence scales can sometimes be used, and the resulting probability and consequence of occurrence values mapped to risk.

If desired, probability distributions can be developed for these risk categories for use in cost and schedule quantitative risk analyses (e.g., Monte Carlo simulations) by defining appropriate (distribution) critical values. For example, the potential impact of budgetary variations on cost may lead to the use of a triangle distribution with low and high values determined by a subjective analysis and associated with a given most likely estimate. The development of such a probability distribution is largely a subjective exercise unless specific cause/effect information is known or can be accurately estimated (e.g., between budget changes and cost variations.) (Note: A triangle distribution was mentioned as an illustration only and does not necessarily represent the correct or only type of probability distribution that could be associated with potential budgetary changes.)

This approach to selecting probability distributions for a Monte Carlo simulation may be fairly subjective. However, it is far better than to develop and/or calibrate ordinal "probability" scales for these risk categories, include the results as part of an approach for estimating the impact on technical risk, then include the adjusted technical risk in a Monte Carlo analysis. As just mentioned, this is because many such risk categories do not have a structured, repeatable process that is representative of ordinal ranking. In addition, it may not be possible to calibrate such ordinal scales with a high degree of certainty (see Sec. IV.A and Appendix H).

The evaluation of some risk categories, such as management, programmatics, requirements changes, and contractor capability, should typically be performed using a subjective risk analysis by key program personnel rather than attempting to develop specific ordinal "probability" scales because of the inability to relate a specific issue clearly and uniquely to a given probability level.

C. Risk from Concurrency

The risk associated with concurrency of development and/or production tasks should not be evaluated with an ordinal "probability" scale because such scales are generally subjective. Similarly, risk adjustment factors that are related to the degree of concurrency should not be used because they too are subjective. Another problem with using concurrency scales or risk adjustment factors is the extent to which they should be applied to the nonrecurring vs recurring portions of cost and schedule. Because concurrency will not affect nonrecurring and recurring components equally, application of a single factor, even one that is derived perfectly, to cost or schedule will introduce an error associated with underlying nonrecurring vs recurring components. If the major component of concurrency risk is related to schedule, then a Monte Carlo schedule risk analysis should be performed that examines concurrent activities as well as other tasks that contain risk. (Here, schedule risk includes schedule estimating uncertainty, cost risk, and technical risk.) This provides a much better method to evaluate the inherent risk present vs using an ordinal "probability" scale. Cost risk associated with concurrency can similarly be evaluated using a Monte Carlo cost risk analysis that includes cost estimating uncertainty, schedule risk, and technical risk. In some cases it may also be possible and desirable to develop a risk analysis that can evaluate both cost and schedule risk in the same simulation.

Risk from concurrency of development and production tasks should not be evaluate with ordinal "probability" scales or risk adjustment factors because they too are subjective. The best approach for evaluating concurrency is often to perform a cost and/or schedule risk analysis using a Monte Carlo simulation.

D. Resource Risk

Estimates of resource risk related to personnel and equipment should generally be explicitly examined. At a minimum these areas should be specifically considered during risk identification activities (e.g., do we have enough moderate skilled personnel to code the real-time display software module). Issues judged to represent risks should subsequently be evaluated as part of the risk analysis. Failure to do so may lead to potential risks not identified until after they become problems and impact the program.

Quantifying the resulting risk level can be much more difficult, and there is no best method to capture the results. One approach is to use a risk analysis methodology specifically related to resources (e.g., a set of ordinal "probability" scales that cover a variety of resource areas such as personnel and equipment). Another approach is to analyze potential resource risks in the categories where they will likely appear (e.g., software design and hardware manufacturing personnel are two common areas). The important point here is that such risks should be explicitly evaluated, regardless of the approach used.

Resource risk related to personnel and equipment should generally be explicitly examined during risk identification, and if potential issues exist, evaluated during the risk analysis. Failure to do so may lead to potential risks not identified until after they become problems and impact the program.

E. Integration Risk

Integration (hardware/hardware, software/software, and hardware/software) risk categories are often not properly examined (identified) or evaluated (analyzed). This is of concern because many moderately to highly complex items (including commercial systems) can have several levels of integration. It is not uncommon for potential integration risk issues to be overlooked in risk identification, which contributes to them becoming problems later in the program with generally far greater cost and schedule impact to resolve.

However, even if integration risk issues are properly identified, the methodology used for risk analysis is often wanting. Using an inappropriate risk analysis methodology to evaluate integration risk issues can lead to substantial errors in estimating the level of risk present, as well as subsequent risk prioritization and the allocation of resources for risk handling activities. For example, applying ordinal "probability" scales developed for hardware or software to integration should only be done as a last resort, and not the desired approach, because of the potential for generating erroneous results.

There are two likely sources of this error. First, the analyst may pick the wrong scale-level value because of an improper fit of an integration activity, when ordinal "probability" scales are used whose definitions reflect hardware or software items. In this case the analyst incorrectly judges what is the appropriate scale level. Second, the actual integration process may be substantially different than the process portrayed in hardware or software maturity based scales. In this case the scales may have limited application because of underlying process dissimilarities.

Finally, separate ordinal "probability" scales may be needed for hardware/hardware, hardware/software, and software/software integration because of dissimilarities in the process flow for each of these types of integration.

Whenever potential integration risk issues exist, a thorough risk identification activity should be performed, and a suitable risk analysis methodology used to evaluate approved risk issues.

F. Threat Risk

Significant components of threat risk are often not included in a risk analysis. Threat risk includes a variety of subcategories, such as security, survivability, and vulnerability. The nature of potential risks may vary considerably depending on the segment or platform examined. (For example, to the first order, vulnerability risk associated with a spacecraft would likely be far different than for a ground station. To the second order, destruction of a ground station could possibly impact the performance of a spacecraft, although likely for different reasons than in the case of direct vulnerability.) Threat risk may not apply to all non DoD and commercial programs. However, it is often critical to a variety of applications, such as electronic funds transfers, homeland defense, information technology, physical security, and telecommunications, given the threat of hackers, industrial espionage, domestic and international terrorism, vandalism, etc.

Threat risk includes a variety of subcategories, such as security, survivability, and vulnerability. Significant components of threat risk are often not included in a risk analysis. Although at first glance threat risk may only seem to apply to DoD programs, it will also apply to a broad range of non DoD and commercial programs as well.

G. Functional Risk

Functional risk is often not properly evaluated or even examined (e.g., the ability to perform and test a critical program capability). Although a design may be generated based on the flowdown of requirements, it is not sufficient to estimate simply the risk of the design and then claim that this presents an accurate picture of functional risk. It will also be necessary to evaluate separately the ability to meet each designated requirement, or at least key requirements, with a suitable risk analysis methodology.

The design-based risk analysis attempts to ascertain requirements risk from a bottoms-up design perspective. However, what is typically needed is a top-down analysis of each requirement. Simplistic means of assessing functional risk, such as an ordinal "probability" scale for requirements suitability or stability, will often times provide little accurate information because of its subjective nature. (For example, a requirement may be difficult to meet, but without sufficient information tailored to a particular program an assessment that simply states this does not provide much useful information to aid in key systems engineering and program management decisions.) More suitable methods, such as an ordinal "probability" scale directly tailored to evaluating the ability to perform functions or a Monte Carlo performance risk simulation, should instead be used.

Another reason to consider functional risk is that it may help the analyst better understand what key technologies associated with the selected design are necessary to meet a given requirement. This is particularly important when more than one moderate- or higher-risk technology is employed and interdependencies between the technologies exist. (This information may prove helpful for planning technology development programs, resource allocation, etc.)

Functional risk is often not properly examined or even evaluated. It will generally be necessary to evaluate the ability to meet at least each designated key requirement using a suitable risk analysis methodology.

H.   Some Consequence of Occurrence Categories to Avoid

Quality is not a suitable consequence of occurrence component because it is often a *cause* rather than an impact to the program. For example, poor quality may decrease performance, increase cost, or increase schedule (cet. par.), while good quality may do the converse. In addition, the reliability component of quality is suitably captured as part of performance consequence and not appropriately treated as a standalone consequence component. Quality should be treated as part of the performance probability term whenever possible (e.g., via reliability, availability and/or failure rate).

Quality is not a suitable consequence of occurrence component because it is often a cause rather than an impact to the program. Quality should be treated as part of the performance probability term whenever possible.

Scope encompasses C,P,S. Hence, scope is not a suitable consequence of occurrence component because of the correlation it may have with C,P,S.

Scope is not a suitable consequence of occurrence component because of the correlation it may have with C,P,S.

Besides C,P,S other possible consequence of occurrence components may be considered but should not be used. This is because the impact of such possible consequence components usually can not be directly and easily measured, and the component can generally be transformed into some mixture of C,P,S. While these two conditions are not universal, they will typically apply and make the introduction of additional consequence of occurrence components both unnecessary and unwise. In addition, some potential consequence components are often subjective (e.g., quality beyond failure rate), and may even imply a "probability" component. Finally, performance, quality, and scope are not interchangeable, and only performance should be viewed as an independent dimension and used together with cost and schedule.

Only C,P,S consequence of occurrence components should be used.

I. Technology Readiness Level

A Technology Readiness Level (TRL) ordinal scales can be helpful in estimating technology maturity. (See for example, National Aeronautics and Space Administration, "NASA Technology Plan 1998," Appendix B, Technology Readiness Levels.) While carefully constructed "probability" maturity scales, such as the NASA TRL scale, can be very helpful in performing a risk analysis, such a scale only addresses the "probability" term of risk, and must be used in conjunction with suitable consequence of occurrence scales. The results from the TRL scale and the consequence of occurrence scales should then be converted to risk level using a suitable risk mapping matrix (see Sec. IX.A). Note also that a TRL scale should be tailored to *your program*. In addition, it will only evaluate the technology maturity dimension of a potential risk issue, and will not address a number of other potential aspects of the probability term for the risk issue (e.g., design/engineering, manufacturing, support, threat).

TRLs are a maturity-based ordinal scale and only encompass the probability of occurrence term of risk. To obtain an estimate of the risk level, C,P,S consequence of occurrence should be obtained from suitable ordinal scales (e.g., Department of Defense, *Risk Management Guide for DoD Acquisition,* 5th ed., Defense Acquisition Univ. and Defense Systems Management College, Ft. Belvoir, VA, June 2002, p. 18) tailored to your program.

The maximum of the three consequence of occurrence scores, together with the TRL value, should then be mapped to a risk mapping matrix.

Department of Defense, DoD 5000.2-R, "Mandatory Procedures for Major Defense Acquisition Programs (MDAPS) And Major Automated Information System (MAIS) Acquisition Programs," 5 April 2002 discusses the use of TRLs (see Sec. C7.5.4 and Appendix 6). The TRL scale given in Appendix 6 of DoD 5000.2-R is an example of an excellent ordinal scale. This is because the definitions are typically single attribute (so they don't confuse the reader), objective in nature (rather than having a lot of subjective verbiage), and relate to specific measurable events (rather than being obtuse or not measurable).

However, as given in Sec. C7.5.4, "TRLs are a measure of technical maturity. They do not discuss the probability of occurrence (i.e., the likelihood of attaining required maturity) or the impact of not achieving technology maturity." While a TRL scale clearly does not represent consequence of occurrence, it does represent a limited form of the probability of occurrence.

The scale only applies to hardware, not to software or integration. For software and integration another version of this scale must be created and used. Attempting to use a hardware scale for software and integration can lead to substantial errors. Since the converse is also true, the bottom line is that an ordinal scale created for one application should generally not be used for any other application without careful examination and evaluation.

The scale only applies to the technology component of technical risk. It does not apply to design/engineering, manufacturing or other possible technical risk components, or, of course, other risk areas. Given that DoD 5000.1, February 1991, contained seven risk areas to cover (cost, design/engineering, manufacturing, schedule, support, technology, and threat), a single hardware TRL scale is quite limited in its application and should never be thought of as an all encompassing "probability" scale.

As most other ordinal probability scales, I use "probability" to indicate that the scale does not represent true probability levels but only indicators of probability. In addition, the scale is raw/uncalibrated, meaning that the true coefficient values for each scale level are unknown. All that is known about the scale levels is that they are monotonic and decreasing (e.g., for a fixed consequence of occurrence, the risk decreases with increasing scale designator number) (cet. par.). Note that this sorting of scale levels is the opposite of almost all ordinal scales—the larger the scale level designator number the higher the risk (cet. par.). Since the scale level designators are only placeholder values (ordered letters like $A > B > C$ and so on are just as meaningful and accurate), then no mathematical operations can be performed on values obtained from such raw/uncalibrated ordinal scales. (See Sec. IV.A.1 for additional information.)

This type of ordinal "probability" scale is related to the maturity of the item. Other types of ordinal "probability" scales I have identified, and discussed in Appendix H, Sec. I include complexity, sufficiency, uncertainty, subjective probability, etc.

TRL scales are unrelated to consequence of occurrence, only probability of occurrence. It is unwise and erroneous to attempt to perform a risk analysis using only a "probability" scale. And anyone attempting to do so will likely generate results that may be substantially incorrect. (This is all the more true when you consider that 1) technology probability is only a portion of the technical probability term, 2) all other potentially relevant probability terms are not covered, and 3) all consequence of occurrence terms are not covered.)

The "bottom line" for a TRL scale: consider using it but understand that it represents only a *very small* part of the probability term of risk, none of the consequence term of risk, and it should never be used as a standalone measure of risk.

A TRL ordinal scale can be helpful in estimating technology maturity. However, a TRL result only captures a small portion of the "probability" term and none of the consequence term of risk. Hence, a TRL scale should never be used as a standalone measure of risk.

VI. Application of Risk Analysis Methodology

A. Selection of the Risk Analysis Methodology

Detailed risk analysis methodologies are sometimes developed before the risk categories and critical process flows associated with the risk categories are known. This can lead to a faulty risk analysis methodology and erroneous results when the methodology is subsequently used. For example, an ordinal "probability" maturity scale should not be generated or used before the development process flow is known for potential risk issues. Because changes in the risk categories or possibly the process flows will occur during the course of the program, updates to the risk analysis methodology may be necessary.

Do not select a risk analysis methodology before the risk categories and critical process flows associated with the risk categories are known.

B. Blind Use of Flawed Risk Analysis Methodologies

Do not be surprised at how poor some methodologies are—some have no mathematical or probabilistic basis whatsoever. In one case risk was estimated to five digits, but because of the completely flawed methodology used, considerable uncertainty existed in the first digit.

Do not be surprised at how poor some methodologies are—some have no mathematical or probabilistic basis whatsoever.

Risk analysis methodologies are sometimes used simply because they appear in the literature, regardless of whether or not they are flawed, out-dated, or even applicable. In such cases there will also be a tendency to use the entire methodology rather than using it as a starting point, identifying flaws present, and developing and implementing solutions to these issues. It is not uncommon for flawed, or obsolete, methodologies to be included 10 to 20 years later in books, journal articles, and, more importantly, in actual programs. This unfortunately leads to the continued propagation of such undesirable methodologies in much the same manner and with much the same damaging effect as a computer virus.

For example, some flawed risk analysis methodologies published by the DoD in the 1980s included performing mathematics on results from uncalibrated ordinal risk scales. These methodologies are still commonly cited and used today even though they have been withdrawn or canceled by DoD, and subsequent (1997+) DoD guidance clearly states that mathematics should not be performed on results from uncalibrated ordinal risk scales.[13]

Unfortunately the propagation of flawed risk analysis methodologies continues because analysts and program managers tend not to question the validity of methodologies in print, those they previously used, or those they are currently using.

Risk analysis methodologies should not be used simply because they appear in the literature, have been previously been used, or are currently being used. The validity of the risk analysis methodology should be challenged and independently assessed, with corrections made as necessary.

Even more disturbing is the case when analysts and program managers are aware that the risk analysis methodology they are using is flawed, options are available to readily correct the problems, but nothing is done to remedy the situation—they continue using the flawed methodology as if nothing was wrong.

Errors in risk analysis results from flawed methodologies can adversely affect both design trades and allocating resources for RHPs against a potentially flawed list of prioritized risk issues. It is extremely unwise to use a known, incorrect risk analysis methodology because of the potential cost and schedule problems that it may contribute to later in the program. This is because misprioritized risk issues may exist and suddenly become problems that require additional resources and/or a priority to resolve.

However, improvements to a flawed risk analysis methodology should be developed in a structured, comprehensive manner. In some cases corrections will be provided in a subjective or ad hoc manner; this may not adequately compensate for known errors and in fact may introduce another set of errors and/or uncertainty into the results.

The continued use of known, flawed risk analysis methodologies should be avoided. Not only is this practice unethical, but it will likely adversely affect both design trades and allocating resources for RHPs. In addition, the potential exists that some key risk issues will be misevaluated and surface later in the program as problems. If the risk analysis methodology is known to be flawed correct the methodology in a structured, comprehensive manner rather than blindly continue to use the flawed approach or perform corrections in a subjective or ad hoc manner.

Those people that blindly defend a risk analysis methodology are usually unaware or unwilling to discuss inherent deficiencies with the methodology. In fact, the more flawed the risk analysis methodology, the more blind the proponents often seem to be about the flaws and the more closed they are to discussing potential limitations and recommendations for enhancement.

Those people that blindly defend a risk analysis methodology are usually unaware or unwilling to discuss inherent deficiencies with the methodology.

C.   Transferring an Existing Risk Analysis Methodology to a New Application

Risk analysis methodologies developed for use with one type of system (e.g., spacecraft) or group of WBS elements (e.g., hardware) are sometimes applied to a very different type of system (e.g., ship) or group of WBS elements (e.g., software) without considering whether or not the methodologies are appropriate or even applicable to the new system. For example, ordinal "probability" scales developed for a spacecraft that uses prototypes may not be representative of a ground system because the term *prototype* may have different meanings in different systems and/or operating environments. Similarly, the integration, assembly, and test procedure is often very distinct for different systems and operating environments. Hence, ordinal "probability" scales developed for one type of system might not apply to another, and the results can be inaccurate. Finally, variations exist between hardware and software development processes so that ordinal "probability" scales developed for, say, hardware should not be used on software without being suitably modified.

If a risk analysis methodology is developed or tailored for one type of system or WBS elements within a system, do not attempt to apply it to other systems or WBS elements without first determining if it applies and what the resulting limitations will be.

D.   Tailoring the Methodology to the Program's Acquisition Phase(s)

The risk analysis methodology should be tailored to the current program phase, but the analyst should also consider developing an approach suitable to future program phases. During the early part of the development phase, the Production, Fielding/Development, and Operational Support phase may not be an immediate concern. The tendency may be to tailor the risk analysis methodology to short-term needs and goals (e.g., preliminary design or perhaps fabrication of an engineering model). However, because critical design decisions affecting the Production, Fielding/Deployment, and Operational Support program phase are typically made early in the development process, it is often beneficial to assess risk categories relevant to these phases (e.g., manufacturing and logistics/support) at that time. Although the fidelity of the information available to support Production, Fielding/Deployment, and Operational Support-based risk analyses will not be high during the early development phase (e.g., Concept Exploration), performing an evaluation of relevant risk categories over potential risk issues may help 1) identify potential risk issues early in the program, 2) shape the design and development process [e.g., Cost as Independent Variable (CAIV) design trades], 3) improve the resulting Production, Fielding/Deployment, and Operational Support program phase, and 4) prevent risk issues from surfacing later in the program as problems. (Because C,P,S cannot be traded perfectly in the short run, it is generally far more cost effective to resolve such issues early, rather than later when they surface as problems.)

If necessary, different risk analyses can be performed to ensure that both near-term and far-term issues are addressed. For example, in one space program two development satellites were anticipated to be fabricated and launched, while dozens would be built and launched during the later Production, Fielding/Deployment, and Operational Support phase. The same risk analysis methodology was applied to both cases. However, two separate risk analyses were performed with ground rules and assumptions tailored to each case (e.g., total quantity, production rate, and technology freeze date). This produced the logical result of relatively low manufacturing risk associated with the two development phase satellites, with relatively higher risk for the subsequent Production, Fielding/Deployment, and Operational Support phase (based on the need for substantially higher throughput and yield vs what existed to satisfy the development phase requirement).

This approach can be expanded if needed, and time and resources permit, to having separate ground rules and assumptions, and possibly risk analysis methodology, tailored to each program phase. This would allow a separate risk analysis to be performed for each program phase. Regardless of the approach taken, it is important that the risk analysis methodology and ground rules and assumptions that are applied be adequately documented to prevent misunderstandings later in the program.

The risk analysis methodology should be tailored to and conducted for the current program phase. However, the analyst should also be consider developing an approach suitable to future program phases and performing a risk analysis for these program phases as desired/needed.

E. Allocation of Risk Scores to Individual Program Phases

The allocation of risk scores (including separate "probability" and/or consequence of occurrence scores) to individual program phases for a given WBS element should generally be avoided because methods for performing the allocations are often subjective and can lead to erroneous results. [For example, 10, 20, and 70% of the risk score is allocated to the program definition and risk reduction (PDRR), EMD, and Production, Fielding/

Deployment, and Operational Support program phases, respectively, for an aircraft inertial navigation system (INS).] Instead, the analyst should evaluate the given WBS element for each program phase in the life cycle, determine which risk categories apply to that program phase, and develop a risk score for the item from the valid risk categories. For example, design/engineering risk often applies to the PDRR and EMD program phases, but not the Production, Fielding/Deployment, and Operational Support program phases (assuming redesign does not occur during Operations and Support). Thus, for an aircraft INS with high accuracy requirements (e.g., very low drift rate), design/engineering risk should be considered for inclusion as one of the risk categories only for the PDRR and EMD program phases. (Note, however, that high accuracy requirements may decrease manufacturing yield if fabrication tolerance or complexity is an issue, which would be appropriate to evaluate as part of manufacturing risk, even though it is not appropriate to evaluate as part of design/engineering risk for the Production, Fielding/Deployment, and Operational Support phase.)

Do not generally allocate risk scores (including separate "probability" and/or consequence of occurrence) to individual program phases for a given WBS element. Methods for performing the allocations are often subjective and can lead to erroneous results. Instead, evaluate the given WBS element for each program phase in the life cycle, determine which categories apply to that program phase, and develop a risk score for the item from the valid risk categories.

F. Top-Down Allocation of Risk Scores to WBS Elements

In some cases a risk issue is identified that encompasses a number of WBS elements (e.g., 20-year design life), yet the customer may want a risk analysis performed on the risk issue rather than simply on the affected WBS elements. Here, at least two very different approaches can be used. The first uses a top-down allocation of risk to individual WBS elements. The second approach is to develop a design that reflects allocated requirements and associated risks, analyze the level of risk for the affected WBS elements, then perform a roll up of the results associated with these elements (see Sec. IX.B).

The first approach involving a top-down, fractional allocation of risk scores (including separate probability and/or consequence of occurrence scores) to WBS elements should generally be avoided because methods for performing the allocation are often subjective and can lead to erroneous results. (This is not to say that a top-down requirements flowdown to lower WBS level should not be performed, only that risk scores should not be arbitrarily allocated to WBS levels.)

For example, assume a transmitter is being developed for an unmanned ocean monitoring probe. If the transmitter is being evaluated and the

probe's available electrical power is an anticipated risk issue, it is not appropriate to subjectively allocate a fraction of the resulting technical risk for
probe electrical power against the transmitter. Here, it would not be correct
to assume that (hypothetically) 20% of the probe electrical power technical
risk score should be allocated to the transmitter by some mathematical
operation, even if 20% of the total probe electrical power requirement is for
the transmitter. Even if this could be done *and* the resulting probe electrical
power risk had a valid cardinal value (e.g., was not derived from uncalibrated ordinal risk scales), it is unclear what type of mathematical operation
would be performed on the transmitter. For example, would the allocated
probe electrical power risk be added to (e.g., 0.20) the transmitter risk,
multiplied by (e.g., 1.20) the transmitter risk, etc.? (In actual cases attempts
may be made to allocate a risk issue across a number of WBS elements: the
more elements used often translates into larger uncertainty unless sound
methods are used to derive the fractional values.)

The second approach for this example would be to analyze probe electrical
power risk for appropriate WBS elements of the selected design and roll up
the resulting risk scores. If the resulting probe electrical power risk level (or
perhaps even its cost) is judged to be too high, then, for example, examine
whether higher efficiency transmitter devices can be used, a higher power
generation density approach is available, or an antenna with a higher gain is
possible (based on C,P,S and risk trades), at an acceptable cost, schedule, and
risk.

In some cases the customer may insist on evaluating risk issues based
upon the first approach. If this occurs, it is incumbent upon the analyst to
develop a range of uncertainty associated with each component of the
fractional allocation, as well as the overall result.

*Different approaches exist for evaluating risk issues that encompass a
number of WBS elements. Although it may appear attractive, the top-down
allocation of risk scores using analyst-derived fractional values should
generally not be used if the allocation approach involves subjective estimates because substantial, unknown uncertainty may exist in the results.
Often, a better approach is to develop a design that reflects allocated
requirements and associated risks, analyze the level of risk for the affected
WBS elements, then perform a roll up of the results associated with these
elements.*

VII. Probability Distributions in Risk Analysis

A. Selection of the Type of Probability Distribution

Probability distributions are often selected for quantitative risk analysis
with no real world basis or method of validation. Simply choosing a probability distribution type (e.g., triangle distribution) because it has been historically used or for the sake of convenience does not address the issue of

whether or not it is valid or should be applied. Even worse is when a probability distribution is selected and the justification is that other uncertainties present will mask potential differences in the results. Although this may ultimately be true, it is sloppy, and no more valid than randomly selecting a distribution type.

The blind selection of a probability distribution will often introduce an unknown uncertainty into the results. If no better information exists, the triangle distribution is often used when a skewed probability distribution is desired, but its selection does not mean that it is the best or even an appropriate distribution for the items (e.g., WBS element) being modeled. In fact, I have not located published evidence in the project management literature to substantiate the use of a triangle probability distribution where the justification is provided by a statistical analysis of real world data. For example, I am unaware of published research that has evaluated the level of actual risk (e.g., cost growth for the development phase) that occurred for a given project (e.g., an integrated circuit), then performed a curve fit on the results to identify types of probability distributions with an acceptable statistical fit (e.g., 0.05 confidence interval).

Distributions that I have commonly used in performing a wide variety of C,P,S Monte Carlo simulations include, but are not limited to, beta beta-PERT, binomial, cumulative, discrete, gamma, general, normal, Rayleigh, triangle, and uniform.[19] The number of options for the analyst is far greater than this. For example, one commercial Monte Carlo simulation package offers more than 30 different probability distributions.

The analyst should never simply default to using a triangle or any other distribution unless it accurately represents the risk event. The danger with blindly presupposing a distribution is that it may be inadequate or completely wrong, leading to erroneous results.[20,21] For example, suppose that the risk event is represented by (only) two possible outcomes. Any attempt to fit a continuous distribution to this event, including assuming the two values correspond to the low and high values of a triangle or uniform distribution, may yield highly erroneous results. Risk events of this type are correctly modeled by a binomial distribution or a histogram composed of two levels that produce discrete outputs, not a range of values from continuous distributions, like a triangle. (See Sec. VII.D for additional information.)

Even more suspect is the case where probability distributions are selected to yield desired, rather than unbiased, Monte Carlo simulation CDF results. In the best case arguments may exist for shaping the selection of the type of probability distribution or the critical values for a given probability distribution. In the worst case distributions and/or their critical values are selected to intentionally bias downward the resulting levels of estimated risk. Clearly, there is no honest basis to warrant this dubious practice.

Because of the widespread abuse of using triangle distributions in project risk management, I conducted a set of experiments to evaluate the effect of using a triangle distribution vs other continuous distribution types in Monte Carlo simulations. A comparison of a portion of the results from four different sets of triangle and uniform distributions is given in Table 6.13. The critical values for the uniform distribution were selected as the low and high values from the triangle distribution. Each simulation was run for 25,000 iterations. This large number of iterations, along with Latin Hypercube sampling, was used to reduce the impact of statistical sampling errors.

From Table 6.13 the magnitude of the difference is small (e.g., a few percent) when a triangle distribution with minimal skew is used (e.g., Case 1) vs a uniform distribution. However, the resulting deviation can reach 10% for a moderate skew (e.g., Case 2) and 25% or more for triangles with a large skew vs a uniform distribution. (Of course, a uniform distribution has an equal likelihood of a event occurring between the low and high values, and this may not be realistic for some applications.) Note that the maximum level of deviation occurs in the range between roughly the 30th and 70th percentiles. This is problematic because the region between the 30th and 70th percentiles may be sampled relatively frequently in the Monte Carlo simulation for a given WBS element or activity vs the tails depending upon the sampling approach used. In addition, many cost and schedule risk analyses typically evaluate the level of risk in the output CDF between the 30th and 70th percentiles, which is the region, in this case, where relatively large deviations between the distributions exist.

By working with knowledgeable project personnel and not suggesting that they provide answers force fit to a specific distribution type, the analyst increases the likelihood of correctly modeling probability distributions (cet. par.). Two continuous distribution types that allow substantial flexibility for use in Monte Carlo simulations are the general and cumulative distributions. The general distribution is often used to approximate an irregular, but continuous, probability distribution, or when a graphic approximation to a probability distribution is formulated. The cumulative distribution is often used to approximate expert opinion that describes an irregular probability distribution.

Probability distributions used in Monte Carlo simulations are often selected without sufficient supporting rationale. This may lead to uncertain, if not erroneous, results. By working with knowledgeable project personnel and not suggesting that they provide answers force fit to a specific distribution type, the analyst will increase the likelihood of correctly developing appropriate probability distributions and increasing the accuracy of simulation results.

B. Some Statistical Considerations

Not all symmetrical distributions have a mode [also known as the most frequent or most likely (ML) value]. So do not assume that the mean,

Table 6.13 Comparison of uniform distribution vs triangle distribution CDF values (percent difference between uniform and triangle distribution results)

Case	0th percentile	10th percentile	30th percentile	50th percentile	70th percentile	90th percentile	100th percentile
1	<1	-1	1	2	3	3	<1
2	<1	<1	5	9	10	8	<1
3	<1	3	11	16	17	13	<1
4	<1	7	20	26	26	19	<1

Case 1: Triangle, L = 0.95*ML, ML, H = 1.15*ML; Uniform, L = 0.95*ML, H = 1.15*ML.
Case 2: Triangle, L = 0.95*ML, ML, H = 1.15*ML; Uniform, L = 0.95*ML, H = 1.50*ML.
Case 2: Triangle, L = 0.95*ML, ML, H = 2.00*ML; Uniform, L = 0.95*ML, H = 2.00*ML.
Case 4: Triangle, L = 0.95*ML, ML, H = 3.00*ML; Uniform, L = 0.95*ML, H = 3.00*ML.

median, and mode are equal for a symmetrical distribution. For example, a uniform distribution does not have a mode, since all values between the minimum and maximum are identical.

Not all symmetrical distributions have a mode. So do not assume that for a symmetrical distribution that the mean, median, and mode are equal.

The mean (expected value or average) is not equal to the median (50th percentile value) unless a symmetrical distribution exists. The expected value is the mean (simple average) of the random variable or probability distribution "X." The median is the value of a variable that has a 50% likelihood of being exceeded and a 50% likelihood of not being reached. For symmetrical continuous distributions the mean and median are generally identical for unimodal distributions. But for skewed distributions, the mean and median will typically be different. For example, for a right-skewed right triangle distribution (Low, Mode, High), the difference between the mean and median is approximately 0.9% $(1, 1, 1.25)$, 1.8% $(1, 1, 1.5)$, 3.1% $(1, 1, 2)$, 5.1% $(1, 1, 3)$, and 7.4% $(1, 1, 5)$. Hence, while the deviation may be small, it is not zero, and it grows as the skewness of the distribution increases. Furthermore, no simple analytic relationship exists for the sum of medians as it does for the sum of means for nonsymmetric distributions. This is important in a variety of applications, including Monte Carlo simulations, where skewed distributions are commonly used. Thus, it is generally not appropriate to assume that the mean and median are identical unless underlying characteristics of the distribution are known.

The mean (expected value or average) is not equal to the median (50th percentile value) unless a symmetrical unimodal distribution exists.

Be careful in making arbitrary estimates associated with the most likely or reference point estimate value assigned by experts. In some cases specific percentiles are equated with the ML estimate when there is no statistical basis to do so. This may be as common as assuming the most likely and the median (50th percentile) are the same. But in one schedule analysis case, the 70th percentile was assumed equivalent to the ML value. This type of unsubstantiated assumption can lead to potentially large errors in risk analysis calculations.

Be careful in making arbitrary estimates associated with the most likely or reference point estimate value assigned by experts, because in some cases potentially large errors may result.

Simple rules for relating probability distribution percentiles to critical values may be incorrect and introduce considerable error into Monte Carlo simulation results. For example, a 15/70/15 rule may not properly specify a distribution and the results may vary considerably among different distribution types and their critical values. Here 1) the value that occurs 70% of the time is the "realistic" estimate, 2) the value that is better than "realistic" but occurs only 15% of the time is the optimistic estimate, and 3) the value that is worse than "realistic" and occurs only 15% of the time is the pessimistic estimate. The "realistic" value (70% of the time in this case) will often be far from the mean, mode, and median for many types of probability distributions (e.g., normal, triangle, and beta PERT). Note that the 15/70/15 definitions appear to assume the 15th, 70th, and 85th percentile values associated with the underlying probability distribution. An experiment was performed with some common distributions to estimate the level of deviation the 70th percentile would be from the mean and mode. Here, the distributions given in the table below were evaluated in a Monte Carlo simulation with Latin Hypercube sampling and 15,000 iterations to reduce sampling errors to an acceptable level. If the resulting percentiles are considerably different than the 70th percentile ("realistic"), then the probability types should not be used to approximate the 15th, 70th, and 85th percentiles unless suitable probability distributions are available (e.g., cumulative). The results of this experiment are given in Table 6.14.

Note that in the case of the normal distribution, the mean, median, and mode should correspond to the 50th percentile, and the resulting error from the simulation is 0.00%, 0.01%, and 0.5%, respectively (which is quite acceptable for this experiment). Hence for the normal distribution, specifying the 70th percentile corresponds to a 20, 20, and 20.5 percentile deviation from the mean, median, and mode, respectively. For the triangle distribution $(0, 1, 3)$, the mean and mode corresponded to the 53.7 and 33.5 percentiles, respectively, and the deviation from the 70th percentile is 16.3 and 36.5 percentiles, respectively. The deviations from the other distributions are also roughly this same amount. In fact, for the two triangle and two beta PERT distributions, the average deviation for the mean and mode versus the 70th

Table 6.14   Evaluation of 15/70/85 rule for allocating percentiles to critical values

Distribution Type	Normal	Triangle	Triangle	Beta PERT	Beta PERT
Critical Values	(10,1)	(0, 1, 3)	(0, 1, 5)	(0, 1, 3)	(0, 1, 5)
15% Percentile =	8.96	0.67	0.87	0.56	0.58
50% Percentile =	10.00	1.27	1.84	1.13	1.38
70% Percentile =	10.52	1.66	2.55	1.46	1.91
85% Percentile =	11.04	2.05	3.27	1.78	2.46
Mean (value) =	10.00	1.33	2.00	1.17	1.50
Mean (percentile) =	50.0	53.7	55.0	52.5	54.8
Percentile deviation from 70th percentile	**20.0**	**16.3**	**15.0**	**17.5**	**15.2**
Mode (value) =	9.99	1.00	1.01	1.01	1.03
Mode (percentile) =	49.5	33.5	20.5	42.5	34.5
Percentile deviation from 70th percentile	**20.5**	**36.5**	**49.5**	**27.5**	**35.5**

percentile was 16 percentiles (mean) and 37 percentiles (mode). Thus, using the 70th percentile value as a mid-value to specify common probability distributions can lead to substantial errors unless this value can be accurately converted to the distribution mean and/or mode. Finally, for irregular probability distributions (e.g., with more than one local minima), simple rules such as using the 15th, 70th, and 85th percentiles may not be effective or meaningful because they may not properly capture the nature of the probability distribution that exists. Also realize that the error term will increase accordingly in magnitude as the percentile associated with the realistic estimate increases (e.g., the error will be 10 percentiles larger at the 80th percentile) and decrease accordingly as the percentile associated with the realistic estimate decreases (e.g., the error will be 10 percentiles smaller at the 60th percentile).

Simple rules for relating probability distribution percentiles to critical values may be incorrect and introduce considerable error into Monte Carlo simulation results.

Percentile values in a probability distribution do not correspond to a specific likelihood of overrun and underrun that will occur and should not be treated as such. For example, assume in the following example involving a triangle distribution that $L = 0$, $ML = 3$, and $H = 9$. Here, the ML corresponds to the 33.3 percentile. However, it is not then sufficient to say that the low value (0) corresponds to a 33% underrun likelihood and the high value (9) corresponds to a 67% overrun likelihood. The key here is that the L and H values are not likelihood around the ML value but critical value points in likelihood and consequence of occurrence space that, along with the ML value, define the probability distribution.

Percentile values in a probability distribution do not correspond to a specific likelihood of overrun and underrun that will occur and should not be treated as such.

C. Use of Multidimensional Probability Distributions

The use of multidimensional probability distributions may appear attractive for modeling C,P,S risk, but there is typically little or no real world basis for selecting or using such distributions for project management applications. For example, theoretical grounds may exist to use a joint lognormal probability distribution for modeling project cost and schedule risk, but I am unaware of any evidence based on *real world data* to rigorously substantiate the existence of this distribution in project management applications. [My own research based on data from defense development programs, albeit at the total program level (WBS Level 1) and not at lower WBS levels, shows cost risk and schedule risk are not well modeled by a lognormal distribution (e.g., the fit is not statistically significant at the 0.05 level), and cost risk and schedule risk are only weakly correlated with each other. Thus, at the total program level for defense development programs, cost risk and schedule risk are not well modeled by a joint lognormal distribution.]

In many instances the nature of risk involves C,P,S dimensions. Hence, a three-dimensional distribution is desirable for modeling purposes. However, it is unlikely that such distributions can be defined for most cases in project risk management. This is because of a number of reasons. First, the distribution(s) that best matches the true nature of each dimension is unknown. It may be difficult to not only select a suitable probability distribution for a single dimension, but in some cases it may not be possible to rule out a variety of possible distribution types. There is rarely if ever sufficient data to clarify the type of probability distribution based on applicable historical information. (Here, the data may be used to develop a general or cumulative probability distribution, but there are typically insufficient data to permit curve fitting to estimate potential types of probability distributions with an acceptable statistical fit, e.g., 0.05 confidence interval.) Second, the presumption that a single type of probability distribution can be used to model jointly multiple variates cannot easily be verified because of the typical lack of suitable historical data. Third, the degree of pair-wise correlation between C,P,S is typically low, and likely much lower in reality than estimates based upon theoretical considerations.

When a joint probability distribution for a pair of variables is considered (termed a bivariate distribution), the presumption is that the third variate is held constant (or cet. par.). However, in the real world this may not be the case. This is particularly important when considering a cost and schedule bivariate distribution because a very slight change in performance may have a large, yet not well explained, impact on cost and/or schedule for many high-technology development programs. In the real world large potential increases in cost and/or schedule will occur if the three-dimensional design point is in the steep region of the cost-performance and/or schedule-performance feasibility curves, as discussed in Chapter 1. Here, a very slight change in performance can introduce a large change in cost and/or schedule, which is not explained by simply assuming that performance is held constant.

Given these limitations, it is typically better to model each dimension separately, accounting for potential impacts in the development of the individual probability distributions than to make a series of unsubstantiated guesses about joint probability distributions unless suitable real world data exist. (For example, consider cost estimating uncertainty, and schedule and technical risk in developing probability distributions for cost risk analysis, and schedule estimating uncertainty, and cost and technical risk in developing probability distributions for schedule risk analysis, rather than attempting to develop a bivariate cost and schedule probability distribution.)

The use of multidimensional probability distributions may appear attractive for modeling cost, performance, and/or schedule risk, but there is typically little or no real world basis for selecting or using such distributions for project management applications. It is typically better to model each dimension separately, accounting for potential impacts in the development of the individual probability distributions than to make a series of unsubstantiated guesses about joint probability distributions unless suitable real world data exist.

D. Development of Probability Distribution Critical Values

It is not uncommon to incorrectly specify probability distribution critical values, and in some cases the critical values may imply a different type of distribution than the analyst had chosen. For example, if you specify a triangle distribution, yet use critical values of say 10%, 50%, and 90%, then only in the case where $X_{50} - X_{10} = X_{90} - X_{50}$, a symmetrical (equilateral) triangle, will this be valid. The more skewed the critical values, $[(X_{90} - X_{50})/(X_{50} - X_{10}) \neq 1]$, the more invalid is such a relationship.

It is not uncommon to incorrectly specify probability distribution critical values, and in some cases the critical values may imply a different type of distribution than the analyst had chosen.

Do not generalize a probability distribution by the maximum, minimum, and most likely (mode), or pessimistic, optimistic, and most likely (mode). This presumes a specific type of continuous distribution rather than first getting people to think more broadly what type of distribution exists, followed by what critical values describe it (e.g., mean and standard deviation for a normal distribution).

Three-point critical value estimates (e.g., Low, ML, and High for a triangle distribution, beta-PERT distribution) should not be specified for a Monte Carlo simulation unless they are appropriate to model the probability distributions that will be used. Otherwise, this will prebias the analyst and experts attempting to develop the critical values and type of probability distribution specified and may lead to erroneous results. In addition, many distributions cannot be described by three critical values. For example, three critical values do not describe a normal distribution; its critical values are the mean and standard deviation, and attempts to relate three critical values to a normal distribution are an approximation at best and may lead to erroneous results. Note, also, that a number of different types of beta distributions are either described by two critical values (shape parameters) or up to four critical values (L, ML, mean, H), not simply by three critical values.

Do not generalize a probability distribution by the maximum, minimum, and most likely (mode), or pessimistic, optimistic, and most likely (mode). This presumes a specific type of continuous distribution. Three-point critical value estimates (e.g., triangle distribution, beta-PERT distribution) should not be specified for a Monte Carlo simulation unless they are appropriate to model the probability distributions that will be used.

Do not presuppose that extreme optimistic and pessimistic values are required or should be used in a Monte Carlo simulation as this may bias the selection of the distribution toward a type where two or three critical values define the probability distribution (e.g., beta-PERT, triangle, uniform) vs others that do not [e.g., beta (non-PERT), gamma, and normal distributions]. If you have already preselected a distribution that explicitly requires extreme optimistic and pessimistic values, fine, but do not let the urge to collect these two points force the distribution to be selected. Similarly, do not assume that the extreme pessimistic and optimistic values together with a most likely value forces a triangle distribution, even though these three values are needed to define the specific distribution (e.g., beta-PERT, triangle).

Do not presuppose that extreme optimistic and pessimistic values are required or should be used in a Monte Carlo simulation as this may bias the selection of the distribution toward one where two or three critical values define the probability distribution (e.g., beta-PERT, triangle, uniform) vs others that do not do so [e.g., beta (non-PERT), gamma, and normal distributions].

In quantitative risk analyses where there are two possible outcomes, such an event should be modeled by a binomial distribution or a two level histogram, and not by a triangle or other simple distribution (e.g., uniform). For example, when a triangle distribution is used to model such an event (e.g., one outcome becomes the Low critical value, the other outcome becomes the High critical value, and the most likely is taken to be the average of the two possible outcomes), a range of possible outcomes will occur, when only two are actually possible. Hence, the resulting outcomes are erroneous for all values except when the Low and High values are drawn. This analogy can be extended to other cases where "n" possible outcomes exist, where "n" is small. In such cases, it is almost always far better to model the data as a histogram rather than picking a simple continuous distribution.

In quantitative risk analyses where there are two possible outcomes, such an event should be modeled by a binomial distribution (or possibly a two-level histogram), and not by a triangle or other simple distribution (e.g., uniform).

When performing a Monte Carlo schedule risk analysis do not select critical values for activity "n" based upon the critical values for activity "n-1." In such a situation, anchoring can bias the critical values associated with activity "n" based upon activity "n-1." It is important in such cases to select critical values independent of other activities unless correlation exists between the activities and it can be accurately quantified. The same holds true for cost analysis simulations (typically with an additive structure) and performance (which may include a variety of structures).

When performing a Monte Carlo schedule risk analysis do not select critical values for element "n" based upon the critical values for element "n-1" unless this accurately represents the model structure.

The critical values, "X%" (or "X" percentile) chance of "Y" impact, defines risk for selected probability distributions. This type is common for triangle and some other bounded distributions. The mean of "X" and standard deviation of "Y" defines risk for other probability distributions. This type is common for normal distributions. While no percent values or percentiles are specified for some distributions (e.g., normal), it is a simple matter to relate the critical values to other values that are percent or percentiles. Here, the critical values specify a distribution that is risk. In cases where raw data exists (e.g., $3, $5) a single data point may be viewed as a consequence, but if "n" data points exist, the individual data points can be related to a probability density function (PDF) via a general distribution model (effectively a histogram). Hence, even in this case the data can be related to a frequency (probability) and consequence, hence risk.

When estimating critical values for a probability distribution the results should be related to risk.

Regardless of how probability distribution critical values are developed (e.g., subjective assessments or ordinal scales), it is important that the development process focus on *probability* information. (For example, there is an X percent chance that the schedule length will be A days, and a Y percent chance that the schedule length will be B days.) On the surface this may seem trivial, but I have seen several tools and techniques for eliciting this information that yield a mixture of probability of occurrence-related data, along with consequence of occurrence, and risk information (e.g., interview questions that discuss impact and ordinal scales related to consequence of occurrence or risk) rather than focusing on probability of occurrence. Using consequence of occurrence or risk information will introduce an error in the estimated probability distribution critical values and should be avoided.

A sensitivity analysis may be helpful in some cases to estimate uncertainty bounds, but this may not be sufficient in and of itself to develop critical values for a probability distribution including optimistic and pessimistic estimates.

A sensitivity analysis may be helpful in some cases to estimate uncertainty bounds, but this may not be sufficient in and of itself to develop critical values for a probability distribution including optimistic and pessimistic estimates. For example, variation around cost estimates (cost estimating uncertainty) can sometimes be estimated by performing a sensitivity analysis, although a more accurate approach is via statistics obtained from a regression analysis of relevant historical data. However, a sensitivity analysis is often not meaningful to describe the optimistic and pessimistic levels associated with schedule risk or technical risk impact around the most likely cost.

When developing probability distribution critical values, avoid introducing information relating to consequence of occurrence and risk. Only data pertaining to probability of occurrence should be used.

E. Some General Risk Analysis Interview Considerations

When collecting risk analysis data do not attempt to highlight potential high risk issues (or prioritize risk issues) before valid, approved risk analysis results exist. Highlighting such issues can lead to faulty results for several reasons. First, it presupposes that the items are high risk when there may be no data to substantiate this (e.g., no prior risk analysis may have been performed). Second, this may place less emphasis on potentially lower risk issues that may nevertheless have substantial influence on the program. (For example, a relatively inexpensive item with 100% cost risk may be of far less importance than an expensive item with 15% cost risk because the risk dollars at say the 50th percentile in the former case may be far smaller than those in the latter case.) Third, although this will not always occur, highlighting potential high risk issues (and possibly prioritizing risk issues) may imply to the person being interviewed that potentially larger and/or biased critical values (e.g., a higher High and a higher Low for a triangle distribution) are warranted than for other issues, yet there may be no basis for such an assertion.

When collecting risk analysis data do not attempt to highlight potential high risk issues (or prioritize risk issues) before valid, approved risk analysis results exist.

When collecting risk analysis data do not provide the interviewee with hints about a potential response, whether a single numerical representation or a range of possible representations. This can lead to potentially erroneous responses, even if it appears in a subtle manner. For example, for a risk issue associated with availability of personnel it is not appropriate to provide the interviewee with hints such as: personnel available full-time, personnel available part-time with high priority to this project, and personnel available part-time with low priority to this project. Note that the above representation "suggests" only one of three responses when in fact many more may be possible, and it also provides the listing of options in a rank ordered manner in terms of desirability to the project.

When collecting risk analysis data do not provide the interviewee with hints about a potential response, whether a single numerical representation or a range of possible representations. This can lead to anchoring and potentially erroneous responses, even if it appears in a subtle manner.

When conducting interviews, the respondents should provide information on probability of occurrence and/or consequence of occurrence, not risk. When risk, rather than probability and/or consequence, is assessed the responses may be subjective, and are often highly uncertain if not erroneous.

When conducting interviews, the respondents should provide information on probability of occurrence and/or consequence of occurrence, not risk.

When collecting quantitative data for use in a Monte Carlo simulation, it is important to achieve a consensus on the type of probability distribution and numerical level for each critical value for each risk issue. For example, it is not sufficient to obtain consensus on just the low and high critical values for a particular risk issue. This is because 1) it is unclear what type of probability distribution is assumed (e.g., cumulative, normal, triangle), 2) what critical values are missing vs just specifying the low and high values, and 3) the data quality associated with any other distribution critical values. In the above example involving a low and high critical value data collection, only a very limited number of probability distributions apply (e.g., binomial, histogram, uniform). Many types of probability distributions can not be fitted with just a low and high value (e.g., normal, triangle). In addition, even if you know the low and high values you do not have any idea what other critical values must be specified and whether the distribution is continuous (e.g., uniform) or discrete (e.g., binomial, histogram) unless you define the probability distribution. Even after specifying the distribution type, it is possible that several critical values may be "missing" (e.g., the mean and standard deviation that specify the normal distribution). Finally, if you do not have high-quality data for each critical value the resulting probability distribution will be uncertain at best, and erroneous at worst. For example, if you assume a triangle distribution and have a consensus on the low and high values, but no consensus on the most likely value, the resulting probability distribution may not accurately model the issue being evaluated.

When collecting quantitative data for use in a Monte Carlo simulation, it is important to achieve a consensus on the type of probability distribution and numerical level for each critical value for each risk issue.

Facilitators need some relevant technical background plus suitable management or social science skills to properly develop inputs for quantitative risk analyses. Ignorance is not bliss when attempting to develop probability distribution critical values. Time and again I have witnessed technical experts poorly estimate probability distribution critical values, and general facilitating skills did not do anything to draw out potentially more accurate information. Only when additional technical information was presented by the facilitator or when the technical expert was questioned did the expert provide a potentially more accurate perspective. For example, this may be important when high and low critical values are based upon expert opinion and an underestimation bias exists for one or both of the endpoints. Purely having a good set of social science skills will often not surface this type of problem or the magnitude of the potential error. (See Sec. VII.F and Chapter 3, Sec VI.B for additonal information.)

Facilitators need some relevant technical background plus suitable management or social science skills to properly develop inputs for quantitative risk analyses.

F. Estimation of Distribution Critical Values
from Subjective Assessments

There is no best way to select probability distribution critical values in many instances for Monte Carlo simulations used for project risk management. When developing distribution critical values, the question exists as to how close the estimated critical values are to the actual probability distribution critical values. This is more than just an academic exercise because inaccurate critical values can lead to erroneous results. Because there is often no best solution to this problem, it leads to at least a modest uncertainty being introduced into each probability distribution.

Subjective assessments of critical values are often performed, but the results may have varying degrees of exactness depending on a number of considerations, including, but not limited to 1) expertise and certainty of the people interviewed, 2) biases of the experts interviewed, 3) inability of experts to properly consider potential extreme values, 4) expertise of the interviewer, 5) structure and setting of the interview, 6) suitability and use of relevant ground rules and assumptions during the interview, 7) the culture of the project and larger organizational groups within the government or contractor units, 8) behavior and biases of upper management, and 9) the organizational structure of the project. (This list was independently developed, but overlaps somewhat with information given in Ref 21. Vose includes eight sources of estimating uncertainty: 1) inexpert expert, 2) culture of the organization, 3) conflicting agendas, 4) unwillingness to consider extremes, 5) eagerness to say the right thing, 6) units used in the estimation, 7) expert too busy, and 8) belief that the expert should be quite certain.[21] The rationale and recommendations given by Vose for several of these items are excellent.)

The following is a brief discussion of each of these numbered items that can affect the accuracy of subjective assessments. Whereas consequence of occurrence information is not separately needed when Monte Carlo simulations are performed, it is needed when performing a subjective risk analysis and when using ordinal scales to estimate risk. Hence, the following items generally apply to subjective estimates for developing probability distribution critical values, subjective risk analyses (both probability and consequence of occurrence terms), and when using ordinal scales (both "probability" and consequence of occurrence terms), even though they primarily address only critical values:

1) If the expert interviewed is not knowledgeable about a specific risk issue or cannot represent the results in a fairly certain manner, then the resulting critical values will be of little use. (Of course, there will be uncertainty in each expert's responses, but if the uncertainty band is very large and related to the expert himself, then the resulting data will often not be helpful.) One way to remedy this problem is ensure to the extent possible that the experts interviewed are qualified to discuss the risk issue. In addition, the interviewer should focus the questions in such a way as to help the expert better bound the level that will exist.

2) Each expert may have his own set of biases related to both technical

and behavioral issues. This may include such things as, whether or not the expert has a personal stake in the development of a particular technology; adjustment and anchoring, availability, representativeness, the tendency to fit ambiguous evidence into predispositions, the tendency to systematically omit components of risk, and overconfidence in the reliability of analyses (see Chapter 3, Sec. XIV); whether he is risk averse, risk neutral, or a risk taker; the expert's perceived vs actual role within the project, prior experiences with risk management on this or other programs, etc. To the extent possible, the interviewer must understand these potential limitations and attempt to account for them in the interview process. Of course, it is very helpful when more than one qualified expert is available to provide inputs on a given risk issue. [If multiple personnel are available, then the interviewer must also be cautious about potential group dynamics issues (see Chapter 3, Sec. XVII.D).]

3) Even experts may misspecify potential extreme values (e.g., the most optimistic and most pessimistic cases). The interviewer must have both suitable technical and behavioral skills in order to recognize and alleviate this potential problem. In addition, it may be necessary to relate or assume that the responses correspond to data less than the extreme values possible and structure the development of distribution critical values accordingly (see the discussion in Sec. VII.H).

4) The interviewer should have suitable expertise both in the relevant C,P,S dimensions of the program, as well as being a trained facilitator with an adequate social sciences background. It is very common to find risk analysis interviewers that either have no relevant technical background, inadequate understanding of cost and schedule estimating, little or no knowledge of risk management, no suitable social sciences background, or inadequate training as a facilitator. When this occurs, the resulting subjective risk assessments can be highly suspect. For example, if the interviewer has little or no technical understanding of the potential risk issues on a high-technology development program, he will generally be unable to ask suitable questions that will prompt the expert being interviewed to estimate accurately the probability and/or consequence of occurrence level present. (Simply asking "what's the probability of occurrence for the risk event" may be one of the necessary questions, but it will often be insufficient to adequately draw out information associated with the type of distribution and its critical values from the expert being interviewed.) Likewise, I have observed on several occasions interviewers who had some relevant technical knowledge, but wholly inadequate social sciences skills. This directly contributed to the risk analysis interviews being poorly conducted, and the results being highly suspect. (See Sec. VII.E and Chapter 3, Sec. VI.B for additional information.)

5) Even if the interviewer has suitable training (as just discussed), the structure and setting of the interview itself can greatly affect the results. In some cases the structure and setting of the interview may appear adequate

on the surface, but in reality are so poorly conducted that the results are highly suspect. Interviews should be structured to elicit from the expert the type of probability distribution and its critical values. The interviews should be conducted in a repeatable fashion between personnel being interviewed, possibly following a script, although recognizing that deviations from that script will likely occur. When the interviews are conducted in a group (rather than individual setting), great care must be taken to prevent group dynamics from adversely impacting the results (see Chapter 3, Sec. XVII.D). Simply having an upper management representative present when the interviews take place may bias the results, even if the manager is silent the entire time.

6) When interviews occur, it is unfortunately common that relevant ground rules and assumptions are absent. Although this may seem a simple oversight without much potential harm, without the use of suitable ground rules and assumptions, how can the expert properly understand exactly what information is being requested? Thus, the resulting critical values may be erroneous. For example, if manufacturing risk is an issue, an accurate assessment of risk cannot be performed without knowing several key pieces of information, such as the a) number of prior, compatible units produced; b) start date for manufacturing; c) ramp-up rate and time; d) total quantity; e) annual production rate; and f) number of lots. Simply stated, if the interviewer and expert are not using the same set of ground rules and assumptions, the results can be severely flawed. Hence, *written* ground rules and assumptions should be available and used whenever possible. And ideally, the expert should be provided with relevant ground rules and assumptions prior to the interview to help familiarize him with the type of information that is being requested.

7) The culture of the project and larger organizational groups within the government or contractor can have a substantial impact on the risk interview results. For example, if there is a tendency across the project to underestimate the level of risk present, the resulting critical values may be biased downward (e.g., lower mean and smaller standard deviation) unless the interviewer can adequately draw out from the expert the true level of risk present. In addition, with some organizational units within the government or contractor there may be a history of poor or inadequate risk management, including risk analysis. In some cases this problem may even exist on an organization-wide basis. In such cases the interviewer should first try to identify the nature and degree of the problems present, and use this to shape the questions asked. For example, a more extensive introduction for the interview may be needed when the organization has a weak record of risk management.

8) The behavior and biases of upper management can greatly affect the resulting risk information. For example, if the program manager views risk management as being relatively unimportant, this signal will tend to propagate to the program's technical experts, thus limiting their involvement or the degree to which they will concentrate on developing accurate responses.

If the program manager states, for example, that there are no high risks on the program, this will tend to bias downward the resulting critical values. In such cases the interviewer should first try to identify the nature of upper management behavior toward risk management and the degree of potential biases present, and use this to shape the questions asked.

9) The organizational structure of the project can also shape the resulting responses to a risk interview. For example, when a strong matrix organizational structure exists, the functional departments play a significant role in managing the program, and technical experts may follow their department manager's perspective on risk management much more so than the program manager (who may be little more than a coordinator). Conversely, when a weak matrix structure exists, the program manager's role is substantially greater, and his perspective on risk management will often influence that of other program personnel. The interviewer should first try to identify the type of organizational structure in place, how different groups within the program interact, and the degree of potential biases present, and use this to shape the questions asked.

Finally, it should be recognized that even if the preceding considerations are incorporated in the subjective assessment, there is still no guarantee that the correct information will be obtained—the results will still be at least somewhat uncertain. For example, in one case I interviewed an expert who leads a truly capable team that integrates, assembles, and tests very complex electro-optical sensors. I asked him based on his prior experience how many alignment iterations would be needed for the sensor in question. He responded that the minimum, most likely, and maximum number of iterations would be 2, 2, and 3, respectively. The program manager later stopped the alignment process after seven iterations when only a very slight improvement in performance would have likely occurred.

Subjective assessments are often performed: for determining probability distribution critical values, for subjective risk analyses (both probability and consequence of occurrence terms), and when using ordinal scales (both probability and consequence of occurrence terms). However, the results may have varying degrees of exactness depending on a number of considerations associated with the experts interviewed, the skills of the interviewer, the quality of ground rules and assumptions used, and a variety of behavioral considerations. Careful planning of risk interviews is essential to ensure high-quality information or else the results may be severely flawed.

G. Computation of Critical Values from Ordinal "Probability" Scales

Ordinal "probability" scales can sometimes be used to estimate probability distribution critical values. There is no best way to estimate the critical values, and some approaches will lead to flawed, if not highly erroneous, results. Even when calibrated ordinal "probability" scales are used, there may be no convincing probabilistic basis to compute the resulting distribution endpoints because the calibrated scale values are almost never probabilities.

I will now examine one approach to estimating critical values for a triangle distribution for cost and schedule risk analyses. (This approach was likely first developed by David Graham, U.S. Air Force, in 1994.) With this procedure the most likely cost or duration (reference point estimate) is selected as the ML value (the triangle mode), then the L and H values are estimated from calibrated ordinal "probability" scale values. (Other approaches exist for estimating the critical values of a triangle distribution, but may be more subjective and less acceptable than the example one given here.)

There are two primary steps for determining the triangle distribution L and H values.

First, the analyst determines the risk score for the nominal design risk (ML), plus that for the most Optimistic and Pessimistic design risk levels. Here, either three different designs (optimistic, most likely, and pessimistic) or three different interpretations of the same design are assumed. Although the former approach is preferred from a risk perspective, it may be impractical due to additional resources required.

Second, the Optimistic value (assumed to correspond to the 0th percentile) is then computed from the ratio of Optimistic/ML "probability" scores, and the Pessimistic value (assumed to correspond to the 100th percentile) is computed from the ratio of Pessimistic/ML "probability" scores. Thus, the critical values for the triangle distribution are Optimistic/ML, ML, Pessimistic/ML. [Note: The Optimistic and Pessimistic values may not actually be the 0th and 100th percentiles, respectively (see Sec. VII.H for additional information).]

Given the preceding approach, I will now present a numerical cost risk analysis example that shows how the critical values are computed, and the potential error that results from using uncalibrated ordinal "probability" scales vs calibrated "probability" scales. In this example, for the sake of simplicity, assume that technology is the sole component of the probability term of risk for a given item. (Although this is overly simplistic, it allows a relatively short example to be developed.)

Assume for a first case that the Pessimistic, ML, and Optimistic values correspond to ordinal "probability" scale Levels 6, 4, and 2, which are equivalent to calibrated values of 0.55, 0.18, and 0.11, respectively. The Optimistic and Pessimistic critical values are then given by L = 0.11/0.18 (Optimistic/ML) = 0.61 and H = 0.55/0.18 (Pessimistic/ML) = 3.06, respectively. The resulting triangle probability distribution critical values are thus equal to Optimistic = 0.61 and Pessimistic = 3.06, assuming a value of 1.0 for the most likely cost. (Note: The most likely cost should not be confused with the ML probability level—they represent completely different items.) In effect, the Optimistic and Pessimistic values become multipliers of the most likely cost in defining the resulting triangle distribution. So if the most likely cost = $100, the L cost is $100* 0.61 = $61, and the H cost is $100*3.06 = $306. Thus, the critical values for triangle distribution used in a Monte Carlo simulation are (L, ML, H) = (61, 100, 306).

Now assume a second case where the Pessimistic, ML, and Optimistic values correspond to ordinal "probability" scale Levels 3, 2, and 1, which are equivalent to calibrated values of 0.11, 0.06, and 0.04. The resulting L and H critical values are then given by 0.04/0.06 = 0.67 and 0.11/0.06 = 1.83, respectively. The resulting triangle probability distribution is given by the Optimistic = 0.67 and Pessimistic = 1.83, assuming a value of 1.0 for the most likely cost. In effect, the Optimistic and Pessimistic values become multipliers of the most likely cost in defining the resulting triangle distribution. So if the most likely cost = $100, the L cost is $100* 0.67 = $67, and the H cost is $100* 1.83 = $183. Thus, the critical values for the triangle distribution that is simulated are (L, ML, H) = (67, 100, 183).

Clearly, the triangle distributions for the first and second example are different, with critical values (61, 100, 306) vs (67, 100, 183). However, notice what would have occurred if both distributions had been derived using uncalibrated ordinal "probability" scales. In the first example the Optimistic and Pessimistic critical values are then given by L = 2/4 = 0.5 and H = 6/4 = 1.5, respectively. Assuming a most likely cost of $100, this would lead to a triangle distribution with critical values of (50, 100, 150). In the second example the Optimistic and Pessimistic critical values are then given by L = 1/2 = 0.5 and H = 3/2 = 1.5, respectively. Assuming a most likely cost of $100, this would lead to a triangle distribution with critical values of (50, 100, 150).

Thus, when the critical distribution values are derived from uncalibrated ordinal "probability" scales, the two example distributions are identical in this case. However, they are substantially different vs distributions derived from calibrated ordinal "probability" scales, particularly for the first example (50, 100, 150) vs (61, 100, 306). In the first example the mean of the triangle distribution estimated from uncalibrated ordinal "probability" scales is (50 + 100 + 150)/3 = 100, whereas it is (61 + 100 + 306)/3 = 156 when derived from the calibrated scale, or a difference of more than 50%! Among other things, this indicates that substantial deviations are possible in deriving distribution critical values from uncalibrated vs calibrated ordinal "probability" scales. (It is not clear whether these deviations solely represent errors even if zero uncertainty is assumed for both sets of critical values because there may be no convincing probabilistic basis to compute the distribution endpoints from values derived from calibrated ordinal scales, which in this case are not probabilities, but ratios. Although deriving triangle distribution critical values from calibrated ordinal "probability" scales eliminates the source of error associated with performing mathematical operations on values derived from uncalibrated ordinal "probability" scales, the resulting values may still not be correct because of assumptions associated with probabilities and distribution endpoints just mentioned. However, the results will likely be far more accurate than those generated from uncalibrated ordinal "probability" scales.) Consequently, critical values for a triangle distribution, as well as other types of distributions, *should never be derived from uncalibrated ordinal scales.*

Ordinal "probability" scales can sometimes be used to estimate probability distribution critical values. There is no best way to estimate the critical values, and some approaches will lead to flawed, if not highly erroneous, results. Uncalibrated ordinal "probability" scales should not be used to estimate distribution critical values because the intervals associated with the scale levels are unknown.

H. Subjective Estimates of Probability Distribution Extreme Values

It may be necessary to subjectively estimate extreme values (e.g., High and Low) to specify a probability distribution for Monte Carlo simulation to bound the magnitude of possible outcomes, or for other reasons. However, subjective estimates of extreme values may contain both bias and random error terms, which can adversely impact the results.

For example, for the triangle distribution the L, ML, and H values correspond to the 0th percentile, the mode (also known as the most likely value, whose percentile varies on a case by case basis), and the 100th percentile. If asked, the values corresponding to the 0th and 100th percentiles, many people will provide a value greater than the true 0th percentile value and less than the true 100th percentile value. If not corrected, this will tend to affect the distribution endpoints, and depending upon the type of sampling used, may reduce the number of draws from the tails of the probability distribution when used in a Monte Carlo simulation. [For example, this may tend to compress both the output probability density function (and CDF) and decrease the standard deviation of the results.]

One approach for reducing the effect of this problem with triangle distributions is to assume that instead of the L and H critical values equaling the 0th and 100th percentiles they correspond to numbers greater than the 0th and less than the 100th percentiles, respectively. I am unaware of any published studies that estimated the actual bias level (in percentiles) of respondents vs the actual 0th and 100th percentile values. However, possible solutions proposed in the literature include the response L and H values equaling the 5th and 95th percentiles (corresponding to a 90% confidence interval) and the 10th and 90th percentiles (corresponding to an 80% confidence interval), respectively. Both the 5th and 95th and the 10th and 90th percentiles have been used in various studies for approximating the true L and H triangle distribution values, and it is unclear which is the more accurate choice. Any other percentile values within reason are also possible, such as the 15th and 85th percentiles, which might be more applicable in some cases. For a triangle distribution there is no simple analytic solution to convert a pair of percentile values > 0th percentile and < 100th percentile to a triangle distribution, where the 0th and 100th percentile values are projected from the supplied values. (For example, given the 10th and 90th percentile values, for a triangle distribution, it is not trivial to estimate the 0th and 100th percentile values for the same triangle distribution.) The solution to this problem is complicated, but modern Monte Carlo simulation packages, e.g., @Risk and Crystal Ball, include the capability to perform this transformation, and a mathematical technique has been separately developed that yields a very close approximation to the 0th and 100th percentile values.

In reality the level of the bias error is almost always unknown. (For example, it is unclear whether the 5th, 10th, or 15th percentile should be assumed vs the 0th percentile for the L value of a triangle distribution.) In addition, a random error term will also likely be present (e.g., because of unclear ordinal "probability" scale definitions or instructions from the facilitator). No attempt is generally made to estimate the level of uncertainty present from both the bias and random error terms when the critical values are selected, which will introduce an unknown error term into subsequent results. Thus, Monte Carlo simulation results are generally less accurate and certain than indicated.

In some cases the bias and random error terms present in deriving the critical values can be modeled in the Monte Carlo simulation. Here, the input distribution critical values themselves are modeled by probability distributions. However, this approach should only be attempted if strong evidence exists, rather than unsubstantiated guesswork.

For example, assume a triangle distribution with (L, ML, H) critical values of (25, 50, 75). In addition, assume a random error term around the L value that corresponds to a normal distribution with a mean = 0.0 and standard deviation = 1.0 and a random error term around the H value that corresponds to a normal distribution with a mean = 0.0 and standard deviation = 2.0. Three distributions would then be used to model this input. First, the adjusted L value (L_a) is given by L_a = L + normal $(0, 1)$, where normal $(0, 1)$ is the draw from the normal distribution with mean = 0.0 and standard deviation = 1.0. Second, the adjusted H value (H_a) is given by H_a = H + normal $(0, 2)$. Third, the resulting triangle distribution critical values are given by [L + normal $(0, 1)$, ML, H + normal $(0, 2)$], which is equivalent to [25 + normal $(0, 1)$, 50, 75 + normal $(0, 2)$]. (For the sake of simplicity the bias error term is assumed here to be zero.)

Subjective estimates of probability distribution extreme values may contain both bias and random error terms, which can adversely impact the results. In some cases it may be possible to estimate the level of these error terms and include them in a Monte Carlo simulation. However, this approach should only be attempted if strong evidence exists, rather than unsubstantiated guesswork.

Another suggested value associated with low and high subjective probability assessments is the 1st and 99th percentiles, respectively. While it may not be certain that this approach is incorrect, it adds little if anything beyond assuming that the L and H critical values are the 0th and 100th percentiles (100% confidence level), respectively. It also falls far short of assuming that a moderate bias exists in defining the L and H critical values vs using the 10th and 90th percentiles (80% confidence level), respectively. Hence, the 1st and 99th percentiles should generally not be used for defining the L and H critical values unless some statistically valid measure exists for estimating data at these levels. (Note also that the 1st and 99th percentile values do not correspond, respectively to the best and worst that has happened before. This is both overly simplistic and incorrect.)

The 1st and 99th percentiles should generally not be used for defining the L and H critical values unless some statistically valid measure exists for estimating data at these levels.

Bias in estimating probability distribution critical values may sometimes lead to a high that is too low and a low that is too low. This is generally not considered when estimating critical values since it is often assumed that if any bias exists, it affects the high and low values in a symmetrical manner (e.g., the high is too low and the low is too high). However, the outcome in such a case will tend to decrease the resulting level of risk since the overall trend is to bias downward the critical values.

Bias in estimating probability distribution critical values may sometimes lead to a high that is too low and a low that is too low. This is generally not considered when estimating critical values.

VIII. Monte Carlo Simulations

A. Some Top-Level Considerations

Risk analysis *is not* performing Monte Carlo simulations. Monte Carlo simulations are but one tool or technique for performing risk analysis. A Monte Carlo simulation is just another tool and technique, it is not universally applicable to project management issues, and it should only be used when the available information and data support its use. As discussed in Sec. II.C, it is applicable in situations where probability distributions of known form are embedded in known models covering known possible states (Class 2). Monte Carlo simulations are not useful or even applicable when 1) probability distributions cannot be adequately defined, 2) the model structure is unclear, and/or 3) the possible states are unknown.

For example, in one case a large commercial entity had developed a

Monte Carlo simulation to estimate budget expenditures by year for integrating large, complex facilities built by other organizations. However, two key variables that drove the simulation had large uncertainty that could not be accurately estimated (or even bounded in one case) coupled with probability distributions that could not be adequately defined. In addition, several key considerations that affected the model structure and/or possible states were not included and could not easily be developed. (Even if this had not been the case, the problems associated with adequately specifying the driving probability distributions could not be resolved.) I recommended in this case that the client terminate development of the Monte Carlo simulation, thus ending my consultation, rather than to continue expending resources to develop a simulation whose output was both highly uncertain and likely inaccurate.

A Monte Carlo simulation is not risk analysis and is just another tool and technique. Monte Carlo simulations are not universally applicable to project management issues, and should only be used when the available information and data support its use.

Even though quantitative risk analysis can help reduce the gaming of key project variables, that in and of itself is no guarantee that the inputs to the quantitative risk analysis (e.g., Monte Carlo simulation probability distribution critical values) will not be gamed.

The use of a quantitative risk analysis does not in and of itself eliminate the likelihood that key project variables will be "gamed."

While a quantitative risk analysis with a Monte Carlo simulation can help communicate a range of values rather than a set of point estimates (e.g., sum of the most likely values) to decision makers, providing an estimate at say the 50th percentile will not be helpful unless the probability distribution critical values have been carefully estimated and the model structure is correct. Otherwise the results may not have sufficient accuracy. Hence, do not blindly believe results from a Monte Carlo simulation—"garbage in, garbage out."

While a quantitative risk analysis performed using a Monte Carlo simulation can convey useful information to decision makers, the results will not be any higher in quality than that of the probability distribution critical values and model structure used in the simulation.

When reference is made to probability distributions for use in a Monte Carlo simulation, it is important that unless the list is exhaustive, that it be represented as a subset of possible distributions for use in project risk management. Simply labeling a chart "Probability Distributions for Simulations" incorrectly assumes that the distributions listed are either the only ones that exist, or the only valid ones that can be used. This is hardly ever the case! In addition, the manner in which the data is presented may dissuade individuals from examining other possible probability distributions (see Chapter 3, Sec. XIV).

When reference is made to probability distributions for use in a Monte

Carlo simulation, it is important that unless the list is exhaustive, that it be represented as a subset of possible distributions for use in project risk management.

Not all elements within a Monte Carlo simulation may have probability distributions assigned to them. For example, not all cost elements, performance elements, or schedule activities may have distributions. This may occur because sufficient accurate information does not exist, the simulation only evaluates a subset of the total analysis, only a finite number of "driver" elements are modeled to estimate an output trend, or an element truly has zero risk.

Not all elements within a Monte Carlo simulation may have probability distributions assigned to them.

Errors will be introduced if you assume a specific type of output Monte Carlo simulation PDF then relate the mean, standard deviation or other statistics to it to estimate percentiles. Instead, estimate percentiles directly from the PDF (or the CDF), not using statistics and assumptions associated with the output distribution. For example, if you assume that the output PDF is a normal distribution, then given the mean and standard deviation you can estimate the value associated with a given percentile using standard tables, equations, etc. However, the fundamental assumption that you've made is that the output PDF is normal, which if examined using a rigorous statistical test will likely not pass at the 0.05 level. Instead, select percentiles computed directly based upon the output PDF from the simulation to estimate the value. (Some Monte Carlo simulation packages also allow you to specify a given percentile and the software package then estimates the corresponding value.)

Do not assume a specific type of output Monte Carlo simulation PDF then relate the mean, standard deviation or other statistics to it to estimate percentiles.

While it may be unreasonable for a technical expert to try to fit existing data into a large number of possible probability distributions on a regular basis, a Monte Carlo simulation that is limited to a single probability distribution or some other relatively small number may be too limited for application to many programs. This is because it forces the analyst to pre-suppose a distribution or data type that may not exist. For example, assume that the following percentile and consequence levels exist for a WBS element: 0th percentile, $0.5 million; 20th percentile, $2.0 million; 50th percentile, $6.0 million; and 100th percentile, $8.0 million. Such a data set can not be accurately modeled by distributions found in some Monte Carlo software packages (e.g., beta PERT, normal, triangle, uniform distribution). However, a cumulative (ascending) distribution can accurately model this data. This is not to say that situations will exist where a single probability distribution will accurately model the data—I have developed and used such specialized simulations more than once when analytical results indicated that a specific distribution type was appropriate. It is also not to say that considerable uncertainty may exist in the data which may to some extent overshadow the confidence in selecting the specific type of probability distribution. It does, however, address the situation where people blindly choose a limited or very limited number of probability distributions (one in the worst case) for a Monte Carlo simulation without having any real basis for their decision.

A Monte Carlo simulation that is limited to a single probability distribution or some other relatively small number (e.g., four) may be too limited for application to many programs.

B. Cost, Performance, and Schedule Simulations

Monte Carlo simulations should not just be blindly limited to cost and schedule risk analyses, but should also be considered for performance risk analyses. Monte Carlo simulations modeling the performance dimension are much more common and consume many orders of magnitude more computer resources than those for cost and schedule combined, yet there is little or no discussion of performance Monte Carlo simulations in the project management literature. (For example, this topic is absent from Project Management Institute literature.) Performance Monte Carlo simulations are often dismissed as just being a design tool, but the resulting output is just as valid an input to program management personnel as cost and schedule simulation results and other relevant data. For one project I helped manage, a set of verification simulations were performed on an application specific integrated circuit (ASIC) design using 40 high-end dual processor workstations, that when mapped to a mid-level performance desktop computer available at that time, would have taken almost 2,450 dedicated computer months to run. Assuming that the average cost or schedule Monte Carlo simulation takes 1 hour to perform on the same desktop computer, this translates to about 1.75 million simulations—something that likely far exceeds the number of cost and schedule simulations performed in the entire United States over the course of many months! The next time you watch satellite television, travel on an airline, watch a movie loaded with special effects, or partake in numerous other daily activities realize that the underlying technology was often designed and/or verified in part using performance Monte Carlo simulations, and just because it isn't discussed in project management literature doesn't diminish its importance or value.

Monte Carlo simulations modeling the performance dimension are much more common and consume many orders of magnitude more computer resources than those for cost and schedule combined, yet there is little or no discussion of performance Monte Carlo simulations in the project management literature.

When performing a Monte Carlo simulation, do not solely limit the cost risk analysis or schedule risk analysis to approved program risk issues. This may considerably underestimate the level of risk present. Also, this approach may preclude including estimating uncertainty.

When performing a Monte Carlo simulation, do not solely limit the cost risk analysis or schedule risk analysis to approved program risk issues.

Cost risk should not be defined as the sum of reference point estimates minus the Monte Carlo simulation output CDF mean. While no purely "correct" approach exists the mean cannot generally be analytically related to a percentile of actual output CDFs, and will have an equivalent percentile value that varies on a case by case basis. A far better approach is to estimate the 30th, 50th, and 70th percentile values (plus any others that are desired or required) from the output CDF and use this to estimate the cost risk present (by subtracting the sum of the reference point estimates). Also, it is not very meaningful to say "on average" there will be $X cost risk. It is more meaningful to say that for the "Yth" percentile the cost risk is $Z.

Cost risk should not be defined as the sum of reference point estimates minus the Monte Carlo simulation output CDF mean.

"Generic" uncertainty should not be used in performing a Monte Carlo simulation. This is because it masks the specific nature of the issues present and may lead to developing incorrect critical values, thus probability distributions, used in the simulation. For example, if you are performing a cost risk analysis, you should attempt to model cost estimating uncertainty, technical risk, and schedule risk rather than just lumping these items into a single category ("uncertainty").

"Generic" uncertainty should not be used in performing a Monte Carlo simulation because it masks the specific nature of the issues present and may lead to developing incorrect critical values, thus probability distributions, used in the simulation.

When performing cost or schedule Monte Carlo risk analyses, it is important to recognize that two different types of terms may be present: some related to estimating uncertainty and the other related to risk. Do not automatically assume that a single probability distribution will adequately address both estimating uncertainty and risk. This should lead to the use of at least two different probability distributions for each item modeled (e.g., WBS element or activity). Although estimating uncertainty and risk are often subjectively combined into a single distribution, this may introduce a random and/or bias error. Typically, estimating uncertainty is better understood than risk, and the possibility exists that the resulting probabilistic estimate for the given item will have a higher degree of confidence when two or more separate distributions are used (although the specific level of confidence may be unknown). This is particularly true in cases where the critical values for the selected distributions are developed from historical and/or measured data.

When performing cost or schedule Monte Carlo risk analyses, it is important to recognize that two different types of terms may be present:

one related to estimating uncertainty and the other related to risk. Do not automatically assume that a single probability distribution will adequately address both estimating uncertainty and risk.

Schedule calculations are generally not simply additive if multiple paths or lead/lag or other conditions exist. This may affect the type of output distributions that result from a Monte Carlo simulation. For example, the resulting output distribution may not be symmetrical, let alone a normal distribution, in some cases no matter how may iterations the simulation is run.

Output distributions that result from a schedule Monte Carlo simulation may not be symmetrical, let alone a normal distribution, in some cases.

C. Verifying and Validating Simulations

Verification and validation of a Monte Carlo simulation should always be performed before the results are used by decision makers. Here, verification is assumed to represent a logic analysis of the simulation structure, and validation is assumed to represent "do the results make sense?" A simple example is now given for evaluating a Monte Carlo simulation involving only additive elements (e.g., a cost risk analysis). First, embed the PDFs for each element containing risk. Second, temporarily select critical values such that the output for each probability distribution will be equal to the input critical values. For example, for a triangle distribution designated by (L, ML, H), the L and H critical values = 1. In this case the critical values are: (ML * L, ML, and ML * H), = (ML * 1, ML, and ML* 1) = (ML, ML, ML). Third, run the simulation and compare the sum of the most likely costs (reference point estimates), and the sum of the simulation elements (adjusted via step 2) above. Are the two sums the same? They should be! If they are not the same, check the underlying logic associated with subtotaling, etc. within the spreadsheet or underlying database. Check not only the two totals but all subtotals until the set of elements that contributed to the deviation are identified and corrected. Fourth, once the underlying logic has been corrected and the sum of the most likely costs equals the sum of the simulation elements, then and only then substitute the "real" probability distribution critical values for the test values entered in step 2) above and re-run the simulation. The same approach can be simply tailored and used with a performance or schedule risk analysis as well, with adjustments made given differences in the model structure (e.g., additive, multiplicative elements). For example, with a schedule risk analysis you compare the duration, finish date, etc. for the network simulation with no embedded probability distributions vs an identical one including probability distributions, where the output for each probability distribution will be equal to the input critical values. The resulting duration, finish date, etc. between the two networks should be identical. This approach is particularly important when two or more probability distributions exist for each element because it would be laborious to calculate the results if "real" values had been used for a single element, let alone hundreds of elements (or activities). In one instance where almost 900 probability distributions were used in a Monte Carlo cost risk analysis model to simulate a program with a life-cycle cost far greater than $1 billion, the approach saved considerable resources and permitted rapid debugging of the simulation whenever changes were made to the most likely costs and underlying logic.

Verification and validation of a Monte Carlo simulation should always be performed before the results are used by decision makers. Without performing verification and validation it is possible that errors will be introduced into simulation results due to a number of possible factors. The likelihood of this occurring grows with the size and complexity of the simulation being performed.

In some cases the analyst may want to verify that the input distributions are properly calculated for a Monte Carlo simulation. While this may seem a waste of time, it is quite possible for the analyst to enter incorrect critical values, especially in large simulations. More unusual errors are also possible. In one case I observed input distributions that were not a good match to the distributions specified with a commercial software package. (Here, I used the maximum, minimum, skewness, and kurtosis of the simulation results to identify the problem.) After some fairly sophisticated sleuthing, the error was identified as a timing interference between the spread sheet, the commercial Monte Carlo spread sheet add-in package and the specific spread sheet function being "called" from the cells in question. On the surface no problem should have existed, but a serious one did: minimum values were 25 to 40% below the theoretical minimum possible for the distribution! The problem was finally resolved by rewriting the spread sheet so that "calls" were made to cell locations that had no direct or indirect reference to the offending function. This is but one simple example that shows the importance of thoroughly debugging each and every Monte Carlo simulation before accepting the model's output.

It is important to verify that the input distributions are properly calculated for a Monte Carlo simulation. This is with large simulations because incorrect critical values can be entered.

Be careful to validate the Monte Carlo simulation that you are using before it is used for production work and the results used by decision makers. For example, in one case two simulation packages were evaluated that were add-ins to the project scheduling package used on a program. Both simulation add-ins either crashed or gave erroneous results using the program's schedule, which included tasks that were inserted in one schedule module from another module that actually physically linked two separate files. Given this unacceptable situation, I worked with scheduling personnel and vendors at the two companies that developed and marketed the simulation packages to understand the cause of the problems and what workarounds might exist. Within a week the source of the problem had been identified; it involved linking tasks across separate project files associated with the project scheduling software (not the Monte Carlo add-in software)—something that neither simulation package could properly integrate with. The workaround developed by the project scheduler was to create a standalone schedule file incorporating all needed tasks for the schedule module being evaluated. With this workaround in place both schedule risk analysis add-ins now worked properly and one was chosen and used to perform a simulation of the schedule about three times a month. However, if the results had been blindly reviewed without trying to understand why one of the two packages crashed, the other package might have been selected, yet it consistently produced somewhat subtle, but erroneous results. The lesson here is not to blindly accept the output from a Monte Carlo simulation—challenge all simulation results—especially those from a nonvalidated simulation.

Be careful to validate the Monte Carlo simulation that you are using before it is used for production work and the results used by decision makers.

D.   How the Number of Simulation Iterations Can Affect Results

After a simulation is developed, it is often wise to run a test case with a relatively small number of iterations (e.g., 100) to ensure as part of a verification activity that the simulation logic is acceptable and the output is not unreasonable. After the simulation debugging is finished, a larger number of iterations are generally necessary to ensure satisfactory results. The potential disadvantage of using a small number of iterations is that the resulting output distribution may be multi-modal and will generally contain moderate uncertainty vs the true output distribution because of statistical sampling considerations. In effect, Monte Carlo simulations represent an estimate, rather than an exact solution, and the estimate varies with each simulation performed unless a constant random number seed value is used to initialize the simulation.

When running a Monte Carlo simulation, sample sizes of roughly 1000 iterations may be sufficient when Latin Hypercube sampling is used for modest-sized simulations (e.g., a risk analysis with 30 elements containing risk). Given the speed of modern microcomputers, there is little time advantage to running Monte Carlo simulations with a small number of iterations (e.g., 250). However, even with 1000 iterations, the resulting output, PDF may still be multimodal. The likelihood of this occurring will tend to increase with the number of elements containing risk, together with the number of dissimilar types of probability distributions and their critical values, (cet. par.) For example, a simulation containing a small number of identical triangle distributions with a modest right-hand skew will likely require fewer iterations to achieve a unimodal output PDF than a simulation with a mixture of distribution types (e.g., triangle, uniform, and beta) that are highly skewed both to the left and right (cet. par.). Multimodal simulation output PDFs may occur even though the mean of the PDF may approach the mean of the true output distribution (which would result with an infinite number of iterations).

By the Central Limit Theorem the mean of a set of n variables (where n is large), drawn independently from the same distribution, will be normally distributed. Thus, the output PDF that results from a series of probability distributions which are added (or subtracted) will approach a normal distribution even if the individual distributions modeled are nonnormal (so long as no single variable dominates).[21] When a large number of positive variables are multiplied, then the resulting output PDF will tend to approach a lognormal distribution. Many quantitative risk analysis models are a combination of adding (or subtracting) and multiplying variables together that contain probability distributions. Hence, the resulting Monte Carlo simulation output PDF tends to be somewhere between normally and lognormally distributed, as the number of iterations becomes large (specifically, approaches infinity).[21] However, the exact nature of the distribution is typically unknown, and my attempts at curve fitting numerous output PDFs indicate that it is uncommon except in trivial cases for one to match a normal or lognormal distribution at a statistically significant level (e.g., 0.05) even when a large number of Monte Carlo iterations are performed (e.g., 15,000+) and using Latin Hypercube sampling. (An example of a trivial case is 10 WBS elements all represented by the same normal distribution in an additive model, e.g., cost risk analysis. Here, the resulting output distribution would likely be normal at the 0.05 significance level.) Finally, whereas the mean may be relatively stationary as the number of simulation iterations is increased, values located at specific CDF percentiles will tend to shift, in some cases more than a small amount.

One approach to selecting the number of simulation iterations is to view a graphical representation of the output distribution and examine a statistical analysis of the output to see if it is multimodal, substantially skewed, or has either a very sharp or very broad peak. Each of these items is a possible indicator that an insufficient number of iterations has been performed when continuous distributions are used.

For example, the third moment of a normal distribution, known as skewness, equals zero, and the fourth moment of a normal distribution, known as kurtosis, equals 3.0. Therefore, substantial deviations from these values for a model composed of additive or subtractive elements may indicate an insufficient number of iterations. (Of course, it is overly simplistic to say that a Monte Carlo simulation output PDF having a skewness $\cong 0$ and kurtosis $\cong 3$ is normal: this can *only* be verified by testing the data with appropriate goodness-of-fit statistics, e.g., Anderson–Darling and Kolmogorov–Smirnoff tests.)

If the characteristics of the output PDF are not acceptable (e.g., multimodal, and heavily skewed), the number of iterations should be increased by a factor of perhaps 3 to 5 and the test performed again until a suitable number of iterations have been identified. Of course, this process should only be performed on verified and validated simulations (whose logic and input distributions are correct). Although such high-quality output may not be needed for draft results, it is important that low-quality output not be used as an input to design trades, program cost estimates, risk handling estimates, and other key analyses to avoid introducing potential errors.

Care should be taken in selecting the number of iterations the Monte Carlo simulation uses. Initial simulation runs should be focused on debugging, and a relatively small number of iterations is often acceptable. After debugging is complete, the number of iterations should typically be increased until the output PDF appears unimodal, with acceptable skewness and kurtosis. Deviations from this may adversely impact the simulation results and their subsequent use by decision makers.

E. Correlation Between Elements in Monte Carlo Simulations

Correlation may exist between WBS elements, activities, or items in C,P,S risk analyses. For example, the weight of the spacecraft structure is generally positively correlated with the total weight of the remainder of the spacecraft. (Thus, as the weight of other spacecraft subsystems increases, structure weight will tend to increase.) Interdependence is often not properly evaluated between risk analysis categories, between WBS elements, or activities for a given risk category. In some cases correlation is not evaluated, made worse by not stating this directly in the ground rules and assumptions. In other cases the impact is handled illogically (e.g., a separate ordinal risk analysis scale for correlation, dependency, or interaction), and the resulting contribution is effectively a noise term in the risk analysis results. Still in other cases where quantitative risk analysis is performed, a correlation matrix is used in the Monte Carlo simulation.

Although the latter approach may yield acceptable results, the correlation magnitudes may be selected in a highly subjective fashion (e.g., a medium-level correlation equals a coefficient value of 0.5). In addition, no sensitivity analysis is generally performed to identify the impact of uncertainty associated with the correlation magnitudes on the results. Both of these considerations can lead to unwarranted overconfidence in the results, if not erroneous results. (For example, one analyst said, "In order to avoid the trap of assuming that no such correlation exists, we have therefore applied a correlation of 0.20 between all elements so that we do not seriously underestimate the impact of correlation on the degree of uncertainty of our estimates.") Furthermore, subjective relationships between correlation level and magnitude generally do not take into consideration the fact that a correlation coefficient between elements can be negative. For example, this can occur when funding (or technical issues) for one WBS element is inversely tied to funding (or technical issues) for another element.

The use of ordinary Pearson (product moment) correlation algorithms should generally be avoided when distributions are nonnormal and/or when items are represented by different distributions, because this can lead to computation errors. (In fact, the underlying probability distribution for most items below the total program level is typically not known with any real degree of confidence.) In such cases correlation coefficients should be implemented using a nonparametric rank correlation procedure (e.g., Spearman correlation) because the results are generally distribution independent or by an enhanced Pearson correlation algorithm.[22] (Additional discussion on how to specify correlation in Monte Carlo simulations is beyond the scope of this book, but suitable references are available.)[21,23]

Arguments are sometimes advanced that a non-zero correlation coefficient should be used to prevent underestimating cost (or another parameter) by using the default correlation coefficient magnitude value (0.0 or uncorrelated) in performing a simulation. While this may seem attractive, two resulting questions are the correlation coefficient that should be selected and the impact on the result. Unfortunately, it is not at all easy to accurately answer these questions.

Finally, substantial variations may exist as to how commercial packages implement correlation coefficients in Monte Carlo simulations. *In some cases the variations in results between software packages (e.g., for a correlation coefficient of "n" where "n" > 0) are much larger than that because of the level of correlation being modeled (e.g., between "n" and 0.0 for a single software package)!*

Tests performed with two leading, current commercial Monte Carlo simulation spreadsheet add-in packages that use a nonparametric rank correlation procedure revealed substantial variations in the effect of correlation, although this was only performed for a system composed of 10 identical distributions (Triangle: L = 0.75, ML = 1.0, and H = 3), with all off-diagonal elements of the resulting matrix having the same correlation coefficient. This is far from universal in terms of the number of elements simulated, their distributions, and the fraction of elements with nonzero correlation coefficients. Nevertheless, the difference in results between the two software packages when a correlation coefficient of 0.2 was selected was greater than the difference between the results for *either* software package between a correlation coefficient of 0.0 (default simulation value, uncorrelated) and 0.2 when computed as the average variation determined at every 5th percentile from the 0th percentile to the 100th percentile. The same outcome also existed when comparing the difference between the same two software packages when a correlation coefficient of 1.0 (fully correlated) was selected vs the difference between the results for either software package between a correlation coefficient of 0.0 and 1.0. However, for correlation coefficients of 0.5 and 0.8, the difference in results between the two commercial software packages was less than the difference between the results for either software package between a correlation coefficient of 0.0 and 0.5 or 0.0 and 0.8. Given the variation in results between these commercial software packages, plus the other considerations just mentioned, *the reader is strongly cautioned against blindly using nonzero correlation coefficients in a Monte Carlo simulation unless solid evidence exists and the coefficients can be accurately quantified.*

Although the effect of correlation can potentially be estimated between WBS elements using a suitable Monte Carlo simulation, no simple procedure exists when ordinal risk scales are used. This is typically accomplished through the use of a risk scale termed correlation, dependency, or interaction, which is then either numerically combined with other ordinal "probability" scales for the same WBS element or added to the resulting risk factor (following incorrect multiplication of "probability" and consequence terms). Two fundamental problems exist with this approach, which is effectively an immeasurable cause and effect between the ordinal "probability" scale definitions and the risk category the scale represents (as mentioned in Sec. IV.M). First, although including a dependency (or similar) scale seems reasonable, several questions exist that cannot be satisfactorily answered, such as 1) how a dependency scale should be structured (e.g., what is being measured), 2) how the levels should be quantified such that the correlation between the risk issue in question vs other related risk issues is mapped to a single value (e.g., the risk issue is dependent on two additional risk issues, corresponds to a scale value $= X$), and 3) how the scale should be combined with other "probability" scales (e.g., is it added, averaged, or mathematically correlated) or the resulting risk factor. Second, as already discussed, no mathematical operations (e.g., averaging) can be performed on values derived from uncalibrated ordinal scales, or else the results are often erroneous. Given these severe problems and the typically subjective wording of scale-level definitions, dependency and similar ordinal "probability" scales *should not be used.* Instead, the analyst should note which other WBS elements the risk issue in question is related to and use this insight for risk identification, analysis, handling, and monitoring purposes.

Correlation may exist between WBS elements, activities, or items in C,P,S risk analyses. Interdependence between risk analysis categories, or between WBS elements, or activities for a given risk category is often not properly evaluated. However, because of variations in how correlation is implemented even in current commercial software packages, nonzero correlation coefficients should not be used in a Monte Carlo simulation unless solid evidence exists and the coefficients can be accurately quantified.

Do not automatically assume that positive correlation exists between risk issues—a negative correlation may exist instead. Evaluate each pair of risk issues without automatically presupposing what the sign of the correlation is. Blindly assuming that all correlation coefficients are positive may introduce error when performing a Monte Carlo simulation and other forms of risk analysis.

Do not automatically assume that positive correlation exists between risk issues—a negative correlation may exist instead.

F. Evaluating the Level of Risk from Monte Carlo Simulation CDFs

The level of risk that results from a Monte Carlo simulation depends on the variable modeled (e.g., cost) and how the program's management views risk. For example, cost risk simulations yield results in dollar values, whereas schedule risk simulations typically yield results in durations (e.g., days), finish date (e.g., calendar date), and/or the percent of time a task is on the probabilistic critical path (from 0 to 100). However, even if identical simulations are run and the same CDF percentiles are evaluated, the level of risk may vary between programs depending on how it is estimated.

For example, some programs view cost risk as the difference between the Monte Carlo simulation result CDF at the desired percentile (e.g., 50th) vs the cost baseline developed as part of the acquisition program baseline.[13] Other programs define cost risk as the difference between the Monte Carlo simulation CDF at the desired percentile (e.g., 50th) vs the sum of the most likely cost estimates. Whereas the latter approach is common, the former approach is sometimes used. Thus, even assuming that the Monte Carlo simulation has been correctly performed, the resulting level of risk reported may vary considerably depending on the methodology used to estimate it.

Because multiple approaches exist, the methodology used to derive the level of risk from Monte Carlo simulation CDFs should be clearly defined and documented.

G. Comparing Cost Risk and Schedule Risk Results from Monte Carlo Simulations

Estimates of cost risk derived from Monte Carlo simulations often represent an EAC, not a particular given snapshot in time unless generated from a bottoms-up or engineering cost analysis. This is because the underlying databases used in the derivation of many parametric cost estimating relationships or expert judgment used to develop analogous estimates often represent completed development or production programs. The same, however, is often not true when estimating schedule risk, which typically represents a given snapshot in time, and may possibly not be true for performance risk, which can represent a varying timescale. Consequently, caution should be exercised when comparing cost and schedule quantitative risk analysis results to ensure that they represent a similar time frame.

Cost and schedule quantitative risk analysis results derived from a Monte Carlo simulation may not be directly comparable because of potential differences in the snapshot in time they represent. Always check the time frame of the estimate to ensure that the results can be accurately overlaid.

H.   Allocation of Results Back to Individual Elements

It may be desirable to allocate Monte Carlo CDF risk dollars or time back to individual WBS elements or activities, respectively to gain additional insight into the nature of risk present within the modeled program.

Some schemes for allocating CDF risk results back to individual simulation elements are clearly wrong. For example, one incorrect method involves a weighting based on the proportion of the most likely (reference point estimate) value without risk for a given WBS element divided by the sum of the most likely values for all WBS elements. In this case the allocation is performed without regard to whether or not risk exists for a given WBS element and the degree of risk that exists assuming the WBS element is modeled with risk (having one or more probability distributions associated with it). Another incorrect method involves subjectively guessing the level of risk that should be allocated to individual WBS elements—this may lead to erroneous and nonrepeatable results.

More correct approaches for allocating CDF risk results at a given percentile back to individual simulation elements are based on the level of uncertainty for a given element (indicated by the probability distribution) vs the total risk present (e.g., the difference between the Monte Carlo simulation result CDF at the desired percentile, e.g., 50th, vs the sum of the most likely estimates). Assume here that the distributions associated with all elements containing risk are triangle distributions. WBS elements without risk or those with a symmetrical probability distribution (e.g., normal distribution) do not receive any risk allocation. Any elements with left-skewed or right-skewed distributions would mathematically receive a negative or positive risk allocation, respectively. Elements with a left-skewed distribution and negative allocation should mathematically exist but are often not implemented. On the surface this may seem acceptable, but it implies or means that, for example, no WBS element gives up cost risk dollars, while all elements with risk receive at least some cost risk dollars. This is not correct when viewed from the perspective of management reserve—at least some dollars from all elements should be subject to evaluation ($+$ and $-$, not just $+$). Otherwise, some items may have excessive reserves, contributing to shortfalls, thus cost overruns, in other areas or the tendency to spend the funds on less than essentials. (In such cases there may be a tendency to hold funds until the last minute rather than release them. Because C,P,S can not be traded perfectly in the short-run, this may lead to inefficient trades, non-zero opportunity costs, etc. in other areas.

Note, also, that this type of allocation approach requires that *the same kind of probability distribution be used for all simulation elements, and that a single probability distribution be used for all simulation elements, which may not be the case.*

Another approach examines the level of accumulated risk, e.g., CDF, at a level of integration below the total program level. Here, output levels at, say, WBS Levels 2, 3, and/or 4 can be calculated in addition to the total program level (WBS Level 1). This will provide insight into how risk is allocated at the program segment and system levels, e.g., Levels 2 and 3, respectively. Of course, the output level can be carried to lower and lower WBS levels, but becomes meaningless when it is at the same WBS level as most of the individual probability distributions, e.g., typically WBS Level 4 or 5 for cost risk analysis. In such cases the resulting output level trivially becomes the probability distribution(s) for the WBS element being examined.

In addition, the allocation of Monte Carlo CDF results back to individual simulation elements is often problematic because the uncertainty level present is likely in the first or second decimal place of the results. Hence, even if the allocation procedure is numerically correct, the results will be uncertain and at least somewhat erroneous. Thus, decision makers should use considerable caution in evaluating the allocation of, say, risk dollars or time back to individual WBS elements or activities, respectively, when such information may impact actual program decisions and not just be an academic exercise.

Considerable caution should be used in attempting to allocate Monte Carlo CDF risk dollars or time back to individual simulation elements because of the number of assumptions typically required that cannot strictly be met, coupled with an unknown uncertainty that typically exists in the CDF results.

Allocation of Monte Carlo simulation results back to individual elements using the mean should not be the first approach used because the mean cannot be readily related to a specific percentile in most cases. In cases where no other approach can be developed using the mean may be acceptable so long as the analyst realizes that except in limited cases (e.g., a normal distribution) the mean cannot be related to specific percentiles.

Allocation of Monte Carlo simulation results back to individual elements using the mean should not be the first approach used because the mean cannot be readily related to a specific percentile in most cases.

I. Consequence of Occurrence and Monte Carlo Simulation Results

With a Monte Carlo simulation the consequence of occurrence term defaults to the units associated with the elements being evaluated. For example, if a cost WBS is being evaluated, then the resulting consequence dimension, as well as risk, will typically be given in a unit of cost (e.g., dollars). Likewise, if a schedule network is being evaluated, the resulting consequence dimension, as well as risk, will typically be given in a unit of time (e.g., duration or finish date). If, in a Monte Carlo simulation, one variable is being evaluated (e.g., cost) while probability distributions associated with other variables are present (e.g., cost estimating uncertainty, schedule risk, and technical risk), the resulting consequence dimension will still be in units of the variable being evaluated. In this case the units relate to cost as influenced by cost estimating uncertainty, schedule risk, and technical risk.

With a Monte Carlo simulation the consequence of occurrence term defaults to the units associated with the elements being evaluated.

J. Commercial Software Packages

It should come as no surprise that the performance characteristics of commercial risk analysis software packages are often over-optimistic, and "bugs" may exist in some cases that the user is unaware of. For example, the vendor claim for a commercial Monte Carlo simulation package was that the update would run substantially faster vs the previous version. Well, using the software package on two different computers (with substantially different throughput speeds) with two different operating systems revealed no difference whatsoever in the processing rate for the same file run under both the new and previous versions of the software package. In another case, computations were performed in a nonstandard manner which, because of poor documentation, could lead the user to grossly mis-interpret the results (in effect, the results displayed were "1 -" the norm for computations of this type). In another case, a highly touted feature of a Monte Carlo simulation package "worked," but because of quirks with the underlying application that it was embedded into, great care had to be taken to set up the application file otherwise erroneous results would occur. (In effect, the Monte Carlo add-in would misinterpret the formulation of the model in the application file and incorrectly compute the results.)

The performance characteristics of commercial risk analysis software packages are often over-optimistic (if not inflated), and "bugs" may exist in some cases that the user is unaware of.

Some Monte Carlo software packages and the associated applications that they "plug into" cannot use more than one probability distribution per cell, element, or activity. Using a single probability distribution may be acceptable in some cases where no separation between components can be made (e.g., for a cost risk simulation no differentiation can be made of cost estimating uncertainty, technical risk and schedule risk). However, this is not desirable in other cases where separate and potentially more accurate estimates of these different distributions exist.

Having a simulation software package that constrains the number of input distributions per cell, element, or activity may be problematic for several reasons. First, the critical values for a single distribution may be difficult to estimate and thus be uncertain. Second, a single distribution may not capture the underlying different types of probability distributions associated with the components present (e.g., estimating uncertainty may be best represented by a normal distribution while technical risk may be best represented by a triangle distribution). Third, in some cases the user is forced to use a very limited number of possible distribution types to represent the single distribution. This too may increase the level of uncertainty and error in the model inputs, thus outputs. (See Sec. VII.B for additional information.)

Some Monte Carlo software packages and the associated applications that they "plug into" cannot used more than one probability distribution per cell, element, or activity. This may be acceptable in some situations but not in others where a separate and potentially more accurate estimate of uncertainty and risk categories is available.

IX. Portraying Risk Analysis Results

A. Some Graphical and Tabular Methods of Portraying Results

A variety of different graphical and tabular methods exist for portraying and ranking risk results. [Risk ranking can be helpful for both risk analysis, (e.g., to help summarize results), and risk handling, (e.g., to help prioritize risks for implementing RHPs given finite resources).] Most of the methods are simple to implement, and their usefulness is primarily governed by the accuracy of the underlying data. However, faulty methods of prioritizing or ranking risks exist and are commonly used. In the worst case a flawed approach can yield erroneous results that may lead to suboptimal designs and focusing scarce program budget, personnel, and schedule resources on the wrong risk issues.

I will now show several common graphical and tabular portrayals. This is not an exhaustive list, but a representative list of those commonly used. (For brevity, I have not included time sensitivity, frequency of occurrence, and interdependence with other risk issues as discriminators in risk ranking. They can be added by the reader and assigned whatever subjective weighting factor desired.)

One of the simplest methods for classifying and portraying risk results is a risk analysis and risk handling priority matrix (risk mapping matrix), as given in Fig. 6.2. This matrix serves three purposes. The first is to convert probability of occurrence and consequence of occurrence scores into risk levels. (While a risk mapping matrix can use results from a variety of meth-

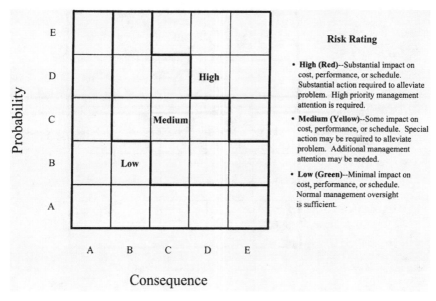

Fig. 6.2 5 × 5 risk mapping matrix.

ods to estimate probability and consequence of occurrence results, it is most commonly applied to results from risk scales, and typically ordinal risk scales.) The second is to permit prioritization of risks based on their assigned risk level. The third, when coupled with the risk rating definitions to the right of the matrix, is to provide a final sanity check on the resulting risk scores. (For example, if a risk is assigned a high level, will it really have substantial impact on C,P,S, etc.?) (Note: I have intentionally used ordinal letter designators on the probability and consequence of occurrence axes to emphasize the point that mathematical operations should not be performed on the results from ordinal scales.)

This type of risk mapping matrix is typically presented as a 5 × 5 or 3 × 3 representation, although many other variations are possible. For example, the 5 × 5 matrix can be made more granular by decreasing the bands associated with the L, M, and H ratings and adding LM (low medium) and MH (medium high) bands to yield five risk levels, as illustrated in Fig. 6.3.

A simple use of the risk mapping matrix is to convert subjective values (e.g., A, B, C, D, E) of the probability and consequence of occurrence terms of risk. Another use is to convert ratings from ordinal probability and consequence of occurrence ordinal scales to risk. In this case the probability and consequence levels (typically more than three) are mapped to equivalent levels on each axis, then converted to an equivalent risk level. For example, if seven level ordinal "probability" and consequence of occurrence

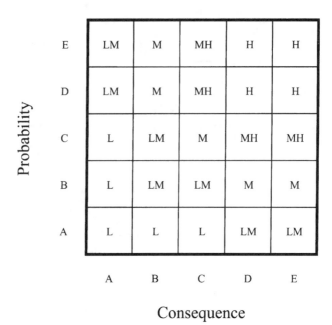

Consequence

Fig. 6.3 Modified 5 × 5 risk mapping matrix.

scales exist, and Level 1 corresponds to A, Levels 2 and 3 correspond to B, Levels 4 and 5 corresponds to C, Level 6 corresponds to D, and Level 7 corresponds to E, then an ordinal score of (4, 6) (probability, consequence) equals a probability score of C, and a consequence of occurrence score of D, which translates using Fig. 6.3 to the (C,D) cell and risk level of MH.

A graphical portrayal of results using a risk mapping matrix is given in Fig. 6.4. Here, the risk issues (denoted with placeholders as Risk 1 ... Risk 10) are placed in the matrix cell corresponding to their risk level.

However, a common problem in portraying results using the risk mapping matrix format is to assign ordering or even cardinal meaning within a cell. For example, in Fig. 6.4 there is no inherent basis to assume by the ordering that Risk 1 > Risk 2, Risk 3 > Risk 4 and so on. Similarly, it would not be appropriate to assume that Risk 1 is X times greater than Risk 2 based on some measure of physical separation (X) between Risks 1 and 2. When risk results are portrayed in a matrix representation, such as in Fig. 6.4, supporting information should always indicate what the results contained within a cell represent. Otherwise, it is not possible to confidently understand the results. (I have seen representations of this type used to portray ordering or numeric factors associated with risk scores where there has been no supporting documentation and where the methodologies used to provide the order-

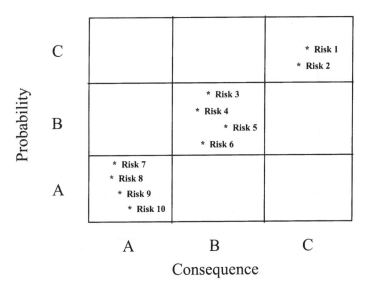

Fig. 6.4   Risk analysis mapping matrix with risk issues.

ing and numeric factors were severely flawed such that the results portrayed were almost meaningless.)

I will now present another risk mapping matrix representation, given in Fig. 6.5, to illustrate a series of problems that can exist. First, this matrix uses definitions for levels that may be confusing to the reader (including minimum, which if construed as the global minimum could be below Low, and significant, which is construed by some people to be above High). Second, the numerical definitions for low (0.1 to 0.3), moderate (0.4 to 0.6), and high (0.7 to 0.9) are subjective and have no cardinal meaning. Third, the scores contained in the individual cells are also subjective and have no cardinal meaning. Fourth, the boundaries separating low and moderate are asymmetric. Unfortunately, this trait is common and appears in a number of risk mapping matrices. In addition, in almost all instances where I have questioned the use of asymmetric boundaries, the reader was unaware that the boundaries where asymmetric, and they had no explanation as to why the boundaries were this way. [One possible explanation is that consequence of occurrence is given a higher weighting than probability of occurrence, which should not generally be the case. (See Sec. I.C for additional information.) However, even if this was the assumption used, this is contradicted by the boundary between moderate and high, which is symmetric.]

Another example risk mapping matrix that warrants comment is given in Fig. 6.6. This representation contains some valid characteristics but also

Probability \ Consequence	Low	Min	Mod	Sig	High
High	0.3	0.4	0.7	0.8	0.9
Sig	0.2	0.4	0.6	0.7 **High**	0.8
Mod	0.2	0.3	0.5 **Medium**	0.6	0.7
Min	0.1	0.3 **Low**	0.5	0.5	0.6
Low	0.1	0.2	0.3	0.5	0.6

High: **0.7 to 0.9**

Medium: **0.4 to 0.6**

Low: **0.1 to 0.3**

Fig. 6.5 Asymmetric risk mapping matrix.

several potential problems, and it should not be used in its present form without correction. On the positive side, the matrix is ordered properly, such that higher-risk issues would appear up and to the right (or northeast) of the origin, while lower-risk issues would appear toward the origin. Although this might seem trivial, I have seen risk mapping matrices that have their highest

Consequence ⟶ Higher

Probability ⟶ Higher	Negligible	Minor	Moderate	Serious	Critical
91–100%					
61–90%					
41–60%					
11–40%					
0–10%					

Fig. 6.6 Example risk mapping matrix.

risk located above (north of) the origin; this type of representation is counterintuitive. (This apparently occurred because the consequence of occurrence scale was reversed—the highest consequence scores were closest to the origin, while the lowest scores were away from it.) Also on the positive side, mathematics and are not performed on results from uncalibrated ordinal scales to derived the matrix locations.

However, there are three potential problems with this risk mapping matrix representation. First, the probability ratings are derived from a five-level estimative probability scale whose levels correspond to the following ranges: $0.0 \leq$ Probability ≤ 0.10 (Level 1), $0.11 \leq$ Probability ≤ 0.40 (Level 2), $0.41 \leq$ Probability ≤ 0.60 (Level 3), $0.61 \leq$ Probability ≤ 0.90 (Level 4), and $0.91 \leq$ Probability ≤ 1.0 (Level 5). There is no apparent real-world basis for using these probability ranges. In addition, the ranges, while symmetric to the middle value (Level 3), have unequal intervals (Levels 2 and 4 the same, Levels 1, 3, and 5 are different). Second, the probability ranges have been embedded on the ordinate, rather than simply replacing the values with suitable probability statements for the five levels (e.g., E, D, C, B, and A). Third, the statements used to describe the consequence of occurrence levels may be adequate, but the same set of statements should generally be used on both the probability (ordinate) and consequence of occurrence (abscissa) axes to avoid confusion. The key consideration for a risk mapping matrix should be that it is *self-explanatory*, rather than requiring interpretation on the part of the reader.

Another potentially incorrect way that risk results are be portrayed is through a numerical representation (typically normalized to 1.0) with risk boundary contours, as illustrated in Fig. 6.7. It is common to find that the underlying probability and consequence of occurrence values used to derive risk scores are obtained from uncalibrated ordinal scales or subjective estimates. For example, a risk factor is determined from the average of one or more probability scale values and one or more consequence scale values. In addition, the numerical risk boundary contours that separate low, medium, and high risks have no apparent basis. (One program that used this risk portrayal included values derived from uncalibrated ordinal scales together with risk contours that had no documented basis. Hence, the results portrayed, although visually appealing, were not meaningful.)

Had the risk factors been derived from calibrated ordinal scales, then such a numerical representation would not have been invalid subject to the following limitations: 1) the probability of occurrence term is not actually probability (unless the scales actually represented probabilities or were calibrated against them), 2) the resulting risk factor values would not have truly been risk but a weighted value of relative importance to the program, and 3) the risk boundary contours should be eliminated unless there is a strong, defensible basis for their use.

Another common portrayal of risk scores is given in Fig. 6.8. (Fig. 6.8 is

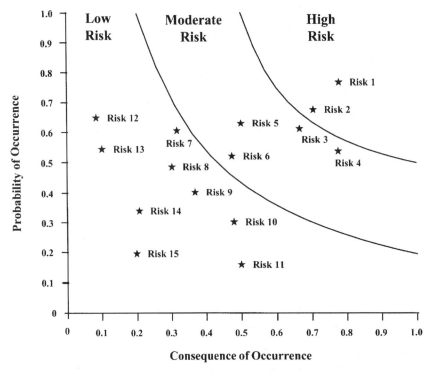

Fig. 6.7   Representation of risks with erroneous numerical values and risk boundary contours.

derived from Ref. 13, p. B-23, "Program Risk Reduction Schedule.") This type of graphical depiction is representative of those often used with RHPs and risk monitoring to track risk reduction progress vs time. (Note: Although this figure represents a single example, there are many different portrayals of this information possible, including the number and types of milestones, the level of detail of risk handling data, and how actual and planned progress are represented.) In Fig. 6.8 the risk rating axis is ordinal (e.g., high, medium, and low), as is the anticipated risk level for risk reduction events. The principal mathematical issue with this representation is when the results portrayed are derived from uncalibrated ordinal scales. In such cases the results are only an *indicator* of risk. Another important consideration in Fig. 6.8 is how the separation between events is estimated within a risk level (e.g., medium). Typically this separation is either based on a subjective assessment or further differentiation of the underlying probability of occurrence and consequence of occurrence scores. However, there is no best method for estimating this separation when an ordinal axis exists. No attempt should be made to quan-

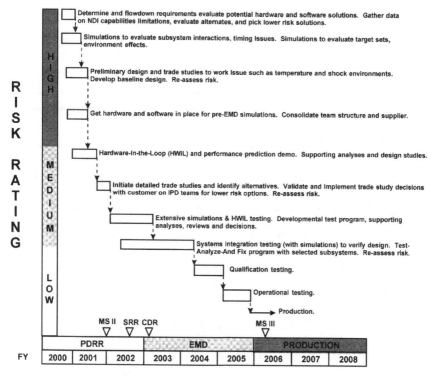

Fig. 6.8   RHP: risk rating portrayal vs time.

tify the vertical separation between risk rating values unless the underlying probability and consequence of occurrence values were derived using calibrated ordinal scales or other sources of cardinal data. Finally, another problem that I have observed with the risk rating vs time plot given in Fig. 6.8 is that the results from one or more uncalibrated ordinal "probability" scales may be used instead of a risk factor computed from probability and consequence of occurrence scores. Although values from neither source are equivalent to risk (because they were derived from uncalibrated ordinal scales), there is *no basis whatsoever* to plot scores solely derived from uncalibrated or calibrated ordinal "probability" scales and term them risk. (Note: When risk analysis results vs time are portrayed, separate probability of occurrence and consequence of occurrence values should also be maintained and separately reported. This is because risk results vs time portrayals, such as given in Fig. 6.8, typically only show the resulting risk level, not the underlying probability and consequence of occurrence levels, which may vary, yet still result in the same risk level.)

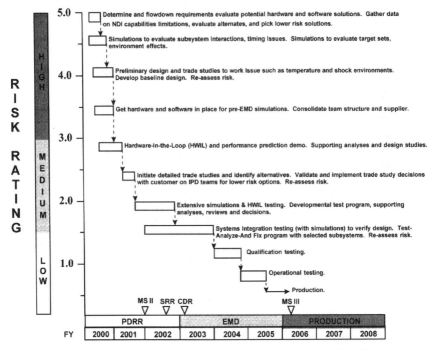

Fig. 6.9   RHP: Generally erroneous risk rating portrayal vs time.

Whereas the portrayal of risk scores in Fig. 6.8 may be acceptable, a generally unacceptable representation is given in Fig. 6.9. (Figure 6.9 is also derived from Ref. 13, p. B-23, "Program Risk Reduction Schedule.") Here, the numerical risk rating axis is typically meaningless because the values are almost always derived from uncalibrated ordinal "probability" and consequence of occurrence scores. For example, an issue with a 5.0 rating is almost certainly not twice as risky as one rated 2.5; the actual factor is *unknown*. As before, no attempt should be made to quantify the vertical separation between risk rating values unless the underlying probability and consequence of occurrence values were derived using calibrated ordinal scales or other sources of cardinal data. [See comments on Fig. 6.8 regarding the validity of the ordinal risk rating axis (high, medium, and low).]

Another less common but widely circulated portrayal is given in Fig. 6.10 (Ref. 24). Here, the plotted risk value (49.1) came from uncalibrated ordinal "probability" and consequence of occurrence risk scales. Unfortunately, this entailed multiplying values obtained from six sets of "probability" of occurrence scales and three sets of consequence of occurrence scales and adding the scores. (This not only led to erroneous results, but because of numerous math errors in the calculations, results not consistent with the methodology

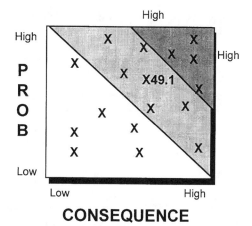

Fig. 6.10 Example of faulty risk level portrayal.

used.) The resulting risk value (49.1) was then transferred into the risk mapping matrix given in Fig. 6.10. Notice that the probability and consequence of occurrence axes of the two-dimensional risk mapping matrix are unitless, simply ranging from Low to High. Yet a single, one-dimensional value (49.1) has been plotted in this unitless two-dimensional matrix! Obviously, this value cannot be assuredly placed in the location of the matrix where it resides even if the probability and consequence axes had been properly scaled. Simply stated, a one-dimensional value cannot be meaningfully placed as a single point in a two-dimensional matrix. In addition to this fundamental problem there are three other issues associated with this representation. First, diagonal risk level boundaries are used which clearly do not correspond to integer increments of the probability and consequence of occurrence axes. Second, the two "High" labels above and to the right of the matrix are both confusing and unnecessary. Third, no labels or legend exists to indicate the low and medium risk level boundaries (although it "appears" that the unshaded are corresponds to low risk and the lightly shaded area is medium risk). Given the numerous issues that exist, this type of portrayal of risk results should not be used.

Several text representation versions are typically used to portray risk results. (In the following examples I have omitted time sensitivity, frequency of occurrence, and interdependence with other risk issues for simplification. For the sake of brevity, I have also only included hypothetical results for only one issue; an actual tabular summary would include risk issues evaluated.) The first representation, given in Table 6.15, includes a separately estimated risk level for each "probability" risk category as well as for C,P,S consequence of occurrence components. This type of representation should

Table 6.15 Example of risk reporting using multiple "probability" and consequence of occurrence components

Probability Term	Consequence Term		
	C_c	C_p	C_s
Design/Engineering	LM	M	LM
Manufacturing	LM	LM	M
Support	LM	L	L
Technology	M	H	M
Threat	M	MH	LM

be used for each issue evaluated. Here, a 5 × 5 risk mapping matrix (not shown here) is used to map probability and consequence of occurrence levels to risk. There is nothing incorrect about using this representation to show risk results (e.g., no mathematical operations performed on results from the underlying ordinal scales).

The second representation, given in Table 6.16, includes a separately estimated risk level for each "probability" risk category, but only a single level across the C,P,S consequence of occurrence components. (As before, this type of representation should be used for each issue evaluated.) Again, a 5 × 5 risk mapping matrix (not shown here) is used to map probability and consequence of occurrence levels to risk. In this case the maximum of the three risk levels derived from C,P,S consequence of occurrence is reported rather than all three values. (This corresponds to the consequence of occurrence dimension corresponding to the maximum risk level.) As in the preceding case, there is nothing incorrect about using this representation to show risk results (e.g., no mathematical operations performed on results from the underlying ordinal scales).

The third representation, given in Table 6.17, includes a single estimated

Table 6.16 Example of risk reporting using multiple "probability" components and maximum consequence of occurrence components

Risk Category	Risk
Design/Engineering	M
Manufacturing	M
Support	LM
Technology	H
Threat	MH

Table 6.17   Example of risk reporting using maximum "probability" components and multiple consequence of occurrence components

Probability Term	Consequence Term		
	C_c	C_p	C_s
Technology	M	H	M

risk level across the "probability" categories, and a separately estimated risk level across the C,P,S consequence of occurrence components. (As before, this type of representation should be used for each issue evaluated.) Again, a 5 × 5 risk mapping matrix (not shown here) is used to map probability and consequence of occurrence levels to risk. In this case the maximum of the risk levels derived from a single "probability" category is reported rather a separate value for all (five) categories. (This corresponds to the "probability" of occurrence dimension corresponding to the maximum risk level.) As in the preceding case, there is nothing incorrect about using this representation to show risk results (e.g., no mathematical operations performed on results from the underlying ordinal scales).

Further aggregation of the results given in Tables 6.16 and 6.17 based on the maximum risk level across the five "probability" categories (Table 6.16) or three consequence of occurrence components (Table 6.17) would lead to a (single) risk level of high being reported for the issue. If such an aggregation is performed, then it is recommended that the risk category (technology) and consequence of occurrence component (performance) corresponding to this risk level can be reported to assist the reader in understanding the results. [Note, that the results in this case should not be viewed as performance risk (taking the maximum of the three consequence of occurrence dimension) or technology risk (taking the maximum of the five "probability" of occurrence dimensions), but technical risk—the top-level risk category associated with design/engineering, manufacturing, support, technology, and threat risk.]

A common mistake in reporting risk is to perform mathematical operations on results, whether or not the operations are permissible. This can include performing risk factor computations on results from uncalibrated "probability" and consequence of ordinal scales, as well as using inappropriate risk factor representations (discussed in Sec. III.A and B). Another common problem is to take the average of risk levels across different consequence of occurrence levels, and/or across different risk categories. (This would be akin to assuming threat risk in Table 6.15 is the average of M, MH, and LM levels for the three consequence of occurrence components, resulting in a value of M.) The results from almost all simple averaging approaches may be erroneous unless the data are based on cardinal risk values (e.g., based on ratio scales) or developed using calibrated ordinal scales. Compounding the problems just illustrated is the case when factors are used to estimate a weighted rather than simple average. Again, the results from almost all weighted averaging approaches may be erroneous unless the data are based on cardinal risk values or developed using calibrated ordinal scales.

When calibrated ordinal scales are used, the resulting risk scores can be directly sorted and presented without mapping. However, even risk scores derived from calibrated ordinal scales have limitations. Three issues will exist that require consideration by the analyst and decision makers. First, the results almost always are a weighted average of relative importance to the program, rather than true risk because actual probability of occurrence data are typically not used. Second, if the results are to be segregated into risk levels (e.g., L, M, and H), then boundaries will have to be determined among the numerical scores. There is typically no objective way to perform this segregation, although statistical clustering techniques and examining results from highly analogous programs can sometimes be helpful. Third, there will be typically an unknown level of uncertainty associated with the results, and rankings based on the second or even third decimal place should be cautiously used when uncertainty may exist in the first decimal place. Hence, as in many risk prioritization schemes, additional engineering and management attention should be placed on any issue that has a medium or higher risk level.

Additional schemes, such as comparison risk ranking, multivoting, and Pareto methods, exist for ranking risks.[25] However, these approaches may have nontrivial limitations and should not be blindly used. For example, comparison risk ranking and multivoting may be viable when used for tie-breaking risk analysis scores derived from a technique such as ordinal "probability" and consequence of occurrence scales and an appropriate mapping matrix. However, they should only be cautiously used with subjective estimates of risk, particularly when risk is estimated directly rather than from separate estimates of probability and consequence of occurrence terms. This is because of the potential nontrivial uncertainty that will exist in the risk estimates coupled with random and bias noise induced by the comparison risk ranking or multivoting process. [For some risk categories, such as management risk, at least part of the risk analysis methodology may be subjective (see Sec. V.B), and the use of a technique such as comparison risk ranking or multivoting may be unavoidable. Such approaches should not be the first choice when a risk analysis is performed with a more sophisticated methodology. Finally, there is no inherent method of estimating the degree of random and bias noise when performing a risk ranking using these approaches. Hence, perhaps more so than with some other risk ranking approaches, the results should not be blindly accepted.]

With Pareto techniques the risks are ranked by a predetermined method (e.g., simple sorting based on risk level), and the analyst develops breakpoints for the top 10%, 20%, and so on risks of the total risk list. (For example, if there were 20 risks, the top 10% would correspond to the two highest risks, etc.) Although this technique provides incremental information beyond just ranking the results, it should not be used if more medium, and particularly high, risk issues exist than the preset percentages that are closely monitored and reported. For example, if five high-risk issues exist out of 20 total, it may almost be irrelevant what the top 10 or 20% (that are closely watched by management) are in this case because 5 out of 25 issues are high risk (25%) and all should have RHPs developed, implemented, and the results monitored.

In addition, there is no guarantee that a Pareto rule of thumb holds for risk management (e.g., 20% of the risk issues cause 80% of the impact to the project)—don't let such rules of thumb "drive" the risk management process. While some risks will not have a substantial impact to the project should they actually occur, it is very unwise to set thresholds on the number of risks that should be examined based upon such heuristics. Also, such an evaluation examines risk vs impact, which is a subset of risk via consequence of occurrence, and risk and consequence of occurrence are correlated, which can lead to biased, if not erroneous, results.

A variety of other approaches exist that can lead to erroneous risk ranking results. For example, on one program a risk percentage (0 to 100) was subjectively developed for each risk issue and reported at program reviews. However, there was no methodology for deriving the value, and the value could not be traced back to either the probability of occurrence or consequence of occurrence risk terms that were developed. On another program risk analysis results for several risk categories were generated from noncardinal methods (e.g., uncalibrated ordinal scales) and subjective assessments and aggregated with results from cardinal methods (e.g., Monte Carlo simulation results). Such aggregated risk values may be uncertain, if not erroneous, and almost never yield risk, which requires actual "probability" of occurrence data.

Two examples of potentially faulty mathematical approaches for risk ranking are now given. First, techniques that involve averaging (whether weighted or unweighted) of "probability" and consequence of occurrence scores derived from uncalibrated ordinal scales should be avoided because they will almost always lead to erroneous results. Second, although it may be valid to use the union representation for combining different probability levels ($P_1 \cup P_2 = P_1 + P_2 - P_1 * P_2$), this too cannot be used with results derived from uncalibrated ordinal "probability" scales, as well as adding values from consequence of occurrence scales (where it does not apply) (see Sec. III.A).

Another technique that performs risk ranking on probability and consequence of occurrence data is Borda risk ranking.[26] Several difficulties exist with this approach. First, the results are rank ordered and it is not possible to generate meaningful numerical ranking comparisons between risk issues as is the case, for example, with results from calibrated ordinal scales. (Although the non-recurring effort to calibrate ordinal scales can be significant, the use of calibrated ordinal scales is a superior approach to Borda risk ranking because it gives direct numerical ranking where the ratios are meaningful as well [e.g., 0.4 is twice as important to the program as 0.2 (cet. par.)]. Second, there is an underlying/inherent notion that rank order is important, even within a risk level. This is true if it separates between say low and medium or medium and high risk, but often not between risk issues that are all high or medium risk. This is because all high risk issues and most medium risk issues will require risk handling to resolve. (Also, if the analyst is using uncalibrated ordinal scales and desires some increase in granularity, low, medium, and high risk levels can potentially be expanded to low, low medium, medium, medium high, and high risk levels using an appropriate risk mapping matrix.) Third, using a Borda approach, there appears to be no way to readily combine or weight preferences across probability terms (e.g., technology, design/engineering)—only a single term is possible whereas an unlimited number of terms are possible with calibrated ordinal scales. The same is true for combining or weighting preferences across the three different consequence of occurrence terms (C,P,S). Fourth, the Borda risk ranking implementation presented has significant limitations. First, in one representation, the single probability scale used is flawed—it is a five-level estimative probability scale, the ranges for each probability level vary with the level and are not based upon measured data or statistical results from a survey. Such a scale is difficult to accurately use and should not be applied to a variety of risk issues (as discussed in Appendix J, Sec. I.) Second, a single consequence of occurrence scale combines cost, performance and schedule components in a subjective manner and with subjective descriptors (e.g., small, moderate, major descriptors for cost/schedule). [In addition, a different Borda risk ranking can be computed using a weighted probability of success for the tasks contained in the RHP (thus a measure of the probability of RHP success) as a means to rank risks. This approach is subjective (particularly given the weighting coefficients) and should not generally be used.]

A variety of different graphical and tabular methods exists for portraying risk results. Most of the methods are simple to generate, and their usefulness is primarily governed by the accuracy of the underlying data. However, faulty methods of prioritizing risks are unfortunately common and may confuse decision makers. In the worst case it can lead to suboptimal designs and focusing scarce program budget, personnel, and schedule resources on the wrong risk issues.

1.　Some Risk Mapping Matrix Considerations

A risk mapping matrix can be presented in four different ways, with risk increasing in quadrant 1 (northwest in map coordinates), quadrant 2 (northeast), quadrant 3 (southwest), or quadrant 4 (southeast). While there is no (mathematically) correct way to present risk mapping matrix results, it is highly recommended that the quadrant 2 (northeast) approach be used, since this is common with other simple graphical representations (e.g., the line y = a + b * X, where X > 0).

A risk mapping matrix should generally have risk increasing in quadrant 2 (northeast in map coordinates).

Rather than displaying the number of risks in each cell of a risk mapping matrix as a single value [e.g., three risks in the (4,4) cell], it is far more helpful to display the individual risks within the cells using a simple identifier for each one. Movement of risk scores vs time can then be portrayed by an arrow for a given risk from one time period to another. If a large number of risks exist, then some cutoff can be used to limit the number of risks portrayed (e.g., all high risks, "Top 10" risks).

Rather than displaying the number of risks in each cell of a risk mapping matrix as a single value (e.g., three risks in the (4,4) cell), it is far more helpful to display the individual risks within the cells using a simple identifier for each one.

Risk issues plotted on risk mapping matrices should be clearly identified. It is not helpful if the items plotted are labeled with an alphanumeric system (e.g., A1) if there is no legend on the risk mapping matrix plot identifying what risk issues are represented by the labels, or if multiple alphanumeric indicators are used (e.g., A1, B1) when there is nothing to differentiate the labels (e.g., does A1 represent a different risk category than B1). The only thing that should be plotted on the chart is risk level, and those values should be tied back to a clear and unambiguous listing (e.g., risks 1 through "n" vs time).

Clearly identify risk issues plotted on risk mapping matrices so that the reader will understand what they represent.

If you use numerical guidelines (e.g., a table of decimal values $\geq$ 0 to $\leq$ 1) for placing step-downs within an ordinal risk mapping matrix don't believe the magnitudes of a step-down or the ratio of step-down levels—the true magnitudes and ratios are generally unknown. For example, assume that the (5,5), (4,4), and (3,3) cells in a 5 × 5 risk mapping matrix have values of 0.8, 0.6, and 0.4, respectively, and the boundary between high and medium passes between the (4,4) and (3,3) cells. There is no basis in this case to place cardinal significance on a step-down activity associated with the (5,5) cell vs the (4,4) cell since both cells correspond to high risk in this example and the underlying risk analysis results were derived from uncalibrated ordinal scales. In addition, you cannot attribute any cardinal significance to the ratio of cell scaling values. For example, it is not meaningful to say that the (5,5) cell is 2.0 times higher risk, more important to the program, and so on, than the (3,3) cell despite the numerical ratio of 0.8/0.4 = 2 because the scaling values are placeholders and the underlying risk analysis results were derived from uncalibrated ordinal scales. Simply stated, unless you have true cardinal risk scores or scores derived from calibrated ordinal scales (leading to a value of relative importance to the program), it is generally better to avoid numerical guidelines and simply label the step-downs as notional within a risk level (e.g., low, medium, high) than to fall into the trap of inferring cardinal significance to the results. Finally, allowing the user to arbitrarily set decimal values in each cell should be avoided because it can lead to an underestimation of the maximum/minimum ratio of the scores and a bias in the scores mapped to a particular risk level across the matrix. This may cause an inadvertent skew across the risk mapping matrix and the resulting cells associated with a given risk levels.

Another potential issue associated with using such decimal values is what value corresponds to the boundary between any two cells? For example, in the above example the (5,5), (4,4), and (3,3) cells in a 5 × 5 risk mapping matrix have values of 0.8, 0.6, and 0.4, respectively, and the boundary between high and medium passes between the (4,4) and (3,3) cells. Given this information, is the boundary between medium and high 0.4, 0.6, or some other value? While you may think it to be 0.4 or 0.6, or even the average of the two scores (0.5) it may be none of these values because the influence of neighboring cells must be taken into consideration in estimating a single boundary value for a given level across the matrix. Techniques such as cubic convolution or bi-linear interpolation will likely provide a more accurate answer than simply using a single value or average of values. However, because of the underlying ordinal nature of the data the results developed will still be inaccurate and potentially arbitrary.

Finally, if decimal numerical guidelines are used in generating step-downs within an ordinal risk mapping matrix it is unwise to portray them numerically in a table or other view because of the potential danger in believing that these values are accurate and cardinal, when in reality they are only placeholder values with unknown uncertainty applied to ordinal results.

If you use numerical guidelines (e.g., a table of decimal values ≥ 0 to ≤ 1) for placing step-downs within an ordinal risk mapping matrix don't believe the magnitudes of a step-down or the ratio of step-down levels, the true magnitudes and ratios are generally unknown.

Attempts at labeling risk mapping matrix cells as a mixture of integer and fractional values should be avoided since it will likely be erroneous, and at a minimum will generally be confusing.

Do not label risk mapping matrix cells as a mixture of integer and fractional values.

While a 3 × 3 risk mapping matrix may be inadequate in some cases, a 2 × 2 matrix should not be used unless binary data [limited to (0,1)] exists. Here there are not even enough cells to lead to low, medium and high levels with more than a single cell in two of the three resulting levels. In addition, a modest amount of uncertainty can then lead to a low risk becoming a high risk and vice versa. Hence, do not arbitrarily use a 2 × 2 risk mapping matrix.

Do not use a 2 × 2 risk mapping matrix unless you have binary data [limited to (0,1)].

Different risk mapping matrices may be used for different risk issues evaluated using the same methodology at the same time. This is confusing at best and erroneous at worst. In one case, different low, medium, and high risk level boundaries were used to evaluate different risk issues within the same IPT, yet this was never described to the reader. The result of this is that some issues reported by the program could have shifted an entire level (e.g., low to medium) because of the use of different risk level boundaries, yet there was no supporting documentation to indicate that this was even possible.

Do not use different risk mapping matrices for different risk issues evaluated using the same methodology at the same time. This is confusing at best and erroneous at worst.

For a risk mapping matrix, L, M, H; or L, LM, M, MH, H; etc. are often acceptable, but don't use "none." It is almost always incorrect to portray a risk level as "none" (particularly in cases where it has been mislabeled in a risk mapping matrix and should be at a higher level than low). The bottom-most risk level in a risk mapping matrix should generally be low. Finally, risks that are closed or otherwise retired should be removed and not evaluated rather than saying "none" is the appropriate risk level.

Do not use "none" as a risk level in a risk mapping matrix—low should generally be the bottom risk level.

Do not set boundaries in a risk mapping matrix by using constrained results from a nonstandard risk factor computation. Such boundaries will likely be uncertain and/or erroneous. For example, if probability and consequence of occurrence are given by ordinal scales of "X" levels each, then Risk Factor = Probability + n * Consequence should not be used to describe a risk mapping matrix, where the resulting risk level boundaries are set by dividing the resulting range of values into "m" equal levels (or some other such scheme). Risk Factor = Probability + n * Consequence is not a good or even valid metric to represent risk. This is because probability and consequence are not contained in the same set mathematically, hence cannot be added. If the "+" sign is replaced by a multiplication "*", then the equation is valid, but not necessarily meaningful when n ≠ 1.0 unless there is an objective, accurate means to estimate the value of "n." (Although it may be mathematically acceptable, I do not recommend this type of risk representation.)

Do not set boundaries in a risk mapping matrix by using constrained results from a nonstandard risk factor computation. Such boundaries will likely be uncertain and/or erroneous.

Effective risk handling will tend to drive a risk to a lower level, reducing the probability and/or consequence of occurrence terms. On a square risk mapping matrix (e.g., 5 × 5), this may manifest itself in two primary ways.

The first is movement toward the origin of the matrix when both the probability and consequence terms can be reduced (northeast to southwest in a typical representation). The second is movement (reduction) in one dimension that is greater than the other (e.g., probability vs consequence) when it is either easier to reduce the magnitude of the term in the (one) dimension vs the other, or when the nature of the ordinal scales do not permit a reduction to take place after an event has occurred unless re-baselining is used. (For example, if cost growth has occurred, then depending upon the scale definitions used it may not be possible to reduce the cost consequence of occurrence until the risk is retired.)

Risk reduction will lead to movement of the probability and/or consequence of occurrence terms toward the origin or one axis of a risk mapping matrix.

The 5 × 5 risk mapping matrix given in Fig. 6.11 is not inherently wrong, but implies that a mathematical relationship exists. Here, high is defined as values between 16 and 25, medium between 10 and 15, and low from 1 to 9. The danger in this case is if the user makes comparisons between numerical levels. This is subtle but can lead to errors (e.g., a score of 20 is almost certainly not twice as high a risk as a score of 10). Also, the number of cells assigned a risk rating of medium and high are relatively small (6 and 4

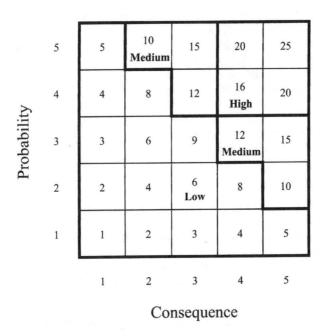

Fig. 6.11   Example 5 × 5 risk mapping matrix for discussion (1).

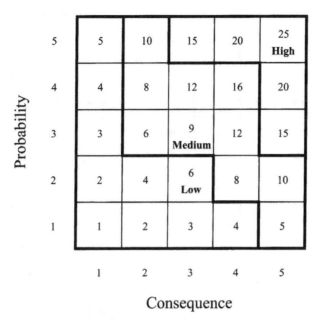

Probability

Consequence

Fig. 6.12 Example 5 × 5 risk mapping matrix for discussion (2).

respectively) compared to the number assigned a rating of low (15) in this example, hence the risk mapping matrix may be imbalanced. In addition, the risk labels have numbers, which although not inherently wrong, may imply that a mathematical relationship exists between cells. Labeling the axes 1 through 5 for probability and consequence is not wrong but I do not recommend it. Instead, use "A" through "E" for both axes where possible to avoid the implication that numerical values exist.

The 5 × 5 risk mapping matrix given in Fig. 6.12 contains a serious problem with the way that the risk level boundaries have been selected. Here, high is defined as values between 15 and 25, medium between 5 and 16, and low from 1 to 5. Note that there a cross in boundaries for L (1 to 6) and M (5 to 16), and for M (5 to 16) and H (15 to 25) which at best will be confusing and at worst lead to erroneous results (e.g., leading to a one risk level shift). Risk level boundaries should never overlap, let alone cross.

The 5 × 5 risk mapping matrix given in Fig. 6.13 should not be used. The decimal probability and consequence scale values and their resulting products are meaningless since they were obtained from uncalibrated ordinal scales. (Here, the risk levels would have greater meaning if the numerical values were replaced by L, M, H, etc.) In addition, note that the consequence

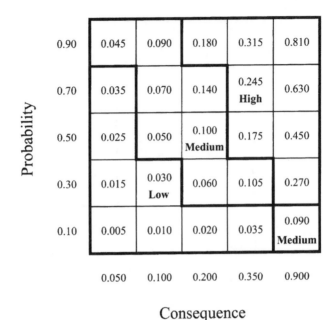

Consequence

Fig. 6.13　Example 5 × 5 risk mapping matrix for discussion (3).

scale contains two different changes in interval values among five levels (0.05, 0.10, 0.15, and 0.55 from lowest to highest), yet there is no basis provided to justify changing the interval values in such a manner. Finally, note that boundaries for L and M are symmetric but those for M and H are highly asymmetric. Asymmetric risk level boundaries should generally not be used, but if necessary or mandated for a particular program should include a discussion of the underlying rationale for using nonsymmetric boundaries.

Similarly, the 3 × 3 risk mapping matrix given in Fig. 6.14 should not be used. Here, the scores are estimated from two, three-level ordinal scales, one for "probability" and one for consequence. As mentioned in Appendix H, Sec. III, three-level ordinal scales should be avoided since they do not have sufficient granularity to properly evaluate many risk issues. The scale definitions used were subjective (e.g., too broad and difficult to measure), definitions for medium and high in each case are defined in terms of the need for mitigation and/or monitoring (which is related to risk handling and should not be included), and the three "probability" scale definitions include reference to the project schedule (which is related to consequence, not probability, and should not be included in a probability scale). Given these

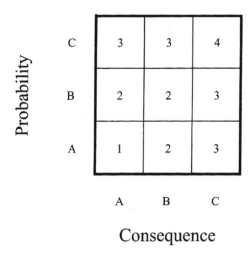

Fig. 6.14 Example 3 × 3 risk mapping matrix for discussion (1).

limitations, the resulting "probability" and consequence scores were then plotted on the following risk mapping matrix. Numerical values were assigned to the resulting risk levels, and these scores were then used to define a risk handling strategy (overly simplistic and incorrect) and in subsequent computations whereby the root sum square (square root of the sum of the squares) of individual risk issues was estimated to develop a project-level risk score. Here, the resulting scores derived from the risk mapping matrix are only ordinal values and have no mathematical meaning (e.g., $D > C > B > A$ is just as valid as 3, 2, 1, and 0), and the RSS of the scores across individual risk issues is also meaningless. A better approach to determine which risk issues have low, medium, and high risk is to use a 3 × 3 risk mapping matrix, such as the one in Fig. 6.15, then develop RHPs tailored to the specific risk issues that are medium or higher. This avoids introducing arbitrary errors into the estimation of both individual risk issues and the total number of each level of risk issue type (e.g., low, medium, or high) that exists.

2. Some Risk Step-Down Plot Considerations

While it may be meaningful to plot probability of occurrence vs consequence of occurrence for a given risk issue, it is generally not relevant or meaningful to plot risk factor vs probability of occurrence or risk factor vs consequence of occurrence. This is because risk = $f(P, C)$, and thus risk factor vs probability of occurrence is not an independent relationship nor is risk or risk factor vs consequence of occurrence.

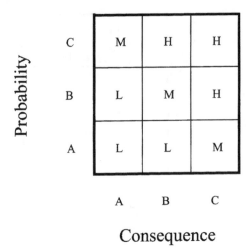

Consequence

Fig. 6.15   Example 3 × 3 risk mapping matrix for discussion (2).

While it may be meaningful to plot probability of occurrence vs consequence of occurrence for a given risk issue, it is generally not relevant or meaningful to plot risk factor vs probability of occurrence or risk factor vs consequence of occurrence.

In plotting a risk handling step-down, use a vertical line rather than a non-vertical line since the event occurs at one point in time (milestone). Use a staircase for multiple events over a period of time, not a single angled line (e.g., −45 degrees).

Use only vertical lines for plotting risk reductions in risk handling step-down plots.

Make sure that potential risk handling step-downs match both the risk level and schedule (time). This should be self-evident, but on numerous programs I've seen step-downs that are erroneous in the risk, time, or both dimensions.

Make sure that potential risk handling step-downs match both the risk level and schedule (time).

In some cases ordinal "probability" and consequence of occurrence scales are used to generate a risk factor (probability * consequence), but subsequent computations used to show milestones and durations associated with an actual or planned variation with time (commonly known as a risk step-down chart) are wholly subjective, no longer using the "probability" and consequence of occurrence scales. This practice is surprisingly common. However, it is an exceedingly unwise practice, since the subsequent risk factors are purely subjective, and they are not accurately tied to RHP milestones and portrays both a level of accuracy and certainty in the results that may be unwarranted. In effect, the resulting step-down plot may be highly uncertain, if not almost meaningless. (For example, risk scores may be linked to milestones, but the level of risk for each milestone is not accurate.) One reason sometimes given for no longer using the "probability" and consequence of occurrence scales after the initial estimate is that they can not be applied to potential RHP milestones. However, this is rationale for developing a better set of risk analysis scales rather than using inadequate scales that can not meaningfully estimate the potential risk level at designated milestones during the course of the program.

If risk scales are only used to estimate the current risk level for a risk step-down plot and other milestones are subjectively estimated, the resulting plot may be uncertain, if not almost meaningless.

When risk handling milestones vs time are plotted it is important to provide both actual progress and planned progress, as well as to clearly label which items correspond to each category. On some plots it is unclear what the information corresponds to. This can be confusing at best, and may lead to erroneous interpretations.

When risk handling milestones vs time are plotted it is important to provide both actual progress and planned progress, as well as to clearly label which items correspond to each category.

A risk mapping matrix with time-varying entries should not be used in place of a risk step-down plot. While the history within such a risk mapping matrix may be helpful for communicating changes in risk over consecutive time periods to decision makers, insufficient information will exist for the decision maker to understand actual vs planned progress and which risk handling activity(ies) are either on track, ahead or behind anticipated progress.

A risk mapping matrix with time-varying entries should not be used as a or in place of a risk step-down plot.

A risk "stoplight" chart (e.g., red = high risk, yellow = medium risk, and green = low risk) vs time can sometimes be helpful for reporting risk levels. Here, the "probability" and consequence of occurrence scores, together with the risk level are reported and a trend is provided as to how the risk has changed vs the previous reporting period, etc. [For example, an "up arrow" ($\uparrow$), "horizontal arrow" ($\rightarrow$), and "down arrow" ($\downarrow$) indicates an increased, constant, and decreased risk, respectively, from the previous reporting period.) (Note: Methods of converting underlying data to "stoplight" charts can be subjective, and scoring rules should be explained. The same issues typically exist as when classifying results from multiple ordinal "probability" or consequence of occurrence scales into a single level.]

A risk "stoplight" chart (e.g., red = high risk, yellow = medium risk, and green = low risk) vs time can sometimes be helpful for reporting risk levels, but methods of converting underlying data to "stoplight" charts can be subjective, and scoring rules should be explained.

If you use three-level probability and consequence of occurrence scales, the resulting step-down charts will be so coarse that only major risk reduction activities will lead to a visible change in the charts. Five-level probability and consequence of occurrence scales are often a practical minimum for generating step-down charts. And risk step-down plots may require seven or more scale levels to have sufficient granularity to capture risk reduction progress. The reason for this is that for a five-level nonestimative probability scale, the upper and lower "probability" definitions usually represent boundary conditions [e.g., most possible (1) and least possible (5) maturity]; thus leaving only three levels (Levels 2, 3, and 4) to represent variation that will likely occur in most programs. And in cases where a program is using relatively mature items, the resulting five-level scale may reduce to three-levels (e.g., Levels 1, 2, 3, whereby Levels 4 and 5 will not exist). However, with a seven-level scale, the number of likely levels in this case will increase on average by one (1, 2, 3, and 4), which provides added granularity for both risk analysis scoring and risk handling step-down plots.

If you use three-level probability and consequence of occurrence scales, the resulting step-down charts will be so coarse that only major risk reduction activities will lead to a visible change in the charts. Five level probability and consequence of occurrence scales are often a practical minimum for generating meaningful step-down charts.

B. Some Issues with Rolling Up Risk Analysis Results

When risk analysis results have gone through multiple levels of roll up, (e.g., by WBS level), the underlying risk issues can be smoothed out and may no longer be visible. This can lead to the possibility that weak or no risk handling strategies are developed for the risk issues.

For example, in one case the government rated the risk for coatings used on mirrors in an electro-optical telescope to be moderate risk because they were not off the shelf and would have to be radiation hardened and tailored to meet the specific wavelength region of operation needed. When the risk was rolled up to the telescope level, the medium risk rating associated with the mirror coating was retained, and the telescope was rated as medium risk even though the other components (mirrors and metering structure) were assessed to be low risk. The contractor developing the telescope came to similar conclusions at the component level (coatings) but analyzed the telescope-level risk to be low. The contractor rationale was that only one medium-risk issue (mirror coating) existed, while several low-risk issues likely existed. Thus, the contractor's detailed risk analysis had been correct, but in the process of rolling up the risk scores, a key risk issue (mirror coatings) was lost.

A conservative approach to obtain a single risk value is to maintain the highest risk score throughout the roll up. An illustration is given in Table 6.18 that demonstrates this principle. Assume the risk score for WBS element

**Table 6.18   Example of risk roll-up
across multiple WBS levels**

WBS number	Risk
3.0	High
3.1	Medium
3.1.1	Medium
3.1.2	Low
3.2	High
3.2.1	Low
3.2.2	High

3.1.1 is medium and the risk score for 3.1.2 is low. Then the roll-up risk score for WBS element 3.1 is medium (assuming no other third indenture WBS elements exist). Assume the risk score for WBS element 3.2.1 is low and 3.2.2 is high. Then the roll-up risk score for WBS element 3.2 is high (assuming no other second indenture WBS elements exist). In this case the roll-up risk score for WBS element 3.0 is high (assuming no other second indenture WBS elements exist).

Even though this will give a conservative answer, such a roll up should generally not be performed beyond two or three higher WBS indenture levels (e.g., 3.2.1 to 3.2 to 3.0) because of the large number of risk scores and risk items that will typically be present. Finally, if such a roll up is performed, the specific issue that possesses the higher risk should be separately handled and tracked if it is a medium or higher risk to ensure that unanticipated problems do not occur later in the program.

When risk analysis results have gone through multiple levels of roll up (e.g., by WBS level), the underlying risk issues can be smoothed out and may no longer be visible. A conservative approach to obtain a single risk value is to maintain the highest risk score throughout the roll up.

When rolling up results, it is important to select the risk score (P * C) or maximum (probability, consequence) pair for values from uncalibrated ordinal scales for each risk issue, rather than the maximum of separate probability and consequence values across risk issues. For example, it is incorrect to pick the maximum probability level from one risk issue and the maximum consequence level from another risk issue and consider this the maximum (probability, consequence) pair. The risk score should be computed or the maximum (probability, consequence) pair should be selected for each risk issue, and the roll up performed across this data for the desired number of risk issues, rather than across separate probability and consequence of occurrence components.

Assume for an FPA, a maximum "probability" value = 3 and a maximum consequence of occurrence value = 3 for five-level uncalibrated ordinal scales. (Assume in this case that scores of "5," "4," "3," "2," and "1" correspond to "E," "D," "C," "B," and "A," respectively on the risk mapping matrix.) Assume for an EPS, a maximum "probability" value = 2 and a maximum consequence of occurrence value = 5 using the same uncalibrated ordinal scales. Given the "probability" and consequence of occurrence values and using the risk mapping matrix in Fig. 6.3 yields a medium risk for both the FPA and EPS. However, if the "probability" value for the FPA (3) is incorrectly combined with the consequence value for the EPS (5), the resulting risk level will be erroneously recorded as medium high.

The risk score should be computed or the maximum (probability, consequence) pair should be selected for each risk issue, and the roll up performed across this data for the desired number of risk issues, rather than across separate probability and consequence of occurrence components.

C. Risk Analysis Documentation

Insufficient documentation may exist to adequately understand terminology in ordinal risk analysis scales. This may lead to uncertain and/or erroneous risk analysis results. For example, terms such as "brassboard," "breadboard," and "prototype" will mean different things to different people (e.g., the term prototype may represent a different item configuration and testing for a U.S. Air Force space subsystem vs a U.S. Army ground subsystem).

Supporting documentation is needed for each risk analysis scale definition to explain what it means.

Risk analysis results are sometimes mapped into broad categories (e.g., low, medium, and high) without sufficient backup documentation to understand the likelihood and potential impact(s) of the risk issue.

Similarly, insufficient documentation may exist to understand why a risk issue received a specific set of ratings. (Although this is not an issue with Monte Carlo simulations, it can be problematic for many other methodologies.) A concise, but clear, rationale should be provided that explains the basis for assigning the probability of occurrence and consequence of occurrence values. Without this supporting rationale, there is no easy way to perform a sanity check on the results, and a weak or inadequate rationale may point to erroneous results. (On numerous occasions I have uncovered erroneous risk scores that resulted from faulty application of the risk analysis methodology. Often I have found that the analyst used incomplete or confusing rationale to justify the probability of occurrence and consequence of occurrence scores. Scores with weak documentation should be challenged to ensure that the results are accurate.) In addition, weak documentation of risk results may provide incomplete or uncertain information to key program personnel, which can adversely affect their decision-making capability. Finally, weeks or months later questions may arise about why a risk issue received specific scores in a previous risk analysis. Without adequate supporting documentation, it is often not possible to accurately and easily resolve such questions.

Risk analysis documentation should include, at a minimum, the risk level, probability of occurrence and consequence of occurrence terms, plus the time to impact and other information if desired for each risk issue. Concise, but clear, rationale should be provided that explains the basis for assigning the probability of occurrence and consequence of occurrence values.

In some cases individual risk scores may be reported, but information relating to prioritization and potential risk issues is not available. However, this is often the very information that key program personnel need for decision-making purposes.

Risk information provided to key program personnel for decision making should include, at a minimum, a prioritized list of risks, a watch list, and possibly a list of retired risks vs the prior RMB meeting. (Detailed risk information, including risk scores and their probability and consequence of occurrence terms, plus time to impact and other information can also be provided if desired.)

References

[1]Alexander, A. "The Linkage Between Technology, Doctrine, and Weapon Innovation: Experimentation for Use," RAND, Santa Monica, CA, P-6621, May 1981, pp. 3–5.

[2]National Research Council, *Improving Risk Communication,* National Academy Press, Washington, DC, 1989, pp. 36, 37, 44.

[3]Department of Defense, *Systems Engineering Management Guide,* 1st ed., Defense Systems Management College, Ft. Belvoir, VA, 1983, p. 12-4.

[4]Hogg, R. V., and Craig, A. T., *Introduction to Mathematical Statistics,* 2nd ed., Macmillan, New York, 1965, pp. 4–5.

[5]Clemen, R. T., *Making Hard Decisions,* 2nd ed., Duxberry Press, New York, 1996.

[6]Pratt, J. W., Raiffa, H., and Schlaifer, R. *Introduction to Statistical Decision Theory,* MIT Press, Cambridge, MA, 1995.

[7]Kerzner, H., *Project Management,* 7th ed., Wiley, New York, 2001, pp. 907-912.

[8]Boehm, B., *Software Risk Management,* Inst. of Electrical and Electronics Engineers Computer Society Press, Los Alamitos, 1989, pp. 310–313.

[9]Shubik, M., *Game Theory in the Social Sciences,* MIT Press, Cambridge, MA, 1982, pp. 431–433.

[10]Clemen, R. T., *Making Hard Decisions,* Duxberry Press, 2nd ed., New York, 1996, pp. 274–281.

[11]Pariseau, R., and Oswalt, I., "Using Data Types and Scales for Analysis and Decision Making," *Acquisition Review Quarterly,* Spring 1994, Vol. 1, No. 2, pp. 146–152.

[12]DoD *System Engineering Fundamentals*, Defense Acquisition University Press, Ft. Belvoir, VA, Jan. 2001, pp. 137-138.

[13]Department of Defense, *Risk Management Guide for DoD Acquisition,* 5th ed., Defense Acquisition University and Defense Systems Management College, June 2002, pp. 20, 63-66, B-24.

[14]Law, A. M., and Kelton, W. D., *Simulation Modeling and Analysis,* 3rd ed., McGraw–Hill, New York, 2000.

[15]Vose, D., *Quantitative Risk Analysis,* 2nd ed., Wiley, New York, 2000.

[16]Gray, S. *Practical Risk Assessment for Project Management,* Wiley, New York, 1995.

[17]Project Management Institute, *A Guide to the Project Management Body of Knowledge (PMBOK® Guide)*, Newtown Square, PA, 2000, p. 204.

[18]Michaels, J. V., *Technical Risk Management,* Prentice–Hall, Upper Saddle River, NJ, 1996, pp. 72–74, 208–211, 223–226.

[19]Evans, M. Hastings, N. and Peacock, B. *Statistical Distributions,* 3rd ed. Wiley-Interscience, New York, 2000.

[20]Law, A. M., and Kelton, W. D., *Simulation Modeling and Analysis,* 3rd ed., McGraw–Hill, New York, 2000, pp. 292-401.

[21]Vose, D. *Quantitative Risk Analysis,* 2nd ed., Wiley, New York, 2000, pp. 41-43, 99-143, 263-312.

[22]Lurie, P. M., and Goldberg, M. S., "An Approximate Method for Sampling Correlated Random Variables from Partially-Specified Distributions," *Management Science,* Vol. 44, No. 2, 1998, pp. 203–218.

[23]Gray, S., *Practical Risk Assessment for Project Management,* Wiley, New York, 1995.

[24]Air Force Materiel Command, "Acquisition Risk Management," AFMC Pamphlet 63-101, 9 July 1997, pp. 21, 22.

[25]Dorofee, A. J., et al., *Continuous Risk Management Guidebook,* Software Engineering Inst., Carnegie Mellon Univ., Pittsburgh, PA. 1996, pp. 317–324, 383–389, 391–398.

[26]Garvey, Paul R, Lansdowne, Zachary F., "Risk Matrix: An Approach for Identifying, Assessing, and Ranking Program Risks," Air Force Journal of Logistics, Vol. XXII, No. 1, June 1998, pp. 18-21, 31.

Chapter 7
Some Risk Handling Considerations

I. Introduction

In this chapter I will briefly look at some key features of how to implement risk handling, including some recommended approaches and traps to avoid.

II. Some Risk Handling Considerations

A. Development of Risk Handling Strategies

If you assess risk, then it is very important to both develop risk handling plans (RHP) and implement them. Having a high-quality risk assessment is almost meaningless unless you follow through with developing a risk handling strategy and implementing RHPs for medium or higher risk issues. Talking about candidate risk handling strategies does no good unless they are selected and implemented.

Talking about candidate risk handling strategies and RHPs does not good unless they are actually developed and implemented.

In organizations without a history of effective risk management risk handling strategies may be developed without any structured approach that examines options, approaches, their suitability, and potential effectiveness. While it may appear that the ad hoc development of risk handling strategies is better than "nothing," the resulting strategies may well be suboptimal for a number of reasons (e.g., the "best" option was not selected, the "best" implementation approach was not selected, and suitable resources were not identified or quantified). While the structured development of risk handling strategies may require some additional effort in the nearterm to formulate, the benefit/cost of doing so may be very high vs selecting an inadequate strategy and later not having the ability to improve it.

Ad hoc development of risk handling strategies is common in organizations without a history of effective risk management. Using a structured method to develop risk handling strategies is a superior approach even though additional near-term effort will be required to develop it.

The risk handling implementation approach should be stated with the risk handling option to create the risk handling strategy (whether primary or secondary). The risk handling implementation approach should not be stated by itself since it is not a stand-alone part of risk handling. Similarly, the risk

365

handling option selected is not stand alone and should be grouped with the selected implementation approach (whether primary or secondary).

The risk handling option and the risk handling implementation approach should both be provided—not just one or the other—because neither are sufficient to achieve effective risk handling.

An appropriate procedure for developing risk handling strategies involves 1) examining each of the four risk handling options [assumption, avoidance, control, (mitigation), and transfer)], 2) selecting the most desirable option, 3) picking the most desirable implementation approach for the selected option, 4) verifying that suitable resources will be available for the chosen option and approach (particularly for the control and transfer options), and 5) ensuring that the selected option and approach (the "risk handling strategy") will have suitable cost (e.g., benefit/cost ratio), performance, schedule, and risk reduction characteristics. In cases where the risk is evaluated to be high, a backup risk handling strategy should also be developed. This may also be advisable in some cases where a medium or possibly even a low-medium risk level exists (e.g., if the risk issue interrelates with other risk issues). Note: The backup risk handling strategy may include a different option and certainly a different implementation approach than the primary strategy.

A structured approach should be used to develop each risk handling strategy that involves evaluating each of the four risk handling options, selecting the most desirable option, picking the most desirable implementation approach for the selected option, verifying that suitable resources will be available for the chosen risk handling strategy, and ensuring that the selected risk handling strategy will have suitable cost, performance, schedule, and risk reduction characteristics.

The primary risk handling strategy can be a multioption/implementation approach. For example, hardware/software partitioning as part of the transfer option, then employing control or assumption or avoidance for one side of the interface vs the other, then selecting an implementation approach for each option on each side of the interface.

A multioption/implementation approach can be used as the primary risk handling strategy. Don't limit your thinking to a single option and implementation approach.

Do not passively depend upon another program, even if it is within your own organization, to provide a solution to a risk issue. For example, do not depend upon another program, then state that this is your risk handling strategy using the control option and implementation approach. This can be a particularly bad situation when the dependent program is passive and not proactive in monitoring the primary program implementing the approach and the progress they are making in implementing their risk handling strategy, when there are no suitable backup risk handling strategies in place, and when the item in question is a relatively high risk issue.

Do not passively depend upon another program, even if it is within your own organization, to provide a solution to a risk issue. This is often not effective risk handling or risk management.

Beware of the "favored supplier" mandated risk handling (parallel development or procurement) situation. In some cases a backup risk handling strategy is wise, even if not otherwise mandated. However, in cases where a second supplier is carried (e.g., parallel development) and when the supplier has limited experience, this can provide little true risk handling backup and may lead to problems later in the program. When the customer mandates the use of such a supplier it may be for other reasons (e.g., increase or maintain the industrial base), but it can drain resources from the organization developing and implementing the RHP.

In cases where a second supplier is carried (e.g., parallel development) and when the supplier has limited experience, this can provide little true risk handling backup and may lead to problems later in the program.

B. Risk Categories in the Risk Handling Strategy

When an RHP is developed, it is important that each risk category be addressed that possesses a medium or higher risk level. In some cases the risk handling strategy may address some, but not all risk categories, leading to a higher than acceptable residual risk level.

Ensure that each risk category with a medium or higher risk level is addressed and included in the risk handling strategy for the risk issue.

C. Risk Handling Strategy Should Consider Probability and Consequence Terms

Risk handling strategies are often primarily tied to the probability of occurrence risk term, even in cases where the consequence of occurrence term may be large. The selected risk handling strategy should include both the probability and consequence of occurrence terms, as warranted from risk analysis results for each risk issue. [Of course, the orientation of the risk handling strategy should be related to the magnitude of the probability and consequence terms: if one term dominates the other, then greater emphasis should typically be placed on the larger term (cet. par.).]

When developing a risk handling strategy, do not automatically emphasize addressing the probability of occurrence risk term, but also consider the consequence of occurrence term. Where possible, the resulting strategy should be related to the relative contribution of the probability and consequence risk terms.

D. Selection of Risk Handling Backup Strategies

Many risk handling strategies employ a single approach or are implemented in a serial fashion when multiple approaches exist (e.g., try one approach, then another approach). Suitable backup risk handling strateg(ies) are often not identified. This can lead to substantial problems if/when the primary strategy fails and no suitable backup strategy exists. This is particularly important for issues that are high risks (and some medium risks) because the program may be adversely affected if the risk occurs. (On one project primary and two backup risk handling strategies were selected. The control option was chosen for each risk handling strategy, and a primary and two backup approaches were implemented in parallel. The primary implementation approach failed a demonstration test and was abandoned. The first backup implementation approach was then selected and passed the same test. However, the second backup approach was continued and made ready because of the possibility that the first backup approach might not pass the subsystem qualification test.) As when choosing a primary risk handling strategy, for each backup strategy the most suitable option is selected, then the "best" implementation approach is chosen for that option. In no case for a primary or backup risk handling strategy should the implementation approach be chosen before all four risk handling options (assumption, avoidance, control, and transfer) are evaluated.

If backup strategies are identified, they are often described in insufficient detail. For the primary and each backup risk handling strategy, cost and schedule estimates (and associated impacts) and risk analyses (e.g., resulting risk level if the approach is successful) should be developed. Ideally, a benefit/cost analysis should be conducted for each risk handling approach. In addition, a prioritized list should be generated of candidate approach(es) to meet any required/desired risk profile vs time. From this information the risk point of contact (POC) and his integrated product team (IPT) should recommend the primary strategy plus one or more backup strategies to Risk Management Board (RMB), which evaluates and approves the desired primary and backup strategies. (Of course, the backup strategy may also include a different risk handling option than used for the primary strategy. Again, a thorough evaluation of options and approaches should be performed.)

When possible, identify one or more backup strategies in addition to the primary risk handling strategy. For each strategy develop cost and schedule estimates (and associated impacts) and risk analyses (e.g., resulting risk level if the approach is successful). The risk POC and his IPT should forward this information to the RMB for evaluation and approval.

E. Correlation Between Risk Handling Strategies

The degree to which the risk handling strategies are correlated with each other should be identified to prevent potential problems associated with shared resources, insufficient budget, etc. No attempt should be made to formally determine a correlation coefficient. Instead, the potential extent of the overlap, plus whether the likely outcome will be negative (e.g., insufficient personnel available) or positive (e.g., addressing problems for one component may lessen the need to address related problems for another component in the same subsystem), should be qualitatively assessed. It may be necessary to take additional action to either alleviate potential problems or examine likely benefits of one risk handling strategy in terms of another. Affected RHPs should then be adjusted as warranted by this information.

Risk handling strategies should not be viewed separately for budget and resource considerations because strategies for different risk issues may be correlated. Attempt to identify the degree of overlap and how it will impact the budget and shared resources between risk handling strategies. It is particularly important to identify cases where sufficient resources may exist for any single risk handling strategy, but insufficient resources will exist across strategies requiring the use of the same resources (e.g., assembly personnel, test equipment, or facilities).

F. Risk Handling Strategy and Schedule Integration

Risk handling strategies may not be tied to or tracked against the program's integrated master schedule [(IMS), or equivalent]. RHP tasks, milestones, and associated schedule dates should be included in the program schedule and used to track actual vs planned progress associated with the risk handling strategy.

Integrate the risk handling strategy with the program's IMS (or equivalent). Include RHP tasks, milestones, and associated dates for the strategy in the IMS.

G. Risk Handling Strategy and Test and Evaluation Integration

Risk handling strategies may not be adequately integrated into the Test and Evaluation (T&E) program. This is particularly important because many risk handling strategies require testing to verify performance and progress in reducing risk. Without a tight coupling between the risk handling strategy and the T&E program, there will be an increased chance of not achieving the desired goals (e.g., from insufficient test planning and procedures; personnel, equipment, and facility availability; or documentation of results). Because of the time often required to plan T&E activities, coupled with the availability of resources, test plans should be drawn up and integrated with the RHP long before they are needed to acquire the needed resources, allocate the necessary budget, and permit resolution of conflicts (e.g., parallel attempts to schedule the same facility).

Integrate the risk handling strategy with the T&E program. Provide sufficient time to plan T&E activities, to ensure that resources will be available, to allocate a budget, and to resolve potential conflicts.

H. Analysis of Risk Handling Strategies

Risk handling options and approaches should be evaluated by cost, performance, and schedule (C,P,S) and risk trade process whenever possible and practical. This may provide useful information on the relative ranking of strategies for each of these variables, as well as overall ranking.

For example, at some point the C,P,S per unit of risk reduction may increase significantly for a given item; hence, the marginal C,P,S for reducing risk becomes unacceptably high. At this stage you might consider 1) reducing (e.g., buying down) risk as needed that is associated with another variable for the item (e.g., cost assuming the marginal performance for reducing risk becomes high); 2) using a different risk handling strategy for the item (e.g., transferring risk from one item to another within a subsystem vs controlling risk for the item); 3) using a different design approach for the item, subsystem, or system; or 4) applying the additional resources to another item within the subsystem or system.[1]

Ad hoc or subjective assessments of C,P,S and risk should be avoided because this may introduce errors and uncertainty into the evaluation and decision-making process to select the optimal strategy, as well as contribute to inadequate documentation for the resulting selected strategy.

In addition, inadequate cost, schedule, and risk estimates of potential risk handling strategies often exist. If an unrealistic budget, schedule, or anticipated risk level exists for a risk handling strategy, its effectiveness will likely be greatly diminished or eliminated (e.g., they may prove impossible to execute). For example, a schedule risk analysis should be considered for activities in the RHP and tied to the IMS to estimate the latest possible initiation date. This is typically needed because uncertainty will almost always exist in the time duration to successfully enact the RHP and reduce risk to the desired level.

The risk POC should perform a C,P,S, and risk evaluation of candidate risk handling strategies and rank the results to identify the optimal strategy. In addition, this evaluation will tend to reveal strategies that have an unrealistic budget, schedule, or anticipated risk level. Ad hoc or subjective assessments should be avoided where possible because errors or uncertainty introduced can adversely affect the risk handling strategy selection.

I. Unwise Risk Handling Strategies

Do not develop and implement a risk handling strategy with a substantial fraction of the risk reduction work near the end of the implementation approach—especially the "all or nothing" (sic, the "big bang") approach that presumes that the level of risk will drop steeply with one or more risk reduction activities late in the program (as shown in Fig. 7.1). This may introduce considerable risk and decrease the likelihood that the strategy can be achieved. It is much better to have, where possible, an incremental approach with meaningful, measurable risk reduction activities throughout

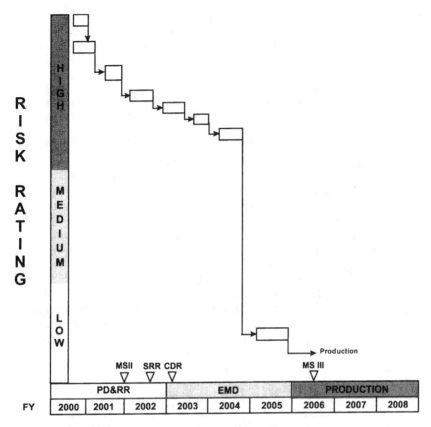

Fig. 7.1   Risk handling plan—risk rating portrayal vs time.

the course of the risk handling strategy (implementation), as illustrated in Fig. 6.8. That way a schedule slip or lower performance for any single test event is more apt to leave room for recovery during the implementation vs an "all or nothing" approach with one or two risk reduction activities near the end of the implementation.

Do not develop and implement a risk handling strategy with a substantial fraction of the risk reduction activity near the end of the implementation approach. This may introduce considerable risk and decrease the likelihood that the strategy can be achieved.

J.   Setting Thresholds for Risk Handling

An objective, repeatable measure should be used to set the threshold for performing risk handling on a given risk issue. Don't use a subjective measure (e.g., "important") to determine which risks should be handled. All risks above a predefined level (e.g., medium or higher) should instead be handled. This is because the boundary (e.g., "important") may be so unclear that some risk issues that should otherwise be handled won't, while others may be handled that otherwise should not be.

An objective, repeatable measure should be used to set the threshold for performing risk handling on a given risk issue.

K. Resources Needed for Implementing Risk Handling Plans

When estimating the resources needed to implement RHPs, the magnitude and type of resources should first be estimated followed by the source of the estimate. Reversing this order may lead to a constrained estimate of the total magnitude and type of risk handling resources needed, whereas if done in the recommended manner, the subsequent requirement from the available sources may show the shortfall that exists and assist in either reallocating resource requirements among the sources, or in seeking additional resources or new sources.

It is also important to consider both the type as well as the level of resources needed. If an incomplete list of resources exist, then RHP implementation may be delayed, the actual vs planned risk level may not decrease as desired, and/or the risk level may actually increase (e.g., if incomplete or flawed information exists when key decisions are made). Similarly, if resource types have been properly identified but insufficient quantity are available (e.g., too few software programmers), RHP implementation may exhibit the same potential issues as mentioned above.

In cases where, for example, nontrivial C,P,S consequence (impacts) may occur there may not be enough resources to reduce all three dimensions to an acceptable level, particularly if a moderate to large number of medium or higher risk issues exist. Here, it is important to obtain management (and often stakeholder) preferences for C,P,S and include this prioritization when developing risk handling strategies. This is not to say that the cost for risk handling actions will be "3X" if it is necessary to address C,P,S vs "X" if only say schedule must be addressed, or that three different sets of risk handling actions must be taken if C,P,S must be handled vs one set of actions if only say schedule must be addressed. However, a knowledge of management and stakeholder preferences for C,P,S given the program constraints that exist should provide valuable inputs to the development of RHPs.

Establishing a suitable level of funding for risk handling strategies should be part of risk handling and general program management and not a separate risk management process step. However, a risk issue should not be assigned for risk handling without adequate resources being available to reduce it to an acceptable level. If there are no funds appropriated or allocated to implement approved RHPs, then the risk handling process step as well as the overall risk management process will be ineffective. Since the funding of RHPs is mainly performed by key project management, this behavior will be negatively viewed by lower-level project personnel. Routinely developing RHPs without subsequently allocating resources to implement the plans can be very damaging to morale across the program—far beyond risk management activities. (Of course, there may be situations where not all RHPs will have adequate resources allocated, but when this becomes routine, then it can be very harmful.)

An adequate level of resources, including funding, should be made available for all risk issues approved for risk handling and, in particular, all risk issues that have RHPs developed. Soliciting management and stakeholder preferences may be helpful in prioritizing aspects of a risk handling strategy when insufficient resources exist to implement the entire, desired strategy. Routinely developing RHPs without subsequently allocating resources to implement the plans can be very damaging to morale across the program—far beyond risk management activities.

When a risk handling strategy is developed, it is important that each relevant risk category be addressed plus resources, such as personnel with suitable training, test equipment availability, and production equipment. In some cases a sufficient budget may be available, but insufficient resources may exist. These resources may not be available at any reasonable budget level. In cases where multiple items require shared resources (e.g., personnel or test equipment), this problem may become acute unless recognized in sufficient time to provide relief (e.g., second shift, resource loading, or temporary personnel). The number of potential solutions to such problems will likely greatly diminish if they are explored shortly before needed because of the inability to trade C,P,S plus other resources perfectly in the short run.

To efficiently implement RHPs, it is important that not only sufficient budget be available, but resources as well. Necessary resources can include a wide variety of items, ranging from personnel, to assembly and test equipment, to facilities. Failure to plan for adequate resources can lead to substantial program impacts, particularly for items on or near the program's critical path.

L. Budget and Schedule Sensitivity of Selected Risk Handling Strategy

The selected risk handling option and approach should be somewhat insensitive to relatively small changes in budget and schedule. The situation you want to avoid is where a small change in the budget or schedule of the risk handling strategy will degrade the results to an unacceptable level. When the RMB evaluates risk handling strategies, budget and schedule considerations, along with the degree to which the strategy can be implemented and successfully completed if less than 100% of the identified budget and schedule are available, should be noted. Risk handling strategies should also be noted that require full budget and schedule to achieve any potential results (e.g., a zero sum situation). Finally, it may be possible to modify the risk handling strategy to achieve substantial results, albeit less than the desired level, for less budget and/or schedule (e.g., the premium price of many insurance policies varies with both the coverage and deductible). If possible, compute the marginal benefit/cost ratio of slight changes in budget and schedule for the desired risk handling strategy plus other candidates to ensure that the optimal strategy is selected.

When possible, do not select a risk handling option and approach that is highly sensitive to exactly obtaining the prescribed budget and schedule to achieve the desired results. Evaluate the feasibility of modifying the risk handling strategy to achieve substantial results, even if less than the desired level, for less budget and/or schedule.

M. Estimating the Probability of Risk Handling Plan Success

It is generally meaningless to try to estimate the probability of RHP implementation success because of substantial uncertainty that may exist at the time the estimate is made plus the fact that risk handling strategies should always be developed and implemented that have a very high likelihood of success. (The latter point is especially important because the opportunity cost of risk handling strategy failure may be very high since there is generally insufficient time and resources to begin anew if the risk handling strategy fails to reduce the risk to the desired level.) Although I do not recommend it and substantial uncertainty will generally exist, a probability of success estimate may provide some benefit as a management indicator in cases where multiple risk handling strategies exist coupled with a time delayed implementation of one or more potential backup strategies. However, don't be fooled by the apparent accuracy of any such probability values given the level of uncertainty that typically exists. (For example, it is often unwise to use these probability estimates in mathematical evaluations of the potential risk handling success for a given risk issue.)

Estimates of the probability of RHP implementation success are generally meaningless because of substantial uncertainty that may exist at the time the estimate is made plus the fact that risk handling strategies should always be developed and implemented that have a very high likelihood of success.

N. Metrics for Evaluating Risk Handling Strategy Effectiveness and Their Uncertainty

Metrics other than cost and benefit/cost ratio may be considered for evaluating risk handling strategy effectiveness. One metric that is sometimes used is related to the degree of risk reduction as measured by the $(RF(i) - RF(f))$/risk handling cost. Here, the lower the risk handling cost for the same level of risk reduction (initial minus final) or the higher the level of risk reduction for the same risk handling cost, or some combination of the two, the "better" the risk handling strategy. However, this approach is fraught with a number of issues since cost and risk factor scores represent fundamentally different entities and should not be intermixed. In addition, how much risk reduction vs cost exists is of far less concern than whether or not the resulting (final) risk level will reach the necessary level (often low). Simply stated, if you have a large risk reduction vs cost, but the resulting (final) risk level is medium risk, then the risk handling strategy may be unacceptable. A better approach is to evaluate the benefit/cost ratio of the different risk handling strategies, particularly if a necessary constraint for each strategy is that the resulting final risk level must be low.

Metrics more elaborate than cost or benefit/cost ratio for evaluating risk handling strategy effectiveness may give uncertain and/or meaningless results and should not be used.

A number of methods exist to quantify the benefit/cost ratio or return on investment (ROI) associated with risk handling. However, the level of uncertainty in the calculations may overwhelm the resulting estimate and thus render it meaningless. For example, one procedure estimates the benefit/cost ratio as $[(Pr_{occ} * C_{costocc})/(RHP \text{ Cost} * Pr_{success})]$. Here, the probability of the event occurring is multiplied by the cost consequence. This product is then divided by the cost of the RHP times the probability of success of the RHP. While this may seem to be a perfectly reasonable calculation, the Pr_{occ}, $C_{costocc}$, and $Pr_{success}$ are often relatively uncertain, if not unknown, and thus the resulting benefit/cost ratio will likely be at least moderately uncertain.

The level of uncertainty in metric calculations associated with risk handling strategies may overwhelm the resulting estimate and thus render it meaningless.

O. Risk Handling Options

Risk handling options should be listed alphabetically: assumption, avoidance, control, and transfer with a statement attached saying they are not given in any order of preference. What is sometimes unhelpful is when the ordering is control, assumption, avoidance, and transfer since control (mitigation) is the option people commonly default to without adequately addressing the other options.

Risk handling options should be listed alphabetically: assumption, avoidance, control, and transfer with a statement attached saying they are not given in any order of preference.

The risk handling avoidance, control, and transfer options rarely if ever eliminate a risk, but generally reduce the resulting level of the risk to an acceptable level by reducing the probability and/or consequence of occurrence terms. (Note: The assumption option can not eliminate a risk in and of itself.)

Risk handling strategies rarely if ever eliminate a risk, but they should reduce it to an acceptable level.

Risk handling options should not be tied to specific probability and/or consequence levels or risk levels. This is often a suboptimal approach for selecting the risk handling option. The "best" option may sometimes be independent of a specific probability score, consequence score, and/or risk level. Some individuals presuppose that for a high probability or consequence score, and/or risk level, control is the "best" option. While assumption may not be tolerable, avoidance by changing a requirement or transfer (e.g., hardware software interface or between contractors or other organizations) may be the "best" approach. Thus, risk handling options should be selected on a case by case basis and not tied to specific probability and/or consequence levels or risk levels.

Do not tie risk handling options to specific probability and/or consequence levels or risk levels. This is often a suboptimal approach for selecting the risk handling option.

Be careful when selecting risk handling strategies when the potential solution may introduce more risk than just assuming, or assuming and avoiding, the existing situation associated with the risk issue. For example, in some cases the risk handling control option may involve a complex development activity that can introduce risk (e.g., schedule risk) and uncertainty, and possibly additional risk and uncertainty through integration and other considerations that would not exist if the assumption and/or avoidance risk handling option was selected.

Be careful when the potential risk handling strategy introduces more risk than just assuming, or assuming and avoiding, the existing the risk issue.

The risk handling control option or any other risk handling option should not just be performed on just the "Top 10" risk issues, but all medium or higher risk issues [or some other level set by the RMB (or equivalent)].

Apply risk handling to all medium or higher risk issues, not just the "Top 10" risk issues.

In earlier Defense Systems Management College (DSMC) risk management guides, specifically the DSMC "Risk Management: Concepts and Guidance," 1989, pp. 4–13, knowledge and research was listed as a fifth risk handling option. "The DSMC guide, 'Risk Management: Concepts and Guidance,' includes a fifth risk-handling option, knowledge and research. The guide acknowledges that this is not a true risk handling technique, but it does complement the other techniques by providing valuable information to further assess risk and expand on risk-handling plans." (Defense Acquisition Deskbook, Section OSD - 3, "Risk-Handling Techniques," Version Final, 31 March 2002.) Knowledge or research may lead to a risk handling option being selected, an implementation approach chosen, and a strategy implemented, but it is not a risk handling strategy in and of itself.

Knowledge and research is not a true risk handling option, but it does complement the four options (assumption, avoidance, control, and transfer) by providing valuable information to develop RHPs.

"Watch" is not a risk handling option—this is what is done for risk monitoring, particularly if it is defined in terms of a monitoring function rather than a proactive implementation.

The four risk handling options are assumption, avoidance, control, and transfer. "Watch" is not a risk handling option, but typically what is done for risk monitoring.

Don't confuse desired risk handling outcomes (e.g., decreased risk level) with a risk handling option (assumption, avoidance, control, and transfer). This confuses cause and effect. Here, the cause is the risk handling strategy (which includes the option and implementation approach) and the desired effect is a decreased risk level.

A risk handling outcome is the effect of a risk handling strategy—the two entities are not the same.

1. Assumption

The following are some observations associated with the assumption risk handling option.

The assumption risk handling option does not affect the level of risk present, while the avoidance, control, and transfer may ideally decrease the risk level (via the probability and/or consequence of occurrence terms) to an acceptable level.

The assumption risk handling option is not and should not be equated to ignorance or denial because it may prevent adequate resources from being made available to deal with the risk should it occur.

The proactive form of the risk handling assumption option (understanding what potential impacts may occur and having resources available to handle potential impacts) is preferable in many cases vs a reactive form, which is to do nothing until the impact occurs.

The assumption risk handling option is not just accepting the consequences of a risk issue, it is accepting the risk level associated with the risk issue—both the probability of occurrence and consequence of occurrence.

The assumption risk handling option should not generally include the idea of a contingency plan to execute once the risk has occurred. At that stage, the risk issue has become a problem, and the contingency plan approach may not be the best possible strategy. In addition, in such cases, it may be better to pursue a different risk handling option to attempt to prevent the risk issue from occurring and becoming a problem (of course this excludes cases where assumption is truly desired).

There may be reluctance to identify management reserve (or similar funds) set aside for risk issues handled with the assumption option in some programs because, depending upon contractual characteristics, such funds may be withdrawn by the buyer. For example, if the buyer will potentially withdraw management reserve, the seller may be reluctant to set aside funds for risk issues handled with the assumption option.

The level of management reserve held for risk assumption will vary on a case-by-case basis, and is not readily mapped to program phases, risk categories, etc. For example, in some cases a relatively small percentage of management reserve may be needed for some risk issues early in the project, while in other cases a larger percentage of potential cost of the risk issue may be warranted. The key here is to examine each risk issue, the program phase, interrelationship with other risk issues, the potential time of risk impact, and other considerations to estimate the level of management reserve needed when applying the risk assumption option.

2. Avoidance

The following are some observations associated with the avoidance risk handling option.

The process of not acting, but doing so consciously, is the risk handling assumption option, not the risk avoidance option. Avoidance best represents changing a design, requirement, etc., not a lack of action.

The risk handling avoidance option may be used to change a requirement, not just when a probability score, consequence score, or risk level is low. The probability score, consequence score, and/or risk level may be high if a risk issue is found late in the development phase as cost/performance/schedule/risk can not be traded perfectly in the short run. However, avoidance should also be considered throughout the acquisition cycle of the program, as well as the other three risk handling options (assumption, control, and transfer) on a case by case basis.

Work done "today" should be treated and grouped under its true risk handling option and not simply termed avoidance (as if since it has been done it does not count or it is ground-ruled out).

3. Control

The following are some observations associated with the control risk handling option.

Most risk handling options are focused on control (commonly known as mitigation), whereas potential assumption, avoidance, and transfer options are typically not thoroughly evaluated or, in some cases, even considered. The control option may be the best option for a given risk issue, but there is no guarantee that this will be the case. In some cases the control option may not be the best strategy. (For example, the transfer option should be considered when hardware and software interfaces exist and the design is not frozen. In this case, the partitioning of functions to hardware and software based on C,P,S, and risk trades may permit a lower risk implementation. However, the arbitrary allocation of requirements across interfaces should not be performed because this may actually increase, rather than decrease, risks.) What should be avoided is the almost automatic selection of the control option without carefully evaluating the pluses and minuses of this option vs the others (assumption, avoidance, and transfer).

Simply adding resources or changing schedules (usually slipping them) may not be an effective implementation approach for the risk handling control option. Unless the existing personnel loading was inadequate or the schedule was unrealistically short, simply adding more personnel or schedule will often do nothing to resolve underlying technical issues that may exist. In other words, having more people or time may present additional opportunities, but unless a structured risk handling strategy otherwise exists and is implemented it will do nothing in and of itself to help resolve these issues. (For example, adding sufficient budget for people and schedule to permit another iteration of microelectronics chip fabrication may be helpful in solving technical issues for a particular chip, but if a new process exists risk handling should also address likely risk issues associated with the process itself.)

The risk handling control option is much more than simply assigning a risk to a risk issue POC—it involves developing a proactive implementation approach to reduce a risk to acceptable levels, etc. Assigning a risk issue POC is important and a risk issue POC should exist for each risk issue approved by the RMB (or equivalent), but this does not necessarily do anything in and of itself to reduce the level of risk present (cet. par.).

The term risk control should not be used to describe the particular risk handling option selected since control is one of the four risk handling options —it is not risk handling in and of itself.

The risk handling control option may be used in order to attempt to prevent a risk issue from occurring, in addition to decreasing the affect of the risk should it occur. The former case is related to the probability of occurrence term, while the latter case is related to the consequence of occurrence term. As previously mentioned, the control option should attempt to reduce both the probability and consequence terms of risk, as well as risk itself, to an acceptable level assuming that the strategy has a suitable benefit/cost ratio, sufficient resources are available, etc.

4. Transfer

The following are some observations associated with the transfer risk handling option.

The risk handling transfer option should not just be considered for risk issues with potentially significant cost risk exist (e.g., when insurance, guarantees, and warranties may be considered), but also as appropriate, in cases where potentially large performance and schedule risk may exist. In effect, the nature of the risk issue (including its consequence component) should not dictate the risk handling option—all options should be evaluated in an objective, unbiased manner for each suitable risk issue (e.g., medium or higher risk).

While the risk handling transfer option is often implemented via insurance, warranties, or guarantees, etc. that primary affect the consequence of occurrence, when this risk handling option is used between contractors or across interfaces (e.g., partitioning hardware and software) it may also lead to a change (and possibly reduction) in the probability term. This is because different contractors have different levels of maturity in the design and fabrication of items. Similarly, variations in the probability term associated with maturity, complexity, etc. may exist across an interface and transferring functions across that interface (e.g., between hardware and software), may lead to changes in the probability term. Hence, the transfer option can lead to potential changes in the probability and/or consequence terms of risk.

It is the practice on some programs to assume that the risk handling transfer option will lead to no change in the overall risk exposure. This may be true in a limited sense for insurance, but it is not necessarily true, for example, for partitioning requirements across interfaces early in the development phase.

Transferring a risk issue can reduce the level of risk present in some cases where hardware and software exist, where one is needed to be state of the art or beyond and the new mix makes both less than state of the art. Another example is where one contractor has insufficient manufacturing facilities or knowledge, yet another has the ability to manufacture the item at rate production.

When a risk issue is transferred between organizations it is important that the transfer officially occur and not be informal. The more organizations involved that have a stake in the risk issue, the more important this may become. This is because the informal transfer of risk issues may lead to inadequate risk handling later in the program and a risk issue becoming a problem because: 1) it is unclear what the roles and responsibilities are between the organizations (e.g., who does what) if each organization thinks another is the lead for risk analysis and handling, and 2) no effective risk analysis and handling may be performed by any organization.

P. Development of Risk Handling Plans

The evaluation of risk handling options and specific approaches, plus the development and implementation of RHPs, is sometimes not initiated or even considered until when they are needed. Ideally, any risk issue analyzed to have a medium or higher risk level should immediately have a risk handling evaluation performed and an RHP developed. Despite the fact that developing an RHP takes resources, it is important not to limit the number of RHPs to some arbitrary value (e.g., for the "Top 10" program risks) because the program impact of only a single missed risk issue may far outweigh the cost of developing RHPs for all medium- or higher- risk issues and implementing many of them. In addition, waiting until later in the program to develop and initiate RHPs is typically less efficient in the short run and long run (in part because some risk handling options and/or approaches may be foreclosed vs time). Worrying about a risk issue without exploring potential risk handling options and approaches is not a suitable risk handling strategy.

Action item lists or similar program-issue tracking devices are generally not suitable substitutes for RHPs for medium- or higher- risk issues. This is because a single summary statement often will not provide sufficient insight for key program personnel into the risk handling option and approach selected, resources required, status of the implementation, etc. In addition, a generally unanticipated benefit of developing an RHP is that it may help identify missing implementation steps, particularly when the control or transfer options are selected. In some cases the responsible engineer may have an understanding of the best risk handling strategy, but may not have thought through the steps needed to achieve the desired outcome. In other instances, laying out the RHP implementation steps may lead to identifying 1) correlation or interrelationship between risk handling strategies for different risk issues, 2) additional resources needed for successful implementation, and 3) backup strategies not already considered. Finally, another potential benefit of developing an RHP is that additional risk issues may be identified that were not considered already (e.g., potential resource limitations).

For risk issues analyzed to have medium- or higher-risk levels, evaluate potential primary (and in some cases secondary) risk handling options and approaches, develop a suitable RHP, and implement the RHP. Do not wait until the last minute to initiate risk handling activities because potentially viable risk handling options and/or approaches may be foreclosed.

Q.   Risk Handling Plans vs Contingency Plans

Managing a risk is not "Can the team do anything to mitigate the impact of the risk should the risk occur?" This is contingency planning at best and problem solving at worst. RHPs should be part of a proactive risk management strategy and not simply contingency plans. Contingency plans by themselves may be reactive and/or assume that the risk will occur. Contingency plans are not RHPs, although RHPs may include contingency plans. Including contingency plans within an RHP may be beneficial in some cases; particularly when a relatively small number of well-defined outcomes are possible. (For example, when a backup risk handling strategy is contingent on a primary risk handling strategy.) The contingency plan should not be performed in parallel with the primary strategy, but is implemented if, and only if, the primary strategy is not successful against a predetermined set of criteria (e.g., performance level of "X" achieved by time "Y" and the resulting risk level is reduced to "Z"). Information as to what circumstances to implement a contingency plan should be included in the RHP (e.g., the latest date to implement the contingency plan). (In cases where the risk issue has become a problem, a fresh look at the risk handling strategy is often needed, and a new risk handling option and/or implementation approach may be necessary vs the original one used.) Assuming that the contingency plan is not ad hoc or unstructured then many, if not all, of the attributes that define the RHP should be common to a contingency plan. As the number of possible outcomes increases, when the nature of the outcomes become unclear, or when potential outcomes are not properly identified, the value of including contingency plans in RHPs diminishes greatly. For example, if the resulting state of the world could not have been previously predicted, developing a contingency plan would not be helpful.

RHPs should be part of a proactive risk management strategy and not simply contingency plans. Contingency plans are not RHPs, although RHPs may include contingency plans.

R. Exit Criteria

There should be clearly stated exit (or success) criteria for each RHP implementation activity so that both participants and decision makers will have an objective method to determine whether or not the goals for the activity were suitably met so that focus can shift and resources applied to meeting criteria for the next activity. Without such a criteria there will often be no objective means to determine whether or not you have properly completed one implementation activity before beginning the next. This may lead to issues not being properly resolved that later become problems and increase, rather than decrease the risk level present.

Clearly stated exit (or success) criteria should exist for each RHP implementation activity so that both participants and decision makers will have an objective method to determine whether or not the goals for the activity were suitably met.

S. Some Organizational Considerations

While a broad agreement is desirable for selecting risk handling strategies and approving RHPs, this is not necessary and may not always be possible. What is important is that the RMB (or equivalent) evaluate and approve each RHP, whether or not decisions pertaining to it are unanimous.

While a consensus is desirable for selecting risk handling strategies and approving RHPs, this may not always be possible.

Risk handling for each approved risk issue should have a single POC.

Having multiple people assigned as responsible for a given RHP will dilute the effort needed and weaken the associated accountability to properly implement it. The POC associated with risk handling should be the risk issue POC assigned by the IPT lead. Of considerable importance is for the risk issue POC to have the authority to not only develop, but to implement an RHP approved by the RMB.

A single POC should exist for each risk issue and associated RHP. Having multiple people assigned as responsible for a given RHP will dilute the effort needed and weaken the associated accountability to properly implement it.

T. Cost and Benefit/Cost Estimate of Risk Handling

When the risk handling control option is selected, a cost estimate should be prepared for the added cost associated with risk handling vs the otherwise anticipated development cost for the item. Similarly, potential cost savings (benefits) associated with implementing the control option vs taking no action should also be estimated where possible.

In many cases the risk handling cost will be in the relatively near term (e.g., the development program phase, such as program definition and risk reduction, that the program is currently in), whereas potential cost savings may not be realized until later in the program (e.g., the Production, Fielding/Deployment, and Operational Support Phase). For example, by having a more sensitive focal plane array (FPA), smaller optics and a lighter spacecraft will result for the same level of system performance (cet. par.). Thus, nonrecurring investments to increase FPA sensitivity may appear as a risk handling, thus development, cost, yet could lead to recurring production *cost savings* that will increase with the number of systems required.

Given this information, a benefit/cost computation can be made, and the ROI can be determined. (Always perform such computations in constant year or base year dollars, not in then-year dollars because the inflation present in the out years will serve as a noise term. Also, the computation can be performed in nondiscounted dollars or dollars discounted to net present value with a discount factor.) When the resulting nondiscounted ROI is very low (e.g., < 1:1), the risk handling strategy is unacceptable from a cost perspective (although there may be reasons to pursue it from a performance or schedule perspective). In general, the cost associated with successfully implementing an RHP should be less than the overall impact to the program if the risk issue occurs. Similarly, an ROI can be estimated for each candidate risk handling strategy for each risk issue (in part by converting potential schedule and/or performance impacts to cost). The ROI estimates can then be used to rank risk issues by the ROI associated with its risk handling strategy(ies) and/or rank risk handling strategies per risk issue (when more than one risk handling strategy exists). However, in some cases this perspective may be too simplistic, such as when the threshold value of a critical performance requirement (e.g., key performance parameter) must be met or the program could be terminated. When the ROI is large (e.g., > 5:1), the risk handling strategy will likely be quite cost effective. Similar calculations should also be performed when the transfer option is selected (e.g., insurance is purchased).

Summing the risk handling option costs vs benefits will provide an estimate of the program-wide benefit/cost of risk handling.

Ideally, risk issues and their associated handling strategies should be rank ordered by risk level, and funds needed to execute the handling approaches are added (if additional funds are available) or subtracted (if a budget cut exists) in a prioritized manner. For example, budget cuts should potentially impact the ability to handle lower priority risk issues before impacting higher priority risk issues, while added budget should be given to higher priority risk issues as warranted before lower priority risk issues. In cases where only partial funding may be available for the risk handling strategy for a risk issue, then management will need to decide whether to fund a risk handling strategy with a lower benefit/cost ratio for the risk issue or fully fund a lower priority risk issue, etc.

The benefit/cost ratio (or internal rate of return) associated with risk handling activities can in some cases be large and can be used by program management to request additional funding to ensure implementation of RHPs and/or fence risk handling funding to ensure its availability. Although a budget element can never be totally protected, the lack of funds to execute risk handling strategies can reduce the risk management process to nothing more than a paper exercise.

Where the risk handling benefit/cost computation becomes somewhat cloudy is when 1) the control or transfer option is used, 2) the program is already underway, and 3) no formal risk management process exists, although some aspects of risk management are nonetheless implemented. In this case risk handling activities may be implemented without being identified as such. The resulting development plan for at least some work breakdown structure (WBS) elements may include risk handling tasks and budgets. Here, the cost associated with risk handling may be embedded in the development phase budget, and it may be difficult to separate out the risk handling cost. (In some cases it may be necessary to verify the adequacy of existing risk handling activities and adjust them accordingly in terms of budget, and schedule as warranted.)

Cost and dollar benefits of risk handling options should be determined, and the ROI computed for each risk handling strategy, as well as at the total program level. This may provide management with additional information and leverage to seek, protect, or expend funds to implement the risk handling strategies.

U. Residual Risk Level

The residual risk level from the anticipated completion of the RHP implementation should be identified to determine if any additional action is necessary. In most cases the risk will be reduced to an acceptable level if the implementation is successful, but this should not be taken for granted. The desired outcomes of the RHP should be verified, a risk analysis performed on this anticipated outcome, and the residual risk level estimated. If the residual risk level is greater than what is acceptable, a change in the risk handling strategy will have to be developed and implemented. This can either be an enhancement to the existing strategy using the same risk handling option and approach or a second-stage activity that may even use a different option and/or approach to reduce the risk to an acceptable level.

Do not automatically assume that the risk issue will be reduced to an acceptable level by implementing the RHP. Estimate the residual risk level, and, if needed, develop and implement an additional risk handling strategy to reduce the risk level to an acceptable value.

V. Risk Handling Documentation and Communication

Inadequate risk handling documentation of such approaches and plans often exists. Unfortunately, the level of detail and completeness often does not increase vs increasing risk level, which should be the case. (In some instances the reverse seems to occur: the level of documentation decreases with increasing risk level.) The RHP should, at a minimum, include 1) responsible individual (and relevant manager), 2) selected option (assumption, avoidance, control, or transfer), 3) specific implementation approach for selected option, 4) initial plan date, 5) status of plan, 6) date when the RHP will be enacted, 7) anticipated completion date, 8) criteria for knowing if RHP has been successfully implemented via measurement or validation, 9) risk level for each relevant risk category if RHP is successfully implemented, 10) risk reduction milestones and success criteria for each milestone (via measurement or validation), 11) backup option(s) and approach(es) and decision date for use, 12) resources required for implementing the primary and backup risk handling strategies, 13) correlation or interrelationship between this RHP and those for other risk issues, and 14) any additional (including stakeholder and user) considerations. This information should be generated by the risk owner and forwarded to the appropriate personnel for review and disposition (e.g., the IPT lead, then RMB).

The completeness of risk handling documentation should increase with increasing risk level for a given issue. In addition, candidate RHPs should include sufficient information to permit RMB evaluation and determine whether or not to approve them. This information may also prove useful to other program personnel who may have additional data to share about the candidate risk handling strategy.

While a short description of the risk handling strategy may be useful as a summary, it should be used in addition to and not replace an appropriately detailed discussion of both the selected risk handling option and implementation approach. Omitting information as to which option was selected and why it was selected along with similar information for the implementation approach may leave out key data needed by decision makers and others that must review risk handling strategies.

An appropriately detailed discussion of both the selected risk handling option and implementation approach should be provided in risk handling documentation.

An RHP should not just be developed for risk handling strategies using the control (mitigation) option, but for all four options (assumption, avoidance, control, and transfer). The threshold set for the RHP should be medium or higher (or whatever threshold is appropriate for your program), not the risk handling option selected. Also, don't call the RHP a risk mitigation plan because this may bias the selection of the risk handling option to control.

An RHP should be developed for risk issues that are medium or higher independent of which risk handling option is selected.

A risk step-down chart (also known as a waterfall chart or a risk reduction chart) is not a risk handling strategy, but may graphically present a risk handling strategy in terms of risk level vs time. However, what often occurs when a graph is used as the sole representation of risk handling strategy is that a suboptimal risk handling option and/or missing implementation actions will exist. This is often times not realized until later in the program when alternatives are foreclosed and the resulting opportunity cost (in terms of C,P,S) may be high.

A risk step-down chart (also known as a waterfall chart or a risk reduction chart) is not a risk handling strategy, and should not be used as the sole representation for a risk handling strategy.

Whether a risk issue is "on" or "off" (equivalently "on" or "behind") the RHP may be somewhat subjective since a risk step-down chart (also known as burndown or waterfall chart) is a two-dimensional representation of risk score (level) vs time, which cannot be accurately reduced to a single word or other descriptor. For example, the actual risk level can be higher, the same, or lower than the planned risk level at a given point in time, and the actual time to achieve this risk level can be ahead, the same, or behind that given in the RHP. Hence, one technique to represent actual vs planned RHP results from a risk step-down chart is to include two text descriptors: Risk Level (e.g., higher, same, lower), and Time (e.g., ahead, same, behind) to address the two dimensions of the plot. (Note: The previous text descriptors are given as examples only and should not necessarily be used on your program.)

Whether a risk issue is "on" or "off" (equivalently "on" or "behind") the RHP may be somewhat subjective since a risk step-down chart (also

known as burndown or waterfall chart) is a two-dimensional represen-
tation of risk score (level) vs time, which cannot be accurately reduced to
a single word or other descriptor.

Attempting to assign simple rating scores or colors to risk issues based upon the status of risk handling actions is generally not meaningful. For example, to assume that the risk handling plan will be successfully completed and to assign a color value to this statement (e.g., green) is at least somewhat arbitrary. Risk issues that are retired should be retired and not have scores or colors assigned to them. Risk issues that are not retired should be reported in terms of the risk level, whether or not they are "on" or "off" the RHP (actual vs planned progress) in terms of risk level and time, and with appropriate risk monitoring techniques (e.g., earned value and technical performance measurements).

Attempting to assign simple rating scores or colors to risk issues based
upon the status of risk handling actions is generally not meaningful.

Reference

[1]Developed in part from Greenfield, M.A., "Risk Management: Risk As A Resource," Second Aerospace Corporation and Air Force Space and Missile Systems Center Symposium on Risk Management, 9 Feb. 1999.

Chapter 8
Some Risk Monitoring Considerations

I. Introduction

In this chapter I will briefly look at some key features of how to implement risk monitoring, including some recommended approaches and traps to avoid.

II. Some Risk Monitoring Considerations

A. Some Desirable Risk Monitoring Characteristics

The risk monitoring process step should provide quantitative information to decision makers regarding progress to date in resolving risk issues through implemented risk handling plans (RHP). As such, risk monitoring data is used to help systematically track and evaluate the performance of risk handling actions. These data can include, but are not limited to, 1) cost, performance, and schedule (C,P,S) metrics data; 2) changes in risk (computed via risk analysis); and 3) other data from tests.

On some programs risk monitoring data may be evaluated using unstructured or subjective procedures, which can lead to interpretation errors. For example, there may not be a suitable methodology in place to evaluate progress in reducing risks when tests provide mixed results (neither a complete success nor complete failure). A structured, systematic approach for collecting relevant metrics data is highly desirable to avoid reactive changes to the risk handling strategy. In addition, objective, quantitative methods of evaluating risk monitoring results are highly desirable to avoid subjective assessments, which can lead to erroneous results.

As in the other risk management process steps, documentation for risk monitoring should be tailored to the individual program. Documentation should be developed and distributed for earned value (cost), technical performance measurement (TPM) (performance), and schedule variation (schedule) results, along with changes in risk levels plus risk issues that could potentially increase to have a medium-or higher-risk rating. (This latter documentation is sometimes called a risk "Watch List.")

Risk monitoring should be more than keeping track of risk issues. This is a passive form of risk monitoring that is nothing more than a bookkeeping function, and one that should be avoided. Risk monitoring should be proactive in terms of generating metrics data to determine the actual vs planned cost, performance, schedule, and risk progress in reducing risk issues to acceptable levels (via implemented RHPs), having both planned and "as needed" updates to risk analyses for given risk issues, identifying candidate risk issues or potential changes in the character of existing risk issues (e.g., via TPMs and other techniques), and identifying potential changes that may be needed for risk planning (e.g., if new risk categories emerge from monitoring progress in implementing an existing RHP).

Risk monitoring feedback should be performed in a cohesive fashion to all other risk management process steps. In addition, the feedback provided should be evaluated across process steps—not just in an uncorrelated manner for individual steps. For example, if an unanticipated change in the risk level is determined from risk analysis (e.g., say, low to medium risk), then it may also be prudent to evaluate the potential impact on the existing risk handling strategy (if one exists), or to develop and implement a risk handling strategy (if one did not previously exist). Here, in this example, it would not be correct to just view the risk analysis impact without also considering the risk handling impact as well. (And of course, there may also be an impact on risk identification if a "new" aspect of the risk issue is revealed, risk planning if a new risk category is revealed, etc.)

Risk monitoring results can potentially provide decision makers with valuable information regarding progress in implementing risk handling strategies. However, to be effective, a structured, systematic proactive approach should be used, coupled with objective, quantitative methods of evaluating risk monitoring results, and reported and distributed in suitable documentation. Risk monitoring feedback should be performed in a cohesive fashion to all other risk management process steps. In addition, the feedback provided should be evaluated across process steps—not just in an uncorrelated manner for individual steps.

B. Some Guidelines for Monitoring Low Risks

Although it is necessary to monitor say medium and higher risks, it may also be beneficial, if not necessary, to monitor selected low risks. This includes cases when 1) the risk issue has recently been assigned a low risk rating; 2) there is considerable development activity yet to complete; 3) other subsystems, components, or processes still under development could affect the issue in question; and 4) final integration and testing has not yet been completed (or even performed). If, however, all objectives in the risk issue's RHP have been met (e.g., the item has successfully completed integration and testing or some other suitable, mature milestone) and the risk issue is retired, then there is generally no further need to monitor the issue.

Although medium and higher risk issues should be proactively monitored, it may also be beneficial to monitor low risks in selected situations.

C. Use of C,P,S Metrics

Risk monitoring should include metrics for evaluating C,P,S progress in implementing the approved risk handling strategy for each risk issue. It is not uncommon that risk monitoring metrics are focused on one or two of the three variables, whereas metrics are typically needed for all three. (For example, on one program TPMs were not collected, and management decisions were sometimes reactive and overshot the desired goals, thus necessitating more iterations to correct hardware development problems than otherwise might have been necessary.)

Unless compelling reasons exist, risk monitoring metrics should provide C,P,S information for each risk issue via the approved risk handling strategy contained in the RHP.

D. Collect and Report C,P,S Metric Data and Risk Scores at the Same Time

C,P,S metrics data and risk scores should be reported at the same point in time to permit overlaying the information. If data are collected from one or more of the metrics or risk scores at different points in time, the resulting picture of progress in implementing the risk handling strategy may be out of synchronization. In some cases data may be collected for one item more frequently than another because it is generated by an automated procedure [e.g., the project's earned value management system (EVMS)]. But for purposes of tracking risk reduction progress, the data should use a common-time baseline to permit overlaying results.

C,P,S metrics data and risk scores should be collected and reported using a common time frame to permit decision makers to evaluate a multidimensional representation of progress in implementing the risk handling strategy.

E. Use of Metrics Information by Decision Makers

C,P,S risk monitoring data should not only be collected, but it should be used by management as an input to making key decisions. Although this may seem rhetorical, on some programs C,P,S metrics data may be collected, but data representing one or more of these dimensions are not used in actual decision making. (For example, on one program earned value was computed, but this information was not used by the program manager to evaluate the degree of progress being made in implementing risk handling strategies.) Similarly, on other programs cost (earned value), performance (TPMs), and schedule (schedule variation) metrics data were evaluated by different groups of people, and the results were often not satisfactorily integrated to provide decision makers with a multidimensional representation of progress in implementing risk handling strategies.

Simply collecting C,P,S metric data will not guarantee that decision makers will use this information. The metrics data should be integrated, and key program personnel should be encouraged to it as an input to their decision-making process.

F. TPMs and Risk Monitoring

For risk issues involving a substantial technical or integration challenge, more than one TPM may be needed for a given item to describe adequately the progress achieved in implementing the risk handling strategy. In some cases, if a single TPM is used per risk issue, it may not adequately capture the progress in reducing the level of risk present. Conversely, a single TPM may not detect an adverse situation, where the level of risk is actually increasing.

A single TPM may not adequately describe either the progress being made in reducing the level of risk, nor the possibility that an adverse situation exists whereby the risk level may actually increase. More than one TPM may be needed for each risk issue when a substantial technical or integration challenge exists.

G. Apply Metrics at Same WBS Level as the Risk Issue

Risk monitoring metrics should be applied at the level of WBS detail associated with the risk issue. It is generally ineffective to have metrics that are at a higher WBS level because they may not provide an accurate representation of the progress being made to resolve risk issues. Having metrics at lower WBS levels requires aggregation to be performed to reach the desired WBS level. Although this may be relatively simple for some cost and schedule metrics (e.g., earned value and schedule variation, respectively), it is more difficult for technical metrics (e.g., TPMs) because it will often be necessary to combine dissimilar measures of performance into higher-level metrics. This may not yield acceptable results for the performance dimension. (Although it is possible to combine TPMs into a weighted measure of progress at higher WBS levels, such methods are typically not objective and directly measurable, e.g., they may represent the desires of decision makers, and should not be used unless necessary.)

Risk monitoring metrics should be applied at the WBS level associated with the risk issue. Applying metrics at higher WBS levels may not provide an accurate representation of the progress being made. Using metrics at lower WBS levels will require aggregation, which may not yield acceptable results for the performance dimension.

H. Use Quantitative Metrics When Possible

In some cases risk monitoring may not use quantitative metrics. Here, the results may be a subjective interpretation of progress made in implementing

RHPs. Because the ability to interpret accurately subjective measures is often limited, the resulting ability to monitor progress may be impeded. In addition, when metrics are not used, the result is often reactive in nature (e.g., workarounds), whereas issues could often have been identified and resolved earlier. A possible exception to this is for very short duration programs when a highly effective risk management process exists.

In one case daily engineering management meetings were held to discuss progress in solving problems and reducing risks. Here, computation of earned value was done on a bimonthly basis and reported monthly, and few TPMs were formally reported. What made risk monitoring work on this program was the daily feedback that provided progress on key risk issues, coupled with the fact that the engineering management team was the program's RMB. However, this is a highly exceptional case, both in terms of program duration (due to a 4:1 schedule compression) and the effectiveness of risk management implementation. Attempts to emulate this approach will likely prove futile in many other programs, and a more formal and structured risk monitoring process (albeit tailored to the program) should generally be used.

Quantitative C,P,S metrics should typically be used for risk monitoring for all but very short duration programs. Subjective assessments should be avoided because of the inherent uncertainty present and possibility of introducing unintentional or intentional biases into the data.

I. Monitoring Risk Solely Using the Risk Probability Term

Graphical representations of risk level vs time are sometimes used for risk monitoring purposes. However, it is surprisingly common that rather than plotting risk on the ordinate the actual variable plotted is the probability term of risk. This is clearly incorrect because risk includes both the probability and consequence of occurrence terms. And in most cases when the probability term is solely used, the reader is given insufficient information to recognize this fact.

This presumes that the consequence term is static during the period of time that bounds the probability estimates (initial to final). For many risk issues this is not the case. Changes—both increases and decreases—in the C,P,S consequence dimensions do occur during a program phase. Hence, the resulting risk score will change *even if the probability term remains constant.* Because both the probability and consequence terms will likely change, representing risk solely by the probability term can lead to substantial errors. This problem is made all the more severe if a single probability measure (e.g., ordinal scale) is used because this will typically only represent a fraction of the true probability term.

To eliminate this issue, simply plot risk instead of solely the probability term. The anticipated risk level vs time can assume a constant consequence term, whereas the actual risk level vs time (given on the same plot) should include updates to both the probability and consequence terms (with both probability and consequence of occurrence estimates updated at the same point in time).

When using risk level vs time as a risk monitoring metric, do not solely plot the probability term of risk, which can lead to substantial errors. Both the probability and consequence terms must be included in the risk computation and resulting plot.

J. Ordinal Consequence of Occurrence Scales for Risk Monitoring

Ordinal C,P,S consequence of occurrence scales should not be separately used for risk monitoring for two reasons. First, they are generally too coarse to be of any benefit for risk monitoring purposes, even if a five-level consequence of occurrence scale is used. Second, uncalibrated scales only represent ordinal ranking, not cardinal values—a scale level value of 4 is not necessarily two times greater than a scale level value of 2 (the exact factor is unknown). Third, such scales typically have either qualitative definitions (e.g., moderate cost growth is possible) or specify a percentage of likely cost growth for the item (e.g., 5% < cost growth ≤ 10%). (In the latter case the cost-deviation range pertains to a given program phase or phases for the item, *not* the cost associated with implementing the RHP.) Neither set of information is truly helpful for evaluating RHP implementation progress. It is far better to use C,P,S metrics that are amenable to continuously tracking progress made (e.g., earned value and TPMs) than to use ordinal scales that were never designed to be used for risk monitoring purposes.

Do not use ordinal consequence of occurrence scales for C,P,S risk monitoring purposes because of inherent limitations associated with the scale-level definitions. Instead, use metrics such as earned value (cost), TPMs (performance), and schedule variation (schedule) that are cardinal and continuous in nature.

K. Risk Scores as the Sole Metric for Monitoring Performance Progress

In some cases, risk scores (or simply the probability term of risk) are used as the sole performance metric for risk monitoring purposes. While this may seem adequate at first glance, it can lead to flawed results for several reasons. First, the risk score typically represents the combination of a number of probability and three consequence of occurrence scores (cost, performance, and schedule) for a given item. Even when results are derived from calibrated ordinal scales, the risk score does not represent a single value, but typically several values. Hence, while the trend in reducing the risk level may well match the plan, it is possible that one or more components of probability and/or consequence of occurrence may actually be increasing instead of decreasing, yet this undesirable affect may be masked by viewing the overall risk score. Second, when risk scores are derived from ordinal "probability" and consequence of occurrence scales, the scales are often too coarse to adequately be used for risk monitoring purposes. Definitions even on "probability" scales with five or more levels may represent considerable variations in time between adjacent levels. The potential danger with this is adverse trends (e.g., an increase in the risk score) may not be identified until a considerable period of time has elapsed, leading to a substantial increase in cost and schedule needed to resolve the issue. Third, while consequence of occurrence scales may permit the identification of a possible adverse trend (e.g., increased cost) if they are suitably devised, this same feature is difficult, if not impossible, for ordinal "probability" of occurrence scales— particularly those related to maturity, complexity, uncertainty, and estimative probability. While ordinal "probability" scales related to sufficiency and true probability can possibly be used, they will typically have the same limitations identified in the first two issues mentioned above.)

It is far better to use cost, performance, and schedule metrics that are amenable to continuously tracking (e.g., earned value, TPMs, and schedule variation) than to use risk scores that were never designed to be used as the sole risk monitoring metric. Simply stated, risk scores should be an adjunct to, not a replacement for, tailored cost, performance, and schedule metrics used for risk monitoring on a given item.

Risk scores (or simply a probability or consequence of occurrence score) should not be used as the sole performance metric for risk monitoring purposes because such scores can mask potentially adverse trends. Instead, use metrics such as earned value (cost), TPMs (performance), and schedule variation (schedule) that are cardinal and continuous in nature, and include risk score variations with time as an adjunct to, rather than a replacement for, values from these metrics.

L.   Risk Monitoring Should Be Tied to the Program's Integrated Master Schedule

Risk monitoring may not be properly tied to nor tracked against the program's integrated master schedule [(IMS) or equivalent]. Without the use of an IMS, it is possible that the resulting C,P,S monitoring data may not be aligned in time (which may not permit overlaying the three-dimensional information) or may not be available to support key program milestones.

Key risk handling strategy milestones in each RHP should be included in the IMS (or equivalent). Progress measured in implementing the risk handling strategy should be tied to the IMS for cost (e.g., earned value) and performance (e.g., TPMs) as well as schedule (e.g., schedule variation).

M. Do Not Use Schedule Variance as a Schedule Metric

One metric that can be derived from the EVMS is schedule variance, which is defined as the budgeted cost of work performed minus the budgeted cost of work scheduled. Unfortunately, schedule variance is only an indicator of actual schedule variation because it is derived from cost data, not schedule data. More accurate schedule metrics include the start date, finish date, and duration of key tasks vs the baseline schedule. (A quantitative schedule risk analysis can be also performed that will yield a probabilistic estimate of the likelihood of meeting key schedule milestones.)

Schedule variance derived from the EVMS provides only an indication of the variation in schedule because it is derived from cost data. More accurate schedule metrics include the start date, finish date, and duration of key tasks vs the baseline schedule.

N. Risk Monitoring Data Should Be an Input to Other Risk Management Steps

Results from risk monitoring may be required as inputs to processes and documents outside of the risk management process. This generally increases both the desirability and need to have reasonably high quality data that can be used for program use. Risk monitoring outputs used by other program processes may include changes to planning, budgeting, scheduling activities, etc. Hence when subjective and/or ad hoc risk monitoring is performed, the results will be of little value not only to risk management-related activities, but to other program processes and needs as well.

The value of risk monitoring results is diminished if the information is not effectively fed back as inputs to the other risk management process steps. This will also tend to reduce the effectiveness of the risk management process (cet. par.). C,P,S risk monitoring data can potentially be used to adjust the risk handling strategy and RHP and provide new information to update the risk analysis (both the risk probability and consequence terms). In addition, risk monitoring results may possibly point to new risk issues or different risk categories associated with an existing risk issue (risk identification) and for updating the RMP (e.g., number of open risk issues).

Results from risk monitoring may be required as inputs to processes and documents outside of the risk management process. This generally increases both the desirability and need to have reasonably high-quality data that can be used for program use. Risk monitoring results should be fed back as inputs to the other risk management process steps and closely coupled with the risk handling and risk analysis steps.

O. Cautions about Metrics

Although the following information was developed for software metrics, it is highly relevant to most metrics used for risk (and program) monitoring.

Some common limitations and constraints associated with metrics include[1]:

1) "Metrics must be used as indicators, not as absolutes."
2) "Metrics are only as good as the data that support them."
3) "Metrics must be understood to be of value."
4) "Metrics should not be used to judge contractor (or individual) performance."
5) "Metrics cannot identify, explain, or predict everything."
6) "Analysis of metrics should be performed by both the government and contractor."
7) "Direct comparisons of programs should be avoided."
8) "A single metric should not be used."

P. Some Top-Level Metrics Considerations

The following are examples of some top-level considerations that should be applied to selecting and implementing metrics for risk (and program) monitoring.[2]

1) Metrics should be a good fit to the item being evaluated.
2) Metrics should be useful to help understand and manage the program.
3) Metrics should increase, where possible, the likelihood of program success.
4) Can the metric values be influenced by process change?

Q. Some Additional Metrics Considerations

A wide variety of metrics can potentially be used for monitoring progress of the risk management process. However, many of these may not be meaningful even if they appear to be quantitative in nature. Rather surprisingly, even on programs with a strong inclination toward metric data collection, it is rare to find that they obtain cost (e.g., cost variance), schedule (e.g., schedule variation), technical (e.g., TPMs), and risk level metrics at the same WBS level and the same point in time and use this information for decision making.

While a wide variety of metrics can potentially be used for monitoring progress of the risk management process, many of these may not be meaningful even if they appear to be quantitative in nature.

Sometimes a metric, such as the number of low-, medium-, and high-risk issues is used as a top-level measure of risk management progress. While such a metric may well have upper management appeal and be easy to communicate, it may not be very meaningful in and of itself, particularly on a large program. In addition, focusing on such metrics may allow other, useful information may go unreported. For example, on one large program

~200 open risk issues existed at the peak that was reduced to ~100 open risk issues six months later. However, even with 100 open risk issues, upper management had no insight into the progress being made (actual vs plan) on any individual risk issue.

First, the low, medium, and high boundaries are almost always somewhat arbitrary (even if measured against or compared to top-level definitions for low, medium, and high). Thus, the actual number is only an indictor of program risk issues at these three levels, not an absolute measure. Second, it is of greater interest to see how individual risk issues change with time (e.g., due to risk handling implementation) rather than how the aggregate of risk issues change with time or how many risks are closed. (In the latter case if risk issues with relatively low levels are retired first, this may give a biased perspective of the remaining risk issues, how many will be retired vs time, and the degree of difficulty in retiring the remaining risk issues.) Of greater interest is how the existing risk issues changed (risk level) vs time for 1) actual vs planned progress, and 2) particularly for those risk issues that increased vs time, especially in cases where a low- or low-medium risk increased to medium or higher risk. Third, even a single medium or high risk may require substantial management attention, and an individual risk cannot be highlighted using top-level risk metrics. Thus, even if the total number of high, medium, and/or low risks decreases with time it is possible that a severe risk to the program may be present, yet not be visible.

If high level risk "roll-up" metrics must be used, also be sure to report risk issues individually where actuals are worse than the plan for cost, performance, schedule, and risk level (e.g., positive cost variance greater than some threshold, schedule variation against the IMS greater than some threshold, TPMs that hit trigger levels by some pre-determined value, and risk levels that increase with time or do not decrease as anticipated in the plan with time), etc.

Metrics, such as the number of low, medium, and high risk issues, are generally subjective and should not be used as a top-level measure of risk management progress.

Cost, performance, schedule, and risk metrics may be generated but not integrated and/or generated but not obtained at the same snapshot in time. The resulting effectiveness of the metrics will not be very high in such cases, and the information they provide may not be correctly interpreted by key decision makers on the program.

Cost, performance, schedule, and risk metrics should both be generated and integrated at the same snapshot in time whenever possible and practical.

Select risk monitoring metrics as part of risk handling and include them in the RHP. Do not wait until after RHP implementing has begun and there is a need for data as part of risk monitoring to select the metrics—this may lead to choosing the wrong metrics and/or lost opportunities for monitoring

RHP implementation progress. Choosing metrics while developing the RHP may also help the risk issue POC better think through what is needed for the risk handling strategy, and possible trends that might exist (e.g., TPM trend vs time).

Select risk monitoring metrics as part of risk handling and include them in the RHP. Do not wait until after RHP implementing has begun and there is a need for data as part of risk monitoring to select the metrics.

References

[1]Rozum, J. A., "Software Measurement Concepts for Acquisition Program Managers," Carnegie-Mellon Univ., Software Engineering Inst., Technical Rept. CMU/SEI-92-TR-11/ESD-TR-92-11, Pittsburgh, PA, June 1992; pp. 9–11.

[2]Derived from Mayer, J., "Performance/Progress Review," Fall 2002 New/Future Ships Semi-Annual Meeting, U. S. Navy, San Diego, CA, 19 November 2002, p. 11.

Appendix A:
Comparison of Risk Management for
Commercial and Defense Programs

I briefly discuss in this appendix some differences in acquisition and risk considerations between commercial (free market theory) and DoD/NASA practices.

I. Some Acquisition Differences

Brief comparisons are provided in the following two subsections between commercial vs DoD and NASA acquisition practices and commercial vs DoD software acquisition practices. Because DoD and NASA are implementing a variety of acquisition reform initiatives, some of their acquisition practices listed in the following subsections may approach or equal commercial practices as a function of time. In addition, DoD's desire for commercial procurement is not limited to small items, but in some cases may even involve whole systems [work breakdown structure (WBS) Level 1 or WBS Level 2]. For example, in one case in the mid-to-late 1990s, DoD procured several launch vehicles under what was basically a commercial contract. (However, there was effectively only one supplier for the necessary launch vehicle, which had previously been developed and flown.)

A. Commercial vs DoD/NASA General Acquisition

In 1980 Gansler developed a comparison between the typical commercial practice (free market theory) and defense market for a number of key characteristics. This comparison was updated by Gansler in 1989 and I have modified it to include NASA and to reflect current practices. This updated and modified comparison is given in Table A.1 (Ref. 1).

B. Commercial vs DoD Software Acquisition

In 1994 Ferguson and DeRiso performed a study comparing numerous aspects of both DoD and commercial software practices, including requirements, acquisition methods, vendor selection, development process, business practices, integration testing and delivery, maintenance, and rights in data. They found that:

"The largest differences between commercial and DoD practices lie in the user-buyer-developer relationship. Industry considers the

Table A.1 Comparison of commercial vs DoD and NASA practices for systems acquisition[a]

Typical commercial practice	DoD/NASA market practice
Many small buyers	Few buyers (DoD and NASA, with overseas market secondary)
Many small suppliers	Typically few, large suppliers of a given item
Market sets price	Differentiated oligopoly pricing, often includes buy-in on the part of both government and industry to available budget
Free movement in and out of market	Typically extensive barriers to entry, lesser barriers to exit
Prices are set by marginal costs	Prices often proportional to total cost
Prices fall with reduced demand	Prices increase with reduced demand
Once funding is secured, it is usually predictable and stable	Unanticipated variations can occur vs the planned budget (year to year and within a year) from Services, DoD, and Congress
Excess capacity may exist, but supply adjusts to demand	Moderate to large excess capacity
Market shifts rapidly with changes in supply and demand	Market shifts slowly; particularly for major systems development
Little or no government involvement	Substantial government involvement
Source selections are often rapidly performed and require few iterations	Source selections are often protracted and costly and require many iterations (despite claims of streamlined acquisition)
Selection is based upon price and features	Historically, selection primarily based upon performance, with cost, schedule, and risk often secondary. Currently, stronger balance between cost and performance (still primary) with schedule and risk secondary.
Profits are a return for risk	Profits are regulated and related to contract type
Competition is for a share of the market, which is often small.	Competition is typically for a larger share of the market
Time to delivery set by firm based upon the anticipated market	Time to deployment often set by higher-level government participants (above program office)

Table A.1 *(continued)*

Typical commercial practice	DoD/NASA market practice
Size of market is established by buyers and sellers	Size of market is established by Congress (third party)
Demand is price sensitive	Demand is only weakly price sensitive. More dominant consideration is threat (DoD) and mission requirements (NASA).
Buyer has the choice of spending now or saving for a later time	DoD and NASA must spend its congressional appropriation or lose it.

[a]Information shown here is derived from Ref. 1. Although some of the items reported by Gansler are not included here, the data still effectively represent his work.

availability of existing products in this phase and is more willing than the DoD to trade functionality with availability to decrease cost and schedule. Systems are thus delivered earlier and are then evolved to include later requirements."[2]

However, since late 1995, under the auspices of the DoD Cost as an Independent Variable (CAIV) initiative, both the government and contractors are now more able to trade performance (functionality) against cost, schedule, and risk—particularly within the bounds of threshold and objective performance levels.[3]

Another important area associated with differences in software development between DoD and commercial practices involves the development process. A summary of some commercial vs defense market software development differences (c. 1994) condensed from Ferguson and DeRiso is given in Table A.2 (Ref. 2).

II. Examination of Some Risk Management Issues

Commercial suppliers are typically driven by price, profit, and market-share considerations related to cost, features or functions related to performance, and time to market related to schedule. As just illustrated, there are a number of differences between commercial vs DoD and NASA market practices, but commercial suppliers also face cost, performance (technical), and schedule (C,P,S) risk. The magnitude of the associated cost risk on a per-unit basis may in some cases be small—literally pennies to dollars, but when very large quantities are involved, the dollar amounts can be substantial. For example, in one case the owner of a commercial supplier producing valve guides for the automotive industry who manufactures items used in relatively simple engines as well as ultra-high-price foreign supercar engines

**Table A.2   Comparison of best commercial and DoD practices
for software development[a]**

Best commercial practice	Defense market practice
Existing systems often used with COTS—fit into a defined product line	Varies with application—some use COTS, but little reuse and many unique systems built
Buyer involvement may be heavy (team member)	Formal development model; buyer oversees development but team role often limited
Informal reviews	Very formal reviews
Heavy user involvement	Limited user, heavy buyer involvement
Vendor uses one or more industry standards	Government and industry standards used
Higher potential for code reuse possible	Tailored system with little focus on code reuse
Prototyping common	Limited prototyping—becoming more popular

[a]Condensed from Ref. 2.

said that a variation of $0.001 to $0.01 price per part can be the difference between winning and losing a contract! In another case a person who performs risk management at an air-conditioning manufacturer said that schedule risk is a key concern for in-home units. He remarked that it is "pretty tough to sell air conditioners in the fall" (in the northern hemisphere) and that a schedule slip of only a month may force a unit to be delayed a year with a large potential loss of revenue and profit.

Contractual requirements to perform risk management for both commercial and government programs can vary from negligible to substantial and are often not well correlated with the true program risk. For example, on one high-risk government program, the entire requirement for performing risk management was "develop a comprehensive, proactive Risk Management Plan."

The need for formalized risk management should be dictated by the true level of program risk. For example, where is the design point relative to the (C,P,S) surface (e.g., the C:P curve given in Chapter 1, Sec. III)? The higher the level of desired performances, coupled with the lower the level of cost and/or shorter delivery schedule, then the higher the resulting level of risk (cet. par.). I will briefly illustrate this issue with an example.

The risk management process used by a commercial aircraft manufacturer on one development program was informal, seemingly ad hoc, and administered by a single manager as a partial responsibility. The development program in this case was limited to changing the shape of an existing wing to upgrade an existing aircraft. Here, an informal risk management process may have been tolerable, although far from ideal, because whereas performance (technical) risk was low, cost and schedule risk were nontrivial. However, as one observer pointed out, if the redesign involved making the entire aircraft virtually invisible to radar, then formal, structured, and far more sophisticated risk management would likely be needed. (In this hypothetical case the necessary design would have involved relatively high levels of performance for a number of subsystems and a new start activity. The resulting solution point for these subsystems would have been in the steep part of the C:P curve, potentially indicative of high risk.)

The C,P,S characteristics of the design and acquisition strategy should affect program risk, which in turn should influence the nature and level of risk management needed. Ideally, this will occur whether or not there is a contractual requirement to perform risk management.

III. Likely Risk Categories for Commercial and DoD/NASA Programs

A summary of different risk categories likely to exist for commercial vs defense and NASA programs is given in Tables A.3 and A.4. These tables are based on the risk categories identified and discussed in Chapter 2, Sec. I.B. The tables illustrate the likelihood that a particular risk category will be relevant for commercial, defense, and NASA programs. The likelihood is coarsely classified into four qualitative levels (unlikely, possible, likely, highly likely), without reference to any specific probability value. (*Note:* For each risk category a range of likelihood will exist for both commercial and DoD/NASA programs. Hence, the likelihood estimates given in Tables A.3 and A.4 *should only be viewed as a relative indicator rather than anything quantitatively rigorous.*)

Although not addressed here, risk categories can be correlated with each other, but this may vary on a case-by-case basis. For example, budget risk and political risk are positively correlated with each other and often with a correlation coefficient > 0. This is easy to understand because (positive/negative) political pressure on a program can lead to (positive/negative) changes in funding. Hence, when developing a matrix of feasible risk categories vs items for the program, the relationship between risk categories should be considered and included as appropriate.

A few of the risk categories listed in Tables A.3 and A.4 can potentially be helpful to the program in some cases, e.g., budget and political. An example of this is the long-range Air Launched Cruise Missile (AGM-86B), Minuteman I, and Polaris A-1 programs named by the Packard Commission as examples of highly successful programs. In each case, because of the high national priority associated with the programs (political), increased funding

Table A.3　Different risk categories for commercial vs DoD/NASA programs

Risk category	Commercial	DoD/NASA	Comments
Cost	Highly likely	Highly likely	Issue for many programs where development needed or replication of an off-the-shelf item does not exist.
Design/engineering	Possible	Likely	Depends upon sophistication of design and degree of evolution/revolution vs existing, available designs.
Functional	Possible	Likely	Issue for most complex programs where the ability to meet each designated requirement, or at least key requirements, must be verified. Risk category often not formally evaluated.
Integration	Possible	Likely	Issue for complex programs. The likelihood of integration risk varies with the number of interfaces, quality of interface definitions, ability to perform early prototyping and testing, etc. Risk category often not formally evaluated.
Logistics/support	Possible	Likely	Commercial may have relatively short life cycle (LC) compared to defense; however, varies from industry to industry, e.g., chemical processing plant (long LC) vs personal computers (short LC).
Manufacturing	Likely	Likely	Possible issue for any hardware production program, but varies with annual production rate and availability of suitable resources, e.g., personnel.
Schedule	Highly likely	Highly likely	Issue for many programs where development needed or replication of an off-the-shelf item does not exist.
Technology	Possible	Likely	Depends upon performance requirements, availability of suitable technology, and trade space between C,P,S. Increased risk likely as necessary performance pushes the state of the art, and technology rather than design is viewed as the solution.
Threat	Possible	Highly likely (DoD), Possible (NASA)	Issue for defense programs. Possible issue for NASA programs (less severe than defense programs). Possible issue for a variety of commercial programs (e.g., information technology, physical security, and industrial espionage).

Table A.4 Different risk categories for commercial vs DoD/NASA programs

Risk category	Commercial	DoD/NASA	Comments
Budget	Possible to likely	Likely to highly likely	Depends upon funding source and mechanism. Can introduce considerable instability, and issues are generally external to the program.
Concurrency	Possible	Possible	Issue for programs where overlapping acquisition phases exist.
Capability of developer	Possible	Possible	Varies on a case-by-case basis depending upon the developer's experience, resources, and knowledge to design, develop and manufacture the specific system.
Management	Possible	Possible	Varies on a case-by-case basis. Potential issue for programs where relatively high performance exists (particularly, integration complexity or scope).
Modeling and simulation	Unlikely to possible	Possible	Potential issue for programs where relatively high performance exists.
Requirements	Unlikely to possible	Possible	Potential issue for programs where relatively high performance exists, coupled with uncertain and/or unstable requirements.
Test and evaluation	Possible	Likely	Varies on a case-by-case basis. Potential issue for programs where relatively high performance exists.
Environmental impact	Possible	Possible	Varies on a case-by-case basis—some industries and programs more likely than others.
Operational	Possible	Possible to likely	Varies on a case-by-case basis.
Political	Unlikely to possible	Possible to likely	Varies on a case-by-case basis. Potential issue is generally external to the program.
Systems safety and health	Possible	Possible	Varies on a case-by-case basis.
Systems engineering	Possible	Possible	Varies on a case-by-case basis. Potential issue for programs where relatively high performance exists.

resulted beyond initially planned levels (budget). In addition, political and budget risk were positively correlated: a high desire to deploy the systems (political) lead to increased funding levels to cover cost growth (budget). For additional information, see Ref. 4.

In addition, although process and personnel availability risks are not separately called out in these tables, they can represent important risk issues that should be addressed on both commercial and DoD/NASA programs. Process risks are typically embedded in several risk categories, including, design/engineering, integration, logistics/support, manufacturing, technology, management, test and evaluation, and systems engineering. In addition, personnel availability is often embedded into several risk categories, including design/engineering, integration, manufacturing, technology, and test and evaluation. (It can also be impacted by the level of concurrency present on the program.) It is important that both process and personnel availability risk issues be carefully considered during risk identification in order that they not be overlooked and later result as problems that adversely impact the program.

According to renowned venture capitalist John Doerr, for high-tech commercial development projects there are four risk categories to look for in every project. These include the following:[5]

1) "People risk: How the team will work together. Because inevitably, one of the founders does not work out and drops out."

2) "Market risk: This is an incredibly expensive risk to remove. It is about whether the dogs will eat the dog food. Is there a market for this product? You do not want to be wrong about market risk."

3) "Technical risk: This risk we are quite willing to take on. Whether or not we can make a pen computer that works, be the first to commercialize a web browser, or split the atom, if you will. That technical risk is one we are comfortable trying to eliminate or take on."

4) "Financial risk: If you have all of the preceding three risks right (people, market, and technical), can you then get the capital that you need to go grow the business? Typically, you can. There is plenty of capital to finance rapidly growing new technologies that are addressing large markets."

Two of the preceding four risk categories (technical and financial) identified by Doerr can be readily mapped into the risk categories given in Tables A.3 and A.4. Technical risk primarily maps into design/engineering, manufacturing, and technology risk categories. One large commercial company with sales more than $10 billion per year stated in a risk management white paper that "technical risks are by far the easiest to handle, because they are, after all, only technical problems; the answers to which are not currently known." This is a very naive view of technical risk! It is not surprising for the company in question because they have had several major development projects in the public spotlight with nontrivial technical issues, leading to cost growth and schedule slippage on the order of 50 to 100%. Technical risk can also map into integration, logistics/support, test and evaluation, plus possibly other risk categories. Financial risk primarily maps into budget and cost risk. (Of course, the budgetary mechanisms for commercial vs government programs are completely different. There may be less than the desired level of funding available for DoD/NASA programs, particularly since the early-to-mid-1990s.) Budget levels are a key program planning input, and variations in funding are often an externally induced event. The negative impact of such variations can often be reduced, at least somewhat, by having a good risk management process that provides insights to key program personnel for decision making.

People risk primarily relates to management risk, coupled with behavioral issues associated with program execution on DoD/NASA programs. (Some behavioral issues associated with risk management implementation are given in Chapter 3, Sec. XIV.) Market risk on defense programs relates primarily to the degree that the relevant user command(s) and stakeholders (including Congress) will accept the system under development and is potentially related to many risk categories given in Tables A.3 and A.4. (Market risk is also sometimes known as business risk. For example, one company defines business risk as "one in which there is no question that the technology exists to develop a system, but it is not clear that the system will satisfy the user's true requirements.") In the case of defense programs, market risk is not necessarily an incredibly expensive risk to remove. However, if the user command(s) are not actively involved in the requirements tradeoff and design activities and stakeholders are not regularly advised about program activities, the resulting penalty to the program can be severe, possibly leading to a major restructuring or cancellation. I will now take a closer look at market risk.

One definition of market risk, developed by Preston Smith and Donald Reinertsen, is the uncertainty of not meeting the needs of the market, assuming that the specification (requirements) has been satisfied. "It is the risk of selecting the wrong target."[6] Market risk can result from having done inadequate market research, from following a specification that fails to define adequately what is needed, or from unclear customer desires, changes in customer requirement, or the introduction of competing products.[6]

Smith and Reinertsen state that many companies are more accustomed to dealing with technical risk rather than market risk. "Compared with how they handle technical risk, most companies do a poor job of managing market risk. This is largely because they consider it less objective and quantifiable than technical risk. However, market risk is also a more important cause of product failure. Typically, companies resolve technical problems, or agree to ignore them, before a product is introduced. In contrast, market problems usually show up only after a product has been shipped."[6]

Smith and Reinertsen suggest that the "most obvious way of resolving market risk is to increase involvement with the customer, either through formal means such as market research or more direct means, such as establishing routine designer contact with customers or actually having a leading-edge customer on the development team."[6] Although market research will always be needed, the direct approach is often desirable because it provides a quick means for the design engineer to receive valuable feedback from the customer. (Market research often does not provide specific answers fast enough, particularly during the development phase when design trades are being performed.) Smith and Reinertsen also suggest that another technique for reducing market risk is to stay flexible on unresolved issues until sufficient, accurate information is available to clearly identify the correct approach that should be taken. Finally, they also suggest that when relatively high technical risk exists that this can delay a program, which in turn increases market risk.[6] This latter problem is also seen in DoD/NASA programs. In this case, cost growth and/or schedule slips induced by problems in meeting performance requirements can lead to further negative perturbations, including major program restructuring or cancellation, typically from variations in 1) cost/funding (budget), 2) requirements (both threat-driven and new requirements), and 3) the level of stakeholder support.

Finally, phased project planning, used in many DoD/NASA programs, does not commit finances to the next acquisition phase until major questions are resolved from the previous one. (On some government programs yearly funding battles between Congress and the executing agent may even occur regardless of what is planned in the budget.) This is suitable for a variety of large-scale programs (e.g., with noteworthy technical risk), but it may not properly address market risk (e.g., missing the market opportunity) on a commercial program.[6]

IV. Discussion

Given the information just provided on commercial program acquisition and risk management, how does this apply to government (including DoD/NASA) programs?

As already mentioned, the need for formalized risk management should be dictated by the true level of program risk. The higher the level of desired performance, coupled with the lower the level of cost and/or shorter delivery schedule, then the higher the resulting level of risk (cet. par.).

The risk management process discussed in Chapter 2 and through the remainder of this book *is valid for both commercial and government programs, but the process must be tailored to each program, depending upon C,P,S issues, managerial considerations, and program constraints—one size does not fit all!* For example, some of these issues, considerations and constraints include, but are not limited to:

1) program budget,

2) program schedule,

3) the level of desired performance relative to the state of the art (see Chapter 1 and Appendix D),

4) the advancement needed for the contractor and/or government to achieve the desired level of performance (see Chapter 1 and Appendix D),

5) contractual requirements for risk management (if any),

6) how formally and extensively one desires to implement the risk management process (see Chapter 3),

7) how much documentation should be performed (see Chapters 2 and 3),

8) the risk categories to be evaluated (see Chapters 2 and 3, plus this appendix),

9) the level of risk planning that should be performed (see Chapter 4),

10) risk identification procedures used (see Chapter 5),

11) the risk analysis methodology used (see Chapter 6),

12) risk handling options and approaches (see Chapters 2 and 7), and

13) suitable risk monitoring approaches (see Chapters 2 and 8).

Of course, as just mentioned, for commercial programs people risk, market risk, technical risk, and financial risk must be carefully addressed. People risk primarily relates to management risk, coupled with behavioral issues associated with program execution. Methods of dealing with technical risk are provided throughout this book. As mentioned, financial risk primarily maps into cost and budget risk (albeit with different funding mechanisms for commercial vs government programs), which is also discussed throughout this book.

Market risk must clearly be considered for commercial programs. It is possible to do this within the context of the risk management process discussed in this book, such that market risk is integrated with the program's tailored risk management process. If you choose to evaluate and handle market risk separately from the described risk management process, at least make sure that the data and outputs from dealing with market risk are compatible with those for other risk categories and that this information can be merged with data from the risk management process and used by key program personnel for decision making.

References

[1]Gansler, J. S., *Affording Defense*, MIT Press, Cambridge, MA, 1989, pp. 159, 160.

[2]Ferguson, J. R., and DeRiso, M. E., "Software Acquisition: A Comparison of DoD and Commercial Practices," Software Engineering Inst., Carnegie-Mellon Univ., CMU/SEI-94-SR-9, Pittsburgh, PA, Oct. 1994, pp. 5, 8.

[3]Kaminski, P., Under Secretary of Defense (Acquisition and Technology), "Re-

ducing Life Cycle Costs for New and Fielded Systems," (memorandum plus two attachments), 4 Dec. 1995.

[4]Conrow, E. H., "Some Common Characteristics of the Minuteman I, Polaris A-1, and ALCM Development Programs," *Acquisition Review Quarterly*, Defense Acquisition Univ., Vol. 2, No. 2, Spring 1995, pp. 104–120.

[5]"Cringely, Robert X, interview with John Doerr, 26 Nov. 1998, "Nerds 2.0.1: A Brief History of the Internet," Public Broadcasting Service.

[6]Smith, P. G., and Reinertsen, D. G., *Developing Products in Half the Time*, Reinhold, New York, 1991, pp. 154, 209, 211–214.

Appendix B:
Current DoD Program Phases and Milestones

I. Introduction

The four major milestone decision points and four phases of the acquisition process, illustrated in Fig. B.1, typically provide a basis for comprehensive management and the progressive decision making associated with program. (Sections I through V were derived from Ref. 1.)

II. Concept and Technology Development

A. Entrance Criteria

After the requirements authority validates and approves a Mission Need Statement (MNS), the Milestone Decision Authority (MDA) [through the Integrated Product Team (IPT) process] will review the MNS, consider possible technology issues [e.g., technologies demonstrated in Advanced Technology Demonstrations (ATD)], and identify possible alternatives before making a Milestone A decision. The decision shall not be made final until a thorough analysis of multiple concepts to be studied, including international systems from Allies and cooperative opportunities (see 10 U.S.C. §2350a), has been completed. If an international system is selected, the program shall enter systems acquisition activities at Milestone B or C.

B. Milestone A

At Milestone A, the MDA shall approve the initiation of concept studies, designate a lead Component, approve Concept Exploration exit criteria, and issue the acquisition decision memorandum. The leader of the concept development team, working with the integrated test team, shall develop an evaluation strategy that describes how the capabilities in the MNS will be evaluated once the system is developed. That evaluation strategy shall be approved by the Director of Operational Test and Evaluation (DOT&E) and the cognizant Overarching Integrated Product Team (OIPT) leader 180 days after Milestone A approval.

C. Concept Exploration

Concept Exploration typically consists of competitive, parallel, short-term concept studies. The focus of these efforts is to define and evaluate the

413

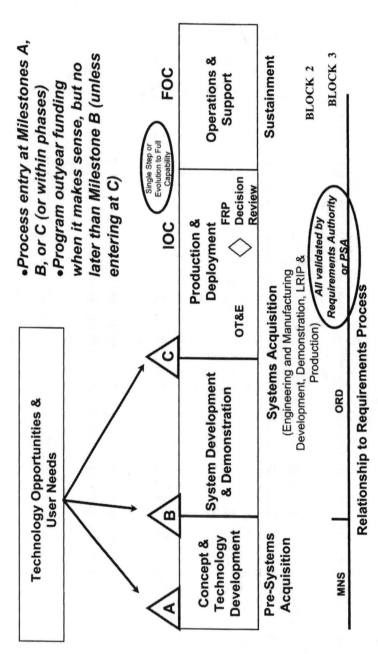

Fig. B.1 Current DoD program phases and milestones.

feasibility of alternative concepts and to provide a basis for assessing the relative merits (i.e., advantages and disadvantages, degree of risk, and so forth) of these concepts. Analyses of alternatives shall be used to facilitate comparisons of alternative concepts.

In order to achieve the best possible system solution, emphasis will be placed on innovation and competition. To this end, participation by a diversified range of businesses (i.e., small, new, domestic, and international) should be encouraged. Alternative system design concepts will be primarily solicited from private industry and, where appropriate, from organic activities, international technology and equipment firms, Federal laboratories, federally funded research and development centers, educational institutions, and other not-for-profit organizations.

D. Component Advanced Development

The project shall enter Component Advanced Development when the project leader has a concept for the needed capability, but does not yet know the system architecture. Unless otherwise determined by the MDA, the component technology to be developed shall have been proven in concept. The project shall exit component advanced development when a system architecture has been developed and the component technology has been demonstrated in the relevant environment or the MDA decides to end this effort. This effort is intended to reduce risk on components and subsystems that have only been demonstrated in a laboratory environment and to determine the appropriate set of subsystems to be integrated into a full system. This work effort normally will be funded only for the advanced development work. The work effort will be guided by the validated MNS, but during this activity, an Operational Requirements Document (ORD) shall be developed to support program initiation. Also, acquisition information necessary for a milestone decision (e.g., the acquisition strategy, program protection plan, and so on) shall be developed. This effort is normally followed by entry into the System Development and Demonstration phase after a Milestone B decision by the MDA.

III. System Development and Demonstration

The purpose of the System Development and Demonstration phase is to develop a system, reduce program risk, ensure operational supportability, design for producibility, ensure affordability, ensure protection of Critical Program Information, and demonstrate system integration, interoperability, and utility. Discovery and development are aided by the use of simulation-based acquisition and test and evaluation and guided by a system acquisition strategy and test and evaluation master plan (TEMP). System modeling, simulation, test, and evaluation activities shall be integrated into an efficient continuum planned and executed by a test and evaluation integrated product team (T&E IPT). This continuum shall feature coordinated test events, access to all test data by all involved Agencies, and independent evaluation of test results by involved agencies. Modeling, simulation, and development test shall be under the direct responsibility of the program manager (PM) or a designated test agency. All results of early operational assessments shall be reported to the Service Chief by the appropriate operational test activity and used by the MDA in support of decisions. The independent planning, execution, and evaluation of dedicated Initial Operational Test and Evaluation (IOT&E), as required by law, and Follow-on Operational Test and Evaluation (FOT&E), if required, shall be the responsibility of the appropriate operational test activity (OTA).

This phase can be entered either directly out of technology opportunity and user need activities or from Concept Exploration. The actual entry point depends on the maturity of the technologies, validated requirements (including urgency of need), and affordability. The MDA shall determine the appropriate entrance point, which shall be Milestone B. There shall be only one Milestone B per program, or evolutionary block.

A. Entrance Criteria

Entrance into System Development and Demonstration is dependent on three things: technology (including software) maturity, validated requirements, and funding. Unless some other factor is overriding in its impact, the maturity of the technology will determine the path to be followed. Programs that enter the process at Milestone B shall have a system architecture and an operational architecture for their relevant mission area.

B. Milestone B

Milestone B is normally the initiation of an acquisition program. The purpose of Milestone B is to authorize entry into System Development and Demonstration.

C. System Integration

The program shall enter System Integration when the PM has an architecture for the system, but has not yet integrated the subsystems into a complete system. The program shall exit System Integration when the integration of the system has been demonstrated in a relevant environment using prototypes (e.g., first flight, interoperable data flow across systems), a system configuration has been documented, the MDA determines a factor other than technology justifies forward progress, or the MDA decides to end this effort.

D. System Demonstration

The program shall enter System Demonstration when the PM has demonstrated the system in prototype articles. This effort is intended to demonstrate the ability of the system to operate in a useful way consistent with the validated ORD.

This phase ends when a system is demonstrated in its intended environment using engineering development models or integrated commercial items, meets validated requirements, industrial capabilities are reasonably available, and the system meets or exceeds exit criteria and Milestone C entrance requirements. Preference shall be given to the use of modeling and simulation as the primary method for assessing product maturity where proven capabilities exist, with the use of test to validate modeling and simulation results. The completion of this phase is dependent on a decision by the MDA to commit to the program at Milestone C or a decision to end this effort.

IV. Production and Deployment

The purpose of the Production and Deployment phase is to achieve an operational capability that satisfies mission needs. The production requirement of this phase does not apply to Major Automated Information Systems (MAIS). However, software has to prove its maturity level prior to deploying to the operational environment. Once maturity has been proven, the system or block is baselined, and a methodical and synchronized deployment plan is implemented to all applicable locations.

A. Entrance Criteria

Regardless of the entry point, approval at Milestone C is dependent on the following criteria being met (or a decision by the MDA to proceed):

1) Technology maturity (with an independent technology readiness assessment), system and relevant mission area (operational) architectures, mature software capability, demonstrated system integration or demonstrated commercial products in a relevant environment, and no significant manufacturing risks
2) An approved ORD
3) Acceptable interoperability
4) Acceptable operational supportability
5) Compliance with the DoD Strategic Plan
6) Demonstration that the system is affordable throughout the life cycle, optimally funded, and properly phased for rapid acquisition
7) Acceptable information assurance to include information assurance detection and recovery
8) Acceptable anti-tamper provisions

B. Milestone C

The purpose of this milestone is to authorize entry into low-rate initial production [for Major Defense Acquisition Programs (MDAPs) and major systems], into production or procurement (for nonmajor systems that do not require low-rate production) or into limited deployment for MAIS or software-intensive systems with no production components.

C. Low-Rate Initial Production

This work effort is intended to result in completion of manufacturing development in order to ensure adequate and efficient manufacturing capability and to produce the minimum quantity necessary to provide production configured or representative articles for IOT&E, establish an initial production base for the system, and permit an orderly increase in the production rate for the system, sufficient to lead to full-rate production upon successful completion of operational (and live-fire, where applicable) testing. The work shall be guided by the ORD.

Deficiencies encountered in testing prior to Milestone C shall be resolved prior to proceeding beyond low-rate initial production (LRIP) (at the Full-Rate Production Decision Review) and any fixes verified in IOT&E. Operational test plans shall be provided to the DOT&E for oversight programs in advance of the start of operational test and evaluation.

D. Full-Rate Production and Deployment

Following IOT&E, the submission of the Beyond LRIP and Live Fire Test and Evaluation (LFT&E) reports (where applicable) to Congress, the Secretary of Defense, and the under secretary of defense for acquisition, technology, and logistics [USD(AT&L)], and the completion of a full-rate production decision review by the MDA (or by the person designated by the MDA), the program shall enter full-rate production (or procurement) and deployment.

V. Operations and Support

The objectives of this activity are the execution of a support program that meets operational support performance requirements and sustainment of systems in the most cost-effective manner for the life cycle of the system. When the system has reached the end of its useful life, it must be disposed of in an appropriate manner.

A. Sustain Systems

The sustainment program includes all elements necessary to maintain the readiness and operational capability of deployed systems. The scope of support varies among programs but generally includes supply, maintenance, transportation, sustaining engineering, data management, configuration management, manpower, personnel, training, habitability, survivability, safety, occupational health, protection of Critical Program Information (CPI), antitamper provisions, information technology (including national security systems) supportability and interoperability, and environmental management functions. This activity also includes the execution of operational support plans in peacetime, crisis, and wartime.

B. Evolutionary Sustainment

Supporting the tenets of evolutionary acquisition, sustainment strategies must evolve and be refined throughout the life cycle, particularly during development of subsequent blocks of an evolutionary strategy, modifications, upgrades, and reprocurement. The PM shall ensure that a flexible, performance-oriented strategy to sustain systems is developed and executed. This strategy will include consideration of the full scope of operational support, such as maintenance, supply, transportation, sustaining engineering, spectrum supportability, configuration and data management, manpower, training, environmental, health, safety, disposal, and security factors. The use of performance requirements or conversion to performance requirements shall be emphasized during reprocurement of systems, subsystems, components, spares, and services after the initial production contract.

C. Disposal

At the end of its useful life, a system must be demilitarized and disposed. The PM shall address in the acquisition strategy demilitarization and disposal requirements and shall ensure that sufficient information exists so that disposal can be carried out in a way that is in accordance with all legal and regulatory requirements relating to safety, security, and the environment. The Defense Reutilization and Marketing Office shall execute the PM's strategy and demilitarize and dispose of items assigned to the office.

D. Follow-on Blocks for Evolutionary Acquisition

Evolutionary acquisition strategies are the preferred approach to satisfying operational needs. Evolutionary acquisition strategies define, develop, test, and produce/deploy an initial, militarily useful capability (Block 1) and plan for subsequent definition, development, test, and production/deployment of increments beyond the initial capability over time (Blocks 2, 3, and beyond). The scope, performance capabilities, and timing of subsequent increments shall be based on continuous communications among the requirements, acquisition, intelligence, logistics, and budget communities. Acquisition strategy considerations for evolutionary acquisition are part of system development and demonstration.

VI.   Previous DoD Program Phases and Milestones

A.   Introduction

The four major milestone decision points and four phases of the acquisition process, illustrated in Fig. B.2, typically provide a basis for comprehensive management and the progressive decision making associated with program maturation.[2] (This section was derived from Ref. 2.) The MDA can tailor milestones and phases to support the specific acquisition situation.

At each milestone decision point assessments should be made of the status of program execution and the plans for the next phase and the remainder of the program. The risks associated with the program and the adequacy of risk management planning should be explicitly addressed. Additionally, program-specific results required in the next phase, called exit criteria, should be established and approved.

B.   Phase 0: Concept Exploration

Competitive, parallel, short-term studies by the U.S. government and/or industry will normally be used during this phase. The focus is on defining and evaluating the feasibility of alternative concepts and providing the basis for assessing the relative merits of the concepts at the Milestone I, New Acquisition Program Approval, decision point. Early life-cycle cost estimates (see Ref. 3, Pt. 5.6) of the competing alternatives should be analyzed during the phase relative to the value of the expected increase in operational capability for each alternative. This analysis of alternatives (AOA), to include estimated costs and operational effectiveness, (see Ref. 3, Pt. 2.4), can facilitate comparisons of the alternative concepts. Tradeoffs should be made among cost, schedule, and performance, as a result of a Cost as an Independent-Variable (CAIV) analysis (see Ref. 3, Pt. 3.3.3.1.). To assist alternative concepts generation, conceptual design, and design tradeoff studies may be performed. The most promising system concept(s) should be defined in terms of initial objectives for life-cycle cost, schedule, and performance (see Ref. 3, Pt. 3.2.2) and overall acquisition strategy (see Ref. 3, Pt. 3.3). Critical system characteristics and operational constraints (e.g., survivability, transportability, interoperability, and security), projected surge and mobilization objectives, and infrastructure support requirements should be defined interactively with users or their representatives. Establishing detailed performance requirements and mandatory delivery dates should be avoided at this time. Premature detailed requirements are counter to evolutionary requirements definition and inhibit cost, performance, and schedule, (C,P,S) tradeoffs. The acquisition strategy should provide for the validation of the technologies and processes required to achieve critical characteristics and

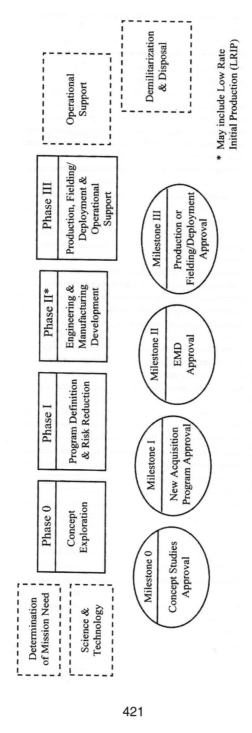

Fig. B.2 Previous DoD program phases and milestones.

meet operational constraints. It should also address the need and rationale for concurrence and for prototyping considering the results of technology development and demonstration. Plans for the next phase should address risk areas.

During Phase 0, the following should normally be done:

1) creation of validated assessment of the military threat;*
2) consideration of technology and technical risk;
3) assessment of advantages and disadvantages of each alternative concept;
4) identification of an acquisition strategy;
5) identification of cost, schedule, and performance for approval;
6) identification of potential environmental consequences;*
7) identification of program specific accomplishments to be completed during the next phase;
8) analysis of any major technology and industrial capability issues;*
9) identification of cooperative opportunities;*
10) ensuring compliance with international arms control agreements;*
11) creation of a proposed oversight and review strategy to include a description of mandatory program information and when this information needs to be submitted for the next milestone decision; and
12) development of the system requirement in terms of measures of effectiveness, measures of performance, and Command, Control, Communications, Computers, Intelligence, Surveillance, and Reconnaissance (C4ISR) support requirement (see Ref. 3, Pt. 2.2.1.).

Note: An asterisk (*) indicates items normally not applicable to ACAT 1A programs.

C. Phase I: Program Definition and Risk Reduction

When warranted, multiple design approaches and parallel technologies are pursued within the system concept(s) during this phase. Supportability and manufacturing process design considerations should be integrated into the system design effort early. This is essential to preclude costly redesign efforts downstream in the process (see Ref. 3, Pt. 4.3). Prototyping, testing, and early operational assessment of critical systems, subsystems, and components should be emphasized. This is essential to identifying and reducing risk and assessing if the most promising design approach(es) will operate in the intended operational environment including both people and conditions.

Cost drivers and alternatives are identified and analyzed. Further, the costs of the design approach(es) should also be analyzed as a function of risk and the expected increase in operational capability. This AOA (see Ref. 3, Pt. 2.4) should provide comparisons of the alternative design approaches and should be the principal basis for establishing or updating CAIV life-cycle-based objectives. Possible cost-saving changes that affect key Operational Requirements document/Acquisition Program Baseline (ORD/APB) performance parameters should be reviewed by the IPT. C,P,S tradeoffs will be made as a result of this analysis. The affordability constraints and CAIV life-cycle-based objectives established at Milestone I should be used in evaluating the results of the analysis.

Consistent with evolutionary requirements definition, the program manager works with the user or the user's representative to establish proposed performance objectives, identify production-rate requirements for peacetime, contingency support, and reconstitution objectives and develop proposed cost-schedule-performance tradeoffs for decision at Milestone II.

During Phase I, the following should normally be done:

1) creation of updated assessment of the military threat;*
2) consideration of technology and technical risk;
3) refinement of cost objectives and affordability assessment;
4) identification of major C,P,S tradeoff opportunities;
5) refinement of acquisition strategy and determination of initial low-rate initial production quantities;*
6) identification of a test and evaluation strategy and appropriate testing;
7) assessment of the industrial capability to support the program;*
8) identification of proposed C,P,S objectives and thresholds for approval;
9) assessment of potential environmental impacts;*
10) verification that adequate resources have been programmed to support production, deployment, and support;
11) identification of cooperative opportunities;*
12) ensuring of compliance with international arms control agreements;*
13) creation of a proposed oversight and review strategy to include a description of mandatory program information and when this information needs to be submitted for the next milestone;
14) refinement of CAIV objectives;
15) analysis of any major technology and industrial capability issues;
16) creation of independent cost estimate and manpower estimate; and
17) refinement (C4ISR) support requirements (see Ref. 3, Pt. 2.2.1).

Note: An asterisk (*) indicates items normally not applicable to ACAT 1A programs.

D. Phase II: Engineering and Manufacturing Development

Effective risk management is especially critical during this phase. To assist in managing risk resources should only be committed during this phase commensurate with the reduction and closure of risk. Configuration control should be established for both the design and the processes. Development and test activities should focus on high-risk areas, address the operational environment, and be phased to support internal decision making and the Milestone III decision review (see Ref. 3, Pt. 3.4). When possible, developmental testing should support and provide data for operational assessment prior to the beginning of formal initial operational test and evaluation by the operational test activity. CAIV analyses from earlier phases should be refined and continued through critical design review.

System-specific performance requirements should be developed for contract specifications in coordination with the user or the user's representative (see Ref. 3, Pts. 2.3 and 3).

Planning for Phase III should address design stability, production, industrial base capacity, configuration control, deployment, and support including, as appropriate, the transition from interim contract to in-house support (see Ref. 3, Pt. 4).

Program budget execution status should be periodically reviewed by both the planning, programming, and budgeting and acquisition management systems during this phase. Changes to the program that result in an actual or projected breach of an established program baseline parameter must be identified. Such changes may require a formal notification to the milestone decision authority (see Ref. 3, Pt. 6.2.1).

During Phase II, the following should normally be done:

1) achievement of design stability;
2) consideration of technology (10 USC 2364) and technical risk;
3) design, coding, integration, and testing of software;
4) creation of updated assessment of the military threat;*
5) creation of an updated test program with required lethality and survivability testing;*
6) production of Initial Operational Test and Evaluation results that realistically portray operational performance;
7) identification of a refined acquisition strategy to include support concept;
8) creation of a refined program cost estimate, independent cost estimate, cost objectives and manpower estimate;
9) creation of an updated affordability assessment;
10) assessment of the technological and industrial capability to support the program;*
11) identification of proposed C,P,S objectives and thresholds for approval;
12) assessment of potential environmental impacts;*
13) verification that adequate resources have been programmed to support production, deployment, and support;

14) identification of cooperative opportunities;*

15) ensuring compliance with international arms control agreements;*

16) creation of a proposed oversight and review strategy to include a description of mandatory information and when this information needs to be submitted for the next milestone;

17) refinement of CAIV objectives; and

18) refinement C4ISR support requirement (see Ref. 3, Pt. 2.2.1).

Note: An asterisk (*) indicates items normally not applicable to ACAT 1A programs.

E. Phase III: Production, Fielding/Deployment, and Operational Support

System performance and quality are normally monitored by follow-on operational test and evaluation during this phase. Program budget execution status is periodically reviewed by both the planning, programming, and budgeting and acquisition management systems. The results of field experience to include operational readiness rates should be continuously monitored, particularly during the early stages of this phase. The objectives are to assess the ability of the system to perform as intended, identify and incorporate into production lots minor engineering change proposals to meet required capabilities, and identify the need for major upgrades or modifications. Support plans should be implemented to ensure support resources are acquired and deployed with the system.

During Phase III, the following should normally be done:

1) full-rate production experience that verifies manufacturing and production processes, confirms the stability and producibility of the design, and provides realistic production cost estimates;*

2) creation of a refined configuration management program;

3) creation of an updated and validated assessment of the military threat;*

4) creation of refined life cycle cost estimates;

5) execution of operational and support plans to include transition from contractor to in-house support, if appropriate;

6) identification of operational and support problems;

7) resolution of system deficiencies and verification thereof in demonstration, test and evaluation, and full operational test and evaluation, if appropriate; and

8) refinement of C4ISR support requirement (see Ref. 3, Pt. 2.2.1).

Note: An asterisk (*) indicates items normally not applicable to ACAT 1A programs.

References

[1]Department of Defense, Department of Defense Instruction 5000.2, April 5, 2002.

[2]Department of Defense, *Defense Acquisition Deskbook,* Dave Anderson (owner), Version 3.0, June 30, 1999, Sec. 2.3.

[3]Department of Defense, "Mandatory Procedures for Major Defense Acquisition Programs (MDAPs) and Major Automated Information System (MAIS) Acquisition Programs," Regulation No. 5000.2-R, May 11, 1999. (incorporating change 4).

Appendix C:
Comparison of the Microeconomic Framework to Actual DoD Program Outcomes

Five hypotheses resulting from the microeconomic framework were tested and confirmed by a statistical analysis performed on a large sample of historic DoD programs.[1] (This appendix was derived from Conrow, E. H., "Some Long-Term Issues and Impediments Affecting Military Systems Acquisition Reform," *Acquisition Review Quarterly*, Vol. 2, No. 3, 1995, pp. 199–212.) Statistical analyses of cost, performance, or schedule (C,P,S) change data derived from DoD major weapon systems can help to determine the degree to which historical data are consistent with the microeconomic framework of military systems acquisition.

I. Data Collection and Analysis

Three different data sets were obtained for the statistical analysis and combined into an overall data set to increase the statistical sample size. The data sets mostly consisted of aircraft and missile programs (46 of 58 total programs). In addition, the programs contained in the data sets were major development programs rather than follow-on or upgrade programs. The data sets and the number of nonoverlapping programs they contain are now discussed.

The Perry et al.[2] data set was originally derived from surveys and follow-up visits to various DoD programs: it represents programs with Milestone II (or equivalent) dates in the 1950s (2 programs) and 1960s (18 programs). The Dews et al.[3] data set was derived from selected acquisition reports (SARs) and represents programs with Milestone II (or equivalent) dates in the 1970s (8 programs). The Conrow data set[1] was also derived from SARs and represents programs with Milestone II (or equivalent) dates in the 1960s (7 programs), 1970s (17 programs), and 1980s (6 programs). The overall combined data set (1950s–1980s) derived from the Perry, Dews, and Conrow data sets thus includes 58 programs $(2 + 18 + 8 + 7 + 17 + 6 = 58$ programs) with a total of 48, 52, and 51 programs reporting cost change, performance change, and schedule change data, respectively.

The ratio between a current estimate (CE) produced at one snapshot in time during a program divided by an estimate produced early in the development phase, known as a development estimate (DE), was defined for C,P,S as a baseline for these estimates. The DE is typically associated with Milestone II. Milestone II is the decision point to determine whether or not

427

a DoD program will enter engineering and manufacturing development (EMD). Some programs in the sample did not go through a Milestone II review because they predated this particular management scheme. In these cases an equivalent time, such as the start of the EMD (or equivalent) phase contract, was used.

The time in the program when a CE was made in the Perry data set[2] spanned a large range from early in EMD to the Operations and Support phase. In the Dews et al. data set[3] the CE spanned a narrower range from the middle of EMD to the middle of the Production, Fielding/Deployment, and Operational Support phases, but only development phase C,P,S change data were included in the data base. In the Conrow data set[1] the CE represented a point in time near the program Initial Operational Capability date. Only development phase C,P,S change data were included in the database. Thus, most of the programs in the overall sample represented the EMD (or equivalent) program phase.

Summary descriptive statistics for the overall combined data set are given in Table C.1. Sample statistics for all three data sets were quite similar, but because the overall combined data set covers a longer time period (1958–1986) and includes more systems, Table C.1 only includes results from this data set. The mean, median, and standard deviation for the cost change and schedule change variables are similar to each other, yet noticeably larger than the corresponding values for the performance change variable.

C,P,S predictions, drawn from the microeconomic framework just discussed, were tested against the statistical results.

II. First Hypothesis

Because of government and contractor utility preferences, relatively few systems will have significant overall development phase performance deg-

Table C.1 DoD program summary statistics

Variable	Cost[a]	Performance	Schedule
Sample size (programs)	48	52	51
Average	1.26	1.00	1.24
Median	1.16	1.00	1.13
Standard deviation	0.28	0.13	0.30
Minimum	0.86	0.65	0.75
Maximum	2.07	1.42	2.25
First quartile	1.06	0.92	1.03
Third quartile	1.41	1.06	1.44
Skewness	1.24	0.38	1.24

[a]C,P,S correspond to cost change, performance change, and schedule change associated with the current program estimate divided by the initial Milestone II (or equivalent) estimate.

radations. In addition, because many U.S. military systems have performance requirements set at or beyond the technical feasibility level, relatively few programs will have large gains in performance from the initial estimated level.

The hypothesis cannot be rejected given the mean (1.00) and median values (1.00) for the performance change distribution, as well as the standard deviation (0.13) of performance change values around the no-change level (1.00). Only 10 of 52 programs had an average slip in performance > 10%, whereas only 9 of 52 programs had an average gain in performance > 10%. In terms of more extreme values, only two of 52 programs had an average slip in performance of 25% or more, and only one of 52 programs had an average gain in performance of 25% or more.

III. Second Hypothesis

Because of a combination of utility preferences and technical feasibility, the variation in performance change for DoD systems is likely to be smaller than corresponding variations in cost and schedule.

The standard deviations of changes in C,P,S are 0.28, 0.13, and 0.30, respectively. Consequently, the hypothesis cannot be rejected given that the standard deviation of performance change is less than half that of program cost change and schedule change.

IV. Third Hypothesis

Because of a combination of utility preferences and technical feasibility, DoD systems will typically exhibit an increase in cost and/or schedule during development.

The hypothesis cannot be rejected given that 43 of 48 programs (90%) exhibited cost growth and that 40 of 51 programs (78%) exhibited schedule slippage. In addition, a number of programs had large cost growth or schedule slippage. For example, 30 of 48 programs had cost growth $\geq$ 25% and 20 of 51 programs had schedule slippage $\geq$ 25%.

V. Fourth Hypothesis

The shape of the development performance distribution will likely be near symmetrical, whereas the shapes of the cost change and schedule change distributions will likely be right-hand skewed. This is because the government and contractor strive to meet performance requirements while typically adjusting program cost and/or schedule to achieve the desired levels of performance. Final performance achievements can be viewed as random variations around the target value.

The hypothesis cannot be rejected given the skewness, mean, and median values for these change distributions. A skewness of zero indicates that the data are symmetrically distributed, whereas a positive value indicates that the distribution has a right-hand skew. The skewness coefficient for the cost change distribution (1.24) and schedule change distribution (1.24) is positive and roughly 3.3 times greater than that for the performance change distribution (0.38). The mean for the C,P,S change distributions was 1.26, 1.00, and 1.24, whereas the median for the C,P,S change distributions was 1.16, 1.00, and 1.13.

The difference in the mean and median for the performance change distribution is virtually zero (< 0.01), while that for the cost change and schedule change distributions are 0.10 and 0.11, respectively. These results, as with the skewness results just mentioned, indicate that the performance change distribution is nearly symmetrical, while the cost change and schedule change distributions have a right-hand skew.

The initially infeasible C,P,S solution point that exists for many systems results from a misspecification of the technical possibility surface caused part by an underestimation bias associated with the level of performance that can be achieved for a given level of cost and/or schedule. This together with the primary government and contractor desire to meet performance requirements, while allowing cost and/or schedule to increase during the course of the program to achieve a feasible C,P,S solution point, causes the cost change and schedule change distributions to have means greater than one, as well as a right-hand skew.

VI. Fifth Hypothesis

Given the complex nature of the C,P,S trades that occur during a military program, no simple relationship will likely exist between the Milestone II date (start of EMD) and C,P,S change.

There was negligible correlation between cost change, performance change, and schedule change vs the Milestone II date. Consequently, the hypothesis cannot be rejected given the limited correlation between C,P,S change and the Milestone II date.

References

[1]Conrow, E. H., "Some Long-Term Issues and Impediments Affecting Military Systems Acquisition Reform," *Acquisition Review Quarterly,* Vol. 2, No. 3, Summer 1995, pp. 199–212.

[2]Perry, R., Smith, G., Harman, A., and Henrichsen, S., "System Acquisition Strategies," RAND, Santa Monica, CA, R-733-PR/ARPA, June 1971.

[3]Dews, E., Smith, G., Barbour, A., Harris, E., and Hesse, M., "Acquisition Policy Effectiveness: Department of Defense Experience in the 1970s," RAND, Santa Monica, CA, R-2516-DR&E, Oct. 1979.

Appendix D:
Some Characteristics of the Cost–Performance Slice of the Technical Possibility Surface

Characteristics of the cost vs performance (C:P) curve presented in Chapter 1, Sec. III can also be demonstrated in a wide variety of commercial and military items beyond the microprocessor example already discussed. [1] (This appendix was derived from Conrow, E. H., "Some Considerations for Design Selection in Commercial, Government, and Defense Programs," 1997 Acquisition Research Symposium Proceedings, Defense Systems Management College, 1997, pp. 195-217.) I will now give some additional examples of cost change related to change in performance for several dissimilar items. (Note: price is assumed to be a proxy for cost in this discussion. This is not completely correct because economic considerations internal and external to the seller can affect price even if cost is fixed. Nevertheless, the term cost is used generically in the remainder of this appendix except in cases where price data exists.) The results of this analysis are presented in Table D.1. (Some of these data were originally presented by Norman Augustine.[2]) A three-step process was used to generate these results.

First, C:P data were normalized against the upper-bound (highest cost and performance) value that existed in each data sample (e.g., a microprocessor). (Consequently, the upper-bound C:P value was always 1.00:1.00.) Second, I examined the second highest C:P value in each data sample and computed the percent deviation in normalized cost and performance vs the upper-bound value. This gives the marginal (or delta) cost and performance between the second C:P value and the upper-bound value (1.00:1.00). For example, in the commercial microprocessor case the last 10% of performance (measured by chip clock rate) led to a 43% increase in price (all else held constant). Third, I determined the slope of the data by taking the ratio of the change in cost divided by the change in performance of the second highest value vs the upper-bound value. This yields the first derivative (slope) of the C:P curve at this location. (Note: The slope is not computed from the percent marginal cost and marginal performance data in Table D.1, but from the normalized, nonpercent values, which are not reported here.)

It is evident from the results in Table D.1 that the marginal cost with respect to performance in the region of the upper-bound C:P value can lead to *huge* potential cost increases for many different types of items. Augustine termed this phenomena "the high cost of a little more."[2] In fact, this might

Table D.1 Normalized marginal cost vs marginal performance for various items— percent deviations between second highest value and upper-bound value

Item	Marginal cost or price, %	Marginal performance, %	Slope	Angle, deg
35-mm camera lenses	167 (price)	50 (focal length)	+1.8	62
Baseball player salary	102 (salary, price)	10 (batting average)	+5.6	80
1960s airplanes	388 ($/lb)	28 (maximum speed)	+3.6	75
Machined parts	52 (price)	25 (log tolerance)	+1.7	60
Radar availability	37 (cost)	3 (radar availability)	+9.4	84
Space detector chip	93 (cost)	2 (specific detectivity)	+30.1	88
Microprocessor	43 (price)	10 (clock rate)	+3.0	72
Commercial CCD	155 (price)	0.00036 (operability)	+168,888.9	89.9997

be better termed "the very high cost of a very little more." Because a slope having a 45-deg angle corresponds to a marginal cost vs performance ratio of 1.00, it is apparent that the C:P relationship for many of the items examined is nearly vertical in the region of the upper bound of the C:P curve.

To quantify this assumption, the angle of line connecting the second highest and upper-bound C:P values was determined and the results given in Table D.1—here, the angle is simply computed by angle = arc tangent (slope). The results indicate that the slope angle of the C:P curve in the vicinity of the upper-bound value is nearly vertical in most cases (e.g., > 80 deg in four of eight cases) and steep in the remaining cases (e.g., between 60 deg and 75 deg for the other four items). In one case, for the commercial charge coupled device the resulting slope angle was effectively identical to 90 deg. This should bring pause to designers and program managers who think by simply using commercial off-the-shelf components C:P related problems will vanish. Clearly, this is not the case when a relatively high level of performance is required!

Finally, not only is the first derivative (slope) of each item given in Table D.1 positive, but the second derivative (computed as the change in slope between the third highest value and second highest value vs the second highest value and the upper-bound value) is positive in each case. Values for the second derivative ranged from +1.1 (35-mm camera lenses) to +5.9 (1960s airplanes), with a mean and standard deviation of the eight-second derivative values equal to 2.8 and 1.6, respectively. Similarly, the microprocessor normalized price vs normalized performance data given in Fig. 1.2 have a positive first and second derivative of C:P for each of the six sample time frames where normalized performance ≥ 0.80.

Consequently, not only is the slope large in the steep portion of C:P curves derived from a variety of different items, but the change in slope is also quite large. Hence, a slight miscalculation in the level of performance that can be achieved can potentially lead to a very large cost, schedule, and risk increases in this C:P curve region. This applies to many commercial and DoD/NASA programs because their designs are in the steep part of the C:P curve, and thus subject to considerable cost growth and schedule slippage and increased risk. *However, by performing balanced cost, performance, schedule, and risk trades, it is possible to decrease cost, schedule, and risk with only a very small decrease in performance, so long as it is consciously practiced.*

References

[1]Conrow, E. H., "Some Considerations for Design Selection in Commercial, Government and Defense Programs," 1997 Acquisition Research Symposium Proceedings, Defense Systems Management College, Ft. Belvoir, VA, June 1997, pp. 195–217.

[2]Augustine, N. R., *Augustine's Laws,* AIAA, New York, 1983, p. 46.

Appendix E:
Changing the Definition of Risk—Why Risk It?

By Robert N. Charette

I. Introduction

A debate has begun among the practitioners of risk management about the definition of "risk." Traditionally, risk has been defined as the likelihood of an event occurring coupled with the negative consequence of the event occurring. In other words, a risk is a potential problem—something to be avoided if possible, or its likelihood and/or consequences reduced if not.

The Project Management Institute, the British Standards Institute, the UK Institution of Civil Engineers, and others have proposed an expanded definition of the word risk. They would define risk as "an uncertain event or condition that, if it occurs, has a positive or negative effect on project objectives."[1] A slightly different definition is that a risk is any deviation from the project plan.

The proponents of changing the definition of risk argue that its traditional interpretation is incomplete and too restrictive, especially with concern to how opportunities are addressed. Some of the arguments made for changing the definition of risk, specifically regarding project management, are that 1) by not including events with positive effects in the definition, opportunities are more likely to be overlooked; 2) by dwelling on just the negative aspects of a project, project personnel tend to reject risk management as a project management practice; 3) if risk is confined to negative consequences, another process would be needed to cope with the likelihood of positive events, which means that again, opportunities are overlooked; and 4) project success rates are lower than they could be because positive events are excluded from risk management.[2]

While I agree that some of these assertions may represent valid examples of (poor) risk management *practice*, they are not reasons to change the very *definition* of risk. For instance, risk management often may be rejected by some project managers because it appears to the uninformed to dwell "too much" on potential problems. However, that is more a management-related educational issue than a risk definitional issue.

In this appendix, I will show that most of the previously stated assertions have little merit, from either a theoretical or practical perspective. I will argue that the proposed change to the definition of risk represents a basic misunderstanding of managing risk and exploiting opportunity and further, it attempts to correct poor risk management practice by entirely incorrect means. I will show that the proposed change in definition will work to weaken risk management practice instead of enhance it, as the proponents of the definition change claim. Finally, I will demonstrate what can be done to overcome some of the deficiencies in risk management practice without accepting the risk of undermining its usefulness as an important project management discipline.

II. What is Risk? What is Opportunity?

To understand my position, I will set the scene by reviewing a few fundamental notions about what exactly I mean when I speak of a risk or an opportunity. The arguments begin with the definitions of risk and opportunity, and then move on to how they relate in the context of defining and executing projects within the confines of an enterprise.

Let's start with a traditional definition of risk, and from this develop a working definition of the word opportunity. For our purposes, risk is defined as the "potential for the realization of unwanted, negative consequences of an event."[3] Consider a few themes contained in this definition.

First, the negative outcome of a specified "risk" event is relative, not absolute. Just because an event has a negative outcome does not necessarily make it a risk. An absolute positive outcome may still be viewed as a relative negative one. For example, one might perceive that making anything less than $1 million in profit per year on a new product is a negative outcome. This means that risk is perception based. Second, the outcome of the event must be unwanted. This seems obvious, but there is an implication that one desires something else to occur if the risk event happens. Third, a threshold distinguishes between desired and undesired outcomes of the event. Without this threshold, one cannot say that an event presents a risk or not. Finally, a risk event is a potential outcome, not a certain outcome. If one knows that such an event will happen, then the event does not present a risk, but a certainty.

We can construct a definition of opportunity from this definition of risk. I claim that an opportunity is the "potential for the realization of wanted, positive consequences of an event." Like risks, opportunities have thresholds that distinguish desired outcomes from undesired outcomes of an event. Similarly, an opportunity is a potential outcome, not a certain one. In addition, like risks, opportunities are perception driven.

Given these two definitions, we can characterize an event as having the potential for 1) only positive consequences (i.e., a "pure opportunity" event where only the magnitude of the positive consequences and the likelihood of the event are in doubt); 2) only negative consequences (i.e., a "pure risk" event where only the magnitude of the negative consequences and the likelihood of the event are in doubt); or 3) a mixture of positive or negative consequences (i.e., a "speculative event" where the likelihood and consequences of both are in doubt).

Typically in projects, we are most concerned with speculative events more than pure risk or opportunity events that are most frequently outside our control. Generally, a fundamental difference between opportunities and risks are that opportunities are events that we must take deliberate action to capture, but risks are events that may be ignored (e.g., assumption risk handling option). With our definitions in place, let's next examine how risk and opportunity are related to projects.

III. Understanding Project Risk and Opportunity

To understand the relationships of risks and opportunities to projects, we need to ask a simple question: Why are projects started? Generally, projects are begun to achieve some change in the present state of the enterprise. For whatever reason, the present operating state of the enterprise or its perceived future trajectory is believed to be unacceptable. Therefore, some expenditure of resources to change the present state is thought necessary.

Enterprises usually have limited funds to invest in improvements in any given year and usually take great care to invest these funds wisely. Such enterprises have an investment decision-making process, either formal or informal that determines which projects are funded. At the enterprise level, there is typically a separate "opportunity evaluation" process to determine potential projects that represent opportunities and those that don't. This effort is given various names within organizations, such as investment analysis, portfolio analysis, and so forth. For purposes of this section, my efforts focus mainly on project management of opportunity and risk.

A change in the enterprise's state sought by taking on a project is achieved usually by the accomplishment of some *project objectives*, which will change the enterprise's present state into a more favorable future state. Therefore, a project is the mechanism through which these beneficial changes can be gained. Informally, we can say that the project represents the enterprise's attempt to realize an "opportunity." In other words, a project is an "enterprise event" that has a potential for some desired positive outcome.

Summarizing, I contend that projects are begun with an expectation by the enterprise of some level of improvement in its operations over the present state. Namely, there is the likelihood that the project, when completed, will provide some range of perceived benefits. I will, in fact, define *project expectation* just in this way. Project expectation is the *minimum* acceptable benefit (i.e., positive outcome) that a project will achieve.

Observe that the minimal acceptable benefit (i.e., a positive result in comparison with the present state) is based upon an enterprise's perspective, which is a fundamental part of the project's context. What I mean is that the benefit is based upon achieving some specified project objectives given certain assumptions and constraints. Notice, however, that the beneficial outcome is *assumed* but not *assured*—the project may fail to produce the beneficial results that are expected. The reasons for such failure may range from poor investment decisions, changing market environments, poor project planning, unrealistic expectations, to poor project execution, and so forth. It is very possible that a project can achieve its objectives but because of other factors, the enterprise gains no benefit. Therefore, the eventual outcome of a project may range from beneficial to neutral to negative.

In Fig. E.1, I have labeled various outcomes of a project. The *y* axis represents the relative likelihood of outcomes of the project. The peak is the most likely outcome (or the mathematical mode). The *x* axis represents the potential outcomes of the project. For the moment, assume that the most likely project outcome matches our project expectation for the project (i.e., our minimum acceptable benefit), and outcomes to the right are undesired consequences, or "risk" events. This means, from our definition, that the outcomes to the left of our expected outcome represent opportunities.

Let's review a few observations concerning Fig. E.1. The value of the project expectation sets a threshold for what is a risk and what is an opportunity. In fact, how we label the distribution of outcomes as risks or opportunities in Fig. E.1 depends entirely upon what we define as the minimum acceptable beneficial outcome (i.e., our project expectation). Consider that if we were to move our project expectation more to the right or to the left, as labels "a" and "b" in Fig. E.2, the sets of risks and opportunities would have different members.

We can say, then, that risks are those events in which the outcomes may be worse than our project expectation and opportunities are events in which the outcomes may be better than our project expectation. Our project expectation itself, as I mentioned before, is an event with a possible positive outcome, or an opportunity in itself. A project risk, then, is *always* defined in relation to our project expectation.

IV. Risk Management in Projects

When a project is planned, different alternative approaches are examined to see which provide the most likely (i.e., best chance) to meet or exceed our objectives. Each approach is one path through the branches of a vast decision tree. The job of the project planners is to select the one series of branches from the various options that will meet the objectives within the project assumptions, constraints, and success or acceptability criteria.

Projects are made up of many interrelated activities each with their own distribution of event outcomes, similar to that shown in Fig. E.1. A project plan assumes (i.e., plans) that each of these interrelated activities will have a (minimum) positive outcome. Each project activity therefore is a unique "local opportunity" that is being pursued. Risk management comes into play

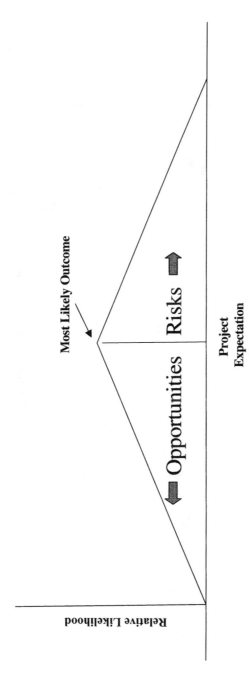

Fig. E.1 Distribution of project outcomes.

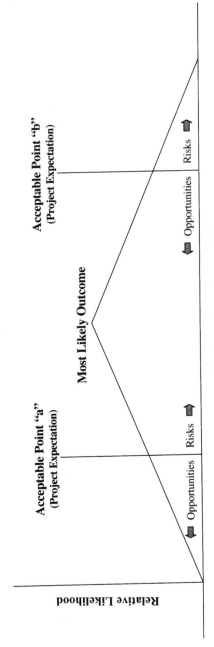

Fig. E.2 Differing points of acceptability.

because we know from experience that the minimum acceptable positive outcomes are not always achieved. The process of risk management looks at selected project activities and determines what situations, circumstances, or events might keep the activities from achieving their expected positive outcomes.

For example, let's assume that there is an information technology (IT) project that will use a particular microprocessor. The risk management process would examine the use of the microprocessor from various perspectives. It would examine which project's objectives it is trying to achieve, what assumptions are being made in its use, what constraint it imposes on the project, what constraints the project imposes on it, and so forth. In addition, the process would examine what events, situations, or circumstances might occur to keep the use of the microprocessor from achieving the expected benefit of its use. For example, the microprocessor might not be able to handle the workload planned for it, leading to consequences that might be detrimental to the project. If this event were perceived as a possibility, it might be viewed as a risk to be managed.

As I mentioned, a project plan assumes (i.e., plans) that each planned activity will have a (minimum) positive outcome. Experience teaches us that this is not always true—sometimes the positive outcome is *better* than we expected, instead of worse as in the previous example. Would the risk management process look for situations where the microprocessor would exceed its expected benefit? Maybe, maybe not. The primary purpose of risk management is to ensure that situations do not get worse (i.e., we meet our minimum expectations), instead of better. Another way of viewing it is to ensure every project activity—each representing a local opportunity—is achieved successfully. However, as the project progressed, the risk management process would be able to determine if the risk associated with an activity were overestimated. If this were the case, a new expected benefit *could* be set if so needed.

In the next section, let's explore further the idea of whether opportunities would be seen by a risk management process based upon a "traditional" definition of risk.

V. Are Opportunities Really Being Missed?

Those advocating a change in the definition of risk voice three major complaints about how opportunities are currently treated in projects. First, they complain that opportunities are being overlooked in projects because the "traditional" definition of risk does not contain the idea of opportunity. Second, they complain that opportunities don't get used to offset risks. Third, they complain that opportunities are not actively exploited. Therefore, they argue that only a change in the definition of risk that includes opportunities as well as "threats" (or "risks" in my terminology) will allow a single, efficient management process to look for and exploit opportunities. Otherwise, a separate "opportunity management" process will be required. I believe that each of these complaints is without much merit.

The proponents offer no data that supports their first complaint that opportunities (from here on out I mean an event, situation, or circumstance that may lead to better-than-expected results, either for a project activity or to the project itself) are being commonly overlooked. Further, they seem to assume that risk management somehow inhibits a project from looking for opportunities. A question then arises whether this means that projects that don't use risk management are less inhibited than those that do, but we will leave this issue for another time.

Instead of inhibiting opportunity seeking, I argue quite the contrary. It seems to me that standard risk management processes provide very effective mechanisms for identifying meaningful project opportunities when they arise if the processes are applied competently. These mechanisms include activities such as monitoring a project's risks and its context as well as risk handling. When these are coupled with normal project status reporting and review procedures, project opportunities are likely to be recognized regularly.

Let's go back to our microprocessor example. Now let's assume that the risk management process is monitoring or actively looking for a means to handle a microprocessor-related risk, (e.g., a risk with its throughput, power consumption, etc.). The arrival of a new microprocessor in the marketplace that promised to address these risks would likely be noticed as a part of the project's risk handling process. The project manager would likely make use of such an opportunity to adjust his or her project activities (assuming the new microprocessor opportunity indeed turned out to be beneficial, of course). It's not reasonable to assume that an opportunity-seeking process would necessarily see events involving risks better than a risk handling process would!

Well, then, what about an opportunity that is not related to a project risk and therefore is not being ordinarily monitored by the project's risk handling activities? Will the traditional risk management process find it? Maybe, maybe not. Let's consider a couple of "out of the blue" opportunities and a more speculative one that is not directly related to a project risk.

Let's assume that the use of the microprocessor in our example was not seen as a source of risk, but a new version of it was introduced possessing a significant performance increase. In this situation, the performance level required by the microprocessor would likely appear either as an assumption or constraint to the project risk assessment. When such a constraint or assumption changes, this information is immediately introduced in project reviews to the project manager because of its importance. In fact, changes to project context—generally external events that relate to a project's objectives, assumptions, and constraints—are the source of the greatest shift in project risk and opportunity, and as such, are high priorities for review. As part of the project context, the microprocessor's status would be continuously monitored during standard risk management activities, and changes related to it would be noticed.

For a second example, let's say that software productivity was estimated for a software subsystem to be three lines of tested code per day per programmer and it turned out to be four lines instead. This increased coding productivity obviously could have the effect of lowering project cost or decreasing the schedule. The people responsible for the delivery of the software subsystem would likely observe this change in productivity and report it. It would be hard to imagine that this situation would be overlooked for long, or all of its implications to the project not considered as a matter of course. For the increase in coding productivity to be overlooked would mean that either it is unimportant or that competent reviews of project activities and their statuses were not happening. It might also mean a proficient project measurement system was not in place. All these "opportunity-identifying" activities should happen even if coding productivity is not seen as part of the project context. If it were, coding productivity would be routinely monitored as part of the normal risk management activities, as I noted before.

Consider a more speculative case: The programmers are coding at three lines of code per day, and the productivity level is considered adequate (i.e., coding productivity is either a very low or no risk event and so doesn't appear on the project's risk watch list). Would an opportunity to code four lines of code per day by using some different approach be seen? If coding productivity was again for some reason not being seen as a project objective, assumption, or constraint, then a risk management process might very well overlook it. Notice, however, for coding productivity not to be seen as either a project objective, assumption, or constraint or be a source of risk, it is conjectural to assume that the chance to increase productivity, as previously noted, would be considered an opportunity to be exploited. One could just as easily assume that increasing coding productivity was not relevant to project success.

Therefore, opportunities that are related to risks are highly likely to be identified by the risk management process. The same is true for those opportunities caused by changes in project objectives, assumptions, or constraints because they are supposed to be identified by the routine monitoring of the project context. Only opportunities not related to these two categories are likely to be missed by risk management activities. However, other standard project management activities very well might discover them. In any case, it is debatable whether these opportunities are generally significant anyway.

Without any data to the contrary, the mechanisms already part of standard risk management processes using traditional definitions of risk, (e.g., *IEEE Std. 1540-2001 Standard for Software Life Cycle Processes—Risk Management*), are likely to identity meaningful opportunities to reduce risk or to improve project outcomes when competently applied.

The proponents' second complaint is that the traditional definition of risk effectively keeps opportunities from being used to reduce risks posed to the project. As the proponents themselves state, for an opportunity to be exploited, the opportunity must be successfully accomplished, and the opportunity either must be "directly useful" or "be capable of being transformed into something that can be used in another area."[4] Let's consider "directly useful" opportunities first and follow that with the situation of "transformational" opportunities.

As I have demonstrated earlier, opportunities that are directly related to a risk are routinely identified and assessed for exploitation by standard project risk handling and monitoring activities. These activities are commonly used to select those opportunities whose exploitation will best address risk.

Let's return to our microprocessor example where a new microprocessor appears in the market that overcomes the risks with the one that is currently used. Before the new microprocessor's arrival in the market, competently applied risk handling will be looking for ways to lower or eliminate the current microprocessor risks, including looking for a replacement (assuming the risks are considered important enough to worry about). If such a replacement appears, and the risks can be eliminated as in our example, great. Moreover, if such a replacement creates additional benefit to the project, I claim that these benefits would likely be used to offset other risks by any competent project manager. It would not be reasonable to assume that a project manager would not consider the implications of such a circumstance. I do not believe that the proponents really believe project managers do not routinely act to exploit such opportunities when they appear.

This leaves us with an opportunity that is capable of being transformed into something that can be used in another project area. This is a case of an opportunity that isn't directly related to a risk again. As I pointed out earlier, these may be missed if they aren't related to the project's context information.

These "transformational" opportunities are therefore unique in character. Because they are not connected to a project risk or important enough to be tracked as part of the project context, these opportunities must be of one of two types. First, the opportunity must be related to those project activities that potentially increase benefit to the project at no increase of risk. Exploiting these opportunities means deliberately acting to increase the benefit of a project activity that is already meeting its expectation or one that is currently exceeding its expectation. Either this, or it means pursuing an opportunity that creates potentially significant project benefit at some agreeable (small) increase in project risk.

The first type of opportunity indeed would be worthy of exploitation, *if* they were present, and *if* in truth they could be exploited in net "cost-free" manner. However, in my experience, precious few of these "risk-free, cost-free" opportunities come along. In addition, those that do are usually exploited as a matter of good project management. Why, then, do the proponents assume that a project manager will overlook the possibility of creating the most benefit from a project activity that is already meeting or exceeding its expectation if it is possible to do so?

Further, acting to make an already successful project activity more successful so that it can be used to offset other project risks assumes many things, such as there is a project risk-opportunity pool that can be easily traded-off against each other in a fungible manner. Even if this could be done successfully with no net additional project resources (this is doubtful), it is speculative that the benefit would be directly translated into something elsewhere in the project. In our coding productivity example earlier, our more productive coders might be finished sooner, but then have to sit on their hands as the rest of the project catches up. Only if the coders were in the critical path would the benefit be useful (and if they were, a coding productivity risk would already be raised about it!). Spending resources to look for these types of opportunities seems rather extravagant to me.

The second type of opportunity is one that promises large gains at only marginal increases in project risk. Again, in my experience, these are quite rare and usually suspect. At the very least, an opportunity of this type requires that the project as a whole is reconsidered, because the assumptions of the project's original benefits, risks and costs would likely be overturned. A new project plan would likely have to be developed, which in turn would likely involve going back to the enterprise to get approval.

Would it be useful for a project to divert resources to look for such rare opportunities? I tend to doubt it, especially if those same resources could be spent on handling known risks. As the old saying goes, "One in the hand is worth two in the bush."

This leads me to the third complaint that the definition of risk needs to be changed to look for all these opportunities, thereby avoiding the need for a separate opportunity management process to be invoked to help identify and exploit them. I look at this issue differently. As I have shown, the number and types of opportunities that are likely to be overlooked or not considered for exploitation by a standard risk or project management process are few, and of questionable importance. I have demonstrated that these standard processes will allow opportunities to be identified, assessed, and exploited for risk handling where useful. I have also shown that opportunities that matter—i.e. are important enough to be in the project's context or on a project's risk list—are likely to be seen and judged for their usefulness. Therefore, I don't believe that a separate opportunity management process is necessary, cost effective, or beneficial at a project level. To me, this complaint like the previous two is moot.

What we have shown is that opportunities are not typically overlooked by traditional risk management. I contend that standard risk and project management processes competently applied, will find, assess, and exploit nearly all opportunities of merit. I fail to see how a change in the definition of risk to include opportunity will make opportunities any more identifiable or exploitable. I do know that changing a definition in a scientific or engineering discipline is a radical solution that is reserved for the time when an existing definition does not work in theory or in practice. The proponents have not made a compelling theoretical case for such a change. As we will see, they do not make a practical case either.

VI.   Practical Issues Opposing the Change in Definition

The argument for changing the definition of risk is flawed from not only a theoretical perspective, but from a practical perspective as well.

For instance, the proponents of including opportunity as part of the definition of risk claim this change will increase project success because project managers will be more inclined to perform risk management. The reason for this claimed potential increase in project success is that risk management won't be perceived to be so negative in its outlook so it will be applied more, and second, opportunities for improvement will be seen more clearly because they must be looked for regularly.

It is interesting to see that the proponents of change believe that the application of traditional risk management increases a project's chance of success. We agree with this view wholeheartedly. However, their argument that by finding more opportunities—for achieving or bettering the project objectives—project success rates will increase is not supported by any data I know of or offered by the proponents. It is pure supposition. I contend that projects fail more often because risks are not addressed correctly, rather than because opportunities are being ignored. It is also interesting to me that the proponents assume that these new found opportunities will have their risks managed better than with the traditional definition of risk.

Further, their argument that opportunities are overlooked seems peculiar to me based upon my experience. I have not yet encountered a project where "opportunities" are customarily overlooked or ignored. Quite the contrary, too often I see projects chasing after so-called "opportunities" at the expense of getting something perfectly acceptable working. Without much effort, it is easy to foresee how the change in definition may exacerbate the current situation of requirements to creep or to project gold plating. Instead of being viewed as risks, you could argue that all the added features are opportunities for improvement. Voltaire's maxim, "The best is the enemy of the good," comes to mind in most of the projects I see.

As we have seen, the opportunities that the proponents speak of are related to how well risk handling is performed by an individual project. This in turn is related to how effectively the process of risk assessment—identification and analysis—is performed. Again, this in turn is based on how effectively the project's context—its objectives, assumptions, and constraints—is defined at project initiation and as part of risk management planning.

Poor risk management practice more often than not can be traced to poor project definition or poor risk management training. Without well-defined objectives and project acceptability thresholds—which are often not defined—risk management is difficult to perform. In a 2002 survey conducted by myself with the Cutter Consortium of over 180 IT project managers, only 33% stated that their projects have explicit thresholds which a project can't exceed.[5] Similarly, formal training in the practice of risk management is often lacking which makes overlooking opportunities for effective risk handling a real possibility. In the Cutter survey, over 50% of IT project managers said they had never attended any risk management training. Changing the definition of risk because of poor training or poor project definition is ill conceived at best.

VII. Risk Management Is for Adults

Moreover, the arguments that risk management will be used more because, through a definitional change, project managers will perceive the management of risk as "more positive" in outlook is curious. Even if such a change were made in the definition, does anyone really believe that risk management would now be embraced effortlessly? The risks or threats in the proponents' terminology—those nasty negative events that scare supposedly professional project managers—still have to be identified, assessed, and managed. Or do the proponents feel that because a few opportunities are identified that the project manager will now feel better about taking on threats to the project? Are we to assume that for every "threat" we need to identify an opportunity to ensure some type of politically correct balance, so the project manager and their team will not have a crisis in self-confidence or self-esteem because risks present the project in a poor light? Some proponents go so far even to state that we should get rid of the term "accept the threat (risk)" because that phrase is seen as being too negative![6]

What is scary to me is that supposedly professional project mangers should need to be treated like children—that they somehow need that spoonful of sugar to make the poor tasting risk medicine go down. Risk management, to quote Tim Lister, is for adults.[7] Project managers that need a change in the definition of risk to make them apply risk management should look for a new profession. We need project managers who are capable leaders and have egos strong enough to look for risks and manage them with a realistic perspective, not to pretend they are not there. I would rather have a project manager with 100 risks than one who pretends that risks don't exist and later has to manage a hundred problems—timid project managers don't make successful project managers.

This leads me to a point about professional hypocrisy. One of the laments of risk management practitioners is that project managers never want to call a risk a risk, but instead "a challenge," "an issue," or yes, "an opportunity." Aren't the proponents doing the same thing by changing the definition of risk? Worse, won't a change in definition just aid and abet the use of these euphemisms, and likely make the current "let's pretend our project is risk-free or low risk" situation worse?

VIII. Conflict of Interest

To successfully sell risk management to project managers, the proponents claim the search for opportunities must be emphasized. This sneaking risk management into the project via the backdoor potentially makes actively managing risk an afterthought, versus a primary project element to be managed. More troubling is the fact that by changing the definition, it places the risk manager in a potential conflict-of-interest situation, similar to the position Wall Street analysts have found themselves in recently. By changing the definition of risk, and emphasizing the need to look for opportunities, we place the risk management professional in a potential "cheerleader" role instead of a neutral analyst role.

Traditionally, risk management practitioners become the dispassionate conscience of the project, verifying that everyone understands the potential problems the project must effectively confront for it to be successful. It is both an unglamorous and thankless role. However, by pressuring the analyst to seek opportunities to offset the real risks of the project, the analyst is no longer a neutral observer. The analyst will be tasked to look for opportunities to improve the project's perceived performance, despite how realistic or beneficial such opportunities may be. Will the analyst be tempted to push for his or her newly discovered opportunity despite the risk it may bring to the project? Will the analyst be tempted to push the opportunity at the expense of managing existing risks? Will there be a need for another risk analyst to review said opportunity to ensure such prejudices do not exist?

Given that the risks (i.e., threats) are considered "bad," will the analyst be tempted to look only for opportunities because they will make the project manager feel good and keep the analyst in good graces with the boss (and thereby allow potential career advancement)? Will resources for "threat management" be shortchanged in the process? Or, will the project manager dislike being second-guessed on both threats and opportunities and kill any form of risk management outright? The proponents of changing the definition haven't thought through the Pandora's box of implications that such a change may bring.

In my experience, I have never encountered a project that was in trouble because a project manager was "too negative." On the contrary, projects get themselves into trouble because project managers are often much too optimistic about what can be accomplished given the constraints and risks that exist associated with cost, performance, and schedule. Also I don't regularly experience projects whose objectives are too easy to attain, but I do regularly encounter those with unrealistic expectations.

The practice of "traditional" risk management is aimed to ensure that this optimism is realistic and to ensure that the planned-for project expectation is reached, not necessarily exceeded. Exceeding project expectations is not risk management's primary purpose, or is it the first duty of the project manager. Exceeding project expectations is a pleasant experience, but trying to do so more often than not leads to disaster. Unfortunately, the proponents of including opportunity as part of the definition of risk encourage decisions and actions that make exceeding expectations "normal practice." This may cause an unintended consequence of the enterprise setting project expectations at such an unrealistically high level that they cannot be achieved, which then forces excessive risk taking on the project manager's part to try to achieve them.

Further, risk management as a legitimate discipline is already under intense pressure from attacks in many quarters. For instance, it is being increasingly described as a "bogus discipline" that is "on its way out" for "rationalizing government decision making."[8] Changing the definition of risk feeds not only into the hands of those who think risk management is bogus, but also into those who wish to abuse it.

Finally, to some cynical outsiders, the proposed change in definition is nothing more than a consultant's ploy to expand the market for risk management practitioners. This perception, fair or not, does not help promote the need for effective risk management to projects.

IX. Improving Risk Management Practice

I do agree with the proponents of the change in risk management definition on one issue—the current poor practice of risk management. Too many projects still do not practice risk management, and many projects that do, perform it unsatisfactorily if not incompetently. The Cutter survey (earlier mentioned), concerning the state of risk management practice, supports this contention. Because of this situation, easy opportunities for risk handling may not be exploited, leading some projects not to achieve their true potential.

Further, because projects often don't perform competent risk management they frequently find themselves in trouble. Consequently, they have to chase relatively high-risk "opportunities" to bail themselves out of their self-created crisis condition. This leads to the gambler's syndrome of doubling each bet to try to breakeven that plagues almost every troubled project I have ever encountered. I am afraid that the changes the proponents' desire will only increase the number of projects in trouble, instead of reduce them.

What is needed is more education of risk management practitioners and project managers on the subject of correct risk management practice. As I have mentioned, few project risk managers, and even fewer project managers, have much formal training in risk management. Moreover, there is a need to educate senior managers regarding risk *and* opportunity, especially concerning the ridiculous notion that all project risk is somehow bad or reflects poorly on a project manager. A fundamental notion of economics is that without risk there is no profit. Therefore, any worthwhile business opportunity has risk associated with it. Without risk, therefore, projects would have no value to the enterprise. Senior managers need to understand that a project will remain at risk until it is delivered, and even then, new risks are created in new forms as the project is rolled out and becomes operational.

Furthermore, as we have shown earlier, most of the opportunities the proponents claim are overlooked are merely sources of risk handling that many risk management practitioners and project managers often do ignore at their peril. Too much effort in the risk management literature is focused on risk identification and analysis and not enough on how to properly handle (e.g., creatively avoid, control, or transfer) risks. Efforts to improve this area of the risk management process would help alleviate this weakness.

The solutions of the problems voiced by the proponents of the change in definition will be found in improving risk management's processes and practice, not in tampering with its theoretical or practical underpinnings.

X. Conclusion

In this appendix, I have shown that most of the assertions made by the proponents of a change in the definition of risk have little or no merit from either a theoretical or practical perspective. A change in the definition of risk to include opportunities will not likely change the behavior of project managers so that they will now use risk management wisely. More likely, it will encourage them only to abuse it or use it more timidly, and thus less effectively. Nor will a change likely make projects more successful because opportunities that are supposedly being overlooked will now be somehow effectively exploited.

To overcome a perceived deficiency in the current definition of risk, it is far easier to educate project managers regarding the purpose of risk management, or better yet, replace the ones who can't or won't manage risk. I believe that changing the definition of risk is the wrong approach to the wrong problem at the wrong time.

Changing a definition in a scientific or engineering discipline is a radical solution that is reserved for the time when an existing definition does not work in theory or in practice. The proponents of changing the definition of risk have not shown either of these situations to be the case.

I believe the change in the risk management definition is ill conceived, and, in violation of the first law of risk management, causes more harm than good. We should work hard to avoid this irony.

References

[1]Project Management Institute, *A Guide to the Project Management Body of Knowledge (PMBOK® Guide)*, Project Management Institute, Newtown Square, PA, 2000, p. 127.

[2]Hullett, David T., and Hillson, David, "Project 'Risk' Includes Opportunities: It's Not Just a 4-Letter Word Anymore," *Cutter IT Journal*, Vol. 15, No. 2, Feb. 2002, pp. 4–10.

[3]Rowe, William, *An Anatomy of Risk*, Robert E. Kreiger Publishing Co., Malabar, FL, 1988, p. 24.

[4]Hullett, David T., and Hillson, David, "Project 'Risk' Includes Opportunities: It's Not Just a 4-Letter Word Anymore," *Cutter IT Journal*, Vol. 15, No. 2, Feb. 2002, p. 5.

[5]Charette, Robert, *The State of Risk Management Practice 2002: Hype or Reality*, Cutter Consortium, Arlington, MA, 2002, p. 17.

[6]Hullett, David T., and Hillson, David, "Project 'Risk' Includes Opportunities: It's Not Just a 4-Letter Word Anymore," *Cutter IT Journal*, Vol. 15, No. 2, Feb. 2002, p. 6.

[7]Lister, Tim, "Risk Management for Software and System Projects: Utterly Doomed," *Cutter IT Journal*, Vol. 15, No. 2, February 2002, pp. 31–33.

[8]Charnley, Gail, keynote speech to the 1999 Annual Meeting of the Society for Risk Analysis. Ms. Charnley is the society's past president. For more, see the *SRA Risk Newsletter*, Society for Risk Analysis, Vol. 20, No. 1, 2000, p. 3.

Appendix F
Program Structure Models

I. Program Structure Models

"Program structure means the phases and milestone decision points established for a program. Phases and milestone decision points facilitate the orderly translation of broadly stated mission needs into system-specific performance requirements and a stable design that can be produced efficiently. They provide the context within which a system is designed, developed, and deployed during its life cycle."[1]

"The program structure is a fundamental building block of the program's acquisition strategy. It provides the point of departure for those developing the strategy to determine how the system will be acquired. As such, the program structure is described in, and approved as part of, the acquisition strategy."[1]

Six program structure models are briefly mentioned next: traditional, grand design, incremental, evolutionary, vee, and spiral. These models, appropriately tailored, describe program structures suitable for the vast majority of major DoD/NASA and commercial programs. Other structures are needed in some cases (e.g., for low-cost commercial items). When other-than-traditional models are used, the resulting program structure must include specific plans for satisfying the statutory requirements in conjunction with appropriate phases and decision points.

II. Traditional Model

"The traditional model represents DoD's typical approach to major acquisition development programs. Because of its widespread use, statutory requirements tend to be associated with this model's phases and milestone decision points (e.g., 10 USC 2434 requires an independent cost estimate and a manpower estimate at Milestone II, as a prerequisite to the Milestone Decision Authority authorizing commencement of Phase II, Engineering and Manufacturing Development)."[1] (The traditional model is also closely akin to the waterfall model.)

453

III. Grand Design Model

"The grand design model is characterized by acquisition, development, and deployment of the total operational capability in a single increment. The required operational capability can be clearly defined, and further enhancement is not foreseen to be necessary. The grand design model is most appropriate when the user requirements are well understood, supported by precedent, easily defined, and assessment of other considerations (e.g., funding, schedule, risks, size of program, or early realization of benefits) indicates that a phased approach is not required."[1]

IV. Incremental Model

"The incremental model is generally characterized by acquisition, development, and deployment of capability through a number of clearly defined system increments that stand on their own. The number, size, and phasing of the increments required for satisfaction of the total scope of the stated user requirement should be defined by the program manager in consultation with the user. An incremental model is most appropriate when the user requirements are well understood and easily defined, but assessment of other considerations (e.g., risks, funding, schedule, size of program, or early realization of benefits) indicates a phased approach is more prudent or beneficial. An example of this model is Pre-planned Product Improvement P3I."[1]

V. Evolutionary Model

"The evolutionary model is characterized by the design, development, and deployment of a preliminary capability using current technology that includes provisions for the evolutionary addition of future capabilities as requirements are further defined and technologies mature. Evolutionary Defense Acquisition (EDA) combines and collapses the Engineering and Manufacturing development and Production, Fielding/Deployment, and Operational Support phases through maximizing the use of proven state-of-the-art technology and concentrating on manufacturing concurrent with design development."[1]

"The EDA strategy differs from the incremental program strategy in that the total functional capability is not completely defined at inception, but evolves as the system is built. This model offers an alternative to the traditional model for those programs not requiring a leap in technology, where the design process includes technology maturation and where a program can make use of an interim solution with successive upgrades. Evolutionary developments are particularly suited to situations where, although the general scope of the program is known and a basic core of user operational characteristics can be defined, detailed system or operational requirements are difficult to articulate (e.g., decision-aiding systems requiring extensive human-machine interaction)." [1]

"Advanced concept technology demonstrations (ACTDs) and evolutionary models share some similarities in that both involve short cycle times and address a requirement for start-of-the-art technology. ACTDs, however, are oriented to the development of an operational concept and do not necessarily result in a production program. Evolutionary models are oriented toward production from the beginning." [1]

VI. Vee Model

"The vee model, which has a V-shaped flow, was introduced to focus attention on the need to consider test or validation and verification issues at each phase of product development. Initial phases of the vee model define the need and how to test on the left-hand leg of the vee, whereas the later phases of the vee (upward right-hand leg) implement these tests." [2]

VII. Spiral Model

The spiral life-cycle model reflects the underlying concept that each cycle involves a progression that addresses the same sequence of steps, for each portion of the product and for each of its levels of elaboration, from an overall concept of operation document down to the coding of each individual program.[3] The spiral model includes each of the objectives, alternatives, evaluation, and risk resolution steps as one revolution around the life-cycle spiral. Although originally devised for software development, it can also be applied to nonsoftware-intensive projects.

VIII. Other Models

"Other models are intended to encompass variations and/or combinations of the program. Models not listed include commercial off-the-shelf, nondevelopmental item, and commercial item acquisitions." [1]

References

[1]Department of Defense, *Defense Acquisition Deskbook,* Dave Anderson (owner), Version 3.0, June 30, 1999, Sec. 2.3. See also: Department of the Air Force (Software

Technology Support Center), *Guidelines for Successful Acquisition and Management of Software-Intensive Systems*, Vol. 1, Version 3.0, May 2000, Sec. 5.6 for additional information.

[2]Mar, B. W., "Does Choice of Development Life Cycle Model Define Program Risk?" Air Force and Aerospace Corporation Second Symposium on Risk Management, Long Beach, CA, Feb. 1999.

[3]Boehm, B. W., "A Spiral Model of Software Development and Enhancement," *Computer,* Inst. of Electrical and Electronics Engineers, Los Alamitos, CA May 1988, p. 65.

Appendix G:
Sample Language for Including
Risk Management in an RFP
and Evaluating It During Source Selection

I. Proposal Preparation Instructions (Section L) for Technical and/or Management Proposal or Presentation— Comprehensive Version[1]

Describe your risk management process, including risk planning, assessment (identification and analysis), handling, and monitoring functions, and how you plan to implement it on the program. (All material in Section I was quoted or derived from Ref. 1.) Describe how the risk management process is related to the program management and systems engineering processes. Describe your risk assessment (identification and analysis) methodology. Identify all medium- and higher-risk issues for your design. Describe your risk handling approach, including option(s) selected (assumption, avoidance, control, or transfer), plus how you plan to implement it, for these medium- and higher-risk issues. Describe your proposed process including metrics for risk monitoring and how this information will be fed back to risk handling, analysis, and identification activities. Describe your methodology for implementing quantitative cost and schedule risk analyses (including Monte Carlo simulations) applied to life-cycle cost estimates and the program integrated master schedule, respectively, to be implemented postcontract award.

A. Evaluation Criteria (Section M)

The contractor's description of the proposed processes, including the approach to the critical processes to risk management, and solution characteristics will be evaluated during source selection against the *evaluation criteria* in Section M of the Request for Proposal (RFP).

Generally, risk management is not identified as a stand-alone factor, but rather as a subfactor or as a standard under a factor or subfactor. Assuming risk management is a subfactor, items in italics may be directly copied and then tailored for use in an RFP (based on the current policy and the scope of your program) as follows: *Subfactor: Risk Management.*

457

B. Source Selection Standards

After the proposals are received, they are compared to the source selection standards (not to each other). The information listed under each standard should be tailored to the solicitation.

1. Standard 1: Risk Management Process

Describes an effective approach for risk management, including risk planning, assessment (identification and analysis), handling, and monitoring functions. The standard is met if:

1) The offeror addresses how it will perform each function and how the risk management process is integrated into the program management and systems engineering processes.

2) The offeror addresses how the risk management process will be implemented at the prime contractor and major subcontractor levels, including roles and responsibilities of individual groups within each organization.

3) The offeror includes a schedule for performing the risk management process during the contract and describes how the schedule is linked to actions (e.g., assessments) and products.

4) The offeror addresses how the contractor will monitor the effectiveness of the risk management process and how the government will access risk identification and risk analysis results, risk handling plans, schedules, and risk monitoring results.

2. Standard 2: Risk Assessment Methodology

Describes the risk assessment methodology for cost, technical, and schedule risk that is appropriate and suitable for the specific design and program-management approach. The standard is met if:

1) The methodology is discussed in sufficient detail to permit evaluation of its suitability.

2) The offeror addresses its approach for identifying potential risks at the system level and at lower work breakdown structure (WBS) levels.

3) The offeror addresses its risk analysis methodology for cost, technical, and schedule risk areas a) that are likely to exist (e.g., design/engineering risk); b) for hardware, software, and integration categories; and c) for system and lower WBS levels.

4) The methodology addresses both probability and consequence of occurrence components of risk.

3. Standard 3: Risk Identification and Analysis Results

Describes the results of a comprehensive risk assessment performed against the specific design and proposed program management approach, using the methodology proposed by the offeror. This risk assessment will be performed for the proposal and subsequently postcontract award. The standard is met if:

1) The offeror addresses risk assessment areas associated with cost, technical, and schedule a) that are likely to exist (e.g., design/engineering risk); b) for hardware, software, and integration categories; and c) for system and lower WBS levels.
2) The offeror addresses and provides documentation for the ground rules and assumptions used in the risk assessment.
3) The offeror provides documentation of all issues assessed as having medium and higher cost, technical or schedule risk, including a) a brief technical description of the issue, b) risk analysis results, and c) rationale discussing why the issue possesses a medium- or high-risk level.
4) Analysis and documentation of risk issues addresses probability and consequence of occurrence components of risk.
5) Information is provided in sufficient detail that the government evaluator can replicate the results for identified medium- and higher-risk issues given the methodology, and programmatic and technical descriptions of the issues provided by the contractor.

4. Standard 4: Risk Handling and Risk Monitoring Approach
Describes risk handling plans and a risk monitoring approach that are effective and suitable for the proposed effort. The standard is met if the offeror:

1) Describes the risk handling option (assumption, avoidance, control, or transfer) for all issues identified as medium and higher risk.
2) Addresses how suitable risk handling approaches will be identified, implemented, and tracked with time for each medium- and higher-risk issue.
3) Describes cost, technical, and schedule risk monitoring metrics to be used to track and evaluate the progress in reducing risk for each medium- and higher-risk issue.
4) Addresses, as warranted, alternate concepts and/or designs along with cost, performance, and schedule impacts to reduce the potential level of risk for each medium- and higher-risk issue.

5. Standard 5: Quantitative Cost and Schedule Risk Analysis Approach
Describes the methodology to be used to perform quantitative cost and schedule risk analyses to be performed postcontract award. The standard is met if the offeror:

1) Describes the quantitative cost risk analysis methodology to be used. This includes performing a Monte Carlo simulation over all program activi-

ties. The methodology should include a method to model cost estimating uncertainty, schedule risk, and technical risk as it impacts cost risk for selected WBS elements. The methodology should also include an approach to permit the evaluation of cost risk at selected percentiles (e.g., 30, 50 and 70 percentiles), and identifying which WBS elements are cost-risk drivers.

2) Describes the quantitative schedule risk analysis methodology to be used. This includes performing a Monte Carlo simulation over all relevant program activities. The methodology should include a method to model schedule estimating uncertainty, cost risk, and technical risk, as it impacts schedule risk for selected WBS elements. The methodology should also include an approach to permit the evaluation of schedule risk at selected percentiles (e.g., 30th, 50th, and 70th percentiles) and identifying which activities are schedule-risk drivers.

II. Proposal Preparation Instructions (Section L) for Technical and/or Management Proposal or Presentation— Highly Condensed Version

In situations where you can only include a single sentence pertaining to risk management in the RFP Section L, I suggest the following sentence: Implement aggressive risk management throughout the effort, including risk planning, assessment (identification and analysis), handling and monitoring steps. A two-sentence version of the preceding sentence is the following: Implement aggressive risk management throughout the effort, including risk planning, assessment (identification and analysis), handling, and monitoring steps. The risk management process should be consistent with the May 1999 (or more recent) Defense Acquisition University *Risk Management Guide for DoD Acquisition.*[2]

References

[1]Conrow E. H. (principal author), "Risk Management Critical Process Assessment Tool (CPAT)," U.S. Air Force SMC/AXD, Version 2, June 1998; in the *Defense Acquisition Deskbook,* Version 2.5, Sept. 1998, and greater. (In the *Defense Acquisition Deskbook* the document is dated Aug. 14, 1998.)

[2]Department of Defense, *Risk Management Guide for DoD Acquisition,* 5th ed., Defense Acquisition Univ., Ft. Belvoir, VA, June 2002. While the May 1999 second ed. of the *Risk Management Guide for DoD Acquisition* includes a number of key corrections over the first ed. (March 1998), additional enhancements have been made since that time and the most current edition (now the fifth ed.) should be used.

Appendix H:
Some Characteristics and Limitations of
Ordinal Scales in Risk Analyses

In this appendix, I provide a more extensive discussion of some characteristics and limitations of uncalibrated and calibrated ordinal scales in risk analyses.

I. Some Classes of Ordinal "Probability" Scales

Based upon having evaluated hundreds of ordinal "probability" of occurrence scales, six classes are commonly used in project risk management. These include maturity, sufficiency, complexity, uncertainty, estimative probability, and probability-based scales. I have intentionally structured each of the uncalibrated ordinal "probability" scales contained in the following discussion with scale values of E, D, C, B, and A, where $E > D > C > B > A$ to underscore the point that numerical scale values are meaningless because the actual values are unknown.

"Probability" scales based on maturity typically involve an underlying, applicable process (e.g., technology or manufacturing maturation). Maturity-based scales generally can be subdivided into two categories: scales that represent a snapshot in time (e.g., a specific type of design approach) and those that correspond to a potentially changing activity (e.g., track the development of a particular technology from concept, breadboard, brassboard, prototype to operational unit). (An example of a maturity scale based on a potentially changing activity is given in Table H.1.) The disadvantage of scales based on a snapshot in time is the "probability" value may not change over the course of the program phase. For example, if a specific design approach is taken, this may remain the same over the development phase. Maturity risk analysis scales will generally yield poor results unless the process is well structured, stable, and repeatable.

"Probability" scales based on sufficiency typically involve resources (e.g., personnel or software development tools). This type of risk analysis scale will generally yield poor results unless a logical flow of the quantity and quality of resources can be adequately described and the identified resources represent a well-structured and repeatable flow. (An example of a sufficiency scale is given in Table H.2.)

"Probability" scales based on complexity typically involve an attribute of performance, e.g., gimbal pointing error (microradians). Such risk analysis

Table H.1 Example of ordinal "probability" maturity scale

Definition	Scale level
Basic principles observed	E
Concept design analyzed for performance	D
Breadboard or brassboard validation in relevant environment	C
Prototype passes performance tests	B
Item deployed and operational	A

scales will yield poor results unless they include a valid method of relating complexity to probability level and the relationship between complexity and probability level is objective and can be validated. [This is often times not the case—most complexity-based "probability" scales do not satisfactorily relate complexity and probability level. An example of an inadequate complexity scale is given in Table H.3, where ICD refers to interface control document. Here, the scale definitions represent an immeasurable cause and effect (see Chapter 6, Sec. IV.M for additional information).]

"Probability" scales based on uncertainty typically involve the level to which key information is available (e.g., requirements) or stable (e.g., requirements stability). Such risk analysis scales will yield poor results unless they include a valid method of relating the information available or its level of stability to probability or at the least a well-documented, consistent manner to rank order the results. (An example of an *inadequate* uncertainty scale is given in Table H.4; note the subjective wording used.)

Probability scales based on estimative probability attempt to relate a probability statement (word descriptor, e.g., high) to a probability value (e.g., 0.80), as discussed in Chapter 6, Sec. IV.A. An example of an ordinal estimative probability scale using point estimates derived from a statistical analysis of survey data is given in Table H.5. This scale is derived from a statistical analysis of survey responses (see Appendix J). In some instances the estimative probability value and score are both given; in other cases only

Table H.2 Example of ordinal "probability" sufficiency scale

Definition	Scale level
Research personnel required	E
Insufficient high-skilled personnel	D
Insufficient moderate/low-skilled personnel	C
Sufficient personnel but training required	B
Sufficient trained personnel	A

Table H.3 Example of ordinal "probability" complexity scale

Definition	Scale level
Greater than 20% of the interface design is altered because of modifications to the ICDs	E
Greater than 15% but less than 20% of the interface design is altered because of modifications to the ICDs	D
Greater than 10% but less than 15% of the interface design is altered because of modifications to the ICDs	C
At least 5% but less than 10% of the interface design is altered because of modifications to the ICDs	B
Less than 5% of the interface design is altered because of modifications to the ICDs	A

the estimative probability is provided. In general, a suitable measure of uncertainty derived from a statistical analysis of the survey information should be presented along with the probability point estimate. (See Chapter 6, Sec. IV.C and Appendix J for additional information.)

Probability scales that represent probabilities typically are based on historical distributions of probability vs event (e.g., schedule length from Milestone I to Milestone II). Such risk analysis scales will yield poor results unless the scale levels are derived from a sample that is both large enough and similar to the item in question (e.g., an estimate derived from an aircraft database should not be used to evaluate the risk of a ground system) and applied at the same work breakdown structure (WBS) level as the underlying database. (An example of a probability scale is given in Table H.6. The procedure for deriving this type of scale is given in Appendix K.)

There are, of course, a wide variety of ordinal "probability" scale classes possible. However, almost all other classes I have examined are severely flawed and should be avoided. I will present an example of one such scale, a hybrid "probability" of occurrence and risk handling scale, used on several programs.

Table H.4 Example of ordinal "probability" uncertainty scale

Definition	Scale level
Frequent, major changes in requirements	E
Frequent, moderate changes in requirements	D
Frequent, small changes in requirements	C
Small, noncritical changes in requirements	B
No changes in requirements	A

Table H.5   Example of ordinal estimative probability scale

Definition	Median probability value	Scale level
Certain	0.95	E
High	0.85	D
Medium	0.45	C
Low	0.15	B
Almost no chance	0.05	A

Hybrid ordinal "probability" scales that also include information on risk handling should be shunned, especially when they are the program's sole "probability" scale because they may be inaccurate, improper, and confusing. An example of a hybrid ordinal estimative probability scale that also includes handling information is given in Table H.7.

There are several problems with this hybrid scale. First, the estimative probability information represents point values with unknown pedigree, but likely not derived from a statistical analysis of survey information because the coefficients are symmetrical around the midvalue (although the coefficient values vary with scale level). Second, the risk handling information provided is both irrelevant and confusing when used with an ordinal "probability" scale (or an estimative probability table) for risk analysis. This is because *the level of risk and other considerations* should determine the need for risk handling actions, *not solely the probability level*. For example, suppose an issue has a highly likely probability (e.g., scale level D from Table H.7), but a very low consequence of occurrence. The net result of this combination could be a low risk, and hardly one where the program "cannot avoid this risk with standard practices." Third, the risk handling definitions point to avoidance as the primary risk handling option, whereas all four options (avoidance, assumption, control, and transfer) should be evaluated for each medium or higher risk. Fourth, the risk handling information includes a somewhat specific approach for implementing risk handling. Again, a variety of strategies should be evalu-

Table H.6   Example of ordinal probability scale

Probability	Schedule length	Scale level
0.80 < probability ≤ 1.00	0.0 ≤ schedule length < 2.4 yr	E
0.60 < probability ≤ 0.80	2.4 ≤ schedule length < 3.6 yr	D
0.40 < probability ≤ 0.60	3.6 ≤ schedule length < 4.4 yr	C
0.20 < probability ≤ 0.40	4.4 ≤ schedule length < 5.5 yr	B
0.00 < probability ≤ 0.20	5.5 ≤ schedule length ≤ 10.3 yr	A

Table H.7   Example of ordinal hybrid "probability" of occurrence and risk handling scale

Chance of occurrence	Your approach and processes	Scale level
Near certainty: 90% chance	Cannot avoid this risk with standard practices, probably not able to mitigate	E
Highly likely: 75% chance	Cannot avoid this risk with standard practices, but a different approach may work	D
Moderate: 50% chance	May avoid this risk, but work arounds will be required	C
Low likelihood: 25% chance	Have usually avoided this type of risk with minimal oversight in similar cases	B
Not likely: 10% chance	Will effectively avoid this risk based on standard practices	A

ated for the selected risk handling option. Fifth, if the analyst using this scale identifies a "probability" level for a given risk issue, the risk handling strategy given in the scale may conflict with that desired or needed for the risk issue in question. If this occurs, then there can be an internal inconsistency while using the scale between the "probability" and risk handling information, and the user may misclassify the scale level. (See Chapter 6, Sec. IV.C for several additional problems with developing and using ordinal scales or tables derived from estimative probability data.)

Six classes of ordinal "probability" of occurrence scales are commonly used in project risk management. These include maturity, sufficiency, complexity, uncertainty, estimative probability, and probability-based scales. Each class of scales includes a different set of limitations, and the results will be inaccurate and/or uncertain unless the proper scale class is used and the specific scales are carefully constructed.

II.   Some Additional Examples of Invalid Mathematical Operations Performed on Ordinal Scale Values

The risk probability of occurrence term is very often not actually probability, particularly if generated from ordinal scales. Unless the term is a true probability there is little or no basis for performing mathematical operations (e.g., Risk Factor = P * C), and the results generated by such operations can be misleading or erroneous. Because uncalibrated ordinal scales can never yield probabilities unless they were originally derived from true probability data, there is almost never any valid basis for performing mathematical operations on results derived from them.

The misapplication of mathematical operations can be obvious, such as when the average is computed of uncalibrated ordinal scale probability and consequence of occurrence values then the risk factor is determined from these averages [Risk Factor = P(average) * C(average)]. However, the errors present may be more subtle, yet may also lead to invalid results.

For example, the data contained in Table H.8 are actually derived from two sets of uncalibrated ordinal "probability" and consequence of occurrence scales. Here, ordinal "probability" scale values (1, 2, 3, 4, and 5) have been normalized by the highest level (5) to yield decimal values (1/5 = 0.2, 2/5 = 0.4, 3/5 = 0.6, 4/5 = 0.8, and 5/5 = 1.0). The normalized "probability" values were then converted to a "probability" range (e.g., 1.0 was changed to $0.8 < p \leq 1.0$). Finally, the "probability" range values were multiplied by uncalibrated consequence ordinal scale values (1, 3, and 5) to yield a risk value range, e.g., $0.8 < p \leq 1.0 * 5 = 4.1 - 5.0$ (upper right-hand cell). *So despite the cardinal appearance, the risk scores (e.g., 4.1–5.0) in Table H.8 have no numerical meaning other than indicating an ordering of results.* [For example, moving from the lower left-hand corner (0.0–0.2) to the upper right-hand corner (4.1–5.0) in the matrix leads to higher levels of risk.]

Given the data in Table H.8, the Risk Factor = P * C was then calculated, and a range of risk values were then mapped into risk summary levels (low, moderate, and high), as illustrated in Table H.9. Here, the result is not truly risk (but perhaps an indicator of risk) because the "probability" values were

Table H.8 Example of risk ranges where probability and consequence of occurrence levels are derived from uncalibrated ordinal scales

Probability of occurrence	Minor = 1	Moderate = 3	Severe = 5
Very likely ($0.8 < p \leq 1.0$)	0.9–1.0	2.5–3.0	4.1–5.0
Likely ($0.6 < p \leq 0.8$)	0.7–0.8	1.9–2.4	3.1–4.0
Probable ($0.4 < p \leq 0.6$)	0.5–0.6	1.3–1.8	2.1–3.0
Unlikely ($0.2 < p \leq 0.4$)	0.3–0.4	0.7–1.2	1.1–2.0
Very unlikely ($0 < p \leq 0.2$)	0.0–0.2	0–0.6	0.0–1.0

Consequence of Occurrence

**Table H.9   Example of risk value
range vs risk level risk value range
derived from uncalibrated ordinal scales**

Risk value	Risk level
3.0 – 5.0	High
1.5 – 2.9	Medium
0 – 1.4	Low

derived from (uncalibrated) ordinal scales and are almost certainly not probabilities. The mapping of risk values into low, moderate, and high levels is acceptable because this could have been accomplished by examining the combination of the two variables in a matrix (e.g., 5 X 3 for probability and consequence in Table H.8) rather than the product of the variables. However, if the resulting risk values are then used in any mathematical operation (including roll ups), the results will likely be erroneous.

Another instance of potential abuse is when "probability" and/or consequence values are obtained from granular ordinal scales (e.g., 10 levels) then mapped into a matrix. The danger in this case is that a false sense of accuracy exists, and the uncertainty present is generally unknown. This is all the worse when numerical decimal scores are used, as if each matrix cell corresponds to a range of "probability" and consequence of occurrence values (e.g., Level $1 = 0 < p \leq 0.1$). In such cases cardinal evaluations or rankings of the results will generally be meaningless, and only ordinal rankings will have any value. (Of course, if the scores that are placed in the matrix are derived by taking the average of a series of "probability" and consequence of occurrence values, then the results will likely be erroneous.)

The risk probability of occurrence term is very often not actually probability, particularly if generated from ordinal scales. Unless the term is a true probability there is little or no basis for performing mathematical operations, and the results generated by such operations can be mislead or erroneous.

III.   Some Specific Deficiencies with Ordinal Scales

A large number of problems may exist with ordinal scales used for deriving "probability" of occurrence and consequence of occurrence, even if no mathematical operations are performed on the results. (Note: As already mentioned, true probability of occurrence, and thus risk, can never be derived from ordinal scales unless the ordinal scales themselves were originally derived from actual probability data or are calibrated with actual probability data.) I will now briefly discuss each of these problems:

1) The scale may include an insufficient number of levels (e.g., three). This can introduce substantial uncertainty into the results. For example, a miscalculation of a single level in the same direction on both the "probability" and consequence of occurrence scales can change the resulting risk level from low to moderate, etc. Three scale levels are generally too few, whereas ten or more levels are generally too many. In the former case there is generally too little granularity, whereas in the latter case too much. The tendency when only three levels are used is to automatically assume they represent low, medium, and high, which may not necessarily be the case. (Three-level estimative probability scales that are based upon point values or ranges should especially be avoided because they are often highly subjective and difficult for the analyst to properly interpret and score.) When a large number of scale intervals are used, the possibility exists that ambiguities between two or three adjacent scale-level definitions may occur. In addition, a large number of scale levels are generally inappropriate unless a well-defined, repeatable process exists that is being evaluated.

2) The scale definitions may be too simple. For example, one-, two-, or three-word scale definitions should also be avoided because they are too subjective even if supplementary material is available. An example of such a definition is "newer technology" for technology risk. This can confuse the analyst and introduce uncertainty in scoring. Although there is no firm rule, based on having evaluated hundreds of ordinal scales, carefully constructed scale definitions with five or more words may be a practical minimum number of words needed to help prevent the analyst from making a potentially erroneous interpretation.

3) The scale definition may include several separate thoughts and/or sentences, which can lead to a variety of interpretation problems for the analyst. These problems can include 1) one part of the definition implying a different level of "probability" or consequence of occurrence than other parts, 2) how results should be interpreted among the parts, and 3) uncorrelated components that may exist within the definition. An example of a multithought and sentence ordinal "probability" scale definition for a moderate level (middle level of a five level scale) is listed here:

> A significant shortfall exists between the system requirement and performance demonstrated in existing systems. The performance requirement is near the state-of-the-art. Only components of the item are currently under development or in the testing and evaluation process. Major change in existing software modules/lines of code. Breadboards/brassboards exist and technical/size/weight/ integration issues have been addressed but may not have been resolved.

Lengthy ordinal scale-level definitions should be avoided because they provide the possibility of multiple attributes per level or ambiguities for a given level or between levels. For example, if three separate attributes must be met to move from a score of C to B, how should the analyst interpret meeting one of the three criteria or two of the three criteria, but not all three? Although the conservative approach is to require all criteria be met to achieve the next lowest score (in this case going from C to B), it may well be better to focus the ordinal scale definition to a single attribute and provide clarifying information in a supplementary write-up.

Similarly, as the number of scale definition attributes increases, so does the possibility of having ambiguities for a given scale level or between two or three adjacent scale levels. For example, if three attributes exist for scale levels D and E, it may be possible that one or more of the attributes for scale level D may actually imply a lower level of maturity than one or more attributes for scale level E, thus violating the underlying assumption that the scale is monotonic and positive in nature. This can lead to a scoring error, the magnitude of which may be more than a single scale level if the analyst is confused and keys on a particular phrase separately, rather than in the context of the entire scale.

Based on having evaluated hundreds of ordinal scales, a definition with generally less than 10 words, or certainly less than 15 words, is likely sufficient to convey the intent of the scale level without creating a multiattribute or ambiguous definition. Additional information to convey nuances and clarify the scale-level definitions can be provided separately. Thus while there are no firm rules, 5 or more words may be a likely practical minimum to help prevent potentially erroneous interpretation, and 15 words or less is a likely maximum without introducing multiattribute or ambiguous definitions (cet. par.). (Of course, a poorly worded 10-word scale definition may be inferior to a carefully worded 5-word definition. Hence, quality of the definition is the primary consideration, and word count is a secondary consideration.)

4) The scale definitions may include terms implying probability (e.g., moderate and high) when none are warranted. An example of a definition containing terms implying probability is "good probability of some moderate deficiencies in personnel availability." In addition, this scale definition is highly subjective and confusing.

5) The scale definitions are subjective, or break points included in the definition are subjective. An example of a subjective definition is "good probability of some moderate deficiencies in personnel availability." An example of a subjective breakpoint within a scale-level definition is "one AC voltage cycle (frequency), one AC voltage levels, and two DC voltage levels" for electronic box integration.

6) The scale definition may imply a higher or lower level (e.g., less mature on a "probability" scale) than the value actually assigned to the scale level. Thus, the definition and scale-level value are inconsistent. For example, on a five-level maturity scale, the lowest level (Level 1) should typically represent an item that is operational, deployed, in high rate production, etc. It

would thus be inconsistent for the next highest scale level (Level 2) to represent scientific research, when it should represent a prototype unit, etc. A somewhat related problem is scale definitions that have an internally inconsistent rank ordering (e.g., does not vary in a monotonic fashion). For example, Level 3 has wording that implies a higher level of maturity, thus lower level of risk, than Level 2, which should be less mature (cet. par.).

7) There is no ideal value that should be assigned for ordinal "probability" and consequence of occurrence scale levels. Because the scales are only ordinal, no single set of values are correct, so long as the ordering of scale levels is maintained (e.g., E > D > C > B > A is just as valid as 5 > 4 > 3 > 2 > 1). My recommendation is to use letters for values (e.g., E > D > C > B > A), which dissuades analysts and decision makers from attempting to perform inappropriate math, which can lead to erroneous results.

Some analysts select decimal interval values between 0.0 and 1.0 (e.g., 0.9) to describe an ordinal scale. This practice should be avoided because it appears to add unwarranted credibility and accuracy to the scale values. For example, scale values are not probabilities but may be labeled as such. When decimal numbers represent the scale values, this may further entice individuals to perform math on the results. In addition, there is no correct rationale for assigning decimal scale values other than preserving numerical ordering (e.g., 0.9 > 0.7 > 0.5 and so on). For example, for a five-level scale the ordered values 1, 0.8, 0.6, 0.4 and 0.2 are no more meaningful than 0.9, 0.7, 0.5, 0.3 and 0.1 or 0.8, 0.6, 0.4, 0.2, and 0, and so on.

8) A range of values may be assigned to a single-scale level (e.g., 0.8 < value ≤ 1.0) when there is no basis whatsoever for assigning a range. In most cases the range used is contrived and has no statistical basis. For example, as discussed in Sec. II, it is improper to normalize ordinal "probability" scale values (1, 2, 3, 4, and 5) by the highest level (5) to yield decimal values (1/5 = 0.2, 2/5 = 0.4, 3/5 = 0.6, 4/5 = 0.8, and 5/5 = 1.0), then convert these normalized "probability" values to a "probability" range (e.g., 1.0 was changed to 0.8 < p ≤ 1.0). In rare instances an estimative ordinal probability scale or probability table may exist that is derived from survey responses and includes valid statistical measures representing a range (e.g., Table 6.5, Chapter 6) or an ordinal scale is based upon actual probability data (e.g., Table H.6 and Appendix K).

9) Inaccurate interval scaling may exist among levels, rather than simply using rank ordering. Attempts to arbitrarily weight ordinal scale levels that were not originally derived from cardinal data by applying binary coefficients,[1] linear or constant weighting,[1] exponential[2], logarithmic,[2] or other scaling types will almost always lead to uncertain if not erroneous results. For example, 1 set of 5-level ordinal "probability" scales used the following relationship between the score and the 11 values contained within the 5 scale levels: score = 0 (value 1, most mature), score = 2 (values 1 and 2), score = 3 (values 3, 4, and 5), score = 4 (values 6, 7, and 8), and score = 5 (values 9 and

10, least mature). In this case the number of values per scale level were 1 (scale Level 1, value of 0), 2 (scale Level 2, values of 1 or 2), 3 (scale Level 3, values of 3, 4, or 5), 3 (scale Level 4, values of 6, 7, or 8), and 2 (scale Level 5, values of 9 or 10). Hence, in this case the relationship between the number of values per scale level varies in a nonconstant, nonrepeatable manner.

In addition, even if a set of reasonable coefficients exist for the levels of one scale, they can almost never be transferred to another scale because of the underlying differences between the definitions associated with the corresponding levels in the two scales as well as differences in the probability or consequence of occurrence categories. Similarly, even if calibrated scale coefficients have been derived through an appropriate technique (see Sec. VII), it is not possible to apply accurately the coefficients from one scale to any other scale.

10) The scale levels may have inappropriate titles, which may connote a false sense of accuracy or confuse the analyst. For example, a scale level titled *low* may confuse the analyst if it is attached to the third level of a five-level scale. It is thus often better not to use level titles than to use ones that can potentially confuse the analyst.

11) Correlation may exist between parts of scales for different risk categories (e.g., technology and manufacturing) or subcategories (e.g., manufacturing process and manufacturing production equipment for manufacturing). This problem often occurs at the highest and lowest scale levels, which imply, for example, scientific research and operational systems, respectively. If the subcategories or categories are correlated with each other, then they are not statistically independent. Statistical independence may be a necessary assumption for performing some mathematical operations on ordinal scale values, particularly if the erroneous assumption is made that scale values are probabilities. However, even if correlation coefficient(s) between scales can be identified, they cannot be used in any meaningful way to adjust the numerical results because of the ordinal, nonprobability limitations present.

12) Some ordinal "probability" of occurrence scales actually represent consequence of occurrence or (overall) risk. This is unfortunately not rare and can introduce an error into estimating probability of occurrence. For example in one case, an ordinal "probability" scale for criticality to mission exists, but from examining the scale definitions, it actually is more closely related to the performance component of consequence of occurrence than probability of occurrence. Other instances exist where scale definitions relate to risk rather than probability of occurrence. However, the analyst should be careful to screen out both scales and definitions related to consequence of occurrence or risk when developing ordinal "probability" of occurrence scales.

A large number of problems may exist with ordinal scales used for deriving "probability" of occurrence and consequence of occurrence. The analyst should be exceedingly careful in recommending ordinal scales for use on a program, whether they are being developed for the program or reused from another program, and should be prepared to edit the scales to remove potential difficulties.

IV.   Estimating Consequence of Occurrence with Ordinal Scales

Consequence of occurrence is sometimes evaluated at the wrong WBS level when ordinal scales are used. Consequence of occurrence should always be analyzed at the WBS level associated with the item under evaluation (unit level), such as a focal plane array detector chip. In some cases there may also be convincing reasons to evaluate consequence of occurrence at a WBS level higher than the unit being evaluated (e.g., a spacecraft payload, a single spacecraft, or even the architecture level), but this should be done in addition to, not instead of, an evaluation at the unit level.

Always analyze consequence of occurrence at the WBS level associated with the item under evaluation. If evaluation at a higher WBS level is also necessary, do this in addition to, not instead of, evaluation at the unit level.

In general, much greater effort is expended developing ordinal "probability" rather than consequence of occurrence scales. This is often times a mistake because probability and consequence of occurrence are equal terms of risk. In addition, an overly simplistic methodology for assessing consequence of occurrence may be used. For example, a three-level uncalibrated ordinal scale is sometimes used, which does not adequately capture the complexity or nature of the consequence of occurrence term for cost, performance, or schedule. Because a three-level scale is coarse, substantial uncertainty can be introduced into the results. In this case an uncertainty of just ± one-half level could lead to a change in the resulting risk level (e.g., from low to medium) (cet. par.). In other cases poorly worded scales are used, which can lead to misscoring the consequence of occurrence, and thus impact the resulting risk level.

Much greater time and effort are usually expended in developing ordinal "probability" over consequence of occurrence scales. Weak or inadequate consequence of occurrence scales can adversely affect estimates of risk. Consequence of occurrence scales should undergo the same level of development rigor and scrutiny as expended on "probability" of occurrence scales.

If ordinal cost and schedule consequence of occurrence scales are used, the boundaries for each scale level should be tailored to the specific program if they are given in actual units (e.g., dollars for cost or time for schedule) rather than percentage values (e.g., 5 to 10%). Using nontailored cost and schedule consequence of occurrence scales can lead to substantial errors in estimating both consequence and risk in cases where the program the scales are applied to is substantially different than the type of program that the scales were derived from.

For example, assume two development programs: a $20-million program and a $200-million program. Also assume a potential cost impact of $2 million for a given WBS element. For the $20-million program this corresponds to 10%, whereas for the $200-million program this corresponds to 1%. If a 5-level cost consequence scale is used with the levels corresponding <5% (level 1), ≥ 5% to < 10% (level 2), ≥ 10% to < 20% (level 3), ≥ 20% to < 30% (level 4) and ≥ 30% (level 5), then the $2-million cost impact for the small program corresponds to a scale level = 3, while for the large program the scale level = 1.

Similar problems exist for ordinal schedule consequence of occurrence scales, when the units provided for scale intervals correspond to time (e.g., months) rather than percentage values. Finally, even if percentage values are used to define scale-level intervals rather than actual units (e.g., dollars or time), the percentage values should be tailored to the program in question to ensure that they are meaningful.

If ordinal cost and schedule consequence of occurrence scales are used, the boundaries for each scale level should be tailored to the specific program; particularly if they are given in actual units (e.g., dollars for cost or time for schedule) to prevent misscoring the resulting consequence and risk results.

A related issue is that ordinal consequence of occurrence scale coefficients should not be selected in an arbitrary manner or the risk analysis results can be adversely affected. For example, in one case for schedule impact on a 10-level scale, the following criteria were used: none (Level 1), > 1% (Level 2), > 2% (Level 3), > 3% (Level 4), > 4% (Level 5), > 5% (Level 6), > 6% (Level 7), > 7% (Level 8), > 8% (Level 9), and > 9% (Level 10). Such a criteria selection is not only arbitrary, but mathematically invalid (e.g., Level 1 should read 0% ≤ value < 1%, Level 2 should read 1% ≤ value < 2%, and so on). Unfortunately, I found this ordinal consequence of occurrence scale being used on a multibillion dollar program! Likewise, I have observed highly nonlinear ordinal consequence of occurrence scale coefficient values that did not appear to have a sound rationale being applied to high-value programs. In one case the four scale levels were assigned values ranging from high (30 to 100), medium (3 to 30), low (0.3 to 3), and negligible (0 to 0.3). Thus in this case the potential range in scale coefficients is 1000 (e.g., 100 / 0.1), in just 1 scale! Scale coefficients should be derived using real world data to the extent possible, especially when such large ranges are proposed or else estimated through a structured process (e.g., evaluating an additive utility function) and not simply guessed.

As in the "probability" of occurrence case, ordinal consequence of occurrence scale coefficients should not be selected in an arbitrary manner, or the risk analysis results can be adversely affected. Scale coefficients should be derived using real world data to the extent possible or else estimated through a structured process (e.g., evaluating an additive utility function) and not simply guessed.

Assuming that ordinal cost and schedule consequence of occurrence scales are used, the analyst must also include, as part of the ground rules and assumptions, what program phase or phases the risk analysis will be performed to avert potential misscoring results. It may also be necessary to adjust the consequence of occurrence range values to a given program phase, particularly if actual units are used (e.g., dollars and time) rather than percentage range values (e.g., $\geq 10\%$ to $< 20\%$). This is important because a level of cost increase or schedule slip for an item measured against a single program phase will often yield a different dollar amount or percentage value vs comparison to the remainder of the life cycle.

For example, if the program is currently in Program Definition and Risk Reduction (PDRR) but if the risk analysis must be done over the program's remaining life cycle, which at that point in time includes PDRR, Engineering and Manufacturing Development (EMD), and Production, Fielding/Deployment, and Operational Support phases, then the resulting potential cost impact will typically be much larger on a dollar basis than if it were measured solely against the PDRR phase. Thus, the dollar and time range values selected for cost and schedule consequence of occurrence scales must also be balanced to the desired program phase or phases that the risk analysis is performed against. The same issue will exist if cost and schedule consequence of occurrence scale definitions are given in percentages. Here, the interval ranges given in each scale-level definition (e.g., level = 3 = $\geq 10\%$ to $< 20\%$ increase in cost and/or schedule) must also be adjusted to the desired program phase or phases that the risk analysis is performed against.

Finally, it is desirable to tie cost and schedule consequence of occurrence scale definitions to specific program issues, else the scale levels will be somewhat arbitrary. For example, a schedule slip > 6 months may correspond to a schedule consequence of occurrence scale level and value of 5. However, there is no intuitively obvious reason why this definition should apply to the maximum scale level. A better approach here is to set the upper-bound scale definition to the period of time when the program would be canceled or substantially restructured. This would more accurately represent the intent of the maximum scale level than a seemingly arbitrary value.

If ordinal cost and schedule consequence of occurrence scales are used, the program phase or phases the risk analysis will be performed to in the ground rules and assumptions prevent misscoring results. It may also be necessary to adjust the consequence of occurrence range values to a given program phase and potential program issues to ensure they accurately represent the program.

Consequence of occurrence scales that are based on either actual values (e.g., $20-million cost growth) or percentage values (e.g., $> 20\%$ cost growth) may lead to a risk level greater than low even after the risk issue is closed. If a nontrivial cost growth or schedule slippage occurred during the course of the program, the corresponding ordinal consequence of occurrence scale level may be large (e.g., a score of 4 or 5 on a 5-level scale). This coupled with even a modest score with an ordinal "probability" scale can lead to a risk level larger than low (e.g., medium low for five risk levels and possibly medium for three risk levels).

The analyst can treat this problem in one of several different ways: two of them are given here. First, the risk can be noted at its computed level (e.g., low medium), and the analyst can include a brief discussion that the risk level is driven by an impact (consequence of occurrence) that has already occurred (e.g., cost growth) and that future anticipated cost changes are $X or Y percent. (A similar approach can also be used for schedule consequence changes.) Second, the analyst can view the changes incrementally so that cost or schedule changes recorded beyond a given point in time are not added to the total cost growth or schedule slippage to date (e.g., if $20-million cost growth has already occurred and an additional cost growth of $1 million occurs, then the result might be scored as a consequence of $1 million). The second approach will tend to lower risk scores for items successfully completed by effectively changing the consequence of occurrence baseline. Although this approach may appear attractive, it should not be used unless the entire program is rebaselined. This is because of the potential for error and abuse resulting from incrementally adjusting the item's baseline and changing the consequence of occurrence score, thus potentially underreporting cost and schedule growth and underestimating risk levels.

When ordinal consequence of occurrence scales are used, risk levels greater than low may result even after the risk issue is closed. Unless the entire program is rebaselined, track the computed risk level and note that the risk level is driven by an impact that has already occurred, rather than adjusting the consequence of occurrence value.

In some instances when using ordinal scales, it may be helpful to instruct analysts to estimate consequence of occurrence assuming that the probability of occurrence equals one. Clearly probability and consequence of occurrence are separate risk terms. However, this approach seems to help at least some analysts to evaluate more accurately consequence of occurrence. One possible explanation is that it removes any doubt from their mind that the consequence (risk impact) will occur.

When using ordinal scales, it may be helpful to instruct analysts to estimate consequence of occurrence assuming that the probability of occurrence equals one.

V. Other Classes of Ordinal Scales

Although it is sometimes appropriate to develop ordinal "probability" and consequence of occurrence scales, other classes of scales sometimes exist in risk analysis. One example is a scale related to time sensitivity (e.g., time before a decision must be made or time before the risk issue becomes a problem). Although such scales may seem helpful, they may present no useful information beyond the raw, underlying numbers. In some cases the raw data may actually be more useful than scores from such an ordinal scale. For example, knowing that a decision has to be made in less than 6 months is far more meaningful in most cases than assigning an ordinal scale value of 4 (or any other such value). Hence, ordinal scales for supporting risk information (e.g., the frequency of occurrence, time sensitivity, and interdependence with other risk issues) should be avoided.

Do not develop ordinal scales for supporting risk information. The underlying raw data associated with supporting risk information (e.g., the frequency of occurrence, time sensitivity, and interdependence with other risk issues) are generally far more valuable than scores derived from associated ordinal scales.

VI.   Upper and Lower Bounds for Ordinal Scales

Ordinal "probability" of occurrence scales should have an upper-bound level that corresponds to the least mature (or most complex, etc.) state that will exist. The lower-bound level should correspond to the most mature (or least complex, etc.) state that will exist. Similarly, ordinal consequence of occurrence scales should have an upper-bound level corresponding to the worst likely impact and lower-bound level for the smallest likely impact that will exist. At a minimum the upper- and lower-scale boundaries must be valid for the program phase under evaluation (e.g., PDRR). If they are not, then biased risk analysis results may occur, particularly when the number of scale levels is small.

For example, if the upper-bound level on a five-level probability scale does not represent the true upper bound (in effect, it is lower than the true upper bound), then the remaining levels are biased downward. Although this may not be an issue for an individual probability level, it is for the entire probability (or consequence) of occurrence scale. When the probability and consequence levels are mapped into a risk matrix (which yields say low, low medium, medium, medium high, and high risk levels, as illustrated in Chapter 6, Sec. IX. A), then this may translate into a risk value that is biased downward (cet. par.) vs the actual level of risk present. Similar arguments apply to the lower-bound level. When it does not represent the true lower bound, then the resulting scale values and risk are biased upward. When both types of problems exist (incorrect upper- and lower-bound values), then the scale levels will be compressed toward the center, and risk values toward either extreme (low or high) will tend to be reduced (cet. par.)

The upper- and lower-bound levels for ordinal "probability" scales should be carefully specified to ensure the they represent the least and most

mature (or complex, etc.) state that will exist. Similarly, ordinal conse-
quence of occurrence scales should have an upper-bound level correspond-
ing to the worst likely impact and a lower-bound level for the smallest
likely impact that will exist.

VII. Calibration of Ordinal Scales

Various techniques can potentially be used to calibrate ordinal scales. However, there is no single, superior method. Typically, these approaches use a form of the additive utility function to estimate the preference or utility among the scale intervals based on the supplied scale definitions or among the risk categories. Effectively, a utility score is calculated for each objective, and the scores are added and weighted appropriately according to the relative importance of the various objectives. (Objectives here include individual scale levels and individual probability and consequence of occurrence categories.) The theory behind calibration and the procedure for calibrating ordinal "probability" and consequence of occurrence scales is complex and beyond the scope of this book. However, there are a number of suitable references available, although several require a solid mathematical background.[3]

Techniques exist based on additive utility theory for calibrating ordinal
probability and consequence of occurrence scales. The calibration proce-
dure and underlying theory is complex and should not be undertaken
without a substantial commitment of resources and well-trained personnel.

The same process and techniques can be applied to calibrate ordinal "probability" scales as well as ordinal consequence of occurrence scales. Similarly, calibration coefficients can be derived between hardware "probability" scales (e.g., design/engineering and technology) just as they can between consequence of occurrence components (e.g., cost, performance, and schedule). It may be tempting to simply say that the various "probability" scales or the cost, performance (technical), and schedule consequence components are weighted equally. However, this assumption is rarely valid. In addition, it is likely that the government and prime contractor (or prime contractor and subcontractors) will have different weightings between "probability" scales and between cost, performance, and schedule consequence of occurrence components because of differences in their objective functions.

Calibration coefficients between ordinal "probability" and consequence
of occurrence scales should also be estimated. It is almost never accurate
to assume that equal weightings will exist between all "probability" scales
or consequence of occurrence components. In addition, the weightings will
likely be different between the government and prime contractor (or prime
contractor and subcontractors).

Results obtained from calibrated ordinal scales will not generally yield risk. This is because the resulting calibrated "probability" of occurrence scale coefficient values *are almost never* probabilities unless either the underlying scales were originally derived from probability data or the scales are calibrated using actual probability data. In addition, the calibrated ordinal scale values are only relative in nature and do not correspond to actual, specific values. However, limited mathematical operations can be performed on calibrated ordinal scale values, which is not true of values from uncalibrated ordinal scales. Even though the results will rarely correspond to true risk, they will often represent a weighted value of relative importance to the program. Hence, a value of 0.80 is twice as important to the program as a value of 0.40 (cet. par.), not considering the level of uncertainty present.

Risk cannot generally be computed from calibrated ordinal scales, unless the scales were originally derived from probability data or such data are used to calibrate the scales. However, limited mathematical operations can be performed on results from calibrated ordinal "probability" and consequence of occurrence scales and can yield a weighted value of relative importance to the program.

Improperly calibrated ordinal scales may yield no better, and sometimes even worse, risk analysis results than what can be obtained from uncalibrated ordinal scales. This assumes of course that the analyst does not attempt to perform mathematical operations on uncalibrated ordinal scales.

When ordinal scales are poorly calibrated the resulting risk ranking results (e.g., "Top 5" and their order) can be adversely effected. For example, in one case "probability" of occurrence scales were adequately calibrated, but consequence of occurrence scales were initially poorly calibrated. When the consequence of occurrence scales were later recalibrated, the #6 risk moved to the #2 risk, etc. for no reason other than the calibration coefficients.

In one large development program ordinal "probability" scales were calibrated using an analytic hierarchy process (AHP), which uses the additive utility function. The first time they were used the results from the calibrated scales provided less separation in scores between risk issues than from uncalibrated scales. (In effect, there was a smaller standard deviation among the scores than had previously existed.) This problem was almost certainly related to rushing the calibration process. Once the calibration had been performed, the people who participated in the process were reluctant to change their opinions about the relative weighting between levels for a given scale and between scales.

Given the amount of time, budget, and need for key personnel necessary to perform the calibration, conducting this process in less than an extremely well-thought-out fashion will often prove very unwise.

Improperly calibrated ordinal scales may yield no better, and sometimes even worse, risk analysis results than what can be obtained from uncalibrated ordinal scales. Calibrating ordinal scales is far more complex than meets the eye, and it may subsequently be very difficult to undo problems created by a faulty calibration.

If you accurately and carefully perform a calibration of ordinal "probability" of occurrence and consequence of occurrence risk scales, be very wary of management statements to the effect: "Do not worry, we will adjust the resulting risk scores up or down to whatever we think they should be." This situation is unhelpful, and potentially disastrous when the results have a substantial noise term because the calibration was not properly performed. In such cases noisy inputs to the decision are then adjusted in a subjective manner. The results are likely to be highly uncertain and erroneous.

Results from poorly calibrated ordinal scales will be uncertain at best and erroneous at worst. However, such results should not then be subjectively adjusted as a method to compensate for the poor calibration activity.

If ordinal scale calibration is performed by personnel well versed with the technique being used for the risk category in question (e.g., design/engineering), the resulting calibration may have high internal consistency (e.g., the derived coefficients for the relative scale levels may have very high certainty), but the resulting calibration values may still be erroneous.

An internally consistent calibration is akin to having a small random noise term, but it does not eliminate the possibility that a nontrivial external inconsistency may exist, which effectively represents a bias of the calibration process. In effect, people may agree that specific values should be used for calibrating scale levels of a given risk category, and these levels may be highly internally consistent. However, people performing the calibration may have biased judgment from a number of considerations, such as the importance of their product vs another or specific knowledge about the risk category being evaluated. In addition, they may have limited experience associated with the maturity of candidate risk issues across the span of possible values (e.g., scientific research to operational for a hardware technology item) or between risk categories (e.g., technology and manufacturing). This is also more likely to happen when people performing the calibration are projecting their knowledge into the future (e.g., judging prototype fabrication when none has yet occurred) than when the program is nearing completion or they have worked on a highly similar program, which, at a minimum, successfully entered the Production, Fielding/Deployment, and Operational Support phase.

Finally, the software used to estimate the calibration coefficients is typically complex and requires considerable expertise to properly operate. In one instance a set of preferences was reversed without detection, and the results, while puzzling, were accepted. The analysts and engineers that performed the calibration then developed rationale to justify the results despite the fact that they did not appear reasonable. These calibrated ordinal scales were then used in several risk analyses before it was realized that some of the preferences had been reversed, hence the calibration coefficients, thus results, were erroneous. In another instance calibration coefficients for several ordinal scales were published and used by a number of people over several years. However, years later the authors still do not realize that they made a serious mistake by not properly normalizing the resulting calibration coefficients for both probability and consequence of occurrence scales. (Although this does not change the risk rankings, it can substantially change the numerical values and the degree of separation between risk scores. For example, on 1 spacecraft risk analysis, the mean and standard deviation of risk values, for 54 items evaluated, was 0.023 and 0.019, respectively, using calibrated ordinal scales whose coefficients had not been properly normalized. When the same analysis was repeated using identical scales, but with normalized calibration coefficients, the mean and standard deviation increased to 0.092 and 0.072, respectively. The change in the mean and standard deviation between the results generated by unnormalized and normalized coefficients was 300 and 279% respectively!) In both cases the problems were undetected because the analysts did not properly challenge the results nor verify what the results were portraying.

The calibration coefficients derived for ordinal scales may contain both random and bias noise terms. It is generally far easier to identify and eliminate the random noise term than the bias noise term, and considerable effort should be made to ensure that the calibration process is performed without intentional or unintentional biases. In addition, the calibration process itself is fairly complex, and there is considerable room for making mistakes. This can lead to erroneous calibration coefficients that can adversely impact risk analysis. Whenever a calibration is performed, both analysts and decision makers should challenge subsequent risk analysis results and verify what the results are portraying.

If ordinal scale calibration is attempted by personnel unfamiliar with the technique being used or the underlying risk category in question, the resulting calibration is likely to be of poor quality. Here it is possible that the resulting calibration may have poor internal consistency (analogous to a random noise term) and external consistency (analogous to a bias term).

It is far better to leave the ordinal "probability" and consequence of occurrence scales uncalibrated and accept the resulting limitations on values generated, e.g., perform no mathematics on results and using a risk matrix for prioritization (see Chapter 6. Sec. IX.A), than to calibrate the scales poorly and place more credence on the results than are warranted.

The importance of this point cannot be emphasized enough! Anyone can purchase software that will enable them to perform the calibration process, yet the results are typically severely flawed the first two or possibly three iterations even when very knowledgeable personnel conduct the calibration! An insufficient calibration process can have an adverse impact on a program because the resulting risk scores will be improperly prioritized, and scarce resources will be wasted for the calibration process and later incorrectly applied during risk handling activities!

Ideally, the calibration should be performed by personnel that are well-versed with both the calibration procedure, the risk category being evaluated (e.g., design/engineering), and have relevant experience with items highly similar to what is being development or produced.

Having inexperienced personnel facilitating the calibration process can lead to potentially harmful results. The faulty nature of the results are often not obvious to the participants. For example, I have even observed people experienced in performing the calibration process routinely make substantial mistakes that led to erroneous calibration results.

When any doubt exists as to the capability and competency of how the calibration process will be performed and the experience of the people leading the process, it is far better to use uncalibrated ordinal "probability" and consequence of occurrence scales and accept the resulting limitations on values generated (e.g., no mathematics on results) than to waste resources, poorly calibrate the scales, and place more credence on the results than are warranted.

Different calibrations of the same ordinal "probability" and consequence of occurrence scales may exist for different parts of a program (e.g., different major subsystems, etc.) Although this may appear to be a reasonable approach, it will often produce inconsistencies between similar items across the program and make interpretation of results difficult. A single set of ordinal scales calibrated across the program is generally far more appropriate. This also reduces the likelihood that the results for a given set of WBS elements will be gamed by the risk POC (cet. par.).

A single set of calibrated ordinal scales should be developed by key personnel across the program. It is generally unwise to use sets of scales calibrated separately by different groups of people within the program because of potentially inconsistent or gamed results.

When calibrating ordinal scales, whether "probability" or consequence of occurrence, it is generally much easier to confidently estimate coefficients within a given scale than between scales. This is because within a scale, the scale levels and their definitions are rank ordered and monotonic. Thus, if scale definitions imply that the level of immaturity for a given risk category (e.g., hardware technology) is C > B > A, where C is more immature than B, and B is more immature than A, it is not possible for A > C (where A is more immature than C). This makes the comparison between levels within a scale one-sided because of the monotonic nature of the ordinal scales. And a one-sided comparison is generally much easier to accurately estimate (assuming that the expert is not just randomly guessing) than a two-sided comparison that exists in the between-scale case. This is because the monotonic constraint does not exist for "probability" and consequence of occurrence between scale relationships since the relative ordering of scales has no meaning on their relative rank. In effect, for all "level one" scales (e.g., cost, performance, and schedule consequence of occurrence; or design/engineering, manufacturing, and technology; but not design/engineering, manufacturing process, manufacturing facilities, manufacturing test, and technology), the ordering of the scales from a between-scale sense is akin to a nominal scale—the ordering does not have any mathematical basis (the same way that numbering freeways does not have any mathematical basis). The standard deviation of responses associated with any given between-scale coefficient are often very large, and much larger than those typically observed when doing within-scale calibrations for any scale level. Hence, particular attention should be paid to the between-scale calibration process, because a wide variety of results may exist, including some obviously unreasonable ones, which must be carefully evaluated.

When calibrating ordinal scales, whether "probability" or consequence of occurrence, it is generally much easier to confidently estimate coefficients within a given scale than between scales.

If you compute a risk factor using calibrated ordinal scales, situations may occur where it is difficult to estimate the between-scale weights because some items in a given risk category (e.g., computer and software in hardware/software integration) may include a different number of relevant "probability" scales than other elements (e.g., WBS) in the same risk category. In such cases, you may need to compute the risk factor associated with each "probability" and consequence of occurrence scale that applies (note that cost, performance, and schedule consequence of occurrence scales always apply) and take the maximum resulting score to represent the overall risk issue. While this is not the ideal situation, it is the conservative approach. Of course, in cases where all items in a given risk category should be evaluated by all "probability" scales defined for that risk category (e.g., typically for hardware items all design/engineering, manufacturing, and technology scales will apply), then a single between-scale grouping will exist and estimation of the between-scale weights is straight forward.

If you compute a risk factor using calibrated ordinal scales, you may have to evaluate the resulting score based upon the number of "probability" scales that apply.

VIII.   Interpolation Between Uncalibrated and Calibrated Ordinal Scale Levels

It is almost never valid to interpolate between ordinal scale levels. In the case of uncalibrated ordinal "probability" and consequence of occurrence scales, the true increments between scale levels are unknown, and interpolation is not meaningful. In some cases, such as estimative ordinal probability scales or probability tables, the resulting scale level will more correctly represent a distribution of values. For example, as given in Appendix J, survey results for the term *high* yielded a median of 0.85 and a range (maximum–minimum values) of 0.8 (0.95–0.15).

Even when calibrated ordinal scales exist, the nature of the relationship between succeeding levels is unknown (beyond the likely case that it is a continuous function). Examination of calibration coefficients from many ordinal scales indicates that across scale levels (e.g., lowest to highest) the relationship is typically nonlinear, generally with a positive first derivative (coefficient magnitude increases with scale level—a condition of the underlying ordinal scale having been correctly formulated is that the levels are monotonic) and often with a positive second derivative. Consequently, although the relationship between adjacent scale levels is also likely nonlinear, no information exists as to what this relationship might be. Hence, a simple linear interpolation such as the average value between two adjacent interval levels is likely to be incorrect, but to an unknown extent.

Do not attempt to interpolate between ordinal scale levels because the mathematical relationship between levels is generally unknown. This is obvious for ordinal scales, where the values indicate only rank ordering. However, interpolation between calibrated ordinal scale levels should also not be attempted because the relationship is typically both nonlinear and unknown.

References

[1]Michaels, J. V., *Technical Risk Management*, Prentice-Hall, Upper Saddle River, NJ, 1996, pp. 90–91.

[2]Abramson, R. L., and Book, S. A., "A Quantification Structure for Assessing Risk Impact Drivers," 24th Annual DoD Cost Analysis Symposium, Sept. 1990.

[3]Clemen, R. T., *Making Hard Decisions,* 2nd ed., Duxberry Press, New York, 1996, pp. 530–575. See the list of references on p. 574 for further reading on additive utility functions.

Appendix I:
Example Technical Risk Analysis

I briefly provide in this appendix an example risk analysis that illustrates how to use uncalibrated ordinal "probability" of occurrence and consequence of occurrence scales, along with a risk mapping matrix. *The example is very simplistic, and the scales provided along with the mapping matrix are only given as an illustration and should not be used on your program.* The ordinal probability of occurrence scale may well be too coarse to yield accurate results. In addition, the consequence of occurrence scales do not have equivalent apparent severity for the same consequence level when viewed across cost, performance, and schedule above scale Level A. For example, for scale Level D, C_p (acceptable, no remaining margin) may be more severe than C_s (major slip in key milestone or critical path impacted), which may be more severe than C_c ($\geq 7\%-< 10\%$ cost overrun). The former issue can be eliminated using a high-quality probability scale with more than five levels, whereas the latter issue can be dealt with by reevaluating and changing the criteria (where necessary) for C_c, C_p, and C_s, along with calibrating the three consequence of occurrence scales. (Of course, a better solution, where resources permit, would also be to calibrate both the probability of occurrence scales and the three consequences of occurrence scales.)

I. Example Risk Analysis Methodology

A single probability of occurrence scale, related to technology maturity, is used and given in Table I.1. (This scale is identical to that given in Appendix H, Table H.1.) In reality, technical risk will typically encompass a number of additional risk categories in addition to technology maturity, such as design/engineering, manufacturing, and so forth. However, the use of a single risk category simplifies subsequent computations and is sufficient for illustration purposes.

Three consequence of occurrence scales, for cost, performance, and schedule, are used and given in Table I.2.[1]

For this example risk analysis, we will use the risk mapping matrix given in Fig. I.1.

II. Example Risk Analysis

I will now evaluate two different items associated with a commercial high-grade digital camera using the preceding risk analysis methodology.

Table I.1   Example ordinal technology "probability" maturity scale

Definition	Scale level
Basic principles observed	E
Concept design analyzed for performance	D
Breadboard or brassboard validation in relevant environment	C
Prototype passes performance tests	B
Item deployed and operational	A

Remember, these risk issues are hypothetical and only used to illustrate how to apply the risk analysis methodology.

In the first case a high-performance commercial charge-coupled device (CCD) exists that is in preprototype development. The CCD will be included in a high-grade digital camera. The risk issue is whether or not the desired signal-to-noise ratio can be achieved to meet low-light operating requirements and avoid an increased level of image grain during operation. The potential cost consequence of this occurring is a 6% cost impact for a third design, fabrication, and test iteration (two iterations are baselined). The potential performance consequence of this occurring is acceptable performance, but no remaining margin. The potential schedule consequence of this occurring is additional resources required, but able to meet the need date. In this example the resulting probability of occurrence score from Table I.1 is Level C (preprototype maturity), and from Table I.2 C_c = Level C, C_p = Level D, and C_c = Level B. Given this information and the risk mapping matrix in Fig. I.1, the risk level relative to cost, performance, and schedule is medium, medium, and low, respectively. Taking the maximum of the three risk scores yields an overall medium risk level for CCD low-light performance.

In the second case a high-density digital storage card is in the concept formulation stage. This storage card will be included in the same high-grade digital camera as the CCD already discussed. The risk issue is the ability to achieve the desired bit density for the card to store the desired number of very high-resolution images. Here, the bit density is presumed to be a factor of five times greater than the existing state of the art. The potential cost consequence of not achieving the desired bit density is a 20% cost impact for additional technology advancement of the storage medium, plus one or more additional redesign, fabrication, and test iterations. The potential performance consequence of this occurring is unacceptable performance because the desired number of high-resolution, high-dynamic-range images cannot be stored with existing density storage cards. The potential schedule consequence of this occurring is a major slip in introducing the digital camera with the desired high-density storage card. (It is presumed here that

Table I.2 Example ordinal cost, performance, and schedule consequence of occurrence scale[a]

C_c	C_p	C_s	Scale level
≥ 10%	Unacceptable	Can't achieve key team or major program milestone	E
≥ 7%–< 10%	Acceptable; no remaining margin	Major slip in key milestone or critical path impacted	D
≥ 5%–< 7%	Acceptable with significant reduction in margin	Minor slip in key milestones, not able to meet need date	C
< 5%	Acceptable with some reduction in margin	Additional resources required, able to meet need date	B
Minimal or no impact	Minimal or no impact	Minimal or no impact	A

[a]Table derived from Ref 1. I corrected the inequalities in this table to prevent the cost consequence of occurrence criteria from overlapping between scale levels.

Consequence ⟶ Higher

	A	B	C	D	E
E	M	M	H	H	H
D	L	M	M	H	H
C	L	L	M	M	H
B	L	L	L	M	M
A	L	L	L	L	M

(Probability ⟶ Higher, along the left vertical axis)

Fig. I.1 Example risk mapping matrix.

multiple lower-density storage cards cannot be substituted for a single high-density card.) In this example the resulting probability of occurrence score from Table I.1 is Level D (concept design analyzed for performance), and from Table I.2 C_c = Level E, C_p = Level E, and C_c = Level D. Given this information and the risk mapping matrix in Fig. I.1, the risk level relative to cost, performance, and schedule is high, high, and high, respectively. Taking the maximum of the three risk scores yields an overall high risk level for digital storage card bit density.

Of the results for the two candidate risk issues, the higher-risk item is the digital storage card.

Had there been n technology risk categories instead of the single one used here (technology maturity), then there would have been n X 3 total scores to report for each risk issue. If desired, this could be reduced to "n" risk scores by using a conservative mapping approach and taking the maximum of the three consequence scores per item. The "n" $\times$ 3 total scores could also have been reduced to three risk scores per risk issue by using a conservative mapping approach and taking the maximum score of the "n" technology risk category scores per item together with each consequence score. Similarly, if desired the "n" $\times$ 3 scores for cost consequence, performance consequence, and schedule consequence could be reduced to one risk score per risk issue by using a conservative mapping approach and taking the maximum of the "n" technology risk category scores per item coupled with the maximum of the cost, performance, and schedule consequence scores per item.

[Note: I generally *do not* recommend reporting separate risk scores associated with cost, performance, and schedule consequence of occurrence. This was only presented as an illustration given that a single probability scale (technology maturity) was used in this example. If you have "n" probability scales together with the 3 consequence scales and use the conservative mapping approach, you should generally either report the complete set of "n" × 3 risk levels (which I don't prefer), or a single risk level (which is typically better). If you do report a single risk level and used the conservative mapping approach (selecting the maximum "probability":consequence pair), it is important to identify which probability and consequence of occurrence categories led to that risk level to assist in developing a RHP.]

Finally, given that a medium- or higher-risk level exists for both the camcorder CCD low-light performance and the digital storage card bit density, risk handling plans should be developed for both risk issues.

Reference

[1]Department of Defense, *Risk Management Guide for DoD Acquisition,* 5th ed., Defense Acquisition Univ., Ft. Belvoir, VA, June 2002, p. 18.

Appendix J:
Estimative Probability Values for Subjective
Probability Statements

I. Introduction

This appendix describes the derivation of estimative probability values for a number of different subjective probability statements. (I use the term *estimative probability* in deference to Sherman Kent, whose well-crafted and thoughtful insights are just as valid today as they were in the early 1960s when he presented his ideas within the U.S. intelligence community.) The use of estimative probability data certainly has its proper place in a number of applications, one being to assist the reader in interpreting subjective terms that are used to describe probabilities.

Unfortunately, estimative probabilities now are commonly used in project risk management either as an ordinal scale (e.g., Appendix H, Table H.5) or as a table of probability values (e.g., Chapter 6, Table 6.5). In the former case the data are commonly used along with ordinal consequence of occurrence scales and a risk matrix (e.g., Chapter 6, Sec. IX.A) to develop ordinal estimates of risk (e.g., low, medium, and high). In the latter case the probability data are often used directly to compute a cardinal estimate of risk (e.g., 0.75 X $100 = $75). In many instances these two approaches are not the best choice and in some cases may not even be applicable. (I personally view the use of estimative probability data for project management risk calculations as almost the last choice—one to be used only when more viable options cannot be identified.)

Several problems exist with developing and using estimative probability data in project management related risk analyses.

First, the definitions for probability statements are interpreted differently by different analysts. If, for example, high is defined as 0.75, but the analyst believes that it is much lower, say 0.45, and medium is defined as 0.50, the analyst may choose to score an item as having a medium probability level because of the potential contradiction between the word definition and the numerical score provided. The broad range of values given by survey respondents for the definitions in Table J.3 indicates that a considerable level of variation will exist for a group of analysts in scoring items based upon subjective probability, which may lead to erroneous results. For example, of the 49 different probability statements evaluated in the survey conducted here and reported in Sec. IV, *only 1 statement had a range of responses (maximum probability score − minimum probability score) less than 0.50! Clearly, a broad range of interpretation exists for subjective probability statements.*

Second, results obtained from estimative probability data will typically have a high degree of uncertainty. For example, when estimative probability data are used to construct an ordinal scale, the increment values between adjacent (scale) levels are generally unknown or highly uncertain. When probabilities are given as point values, this can convey a false sense of accuracy. *Hence, a range around the median (or mean) value should always be reported (e.g., quartiles). (Median values are preferable to the mean because the distribution of responses will typically be skewed and nonnormal.) Note: A range around the median (or mean) that is contrived (e.g., guess) or devised without the use of a statistical analysis of underlying data should never be used because it too conveys a false sense of accuracy. Unfortunately, when ranges are given for estimative probabilities, the source of the range information is often not provided. Hence, the analyst or decision maker is unsure whether this information was derived from a sample of actual data (e.g., real world programs or survey responses) or a guess.*

Third, candidate risk issues often evaluated with estimative probability data (e.g., an ordinal scale or a probability table) may actually be related to maturity (e.g., potential development status of an item) or some other criteria different than probability. *This forces the analyst to choose a probability level that may not at all apply.* For example, assume a prototype item has been fabricated and is awaiting test. Here, the application of estimative probability data is not particularly meaningful when the underlying risk issue is will a suitable unit be available for deployment. Perhaps a probability estimate can be made based on previous experience that after a prototype unit has been developed, there is an X percent likelihood that a suitable unit will be deployed. Unless those data are available, and from directly analogous systems, the resulting analysis may be nothing more than a fairly poor guess. (This will likely be the case whether the estimative probability data are directly applied via a probability table or used in an ordinal scale.)

Fourth, probability data of this type *almost never represent probabilities associated with actual measured values* (e.g., real world data or survey results), but typically only subjective estimates made by the author of the estimative probability ordinal scale or probability table and later the analyst attempting to use it. For example, few if any of these data are derived from extensive surveys. Thus, a subjective evaluation is often made by the author to generate the probability values associated with a statement, and a subjective interpretation is made by the analyst using the statements and their associated probability values. The pedigree of estimative probability data, whether used in ordinal scales or probability tables, should always be disclosed. This will help the user decide how confidently he should interpret probability statements linked with probability values or whether he should even use the data.

Fifth, in cases where the probability representation of a risk issue may actually be valid, the analyst often has *little or no knowledge* how to score the given issue. (For example, the analyst may have to rate the reliability of an item that has not been developed, where reliability predictions do not exist.) Thus, without relevant supporting data, the result will typically be nothing more than a guess, and one that may be erroneous. In addition, because the uncertainty associated with the estimate is typically not recorded, the result is generally a point estimate rather than a range of values that may be more appropriate.

I will now digress a bit and discuss a pioneering work on estimative probability, then introduce the research I performed for this book. (This work was not examined until *after* the survey in Sec. III was performed and results were analyzed.)

II. Background

The following extracts from an intelligence community publication serve as excellent background to the issue of estimative probability.[1] The briefing officer was reporting a photoreconnaissance mission. Pointing to the map, he made three statements:

1) "And at this location there is a new airfield. . . Its longest runway is 10,000 ft."
2) "It is almost certainly a military airfield."
3) "The terrain is such that the XXXs could easily lengthen the runways, otherwise improve the facilities, and incorporate this field into their system of strategic staging bases. It is possible that they will." Or, more daringly, "It would be logical for them to do this and sooner or later they probably will."

The preceding are typical of three kinds of statements that populate the literature of all substantive intelligence. The first (type one) is as close as one can come to a statement of indisputable fact. It describes something knowable and known with a high degree of certainty. The reconnaissance aircraft's position was known with precision, and its camera reproduced almost exactly what was there. The second (type two) is a judgment or estimate. It describes something that is knowable in terms of the human understanding but not precisely known by the man who is talking about it. The third statement (type three) is another judgment or estimate made almost without any evidence direct or indirect.

In March 1951 appeared NIE 29–51, "Probability of an Invasion of Yugoslavia in 1951." The following was its key judgment, made in the final paragraph of the conclusions: "Although it is impossible to determine which course the Kremlin is likely to adopt, we believe that the extent of satellite military and propaganda preparations indicates that an attack on Yugoslavia in 1951 should be considered a serious possibility." Clearly this statement is either of type two, a knowable thing of which our knowledge was very imperfect, or of type three, a thing literally unknowable for the reason that the Soviets themselves had not yet reached a binding decision. Whichever, it was our duty to look hard at the situation, decide how likely or unlikely an attack might be, and having reached that decision, draft some language that would convey to the reader our exact judgment.

A few days after the estimate appeared, I was in informal conversation with the policy planning staff's chairman. We spoke of Yugoslavia and the estimate. Suddenly he said, "By the way, what did you people mean by the expression serious possibility? What kind of odds did you have in mind?" I told him that any personal estimate was on the dark side, namely, that the odds were around 65 to 35 in favor of an attack. He was somewhat jolted by this; he and his colleagues had read serious possibility to mean odds very considerably lower. Understandably troubled by this want of communication, I began asking my own colleagues on the Board of National Estimates what odds they had had in mind when they agreed to that wording. It was another jolt to find that each Board member had had somewhat different odds in mind, and the low man was thinking of about 20 to 80, the high of 80 to 20. The rest ranged in between.

There is a language for odds; in fact there are two—the precise mathematical language of the actuary or the racetrack bookie and a less precise though useful verbal equivalent. We did not use the numbers, however, and it appeared that we were misusing the words.

We began to think in terms of a chart that would show the mathematical odds equivalent to words and phrases of probability. Our starter was a pretty complicated affair. We approached its construction from the wrong end. Namely, we began with 11 words or phrases that seemed to convey a feeling of 11 different orders of probability and then attached numerical odds to them. At once we perceived our folly. In the first place, given the inexactness of the intelligence data we were working with, the distinctions we made between one set of odds and its fellows above and below were unjustifiably sharp. Second, even if in rare cases one could arrive at such exact mathematical odds, the verbal equivalent could not possibly convey that exactness. The laudable precision would be lost on the reader.

So we tried again, this time with only five gradations, and beginning with the numerical odds. The chart that emerged (given in Table J.1) can be set down in its classical simplicity.

Table J.1 Example scores for probability statements

Definition	Probability score
Certainty	1.00
Almost certain	0.93 give or take 0.06
Probable	0.75 give or take 0.12
Chances about even	0.50 give or take 0.10
Probably not	0.30 give or take 0.10
Almost certainly not	0.07 give or take 0.05
Impossibility	0.00

Important note to consumers: You should be quite clear that when we say "such and such is certain" we mean that the chances of its *not* happening are in our judgment about nine or more to one. Another, and to you critically important, way of saying the same thing is that the chances of its happening are about one in 10 or less. If the estimate were to read, "It is almost certain Mr. X will not . . . ," we would mean there was still an appreciable chance, say 5% or less, that he would attempt. . . . (I have modified this paragraph by using the term *almost certain* from Table J.1, rather than the example used by Sherman Kent, *unlikely,* which was not included in the table and might, therefore, lead to confusion. The meaning of the paragraph is retained, *and I believe it is very important and warrants being presented* because often times people only perceive probability as being one-sided [e.g., the odds something *will* happen], rather than two-sided [e.g., the odds that something *will* happen, and one minus this value (the odds that something *won't* happen) or the converse depending on how the wording is given].

III. Development of the Survey

A survey was developed to quantify probability values associated with different subjective probability statements. Initial attempts on my part indicated that potential respondents in the project management community were less likely to complete such a survey longer than two pages, nor when they themselves had to supply the probability estimate. The result was a somewhat constrained survey that did not entirely satisfy my desires, but one that was far better than nothing (given the likelihood of respondents balking at a more extensive questionnaire).

The resulting questionnaire contained 50 statements. One statement (occasional chance) was repeated twice—it was a control statement. This was done intentionally. I wanted to see how the respondents would score the same term two different times when the statements were located in different parts of the survey. (For example, were the resulting scores close to each other? If the scores for this repeated statement were wildly different, then the credibility of the survey would be seriously in question.) Thus, the questionnaire contained 49 *different* statements.

The following written instructions were given to the respondents: "Please put an X in the box for the probability value that best describes each statement. All questionnaires are anonymous. There is no correct answer, and your opinion is highly valued for this research." The exact question asked was this: "(Statement) . . . that this risk *will* occur," implies what probability? The emphasis added to *will* occur was intentionally done and included on the survey to instruct the respondent that this form of the probability was being elicited, rather than *will not* occur.

The survey was structured with the statements randomly ordered (although a random number generator was not used to assign the placement). I believe that this was *critically important* because I have witnessed several surveys being developed and administered whose results have been biased because the questions were ordered in a particular manner that influenced responses. For example, if the statements had been ordered ascending or descending according to the estimated probability value I placed on each term, at least some respondents would have anchored a probability estimate for a given statement from the estimate given from the previous (descending) or the next (ascending) statement. (See Chapter 3, Sec. XIV and the associated reference for a discussion of anchoring and other considerations that can affect subjective probability estimates. Also see Chapter 6, Sec. VII.F for some additional considerations.) Twenty-five statements were included on each page (with occasional chance included twice).

The respondents placed an X or checkmark in 1 of 10 columns for each statement. These columns were a probability (%) from 0 to 10, 10 to 20, 20 to 30, 30 to 40, 40 to 50, 50 to 60, 60 to 70, 70 to 80, 80 to 90, and 90 to 100. From the completed questionnaires with X or checkmarks, numerical values were assigned to the midpoint of each response, e.g., a value of 0.05 was given to an X corresponding to the column 0 to 10 probability (%).

The survey results were not as granular as I would have liked: 10 total values were possible, and 20 would have been preferable. However, the tradeoff I made was coarser responses vs fewer properly completed surveys, which I viewed as likely and a more negative situation. In any event this was the dilemma, and the path that I chose.

Incomplete surveys (roughly 10%) were typically discarded because they were often completed anonymously, and I did not want respondents modifying other results. [In three cases I did know the respondents because they e-mailed me their forms and I e-mailed them the statements that they had not answered (completed). The respondents answered the statements and e-mailed me the probability values solely for these statements. This information was used to complete the surveys.] The most common source of eliminating an incomplete survey (and one performed anonymously) was because the respondent could not develop an answer for the following statement: "reduced chance . . . that this risk *will* occur," implies what probability? Several respondents, quite correctly pointed out, reduced from what (e.g., what was the initial level considered)? Unfortunately, because this statement was included in the survey, I was forced to discard those that were incomplete and anonymous. Given the trouble by a number of respondents in evaluating this statement, I strongly recommend that it not be used in the future.

The sample of respondents included 151 completed surveys. Approximately 3/4 of the respondents were engineers, and the other 1/4 were project managers. The sample was composed of people in the aerospace profession (about 2/3) and nonaerospace professions (about 1/3, which included a variety of commercial engineering and project management work).

These numerical values were then statistically analyzed, and the raw results were reported next in Sec. IV.

IV. Survey Results

The data from each participant's survey were converted to numerical values (just described) and manually entered into a spreadsheet. Each converted value was checked twice to catch entry errors (and yes, some did exist). All totaled, 151 surveys were included, and with 50 statements per survey this came to 7550 numbers that had to be entered and double checked—a very time-consuming activity!

A variety of statistical analyses were performed. The primary statistical measures computed for each *statement* (across the 151 responses) include the mean, mode (most likely), standard deviation, median, maximum, minimum, range (maximum–minimum), 3rd quartile (75th percentile), 1st quartile (25th percentile), interquartile range (75th–25th percentiles), 90th percentile, 10th percentile, 90th–10th percentiles, coefficient of variation, skewness, and kurtosis. In addition, the mean, standard deviation, range (maximum–minimum), 3rd quartile (75th percentile), 1st quartile (25th percentile), and interquartile range (75th–25th percentiles) were estimated for each *respondent* (across the 50 survey statements).

Statistical results reported here for each *statement* include the median, 3rd quartile (75th percentile), 1st quartile (25th percentile), interquartile range (75th percentile–25th percentile), range (maximum–minimum), maximum, minimum, the percent respondents whose estimated probability value was within the mode ± 0.10, the percent of respondents whose estimated probability value > 3rd quartile, the percent of respondents whose estimated probability value < 1st quartile, the percent sum of the total number of responses > 3rd quartile and < 1st quartile, the percent of respondents whose

**Table J.2a   Median, third quartile, first quartile, and range
for probability statements**

Probability statement	Median (50th percentile)	Third quartile (75th percentile)	First quartile (25th percentile)
Certain	0.95	0.95	0.95
Almost certain	0.95	0.95	0.85
Nearly certain	0.85	0.95	0.85
Very high chance	0.85	0.95	0.85
Very probable	0.85	0.85	0.75
Highly likely	0.85	0.85	0.75
High probability	0.85	0.85	0.75
High likelihood	0.85	0.85	0.75
High chance	0.85	0.85	0.75
Large chance	0.85	0.85	0.75
Extensive chance	0.85	0.85	0.75
Very good chance	0.75	0.85	0.65
Probably	0.75	0.85	0.65
Major chance	0.75	0.85	0.65
Believe	0.75	0.85	0.65
Significant chance	0.75	0.85	0.65
Likely	0.75	0.85	0.65

estimated probability value > 90th percentile, the percent of respondents whose estimated probability value < 10th percentile, and the percent sum of the total number of responses > 90th percentile and < 10th percentile.

Results from the statistical analysis are given in Tables J.2, J.3, J.4, and J.5. The statements are sorted in descending order based upon the median response, with the mean response being used as the tiebreaker.

From examining skewness and kurtosis results for each *statement* (not provided here), it was clear that in no case were the responses likely normal. (A normal distribution has a skewness of 0 and kurtosis of 3.0. Having such values does not prove that a distribution is normal, but when the values are clearly far from these, it indicates that the distribution is likely non-normal.) Thus, statistical analyses that depend on normality (e.g., difference in means) could not be performed.

The mean and standard deviation of each probability statement are not reported to prevent them for being used in developing point estimates and ranges, respectively. Given that the distribution for each probability statement was nonnormal, the median (50th percentile), 3rd quartile (75th percentile), and 1st quartile (25th percentile) values provide better estimates

**Table J.2b   Median, third quartile, first quartile, and range
for probability statements**

Probability statement	Median (50th percentile)	Third quartile (75th percentile)	First quartile (25th percentile)
Probable	0.75	0.85	0.65
Almost likely	0.65	0.85	0.55
Frequent chance	0.65	0.75	0.55
Better than even chance	0.65	0.65	0.55
Better than 50/50	0.55	0.65	0.55
Moderate probability	0.55	0.65	0.45
Even chance	0.55	0.55	0.45
Possible	0.55	0.65	0.35
Potential	0.55	0.65	0.35
Medium probability	0.45	0.55	0.45
Reduced chance	0.35	0.35	0.25
Occasional chance (1)	0.25	0.45	0.25
Some chance	0.25	0.45	0.15
Occasional chance (2)	0.25	0.45	0.15
Limited chance	0.25	0.25	0.15
Probably not	0.25	0.35	0.15
Not likely	0.25	0.30	0.15

**Table J.2c   Median, third quartile, first quartile, and range
for probability statements**

Probability statement	Median (50th percentile)	Third quartile (75th percentile)	First quartile (25th percentile)
Low likelihood	0.15	0.25	0.15
Unlikely	0.15	0.25	0.15
Improbable	0.15	0.25	0.15
Slight chance	0.15	0.25	0.15
Minor chance	0.15	0.25	0.15
Low probability	0.15	0.25	0.15
Doubtful	0.15	0.25	0.15
Little chance	0.15	0.25	0.15
Very limited chance	0.15	0.25	0.05
Small probability	0.15	0.15	0.15
Highly unlikely	0.15	0.15	0.05
Very unlikely	0.15	0.15	0.05
Negligible chance	0.15	0.15	0.05
Very low probability	0.15	0.15	0.05
No significant chance	0.05	0.25	0.05
Almost no chance	0.05	0.15	0.05

Table J.3a Interquartile range, range, maximum, minimum, and percent respondents within mode +/− 0.10 for probability statements

Probability statement	Interquartile range (75th–25th percentiles)	Range (maximum–minimum)	Maximum	Minimum	Percent respondents within mode +/− 0.10
Certain	0.00	0.9	0.95	0.05	86
Almost certain	0.10	0.9	0.95	0.05	89
Nearly certain	0.10	0.9	0.95	0.05	81
Very high chance	0.10	0.9	0.95	0.05	89
Very probable	0.10	0.8	0.95	0.15	85
Highly likely	0.10	0.9	0.95	0.05	90
High probability	0.10	0.8	0.95	0.15	87
High likelihood	0.10	0.8	0.95	0.15	82
High chance	0.10	0.7	0.95	0.25	85
Large chance	0.10	0.9	0.95	0.05	87
Extensive chance	0.10	0.8	0.95	0.15	77
Very good chance	0.20	0.8	0.95	0.15	74
Probably	0.20	0.8	0.95	0.15	69
Major chance	0.20	0.8	0.95	0.15	72
Believe	0.20	0.9	0.95	0.05	67
Significant chance	0.20	0.9	0.95	0.05	83
Likely	0.20	0.9	0.95	0.05	79

Table J.3b Interquartile range, range, maximum, minimum, and percent respondents within mode +/− 0.10 for probability statements

Probability statement	Interquartile range (75th–25th percentiles)	Range (maximum–minimum)	Maximum	Minimum	Percent respondents within mode +/− 0.10
Probable	0.20	0.9	0.95	0.05	77
Almost likely	0.30	0.8	0.95	0.15	60
Frequent chance	0.20	0.9	0.95	0.05	78
Better than even chance	0.10	0.8	0.95	0.15	95
Better than 50/50	0.10	0.4	0.85	0.45	90
Moderate probability	0.20	0.7	0.85	0.15	79
Even chance	0.10	0.7	0.85	0.15	95
Possible	0.30	0.9	0.95	0.05	58
Potential	0.30	0.9	0.95	0.05	52
Medium probability	0.10	0.7	0.85	0.15	94
Reduced chance	0.10	0.8	0.85	0.05	79
Occasional chance (1)	0.20	0.9	0.95	0.05	69
Some chance	0.30	0.8	0.85	0.05	66
Occasional chance (2)	0.30	0.7	0.75	0.05	66
Limited chance	0.10	0.8	0.85	0.05	77
Probably not	0.20	0.8	0.85	0.05	74
Not likely	0.15	0.9	0.95	0.05	75

Table J.3c Interquartile range, range, maximum, minimum, and percent respondents within mode +/− 0.10 for probability statements

Probability statement	Interquartile range (75th–25th percentiles)	Range (maximum–minimum)	Maximum	Minimum	Percent respondents within mode +/− 0.10
Low likelihood	0.10	0.9	0.95	0.05	79
Unlikely	0.10	0.8	0.85	0.05	77
Improbable	0.10	0.8	0.85	0.05	76
Slight chance	0.10	0.8	0.85	0.05	79
Minor chance	0.10	0.8	0.85	0.05	76
Low probability	0.10	0.8	0.85	0.05	75
Doubtful	0.10	0.8	0.85	0.05	83
Little chance	0.10	0.7	0.75	0.05	88
Very limited chance	0.20	0.8	0.85	0.05	85
Small probability	0.00	0.7	0.75	0.05	92
Highly unlikely	0.10	0.9	0.95	0.05	91
Very unlikely	0.10	0.8	0.85	0.05	79
Negligible chance	0.10	0.8	0.85	0.05	81
Very low probability	0.10	0.8	0.85	0.05	80
No significant chance	0.20	0.8	0.85	0.05	74
Almost no chance	0.10	0.9	0.95	0.05	89

**Table J.4a Percent respondents > 3rd quartile, percent
respondents < 1st quartile, and percent sum > 3rd quartile
and < 1st quartile for probability statements**

Probability statement	Percent respondents > 3rd quartile	Percent respondents < 1st quartile	Percent respondents > 3rd quartile and < 1st quartile
Certain	0	25	25
Almost certain	0	11	11
Nearly certain	0	19	19
Very high chance	0	25	25
Very probable	23	15	37
Highly likely	21	10	30
High probability	13	13	26
High likelihood	10	18	28
High chance	9	15	24
Large chance	10	13	23
Extensive chance	13	23	36
Very good chance	8	9	17
Probably	19	13	31
Major chance	4	14	18
Believe	16	17	33
Significant chance	9	17	26
Likely	7	15	21

for a central value and a symmetrical (percentile) variation around the central value than would be given by the mean and standard deviation. (For example, the standard deviation cannot be related to a percentile value among probability statement distributions because each distribution is non-normal and different from the others.)

Both responses for the control statement, occasional chance, had a median of 0.25. In addition, one had a mean and standard deviation of 0.33 and 0.16, respectively, while the other had a mean and standard deviation of 0.30 and 0.15, respectively. These responses were surprisingly close, although likely not statistically significant at the 0.05 level.

V. Discussion

The broad extent of values given by survey respondents for all 50 statements indicate that a considerable level of variation will exist for a group of analysts in scoring items based upon subjective probability. This will likely

Table J.4b Percent respondents > 3rd quartile, percent
respondents < 1st quartile, and percent sum > 3rd quartile
and < 1st quartile for probability statements

Probability statement	Percent respondents > 3rd quartile	Percent respondents < 1st quartile	Percent respondents > 3rd quartile and < 1st quartile
Probable	5	18	23
Almost likely	7	18	25
Frequent chance	8	14	22
Better than even chance	10	4	14
Better than 50/50	10	7	17
Moderate probability	4	17	21
Even chance	6	2	8
Possible	14	20	34
Potential	13	20	33
Medium probability	4	10	14
Reduced chance	23	11	34
Occasional chance (1)	18	21	39
Some chance	19	5	24
Occasional chance (2)	13	7	20
Limited chance	23	3	26
Probably not	18	11	29
Not likely	25	12	37

lead to erroneous results if a point estimate (single value) is used, particularly in light of how large the ranges (maximum–minimum) were for all statements.

A summary of the range data for each of the 50 probability statements is given in Table J.6. Surprisingly, the range was quite large for *all* statements. Of considerable surprise was that for 49 of the 50 statements included in the survey, *all but one (better than 50/50) had a range* ≥ 0.70! In addition, 42 of the 50 statements had a range ≥ 0.8! (One occurrence of occasional chance had a range of 0.9, and the other had a range of 0.7.)

It can be argued that the range (maximum–minimum) may contain statistical outliers. Hence, even though all but one of the 50 probability statements had a very large range, this could have occurred because of a few respondents that were outliers. No formal statistical analysis for outliers was performed.

Table J.4c Percent respondents > 3rd quartile, percent
respondents < 1st quartile, and percent sum > 3rd quartile
and < 1st quartile for probability statements

Probability statement	Percent respondents > 3rd quartile	Percent respondents < 1st quartile	Percent respondents > 3rd quartile and < 1st quartile
Low likelihood	21	11	32
Unlikely	23	13	36
Improbable	24	23	47
Slight chance	21	19	40
Minor chance	15	9	24
Low probability	15	9	25
Doubtful	17	19	36
Little chance	12	15	27
Very limited chance	15	0	15
Small probability	25	22	46
Highly unlikely	20	0	20
Very unlikely	21	0	21
Negligible chance	19	0	19
Very low probability	20	0	20
No significant chance	16	0	16
Almost no chance	11	0	11

However, the results given in Table J.4 indicate that more than a few respondents were typically outside the range of the 75th percentile to the 25th percentile. In fact, on average, 26% of the respondents had estimates for each probability statement that were > 3rd quartile (75th percentile) and < 1st quartile (25th percentile). A complete set of statistics across the 50 probability statements for the percent respondents > 75th percentile and < 25th percentile is given in Table J.7.

In addition, the results given in Table J.5 indicate that more than a few respondents were typically outside the range of the 90th percentile to the 10th percentile. On average, 11% of the respondents has estimates for each probability statement that were > 90th percentile and < 10th percentile. A complete set of statistics across the 50 probability statements for the percent respondents > 90th percentile and < 10th percentile is given in Table J.8.

Another method was proposed by David L. Wark to screen the viability of estimative probability results.[2] This approach involves determining the

Table J.5a Percent respondents > 90th percentile, percent respondents < 10th percentile, and percent sum > 90th percentile and < 10th percentile for probability statements

Probability statement	Percent respondents > 90th percentile	Percent respondents < 10th percentile	Percent respondents > 90th percentile and < 10th percentile
Certain	0	10	10
Almost certain	0	7	7
Nearly certain	0	9	9
Very high chance	0	5	5
Very probable	0	7	7
Highly likely	0	10	10
High probability	0	5	5
High likelihood	10	7	17
High chance	9	9	19
Large chance	10	9	19
Extensive chance	0	11	11
Very good chance	8	9	17
Probably	0	6	6
Major chance	4	5	9
Believe	0	5	5
Significant chance	9	5	15
Likely	7	7	13

mode for responses to each probability statement, creating a range around the mode of the total number of scores by adding ± 0.10 to the mode, then determining the percent of the respondents whose probability score fell outside of this range. Wark suggested three categories of agreement for complete surveys, namely, super consensus, consensus, and no consensus. The criteria for each category are given in Table J.9.[2]

The results in Table J.2 (sorted by median, then by mean values) were then mapped into the super consensus, consensus, and no consensus categories with the criteria given in Table J.9. The resulting super consensus, consensus, and no consensus listings are given in Tables J.10a, J.10b, and J.10c, respectively.

Of the 50 probability statements, 7, 35, and 8 met the super consensus, consensus, and no consensus criteria, respectively. Because occasional chance was listed twice and both statements met the no consensus criteria,

Table J.5b Percent respondents > 90th percentile, percent respondents < 10th
percentile, and percent sum > 90th percentile and < 10th percentile
for probability statements

Probability statement	Percent respondents > 90th percentile	Percent respondents < 10th percentile	Percent respondents > 90th percentile and < 10th percentile
Probable	5	9	15
Almost likely	7	7	14
Frequent chance	8	6	14
Better than even chance	10	4	14
Better than 50/50	10	7	17
Moderate probability	4	5	9
Even chance	6	2	8
Possible	3	10	13
Potential	5	10	15
Medium probability	4	10	14
Reduced chance	10	1	11
Occasional chance (1)	6	2	8
Some chance	9	5	14
Occasional chance (2)	3	7	10
Limited chance	9	3	13
Probably not	6	0	6
Not likely	9	0	9

the number of no consensus statements was reduced from 8 to 7. Thus, 14, 72, and 14% of the probability statements correspond to super consensus, consensus, and no consensus categories, respectively. Wark's analysis included 33 statements that had complete scores. (Wark rejected 8 statements where 90% or more of the respondents marked the score as "not applicable.") Of these 33 statements 3, 13, and 17 met the super consensus, consensus, and no consensus criteria.[2] Thus, 9, 39, and 52% of the probability statements correspond to super consensus, consensus, and no consensus categories, respectively. Of the 16 probability statements that Wark identified as having super consensus and consensus, 6 matched the exact wording in my survey. They were also in the super consensus and consensus categories in my survey. Of these 6 matching statements all statements had mode values within 0.05 when comparing my results to that of Wark's. (These statements were almost certainly, probably not, likely, highly likely, unlikely, and better than even chance.)

Table J.5c Percent respondents > 90th percentile, percent respondents < 10th percentile, and percent sum > 90th percentile and < 10th percentile for probability statements

Probability statement	Percent respondents > 90th percentile	Percent respondents < 10th percentile	Percent respondents > 90th percentile and < 10th percentile
Low likelihood	9	0	9
Unlikely	9	0	9
Improbable	9	0	9
Slight chance	9	0	9
Minor chance	8	9	17
Low probability	7	9	17
Doubtful	9	0	9
Little chance	5	0	5
Very limited chance	8	0	8
Small probability	8	0	8
Highly unlikely	9	0	9
Very unlikely	7	0	7
Negligible chance	9	0	9
Very low probability	9	0	9
No significant chance	8	0	8
Almost no chance	7	0	7

Unfortunately, I did not receive Wark's paper until *after* my survey was concluded. Thus, there was no way to incorporate the additional statements used by Wark into my survey. However, as already mentioned, I intentionally limited my survey to 50 probability statements contained on two pages in an attempt to minimize the number of incomplete surveys. (Roughly 20% of

Table J.6 Range vs number of probability statements

Range (maximum - minimum)	Number of probability statements
0.9	18
0.8	24
0.7	7
0.4	1

Table J.7 Summary statistics for percent sum > 3rd quartile and < 1st quartile. (Statistics calculated across all 50 probability statements.)

Statistic	Percent value
Mean	26
Standard deviation	9
Median (50th percentile)	24
Maximum	47
Minimum	8
Range	39
Third quartile (75th percentile)	33
First quartile (25th percentile)	20

Table J.8 Summary statistics for percent sum > 90th percentile and < 10th percentile. (Statistics calculated across all 50 probability statements.)

Statistic	Percent value
Mean	11
Standard deviation	4
Median (50th percentile)	9
Maximum	19
Minimum	5
Range	14
Third quartile (75th percentile)	8
First quartile (25th percentile)	6

Table J.9 Definitions for super consensus, consensus, and no consensus

Descriptor	Definition[a]
Super consensus	≥ 90.0 percent
Consensus	≥ 70.0 percent to < 90.0 percent
Non consensus	< 70 percent

[a] Percentage of respondents having scores equal to the mode of the total response +/− 0.10.

Table J.10a   Probability statements meeting super consensus criteria

Probability statement	Percent respondents within mode +/− 0.10
Highly likely	90
Better than even chance	95
Better than 50/50	90
Even chance	95
Medium probability	94
Small probability	92
Highly unlikely	91

Wark's 41 total probability statements, 8 of 41, contained 90% or more responses marked "not applicable." I included none of the 7 statements he listed for this category, of the 8 statements total he indicated, in my survey.)

The reader should be somewhat cautious in interpreting the results given in Tables J.4, J.5, J.7, and J.8 (as well as Table J.10). This is because the survey data *is not* a continuous distribution, but a distribution of 10 sets of discrete values (0.05, 0.15, 0.25, 0.35, 0.45, 0.55, 0.65, 0.75, 0.85, and 0.95).

The recommendation is strongly made that any estimative probability ordinal scales or probability tables derived from the data given in Tables J.2, J.3, and J.4 include the median (50th percentile), 3rd quartile (75th percentile), 1st quartile (25th percentile), and the percent responses above the 3rd quartile (> 3rd quartile) and below the 1st quartile (< 1st quartile). Solely using the median value should not be done—it is tantamount to refusing to recognize that a range of responses exists and can cause erroneous results. This is particularly inappropriate given the broad range of responses for each probability statement, as illustrated in Table J.6. It is also recommended that the percent of responses outside the third and first quartiles be separately reported, along with the sum of these two values. In addition, it is recommended that the seven probability statements given in Table J.10c (probably, believe, almost likely, possible, potential, occasional chance, and some chance) not be used in estimative probability ordinal scales or probability tables given the lack of consensus of survey respondents (average of only 63% for the mode ± 0.10). (As previously discussed, it is also recommended that the probability statement reduced chance not be used in estimative probability ordinal scales or probability tables.)

An example of the recommended estimative probability table structure is given in Table J.11 for the probability statements: certain, high probability, medium probability, low probability, and almost no chance.

Table J.10b   Probability statements meeting consensus criteria

Probability statement	Percent respondents within mode +/− 0.10
Certain	86
Almost certain	89
Nearly certain	81
Very high chance	89
Very probable	85
High probability	87
High likelihood	82
High chance	85
Large chance	87
Extensive chance	77
Very good chance	74
Major chance	72
Significant chance	83
Likely	79
Probable	77
Frequent chance	78
Moderate probability	79
Reduced chance	79
Limited chance	77
Probably not	74
Not likely	75
Low likelihood	79
Unlikely	77
Improbable	76
Slight chance	79
Minor chance	76
Low probability	75
Doubtful	83
Little chance	88
Very limited chance	85
Very unlikely	79
Negligible chance	81
Very low probability	80
No significant chance	74
Almost no chance	89

Table J.10c   Probability statements meeting no consensus criteria

Probability statement	Percent respondents within mode +/− 0.10
Probably	69
Believe	67
Almost likely	60
Possible	58
Potential	52
Occasional chance (1)	69
Some chance	66
Occasional chance (2)	66

Table J.11a   Example of estimative probability table

Definition	Median (50th percentile)	3rd quartile (75th percentile)	1st quartile (25th percentile)
Certain	0.95	0.95	0.95
High	0.85	0.85	0.75
Medium	0.45	0.55	0.45
Low	0.15	0.25	0.15
Almost no chance	0.05	0.15	0.05

Table J.11b   Example of estimative probability table

Definition	Percent > 3rd quartile (75th percentile)	Percent < 1st quartile (25th percentile)	Percent > 3rd quartile and < 1st quartile
Certain	0	24	24
High	13	13	26
Medium	13	20	33
Low	15	9	24
Almost no chance	11	0	11

Between 11 and 33% of the respondents were either above the 3rd quartile or below the 1st quartile for the 5 probability statements in Table J.11. Thus, a notable fraction of potential analysts may assess the subjective estimate of probability *differently* than given by the median value or even the median value bounded by the third quartile and the first quartile values! *(Note: The information contained in Table I.11b is backup data for Table J.11a, but nevertheless should be available to both analysts and decision makers to help them understand the range of underlying survey responses.)*

References

[1]Kent, S., "Words of Estimative Probability," *Studies in Intelligence,* Center for the Study of Intelligence, Fall 1964, (declassified and released for public distribution and use Sept. 22, 1993), pp. 49–65.

[2]Wark, D. L., "The Definitions of Some Estimative Expressions," *Studies in Intelligence,* Center for the Study of Intelligence, Fall 1964, (declassified and released for public distribution and use Sept. 18, 1995, pp. 67–80.

Appendix K:
Development of Ordinal Probability
Scales from Cardinal Data

Suitable historical program data may exist to permit development of ordinal risk analysis probability scales that are indicators of actual probability. However, ordinal probability scales derived from actual probability data are rare for three reasons. First, most risk categories (e.g., technology) do not lend themselves to quantitative measurement that directly supports development of probability scales. Second, even if quantitative measurements can be made, there is typically insufficient data to provide a reliable and statistically sound basis for constructing an ordinal probability scale. Third, if the necessary data existed, they could often be more effectively used to help estimate project risk through other techniques, including developing representative distributions for Monte Carlo simulations and performing Bayesian statistics.

I. Data Collection and Reduction

An example is now given that illustrates the development of an acceptable ordinal probability scale when suitable and sufficient data are available. The example uses schedule length (years) from Milestone II to first delivery at the vehicle level (e.g., aircraft) from historical DoD aircraft, helicopter, and missile programs that were developed during the 1940s through the 1980s. (Whereas this example uses DoD-related data, the methodology given for constructing the ordinal probability scale can be just as readily applied to data from commercial items.) These data were collected and published by Michael B. Rothman and Giles K. Smith of RAND.[1] It was then edited, including minor corrections and adding some new data points, with the help of Smith. The resulting database for this schedule attribute is composed of 90 programs (data points).

The data were first sorted from shortest to longest schedule length. Software was developed to estimate the resulting schedule length for a user-specified fraction of programs (0.0 to 1.0) contained in the database. (This software was developed at no charge to the government in early 1987 and given to the deputy director of a major defense organization to support a series of DoD milestone reviews and is not available for distribution.) This is akin to estimating percentiles for a given probability distribution. For example, a fraction of 0.20 (or the 20th percentile of programs) corresponds

515

to a schedule length of 2.4 years. Thus, only 20% of the programs in the database have a Milestone II (beginning of Engineering and Manufacturing Development) to first delivery schedule length ≤ 2.4 years, while 80% of the programs have a schedule length > 2.4 years. A cumulative distribution function (CDF) plot of the actual (not estimated percentile) data is given in Fig. K.1.

Two underlying assumptions are needed to equate this data to probability information. First, the fraction of the underlying database corresponding to a given schedule length is equivalent to the probability of occurrence for that schedule length. This assumption is not unreasonable because the data represent individual development programs that are typically not directly dependent on other programs in the database. Second, the statistical characteristics of the underlying database sample are representative of the population of DoD aircraft, helicopter, and missile programs. This assumption is also not unreasonable because the database sample is likely close to the population of DoD aircraft, helicopter, and missile programs during the 1940s through the 1980s that reached first delivery. [Note: In many instances a much smaller sample size will exist than available here (90 data points). Attempts to 1) interpolate between existing data points or 2) assume a given probability distribution, perform a simulation, and examine the resulting

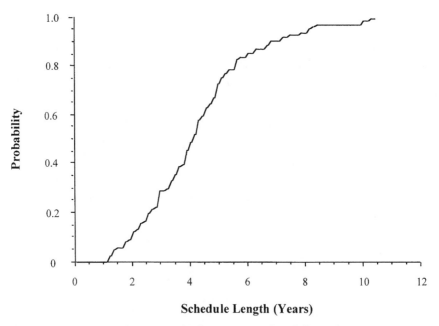

Fig. K.1   CDF plot of Milestone II to first delivery data.

CDF to derive percentile information in such cases may lead to considerable estimation error because of the inherent limitations of performing analyses on small data samples.]

II. Probability Scale Development

These data will now be used to develop a five-level ordinal probability scale. The CDF was divided into 5 areas of equal probability, namely 20th percentile intervals. The schedule length estimation software (already mentioned) was used to calculate schedule lengths for the 20th, 40th, 60th, 80th, and 100th percentiles. (This was necessary because the data were not uniformly distributed in terms of schedule length and frequency of occurrence, e.g., not all points corresponded to single percentile values and there was sometimes more than one program having the same schedule length. Of course, the 100th percentile value was simply the upper bound of the data, which corresponded to a single program with a schedule length = 10.3 years. However, the 0th percentile, needed to bound the data on the lower end, is assumed to correspond to a schedule length = 0.0 years.) The calculated schedule lengths are given in Table K.1 and compare closely to the CDF plot of the actual data in Fig. K.1.

Note that the 20th percentile (2.4 years) actually represents having an 80% chance that the schedule length $\geq$ 2.4 years. This is not unrealistic because there is a low probability of achieving a very short schedule length in an actual development program because of inherent programmatic (e.g., budget and political) and technological considerations. Hence, attempting to implement a program schedule that is very aggressive (short) will increase schedule risk and the likelihood of some resulting schedule slippage vs a less aggressive schedule (cet. par.). From a risk analysis perspective a high probability of occurrence is more undesirable than a low probability of occurrence (cet. par.), except when the consequence of occurrence is vanishingly small, because the product of probability and consequence terms yields risk. Consequently, when transferred to an ordinal probability scale, an event that

Table K.1 Milestone II to first delivery schedule length vs database percentile

Percentile	Schedule length, yr
20	2.4
40	3.6
60	4.4
80	5.5
100	10.3

Table K.2   Milestone II to first delivery schedule length ordinal probability scale

Scale level	Probability	Schedule length
E	$0.80 <$ probability ≤ 1.00	$0.0 \leq$ schedule length < 2.4 yr
D	$0.60 <$ probability ≤ 0.80	$2.4 \leq$ schedule length < 3.6 yr
C	$0.40 <$ probability ≤ 0.60	$3.6 \leq$ schedule length < 4.4 yr
B	$0.20 <$ probability ≤ 0.40	$4.4 \leq$ schedule length < 5.5 yr
A	$0.00 <$ probability ≤ 0.20	$5.5 \leq$ schedule length ≤ 10.3 yr

has a high probability of occurrence (sometimes termed probability of failure) should have a high scale-level designator (e.g., E rather than A, where E > A on a five-level scale).

Similarly, the 40th percentile corresponds to having a 60% chance that the schedule length is ≥ 3.6 years, the 60th percentile corresponds to having a 40% chance that the schedule length is ≥ 4.4 years, and so on.

The range in years corresponding to schedule length that borders the percentiles (in Table K.1) defines the five ordinal probability scale levels given in Table K.2, where the probability of scale level E > D > C > B > A. Similarly, the range in probability values that border the percentiles (in Table K.1) are also given in Table K.2. (Note: To bound the data, the assumption is made that the 100th percentile corresponds to a having a 0% chance that the schedule length > 10.3 years, whereas there is a nonzero chance that the schedule length $= 10.3$ years.)

The use of probability and schedule length ranges (e.g., $2.4 <$ schedule length ≤ 3.6 years) instead of point values (e.g., 3.6 years) is warranted because the underlying database contains numerous values, is not multimodal, and approaches a continuous distribution.

Note that the scale-level designators in Table K.2 are intentionally provided as letters rather than numbers to dissuade the reader from performing mathematical operations on the results. Even in this rare instance where the ordinal scale levels directly map to actual probability values, the analyst is better served not to attempt mathematical operations on the resulting scale-level values. This is because the scale-level value cannot be accurately mathematically combined with values from other ordinal "probability" scales (which will almost never be derived from actual probability data), nor can it be accurately mathematically combined with ordinal consequence of occurrence scale values.

The ordinal probability scale given in Table K.2 may be used for a program risk analysis assuming:

1) the schedule probability category of interest is Milestone II to first delivery,

2) the schedule probability term was only being evaluated at the total program level—the same level the historical data represents,

3) the program performing the risk analysis had similar technical characteristics to those included in the underlying database (e.g., aircraft, helicopter, and missile programs, not a ship program, plus few if any technological breakthroughs needed),

4) the program requiring the risk analysis had comparable acquisition characteristics to those included in the underlying database,

5) the item being acquired is a developmental item (not a nondevelopmental item), and

6) the schedule for the item being acquired meets program and related stakeholder objectives.

Of course, because every program is somewhat unique, there will be uncertainty associated with the resulting probability scale level even in this fairly optimal (extensive underlying database) and simple (only five scale levels) illustration.

Reference

[1]Rothman, M. B., and Smith, G. K., "Aerospace Weapon System Acquisition Milestones: A Database," RAND, Santa Monica, CA, N-2599-ACQ, Oct., 1987.

Index